Seizing
Destiny

SEIZING DESTINY

How America Grew
from Sea to Shining Sea

RICHARD KLUGER

ALFRED A. KNOPF · NEW YORK 2007

THIS IS A BORZOI BOOK
PUBLISHED BY ALFRED A. KNOPF

Library of Congress Cataloging-in-Publication Data

Kluger, Richard.
Seizing destiny : how America grew from sea to shing sea /
by Richard Kluger.—1st ed.
p. cm.
ISBN 978-0-375-41341-4
1. United States—Territorial expansion.   2. United States—History.
3. United States—Foreign relations.   I. Title.
E179.5.K56 2007
973—dc22   2006037733

Manufactured in the United States of America

First Edition

For Josh, Ben, Nick, Than, Zack, and Will—
may they help make their world
and their country (in that order)
better places

CONTENTS

List of Maps   ix

Preface   xi

1 An empty sack cannot stand upright (*1500–1750*)   3

2 The Poor Richards arise (*1750–1776*)   52

3 Thinking large (*1776–1782*)   84

4 The kings outfoxed (*1782–1783*)   129

5 Owning the wilderness (*1783–1800*)   181

6 For a nice little kingdom in Tuscany (*1800–1803*)   232

7 Everything he does is rapid as lightning (*1803*)   270

8 From motives of purest patriotism (*1803–1823*)   301

9 Big Drunk wins the day (*1821–1836*)   351

10 Polking John Bull in the eye (*1836–1847*)   400

11 The lost virtue of their better days (*1846–1850*)   432

12 A wolf couldn't make a living on it (*1850–1854*)   482

13 The great white elephant sale (*1854–1867*)   505

14 Treachery in the tropics (*1869–1902*)   543

15 The so-called mandate of mankind (*1903–1999*)   579

Appendix: Principal Acquisitions of Territory by   605
the United States

Acknowledgments   607

Bibliographical Notes   609

Index   625

MAPS

25   Boundaries of Colonial Virginia

149 Creating Boundaries of the New United States

190 State Land Claims and Cessions to Congress

283 Louisiana Purchase

343 U.S. Western Boundary

386 Texas, 1830–1850

421 The Oregon Country

472 The Mexican Cession

522 Alaska

582 The Gulf of Mexico and Caribbean Sea

PREFACE

O N THE SIXTH OF MAY, 1997, two months into his fifth year in office, President Bill Clinton made his first state visit to his nation's immediate neighbor to the south. His aides were not elated to learn that Mr. Clinton's host, President Ernesto Zedillo of Mexico, had arranged for the two heads of state to pay a ceremonial visit of homage to a monument, a pink marble terrace with six memorial columns, at the edge of Chapultepec Park three miles from the heart of Mexico City. At this place, 150 years earlier, in the closing battle of the American invasion of Mexico, U.S. troops had bloodily fought their way to the top of the hill commanded by Chapultepec Palace, then serving as Mexico's military academy. Among its last, fiercest defenders were six teenage cadets, one of whom, rather than surrender or be skewered by American bayonets, wrapped himself in the red, white, and green flag of his country before leaping off the castle ramparts to his death. Ever after, these defiant young martyrs have remained, in Mexican eyes, a constant reminder of the unjust onslaught by the bullying gringos from the north.

The Clinton advance team, reluctant to stir up the faint but unextinguished embers of animosity, voiced distress over this wreath-laying stop on the schedule. "So we said it's just a sign of respect, part of the protocol," a senior Mexican official told a *New York Times* reporter. Indeed, many heads of state had visited the monument to Mexico's Boy Heroes of Chapultepec, marking the hallowed battleground where 1,800 Mexicans (as well as 450 Americans) died.

But only once before had an American President appeared at the spot. Harry S. Truman came on the hundredth anniversary of the battle, silently laid a wreath, turned around, got back into his limousine, and drove off.

Clinton, a more voluble and gladhanding sort, dealt with it more graciously. "I'm going there as a gesture of respect, not only respect for their lives but respect for the patriotism and integrity of the people who have served this country," he said at a news conference prior to the ceremony. (Presumably "this country" referred to Mexico.) "We are trying to heal the wounds of war with nations with whom we fought even more recently," the President added. At the event itself, however, no words were spoken; Clinton placed a wreath, the two chiefs of state stood at attention while their respective national anthems were played, and that was that. Afterward a history professor at the Colegio de México remarked to a *Newsday* reporter, "President Clinton's visit is in a way a recognition of this symbol of an unjust war. The visit is a sign of historical sensibility on his part."

Sensibility, *sí;* regrets, no—not even for what posterity (and more than a few contemporaries) recognized as America's biggest, boldest act of territorial plunder, under the guise of a war trumped up by a President of engorged willfulness. Even the all-embracing humanist poet of his age, Walt Whitman, celebrated the martial rampage, ignoring—like most of his countrymen—that Mexico in 1847 was a pitiably weak sister republic of the United States, an anarchic invalid that had run through eighteen presidents in the two dozen years since it had declared itself an independent nation. Yet America, with the full license of Congress, raped it, making off with more than 500,000 square miles, nearly half of its southern neighbor's territory. Most of it, to be sure, was loosely held and yielded without a fight. But at times and in places the Mexicans, though poorly trained and ineptly led, fought proudly and determinedly.

For the United States, the decisive savaging of Mexico was the most brazen chapter in an ongoing saga celebrating what some of the nation's most forthright statesmen had dignified as its providential mission. Lions like Henry Clay, Daniel Webster, and John C. Calhoun had asserted their country was hewing to a divinely guided trajectory, fated to extend its dominion from Hudson Bay to the isthmus of Panama. Some even proposed Patagonia as the only logical southern terminus of a hemispheric union under America's enveloping benevolence. While managing to contain itself within more modest boundaries, the United States did not tire of trumpeting its "manifest destiny," a luminous slogan minted shortly before the Mexican war by a New York journalist on the make and hell-bent on propagating expansive dominion as a national virtue.

To label the happy progress of the United States of America evidence of destiny's smile did not make it so. But an incurable case of triumphalism had led Americans to assume that their singular success as a nation was not only foreordained but also deserved—why else would the Universal Overseer have rewarded them so amply? Dumb luck was not an acceptably ennobling explanation. A more measured, less self-serving assessment of America's achievements might suggest that, in pursuit of their mission, its supercharged people overlooked no opportunity to maximize every advantage that nature, geography, history, economics, and, yes, dumb luck presented to them. Crafting their own destiny with whatever tools were at hand, they gained a continental expanse by means of daring, cunning, bullying, bluff and bluster, treachery, robbery, quick talk, double-talk, noble principles, stubborn resolve, low-down expediency, cash on the barrelhead, and, when deemed necessary, spilled blood. Within ninety-one years—the blink of an eye by historical measurement—a league of thirteen lately British coastal colonies, starting without an army or a design for their collaborative future operation, had by 1867 extended their boundaries to encompass 3.7 million square miles, from the western shore of the Atlantic to the eastern shore of the Bering Strait at the tip of Alaska. And then they stopped manifesting their destiny by seizing someone else's real estate. What they had gathered up, except for the future addition of some strategically located islands, was sufficient for their purpose. Today only Russia and Canada occupy more of the earth's surface, and only China and India are more populous. No other sovereign entity ever grew so large so fast to become so rich and so strong.

The main dynamics of this growth process were these: a spectacular virgin landscape of immeasurable expanse and superlative fertility greeted invaders from the Old World, and nobody occupied it but scatterings of nomadic, Stone Age tribes shy on the organizational skills or death-dealing tools to repulse the newcomers. And why bother? Mother Earth was vast. How could the natives have guessed, until it was too late, that the white interlopers were only the first wave of what would shortly prove an ocean swell of humanity, come there to stay? The willful kings of Europe who had licensed the transatlantic expeditions presumed they could buy dominion on the cheap over this largely empty New World. The sovereigns simply announced their proprietary rights to all the territory that their intrepid explorers could see—and far, far beyond—as though the mere act of proclamation somehow legitimized the claim. What the masters of the Old World could not have foreseen was how an unprecedented confluence of liberties and incentives, grounded on the availability of cheap, bountiful, and accessible land on every side and beyond every horizon, would result in the emergence of an unpredictably feisty breed of restless colonials, scornful of authority and orthodoxy.

The land itself was the true treasure of this gorgeous, if nettlesome, new world. And the American colonizing experience advanced fresh ways of thinking about the ownership and value of real property. At the 1961 inauguration of President John F. Kennedy, Robert Frost recited one of his poems, which, given the occasion, immediately earned the lines a place in the annals of the most memorable American verse. Called "The Gift Outright," it begins:

The land was ours before we were the land's.
She was our land more than a hundred years
Before we were her people. She was ours
In Massachusetts, in Virginia;
But we were England's, still colonials,
Possessing what we were still unpossessed by. . . .

The American colonists by their tireless labor and dauntless staying power had embraced the good earth all about them as their own long before they declared it free from the distant sovereign who, with belated insistence, asserted his rule over that land and all who dwelled thereon. Frost's lines assigned a metaphysical content to the passage from colony to nation, as if the American soul and the American soil were inextricably linked. No doubt it was faulty wiring, not a supernatural visitation, that caused a puff of smoke—in fact, several puffs—to arise around the lectern while the flinty old poet read these lines, as if the departed souls of millions of native Americans had suddenly materialized in protest of his bland racism.

For countless millenia, dating back to well before the Christian era, so-called Indian tribes had lived unchallenged on this land and revered it for the beauty and nourishment it provided them, for its immanent life force, for the omnipresent spirits that ruled the weather and inhabited every meadow, brook, tree, rock, beaver, and plover. But the notion that they held title to the land—that it was somehow *theirs* to possess and deny to all others—was plainly absurd, to the Indian manner of thought. How could mere mortals, who passed their short span on earth and soon returned to dust, claim title to the land, which lived on forever? It would be as foolish as claiming ownership of the sky, the sea, the moon, or the stars. Land could not *belong* to any person or people, for the land abided and superseded man. The most that any native American tribe would have claimed was a right of custom to dwell in some more or less defined territory and partake thankfully of its fruits, hoping that habit would certify habitation and fend off others aroused by evil spirits to displace them. Thus, when the white men came and asked—if they bothered—to purchase title to great expanses of the earth's surface from them, the natives had difficulty fathoming the concept. How to assign material value to a priceless thing? One might as well have tried to strike a bargain for life itself.

In the Old World, by contrast, human ownership of the land was not in the least an unnatural idea and had a fateful impact on all daily life. Title to it, however and whenever obtained, was the measure of standing for nations, communal units, and individuals alike. Over long ages men had fought and died to gain and hold territory they judged essential to their well-being. Proprietorship may have been ephemeral and illusory, but it nevertheless defined temporal power. Wealth, grandeur, and hegemony, though, were not defined by acreage alone; the number of vassals and villeins dependent on and paying allegiance to an overlord, rendering him homage in crops, labor, or combat when called upon, was as telling a measure of his importance. In medieval Europe and long after, ironclad feudal control of the land had the virtue of clearly marking where almost every living soul ranked in the community and defining his or her daily duties. In the system's purest form, absolute monarchy, all ownership of the land flowed from the throne downward. The king or emperor alone embodied the realm and, by custom (invariably derived from battles won long before), held ultimate title to all the territory therein; anyone else awarded or claiming title to real estate enjoyed it through the sufferance of the monarch. This privilege, reserved for the nobility, the church, or, on occasion, particularly useful members of the mercantile class, came with a price attached—fees, loyalty, and military and other forms of service in perpetual tribute—and could be withdrawn at the sovereign's whim. At each generational passage a renewal of the vows (and payment) of fealty to the crown was mandatory. It was a system based less on monetary value or other material considerations than on social and, when required, physical domination.

All of which pretty much left the common man with no land to call his own, or much else to his name beyond the shredding clothes on his back, a few sticks of furniture, and basic tools to tend his lord and master's fields. Under the circumstances, those who struggled to wring their meager sustenance from the land did not revere it, for it was not theirs, only assigned to them to toil over. The landless peasant either complied with this grinding regimen or was ground under by it; protest would have availed him little beyond heightened anguish over his lot. The want of land to call their own, in short, doomed the farming masses everywhere to a lifelong struggle for survival without hope of consolation that their labors might someday redound to the betterment of their progeny.

From the fourteenth through the sixteenth centuries, revolutionary thoughts began to stir in the minds of people at all levels of the social hierarchy. Its humblest members, long counseled by their parish priests to suffer silently while clinging to piety as their latchkey to eternal salvation, started to question the holy fathers' call for forbearance. Reformers like Luther and his followers began to pry open the minds and hearts of the laity, inviting their direct address to the Heavenly Father and closer examination of the orthodoxies purveyed by the closed-minded, widely corrupt ecclesiastical establishment. Equally heretical was the embryonic notion that states and their rulers deserved the common man's allegiance only to the extent they served the needs of the people, not the other way around. By the mid-seventeenth century Europe was edging toward its Age of Enlightenment, and an advance cadre of philosophers and social commentators proclaimed that mankind had "natural rights" to a life of liberty, dignity, and self-realization. Central to the fulfillment of this aspiration was every man's right to hold real property in his own name and for whatever disposition he chose to make of it.

But land was finite, in short supply, and few who had it were eager to part with it. Accordingly, the "natural" right to title and conveyance of land—meaning possession that did not have to be granted by any temporal authority, civil, royal, or ecclesiastical—was little more than a wishful invo-cation of God's universal blessing and was met scornfully by those atop the rigidly stratified social system. Indeed, the throttling premise at the core of of feudalism had been that only the divinely anointed ruler, no matter how much given to skullduggery, held a "natural" right to own land—and only he could assign title to it. In truth, even the most enlightened of monarchs (and they were few and far between) ultimately owed their legitimacy to the gleaming edge of a sword or the business end of a musket. Panoply parading as omnipotence certainly helped, but it was earthly power—manpower, horsepower, and firepower, not prayer, reason, or eloquence—that in the end determined who got to own what. "Natural rights" could not compete with the willful wrongs of despots.

When a new world was found across the sea, the set ways of the old one began to be thrown into question. Land on the far side of the ocean was said to be going begging for want of men to take it up. And those who did so might thereby free themselves from the cruelty of perpetual servitude. And, if heaven smiled on their labors, they might arrive at a standard of living they and their families had scarcely dreamed of. Still, it was all designated the king's realm.

By what pretension of legitimacy, though, had the kings and princes who sponsored the expeditionary voyages of the Age of Discovery tried to extend their sway across the wide Atlantic? Since there was no historical basis for any claim of possession, they coined a "right of discovery and set-tlement," premised on the likelihood that any occupants of this looming terra incognita were nullities, possibly monstrous, and at best marginally human by Europe's lights. But was the symbolic gesture by a sailing cap-tain, planting his monarch's flag on misty shores months' travel time from home, sufficient to establish a royal entitlement? Entitlement to what? And

by whose authority and with whose assent? The sovereigns themselves
seemed to understand the dilemma and turned for sanction to Pope Alexander VI, who in 1493, with a shake of his crook and miter, declared the kings
of Spain and Portugal, Their Catholic Majesties, invested to divide the
unexplored pagan world between them along two clearly designated longi-
tudinal lines. But since when and by what sanction was the papacy infallible
or omnipotent when addressing temporal matters? Why should Catholic
France have been excluded from that spectacular papal indulgence? And
why should England and the states of northern Europe that would shortly
turn against the Roman church have been obliged to honor a worldwide
Iberian hegemony? And in fact, five European kingdoms were to make
overlapping claims and issue charters of title to courtiers and clients, granting them immense portions of the barely glimpsed new hemisphere. In
truth, no European sovereign could plausibly claim a mandate of entitlement—his manifest destiny, so to speak—from on high. There was no "on
high" governing the New World; that was one of the delightful things that
was new about it. Only the dispatch of soldiers and settlers could certify
sovereignty.

Nearly all of those who came from the British Isles, whether gentry or
commoners, king's cronies or desperate paupers, the God-fearing or the
God-forsaken, came for the enchanting land, so abundant, so empty, so
fecund. Because the soil was blessedly rich and there was so much of it—
often beyond a family's collective strength to work it—many settlers were
able to reap harvests well in excess of their needs, an unimaginable luxury
for most European peasants scratching away at tired old fields primarily to
benefit a hated overlord. Such hard-won liberation from ancient thralldom
brought the dignity of independence and with it a new breed, the self-
validating American colonist, whose ambition was often as expansive as the
landscape.

The lure of all that land with its robust yields ensured a constant inflow
of settlers, and the more who came, the more who followed. The demand for
fresh territory steadily grew, no matter the sacrifices required to get it and
hold on to it, however painful its clearing and cultivation or furious the
response by the displaced natives. Ineluctably the frontier etched its way
west from the seaboard, up river valleys to the piedmont and the mountains
beyond, then through or over that long rugged barrier to the sweeter mead-
ows, thicker forests, and crystal streams awaiting.

After these irrepressible Americans consecrated their land as a nation,
no longer the provinces of an exploitative absentee power, their territorial
cravings only grew. Americans' passion for space to embrace as their own

private preserve, safe from prying authorities and promising a decent livelihood, animated the nation-building process from the first. What affected
individual families applied with equal force to the country's collective conduct as a sovereign commonwealth. The unbridled United States would forever be in need of new land for its ill-disciplined, hard-charging people. The
land would be needed, if not tomorrow, then one day soon. And so an exuberant national policy emerged more or less spontaneously, aimed at gathering in as much as possible of the earth's adjacent surface and bringing it
under the United States' jurisdiction—as inventory awaiting future settlement—whenever the opportunity arose. And it seemed to arise with remarkable frequency, stirring the nation's political leaders to pursue immense
territorial accretions that, as some wary European observers had feared,
were creating an infant colossus, soon to bestride the full ambit of the New
World.

    This greatness—of size, wealth, and power—did not, of course, spring
forth full-blown; it had to be planted, fertilized, tended to, gathered up, and
processed, all obstacles be damned and, if need be, demolished. Although
self-justifying throughout the process, those early generations of Americans
had no exclusive call on heaven's blessing for their venture. They were simply all too human in confusing opportunity with entitlement and mistaking
the abundance of liberty doled to them by history and geography for a
license to have their way. Those Americans given to blind chauvinism
would do well to consider the darker side of the tale as well.

SEIZING DESTINY

CHAPTER I

An empty sack cannot stand upright

1500–1750

FIVE HUNDRED YEARS AFTERWARD, who of us can summon more than the faintest sense of how the North American continent must have filled the eyes and stirred the minds of the earliest European voyagers? Some, to be sure, recorded their impressions of the primeval setting, with its wild beauty, its web of glinting waterways that wound navigably deep into the hinterland, its brooding and endless woods, its lush soil, its abounding fauna, its mostly temperate climate, and its native peoples, so benign and hospitable at first. None of the newcomers could hazard more than a fanciful guess as to the ultimate scale of that seductive land mass. And almost all of their estimates were to prove laughably, if understandably, inaccurate.

Still, given the lack of engines to help conquer time, distance, and the ruggedness of the terrain, knowledge of the true expanse of North America was gathered rapidly. The opening of the Western Hemisphere to its Old World discoverers at the end of the fifteenth century had been a signal event in the process of unshackling Europe's mental, physical, and spiritual energies. Among the most useful gains in the advancement of scientific thought and instrumentation was the development of the compass, which, as refined over several centuries, allowed more and better ships to sail out in every direction with enhanced prospects of returning safely. The result was a great surge in commerce, a sharp stimulus to manufacturing, heightened cultural interchange, and, with the emergence of guns and gunpowder, a quantum rise in killing power, which in turn aroused military adventurism. Rulers now relied less on the consecrating support of the church and more on the newly enterprising mercantile class to help their regimes prosper.

The development of Protestantism, inviting the laity to veer from cor-
rupted orthodoxy and make personal choices in the form and content of
worship, also cast the beam of doubt on economic, dynastic, and territorial
assumptions. Soon Europe was plunged into an endless series of wars,
chronically destabilizing the continental balance of power that the crowned
heads claimed to favor. Their contest grew decidedly more complex and
heated with the spread of overseas exploration and settlement by the
Atlantic monarchies, engaging the imagination and passions of all Europe
and, for a time, yielding a stream of treasure from the New World.

Earlier, between the eleventh and thirteenth centuries, Europe had also
turned outward in a collective enterprise, toward the East, to liberate the
birthplace of Christianity from what it disparaged as infidel Islam. Like so
many efforts undertaken in the name of religious purification, the Crusades
profaned rather than exalted the tenets of their faith in a travesty of Christian love. In coming to the New World two centuries later, when Europeans
turned outward again, they could not pretend to be reclaiming holy ground
for the church. The Europeans' mission was frankly materialistic: shorter
trade routes, more profitable markets, and whatever booty they could haul
home. To cloak it in the raiment of a moral mandate as well, the venture was
carried out under the banners of heaven, to redeem for Christ the souls of
the pagan natives, whose chief sin appears to have been their otherness, and
to appropriate whatever unconsecrated lands they came upon for the greater
glory of the kings who sent them searching. In the beginning, which is to
say for more than a hundred years, few conceived that the newfound lands
might provide a suitable asylum for those victimized by the Old World's
social afflictions.

THE SPANIARDS CAME FIRST tracking the southerly latitudes and, after
finding little to loot in the Caribbean isles, their first landfall, they reached
the midsector of the hemispheric mainland, which most resembled the
warm, arid, and often jagged setting of their homeland. It was also the
most densely populated region of the New World. Some authorities have
estimated that at the outset of the sixteenth century as many as 25 million
Indians inhabited the Aztec empire and its surrounding civilizations in
modern-day Mexico, Central America, and the northern Andes. But so
horrific was the collision of the indigenous culture with the whites' that,
according to the grimmest calculations, less than 10 percent of the aboriginal total remained a century later.

While such figures are necessarily approximations, there can be little doubt of the genocidal effect of the Spanish invasion almost from the first. Seafaring curiosity and intrepid adventurism may have added wind to the sails of Columbus's three small ships on his monumental first voyage of discovery, but his second sailing west, consisting of seventeen ships and 1,200 men, was undertaken in the hope of finding easy riches—jewels, precious metals, and slaves were the return cargo he and his royal patrons sought—and not to garner knowledge in naval science. Violent clashes soon occurred, the natives could not compete with their brash and notably brutal assailants in lethal weaponry, and even less could they resist the ravaging effects of the previously unknown diseases with which the Europeans infected them on an epidemic scale.

Most modern assessments discredit the Spanish imperial enterprise in the Americas by labeling it a protracted atrocity, marked by contempt for the indigenous peoples and the harsh subjugation of their folkways. While there is no denying the Spaniards' insolence and inhumanity, the success and efficiency of their wholesale thuggery must be noted. Indeed, it was a perverse marvel of heartless conquest and systematic suppression. The Spanish strategy was not to settle the land and drive the natives from it but to control their New World provinces, rather as the Romans had done in creating their empire, and harness the captive peoples to do all the heavy lifting in the newly configured society. The Spaniards came in daringly small numbers, armies of just hundreds, floating across the waves in craft larger than the wide-eyed natives had ever seen, coming ashore like white demigods, sheathed in glittering armor and brandishing fine blades of tempered steel, a weapon that the natives had never encountered or felt, and astride snorting horses, creatures the natives had likewise never beheld.

The early Spanish finds of gold and silver in Mexico and the Peruvian highlands stirred dizzying visions of bottomless treasure. Those who crossed the ocean to get it were neither religious dissenters nor cultural misfits; neither were they the cream of Castile. Most, rather, were the disinherited second and third sons of the nobility, wastrels and idlers in need of a pastime, nothing-to-lose daredevils, and killers for hire—collectively dignified as "soldiers of fortune," whose unbridled conduct escaped the scrutiny of their strict elders back home. Their accompaniment to the New World by a sizable cadre from the priesthood, hungry for converts, has not seemed to soften history's judgment that, like the Crusaders of yore, the *conquistadores* made a mockery of the Christian precepts they vowed to impart to the natives. Whether because of or despite their unscrupulous behavior, it is remarkable that so few full-blooded Spaniards—there were probably never more than 200,000 of them even at the peak of their 300-year colonial dominion—managed to gain sway over more than 2 million square miles of the Americas, some twenty times the size of Spain.

It was as much a triumph of methodology as malevolence. Their means of conquest were essentially two: a totalitarian regime with a single official ethos (one language, one religion, one ruler) and a frank acceptance (if not active encouragement) of racial mingling. The Indians were declared wards of the Spanish state, their activities placed under the strictures of layered civil, military, and clerical authorities. This monolithic imperial system, following directives from Madrid, was overseen from Mexico City, the New World's metropolis, with its broad boulevards, elaborate architecture, and a university that was thriving long before the first English settlers reached the American shore. Army presidios and Catholic missions were installed in each province, from what is now Pensacola, Florida, to Santa Fe, New Mexico, at the northern end of New Spain to as far south as Río de la Plata, three-quarters of the way down the South American continent. Those among the aborigines ungrateful enough to reject the benefits of Western civilization or to refuse the Cross were at dire risk of being dispatched to their pagan purgatory by sword or flame. Submission, under the circumstances, was widespread.

So, too, was intermarriage. Since only one in ten of the Spaniards who came to Mexico and its vicinity was female and official imperial policy discouraged residents of Spain from abandoning their homeland to populate the overseas colony, the lusty *conquistadores* had little option but to cohabit with the Indian natives, who could ill resist being sexually abused en masse. The result was a new breed, the *mestizos,* who in time became the core of the emergent Mexican people within a rigid social hierarchy. At its apex was the narrow, pure-blooded (or mostly so) Spanish *hidalgo* aristocracy to whom the home government and its far-reaching bureaucratic arm parceled substantial grants of countryside under an unmistakably feudal arrangement. This ruling class, more devoted to status and the pleasures of their baronial *hacienda* lifestyle than cultivation of their holdings or other forms of gainful employment, largely delegated the daily business of empire to the *mestizo* population and imposed a close approximation of slavery on the Indians and the growing influx of African blacks laboring in fields, mines, and household service.

For a century and a half, the Spanish hegemony in the New World was not seriously challenged, except for occasional outbursts of Indian discontent, mostly in the outlying provinces. The flow of mineral treasure back to Spain greatly enriched the kingdom, whose gold coinage became the prized standard for Europe's commerce and much of the world beyond, and allowed the nation to field a large army, much of it composed of foreign hirelings. Yet for all the glitter and swagger, the Spanish empire was a stucco castle built on sand.

Based on brute force and the windfall wealth torn from the Mexican and Peruvian earth, the Spanish exploitation of the New World had a corrosive effect on the social fiber of Spain itself. The country feasted on its imperial success, grew vaingloriously self-indulgent, and spent most of its purloined riches on private luxury and a wasteful war machine instead of investing in economic growth and civic improvements. As a result, Spain failed to produce enough food and goods to fill its domestic needs because it could afford—for quite a while—to import them from elsewhere. Worse still, it fell under delusions of racial superiority and, with the arrival of the Protestant Reformation, adopted a religious orthodoxy that shaded into fanaticism unmatched in the rest of Christendom. An intolerance of foreigners served to shut off the economic system from the stimulus of non-Spanish traders and craftsmen. New ideas and unconventional thinking were branded as heresy, sinking the intellectual community into darkness impenetrable by the philosophical and scientific Enlightenment blazing across much of the rest of Europe. With little merchandise of its own creation to offer for sale or barter, Spain began to suffer from a ruinous inflation and imbalance of trade brought on by indolence and improvidence. Thus, by the early seventeenth century, when the flow of bullion back to Spain slowed to a trickle, the country turned into a chronic fiscal invalid for having been spendthrift for so long. Yet Spain would remain a formidable, if fading, global power for the better part of two more centuries, blindly defiant of the reality that its season in the sun had been squandered by vanity, xenophobia, and a dogma-driven incuriosity about whatever it did not fathom. Only an occasional display of martial derring-do would remind the world of Spain's faded glory.

It was along the northern sector of New Spain's distended frontier that the empire's vulnerability became most apparent. Because the early Spanish expeditions crisscrossing the southern regions of the future United States failed to uncover mineral treasure, the empire exerted only minimal effort to garrison that portion of its claimed New World dominion. Isolated presidios, missions, and trading posts had little contact with and marginal impact on the Indians, and aside from early, abortive attempts to introduce ranching in Texas, there was scant commercial activity to lure settlers from Mexico or Spain to the fringes of empire. Only after French explorers and traders encroached on New Spain's northern extremities in the latter part of the seventeenth century by navigating the full length of the Mississippi River did the Spaniards bestir themselves. The French drove a sharp wedge

into their territorial monopoly along the Gulf of Mexico littoral and succeeded, as Spanish sailing captains had not, in probing the Mississippi's
muddy, weed-thick, weblike delta to find the cleanest route to the Gulf and
the world beyond. France's founding of New Orleans, which served as the
natural downriver depot for the surplus produce of the American interior,
was an added throbbing irritant to the Spaniards. French enterprise undermined Spain's hold on the region, and even though Madrid ordered the bol-
stering of its empire's military posts along the Gulf and in east Texas in
order to discourage further French penetration, it was too late to reverse the
pattern.

Had they not terrorized the native peoples and reduced them to a permanently degraded caste, the Spaniards might have used them to help fend off
their approaching rivals. And had they been less bent on imposing conformity and allowed private enterprise some breathing room, their empire
might not have atrophied into a series of decrepit dependencies. By 1750
Spain had receded to a distant last place in potency among Europe's three
leading powers with imperial holdings in the Americas.

FRANCE, COMING TO THE NEW WORLD later than Spain, made a more
gradual and less spectacular appearance and chose not to throttle the natives
in order to make its presence felt. French ambitions were commercial, not
territorial or political, and France's quest was primarily for trading zones
and partners with whom it hoped to make exclusive arrangements.

Deferring to the Spanish presence in the sunnier climes of North America, the French reconnoitered the upper part of the continent, starting in the
1530s, and worked their way from the teeming coastal fishing waters off
Newfoundland up the St. Lawrence and Ottawa river valleys and eventually
into the Great Lakes basin, heart of the Indians' fur-trapping paradise. To
better harvest beaver and other pelts for plump profits in Europe, France
tutored its New World adventurers to embrace the natives, whose mastery of
wilderness living they did well to emulate. Soon French woodsmen became
adept at navigating the pristine streams in light but sturdy birch-bark canoes
and moving through the snow-carpeted forests in wide shoes of Indian
design. Instead of disparaging Indian folkways and spiritual beliefs as the
Spaniards often did, the French tried to understand them, learned their languages, offered them well-made goods of practical value from their own
civilization—metal implements for hunting, cooking, and sewing, and wool
for clothing warmer and more comfortable than animal hides—and bargained with them more or less fairly. In propagating their own mores and

morals along with the blessings of Christianity, the French trod lightly and rarely insisted that theirs was the sole path to salvation.

As a result, the Indians came to trust the French more than the other white men from Europe who seemed bent on taking away their lands, their customs, their dignity, and, to be plain about it, their lives. The bearded Frenchmen asked only to dwell alongside the Indians on the edges of their domain, in small farm communities to sustain their colony, and to conduct business with the tribes. In time they succeeded in enlisting the natives as scouts and warriors against the British frontiersmen to the east and south. To help seal the transcultural bond, the French regularly plied the natives with gifts as a gesture of respect toward the host peoples—precisely the opposite of the Spanish approach. By the opening years of the seventeenth century, as English settlers gingerly approached North America, a thousand French ships a year were trading along its northern coast and in its river valleys, French fishermen trolled the rich ocean banks nearby, and Samuel Champlain had founded a trading post on the St. Lawrence at Quebec, the largest in a chain extending upriver deep into the wooded heartland of the north country.

But the French, like the Spanish in this regard, were not eager to encourage their people, even Protestant dissidents whom France avidly persecuted, to resettle in the New World. Theirs was a highly calculated imperial policy, seeking maximum influence and the highest profitability at the lowest possible cost in money, matériel, and lives. And, like Spain, France adopted feudal methods in making highly conditional land grants to *seigneurs* favored by the Bourbon court. These often absentee landlords enlisted a rentier class of imported Frenchmen and *habitants* of mixed French and Indian blood—many of whom were closer to serfs than freeholders—to tenant-farm the narrow valleys without manifesting an appetite for territorial aggrandizement. It was a mostly benign arrangement between two very different cultures sharing a single ecosystem and cooperating commercially. That the French connection was subtly but inevitably eroding the native culture and seducing it into a dependent relationship did not become apparent for several generations. The French imperial scheme, while avoiding the bloodshed and ill will that deeply scarred the Spaniards' New World presence, shared with theirs an admirably efficient use of emigrant manpower. At the close of the seventeenth century, the number of French officials, traders, trappers, farmers, soldiers, and priests in the New World probably did not exceed 15,000, a fraction of the Spanish presence; France had not come as a blatant conquerer or looter.

By then, nonetheless, nervy New France was claiming its broadest boundaries in North America, a reflection of the expansive statism of Louis XIV, the nation's power-driven ruler. In the spring of 1682, in the wake of the harrowing journeys by the trapper and trader Louis Jolliet and the priest Jacques Marquette, who had found a route linking (with the help of short canoe portages) the Great Lakes and the Mississippi, Robert Cavelier, Sieur de La Salle, became the first European to travel the mighty heartland river's course all the way to the Gulf of Mexico. La Salle grandly claimed the entire Mississippi basin and all adjacent lands drained by its tributaries (among them the beautiful Ohio and churning, red-silted Missouri) for his monarch and named the core of the continent in his honor—Louisiana. It was a confrontational event, placing in dispute territorial rights that Spain had long before declared but done little to reinforce.

This gross French impertinence also constituted a direct challenge to claims made by British mariners and royal charter grants to English landlords and settlement companies that had blithely set the western boundaries of their Atlantic seaboard colonies at the next seashore, wherever that might be. All such claims were, essentially, no more than expressions of national and dynastic hubris. Without fighting forces to transform proprietary claims on paper to possession on the ground—and without settlements to validate and safeguard that ownership—grand declarations of sovereignty over immense stretches of wilderness were literally groundless. Beyond the stretch of British coastal settlements, extending at most 200 miles inland to the Appalachian ridgeline, the American interior at the dawn of the eighteenth century belonged to no European nation, though to varying extents three contenders claimed it. The natives sensed now that their best and perhaps only hope for survival was to play off the oncoming white settlers, pitting each nationality against the others. If one prevailed, the Indians' doom was sealed.

In the looming encounter for North American dominance, the French were not unjustified in believing that, despite their small numbers, they held a strategic advantage over their two rivals. On the strength of their title claims to the principal waterways of the eastern half of the continent, they had built, or were in the process of establishing, enough forts and trading posts to lend credibility to their boast. Taken at face value, New France extended from Hudson Bay to the mouth of the Mississippi and from the western portion of Pennsylvania, Virginia, the Carolinas, and Georgia to the farthest reaches of the Missouri across the Great Plains. For a while, mindful of the great distances involved and the scarcity of European people within this immense region, the Old World monarchs were in no hurry to resolve the jurisdictional dispute. The British did not build their first fort on the Great Lakes until 1722, by which time the French were turning New Orleans into a going operation, with settlers streaming in from France, Canada, and the West Indies. Before long the newcomers headed upriver to establish a fort at Natchez, about 150 miles above the delta, and opening inland trade routes with the Indians along the Alabama River and other southern waterways. Other Frenchmen, mostly hunters and farmers, were fanning out between the Great Lakes and the Ohio River—the western portion of which they called the Illinois Country, or Upper Louisiana—and in that virgin soil planted crops that they soon began shipping down the Mississippi to sustain their countrymen along its banks. The flow of cargoes trafficking both ways over the great inland waterway between Quebec and New Orleans grew steadily—furs, fish, and timber from the northlands and, in time, tobacco, sugar, and rice from the southern tier, where French-run plantations were taking root.

To impose a semblance of social order and restraint on this vast territory, France, like Spain, established a field operation with clear lines of command issuing from a central point to the widely dispersed imperial outposts. A superior council under the royal governor of New France, consisting of Canada above the Great Lakes and the Louisiana territory, acted as the chief administrative agency, with civil authority in the hands of the intendant for each region and the bishop of Quebec charged with winning Indian converts and discouraging debauchery and chicanery, constant menaces in that wilderness setting. The extensive trading network was placed under close bureaucratic vigil in the form of licenses, fees, and rules governing transactions, to protect the Indians from being swindled and to ensure the royal French treasury a hefty cut of the proceeds. The net effect of these exertions made France a formidable claimant to dominion over the North American interior, applying steady pressure against the territorial ambitions of the Spaniards to the south and British settlers to the east.

For all the acumen and energy that infused it, the French program in North America suffered a critical shortcoming. There were simply not enough Frenchmen both willing and encouraged by the state to emigrate in order to carry out so ambitious a design. Like Spain, France would not allow religious dissenters and other malcontents to take refuge in the wilds of a new world, where their conduct might readily become uncontrollable and perhaps present an incendiary example for restless compatriots back home. But the Spaniards, abusive as they were toward the Indians, saw no alternative to mass interbreeding with them. The French, not above racial mixing, as the emergence of the métis demonstrated in Canada, preferred a more removed, albeit congenial, link to the aborigines. With access to and from

New France tightly controlled and the rewards of frontier commerce strictly policed, Frenchmen were not exactly queuing up to endure the risks and discomforts of raw wilderness life. By the time the British drove their government's official presence from the continent, the number of Frenchmen in North America probably did not exceed 75,000.

Behind the ultimate collapse of France's imperial designs on America was another problem that would eventually bring down the whole *ancien régime* before the end of the eighteenth century. Quite simply, Frenchmen who could most afford to pay taxes steadfastly refused to. The nobility had long thought it degrading to be taxed. The French clergy regarded the very concept as a profaning intrusion by man's realm into God's. And the rising bourgeoisie devised countless ways, cronyism and bribery prominent among them, to avoid the crown's dunning collectors and rationalized their evasion by the far from groundless argument that since they had no effective voice in shaping or approving the policies of the king's absolutist rule, they had no obligation to pay his bills. So the peasantry, as powerless as it was numerous, bore a disproportionate share of the cost to run the French state.

What exacerbated the resulting financial strain on the crown treasury was that, unlike Spain's monarchy, French kings from Louis XIV on were not only spending lavishly on themselves but also busily reforming and expanding the role of the state. They were building roads and bridges, improving the postal service, upgrading the judicial system and gendarmerie, fielding the largest army in Europe, and trying to assemble a navy and mercantile fleet to rival the Spanish, British, and Dutch presence at sea. But neither the Sun King nor his less scintillating successors had the determination to effect genuine tax reform, even when more equitably formulated. The failing traced in large measure to the crown's refusal—in contrast to the British monarchy's willingness—to yield to the growing clamor by the aristocracy, commercial class, and yeomanry to be respectfully heard about how their country should be run. So long as the French king insisted that the state was his private fiefdom to rule as he chose, his subjects—at least the ones in a position to—argued that paying for it was his personal problem, not theirs.

Thus, France's imperial effort in North America was underfunded, even though the crown was skimming a sizable share of the trade revenues generated by New France in order to swell the royal treasury. Such a policy, reducing incentives for the venturesome French in Canada and Louisiana, prevented the seeds so carefully planted along the St. Lawrence and Mississippi valleys from ever germinating fully. Still, by 1750 France exercised a strong enough commercial and military presence to sustain a formidable enterprise in America, even if it was more scaffolding than structure.

·   ·   ·

FIVE YEARS AFTER COLUMBUS'S first voyage under the flag of Spain, the British king, Henry VII, grasping the immense implications of the discovery, enlisted another Italian-born mariner to undertake a similar expedition to win England its own stake in the New World. John Cabot's route took him far north of the Spanish zone of exploration, to colder, bleaker shores. He touched the North American mainland at Cape Breton Island on the northeastern tip of Nova Scotia and dutifully claimed it for the British king, along with all the other lands he glimpsed as he sailed south for a time, holding close to the coast before turning back for his adopted home.

This fleeting contact became the basis for all of Britain's future claims in the Western Hemisphere. Like Columbus, Cabot embarked on a follow-up voyage the next year, but his expedition was never heard from again—and for the better part of a century, while Spain was growing rich and fat on its New World exploits, Britain failed to sponsor further serious exploratory efforts or an attempt at American settlement. Its principal, unofficially sanctioned form of maritime enterprise was the bedevilment of Spanish shipping by English sea hellions, of whom Francis Drake and John Hawkins were the chief perpetrators, seizing treasure and torching Spanish vessels and ports in both hemispheres.

Gratifying as these exercises in swashbuckling vandalism may have been to Queen Elizabeth I (and infuriating to the Spanish king, Philip II), they did not advance any British imperial longings. Not until 1583 was the first tiny English settlement planted in North America—in Newfoundland by Humphrey Gilbert, who, in reinforcement of Cabot's earlier, wishful claim, made one of his own that was still more expansive. All lands adjacent to this tiny new perch on the easternmost edge of the continent, Gilbert declared, for as far as they might extend and not in the actual possession of a Christian monarch, were now part of the rightful dominion of the British crown. But what did "possession" mean? Spain, after all, claimed to "possess" rights to the entire Western Hemisphere based on its papal license of 1493. Without settlers, military force, and a sustained commercial presence to support it, Gilbert's gesture had the same practical effect as a flea spitting into a hurricane. The following year, however, Elizabeth was presented with a document that caught the attention of the British court and the realm's burgeoning mercantile community.

Since his childhood in the west of England, Richard Hakluyt had been entranced by the voyages of discovery—the great global drama of his age—and he set out, while a student at Oxford, to steep himself in all the stunning new knowledge of world geography. Trained as an ordained clergyman and armed with a reading knowledge of six languages, Hakluyt scoured every map, diary, ship's log, and any other documents he could find that dealt with the thrilling overseas explorations. In the process he gained the acquaintance of a leading royal courtier and fellow sailing enthusiast, Walter Raleigh, who had been his contemporary at Oxford, and of other prominent naval officers—connections that helped Hakluyt win assignment as chaplain to the British ambassador to France. There he gathered fresh revelatory material by and about the bold explorers, none of them British subjects. The result was the first classic work of travel literature in English, *Divers Voyages Touching the Discovery of America,* issued in 1583.

The greater his knowledge, the more urgently Hakluyt sensed the need for Britain to challenge the Spanish hegemony in the New World, and in Raleigh he found a like-minded advocate. By then a court favorite shortly to be named captain of the queen's guard, Raleigh urged Hakluyt to set down in writing a reasoned argument for the crown's energetic patronage of American colonization. In 1584, at the age of thirty-two, Hakluyt delivered his memorandum, *Discourse on Western Planting,* laying before his sovereign some twenty arguments in favor of what would likely prove a costly business. It was a prescient document.

As a cleric, Hakluyt naturally enough recommended the colonial undertaking to "inlarge the glory of the gospel and plante sincere religion" among the heathen natives. A less spiritual motive was to "halt the Spanish from . . . flowing all over the face of America," to which Britain arguably had as much claim as the Catholic kingdom, and thereby "abate the pride of Spain and put King Philip down." Allowing her "sea dogs," Drake and others like him, to snap at the Spaniards' heels and then knighting them for their efforts was no substitute for colonization. Here was an obvious appeal to Elizabeth's long-standing antipathy toward Philip, a devout Catholic and patron of the Inquisition, who had been married to Elizabeth's frail half-sister, Queen Mary I. A Catholic out of devotion to her mother, Catherine of Aragon, Henry VIII's discarded wife, Mary had joined Philip in reestablishing Catholicism as Britain's state religion, and, but for Parliament's resistance, the Spanish king would have ascended the British throne and further solidified his power as Europe's leading monarch. The history of the New World might have been radically different if Mary had not died in 1558 at forty-two and her twenty-five-year-old half-sister Elizabeth, a deeply committed Anglican, taken the throne. No fancier of Philip, who was the very model of a benighted despot, she refused his marriage offer and became his avid adversary over much of her forty-five-year reign by opposing Catholicism in general and Spanish interests in particular.

But Hakluyt's instructive paper did not limit itself to emotional catharsis. The real burden of his message was to stress the practical advantages of a royal initiative to colonize America. Rather than just plundering the precious minerals of the New World, Britain could harvest its agricultural bounty and ship it home for both domestic use and sale of the surplus on the world market, thus reducing the kingdom's expenditure for needed commodities and improving its balance of trade. Britain's manufactured goods might also, in time, find a growing market among the native peoples in America, who would welcome such wares as they became more civilized through increasing contact with the British colonists.

To achieve these goals, Hakluyt urged the creation of a network of forts, trading posts, and missions, a hybrid of the Spanish and what would later become the French model of empire-building. But he had a more ambitious design in mind. To people the crown's representation in the New World, he favored the enlistment of the unhappiest among Elizabeth's subjects—the growing masses of displaced farmers and urban poor, soldiers mustered out of service and left without other work, debtors, petty criminals, religious dissenters, and separatists—who were clearly available and highly dispensable (given the risks of the venture). As important fringe benefits, the colonizing process might well lead to the discovery of a westward and, presumably, shorter passage to China, with its potential for highly lucrative two-way commerce, and greatly improve the seafaring skills of the kingdom—no small matter for an island nation.

Hakluyt's otherwise farseeing imperial design failed to raise only one eventuality that would pay the nation a rich dividend. He had erred in predicting that the American natives would, over time, become significant consumers of British manufactured goods. It would prove to be the British colonists themselves who, increasing much faster and sooner than anyone could have foreseen, would became a valuable—and captive—export market for London's merchants.

So persuasive was Hakluyt's reasoning that Walter Raleigh, as if to demonstrate to his sovereign the wisdom of such a colonizing initiative, organized and helped fund a private expeditionary settlement on Roanoke Island off the coast of North Carolina. After three struggling years, the colony was found without survivors or their remains—a never-solved mystery that pointed up the perils of exposure to a wilderness an ocean away from home. A much larger, crown-sponsored undertaking seemed the wiser alternative. Yet Elizabeth would never lend her financial backing to such an effort. She was no longer young or eager to challenge Spain's grip on the New World, especially at a time when King Philip, vexed by the queen's hectoring anti-Catholic policies, was known to be contemplating a vengeful blow against—in fact, a full-scale invasion of—England itself. Britain's naval forces were growing, but Spain's power on land and sea remained formidable. Saving Albion from the clutches of an intolerant (and intolerable) would-be conqueror was of far greater urgency to the queen than colonizing America. And so the most glorious moment of her reign was Britain's routing of Philip's so-called invincible armada of 130 ships, carrying 20,000 soldiers, intent on reducing England to a vassal state. Afterward, Spain would never regain its standing at the apex of the European powers. But still, over her last fifteen years on the throne, Elizabeth did not order any royally subsidized colonization of the New World. Nor would any of her successors; they did not need to. The task would be taken up instead by a new breed of Englishmen, venture capitalists from the fast-rising commercial class, which hardly existed in Catholic Europe.

The Reformation, unfolding as Spain was living off its riches from the New World, had a liberating effect not only on the minds and hearts of the laity by denying the tyranny of delivered truth but also on the commercial spirit and practical affairs of the secular world. In celebrating the sanctity of the individual soul, the Protestant sects held that all human beings were equal in the eyes of God—a radical rebuke to the entrenched social system grounded in hereditary privilege. Everyone, moreover, was capable of addressing his or her prayers directly to the Almighty, without need of priestly intercession, and salvation could be won by good works as well as purity of faith and moral deportment. The Protestant offshoots of Calvinsim and Puritanism in particular enshrined industriousness and thrift as high virtues, and the acquisition of wealth through earnest labor was taken for a sign of indwelling grace. A new spirit of individualism began to awaken, and with it possibilities of a better material life for those bold enough to chance them. New ways of thinking and behaving, inherently antiauthoritarian, surfaced in everyday life, relieving its drudgery and making work more productive. New ways of farming raised crop yields and nutrition levels. Improved techniques for mining metals, casting them, and making stronger and more precise tools helped develop more efficient machines and methods for spinning, building homes and ships and port facilities, and practicing medicine. Printing with movable type was a powerful purveyor of fresh ideas that aroused questing scholars and curious laymen. Together, these epochal advances fostered the growth of a more assertive class of merchants, manufacturers, bankers, speculators, artisans, mechanics, and shopkeepers. As a result, new wealth was generated, especially in England, Holland, and northern Germany, and those with accumulating capital sought out new ventures and markets. For England, the rising maritime power, America now beckoned, and investors in London, Southampton, and Bristol were prepared to finance sizable settlement enterprises with a realistic prospect of survival and profitability.

Would-be colonizers would have to endure the months-long, gutwrenching ocean crossing and the rigors of life in a wilderness. Surely those comfortable in English society were not about to risk their necks in such an ordeal and for dubious gains. Willing bodies, though, were available as a result of profound changes in England's social structure, and willing minds were enlisted in response to schismatic strife within England's Protestant movement. Both the landed nobility and the untitled farmer squirearchy found themselves newly powerful after Henry VIII had seized and sold off to them and to favored mercantile interests the Roman Church's vast property holdings, which had comprised perhaps a quarter of the arable land in the realm. Henry used the revenue to improve the royal navy, homeland fortifications, and governmental services. The manorial class, never afraid to get its boots dirty (in contrast to the languorous landed aristocracy in much of the rest of Europe) and glad to try new farming techniques, at first enjoyed unprecedented growth as its crop surplus found markets abroad. But in time, the commodities market grew glutted, wage demands by hired hands and other costs rose, and landlords leasing their fields could not materially increase rents long fixed by custom. The old feudal requirement for the nobility to come to the king's aid by providing soldiers—usually in the person of villeins who farmed their estates—was vanishing as the crown, with the help now of a larger tax base from the growth of commercial enterprise, could afford to hire professional soldiers to fight its wars. England could get by with fewer farms and far fewer farmers, as landholders calculated they would better prosper by converting cropland to pastureland. In the course of the seventeenth and eighteenth centuries, nearly half of England's arable land was converted to raising sheep, while exported English wool supplied Flemish looms and became an international staple.

All of these changes benefited the landed and mercantile classes but threw tens of thousands of English farmers off the land. Few of them had the means to buy their own farms, and, at any rate, landholders were rarely willing to part with their property. With nowhere else to turn, waves of displaced farm laborers crowded into the cities, their numbers far exceeding the jobs being created in the earliest stage of industrialization. Squalor, hunger, disease, and lawlessness turned rampant, and Elizabeth's new poor laws were unable to alleviate much of the misery. Nor, for that matter, was her relative tolerance of deviation from Anglican orthodoxy of much comfort to the victims of Parliament's laws dictating uniformity of religious belief and practice. Dissenters who accused the crown's established church of corruption and hypocrisy and called for simpler, purer forms of worship were denounced as cranks, traitors, and heretics, penalized and imprisoned, and finally threatened with exile by Parliament if they were found guilty of too noisy a dissent and failure to recant.

Early in the seventeenth century, a new law was framed allowing religious separatists to retain the full rights of Englishmen if they enlisted for the American colonization. Another far smaller but important category of new settlers was composed of poor-cousin aristocrats or the second and third sons of large landholders and merchants who, under the still prevailing feudal laws of inheritance, were unlikely ever to come into wealth. For them as well—actually, for them in particular, given their advantage of family connections—America held the promise of material well-being and status they could not have hoped to win at home. Whether a jobless Midlands father of a hungry brood, a redundant Berkshire yeoman seeking gainful farm work, a Puritan bootmaker reviled by his London neighbors, or the besotted fourth son of Lord and Lady Periwinkle in quest of respectability, scarcely any prospective settler in the new British America was short on motivation. Most had little to lose except, of course, their very lives—a distinct possibility, as Raleigh's ill-fated Roanoke colony had demonstrated.

With such financial and human resources accumulating at the outset of the seventeenth century and Spain's naval strength materially reduced, the British monarchy did not have to dig into its own pockets or employ its own military forces to participate in the colonization of the New World. Instead, the crown had the luxury now of simply licensing the settlement ventures that presented themselves for chartering—that is, employing surrogates willing, at their own expense, to bear the royal ensign to America and risk all in the hope of private gain, not just for the greater glory of the king. Devising ways to advance this enterprise, however, while retaining crown oversight and ultimate homeland control took several generations of trial and error.

IF THE LURE OF A NEW LIFE in the colonies was as plain as its risks, the latter nevertheless discouraged experiments in survival by intrepid individuals or even by small groups. Royal grants of territory were therefore reserved in the first instance for syndicates of substantial investors, usually from the landed and mercantile classes, and later for aristocrats, usually titled, who had the wherewithal to carry the costs of multiyear ventures involving large groups of colonists. The earliest crown charters authorized settlement activities within an immense swath of territory, often with trading monopolies included (in case there turned out to be something to trade for and somebody to trade with). These grants came with limited rights of self-government, a specified duration (to ensure the settlers' good behavior and fealty to the crown), and the requirement to pay the king 20 percent of any gold or other treasure discovered.

The early land settlement projects took two forms. One was the joint-stock company, rather like a modern corporation, in which each investor—sometimes referred to in the apt parlance of the day as an "adventurer"—was eligible for profits proportionate to his investment. Typically, these adventurers remained in England, where they were among the well-to-do and thus able to speculate that precious minerals, exotic foods and luxuries, and who knew what other wonders would be forthcoming, perhaps sooner rather than later. Such hopes would prove illusory in the case of Virginia, the first colony to be settled with this form of backing. In the nine years after its establishment in 1607 under a charter from James I, Elizabeth's nephew, some 1,650 people had come there, 1,000 or so died, and 300 had returned to England. Other than the early cultivation of tobacco, a hard plant to raise but promising in its commercial value, there was slim prospect of profits from the hard-pressed Jamestown colony. The other form of settlement, adopted a decade and a half after the founding of Virginia, was the voluntary communal association, a crown-authorized political corporation composed largely of the settlers themselves and concerned less with profits than with establishing a refuge on the virgin continent, where they might worship as they wished unharassed. These communal charters, granting collective rights to far more narrowly delimited tracts in New England and a considerable degree of self-rule, left the distribution of the land in the hands of the community elders, who parceled it out with an eye toward the wealth and eminence of the settling families but not, for the most part, in blatantly unfair portions.

The joint-stock ventures in the Chesapeake and Tidewater regions of Virginia were short-lived. The sources of adversity proved to be many—hunger, disease, dissension, absentee oversight, weather that turned both hotter and colder than in temperate England, and natives who grew bloodily irritable when provoked—and the numbers of settlers and the financial resources to sustain them too few. Before the second decade was out, three charters had lapsed or been canceled, and Virginia was designated England's first royal colony. The communal cooperatives of New England fared better, largely because they ran themselves and were not dependent on profit-minded patrons back in England. But even in the lonesome wilderness, the Puritans did not escape dissension over matters of faith. The more liberal-minded among them, pressing for tolerance toward all sects and fair play toward the native tribes, soon found themselves ostracized. The establishment of breakaway colonies in Connecticut and Rhode Island followed.

The early disappointments in the southerly regions suggested to the mercantile interests that they did not need a costly proprietary stake in the colonizing scheme. Profits might well eventuate from commerce and land sales, but first a more stable structure of ownership and management was required. The crown, accordingly, altered its licensing approach, as the beauty, fertility, and likely future prosperity of the lands along the Atlantic seaboard grew more evident. Large proprietary grants based on early, crude surveys were made to individual, usually titled, English aristocrats and courtiers, sometimes as a favor, other times to discharge an obligation, or perhaps frankly to get them (and their anti-Anglican sympathizers) out of England. A Catholic, Cecil Calvert, Lord Baltimore, was named proprietor of all of what is now Maryland, with remarkably wide latitude to conduct its affairs and subdivide its land to grantees of his choosing (if not obnoxious to the crown). Charles II handed his brother, James, Duke of York, a military man and a Catholic, an immense holding from the Connecticut River southwesterly to the Delaware. When British ships, at war with the Dutch, threatened their settlement at New Amsterdam, it meekly surrendered and was renamed New York, referring as well to the surrounding colony (including contiguous New Jersey), in honor of its royal proprietor. Soon after, a comparably large grant was made to William Penn, son of a British naval hero who had led the capture of Jamaica, the empire's most valuable Caribbean possession, and was owed £16,000 by the Duke of York. In discharging the crown's debt to Penn's family, the grant of more than 40 million acres, comprising most of modern-day Pennsylvania and all of Delaware, provided a sphere of influence for Penn, an ardent Quaker whose tracts and preaching on religious tolerance had earned him a stay in the Tower of London, and created a land of asylum for his sizable band of Friends.

Penn's property, which came, like Baltimore's, with sweeping, practically autocratic, administrative powers, was said to have made his dominion the largest on earth then held by a private individual (that is, not a sovereign ruler or a relative of one). Similarly empowering grants were given in joint proprietorship for the colony of Carolina, not yet subdivided into northern and southern segments, to a group of eight aristocrats, who, unlike Penn and Baltimore, were bent on feudally oppressive domination. New Jersey, separated from New York with its proprietor's approval, was divided with the eastern half given in shared ownership to a pair of titled British lords and the western half to a larger group of aristocrats close to the crown. Most of these proprietors hoped to profit by the gradual sell-off of their holdings to large-scale planters, settlement syndicates, and private land developers.

The most striking feature, in retrospect, of these gigantic baronial colonies, and still more so in royal Virginia and the crown-chartered private cooperative settlements of New England, was the extent of sovereign power delegated to the New World entities. Virginia set the model and, except for the New England colonies, was the closest polity in the New World to a democratic republic, even if run chiefly by and for its largest landholders and answerable for any gross insults to the crown, Parliament, and the English common law. Virginia's governor was, to be sure, the king's designated surrogate, but with the power to make land grants and appoint the colony's ranking officials. Both functions were subject to the approval of the governor's twelve-member executive council (also doubling as Virginia's high court), drawn mostly from the colony's biggest property holders and their relatives. Legislative power was vested in the House of Burgesses, as the colonial assembly was known, established in 1619 and freely chosen by the more substantial property owners of the colony. It was the first representative body in the European settlements of the Western Hemisphere. The governor retained the power to summon the burgesses into session and dismiss them at will and to veto their enactments. Yet he dared not use his prerogatives rashly because it was the assembly that held the exclusive power to levy taxes on the colonists and pay the salaries of the governor and all colonial officials including judges. This critical empowerment relieved the crown and Parliament of the need to subsidize the colonial governments and forced them, in tacit reciprocity for their home rule, to pay their own way. Tax collecting was the governor's job, carried out for him by the colonists; there were next to no crown officials or soldiers at large in the new land to enforce its laws.

Virginians, and those in other colonies who had governments more or less resembling theirs, came to think of their political system as the rough equivalent in miniature of British homeland rule. The royal governor corresponded more or less to the king and his ministers, the governor's council functioned like the House of Lords as a sounding board for the large propertied interests and a check on the governor's conduct, and the burgesses acted as a little House of Commons representing freeholders and the public at large, with control over taxes. As the population grew and county government evolved, local men—not crown appointees—were chosen to serve as sheriffs, justices of the peace, registrars, treasurers, and surveyors. The colonial system was a far cry, certainly, from truly representative democracy, except perhaps in New England, where the communal nature of the settlements and regular town meetings to address common concerns invited—indeed, nearly necessitated—wider civic participation than in the other colonies. The right to vote for assembly members and other officials was restricted everywhere to free white males who owned a fixed minimum of debt-free property—typically fifty acres, although the amount varied from colony to colony. This qualification, aimed at ensuring that political power would not be shared with the unpropertied masses who presumably did not have the same vested concerns as the landed class and therefore ought not to determine public policy, served to limit the franchise to between 10 and 20 percent of the adult population in most colonies. While this de facto minority rule seems harshly unfair now, it was substantially less restrictive in the American colonies than in the British home isles.

The crown's concession of functional home rule in the colonies—the polar opposite of the Spanish and the later French system—was grounded less on a liberality of spirit than on the practicalities involved. Not only was it cheaper for the crown to let the colonists run their own affairs so long as they paid for the privilege with their own tax money, but it was more prudent as well. It allowed the king's ministry to delegate administrative functions to those on the spot, familiar with problems and needs of a frontier existence, rather than to attempt to micromanage the colonial outposts at a distance of 3,000 miles and six to eight weeks' travel time from England. That this arrangement would feed a hunger for freedom of space, thought, and action among the settlers and strengthen their incentive to persevere unhindered by the long reach of royal authority did not concern many British officials during the first century of the American settlement. However much slack the colonies were given, they remained dependencies, creations of the crown for the betterment of the realm as a whole, and ultimately subordinate to the dictates of Parliament and the king. Whether Parliament could, if it chose, tax the colonists directly for the greater good of the nation, as it did Britons in the home isles, was not at issue for most of the colonial period; it was simply assumed but not resorted to. The home government, mindful that it was not being called on to provide military protection or almost any other services for the settlers, was content to let the colonial assemblies do all the taxing needed to keep their settlements operating. Britain's rewards would presumably materialize as commerce grew, but meanwhile the monarchy could engage in empire-building in America on a nearly cost-free basis.

Expediency, then, and not any grand imperial design, governed the colo-

nizing process that the crown was glad to license without trying to orches-
trate. The result was a patchwork creation, without an overall plan or vision,
centralized administration, or master set of restraining regulations and lockstep procedures of the Spanish sort. No two colonies had exactly the same
code of laws or governmental structure. In Massachusetts, the governor's
council was chosen not by the crown and governor together—the more
common practice—but by the colony's elected assembly. In Pennsylvania
the proprietors' (that is, the Penn family's) choice for governor had the
power to appoint all the colony's officials including judges, but the crown
retained the power to hear any judicial appeals by the colonists. And while
the Penns could formulate the laws and rules, they had to consult with the
elected assembly in doing so and submit all their statutes to London lest any
of them offend English customs and laws. But in keeping with the crown's
relaxed standards of supervision, Pennsylvania could dawdle for up to five
years before having to submit the statutory language to royal review, and if
not voided by the ministry within six months, it became the enduring law of
the colony. Maryland, by contrast, did not have to submit its laws to London
at all, while Massachusetts had three years to do so. Virginia, a paradise for
those with baronial aspirations, had no limitation on the size of any individual property owner's holdings, while Georgia, created to benefit the indi-
gent, had a restriction of 500 acres per family. In South Carolina, a man had
to own at least 500 acres to be elected to the colonial assembly—five to ten
times more than required in most colonies. And so the variations went.

Further evidence of the haphazard patterning of British colonial America was the idiosyncratic way that boundaries were projected as new
colonies were chartered and their territory defined. Their lines and reference
points were sometimes vague or ambiguous—often unavoidably so, given
the difficult logistics of surveying in the wilderness—and occasionally
overlapping or conflicting, due in part to bureaucratic carelessness and in
part to the fickle preferences of the crown, which could take away what it
had bestowed earlier. The result was wide confusion.

The most telling example was the first colony to be chartered, Virginia,
which would remain, even after its boundaries were repeatedly redefined,
the largest of the thirteen American colonies. Virginia's first charter in 1606
did not indicate how far inland its northern and southern borders extended;
only its coastal length was given. But its second charter three years later
defined Virginia's boundaries this way: "Land 200 miles north and south of
Point Comfort [on the western shore of the southern entry to Chesapeake
Bay], lying from the seacoast up into the land from sea to sea, west and
northwest."

But what did that mean? Were the 200 miles to run due north and south from Point Comfort or were they to be calculated by tracing the coastline that far in both directions? It was the former, presumably, because the jaggedly irregular Atlantic coastline in the Tidewater/Chesapeake region, with its countless bays and inlets, would have made the calculation dauntingly—and pointlessly—complex. But a line drawn 200 miles due north of Point Comfort ended well inland and one due south loomed up far out in the Atlantic Ocean. Apparently, then, the easterly terminal points of Virginia's east-west boundary lines, which fell approximately on the thirty-fifth and fortieth parallels, were to run west from the seacoast, where they would follow a course "up into the land from sea to sea, west and northwest." But how could the lines run both west and northwest at the same time? And how far west before turning northwest? More logically, the charter probably intended to say the northern and southern borders were to run "west and northwest respectively"—or was it supposed to be the other way around? Examination of a map strongly suggests that the 1609 charter must have intended the southern border of Virginia to run due west, because otherwise it would never have reached the "sea," that is, the Pacific Ocean; if the southern border had been the one intended to run northwest, presumably at a 45-degree angle from the Atlantic coast, it would have severely truncated the colony, not expanded it as was evidently intended. So authorities in the seventeenth century understood that Virginia's ambiguous charter meant that the northern border would run northwest at a 45-degree angle, which would have included a healthy chunk of western Pennsylvania (chartered seventy-two years later) before striking Lake Erie, the closest thing to a sea it would encounter for another 4,000 miles. The Great Lakes were thus taken to be Virginia's northwestern boundary.

Subsequent grants, like the one to Lord Baltimore in 1632, carving Maryland out of the northern sector of Virginia, reduced the immense bulk of the older colony's charter grant, which conflicted (as noted above) with the still later proprietary grant to Penn, which, in turn, took a slice off the northern border of Maryland. In such boundary disputes, the colonies naturally disagreed about which grants took precedence, each invoking the grant or charter that favored it. Virginia and Pennsylvania were long at odds over the extent of the latter's western border. Connecticut's earlier sea-to-sea grant was superimposed upon by the grant creating the Duke of York's colony, and what was to be made of the grant provisions that theoretically extended the colliding western boundaries of New York, Virginia, and Connecticut, as well as the Carolinas', to the next "sea" they came to?

Such territorial squabbles, along with political, commercial, cultural, religious, and ethnic rivalries and jealousies, abounded among the colonies.

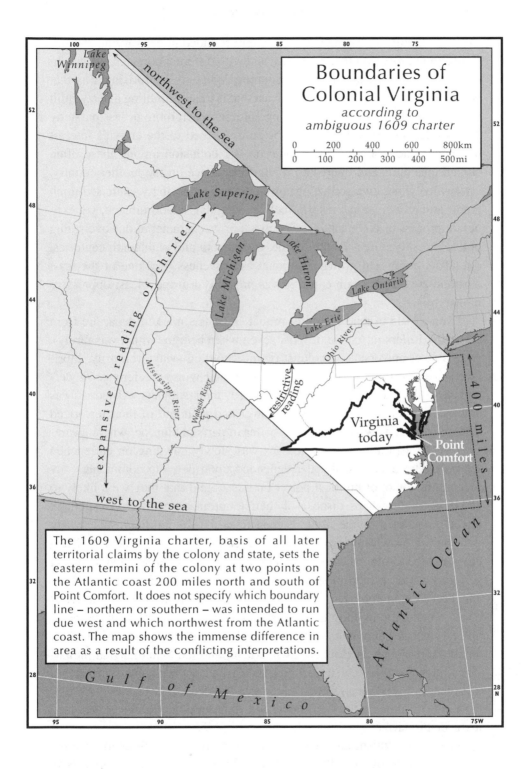

Boundaries of Colonial Virginia
according to ambiguous 1609 charter

Lake Winnipeg

northwest to the sea

Lake Superior

Lake Michigan

Lake Huron

Lake Ontario

Lake Erie

Ohio River

Mississippi River

Wabash River

expansive reading of charter

west to the sea

restrictive reading

Virginia today

Point Comfort

400 miles

Atlantic Ocean

Gulf of Mexico

The 1609 Virginia charter, basis of all later territorial claims by the colony and state, sets the eastern termini of the colony at two points on the Atlantic coast 200 miles north and south of Point Comfort. It does not specify which boundary line – northern or southern – was intended to run due west and which northwest from the Atlantic coast. The map shows the immense difference in area as a result of the conflicting interpretations.

This was hardly surprising since they were founded under varying circumstances and evolved at their own pace and with different climates, geographical configurations, and human resources. What was surprising was that Britain did not seem to mind in the least that it was assembling a crazy-quilt empire in America of nonconforming colonies, each more or less pursuing its own destiny. This diversity, to be sure, worked to the crown's interest because it encouraged neither cohesion nor collusion among these often contentious units and invited a primal dependence on the mother country, always the generative source of power (however sparingly exercised upon them) and arbiter of last resort. Such an irregular, uncoordinated, yet exuberant process of colonization owed much of its character to one overriding political reality: Great Britain in the seventeenth and eighteenth centuries, for all its pomp and growing national assertiveness, had one of the least despotic governments on earth. It was probably Europe's least oppressive monarchy.

Even a little official liberality in that era was a marked departure from the norm. Rulers in Asia and Africa, even when benign (which was rarely), were almost universally absolutist tyrants, holding sway arbitrarily, capriciously, and often barbarously. They governed without reference or deference to the multitudes they commanded; their subjects existed, it was understood, mainly to enhance the power and grandeur of their terrorized states. Conditions were marginally better in parts of Europe, where awareness of the aspirations of the masses was slowly dawning on entrenched regimes. The fixed social order depended upon denying commoners any meaningful share of political power on the ground that they were likely to abuse it—and perhaps dispose of their longtime tormentors. Despotism, under proclaimed divine right, reigned from the Iberian Peninsula, where the Spanish crown imposed a deadening conformity on the land, to Muscovy and the Urals, where the autocracy of the tsars perpetuated an abject serfdom while an inert bureaucracy lay mired in lethargy and corruption. The French monarchy, awakening to the concerns of the rising commercial class, remained unwilling to share power with it, let alone with the peasantry, which it continued—perhaps a bit less avidly now—to grind. Only small nations such as Holland, Switzerland, and the Scandinavian monarchies, along with a few Italian city-states, had governments with even a semblance of republican form.

England, though, was different, and its American colonists benefited disproportionately.

Feudal absolutism had begun to recede early in the thirteenth century, when the barons of the realm forced King John to curb his more oppressive practices against them. To be sure, the barons themselves were scarcely less oppressive toward their vassals and villeins, but the mitigation of despotism in the Magna Carta was understood to extend at least a few basic human rights and liberties, including trial by jury and habeas corpus, throughout the realm. The glacial evolution of a representative parliament as a check against royal and baronial tyranny was advanced, philosophically at least, by the Reformation's radical insistence that all souls were equal in the eyes of God. But few magistrates were prepared to extend that beatific premise by holding that all subjects ought to be similarly regarded as equals in the eyes of the state. The landless masses remained voiceless in the political process and prey to abuse and neglect.

Not until the seventeenth century, corresponding with England's colonial outreach to the New World, was there a tidal shift away from the reign of unchecked royal power and toward the supremacy of Parliament. The consent of the governed as a guiding precept of the state slowly but steadily gained favor as the gloom-ridden tenets of Thomas Hobbes, who viewed mankind as irredeemably brutish and best ruled by the lash, were countered by the far more sanguine credo of John Locke. Writing toward the end of the century, Locke asserted that all men were born free, equal, and happy, each of them a tabula rasa capable of wide learning and noble works, with a natural right to enjoy his "life, health, liberty, and possessions." The Lockean state existed to improve the welfare of its people, not the other way around. This concept, a direct rebuke to the folk culture of submission to hereditary privilege and the impenetrable mysteries of God, began to filter through the consciousness of a growing body of Englishmen who were now as resentful of corrupt secular authority as they had been of an intolerant, bullying, and extortionate religious establishment based in Rome.

These ideas resonated with particular force among Puritans, Quakers, Baptists, and other dissenters and those driven to the margins of society. From their ranks were drawn many who made their way to Britain's settlements in America over the course of the seventeenth century, and neither their numbers nor their convictions receded. This is not to say that the first century of settlers in America consisted of outspoken ideologues, conversant with Lockean political philosophy. Many, though, were driven by deep-seated grievances and receptive to teachings that addressed them, and it helped that almost half the men and a quarter of the women among the colonists were literate; in New England the figures were 85 percent for men and half of the women—far above the literacy rate in their mother country.

IF BRITAIN'S RELAXED OVERSIGHT helped drive the settlement process, another calculated social policy would prove still more of a stimulus soon after it had become evident that the real wealth to be found in the American colonies was its rich virgin soil. The heavy labor of cultivating it was not the way that either the Spaniards or the French chose to profit from their incursions in the New World, and they ultimately paid the price for it. A generous application of ingenuity made the British approach workable and enduring.

The English caste system prevailing in the seventeenth century, while somewhat more receptive to emergent commercial interests, remained grounded in tight control and narrow distribution of the land. Land in Britain was precious because it was finite, while those living off it kept multiplying; land ownership, therefore, was the key to sustenance, wealth, and power, and in a fertile, temperate island kingdom, all the more so. The feudal laws of inheritance, such as primogeniture (dictating passage of title to the first-born male in each succeeding generation) and entail (restricting ownership to the lineal descendants within a given family), effectively limited land distribution. Most who worked the land did not own it and knew they never could. And as the seventeenth century lengthened and more and more farmland was converted to sheep pasturage, the common farmers' lot grew still more hopeless. Where could they go and what could they do? The colonization of America seemed to offer a ready answer for a society that reserved landholding for those born to wealth and privilege. Here was an immense, trackless land mass ripe for the taking. The crown, however, while disinclined to finance its settlement, could not let whoever managed to get across the ocean just roam helter-skelter all over the place, so some mechanism had to be devised that would allow this wild dominion to be more or less systematically parceled, tamed, cleared, cultivated, and sustained against the adversities of nature and the indignation of the cranky natives.

This formidable task could not be accomplished by the commands of a thin upper crust of landed gentry, as in England, where the presumptions and prerogatives of wealth were little questioned. The farming of America could not proceed on the same terms and conditions that had applied for centuries in England, where land was scarce and those willing or forced to work it were in oversupply. The circumstances in America were just the reverse and might remain so for generations. To assemble enough nimble hands and brawny backs to undertake the superhuman task of cultivating the American colonies would require overturning the English caste system so that most of those who worked the soil would have title to it and thus enjoy the fruits of their own labor. The American colonies became one vast experiment in land tenure relations, breaking the customary rules of title and occupancy.

At first, the settlers were invited or permitted to create communities of their own in land chartered and donated by the crown. The land companies hoping to colonize Virginia promised would-be emigrants passage to the New World, where, according to one recruitment pamphlet,

> they will have houses to live in, vegetable gardens and orchards, and also food and clothing at the expense of the Company and besides this, a share of all products and the profits that may result from their labor, each in proportion, and they will also secure a share in the division of the land for themselves and their heirs forever more.

The settlers, that is, were supposed to be sustained until they could survive on their own. In New England the cooperative communities of religious dissenters were helped into being by patrons who often shared their convictions and were willing to pay for the ocean passage of those who could not afford it; the land was owned from the start by the community as a whole, its survival dependent on their own material and spiritual resources. These were the beachhead ventures that the crown was glad to permit, so long as they entailed no royal expenditures.

The seedbed settlements took better root in New England, where the rocky soil and shorter growing season did not invite intensive, wide-scale farming; rather, the land was worked for subsistence. Many Puritans, who came disproportionately from the artisan and commercial classes, pursued their livelihood in the crafts and trades, timber, and the maritime professions of fishing, cargo transport, and shipbuilding. In far more fertile Virginia, the crown was amenable to a highly varied and flexible program of land grants, both large and small—gifts of the king, sometimes with a nominal annual per-acre fee, or "quit-rent," attached—to encourage the settlement process. Other than some bureaucratic paper shuffling, these gifts cost the king nothing—and how else to grow colonies except with colonists?

The largest grantees, invariably court favorites, were handed title to estates ranging from hundreds to thousands of acres—and in one extreme case, that of the Fairfax family, roughly 5 million acres in northern Virginia. A generation later, the crown began making even larger grants, for example, all of Maryland to the Calvert family dynasty, leaving it to these recipients of royal largess to figure out how to get the land distributed, settled, and into cultivation, so the kingdom could better prosper from the resulting commercial activity. Since these New World holdings were of little worth to their owners without the labor to transform them, they gladly paid to transport any of England's idled farmers and their families who were up for the voyage. The emigrants were assigned to their benefactors' fields either as hired hands or as indentured servants, who after a fixed period of unpaid labor (typically, five to seven years), were set at liberty and given title to fifty or a hundred acres of their employer's property, usually with the small yearly quit-rent attached, a remnant of feudalism that rendered the new property owner quit of all other payments or tributes to the crown such as day labor or military service.

Those without connections that would allow them to obtain sizable direct grants from the crown had another, more enterprising method of winning a goodly wedge of the mouthwatering real-estate pie. The crown introduced wide use of "headright" grants in nearly all the colonies outside of New England, starting in Virginia, where they proved far more attractive and successful than the earlier chartered farm cooperatives. Anyone who wished to come to America as a working farmer and could pay his way was awarded fifty acres of farmland by the crown (again, usually with a quit-rent, averaging a shilling a year) and another fifty acres for each family member or other person he could afford to bring along. The privilege was extended as well to English proprietors and land settlement companies willing to sponsor emigrant farmers who could not pay for their passage. In these cases, the paying party was awarded the fifty-acre headright—and sometimes both the settler-farmer and his paying patron were each awarded fifty acres, so eager was the crown to stimulate colonization. The more farmers and their families the land companies or individual entrepreneurs could enlist, of course, the larger their cumulative holdings. In some instances, the grants were made prospectively, as in the case of one Virginia proprietor who was awarded 12,000 acres on the condition that within five years he would oversee the building of a settlement of thirty homes; that worked out to 100 acres per head if the average household consisted of a couple with two children.

Since the land dealers were in business to turn a profit, they would generally extract payment from the farm families they had transported in the form of indentured servitude—in effect, bartering eventual title to the property for their labor—or, for those who wanted their freedom sooner and could pay for the privilege, the dealers would sell them land outright. Prices varied with the location and quality of the land, but in an age when the supply of soil hugely outstripped the demand, it was decidedly a buyer's market. Typically prices ranged upward from one pound sterling per fifty acres, plus a quit-rent of an additional shilling per year; if the buyer wished to own the land "in fee simple"—that is, outright with no quit-rent or other obligation—the price was 50 to 60 percent higher. In terms of currency values at the beginning of the twenty-first century, that would translate to somewhere between three and four dollars per acre. As the better land got gobbled up throughout the seventeenth century, headright grants lost value, and by the early 1700s, most land titles were purchased, not gifted by the crown.

These inducements succeeded. Farm laborers, eager for the chance to own land of their own, willingly accepted indentured servitude for periods up to seven years. By some estimates, 75 percent of the men who migrated to the Chesapeake region during the seventeenth century entered into such an arrangement, and outside of New England nearly half of all settlers fell into this category. At the other end of the economic scale, those who could afford to transport farmworkers and gather up their headright grants in return were soon assembling plantations, and as long as they could afford to cover their imported laborers' living costs during servitude, their holdings could continue to grow. The average estate in Virginia in 1650 was 750 acres, and 10 percent of all holdings were between 1,000 and 8,000 acres.

Even the irksome quit-rents, amounting to between a quarter penny and a half-penny per acre annually, did not present much of an impediment to the pioneering process, because more often than not they were never paid. Resentful that whoever had given or sold them their land—whether the crown or titled favorites of the crown or land dealers or the planters they had formerly labored for—had paid nothing for the land in the first place but were now extracting an annual fee from them for it, many farm owners were intentionally delinquent in paying their quit-rents or conveniently forgot about them. In the New World it took far more time and trouble than the quit-rents were worth to track down the nonpayers. Enforcement officers, moreover, were few and far between. Defiance of quit-rent obligations, a not inconsequential source of revenue in the aggregate to the crown and its proprietary grantees, was one early sign of a stubbornly antiauthoritarian attitude that took hold among the American colonists and would one day flame into open rebellion against those they accused of ill-using them.

Britain's American empire relied heavily, then, not on conquest or befriending the natives but on the encouragement of emigration. The English understood, as the Spanish and French regimes seemed or chose not to, that the more who were attracted to settle in their overseas colonies, the sooner the day when the realm would be enriched, provided that the process did not strip the homeland of an adequate labor supply. In offering sanctuary across the waves for dissenters and those otherwise disaffected, the rulers of the British kingdom were confident that the emigrants' grievances would be subordinated to the tasks of empire-building.

Other socioeconomic factors at work in the British colonies further stimulated emigration early on. In a society where acquiring land was purposely made easy, where there was so much work to be done that almost every non-farming laborer could earn good wages, and where there was no imbedded or titled aristocracy or ground-down peasantry, even the smallest landholder and the least skilled tinker was granted a degree of respect. In such a setting, while far from an egalitarian paradise, a marked degree of social leveling was inevitable and contrasted sharply with Europe's rigidly stratified societies. Feeding this tendency was a liberty of conscience in many parts of the new colonies, with all their space to breathe, act, and think unhampered by the ever-lurking oppressions of the Old World. Not only were growing numbers of Englishmen being lured across the sea, but their fellow Britons—the Scots, the Welsh, the Irish, and the Scots-Irish—were also being enticed, as well as Protestants from the other side of the English Channel, Dutch, Walloon, and Huguenot refugees unhappy or unwelcome at home. Land developers vied for emigrant homesteaders they could carry to America to work their holdings before they became property owners in their own right. By the last two decades of the century, when William Penn came into his great proprietary grant, he and his agents were avidly soliciting the disaffected at home and abroad, even advertising with foreign-language pamphlets and recruiting German Protestants and Moravians—the so-called Pennsylvania Dutch—to work the fecund valleys that veined the eastern half of his colony. The crown helped stir this cosmopolitan brew by its liberal naturalization practices. Most able-bodied foreigners who wanted to head for Britain's American colonies with the assurance of full citizenship rights had only to embrace the Protestant faith and swear an oath of loyalty to the king of England.

Given all the auspices, it is tempting—but misleading—to overstate the success rate among settlers during the first century of British colonization. The achievements were impressive but far from universal. Half of those who had come to America as indentured servants remained landless laborers afterward. As everywhere, natural selection worked against the timid, the lazy, the improvident, the incompetent, and the luckless. Many, cursing their bonded servitude (even if voluntarily entered into) in a place where freedom abounded, violated their contract well before their term of service expired and fled to the backcountry with the hope that their property owners, often absentees, would not bother to pursue them. Usually they did not—in a frontier society you could not indefinitely force a free man to do what he chose not to. Those who became squatters had, of course, to endure the same frontier hardships, in particular the aching loneliness and constant threat of Indian violence, as those who came by their land legally. Still, relatively few settlers gave up and returned to Europe.

· · ·

THE BENEFITS OF THE HEADRIGHT GRANTS were almost immediately evident; their toxic effects took a generation to surface.

The warmer colonies, which lent themselves to commercial cultivation on a scale far beyond mere subsistence farming, began to pay their way by growing tobacco and supplying a waiting global market with the large, sundried golden leaves. The tobacco plantations, many assembled with the headright device, extracted a heavy toll on both the soil, which it drained of nutrients faster than nature could replace them, and the indentured laborers who tended the finicky crop. The conscientious ones among them were quick to leap to freedom when their terms of servitude expired; the ones who could call no man master for long or who could not endure the backbreaking toil for another man's profit often deserted the plantations. As a result, the planters faced the almost constant need to replace their indentured workers, and there were never enough willing hands to meet the demand. Even owners of smaller farms faced the problem, because, as Jefferson was later to remark in his *Notes on the State of Virginia,* "[I]n a warm climate, no man will labor for himself who can make another labor for him."

What was required to ensure the large-scale planters both growth and prosperity—and to spare the small-farm owners from sunstroke and make them feel more lordly—was a reliable supply of captive drones, laborers who could not look forward to release from involuntary servitude or run away with virtual impunity. By the second half of the seventeenth century southern planters, big and small, were purchasing imported African blacks as personal property, with no more rights or hopes than a mule. Slaves may have been wanting in motivation, but their owners counseled one another that coercion worked wonders with creatures who, in their masters' view, did not know enough to resent the pain inflicted on them. To ease any qualms over the morality of the highly useful practice, slaveholders rationalized that their dark chattels may have been human in form but came from a decidedly lower order in the animal kingdom—bestial beyond any possibility of refinement. For masters who treated them with a modicum of humanity, slaves could turn into a very profitable investment. James Madison, Virginia planter and politician par excellence, once revealed that the revenues he reaped from his slave-grown crops were twenty times what it cost him to care for his dark bondsmen. The crueler their treatment, on the other hand, the balkier and less productive they grew, lash or no lash. Still, slavery was judged a more reliable source of labor than indentured servitude, from which escape was less perilous, and the practice rapidly took hold.

By 1750, a century or so after the practice began, slaves constituted some 40 percent of the population in the southern colonies, and their presence was viewed as indispensable not only to the lifestyle of the region but also to the collective economic health of the British domain in America. Amid the rush for prosperity, compunctions about reliance on a vicious and morally indefensible expedient were swept aside. Even righteous New Englanders who did not themselves indulge in it to the same extent managed to suppress their guilt while helping conduct the slave trade and carrying cargoes of slave-grown produce, which represented fully 80 percent of the value of exports from the American colonies. And the greater their output, the more ravenous plantation owners became for fresh soil to add to their dominion. Land was the true currency of colonial America, a fungible commodity readily convertible to specie or credit as well as prized evidence that its owner amounted to something.

Land was the catalyst as well behind the British colonists' equally deplorable treatment of the other race with whom they shared the continent. By and large, they dealt with the native American peoples even more contemptuously than did the Spaniards, who intermarried with the Indians to sustain their imperial domain, and far more harshly than the French, who artfully befriended them as trading partners and military allies. Most British colonists spurned the Indian tribes as nothing but an impediment to their settlement efforts. Since they were not Christian, literate, numerous, well armed, purposefully organized, or otherwise worthy of regard, the newcomers wasted little time or effort trying to gain the natives' friendship or reach a territorial accommodation between their races in that vast landscape, where there was plenty of room for all of them.

There were some, to be sure, who saw both practical necessity and moral value in treating the natives with civility. Without patronizing them, one could admire the simplicity of their ways and beliefs, even if stopping short of embracing the Enlightenment notion of the American Indian as a noble savage, living lightly off the land in harmony with unspoiled nature. A few seventeenth-century colonial leaders such as Roger Williams and William Penn preached and acted with kindness toward the native peoples and insisted that they be regarded as the rightful, long-established possessors of the land, whose title to it had to be purchased or fairly bargained for and not forcibly wrenched away.

But such leaders and their respectful attitudes did not prevail. It was less troublesome and more comforting to brand the natives as ignoble savages, irredeemably primitive, and thus readily disposable on four certifiable grounds. First, they could not be considered true owners of the land they roamed because there was no evidence that it was rightfully theirs. They held no charters, grants, or other documents, of course, since theirs was a preliterate civilization in which even the wheel was unknown. They had no measured or enclosed fields, few crops beyond some scattered plantings, no permanent dwellings, cattle, or enduring monuments, and they had failed to carry out God's commandment to mankind to work the land and make it flourish (see Genesis 9:1, in which the Lord tells Adam, "Multiply, and replenish the earth and subdue it"). By this standard, the Indians were merely Stone Age hunters, gatherers, and warriors who shifted about each season, like herds of grazing animals.

Second, when the error of their ways was pointed out to the Indians, they stubbornly declined to renounce their nomadic habits and take up the ethos of Christian gentlefolk. They would not become farmers and herders, assign ownership to property and learn to hoard it, build permanent settlements, or abandon what the colonists considered pagan animism and superstition for the transcendent worship of the European God. In lamenting the Indians' moral degradation, the colonists' spiritual leaders found ample justification for punitive acts toward them. A leading Puritan divine, the Reverend Increase Mather, wrote of "the Heathen People among whom we live . . . whose land the Lord God of Our Fathers hath given us for a rightful possession." There was no compassion for these godless creatures, only fear and loathing of them. John Winthrop, the first governor of the Massachusetts Bay Colony, spoke glowingly of their immolation by fire when an Indian village was set ablaze by his fellow colonists. The most celebrated and learned clergyman of his day, Increase Mather's son, Cotton, minced no words in calling the Indians "miserable animals." That the British, almost from the first, viewed the natives as vile wretches, best put out of their misery at the earliest opportunity, is suggested by the sentiment of no less an eminence than King James I of Great Britain—the very patron of the peerless English translation of the Bible—who referred to the devastation of Virginia's Indian tribes by white men's diseases as "the wonderful plague."

Third, unlike the imported blacks, the natives refused to be enslaved and do the white man's work for him; death was preferable to such a defilement of their beings and culture. And since they would not make themselves useful to the colonists or take up civilizing practices, death and destruction were dealt to many of them, and their uncultivated lands usurped.

Finally, refusing to slip away without protest—indeed, each time they gave ground to the whites, they soon found themselves newly intruded upon—the Indians were declared agents of the devil for resisting when provoked. Being such, they were regarded as fair prey, to be dealt with in bad

faith following every treaty agreement with them, to be cheated in commercial dealings, and to be driven off and ultimately exterminated for their sins.

The result of such unremitting hatred and circular logic, manifested
almost from the founding of the English colonies, was a constant bloody
struggle along the whole frontier. The British, unwilling to share territory
and a cultural matrix with the aborigines and equally unable to enslave them
or convert them to Christian civility, opted for genocide as their policy of
choice. Whereas an estimated 10 million natives were thought to be living
north of the Rio Grande when Columbus arrived, only 1 million of their
progeny were believed to be living three centuries later in the wake of the
white man's diseases, deceptions, and death-dealing vehemence.

The blame-the-victims animus that ruled the British colonists' conduct
toward both the natives standing in their way and the Africans they
imported in chains to work the land robbed the great pioneering venture of
its virtue. You could not parade your purity of faith upon arrival in the New
World and then, in short order, cite the Indians' hostile response to your
provocations as conclusive evidence of their barbarity. Nor could you cite
your own disadvantaged past to justify heaping indignities on your African
chattels, forcibly denying them literacy and education, nutrition, sanitation,
holy matrimony, family life, and almost every other semblance of dignity.
They who had been deprived, despised, degraded, and rendered powerless
in Europe did not scruple at turning the tables on whomever they could most
easily and usefully dominate. The lesson of compassion had not been carried across the racial chasm. Slavery, though an atrocity, was not deemed a
sin if it turned colonists who were formerly oppressed in the Old World into
masters in the new one. Genocide, though a misfortune, was no crime if it
was the swiftest route to territorial supremacy.

Their gross racist abuses would haunt the British settlers and their issue
as nothing else in the colonial and American national experience. Instead of
tolerating the native peoples and accepting slower and delimited expansion
of white settlement, the colonists turned them into desperate enemies, guaranteeing deadly, endless strife all along the westering trek. In dehumanizing
their living black property, also by way of satisfying their voracious appetite
for the land, they implanted an undying resentment in their victims, caused
a nearly fatal schism within the successor nation, and bred social patholo-
gies that have yet to heal.

BRITAIN'S GENTLE GRIP ON ITS colonial reins, while encouraging private
initiative, did not come without a high price in social volatility. It may not

have been a free-for-all, exactly, but the settlement process in the English colonies was, to say the least, disorderly. Rampant dynamism unchecked by civil authority could spill over into chaos, even anarchy, confirming the Hobbesian belief that people were naturally venal and incapable of self-regulation. In British America, where incentives abounded and endeavors were often lavishly rewarded, widespread chicanery was perhaps inevitable. In that raw frontier society, the fittest did far better than survive, the grasping had a field day, and those of faint heart or will won scant sympathy.

Those who had been most generously treated by the crown in the form of land grants in the colonies were often the quickest to press their advantage there. The handiest way was for them to seize and manipulate the rudimentary machinery of government in order to secure their social position and economic power. Land was the prime source of that power, and control of land grants—other than for the huge proprietary gifts, made directly by the king—resided with the royal governors, who as often as not turned into rank fortune-seekers after having gone unrewarded by Britain's feudal laws of inheritance. Most helped themselves to sizable portions of ungranted crown real estate, but so long as the governors caused London minimal grief and ran their fiefdoms on a pay-as-you-go basis, hardly a peep arose from the king's ministry.

To be charitable, the colonial governors might be described as highly opportunistic rather than larcenous, since their power was usually tethered to their executive councils. But these bodies were composed mostly of landed gentry ever hopeful of adding to their holdings and gaining other favors through the governor's discretionary powers, so they were predisposed to work hand in glove with him in advancing oligarchic rule of the colony. While smaller landholders had their say through the elected colonial assemblies, their public-spiritedness was inconstant and their cooperation purchasable, with goodly land grants as the customary form of lagniappe. At one term of the House of Burgesses, each member of the Virginia legislature was slipped 6,000 acres, courtesy of the governor and his henchmen.

Over time, oligarchic control of affairs in most colonies outside of New England was refined to a degree approaching the conspiratorial. At any given moment, half the members of the Virginia executive council were likely to be related to one another. Between 1680 and the close of the colonial era, 60 percent of the seats on the council were held by members of just twenty-four families. These insider cliques benefited by both upfront and backdoor land grants, friendly legislation, low to nonexistent taxes, and the appointment of relatives, friends, and allies to colony and county administrative jobs, lucrative in themselves and also providing valuable insider knowledge to the officeholder. Colonial surveyors, for example, were uniquely situated to gather intelligence on the most desirable tracts within their jurisdiction and to apprise confederates of their location or even to register preemptive claims of their own, often through a surrogate to cover their conversion of a public trust into private advantage.

Such abuses of office continued throughout the colonial era, escalating in the first half of the eighteenth century to a boldness nothing short of felonious—if some authority had been inclined to press charges. William Byrd, for example, was retained as a surveyor by the colony between 1728 and 1742, during which period he was assigned to lay out a straight boundary line between Virginia and North Carolina. In the process, he was able to purchase more than 212,000 prime acres, or 330 square miles, in the border region for a penny an acre, a fraction of the going price. In North Carolina, Henry McCulloh, the colony's supervisor of royal revenues and land grants in the 1730s, feathered his nest by granting himself and several associates a patent of 1.2 million acres, nearly the size of Delaware. William Johnson, who came to America in 1738 as a shrewd young Irish immigrant, parlayed his social connections, charisma, ruthlessness, and a knack for dealing with native Americans—not a few of whom he took as concubines—to win appointment as royal superintendent of Indian affairs in the colonies north of Maryland. While so serving, Johnson eventually managed to assemble for himself, mostly in what is now upstate New York, the second largest cumulative private holding in the British colonies. In New Hampshire, Benning Wentworth, who became royal governor in 1741, blithely disregarded crown-designated boundaries in making some 200 grants, many of them on the western side of the Connecticut River, part of the domain given to the Duke of York three-quarters of a century earlier. In each case Wentworth reserved for himself 500 of the choicest acres.

Other common abuses of office involving land included failure to enforce quit-rent payments, issuing headright grants in the name of fictitious settlers to allow the accumulation of outsized estates, inaccurate or fraudulent recording (or nonrecording) of deeds, and steering smaller and poorer would-be property owners (usually without social or political connections) to settle on frontier land in the hilly, less fertile backcountry and serve as a buffer against Indian raiders. These westernmost settlers were invariably underrepresented in their colonial assemblies, which convened near the Atlantic coast and were notoriously unresponsive to appeals for protection by militiamen on the far side of the colony.

Even men of demonstrated rectitude succumbed to the temptations of loot when there was so much of it to be had and so little risk of rebuke. A classic instance was the twelve-year career of Alexander Spottswood as governor of Virginia, starting in 1712. A haughty soldier-aristocrat, he fearlessly set out to meet his responsibilities with diligence and enlightenment. He saw to the construction of the governor's handsome palace and expansion of the colonial capital at Williamsburg. He promoted iron mining and smelting as an infant industry, discouraged the rapid growth of the slave trade, and treated the native tribes more kindly by imposing fairer trading rules and opening a school for them (soon shut down by the burgesses, who preferred to annihilate the Indians). He led a quasi-military expedition across the Blue Ridge mountains to thwart French probes into the western sector of the colony, and he cracked down on piracy off the Virginia coast, succeeding well enough to order that the severed head of the infamous Blackbeard be displayed around the colony as a hirsute trophy.

But Spottswood's good deeds soon won him detractors clamoring for his head as well. His fight to reform corrupt practices—in particular, evasion of quit-rents, abuses of headrights, and the executive council's blatant cronyism in issuing excessively large land grants—stirred more reproach than applause. The interlocking family clique that controlled the powerful governor's council took its stand when Spottswood chose to make an example of one tax-evading aristocrat by prosecuting him. When the case was due to be heard by the governor's council in its other capacity as General Court, the colony's high tribunal, a quorum failed to materialize. The accused was related to one of the councilmen, who were past masters at mutual backscratching. Spottswood growled that he had been foiled by a "hereditary faction of designing men," but instead of resigning in protest and carrying his just case to the crown, he astutely concluded that incessantly locking horns with the landed potentates of Virginia would gain him nothing—not even his salary, probably, if he kept it up. For seeing the light and thereafter stringing along with the council and the burgesses, he was able to leave office with ample compensation for his compromised integrity: 85,000 acres of rolling countryside, largely obtained through the issuance of dummy (blank) patent grants with the connivance of the governor's council.

In New York, the land barons were even nervier than in Virginia. The royal governor and his collaborators would see to it that, for a small but obligatory bribe, grants running into the hundreds of thousands of acres were spread among the owners of the duchy-sized Hudson River manors, so tightly held that the common farmer was permitted only to work the land for wages or a pricey rental; labor-for-land or outright purchase was denied. As a result, the colony's agricultural development and population growth languished. In the Carolinas, land was hoarded even more defiantly by the self-styled patricians who had been given proprietary license to treat their colonies like their private property. Only when the downtrodden finally rose up in armed objection did they rouse the attention of the crown, which stripped the offending land barons of their power and placed both colonies under direct royal authority. Even in New England, its officialdom morally immaculate by comparison, advantages were commonly taken and favoritism played. Because the rocky soil and short growing season were not conducive to large-scale farming, the amassing of large tracts was not zealously pursued, but in the cooperative communes, the elders did not dole out the lots with strict impartiality; the biggest and best ones usually went to the wealthiest and most influential among them.

Abuse of power, private as well as official, was widespread largely because there was no machinery for reining it in, no media to stir public outrage, and London was far away and, at any rate, more likely than not to turn a deaf ear to colonial malcontents bawling about unfair advantage being taken by relatives of crown intimates. But it was by no means only the best connected and most favorably positioned who succumbed to the temptations abounding in a slackly policed frontier society. The small farmers, laborers, artisans, and shopkeepers who made up the bulk of the white population understood that the grant system, while permitting wider land distribution than in Britain or anywhere in continental Europe, hardly eradicated the same pathogens of privilege and favoritism that had long infected the Old World's highly stratified societies. Accordingly, resentment incubated over the enormity of the crown's preferential treatment in the form of outsized gifts of land to those who had not lifted a finger to earn it, especially when there were so many earnest, hungry, God-fearing men ready to apply their hands-on energies and risk their lives to turn the king's claimed domain into productive farmland. Why should these stout yeomen have to bond themselves over for years of indentured servitude or buy land from the crown or its pampered grantees or dealers licensed to sell off the wilderness? Besides, the king had no plausible claim to the American soil through inheritance, conquest, purchase, or treaty—only by theft from the aborigines.

Such subversive thoughts prompted the more daring, impatient, and otherwise disgruntled among the settlers to circumvent the rules put in place by the landed oligarchy. Why invest five or seven years of hard labor to win a tract of 100 or 200 acres or pay through the nose for it—along with the quitrent, an added dose of extorted tribute money—when you could stake out a promising piece of property in the hinterland in ungranted crown territory? How could it be just to place great holdings in the hands of absentee landlords dedicated only to profiteering from their windfall titles? It was the squatters who struggled long and hard to transform forest and thicket to thriving fields, so who had a more morally justifiable claim to the land? No king, no lord in a powdered wig, no grubby speculator in a London countinghouse.

These impassioned convictions would, of course, drive the certified grantees or their agents to distraction. But trying to dislodge squatters who were usually a far piece from settled communities was a dicey business, especially when the open regions had more than their share of others also without certified title to their land but with rifles at the ready. The squatters' creed boiled down to the in-your-face homily—indeed, may have inspired it—that possession was nine-tenths of the law. And since they had space and time on their side, years might pass before the law, in the form of certified deeds to the squatters' tracts, caught up with them. By then, though, the industrious squatter might well have made a go of his unrecorded holding and, if pressed enough by the legal titleholder, could pay fair market price for the land (or at least come close). Often the successful squatter sold off his crudely maintained farm to a newcomer long before anyone appeared to challenge the legitimacy of his presence and, with a tidy profit in his pocket, headed west to find another place in the woods and dig in all over again.

Squatting was no minor phenomenon, and squatters' seizure of property, whether from the king's preserve or from others to whom it had been granted or sold, was no random act of piracy. It was, arguably, an authentic form of protest and heartfelt defiance of the crown's customary preference for those in the realm least in need of further advantages. By the first quarter of the eighteenth century, there were an estimated 100,000 squatters residing in Pennsylvania alone and said to be in effective possession of two-thirds of the colony. The practice grew similarly elsewhere, if not as extensively everywhere, frequently reinforced by the argument that the king of England was himself just a squatter in ermine-lined robes, usurping the natives' age-old dominion. Sympathy for these mass infractions took hold over time, and eventually some colonial legislatures (and finally the United States Congress) bowed to the common practice by voting to confirm squatters' preemptive rights so long as the government was recompensed for the land taken from the public domain and the taxes on it were paid regularly thereafter.

Even those inclined to play by the rules, though not favored by them—all, for example, who bought, leased, or bartered their labor for land instead of being handed it by the crown—were often sorely tempted to cut corners. Determining property lines was at best still a crude science, colonial record keeping by untrained clerks was far from fastidious, and colonial land offices were usually close by the Atlantic coast or in county seats not within easy reach for filing a claim or deed, so lapses in title execution were common. So, too, were adjustments after the fact. Property surveys, the surest way to avoid boundary disputes and other bones of contention, were costly, and the surveyors corruptible. In the southern colonies surveys were less used than the informal "metes and bounds" system, the laying out of a tract by reference to natural features such as streams, trees, mounds, and rock outcroppings or by hammered stakes. But trees could be cut down and rocks and stakes moved to reconfigure a challenged claim. The potential for rascality was endless.

It may therefore be safely ventured that the British colonists in America did not suffer a progressive loss of innocence as their settlements took root and spread. Rather, there was little or no innocence to begin with—only ambition and the resolve to make the most of what destiny had kindly dealt them.

WAS THE CHARACTER OF THE BRITISH settlers in America of a low order, then, or any lower than elsewhere? Many of them, having hardly been destiny's favorites back home, must surely have felt justified, when suddenly surrounded by land in endless abundance, in exercising their acquisitive impulses to the limit—and, when undetectable, beyond. Just as many, probably, aspired to a standard of social justice within their community and goodness in their own and their neighbors' private conduct beyond the Old World norms. But all that can be safely ventured about these early generations of colonists is that while they may have wished, or professed, to occupy moral high ground and even to cast themselves as exemplars to the world—to erect what Massachusetts Governor Winthrop called, even before his ship dropped anchor, "a shining city upon a hill"—what they were most devoted to advancing was, of course, their own well-being. Sprung loose in the boundless New World, they were willing, by and large, to do whatever it took to reverse their fortunes. Virtue uncompromised would not have achieved that goal.

We can identify, or certainly infer, some other prominent features of their collective character. To break totally with their past, however torturous it might have been, and withstand the varieties of adversity awaiting them in America meant they were by definition no longer a people submissive to their fate. They had to possess courage, physical and mental stamina, and a positive outlook on life no matter how it might have beaten them down before they set sail. Once landed, they were quick to adapt to the common denominator in their dramatically transformed social condition—survival was the first desideratum; getting ahead required getting along. In a place where everybody was somebody, all hands were busy, and nobody's basic humanity was spat upon, the striving newcomer could measure his good fortune not just in sterling or acreage but as well by the self-respect derived from being answerable to no one. Owning and working your own land for your own benefit brought a liberating independence, the fairest harvest of all in the eyes of that celebrated singer of the good agrarian life, Thomas Jefferson. Looking back on 150 years of the colonial experience, the sage of Monticello argued that liberty and equality were not obtainable in the Old World's stratified societies, where the concentration of economic power allowed one class of men to dominate the rest, to hog the land and impose a tyrannical wage system on idled farmers forced to enter the commercial trades and rely for their survival on what Jefferson called "casualties and caprices of customers." He added: "Dependence begets subservience [and] venality suffocates the germ of virtue." The ideal polity, in his view, was composed largely of independent, freeholding property owners, answerable to no master, landlord, or creditor, with a vested interest in the creation of an orderly community and a duty to see to its health and welfare. Thus would liberty and democracy best thrive.

But Jefferson went a step farther in apotheosizing anyone who farmed for a livelihood. No other occupation could cleanse the soul in a similar fashion, he insisted, because none permitted such independence of action and thought. "Those who labor in the earth are the chosen people of God," he wrote, "if ever he had a chosen people, whose breasts He has made His peculiar deposit for substantial and genuine virtue." He went on: "While we have land to labor then, let us never wish to see our citizens occupied at a workbench, or twirling a distaff [spinning thread]. Carpenters, masons, smiths, are wanting in husbandry. . . . [F]or the general operations of manufacture, let our workshops remain in Europe."

So passionately was Jefferson convinced of the blessings of the farmer's life that upon taking office as the governor of Virginia during the Revolutionary War, he urged the state assembly to grant free acreage to any man who could not afford to buy some. (The legislators were less charitably disposed.)

It is easy in hindsight to mock Jefferson for his unabashed romanticism about the farming life. Why wasn't the village blacksmith, say, or a self-employed cooper equally as free and independent as the farmer and as blessed in his physical labors? And if tradesmen were, as he wrote, subject "to casualties and caprices of customers" (that is, dependent on the whims of the marketplace), weren't farmers equally dependent on the prices their produce could fetch at harvest time and, even more so, on the caprices of nature? And if the truly ennobling element in God's blessing came from the farmer's direct contact with the soil—from running his hands through its life-nurturing granules, as if partaking in a variant of Holy Communion—why did Jefferson himself forgo that joy and bestow it (not to mention the pain, sweat, and fatigue) on the 200 slaves who worked the 7,000 acres he inherited?

Such cavils aside, Jefferson's central premise—that the wider the distribution of land and the wealth it could provide, the freer and more egalitarian American colonial society would become—is undeniable. The land was the great facilitator, and certainly the entire colonial economy depended on it. But we need not apotheosize these British settlers as altogether innocent babes in the woods bent over their plows and dreaming of social equality and perfect democracy. That other eminent Meistersinger of the farmers who carved America from the wilderness, historian Frederick Jackson Turner, saw them locked in a contest with nature rather than achieving a state of grace by immersion in it. Written more than a century after Jefferson's ode to his native state, Turner's famous essay on how the frontier supposedly shaped the American character delved into other, more alloyed qualities in those pioneer farmers: "their coarseness and strength," their "practical inventive turn of mind, quick to find expedients," their "masterful grasp of material things," and their "restless, nervous energy."

But along with "the buoyancy and exuberance that comes with freedom" and a self-reliance and resourcefulness essential to their often isolated existence, Turner saw something else that was less appealing in that archetypal American character: "The first ideal of the pioneer was conquest." Just as they had been no longer willing to submit to the degradations of the Old World, where many of them were bottom-feeders, so, too, they would not shrink before the obstacles and privations that the colonial world set before them. "Facing each generation of pioneers," Turner wrote, "was the unmastered continent. Vast forests blocked the way; mountainous ramparts interposed; desolate, grass-clad prairies, barren oceans of rolling plains, arid deserts, and a fierce race of savages, all had to be met and defeated." The rifle and axe were the settler's primary tools, not the rake and hoe; "directness and destructiveness" were his posture and mission, and a will to domination was the driving passion behind his yearning for peace and well-being on his own terms—not the king's or his officers' or some landlord's or a prying neighbor's or a scolding cleric's. These British colonists were a different variety of *conquistador*—conquerors not of the native peoples, whom they mostly wanted just to vanish, but of space. They were aggressors impelled by what anthropologist Robert Ardrey called the "territorial imperative" driving all members of the animal kingdom to win and hold their own scent-marked dominion in miniature. In the British colonists' case, they destroyed in order to make use of what the Lord had wrought. Later generations of Americans would contemplate their ongoing wholesale disturbance of untrammeled nature and label it the lamentable price of progress. For most of the colonial era, the conservationist mentality was unknown; it was a case of paradise found (but in need of domesticating), not paradise lost, and set the Americans apart from other Englishmen of their age.

Their very success, though, was harped upon in a way that sounded a sour note still echoing down the generations. The bounty visited upon them, some of the colonists insisted, was no fortuitous stroke but, rather, heaven's benediction. The Puritans in particular (but not exclusively) voiced this sentiment, claiming they had been chosen to demonstrate "the right and perfect way" of worship and living, and their prosperity in the new land bore witness to their fidelity to that path of virtue. There was no contradiction in answering the simultaneous calls of the Lord and of commerce (except on Sundays); doing good and doing well were the reverse sides of the same coin of moral currency. Writing 120 years after John Winthrop spoke of his brave band's aspiration to raise its gleaming hilltop city to inspire mankind, the eloquent Congregationalist preacher Jonathan Edwards reminded his fellow colonists that they had been put in that special place to stir the moral regeneration of the world. Fulfillment of that mission implied entitlement of reward.

There were at least two small flaws in the attribution of the colonists' immense good fortune to divine intercession. Almost every other highly successful society that preceded the American colonists—the Egyptians, the Babylonians, the Persians, the Romans, the Chinese, and the Turks, to cite several—had vented identical claims of heavenly sponsorship and transcendent purpose. History might have taught the British settlers that their advancement owed more to their own exuberance and enterprise than to fickle providence and that the stars had not in fact been realigned for their convenience. Humility, though, was not the virtue of the hour. Self-certifying insistence on their exalted standing, moreover, served to justify—indeed, actively encourage—the colonists' beastly behavior toward other races they took to be less beloved by heaven. Since these breeds seemed so demonstrably deficient in mental capacity and cultural accomplishment when compared with even the lowliest Europeans, it followed that these unfortunates had to be among God's unchosen people, who were therefore highly disposable, as in the case of the native Americans, or deservedly exploitable, as with the African blacks. Missing from this syllogism was a sense of charity and moral accountability. For, even assuming that these pathetic creatures were certifiably the most vile and worthless on earth, how did it follow that the British colonists, as beneficiaries of God's grace, had been granted *the right* to brutalize those disfavored by heaven?

The self-justifying nature of the emerging American character was neatly rendered by the leading epigramist of the colonial age, Benjamin Franklin, explaining how his fellow colonists could profess their righteousness while dog-eat-doggedly grubbing after life's material rewards. "An empty sack," Franklin abbreviated, "cannot stand upright." Moral improvement was an attainable ambition but sprang no less from the soil of solvency than from the soul of piety.

To the onlooking Britons of the seventeenth century, their New World settlements existed primarily as an appendage—and for the benefit—of the mother country, under whose thumb, however lightly it pressed, they emphatically remained, regardless of the ocean in between. To varying degrees, the colonies were all getting on nicely, though the crown had done little to bring about their flowering beyond licensing the seed bearers to plant the garden at their own expense and cultivate it in their own way. But if the overseers of Britain's spreading empire seemed benignly withdrawn from their American colonies, they did not remain passive when it came to turning the settlers' good fortune to the overall advantage of the realm.

Starting at the close of the Cromwellian interlude and extending over the latter part of the century, Parliament passed what came to be called collectively the Navigation and Trade Acts, imposing government restrictions on the shipping industry and geared to the combative strictures of mercantilism. This policy derived from the arguable theory that there was a fixed quantity of wealth in the world, a zero-sum condition that meant Britain's relative economic strength would grow to the extent it could control global trade and hoard the resulting profits. British mercantilism was aimed at gaining the most favorable balance of trade possible in two ways primarily: (1) protection of domestic growers and manufacturers from foreign competitors by charging punitive, if not prohibitive, duties on imported merchandise, and (2) regulation of the worldwide marketing of colonial products through compulsory pricing, shipping, and credit practices. The linchpin of the latter policy was the requirement that all goods trafficking to and from the British colonies be carried on British-flag vessels, thus placing the American settlements off-limits to non-British ships and ensuring British carriers and merchants maximum opportunity to profit from their monopolistic advantage. France under Louis XIV had adopted a similar system, but the British refined it, pressed it harder, and had the advantage of owning the agriculturally productive Atlantic seaboard colonies, whose output was steadily gaining buyers in the ever broader world market.

Here now was the one glaring exception to Britain's otherwise generous grant of freedom to the colonists. They could not sell their surplus work product to whomever they chose. Instead they were presented by London with a list of "enumerated goods," including those in the greatest global demand (tobacco, rice, sugar, indigo, molasses, rum, and furs) and those of importance to British maritime and military operations—such as New Hampshire white pine for the mainmasts of ships, and naval stores (tar, pitch, resin, and turpentine) from the Carolinas—and told these could be sold abroad only to Britain and carried there only on British vessels or those belonging to the colonists. Since foreign-flag carriers were now expressly forbidden to put in at British colonial ports, all manufactured goods the colonists wanted to buy had to be routed through England, a requirement adding to their cost. Colonial assemblies, moreover, were forbidden from levying import duties on British goods, which would have made them pricier than locally made wares. As the colonial period lengthened, the increasingly protectionist Parliament denied Americans the right to manufacture woolen goods, hats, and iron products, among others.

Colonial distress over these arrangements was relatively muted. The planters in America were compensated for being denied direct dealings with the world market by the mercantilist benefit of forced selling into a British marketplace that protected them against both competing foreign importers, through high tariffs, and British producers. Homeland farmers, for example, who began raising tobacco in the Midlands soon had their crop banished by the crown, fearful of killing the colonial goose laying the proverbial golden egg. Still, the colonial growers were at the mercy of the London commercial houses that dictated the purchase price, set low enough to yield a healthy profit margin when they turned around and sold American products to British customers and the export market. Britain's financial middlemen were equally adroit at milking the colonies by requiring their planters to bear practically all the costs and risks of the transatlantic trade, making them pay for carting, warehousing, shipping, inspections, insurance, damage to uninsured merchandise, and sales commissions—a nasty service charge—to the British importers.

Because the colonists were also captive customers for British manufactured goods, rarely offered at bargain prices, many planters—especially the high-living ones, like Thomas Jefferson—eventually found their accounts with British merchants in arrears and began to operate on credit secured by their next crop. To expand profits or, more to the point, to reduce their debts to London, the planters acquired more land and more slaves for a larger harvest. But in the process they ran the risk of flooding the world market, thus lowering prices and their per-acre income and going still deeper into debt to pay for their expanded plantations and slaveholdings. The more intensively the colonists worked their soil, the more quickly they exhausted it, especially with the key staple, tobacco, and since a more scientific management of the older land was costlier than abandoning it for new fields, the southern plantocracy kept reaching out for territory and political leverage even while leaving itself still more financially beholden to London.

In short, Britain dictated the terms of the colonial trade, banked fat profits from the markups and service charges on American exports and from exclusive access to colonial buyers, and was smart enough not to leave its imperial milk cow malnourished in the bargain. Why foreclose on colonial debtors, for example, when you could just pay them less for their next crop and resell it at yet higher profit margins? And why tax the settlers and risk their ire when they cost the realm nothing? The whole mercantilist apparatus functioned so well that the crown ministry was able to tolerate considerable smuggling, both by foreign craft delivering cargoes to colonial harbors and by American vessels supplying surplus foodstuffs to the West Indies in exchange for proscribed sugar and thus helping establish a rum-manufacturing industry in New England. The American colonists' carrying trade also enjoyed thriving coastwise traffic—especially between flush Pennsylvania and New York farms and southern single-crop plantations—in grain, flour, and other durable foods. It was the harbinger of a phenomenon that would one day make the American economy a powerhouse: a booming domestic demand that far surpassed sales abroad.

The net effects of Britain's mercantilist initiatives toward its American colonies were the intended ones; they enriched the kingdom and imposed economic dependency on the colonists in international commerce. But the Americans probably gained more than they sacrificed in the bargain. Mercantilism sped their commercial development and the influx of settlers. And since Britain stuck by its hands-off policy in most other aspects of the colonists' daily lives and ceded them virtual self-governance within the crown's purview, swallowing the mother country's dictates on trade did not seem an exorbitant price to pay.

The consequences of Britain's pushing its confrontational mercantilist policy in the faces of its Old World rivals were more dire than in America. Enforcement of its claimed right to prohibit other nations from trading with British colonies provoked constant naval warfare in Atlantic and Caribbean waters, while Britain's appetite for trade monopolies led to the establishment of large-scale, crown-chartered operations such as the East India, Royal Africa, and Hudson's Bay companies all in hot pursuit of exclusive commercial rights at the expense of France, Spain, Holland, and Portugal. With so many flashpoints of antagonism erupting across the global map, full-scale combat over trade and related issues became inevitable as the eighteenth century began. Britain gained ground in the first such multinational struggle, the War of the Spanish Succession, strategically advancing its position in North America by rousting the French from their lightly populated but commercially active fishing settlements in Nova Scotia and Newfoundland, which became new British crown colonies, and winning sovereignty over the bleak Hudson Bay Territory. But Britain's commercial and territorial rivalry with France in India, the West Indies, and North America was just warming up.

BY 1750, NEARLY A CENTURY and a half after the first sustained English settlement in North America, the population of Great Britain and its thirty colonial entities, half of them in North America, came to about 15 million, 5 million fewer than France's total. But commercially and militarily, Britain was unmistakably bidding for first rank in global power. No kingdom was richer, and no naval force ranged farther.

The British did not establish their imperial hold by timidity. They treated their Catholic Irish like a subjugated race, even though granting them a modicum of home rule, as absentee English landlords siphoned off heavy rentals from the native Celtic tenant farmers and ran Ireland as one large, supine fiefdom. On the other side of the world, the crown's quasi-official trading monopoly, the East India Company, operated like a sovereign force from outposts in the big seaports of Bombay, Calcutta, and Madras. The freewheeling company bested French interests by meddlesome maneuvers in the endless wars and turbulent politics of the ethnically fractious subcontinent. In playing off one principality against the next and exploiting deep-seated religious, cultural, and dynastic divisions, the British operatives resorted to trickery, bribery, deceit, extortion, intimidation, and mercenaries under arms who shot when necessary to promote the company's commercial intrigues. And the riches flowed back to England. In the West Indies, a heated cockpit of smuggling and piracy, the British struggled less success-

fully for dominance as European rivals contested their mercantilist hegemony and maintained their own successful outposts. But Britain harvested
particularly large profits from sugar and tobacco grown on the slave-labor
plantations of Barbados and Jamaica. Along the African west coast British
and Dutch vessels had supplanted the French and Portuguese as the principal European operators, dominating the lucrative ivory and slave trades.

None of Britain's overseas holdings, though, could rival its thirteen
American colonies, by far the most successful of all the European colonial
settlements since the Age of Discovery began. It was the most accessible,
abundantly endowed, easily captured, and painlessly managed part of
Britain's empire, and its future promise was stirring many an imagination.

Due in part to the crown's open immigration and naturalization policy
on top of its frank encouragement of the discontents in the home isles to
help build the new overseas enterprise, the population of the thirteen
colonies increased by a million people during the first half of the eighteenth
century, reaching about 1.3 million by its midpoint. It was growing at a
compound rate of 3 percent a year, or three times the figure for Europe, as
large families were needed for tending to the endless labors of a frontier
society. While the crown cracked the whip smartly elsewhere, in America it
chose to keep the reins slack and let the stallion gallop at its own pace. The
results were stunning. Prosperity abounded, from the spreading southern
plantations to the fertile farm country in the middle colonies to New England's bustling harbors and commercial districts. Boston was the largest
seaport in the empire outside of England, and Philadelphia the largest city.
As time passed, the colonies grew more diverse in their makeup. The New
York environs included the Dutch in Brooklyn and the Hudson Valley,
Huguenots in Westchester, Scots and Flemings in New Jersey, and Irish,
blacks, Jews, and adherents of every Protestant sect and no sect at all in
Manhattan. In Pennsylvania, those of German extraction soon outnumbered
those of British origin, and in the southern colonies, two of five residents
stemmed from Africa. Such a porridge of diverse peoples was not free of
lumpiness, but tensions and hostilities were diluted by the resulting commercial vibrancy, cultural ferment, social mobility, and widespread freedom
of thought, expression, association, and location. Opportunity, not paro-
chialism, was their common passion.

No longer were the colonies crude settlements clinging to the edge of an
engulfing wilderness. New England's mercantile aristocracy and many a
southern planter lived in a gracious home; even modest farmhouses
throughout the colonies had a full larder, a snug hearth, and no shortage of
reading matter or candlelight. Three out of five colonial families lived a

middle-class existence, a notably higher proportion than in Britain or any-where else. The average American colonist was better fed, housed, and clothed than his or her counterpart in England (and almost everywhere else), and with more nutritious food, cleaner air, and a lower urban popula-tion prey to city-incubated diseases, Americans were living 15 to 20 percent longer than Europeans. Taxes were low to nonexistent, crown and colonial officials rarely hovered, and even though the colonists were not allowed to buy and sell in the world marketplace, there was more than enough profit generated by their collective enterprise to afford them a remarkably high level of well-being.

What had made all of this possible, of course, was the land. It was the continent's miraculous treasure, in seemingly endless supply, and it cost next to nothing to get enough of it to sustain life and hope. And they came and got it. If they had been the wretched remnant of the Old World before embarking, in the new one they became a high-spirited, self-reliant people, irreverent toward wisdom and authority from times and places that seemed hardly to apply to them or to their special setting. The land transformed them into a people awash in optimism based on their hard-won achieve-ments, a people unapologetic for the transparency of their abuse of the red and black races. Without anyone noticing it, they had turned into a people whom the far-off king of England could no longer hope to reclaim as sub-jects more loyal to his crown than to their own commonwealth.

To be sure, their shining city on a hill had its dingy days, their enchant-ing Eden had its fallow patches and miserable seasons, and their tamed wilderness could erupt with violence at any moment. But the thirteen colonies were by any gauge a stupendous work in progress, almost exclu-sively the product of the colonists' own virtues and predilections—and they were turning less British by the year. Still, as long as each colony remained proud, insular, jealously protective of its individuality, and ultimately dependent on its mother country for economic security, the lot of them had yet to become a viable sovereign whole. The colonists' driving concern was their private property, not the public weal.

CHAPTER 2

The Poor Richards arise

1750–1776

I N 1751, THE LEADING CITIZEN of the foremost city in Britain's American colonies, Benjamin Franklin of Philadelphia, decided at the age of forty-five to delegate the management of his thriving printing and publishing business and devote himself primarily to public service. That year he entered the Pennsylvania colonial assembly and from then on would be the single most forceful advocate for a union of the thirteen British colonies.

In the course of the events transforming them into a sovereign nation, others were more incendiary, and that supreme stoic, George Washington, has been garlanded as the father of the new country for his perseverance in keeping a ragtag little rebel army in the field for seven years against the mightiest military force on earth. But Franklin, a generation older than the Virginia planter-turned-generalissimo, was surely the grandfather of his country. He was moved by the vision of a federated colonial America while the other Founding Fathers were still in their boyhood, and he began championing the commonality of their interests sooner and more vigorously than anyone else. A loyal British subject, he did not call for the allied colonies to break away from the kingdom until two years before the event—and did so then only after being rudely punished by Parliament as a principal instigator of the fury directed against his monarch and an ungrateful enemy of the realm. Nothing could have been further from the truth.

Franklin was the very embodiment of the fresh spirit coursing through the colonies; he won high eminence without benefit of inherited wealth or status. Fully exploiting the twin hallmarks of British America—economic opportunity and social mobility—he willed himself to become the model self-made man. It was a notable feat considering that, in a land where nine out of ten people lived on farms and the soil was the primary source of wealth, he was a singularly urban (and urbane) creature, a man of commerce, science, and the arts. Where most colonists of humble origin relied on their axe, their rifle, and their physical prowess to get ahead, Franklin used a ceaselessly questing mind, remarkable for its range, depth, and acuteness of observation, and a genius for the practical application of his studied insights. These rare aptitudes were embedded in a personality calculating in outlook and disarming in manner. His powers of persuasion were amplified by a gift for communicating complex subjects in a way easy to grasp and hard to forget. No contemporary wrote more pointedly, purposefully, and tirelessly, blending clarity, logic, and wit with a special fondness for the parable to convey his home truths. Son of a Boston candlemaker and the last of a dozen siblings, he rarely lost the common touch as he rose to become the most accomplished and celebrated man in colonial America and then its wildly admired ambassador when he traveled abroad to plead the cause of his fellow colonials before the British and French courts. None of his down-to-earth insights served him—or the American people—better than understanding that a velvet glove was of far more utility than a battering ram to gain his ends, whether modest or monumental.

Franklin's fame, wealth, and influence stemmed first of all from his position as the leading media mogul of the colonial age. His *Pennsylvania Gazette* was almost surely the most widely read newspaper on the continent, and his *Poor Richard's Almanack,* issued in three regional editions and featuring Franklin's deadpan drolleries, was a perennial bestseller. The great popularity of these publications was abetted by his ubiquitous activities as a public-spirited citizen par excellence, spearheading efforts to bring to Philadelphians such civic amenities as better paved and lighted streets, improved police and postal service, a hospital, a subscription library, a volunteer firefighting company, an insurance society, a university, and a forum for prominent thinkers to exchange ideas—the American Philosophical Society. Typical of the practicality of his brainpower was how he addressed a basic deficiency of the colonial economy. While land, the basis of colonial wealth, was plentiful, America was chronically short of cash in the form of gold and silver specie, in which most London merchants insisted on being paid by their colonial customers. This lack of liquidity stymied the growth of commerce. While still in his twenties, Franklin argued in print and in person that Pennsylvania ought to issue paper currency backed not by precious metals but by the colony's immense supply of ungranted real estate—"coined land," so to speak—to serve as a more plentiful and much needed medium of exchange. So cogently did he present this innovative notion that the Pennsylvania Assembly not only adopted it, with a resulting steady rise in commercial activity, but also awarded Franklin's firm the job of printing the new currency. Ingenuity and profit went hand in hand with him.

Franklin, then, was a unique amalgam of civic virtue, channeled energy, and bottomless curiosity about the phenomena of nature. His experiments and widely published reports between 1746 and 1752 on the little-understood properties of electricity made him the most famous scientist of his day, a modern Prometheus who lured lightning down from the gods and then managed to harness it. These studies won him honorary degrees from Harvard, Yale, and Oxford and membership in the most exclusive academic societies of Europe. Thus, the honorific "Dr." became attached to his name and lifted him beyond the mercantile class in social standing, though he was at pains not to affect airs, wear wigs and finery, or strut across the ever-widening stage open to him. Franklin was truly the pioneer in what would become American civilization's most fruitful field of achievement—applied science. He didn't just discover that lightning was indeed a spectacular manifestation of electricity; he devised a simple metal rod connected to a grounded wire that, when properly mounted on a building, cheaply and efficiently diverted the destructive force of the bolt. To improve on open fireplaces that irritated the eyes and skin of those nearby and sucked drafty outside air through every chink in the walls of a warmed room, he designed metal stoves that gave off more comfortable and healthful radiant heat. He studied the principles of optics and devised bifocal lenses, a boon to the visually impaired. On his not infrequent voyages to and from England he put his idle time to use by learning all he could about the Gulf Stream—its course, its swiftness, its temperature—and then proposed, correctly, that mariners could save a good deal of sailing time if they rode the stream on their eastward Atlantic crossing. His mind did not rest for long.

The compass of that mind was by no means restricted to practical uses of his physical observations; ulterior purposes were always nagging at his thoughts. Not a profound philosopher, Franklin was nonetheless a keen student of human behavior and its group consequences. In his 1751 essay "Observations Concerning the Increase of Mankind, Peopling of Countries, Etc.," he wrote, half a century before Malthus, that nations grew populous to the extent their social conditions were conducive to early marriage—a premise he then applied to the experience of colonial America, where general prosperity and freer social mores invited couples to wed young and produce offspring at a rate that was causing the colonies to double in population every generation. At that rate, which he did not foresee slackening, given the New World's territorial abundance, Franklin calculated that within a century, "the greatest number of Englishmen will be on this side the water," and since the growth would not result from depopulation of the home isles, the mother country ought to exult, not lament, over the prospect: "What an accession of power to the British Empire. . . . What increase of trade and navigation!" Britain, accordingly, ought to act with generosity toward its colonists, he wrote, and not try to hamstring them by shortsighted measures such as Parliament's 1750 dictate requiring Americans to purchase all their iron products from the home country even though their own land was rich in deposits of the mineral. How much wiser, Franklin urged, to encourage all phases of the colonial economy and thus invite British subjects on both sides of the ocean to prosper from the steadily rising commercial traffic between them. Britain's American enterprise would blossom still more spectacularly, he added, if, as, and when the separated colonies overcame their isolation and resulting provincialism by pooling their shared interests, talents, and energies in an intercolonial union that could address their joint concerns. Each colony would still run its own affairs, while its territorial extension, however wide, would remain within the ambit of the British empire and the orbit of its mercantilist economy.

This vision of a unified British America was no gauzy dream of Franklin's; he may have been wishful at times but was almost never a dreamer. By the time he began urging a limited American union, he was probably better acquainted with the folkways and byways of the thirteen colonies than anyone else living in them, in part because he had sought and gained appointment by the crown as overseer of the one essential public service they had in common—the mails. As postmaster of Philadelphia, the metropolis among Britain's American settlements, he had overhauled its mail system, remapping routes for speedier and more efficient delivery and making it pay for itself with the introduction of the penny post. But improving the mail in a provincial city was child's play compared with trying to revamp the slow, costly, and unreliable service over hundreds of thousands of square miles linked by primitive, poorly tended roads and riddled with often uncrossable rivers. As the royal postal chief for the colonies, Franklin made it his business during the early and mid-1750s to meet with virtually every local postmaster from Maine to the Carolinas and, as the paragon of bureaucrats, help them solve route problems, expand their service areas, regularize their accounting, and take pride in the importance of their function. By his fourth year at the helm of the colonial mail service it had gathered in more revenue than in the previous three years combined. "No man before him," Franklin's best biographer, Carl Van Doren, wrote, "had ever done so much to draw the scattered colonies together."

In familiarizing himself with the length and breadth of British America,

Franklin became convinced that the colonists shared a binding ethos far stronger than whatever local idiosyncrasies, regional animosities, or juris-dictional disputes were driving them apart. And their churning energies forecast a boundless future that he saw threatened by only two hostile forces, the French and their native American allies, who together seemed intent on confining the British colonists to their strip of settlement between the Atlantic coast and the eastern slope of the Appalachians. It was there-fore essential for the British to project their domain beyond the mountains, where the French had claimed sovereignty over the course of the previous century and were lately extending their trading and military posts far up the Mississippi and Ohio valleys. Their spreading presence and amicable rela-tions with the Indian nations, who preferred them to the land-grabbing British settlers in the east, had cast into doubt the expansive territorial claims of English explorers and the crown's old colonial charters. As the British and French frontiers converged from opposite directions, tensions and the number of violent incidents grew, especially after the Ohio Com-pany, the first large-scale British American land settlement syndicate, com-posed of Tidewater planters, speculators, and their London allies, won a royal grant in 1749 for a huge tract beyond the mountains in western Penn-sylvania and Virginia—territory the French and Indians claimed as well.

To remove this sizable impediment to their advance into the beckoning continent, especially the gentle, fertile valleys of the lovely Ohio River and its many tributaries, Franklin proposed a coordinated effort by the British colonists. Hardly alone in perceiving the need for such joint action, he was the first to render a concrete plan and circulate it. Focused on the need to protect settlers in frontier regions whom the colonial governments had largely ignored, Franklin's "Short Hints Towards a Scheme for Uniting the Northern Colonies" reassured his fellow colonists that such an undertaking need not compromise their separate sovereignties. A council of representa-tives chosen by their colonial assemblies could operate under the direction of a royally appointed and paid "president general," charged with carrying out the will of the yoked colonies. The colonists themselves would foot the bill for the endeavor, with a tax on hard liquor as perhaps the least onerous way to meet the expense.

The scheme was not openly disparaged in London by the Board of Trade and Plantations, imperial overseer of colonial activities, which gave its blessing to a congress of the northern colonies to be held in Albany in mid-1754 to consider ways to cope with the French and Indian peril. At the top of the agenda was a treaty with the six Iroquois nations who held or claimed dominion over lands directly in the likeliest path of oncoming

British settlers. To make sure his plan for an intercolonial defense alliance was given consideration, Franklin, one of the four Pennsylvania delegates to the unprecedented gathering in Albany, publicized it in his *Pennsylvania Gazette.* To stress the need for cooperative action he accompanied his proposal with the first political cartoon ever seen in America—a drawing of a chopped-up snake with each segment bearing the initials of one or several of the colonies and the hortatory caption "Join or Die."

As the date for the Albany Congress drew near, the pressing purpose behind it was underscored by the farthest advance yet of French forces. After rebuffing the twenty-one-year-old George Washington, a major in the Virginia militia sent in the interests of the Ohio Company to protest their incursion, the French seized the British post at the confluence of the Monongahela and Allegheny rivers, forming the Ohio, and in its place built their own, more formidable Fort Duquesne. A month before the Albany Congress, Washington returned as part of a joint British and colonial force that stormed the French fort, plunging the two nations into a seven-year worldwide struggle known in America as the French and Indian War.

With only minor revisions, Franklin's plan for an intercolonial union was endorsed by the delegates from the seven colonies attending the Albany conclave. But even with open warfare under way in the Ohio Valley and other frontier areas, none of the colonial assemblies—including Franklin's own—was willing to embrace such an enlightened measure if it meant yielding an ounce of sovereignty to a cooperative council with potentially coercive, crown-backed powers over them. One colonial governor, William Shirley of Massachusetts, the most democratic and politically independent of the colonies, was surprisingly friendly to Franklin's plan and even proposed acceptance of a tax by Parliament to better safeguard the American colonies. In a series of letters between him and Shirley while the Massachusetts assembly was pondering his Albany proposal, Franklin took issue with the governor's ideas on taxation and sketched out what would become the essence of the American colonists' case against British policies toward them a decade later that would ultimately excite open rebellion.

While remaining steadfast loyalists to the kingdom, Franklin argued to Shirley, the American colonists were (1) better qualified than members of distant Parliament to determine their own needs and how to pay for them, and (2) entitled to enjoy the long-established right of Englishmen not to be taxed except by their own consent as registered by their duly chosen representatives. Britain, moreover, deluded itself if it believed its colonists had fashioned a tax haven from levies that were imposed on the home isles. On the contrary, the Americans paid a steep indirect tax as a result of the Navigation and Trade Acts that forbade their conduct of commerce with other nations and the manufacture of finished products for their own use. As a result, the colonists earned less for their exported commodities and paid more for imported goods than they would have under free market conditions. The colonists, in short, were captive suppliers and customers of Britain's commercial community, whose taxes were thus paid in substantial part out of American pockets. The colonists' right to self-determination, Franklin further stressed, was fully justified because neither the crown nor British banking and other business interests had invested extensively in the settlement and growth of the colonies. The feat was achieved almost entirely by the men and women who had hazarded their all in the perilous struggle, thereby extending the dominion—tree by tree, field by field, valley by valley—and multiplying the wealth and commerce of their mother country. If the colonies were given the dignity of unity under the British banner, Franklin concluded, the king's subjects on both sides of the ocean would come to view themselves "as not belonging to a different community with different interests, but to one community with one interest, which I would imagine would contribute to strengthen the whole and greatly lessen the danger of future separations."

The men who ruled the kingdom, though, were uncomfortable over the prospect of even a loosely federated colonial union many times larger than Britain itself. The colonies could be better controlled and exploited if the constituent parts were kept separate. And so the colonists were urged as transplanted Englishmen, not a union of Americans, to join the battle now to protect the empire's interests against the designs of Britain's chief European maritime rivals. The first truly global conflict, the Seven Years' War, raged from Bengal to well-worn battlegrounds in Germany and Italy, the west coast of Africa, the sugar islands of the Caribbean, up and down the length of the St. Lawrence River, and along the contested shores of the Great Lakes and banks of the Ohio River.

After initial French victories, the tide began to shift as the British loosened French ties with their Indian allies by promising the tribes that the crown would establish "clear and fixed boundaries" between any future British settlements and the natives' hunting grounds. In the field the outnumbered French now faced 50,000 British troops, about half of them rough-hewn and not very obedient American colonists who marched mostly as militiamen with their fellow colonists rather than under the command of the king's officers. Although reluctant contributors at first, the American colonial assemblies authorized war taxes, with Pennsylvania raising half a million pounds to support the crown's broad effort. On the seven seas the

English fleet routed its foes, and to clinch the contest in North America, joint British naval and land forces seized the French stronghold of Louisbourg at the mouth of the St. Lawrence and rolled up the river valley to deal the Marquis de Montcalm's gallant army the decisive blow on the Plains of Abraham below Quebec in 1759. When Montreal fell the next year, the fleur-de-lis banners were swept from the continent.

CAPPED BY GLORIOUS TRIUMPH, the far-ranging war had also proven a hugely expensive one for the British empire, doubling the national debt. With the French surrender of all its Canadian claims as well as title over the Mississippi and Ohio river basins, the crown now began to suffer a continent-sized headache brought on by the imminent financial burden it would have to shoulder to defend and govern its vastly expanded North American domain.

For the previous century and a half, the British colonial enterprise in America had prospered because it was undertaken gradually, in periodic increments, by subjects of the crown at their own physical and financial risk and without requiring the royal army or navy or governmental apparatus except by the colonists' own installation. Whatever the incidental costs to the kingdom for its American possessions, they were more than defrayed by profits from their agricultural bounty and their purchases of manufactured goods from homeland purveyors. Now, though, the crown had come into undisputed possession of an immense interior land mass inhabited by some 75,000 largely Catholic Frenchmen, abandoned by their nation and uneasy about their prospects under British rule, and perhaps three times that many Indians who had sided with the French and feared an onrush of British subjects eager to displace them, brutally if necessary.

What to do with this new war-won territory, home to only a scattering of British settlers—how to pacify it, how to exploit it, how to settle it and when and by whom, and how to pay the price without gravely burdening the royal exchequer—represented a major custodial challenge like nothing the empire had confronted before. Indeed, not a few Britons believed, since the French military threat had been eliminated, that the boundaries of British America ought not to be distended grotesquely. Yes, some forts and garrisons had to be maintained to show the flag and regulate the Indian trade in the western lands claimed by the old American colonial charters and running to the Mississippi, the new boundary between Spanish and British America. But there was no need to swallow the whole of Canada surrounding the confined French settlements. Canada, many in the British ministry and court circles supposed, was best left undisturbed so the placated natives could continue to hunt it and exchange pelts at posts along the Great Lakes for small articles of British manufacture. Trying to create commerce of any real volume so far from civilization made little sense. More useful was for Britain to apply its entrepreneurial skills instead in the Caribbean and to develop the easily accessible sugar fields on tropical Guadeloupe, newly won from the French.

While crown officials debated how far to cast the mantle of empire, the issue hardly troubled the exultant colonists who had fought alongside their British countrymen—4,000 or so colonials fell in the war—and now favored maximum extension of the imperial boundaries westward and northward. Now that the restraining threat from the French military had been lifted and their Indian allies were no longer being armed and incited to mayhem, American settlers anticipated an imminently expansive future. Their aggressive intention to push the frontier westward was forthrightly discussed around London by the colonists' unofficial spokesman, the king's postman in chief for North America, the irrepressible Dr. Franklin.

Already a familiar and acclaimed figure around the city, the wigless and modestly attired Franklin had been sent to London by the Pennsylvania assembly to plead with the crown to lighten the Penn family's proprietary stranglehold on the colony's ability to run its affairs for the common good. To sway the councils of government and public opinion on the question of imperial reach in the New World, Franklin turned his facile pen to pamphleteering in 1760 with the first London publication, now suitably updated, of his 1751 tract on population growth and the certain emergence of North America as the true engine of the British empire's future prosperity. Alongside it he weighed in unabashedly with *The Interest of Great Britain Considered: With Regard to Her Colonies and the Acquisitions of Canada and Guadaloupe.* Canada and the charter-claimed backlands in the American colonies ought to be actively integrated within the bounds of empire, Franklin wrote, as a military necessity. At the same time it was a prudent business investment that would pay off handsomely, he added, rather like a chamber of commerce pitchman, and painted a radiant picture of the riches certain to accrue from the newly expanded arc of British settlement rimmed by the St. Lawrence, Mississippi, and Great Lakes basins and offering a superb system of inland waterways for carrying the agricultural abundance of the interior to world markets. The colonial population, so long as there was so much readily attainable land, was likely to remain rooted in the soil, even when its numbers surpassed 100 million, he predicted, and to become an immense market for British manufactured goods carried on British ships—the ultimate flowering of mercantilism.

As important, to Franklin's way of thinking, as assuring the mother country that America would not turn into a serious manufacturing rival was the need to avow that the colonists would not march off on their own at the earliest opportunity. He reminded his British readers how, only six years prior, the American settlers had spurned the chance to form even a loosely binding union to fight off the French and Indian menace on their doorstep. Plainly the colonists prized their ties to their homeland far more dearly than to one another. "When I say such a union is impossible," he went on with a cautionary note, "I mean [in the absence of] most grievous tyranny and oppression. While the [British] government is mild and just, while important civil and religious rights are secure, such subjects will be dutiful and obedient. The waves do not rise but when the wind blows."

It was an argument well crafted to please Britain's commercial soul. Now that peace had returned and normal trade was in the offing, the importance of the American market was becoming so evident that Franklin's exuberant prophecy could not be ignored as a siren song. As the 1760s began to unfold, the American colonies accounted for 25 percent of all domestic products exported by Britain. Franklin's tune was taken up by many in government and commerce who felt the realm was surely robust enough to absorb the immense increment of New World territory that would over time only enhance Great Britain's wealth, power, and glory. Thus, the acquisitive imperial impulse was heeded, while Ben Franklin's warning against crown oppression of the colonies was lost in the celebratory din.

Under the peace terms finally set in 1763 and formally ending the French and Indian War, the British now held all of eastern America from the Atlantic to the middle of the Mississippi River and all of Canada, whatever "all" might mean. Badly beaten France was allowed to retain fishing rights off Newfoundland, was handed back Guadeloupe and several other Caribbean trophies, and was permitted to keep trading at posts in India provided it undertook no further military escapades or political entanglements on the subcontinent. Eager to deny Britain total dominion over North America, France readily agreed to cede to Spain, its Bourbon ally, the western half of Louisiana province, a vast, loosely defined entity running from the west bank of the Mississippi to the farthest reaches of the Missouri River basin, as compensation for joining the war and losing boggy, poorly defended Florida to Britain. Spain, then, held nominal title to North America for the full length of the Mississippi westward, though no one said, or knew, just how far that was. For Spain this gigantic addition of territory, much of it arid and empty except for widely dispersed Indian settlements, was almost worthless except as a buffer for New Spain against the looming threat of Britain's grabby American settlers. The deal with France allowed

Spain to gain the sleepy but awakening port of New Orleans, strategically poised to handle the tide of commerce that would soon begin flowing down the Mississippi Valley. But Spain, for all its bluster, was a spent military power without France to prop it up; at most, it could cause mischief, at which it now and then excelled.

These new arrangements left the native people on the fringes and west of the British region of settlement at the mercy of one imperial superpower. Some Indians believed the British promise that once they prevailed over the French, they would stake out clear boundaries separating areas of permissible future settlement from the natives' hunting grounds. These Indians no longer paid allegiance to the doomed French. Now, though, in the immediate wake of victory, British settlers were already on the move all along the frontier. They were moving west in New England, west in New York and Pennsylvania, west over the Blue Ridge and Cumberland mountains into Virginia's deep interior, west in the Carolinas and Georgia, pressing against the Cherokee, Creek, Choctaw, and Chickasaw.

The Indians did not like these palefaced settlers who dealt with them contemptuously, traded with them stingily, and meant them no good. But other than the Iroquois nations, never had the tribes united to sustain their resistance to the British settlers' steady incursions. Sensing, though, that their vulnerability was growing by the day, the tribes in the Great Lakes region rallied behind a charismatic Ottawa chieftain, who in the spring of 1763 launched the bloodiest, most determined Indian uprising in colonial history. In a series of assaults over a 1,000-mile stretch, Pontiac's braves captured every British fort along the Great Lakes and the Ohio Valley save Detroit and Fort Pitt (France's former Fort Duquesne), which survived punishing sieges, and ravaged civilian settlements from Niagara to outer Virginia.

Pontiac's rampage, taking the lives of some 2,500 British soldiers and settlers, arrested London's attention. Having opted to include interior America and Canada as imperial territory, the crown had urgent need now to forge a policy for avoiding deadly conflict between natives and settlers. The latter could not be left to their own devices to solve the problem, which was exacerbated by their raging appetite for land. For not only had the colonial assemblies failed to provide protection for their frontiersmen against Indian violence—leave aside that much of it was brought on by their own provocative conduct—but they had also declined the chance to pool their martial resources under Franklin's Albany Plan. During the lately concluded war, moreover, the colonies' participation in their own defense was found seriously wanting by British officials. Their elected representatives—or so the charges went—had dragged their feet about appropriating funds to assist the war effort; local merchants had blatantly profiteered when selling wagons and other supplies to the redcoated regulars, and those colonials who did join the fight were insubordinate, shockingly unsanitary, and prone to wander off from formation to take target practice. All that freedom in the wilderness did not a soldier make.

Thus, to defend the vast territory beyond the Appalachians, restrain the settlers' aggressiveness, minimize unrest among their new French Canadian subjects, and police the expected increase in trading with the Indians, many in the British government concluded that it would need to impose an extensive military and administrative command, perhaps not permanently but surely for the time being. Fortifications would have to be repaired and expanded, new rules and regulations promulgated and enforced, and no fewer than 10,000 troops assigned to patrol hundreds of thousands of square miles of lightly populated terrain—all at a cost likely to exceed 1 million pounds a year, no small nut when added to the 5 million in annual interest on the bloated national debt. Primary responsibility for fashioning specific policies to carry out this nettlesome colonial program was handed to a precocious lord of the realm, twenty-six-year-old William Petty Fitzmaurice, president of the Board of Trade and Plantations, who would shortly succeed to his father's title, Earl of Shelburne. An anomalous figure in British public life, with useful acquaintances on both ends of the political spectrum but few close friends in either the antagonistic Whig Party or the king's camp, the brainy, enigmatic, rather secretive aristocrat was an unlikely choice for the assignment. It was less likely still that two decades later, fate would finger Shelburne, never more than a marginal participant in the British government, to play the decisive role in securing the American colonies' transition to nationhood.

He was the product (by his own account) of a loveless childhood on the 100,000-acre estate of his maternal grandfather, the tyrannical Earl of Kerry, in southwest Ireland while his weak-willed parents lived on his father's holdings in England. Shelburne was rescued from the intellectual vacuity of a feudal upbringing by the attentions of a tender, auntlike neighbor and a Huguenot tutor who taught him fluent French. Sent at sixteen to Oxford's Christ Church College, he was awakened to public affairs by Sir William Blackstone's renowned lectures on the common law. Restless after two years, he went off without a degree to military service, distinguishing himself during the Seven Years' War as an infantry officer on the battlefields of Germany and Italy. By the time he returned to civilian life, he had been rewarded with the rank of colonel, appointment to the king's court as an aide-de-camp, and membership in the House of Commons for the family borough of High Wycombe in Buckinghamshire—a hereditary seat under the prevailing practice. Later he would speak out for reforming such undemocratic practices in Parliament, but his career in Commons ended before he could take his seat there because his father's death resulted in Shelburne's transfer at twenty-four to the House of Lords.

A glib speaker with a tongue known to turn acid in private assessments of his colleagues, he was also a facile writer and a shameless flatterer who was taken under the wing of Prime Minister John Bute, mentor to the new young king, George III. Shelburne advanced himself by running nasty errands for Bute, who made it his mission to promote the king's ascendancy vis-à-vis Parliament and diminish the Whigs' monopoly on power and policy making. Shelburne, though, was no mindless henchman; he got on not only with the "king's friends," as the royal inner circle was termed, but as well—indeed, even better—with William Pitt the Elder, the "Great Commoner" and reform-minded Whig, who had been forced to retire as prime minister after George III took the throne. Shelburne's townhouse in Mayfair attracted a circle of prominent intellectuals and artists who helped liberate him from lockstep thinking. He was smart, suave, and duplicitous when the occasion required it—perfect credentials for a brilliant ministerial career. Only deficient force of character would deny him greatness. For America, he would prove a godsend.

As the new president of the Board of Trade, Shelburne was asked in May 1763 by Charles Wyndham, the Earl of Egremont, who as Secretary of State was his immediate superior among the cabinet members, to draw up a detailed program for coping with Britain's expanded and potentially combustible North American empire. To keep the tinder from igniting, Egremont suggested that the government ought "to fix upon some line for a western boundary to our ancient provinces beyond which our people [the American colonists] at present should not be permitted to settle." As their numbers grew and pressure rose for new homesteads, the settlers might be directed not westward but north toward Nova Scotia or the newly designated crown colony of Quebec, where British colonists were needed as a counterweight to the largely French population, or south toward the other new and equally open colony of Florida, where British subjects were wanted to fend off Indians and Spanish interlopers.

The more closely Shelburne studied the new challenge to the empire, now that the Ohio Valley and the eastern half of the Mississippi Valley were certifiably British, the more keenly he sensed the prospect for disaster if measured steps were not soon taken. An influx of settlers was certain to stir a tidal wave of rancor over conflicting jurisdictional claims by the colonies and the legitimacy of treaties and contracts for the purchase of Indian lands. Certain to inflame the turmoil would be speculators, the colonial governors and their councils, and royal officials and court-connected aristocrats in England, all after a free helping of American soil. Southern planters, too, driven by favorable market conditions, were eyeing new farmland to replace their exhausted fields, and squatters would rapidly proliferate to claim land they thought they had as much right to as the king. All that activity would whip the native tribes into a desperate frenzy and inevitably result in extensive bloodshed. But the costs of installing truly effective governmental machinery over so broad an expanse threatened to exceed by far whatever the empire could hope to reap from it in the foreseeable future.

To reason his way out of this quandary, Shelburne's agile mind seized on the rough proposal submitted to him for the government to erect a temporary barrier—on paper, anyway—against further western settlement. The quarantined territory could remain Indian land, provided that the tribes recognized it as under the British king's sovereignty and swore their loyalty to him. The eastern colonies' charter claims beyond the line of permissible settlement would not be extinguished, but no new royal grants would be permitted there, nor sales by speculators who alleged they had bought titles in good faith from the Indians, putting a halt to the scandalous land plundering that had become common throughout the colonies with the crown's complicity. Under Shelburne's approach, conditions could be stabilized, the Indians calmed, and an orderly extension of empire planned for and gradually, peaceably carried out.

The boundary line Shelburne favored was to run along the crest of the Appalachian range, slicing obliquely south by southwest from New England to Georgia. New settlement on ungranted tracts east of the line would still be allowed. The language of the proclamation, issued in the king's name and pointedly suggesting that it was an emergency measure rather than a permanent abolition of westward settlement, prohibited all colonial governors and military commanders "for the present, and until our further Pleasure is Known, to grant Warrants of Survey, or pass Patents for any Lands beyond the Heads of Sources of the Rivers which fall into the Atlantic Ocean from the West and North West." Those frustrated by the ruling would be directed to the new colonies of Quebec and Florida, with its panhandle then extending nearly to the gates of New Orleans—a coastline of a thousand miles, so long that Shelburne broke the colony in two, East and West Florida.

If the proclamation of such a cordon sanitaire served its purpose of slowing western colonization while preserving, at least temporarily, the interior of the continent for its natives, relatively few British troops and officials would be needed to keep order across that immense wilderness. Then Parliament would not have to consider an expedient it had long avoided—imposition of a direct tax on the American colonists—to help pay for crown supervision of the frontier regions. To keep Canada from turning into a sprawling garrison colony that would become an administrative nightmare and threaten the older Atlantic seaboard colonies by its sheer bulk, Shelburne rejected the suggestion by the British military high command that the Canadian boundary be extended south of the Great Lakes to the Ohio River, a region encompassing more than 300,000 square miles (comprising the modern states of Ohio, Indiana, Illinois, Michigan, Wisconsin, and part of Minnesota).

Shelburne's Proclamation Line, as it came to be called, and his related proposals to discourage western settlement were met with favor by his fellow cabinet members, but their consensus was that his hope to limit the crown's military and administrative presence was unrealistic. The ban on new settlement would need considerable enforcement, while disgruntled Indians and Britain's balky new French subjects would have to be contended with—functions likely to cost a lot more than Shelburne's rosy outlook was anticipating, so new revenues would have to be raised. Chancellor of the Exchequer George Grenville, a hard-bitten veteran of Parliament and champion of a greater British empire, called for a strong, sustained show of military power in America, with troops garrisoned near busy towns as well as in remote inland areas. Since this prominent flexing of military muscle would be primarily for the colonists' benefit, Grenville and his allies argued that the Americans ought to bear 30 to 40 percent of the cost in the form of direct taxes levied by Parliament and earmarked for expenditure in the colonies. When growing Whig objections to Bute's efforts to enhance the king's power at the expense of Parliament forced him to retire, the wily, poker-faced Grenville succeeded him, leaving Shelburne in an untenable position. He left the cabinet after just half a year in office.

Under Grenville's stricter ministry, the Proclamation Act approved by Parliament and signed by the king in October 1763 was notably more intrusive than Shelburne's plan. It ordered British subjects already settled west of the line to surrender their holdings and retire to the eastern side of the mountains (or go north or south to the newly won colonies). The colonists were barred from making purchases from, or having private dealings with, the Indians. Only crown-licensed agents operating at official trading posts could do business with the Indians, and all further sales to them of guns and rum were outlawed.

Even though nothing was yet said about a greater military presence or a new tax on the colonists to help pay for it, the Proclamation Act was the first overt sign that the crown's long-standing hands-off policy toward the spirited Americans would no longer apply. The colonists' decentralized jurisdictions were not up to the new, harder job of empire-building; British America needed to be systematized and policed. But what seemed like prudent, unassailable reasoning to the king's ministry churned up an unhappy response in America. The expulsion of the French and the resulting diminished strength of the Indian nations should have translated into still greater freedom from Britain's oversight, according to the colonists' way of thinking, and, by opening the way west, licensed them to multiply the remarkable prosperity they had generated. They had little need for protection now and even less desire for British soldiers permanently quartered among or close by them in peacetime—unless, of course, they would like to drive off the Indians and allow the colonists to take their virtually unused lands. The last thing the Americans had in mind was that the inviting western region of the continent would be withheld from them indefinitely and reserved for the worthless Indians' pleasure. Yet no sooner were the colonists done celebrating the peace treaty of 1763 and their proud place in the incomparable British empire, so militarily mighty yet so sparing in its civil oversight, than their rulers in far-off London were putting on a very different face.

The Proclamation Act, then, came as a jolting reminder of feudal prerogatives that the colonists thought, or certainly hoped, they had left behind them forever. Here were the king and Parliament telling them that the American interior belonged to the crown, not to them, and that the monarch could impose his imperial will on their duly elected assemblies and check their collective and individual ambitions when and how he chose. The imperial message was as clear as it was unwelcome: your fine settlements were never meant to be sovereign entities.

Charles Gravier, the skilled French ambassador to the Turkish Ottoman court in Constantinople, studied the final terms of the 1763 Treaty of Paris ending the Seven Years' War and foresaw that the defeat his countrymen had just suffered would give Britain much cause to regret it. The thirteen British colonies, Gravier wrote home, were "no longer in need of her protection. She will call on them to contribute to supporting the burdens they have helped to bring upon her, and they will answer by striking off all dependence." Two decades later, Gravier, by then the Comte de Vergennes and the foreign minister of France, would contribute decisively toward bringing about that outcome.

SOME IN THE COLONIES DELUDED themselves with the hope that the Proclamation Line was conceived as a passing gesture to soothe the Indians' distress over the results of the war and what it portended for them. The measure was accordingly dismissed as a mere formality, more of a plea to the colonists than a command, rather like the import duties that the crown not infrequently enforced by benign neglect.

But there was no mistaking the intent of the new policy when Parliament followed up the Proclamation Act over the next twelve months with a series of measures requiring the colonists to help pay for enforcement of the territorial embargo in the West and other anticipated military costs—a doubly painful blow. And there was no pretense by Grenville's haughty ministry of soliciting the colonies to help formulate the revenue-raising program despite the Americans' recent cooperation in financing the war without being coerced. For the colonies were, after all, only colonies and did not have to be deferred to in such matters, or so His Majesty and his ministry had decided. At any rate, to whom would they have broached the matter of a blanket tax on the colonies? By imperial design there was no intercolonial executive body to coordinate policy among the thirteen American provinces, and it would likely have proven easier to wring nectar from Plymouth Rock than win unanimous compliance from the bumptious colonial assemblies.

The brainchild of Prime Minister Grenville, the American Revenue Act of 1764, better known as the Sugar Act, introduced or increased duties on refined sugar, coffee, textiles, and wine, among other commodities and luxuries imported by the colonies. Because Grenville, a demon with figures, had discovered that the costs of the existing British customs service for America exceeded revenues, he was determined that the new duties would not likewise be blithely disregarded or evaded by smuggling, bribery, and other forms of colonial impertinence. More manpower was to be enlisted for the reorganized and more tightly supervised customs service, and those who defied it would be hauled in front of the crown's own Admiralty courts and tried without benefit of a jury—a sharp slap at colonial juries notoriously disinclined to return guilty verdicts against their peers in such cases. Thus, Britain was signaling across the ocean that it would no longer tolerate funny business over taxes, and not just to put the colonists in compliance with the imperatives of mercantilism but also to save the empire from tumbling still deeper into debt. Remote from New World realities and the bracing air of self-determination, the ministry in London somewhat obtusely supposed that after a bit of initial grumbling, the colonists would obey the Sugar Act, especially since its burden fell most heavily on the merchants, who were the chief miscreants in the smuggling game.

No sooner did the colonists learn of the Sugar Act than they sent up a prodigious outcry. Among the loudest and most eloquent protesters was the admired Massachusetts lawyer James Otis, who told a Boston town meeting that their mother government was defiling the long-honored British principle of no taxation without representation by imposing the sugar duties on the colonies, which were not allowed to send anyone to speak and vote for or against them in Parliament. It was an anguished protest that would resonate across British America over the next dozen years. Otis appealed to the other colonies to join his own in objecting to the grave offense, and before long hundreds of merchants in Boston and New York were slashing or canceling their orders for luxury items like ruffles and lace in order to signal their counterparts in London that the colonists believed they were being sorely used.

Beyond his certainty that the uproar would soon subside, Grenville felt the Americans had long been spoiled by the minimal taxes their own legislatures and local communities levied, and why should mere colonists be permitted to escape paying the same sorts of taxes as Englishmen did back home? The following March, Grenville imposed a far more sweeping revenue-generating tax designed to impinge on almost every commercial and legal transaction conducted in the colonies. The 1765 Stamp Act dictated that all printed matter and official written documents—broadsides, pamphlets, newspapers, books, contracts, deeds, licenses, wills, diplomas, ships' logs, even playing cards—were to be produced on specially stamped paper shipped from a central stamping office in London or to carry the tax stamps purchased from official agents in the colonies. Such a tax, crown officers noted, had long been used in England, where it was higher than the planned colonial version. Some of the American colonies had even turned to tax stamps as an emergency revenue measure during the French and Indian War.

Such rationales, however earnest, failed to take into account just how radical a departure from long custom the Stamp Act constituted: a direct tax, ordered by their absentee ruler, on the colonists' everyday purchases and services. The government's insensitivity to the impact of its action, which was perhaps greater on the colonists' collective psyche than on their purse, was conveyed during the parliamentary debate on the Stamp Act by the remarks of Commons member Charles Townshend, who was shortly to join the ministry in the key post of Chancellor of the Exchequer. The colonists, Townshend remarked with towering paternalism, were Britain's "children planted by our care, nourished up by our indulgence," who had jolly well better help their parents shoulder the cost of protecting their American brats. Other British officials said it was specious for the colonists to whine that they were being taxed without the consent of their own elected representatives. They explained, in an early display of political spin-doctoring, that the colonists enjoyed the benefit of "virtual representation" because Parliament was charged with looking after the welfare of everyone in the realm, the disenfranchised included. Given that half the seats in that kindhearted Parliament were held by dependents of the crown (as ministers, court officers, civil servants, military brass, government contractors, et al.), that many of the remaining seats represented "rotten boroughs" (with small populations and therefore overweighted power) and "pocket boroughs" (controlled by local gentry, such as Shelburne's High Wycombe), and that less than 10 percent of the adult population was eligible to vote, this sort of Olympian head-patting served only to stoke the colonists' unhappiness. Nor was their pain soothed when Parliament followed directly on the heels of the Stamp Act with passage of the Quartering Act, requiring the colonists to provide food, housing, and supplies for the reinforced British soldiery posted to America—troops the Americans did not want to look at, let alone have to feed and lodge.

The resulting hullabaloo, led by the most vocal members of the colonial community—lawyers, editors and publishers, and merchants whose routine business would feel the Stamp Act's pinch—managed to instill a shared public purpose in the colonists that their geographical adjacency had never inspired. Their common grievance was vented at protest meetings, in angry editorials and letters to the editor, by the colonial assemblies petitioning the crown to withdraw the new taxes as a gross infringement on their liberties, and through the intensified boycott of manufactured products imported from Britain. Abstinence from luxury goods became an ennobling form of defiance as homespun garments replaced calico and silk.

The protest soon swung from passive to active resistance. Not only did many colonists refuse to buy and affix the hated tax stamps, but the rowdiest ransacked the offices of the stamp vendors and harassed officials who declined to process unstamped documents. And the heat of the protest rhetoric rose. Two months after the Stamp Act was signed, attorney Patrick Henry, newly elected member of Virginia's House of Burgesses, introduced resolutions loudly decrying the crown's action as an illegal intrusion into the affairs of the colony and added famously, "If this be treason, make the most of it." In Boston, James Otis skewered London officials' toplofty reassurance that the colonists had "virtual representation" in Parliament by replying that one could "as well prove that the British House of Commons in fact represents all the people of the globe." For that matter, he might have said the Parliament could be dispensed with entirely since His Royal

Majesty was supposed to look after the interests of all his subjects with infinite love, wisdom, and impartiality. By late October, six months after the revenue bill became law, delegates from nine colonies gathered in New York at a Stamp Act "congress" to ask Parliament to repeal the hated measure.

At the root of the deepening transatlantic quarrel was the suddenly urgent need for determining to what extent Parliament could impose its will on the unrepresented colonists. An obvious solution might have been to invite the Americans to send representatives, perhaps one per colony, to sit in Parliament. But time and distance made such an arrangement impracticable, and, anyway, the crown was disinclined to bestow such a privilege on its overseas subjects, who themselves had doubts that their participation in such disproportionately small numbers would have any real effect on Parliament's deliberations. It followed, then, as the colonists argued, that if actual representation in Parliament was not viable and "virtual representation" was a sham, the American colonies could not be taxed directly except by their own elected assemblies. It was a position that some in high places in Britain, though decidedly a minority, accepted. No less a luminary than William Pitt, an ailing but still magnetic figure soon to reassume the post of first minister, spoke out admiringly of the colonists' accomplishments and in defense of their liberties, but he was careful to underscore "the sovereign authority of this country over the colonists," which Pitt said extended "to every point of legislation whatever . . . [Britain] may bind their trade, confine their manufactures, and exercise every power whatsoever except that of taking their money out of their pockets without their consent." The Stamp Act, he agreed with the colonists, should be scrapped "absolutely, totally, and immediately."

It was left to the most influential colonist then residing in England to deliver the most telling case for repeal—and in the process shred British presumptions about the extent of the empire's authority over crown subjects in America. Having acquired an encyclopedic knowledge of the colonies' social, economic, and political concerns, Benjamin Franklin had been newly dispatched to London as an official spokesman for Pennsylvania, Massachusetts, New Jersey, and Georgia, and as such was without peer as a conveyor of the colonists' point of view.

Campaigning in person and by articles in the newspapers, many of them anonymous and some satirically lacerating, Franklin asserted that the Stamp Act was a misguided and hostile measure that served the best interests of neither Britain nor its American settlers. The former, he conceded, held sway over the latter, who might not—or might very well—have thrived without the protection and friendship of their parent country. But there was no reason for the empire now to start treating the colonists as if they were a conquered race and oppressing them with unjust taxes when the fact was that "[o]ur whole wealth centers finally among the merchants and inhabitants of Great Britain." To argue that the colonists were duty-bound to pay the same taxes as all other Englishmen was to ignore that they were denied access to free trade and representation in Parliament and were already taxed by their own governments.

Given the courtesy of testifying before Parliament in February 1766, Franklin was more than a match for his inquisitors as he neatly dissected the arguments for the colonists' compliance. Asked if the Americans failed to understand that the stamp revenues were to be spent in the colonies for their residents' own good, he begged to disagree. The money was to be spent, Franklin pointed out, "in the conquered colonies [Quebec and the two Floridas], where the soldiers are, not in the colonies that pay it." As to the benefit derived, he added, "Numerous as the people are in the several provinces [the American colonies], they cost you nothing in forts, citadels, garrisons, or armies to keep them in subjection. They were governed by this country at the expense only of a little pen, ink, and paper. They were led by a thread. They had not only respect but an affection for Great Britain." As to the need for troops to pacify the Indians and supervise trade with them, such commerce, "though carried on in America, is not an American interest. The people of America are chiefly farmers and planters; scarce anything they raise or produce is an article of commerce with the Indians. The Indian trade is a British interest; it is carried on with British manufacturers, for the benefit of British merchants."

Flirting with the dark arts of deception, Franklin wound up his disquisition by suggesting the colonists were by no means dead set against paying the crown any taxes whatever. In an adroit piece of flummery, he said the colonists distinguished between paying an *external* tax, such as duties levied against imported commodities, which could be added on to other expenses in determining the final price that merchants charged their customers—who were then free to pay it or not, as they chose—and *internal* taxes such as the Stamp Act imposed, an excise on goods consumed domestically within their own colonial jurisdiction. Unconvinced, his parliamentary examiners wondered why, since the colonial consumers were free in either instance to buy or not to buy at the selling price, they did not object equally to both categories. Because, Franklin said, "the sea is yours, you maintain by your fleets the safety of navigation on it and keep it clear of pirates; you may have therefore a natural and equitable right to some toll or duty on merchandise carried through that part of your dominions, towards defraying the expense . . . of that carriage."

Franklin's argument was a bit light on logic. The British government that operated fleets to keep the seas open for commerce was the same government that had chartered the colonies in the first place, granted their people land, and empowered their assemblies to operate an orderly society under the kingdom's watchful and benevolent eye. Either the American colonies were a loyal part of a larger sovereign entity, or they were not. Franklin was telling Parliament, more or less, that the Americans wanted it both ways.

A MONTH AFTER FRANKLIN'S TESTIMONY, which doubtless had had some influence but not a fraction as much as the importuning of Britain's mercantile interests that were hurting from the American boycott of their goods, Parliament withdrew the Stamp Act. It had managed to be both uncollectable and harmful to the home country's balance of trade. In bowing to expediency, though, the House of Commons petulantly issued a Declaratory Act, lest its overseas provincials should unduly celebrate their triumph. It stated that Britain had—"and by right ought to have—full power and authority to make laws and statutes of sufficient force and validity to bind the colonies and peoples of America, subjects of the crown of Great Britain, in all cases whatever." Taxes were not specified, but "all cases" seemed a sufficiently stout thumb in the colonists' eye.

Still, in a strident clash of colliding principles, British majesty had been challenged and had given way. The colonists' satisfaction, however, was short-lived. Prime Minister Pitt's health failed, and his cabinet fell increasingly under the sway of its chief finance minister, the bright, willful bureaucrat Charles Townshend. A volatile mixture of energy, vanity, and perversity, Townshend pushed through a popular measure to reduce Britain's realty tax by 25 percent, a boon to the gentry but one with the predictable effect of leaving the government strapped for funds. Searching for economies and chafing from the rebuff by the colonists over the tax measures and their reluctance to billet and supply British troops, Townshend found his target in the £700,000 the crown was spending for forts and trading posts in the American interior. He ordered the administration of Indian affairs returned to the individual colonies—a step that Shelburne also favored but which had the practical effect of canceling the government's resolve to intervene actively so that the vast western frontier region would not deteriorate into a strife-torn cockpit of colliding claims and ambitions.

Still hungry for revenues, Townshend then displayed an abysmal lack of judgment by deciding to test Franklin's artful dodge that the colonists distinguished between external and internal taxes—a distinction the finance minister himself thought nonsensical—and would thus acquiesce on import duties because they fell under Parliament's conceded right to control the empire's trade. The result was the 1767 Townshend Revenue Acts, imposing duties on glass, lead, paints, paper, and tea. Only the last of these products was imported in heavy volume, and the duty on it was not high, but Townshend was determined to act upon the principle enunciated by the Declaratory Act—that Parliament was not beholden to the colonists or their assemblies in carrying out its imperial responsibilities. Townshend's position reflected a growing belief in London that the government would either have to tame the colonies or lose them. Accordingly, a customs commission was installed in Boston's commercial hub to oversee enforcement of the new duties, the number of inspectors was substantially raised, and their powers were expanded, most notably (and offensively) by so-called writs of assistance issued by the highest court in each colony and authorizing the crown's paid snoops to barge into homes, offices, stores, warehouses, and ships to root out evidence of smuggling.

Townshend, who died before he could witness the consequences of his confrontational strategy, had been right to suspect that Franklin's reassurance about American acceptance of external taxes was bogus. It was the very principle at the heart of the Declaratory Act that the colonists most fiercely objected to—that Parliament could impose *any* laws, rules, or regulations on them that it chose, however misguided or punitive. The response to the Townshend Acts was swift and the howls of anguish louder than ever as Britain seemed determined to put the colonists in their place. Sparks flew from the pens of firebrands such as Samuel Adams and Franklin's Philadelphia rival, John Dickinson, an ally of the Penn family, whose widely reprinted *Letters from a Pennsylvania Farmer,* while conceding Parliament's right to monitor British commerce, rejected all taxes on the colonists if their purpose, as bluntly stated in the very title of the Townshend duties, was to extort revenues from them. Again the Americans began boycotting English imports, massively this time from New England to Virginia, and the only tea they were drinking was what Dutch ships could smuggle in from the West Indies. Aroused colonists formed underground intercolonial networks of protest, began hectoring British customs agents, and vandalized crown offices. In response, a British warship appeared in Boston harbor, guns bristling, and by the autumn of 1768 two regiments of redcoats were garrisoned on Boston Common.

That the crown had set in motion the whirlwind now threatening to veer out of control was acknowledged by few among Britain's ruling class. One of those few was the young Earl of Shelburne, who, in exile from the ministry when the Sugar Act and Stamp Act were passed, spoke up against them in the House of Lords as unjustifiable and unenforceable and scored the Declaratory Act as unnecessarily provocative. Without any troops to enforce it, Shelburne's Proclamation Line, though well intended, had proven an exercise in futility, rather as if the crown had commanded the sun to stand still. The colonists' angry response to the prohibition on new western settlements and the tax and troop-quartering acts dramatized for Shelburne the hard truth that Britain's willful government chose to ignore: the American colonies were no longer a frail dependency but a junior partner, to be dealt with equitably, not dictatorially.

Lonely among his peers for this insight and unbeloved for voicing it, Shelburne had taken a position remarkably close to the one that Benjamin Franklin had been advocating for several years among government officials, leaders of his own mercantile class, and London's intellectual elite—that America was Britain's brightest hope for enhanced wealth and power, the empire's outsized diamond in the rough, whose residents ought to be dealt with not as rustic suppliants but as enterprising Englishmen faithfully serving both the kingdom and themselves. It was no accident that Shelburne's views seemed to coincide so closely with Franklin's and that the young aristocrat was about to act to translate them into a revised and more sensible British policy.

During his years out of office, Shelburne had busied himself tending to his large landholdings in Ireland, Wiltshire, and Buckinghamshire but remained in steady touch with the social, political, and cultural scenes in London. He turned Bowood, his chief English country estate, into a showplace with the guidance of famed landscape architect Lancelot "Capability" Brown, installing delightful terraces and planted courtyards, an artificial lake, and a clock tower, and building a magnificent library replete with rare manuscripts. To his townhouse on the south end of Berkeley Square he drew the leading artists and most advanced social thinkers of his day, including Adam Smith, Jeremy Bentham, David Hume, Samuel Johnson, Oliver Goldsmith, William Blackstone, Joseph Priestly, Joshua Reynolds, and Benjamin Franklin. Disdainful of party politics and in a social position to go his own way, Shelburne was likely drawn by such an accomplished crowd toward relatively radical and, for his class, nonconformist views, some of which he expressed in the House of Lords, where he had few superiors as a speaker and debater. His favoring of free trade (over combative mercantilism), reform of Parliament (through more frequent elections and an extended franchise), purging of the crown's encrusted patronage system (producing a grossly inflated, sedentary civil service), an end to the abusive practices of the East India Company, and leniency toward the American colonies were evidence of his liberated mind. Whether Franklin helped shape that mind or it was already highly receptive to his arguments, the American sage found in the young man, who was less than half his age, a generous spirit and fertile turf for cultivation.

Called back to the cabinet in 1766 by Pitt, now Earl of Chatham, Shelburne was made Secretary of State in charge of the Home and Colonial Department and sought to regain the goodwill of the Americans, a policy surely nurtured by his friendship with Franklin, who saw more of him than of any other government minister. Chatham's poor health led to his frequent absence from cabinet meetings and left Shelburne with no staunch ally in his pro-American, antitax position. But Chancellor of the Exchequer Townshend's death in 1767 gave Shelburne more room to maneuver. He began formulating a proposal to encourage British America's westward settlement—beyond the Proclamation Line but within new parameters to be set by the government. Such expansion, Franklin and many colonists were arguing, would create new commercial opportunities for the empire. But under the Proclamation Act, Americans with land fever—and there were many—could take up property beyond the Appalachians only if they were willing to chance the crown's wrath as squatters or were able to convince the government that extending them a grant would somehow advance the overall British position in North America. Just such a large-scale settlement plan was being hatched at the time by a group of leading Pennsylvania merchants, who happened to have a close acquaintance in London on congenial terms with potentates of the realm. Ben Franklin, public-spirited and high-minded as he was, had never been mistaken for an angel. If he could latch on to a bucket or two of gold for himself while serving the rest of mankind, so much the better—and the Illinois Company, as the speculative venture dreamed up by his Philadelphia business pals was named, seemed well suited for both purposes.

Franklin's merchant friends in Philadelphia had set out to buy land northwest of the Ohio River in Illinois Country, a region of active commerce with the natives. To circumvent the Proclamation Act, they planned to buy property titles in Illinois from French settlers, a stratagem not explicitly disallowed under crown rules. Prominent among the backers of the scheme was Joseph Galloway, said to be the richest merchant in Philadelphia and perhaps Ben Franklin's closest business associate. Not surprisingly, then, among those also invited to join the big realty deal were Franklin himself, who could open many doors in London for the Pennsylvanians; his illegitimate son, William Franklin, then the royal governor of New Jersey, thanks to his father's pull; the royal governor of New York, and, probably through him, the superintendent of Indian affairs for the northern colonies, William Johnson, who lived in baronial splendor in a frontier palace in New York's Mohawk Valley, had an Indian wife, and was widely regarded as the most knowledgeable man in the British colonies when it came to getting along with the natives. Here, then, was a formidable land syndicate, not a gang of fly-by-night operators.

They were so well connected, in fact, that William Franklin urged the Illinois Company not to bother buying up French-owned farms and estates but instead to approach the British government directly for a grant, seeking 1.2 million acres between the Illinois and Mississippi rivers and promising to settle at least one white Protestant for every hundred acres—a way to counter the largely Gallic population in that far western end of Britain's newly extended territory. The plan was forwarded to Franklin in London.

Whether Franklin was the mastermind behind Shelburne's reshaped thoughts on westward expansion or was simply adroit at exploiting them, there is documented evidence that the king's minister in charge of colonial affairs and the distinguished American lobbyist discussed the Illinois land project at length during 1767. Since Shelburne's sudden enthusiasm for new colonial settlements marked an abrupt turnaround from his earlier position, suspicion that Franklin may have been the instigator—or, at the least, an active proponent—can hardly be dismissed. His own account suggests that he played a somewhat less guileful role. In correspondence with his son, Franklin reported discussions with Shelburne about new western settlements, which, in fairness to the British minister, may now have seemed a timely policy to regain goodwill for the crown among the aggrieved colonists. When Shelburne confided his concern that any substantial new settlement initiatives licensed by the crown would require extensive efforts to control the Indians and prevent friction in trading with them, Franklin enlightened the young Secretary of State about the difficulties of keeping the natives subdued over so vast a terrain. Later, probably feeling budgetary pressure from Townshend, then the cabinet heavyweight, Shelburne conceded that the only practical way to proceed was to take the costly regulation of Indian affairs out of British military hands and turn the task back to the individual colonies. Franklin pounced. "I took the opportunity," Franklin wrote William on August 24, 1767, "of urging it [the transfer of Indian oversight] as one means of saving expense in supporting the [British military] outposts, that a settlement should be made in the Illinois country [and] expatiated on the various advantages." Such an enterprise, Franklin suggested, could make the region more secure, enhance British trade with the Indians, and provide a useful military base on the Mississippi, of potentially great value if British forces were ever required to be shipped downriver to halt incursions by Spain or some other foreign power. Then, according to his version of their exchange, Franklin pulled his rabbit out of the hat and revealed the Illinois Company's plan to seek a government grant that could form the nucleus for a new crown colony, adding that he understood the formidable William Johnson was amenable to serve as its governor.

How decisive Franklin's intervention was in affecting Shelburne's actions can only be surmised, but scholars have detected a causal connection. Thomas P. Abernethy, in his classic study *Western Lands and the American Revolution,* wrote: "The Philadelphia philosopher carried out his functions with remarkable success," to the extent that not only did the Secretary of State support the Illinois enterprise but "Shelburne converted the [Privy] Council to the plan." Perhaps to avoid the appearance of special pleading on behalf of Franklin and his associates, Shelburne's endorsement was part of a grander plan that he formulated for the cabinet's approval. To encourage orderly settlement and promote commerce, he called for the establishment of three new, self-sustaining colonies, one along the upper Ohio River, a second in the region around the fort at Detroit, and the most westward one in the Illinois Country.

But Shelburne remained a lone wolf in the cabinet. His poorly masked scorn for others' petty political motives won him little leverage, and his opposition to a tough anti-American policy, emblemized by Townshend's new import duties, and his stance—solitary within the ministry—against expelling the iconoclast John Wilkes from the House of Commons for allegedly slandering the king were too radical to be tolerated. With the resignation of Pitt the Elder for ill health, Shelburne's survival in the cabinet was untenable, and his ambitious program for new western settlements wilted on the vine. Subsequent efforts to revive and reconfigure the Illinois Company's application for a grant as well as similar large-scale projects proposed by other groups of speculators would all prove unavailing despite Franklin's best efforts. Up to the eve of the colonies' rebellion, Shelburne continued to call for conciliation with the Americans and thought it madness to go to war with them. After Franklin left London in 1774, the two men were never to meet again. But when they renewed contact in writing and through intermediaries eight years later, the future course of their nations would ride on the outcome of their dealings.

. . .

THROUGHOUT THE 1760S, the most powerful figure in Massachusetts was its governor, Thomas Hutchinson, scion of a leading mercantile family dating back to the Puritans—his ancestor Anne Hutchinson had boldly advocated religious toleration—and a Harvard alumnus of genuinely intellectual bent. An accomplished author (of, among other works, a reputable history of his colony), he had served as chief judge of Massachusetts's high court before being chosen acting governor by the colonial assembly. He was also a rabid crown loyalist, and when he called for compliance with the Stamp Act, his home was sacked by protesters—an act that no doubt intensified his alarm that a radical rabble was loose in the land. Toward the end of the decade, as many in his colony joined to protest the Townshend duties as evidence of unceasing British oppression, Hutchinson wrote to a number of well-placed friends in London, advising the ministry that in order to quell the growing turmoil in the colonies "there must be an abridgment of what are called English liberties."

Hutchinson's views were well regarded in London, and before long 10,000 British troops were posted in the colonies, the heaviest concentration of them around Boston. Their presence served only to intensify colonists' resentment, spilling over into bloodshed in the so-called Boston Massacre of 1770, which claimed five lives and raised American tempers to the boiling point. A cooling-off period followed, due in part to conciliatory gestures by the new prime minister, Lord Frederick North, who ordered the Townshend revenue acts dropped—except the one covering tea imports—and allowed the Quartering Act to lapse.

Once again, though, the British government was not content to leave well enough alone. It took the powerfully symbolic step of ordering Governor Hutchinson and the colony's judges to be paid out of import duties and not directly by the legislature, thereby reducing public influence over its ranking magistrates. Cries of tyranny were renewed. Two developments in 1773 further fueled the lurking conflagration. In order to rescue the East India Company, a crown-chartered monopoly, from financial collapse due to stupefying mismanagement and rampant graft, Parliament passed the Tea Act, which designated the company as the sole licensed exporter of tea to America and allowed it to dump its large surplus of the commodity on the captive colonial market instead of having to auction it off at ruinous prices. To foil persistent smuggling of tea by non-British vessels, the East India Company was empowered to sell its tea to the colonies only through retailers known to harbor strong Tory sentiments. These selected merchants, freed of having to deal with profit-leeching wholesalers, were thus able to underprice all vendors outside the monopoly arrangement. Besides tea, the East India Company held a monopoly on other heavily imported goods such as silks, drugs, spices, and chinaware. Would the crown soon hand its semi-official trading company still greater monopolistic power over colonial commerce with America in order to stabilize its operations and thereby further enrich the British economy?

As aroused Massachusetts patriots vowed to undermine the Tea Act, their ire was fed by the disclosure, through public reading in the colonial assembly, of the letters Governor Hutchinson had sent to London some years earlier, calling on the home government to take repressive measures against his unruly colonists. The latter, on learning of the governor's treachery, now wanted his head. But when the Massachusetts assembly dispatched a petition to London, demanding Hutchinson's removal, ministry officials were incensed that the loyal governor's private letters had been stolen and placed in mischievous hands for shipment to Boston, a veritable powder keg of subversive sentiment. Who had done so dastardly a deed?

Only after one nearly fatal duel had been fought in London over that question and another one scheduled did the true culprit stand forth to prevent an unmerited loss of life. Benjamin Franklin confessed that the incendiary letters had been given to him—he steadfastly refused to identify the intermediary beyond vindicating those who had been falsely accused—and explained that he had sent them to friends in Boston not to inflame public sentiment against the crown but to let it be known within the most actively anti-British circles who had been the chief fomentor of the repressive measures. To prevent the letters from stirring an outbreak of antiroyalist violence, Franklin added—perhaps disingenuously, to minimize his culpability—that he had instructed the recipients of the letters not to publish them. If so, he surely should have known better; if not, the comeuppance soon visited upon him could hardly have been a surprise.

Franklin's revelation, feeding latent suspicion around London that he had always been an American first and an Englishman second, required an official rebuke. While one was being contemplated, word reached the British capital of the epic vandalism perpetrated by stealth at Boston harbor on the evening of December 16, 1773. The first of the ships loaded with the East India Company tea had arrived, touching off a series of mass meetings to prevent the obnoxious cargo from being landed and the three-pence-a-pound duty on it from being paid. After Governor Hutchinson ruled that the tea-laden ship *Dartmouth* could not leave the harbor still loaded and with the tea duty unpaid, Samuel Adams denounced him before 8,000 seething colonists gathered at Old South Church. Later that night a band of activists masquerading as Mohawk Indians boarded the *Dartmouth* and dumped 342 casks of tea into the drink. So curt a message to the crown would have to be met by harsh reprisal, Lord North's tone-deaf ministry reflexively concluded, or there would be no end to the colonists' incorrigible tantrums.

In need of a scapegoat, the government found a handy one in the eminent Dr. Franklin, who had plainly betrayed the trust expected from a crown officer by conspiring to transmit the inflammatory Hutchinson letters. Ordered before the Lords' Committee of His Majesty's Privy Council on Plantation Affairs at the end of January 1774, Franklin stood for two hours while he was assailed as morally reprehensible for having obtained the Hutchinson letters by fraud and corruption—a charge without a molecule of evidence to support it—and labeled by the solicitor general, a renowned maestro of vituperation, as "the first mover and prime conductor of the whole contrivance," whose "mind may have been . . . possessed with the idea of a Great American Republic." In fact, no one in the kingdom had tried harder than Franklin to calm the troubled waters between the mother country and its headstrong colonies and emphasize the mutual benefits of amicable relations. Even his ultimately fruitless efforts to win land grants for the Illinois Company and successor ventures, involving many prominent British backers in and out of government in his plan to establish new western colonies—certainly censurable as attempted seduction of crown officials to advance a private interest for financial gain—had the public-spirited rationale of fusing British and American commercial interests.

A few days later, the government formally reprimanded Franklin for disloyalty, stripped him of his colonial postmastership, and thereby succeeded in turning the crown's most constructive ally and advisor among the colonists into a henceforth unshakable enemy. Britain's loss was Franklin's—and the colonists'—immediate gain. There were some in America, most of them no doubt envious of Franklin's remarkable standing, who thought him too cozy with the royal establishment; a few had even accused him of helping draft the Stamp Act in return for a patronage grant to appoint sales agents and enforcement officers for the tax. Flagellated by the crown for the Hutchinson affair and officially defrocked, Franklin returned home a hero, the venerable solon about to play a titanic role in winning the colonists' independence.

The chain reaction of events, each new crown act of repression met by heightened colonial defiance, quickly played itself out. In a series of progressively more coercive acts, Britain shut down the port of Boston, commercial nexus of the continent; suspended many civil liberties, including the right of assembly and habeas corpus; and took over effective control of the government of Massachusetts, which fell under the direction of General Thomas Gage, formerly military commander for British America. The greatest blunder and most potent incitement to rebellion was Parliament's passage of the Quebec Act of 1774, which stoked outrage in Virginia, the largest colony and most important agriculturally.

The Quebec Act, partly intended and certainly perceived as a punitive step by Britain against the American colonies for their vehement objections to the Stamp Act and other revenue measures, extended the southern border of Quebec province all the way south to the Ohio River, thereby removing some 300,000 square miles of territory claimed by Virginia and, in parts of the northern sector, by Connecticut and Massachusetts under their conflict-ing charters. Denied American tax revenues, the British government had withdrawn troops and dismantled or abandoned forts in this sprawling northwest sector of Virginia's claimed territory above the Ohio, so that the mostly French settlers were left without a civil administration and prey to Indian misconduct (and vice versa). To stabilize the region, the crown estab-lished civil rule more like an imperial French or Spanish regime than the self-governing—and now increasingly unmanageable—ones in the thirteen Atlantic colonies. Quebec would now be run by a royally appointed council with the king retaining veto power over all its legislative acts and Parliament empowered to levy all but local taxes. Although denied a freely elected assembly and other basic democratic rights, the mostly French Catholic population was granted freedom of worship and the retention of their cus-tomary semifeudal seigneurial laws of land tenure, a concession to larger property owners. In a companion enactment, Parliament and the Board of Trade ordered a halt to the systematic corruption of colonial land grant pro-cedures by self-serving royal governors and their executive councils. This customary abuse of power by private dealings that most notoriously took the form of enormous grants to officeholders and their favorites was to give way to regularized procedures that required surveys of crown lands being put up for public auction at not less than sixpence per acre. There would be no more giveaways, and the crown would no longer recognize titles obtained by speculators in spurious private deals with the Indians.

Reforms, even if greatly belated, in the land distribution system might have been welcomed if they had not been coupled now with the trans-parently punitive effects of the Quebec Act. At a stroke, these sweeping changes seemed to deny Virginians their chartered territorial rights—or claims, at any rate—and their destiny as the dominant British American colony. Farmers, speculators, and squatters afflicted with land fever were angered by the brute force of the directives from London, and large planters in debt and in thrall to the British mercantile system, including many of the leading aristocratic families in the southern colonies, bonded as never before with their New England brethren in denouncing crown despotism. Quebec and the rest of Canada, they feared, might now become the base for a repressive onslaught against the American colonies, whose citizens might wind up with governments as undemocratic as the one about to be imposed on the French Canadians. One prominent Virginia planter and soldier, George Washington, wrote at the time: "The crisis is arrived when we must assert our rights or submit to every imposition . . . that can be heaped on us, till custom and use shall make us as tame and abject as the blacks we rule over with such arbitrary sway."

In London the Earl of Shelburne sounded a sympathetic note, drowned out amid a ruling class unshakable in its certitude. Though powerless, he decried "the madness, injustice, and infatuation of coercing the Americans into a blind and servile submission." Franklin may not have put the words into his mouth, but they surely echoed his own and his countrymen's sentiments. Shelburne's (and Franklin's) friend, the Scottish economist Adam Smith, captured the essence of the American grievance in his most famous work, issued the same year the colonists declared their independence—*The Wealth of Nations,* a treatise on the virtues of laissez-faire and the eventually deadening effects on commerce of government-sanctioned monopolistic practices. In diagnosing the American colonists' pain, Smith wrote: "To prohibit a great people from making all they can of every part of their own produce . . . in a way they judge most advantageous to themselves, is a manifest violation of the most sacred rights of mankind."

The rulers of Great Britain, though, saw in their American colonists not a great people but indulged upstarts who owed the crown eternal tribute for all the blessings it had bestowed upon them. That the tribute had never been formally demanded before was beside the point, and when the empire had need to call in this due bill of gratitude, the overseers of the realm were dismayed by the colonists' denial of its validity. Whatever feelings of gratitude the British may have once been entitled to for permitting the Americans to enjoy the fruits of their own labor and fortitude had long since worn off. Like Lear, King George III could only rant how sharper than a serpent's tooth it was to suffer an ungrateful child. But to the Poor Richards of the colonies, the crown's demand for obedience and tribute money symbolic of their subordinate status was a clear case—no matter how dressed up—of child abuse.

CHAPTER 3

Thinking large

1776–1782

I F ALL OF BRITANNIA DID NOT EXULT at the prospect of its American colonies someday dwarfing the home isles in population, wealth, and power, as they already did in acreage, more and more of the colonists themselves were coming to share Benjamin Franklin's expectation of their infinitely expansive future. Their vision was based on a vast territorial dominion in the offing. That the crown had lately adopted land settlement policies to discourage that process—at least temporarily—served only to whet the Americans' appetite for space while arousing protest over their enclosure. Their undaunted aspirations echoed in the excited young voices of two graduating members of the class of 1771 of the College of New Jersey at Princeton who delivered a collaborative poem at their commencement exercises. Titling their work "On the Rising Glory of America," Philip Freneau and Henry Brackenridge wrote:

> Shall we ask what empires yet must rise,
> What kingdoms, pow'rs and states where now are seen
> But dreary wastes and awful solitude,
> Where melancholy sits with eye forlorn
> And hopes the day when Britain's sons shall spread
> Dominions to the north and south and west
> Far from the Atlantic to Pacific shores?

Four years later, on the eve of the American rebellion, another equally young man—and still a newcomer to the colonies—named Alexander Hamilton left King's College (Columbia) in New York to begin writing pamphlets for the cause of independence. In one tract, Hamilton charged that British oppression of the Americans was readily traceable to "a jealousy of our dawning splendour . . . The boundless extent of the territory we possess, the wholesome temperament of our climate, the luxuriance and fertility of our soil, the variety of our products, the rapidity of our population [growth], the industry of our country men" all foretold a destined greatness.

But what exactly was that "extent of territory" to which Hamilton alluded and the young Princeton poets blithely laid transcontinental claim more than a generation before anyone knew the true distance? The War for Independence would determine who should wield civil power over that indeterminate terrain; the peace treaty—assuming the colonists' success— would fix its boundaries, which the Old World nations wished to confine as narrowly as possible. Contesting the issue at the bargaining table would be the infant republic's first great challenge.

From the first months of their ringingly proclaimed nationhood, the Americans were consistently clear about the extent of the country they claimed was theirs. According to John Adams's text for a contemplated "model peace treaty" of alliance with France that Congress approved in September 1776, the federated American states intended to secure "the sole, exclusive, undivided and perpetual possession of the Counties, Cities, and Towns on the said Continent, and of all the lands near to it, which now are, or lately were under the Jurisdiction of or subject to the King or Crown of Great Britain, whenever they shall be united or confederated with the said United States." That meant the new nation would extend not only westward to the Mississippi River but northward as well to enclose all of Canada as then understood (most of modern Quebec and Ontario provinces) and the Maritimes, Nova Scotia and Newfoundland, and southward to ensnare East and West Florida, too—that is, all of British America as established by the empire's sweeping victory in the French and Indian War. Never mind that the sparsely settled Canadian provinces and Florida were not part of the rebellious thirteen colonies and had registered not the slightest wish to separate from Britain; Americans were thinking large, grandiose thoughts from the outset.

None of them had more incandescent dreams and a greater territorial grievance against Britain than the Virginians. The Proclamation Act of 1763, which had barred all settlements beyond the Appalachians, affected more than half of the undisputed area of colonial Virginia (comprising the westernmost section of modern Virginia and all of West Virginia and Kentucky), while the Quebec Act of 1774 had peremptorily assigned the huge Old Northwest section of the colony above the Ohio River to the Canadian province. As a practical matter, the two acts together had taken away about 75 percent of the land over which Virginia had claimed jurisdiction under its charter of 1609. To grasp the scale of this diminution, it should be added that Virginia's boundaries as claimed by its charter grant, the first awarded in America, constituted close to half of all the land claimed by the original thirteen colonies. Virginia was more than four times as large as the next biggest colony, North Carolina (then including Tennessee). Is it any wonder that so many of the ablest Revolutionary-era statesmen were aroused members of Virginia's planter aristocracy, whose fortunes and standing had everything to do with real estate?

To lay the groundwork for an assertion of their sovereign status, the American colonies had sent delegates to Philadelphia in 1774 to an initial conclave they grandly dubbed the first Continental Congress. To lend credibility to what struck most European observers as its absurdly ambitious claim to all of King George III's North American holdings, the second Continental Congress convening in 1775 ordered a bold military strike a full year before formally declaring itself independent of the crown. When the colonial forces under their new commander, Virginia's George Washington, began to besiege Boston, the British had reinforced their New England garrison with troops shifted from Canada, leaving little more than a token defense there. If American soldiers could strike unexpectedly and exploit the less than ardent fondness for the British among the French Canadians and the native tribes making up most of the sparse population, the United States could deny Britain its base for assaulting the insurgent colonies from the north and west. Out of gratitude—or so Congress calculated—the liberated Canadians would flock to the new American confederation and participate in its rebellion.

In the autumn of 1775 an American army of 2,000 pushed north from Fort Ticonderoga, recently captured by the bold Ethan Allen and his band, as George Washington addressed an appeal to the Canadian people, urging them to rebel and "range yourselves under the standard of General Liberty, against which all the force and artifice of tyranny will never be able to prevail." If ever received and circulated, the message made little impact on Montreal, where the British garrison of 800, aided by the locals, held out valiantly for fifty-five days before yielding to the invaders. Leaving behind enough troops to control the town, the main body of Americans moved down the St. Lawrence to the provincial capital of Quebec City, where they rendezvoused with a smaller force of fellow rebels, led by Benedict Arnold, who had suffered a punishing march through the Maine woods. To deal imperial Britain a severe blow at the very outset of their uprising, all the

Americans had to do was overcome the outnumbered defenders of Quebec. The latter, though, held the high ground, looking down from their stout, stone triangular bastion that only ceaseless bombardment could have tumbled. But with winter coming on, the frozen ground would not allow the attackers to raise earthworks for mounting their big cannons. The alternative of trying to starve the defenders into submission would have required the Americans to endure a Canadian winter outside the city gates—and, at any rate, many in their ranks were due to finish their term of service at the end of the year.

With the clock, the topography, and nature—in the form of a swirling snowstorm—all against them, the Americans stormed the heights above the Plains of Abraham on the next to last day of the year and were decisively repulsed. American forces hung on through the cruel winter months but failed to win over the sympathies of the locals. Only the year before, under the Quebec Act, the British regime had appeased the most powerful elements in the province by restoring the historic rights and privileges of the landed seigneurs and the Catholic clergy and extending the fur traders' hunting grounds south of the Great Lakes. Since Canada, unlike the lower thirteen colonies, had never been allowed to indulge in democratic practices and a substantial measure of self-rule under either French or British governance, the Americans' appeal to join them in throwing off the yoke of colonial subjugation fell on deaf ears. Besides, Congress had not supplied enough money to sustain its first military incursion through a long frigid campaign so far from home, forcing its soldiers to live off the countryside and its increasingly resentful inhabitants. As heavy British reinforcements moved upriver with the first thaw of spring, the spent invaders withdrew, and America had lost its chance to seize the military initiative. Six years of often hopeless struggle had to be endured before that chance would come again.

ON THE FACE OF IT, the colonists did not have even the faintest prayer of victory.

Ranged against them were the most powerful military force and flourishing economy in the Old World. Britain had lately routed its European rivals on the battlefield and the open seas. It enjoyed stable social institutions, the semblance of representative government, and a tax revenue system that made its currency and credit the world's strongest. Its merchant fleet, the largest and best afloat, carried the trade that generated the wealth that kept the whole imperial edifice growing. That such a majestic power might let its most lucrative colonial possession slip from its grasp was unthinkable, especially to its monarch, George III, thirty-eight years old and in the sixteenth year of his reign at the time the colonies declared him an incorrigible oppressor. He ruled over some 11 million subjects in the home isles, nearly four times the population of the American colonies (one-fifth of whom were slaves), and kept a standing army of 50,000, which he could afford to supplement at will to meet emergencies, such as the American uprising, by enlisting foreign mercenaries—much cheaper than adding permanent recruits and swelling the ranks of crown pensioners.

By contrast, the Continental Congress, without a standing army or navy at its disposal, had to scrape together a force from the ranks of the unemployed, indentured servants and tenant farmers who wanted relief from their grinding labors, and militiamen willing to take up arms for a season to free themselves and their neighbors from the royal yoke. The newly declared American nation, moreover, had no government, no revenues except what it could coax from its stingy constituent states, no industry to produce the weaponry required to wage a protracted war, no universally accepted currency, and little credit. Its overseas trade was immediately subjected to British blockade and seizure. It was surrounded on three sides by British territory, from which it could be attacked, and on the east by the ocean, from which the unassailable enemy could launch strikes where and when it chose. America was a sprawl of loosely linked provinces, rather like a well-fed but laughably uncoordinated infant trying to propel itself on the wobbliest of appendages, all the while furious at a suddenly intolerant parent. It seemed, in short, a contest between grotesquely mismatched antagonists.

That very fact, though, would work in the Americans' favor by inspiring overconfidence and miscalculation by the crown's ministers and generals, who failed from the outset to grasp the physical challenges of a protracted overseas war and the staying power of the colonists' alienation. King George persuaded himself that the bulk of his wayward American subjects had been temporarily led astray by hotheads who would cool down at the first real show of British military might. Surely there were plenty of crown loyalists among them who, once his troops were on the march, would rally to the king's colors and bring their fellow colonists back to their senses.

The sovereign, if badly self-deluded about the colonists, was far from a fool. Though garrulous, moralistic, self-congratulatory, temperamentally volatile, prone to pigheadedness, and overproud of his spreading dominion, George III was also dedicated to his duties, more sensible than most of his ministers and retainers, and bent on reducing the rampant corruption and influence peddling that riddled the royal administration. As a young ruler, the king had resolved to tame the ascendant Whig aristocrats in Parliament who for a generation had eroded the crown's influence. But in so doing he had to dispense patronage freely and rely on ministers who, while dependably faithful, lacked talent for statecraft. The result, during his first decade as king, was an unstable, chronically bickering government that often pursued erratic and imprudent policies, such as those meant to force the tax-loathing American colonists into submission.

Once hostilities were under way, it was naturally supposed throughout Britain that its army's great advantage in numbers, training, equipment, and discipline would make quick work of the rebels. But the latter, holding the heights above Boston in the earliest days of the conflict, soon let the masters of the empire know just how irritating it would prove to quell them, however unschooled they were in the ways of war. Their amateur status forced the Americans to improvise. From adjacent lanes and alleyways and whatever enclosures were handy they directed their disorderly rifle fire at the lines of redcoats advancing in rigid formation up the environs of Bunker Hill. It took the British troops three bloody charges and cost them nearly half their 2,400-man force to dislodge the defenders, who suffered far fewer casualties and retreated largely intact.

The encounter set the pattern for what followed. Because the British generally had at least twice as many men in the field at any one time and commanders experienced in troop deployment, they were able to prevail whenever clashes occurred on conventional, open battlefields with room to maneuver and no place to hide. Thus, in the first autumn of the war after the United States declared its independence, the British professionals badly battered Washington's ill-trained Continental Army in a series of routs in and around New York City and sent them reeling across New Jersey to eventual refuge beyond the Delaware River in eastern Pennsylvania. An army less cocksure than the British might have given chase and obliterated the wounded rebel prey, effectively ending the armed insurgency. Washington, though, learned his lesson, and for the rest of the war did his best to avoid presenting his troops as targets for the enemy's massive firepower and cruel bayonets.

In practical terms, that decision meant waging most ungentlemanly guerrilla warfare, ever on the move against a far less agile foe, stealthily exploiting the American terrain with its deep, bosky recesses and striking when least expected, sometimes at night or in foul weather, as in the morale-building victory at Trenton and its aftermath at Princeton. Here was the great leveling factor in the war: the Americans were defending their homeland, and it was vast by European standards, affording Washington and his men a depth of countryside to fall back on, ample cover from which to spy on every British movement, and ideal conditions to ambush the enemy when it tried to pursue at less than full strength. In an age when the foot soldier was the core of the army and cannons had to be tiresomely dragged over crude roads, America's great distances worked much to the advantage of the Continental Army. The British, as a result, kept their forces in or close by the seaport cities and larger towns, but controlling these areas brought them no decisive benefit (beyond, that is, more easily extinguishing the colonists' seaborne trade). For America had no real center, no true capital; it was farmland, by and large, its spirit of resistance dispersed among hundreds of villages and countless crossroads hamlets and their surrounding, unconquerable countryside.

The ultimate folly of the British endeavor was dramatized for the watching world in the second summer of the war. In a carefully planned but misguided—and disastrously executed—attack intended to cut off New England, the seedbed of the insurrection, from the rest of the colonies, jaunty, disdainful General John Burgoyne led an army of heavily equipped British regulars and German mercenaries south from Canada through the thickly wooded Hudson Valley on a projected 300-mile march to meet a second British force driving north from New York harbor. Oblivious at first of their largely invisible adversaries lurking in the bush, Burgoyne's troops soon enough discovered the Americans' shadowy presence by the man-made obstacles—tangles of felled trees, destroyed bridges, dammed and diverted streams—slowing their advance to a mile-a-day crawl in the summer heat. The farther south they ventured and the longer their supply train, the greater the redcoats' exposure to the dogged Continental regulars and the ever-growing legion of militiamen from surrounding New York, Massachusetts, New Hampshire, and Connecticut who now swarmed nearby. Their rifle fire from the cloaking summer foliage, out of murky swamps, and behind stone walls began to pick off the marchers in full battle regalia, their swords dragging in the mud. And it was well-aimed gunnery, for in a mostly agrarian, prospering society like colonial America, rifles were ubiquitous—as they were not in Europe—and almost every lad was taught how to use the family weapon for hunting and repulsing Indian attackers and other intruders. Not that every American recruit was a crack marksman—far from it—but colonial civilians were highly familiar with the rifle, and the kind they favored was often faster-loading and more accurate than their invaders'. In time, the encircling colonists began to skirmish with the thinned and exhausted British forces, producing a critical American victory near Saratoga, where "Gentleman Johnny" Burgoyne surrendered his 6,000 surviving troops, 7,000 muskets, forty-two brass cannon, and his personal featherbed that the baggage train hauled.

It is only a slight exaggeration to suggest that the land itself was the best weapon at the disposal of the colonists, even as the prospect of owning a piece of it had been the prime incentive for the settlement of British America. As important to the revolutionary cause as its backers' somewhat hyperbolic outcry against imperial tyranny and their noble rhetoric about liberty denied and theoretical equality among all (white) men was the pressing practical question of who would control the immense supply of America's ungranted—indeed, unmapped and largely undiscovered—territory. During its two pre-Revolutionary years in session, the Continental Congress had never insisted that the crown hand it sovereignty over the colonies' commerce, specifically acknowledging the mutual benefits of the monopolistic Navigation and Trade Acts to America as well as Britain. And the fiery language of the Declaration of Independence, with full poetic license, conveniently failed to note that the imperial crackdown had begun only after a century and a half of virtual self-rule, that Parliament and the crown had offered to cancel all offending enactments in order to avoid the American secession from the empire, and that the colonists paid but a fraction of the taxes burdening the average landholder in the British Isles. But there was no equivocation, ambiguity, or artifice in the Americans' conviction about who owned their land and who held the power to distribute and govern it. The British king and Parliament had long ago lost their claim to it and the right to parcel it arbitrarily among the favored few on the basis of hereditary privilege and political allegiance. Jefferson spelled out the subversive principle at the core of the colonists' grievance in his 1774 treatise "Summary View of the Rights of British America," which placed him in the forefront of the revolutionary movement:

> America was conquered, and her settlement made, and finally established, at the expense of individuals, and not of the British public. Their [the American colonists'] own blood was spilt in acquiring lands for their settlements, their own fortunes expended in making that settlement effectual; for themselves they fought, for themselves they conquered, and for themselves alone they have right to hold.

Completely rejected was the British contention that the American colonial success had been won through the sufferance of the crown, which had benevolently licensed its subjects to settle the New World. On the contrary, Jefferson and like-minded thinkers argued, invoking the Enlightenment social philosophers, America was virgin earth, where man, in his natural state, enjoyed his unalienable rights to live free and do what he wished in the pursuit of happiness. Those who applied their unfettered energy to transforming wilderness to arable fields earned their land and deserved to have it protected from encroachment by others. In this hope they entered into a social compact creating a government, the first function of which was to safeguard the property of similarly enterprising members of the community. It was their frankly vested interest in perpetuating the well-being of this commonwealth, through their participation in and consent to the process, that was for Jefferson the bedrock of republican democracy. Such thoughts were a radical departure from imperial doctrine, under which royal prerogatives and hereditary privilege overruled the rights of ordinary people. In America the untitled masses owned land in far greater proportion than they did in the Old World, and their land—both what they owned individually and laid claim to collectively—would now help free them from the crown's jurisdiction.

Political philosophy aside, in terms of economic reality American land not yet in private hands was the new nation's chief financial resource, and with their commerce stymied by the British navy and normal social transactions in turmoil, the crown's real estate had to be utilized somehow to pay for the war. But there were complex questions that stood in the way, starting with who owned the lands and who had the power to award and administer them. There were three categories of land involved. First were the tracts within any given colonial jurisdiction that had not as yet been granted or sold by the crown, its royal governors, or their councils. Did these lands, once independence had been declared, automatically become public property belonging to the states under their newly declared sovereignty? Second was the property confiscated, with the explicit encouragement of Congress, from colonists who remained loyal to the crown and were now branded traitors to the patriot cause. Were such takings by the states and their subsequent sales thereof legitimate public entitlements by the new governments or simply sanctioned mob looting? Third were the so-called backlands beginning on the western slope of the Appalachians and running to the Mississippi River, over which Parliament had withdrawn jurisdiction from the American colonies starting in 1763 despite their long-standing colonial charter claims to them.

This western territory was the most important and tangled of the land issues. It was an immense area, encompassing the eastern half of the Mississippi River basin, with as much square mileage as the combined thirteen rebel colonies occupied—uncontested by the crown—between the Atlantic coast and the Appalachian ridgeline proclaimed in 1763 as the permissible extent of western settlement. Which was to say that the land between the mountains and the great midcontinent father of rivers, if won from Britain in the war or at the peace table, would effectively double the size of the new United States.

POTENTIAL REVENUE FROM THE immediate or future sale of the undistributed American land, much of it wonderfully fertile, became at once the primary form of collateral for the struggling new republic as the war began. The money from such sales (and the promise of a great deal more) was badly needed to supplement the states' waning tax revenues and sustain their functioning governments throughout the revolutionary crisis. Bonds had to be issued and interest paid on them as the supply of coinage tightened and the value of paper currency was eroded by inflation and the states' dwindling treasuries.

The ungranted land had equally urgent use in lieu of pay to keep George Washington's patchwork forces in the war. Instead of taxing themselves enough to maintain even minimal troop levels and supplies, the states turned to promised gifts of their frontier lands as compensation to recruits, especially indentured farmworkers and artisans hopeful of cultivating the soil as a decent future livelihood in their liberated new nation. The land bounties offered instead of pay rose with the recipient's rank in the service and varied in generosity from state to state. Virginia, with the most territory to dispense, was the most liberal, its grants reaching as high as 600 acres per soldier for the noncommissioned ranks and up to 15,000 acres for generals. Some farsighted and fairminded members of the patriot leadership saw yet another important potential use for these wilderness lands—as indemnification to the crown loyalists whose homes and other property were confiscated, in case Britain were to demand such a payback as part of a peace pact.

Thus, the Americans needed to win, either on the battlefield or at the bargaining table, clear title to the western lands if the new nation was to avoid insolvency and acquire enough growing room to ensure its future prosperity. But even assuming the war eventually went their way, the states would have to decide which of them, if any, already held or should be awarded jurisdiction over the land beyond the mountains. Seven of them had expansive (most of them "sea-to-sea") claims westward—Massachusetts, Connecticut, and New York in the north; Virginia, the Carolinas, and Georgia in the south—either by their crown charters or, additionally in New York's case, by crown treaties extracted from the Iro-

quois and other Indian nations. The trouble was that all these claims were
open to challenge based on subsequent and sometimes conflicting crown
grants and regulations that were issued as geographical knowledge and
political exigencies dictated. Administrative carelessness or indifference
within the British ministry left many colonial titles and boundary disputes
unresolved. Thus, Massachusetts and Connecticut claimed that their western boundary extended, as their charters said, to the nearest ocean (that is,
the Pacific), but when New York was chartered after them in the seventeenth
century, it was plunked down directly in the path of the New England
colonies' expansive claims. Both of them insisted, apparently with a straight
face, that their legitimate territory resumed beyond New York's western
boundary (and Connecticut further said it had a prior claim to a sizable
piece of Pennsylvania). For its part, New York rejected the New England
states' claims, arguing that it had jurisdiction over all the territory within its
boundaries and was heir to all adjacent land ceded to the crown under
treaties with the Indian nations—or, as one skeptical contemporary put it, to
"every mountain, forest, or prairie where an Iroquois has taken a scalp." But
this claim by New York, in turn, poached on a sizable piece of the Old
Northwest above the Ohio River, which Virginia said it owned under its
1609 charter, the oldest in the colonies but also the most ambiguous and
often challenged by subsequent grants and charters. And the claims westward to the Pacific by the Carolinas and Georgia had been massively compromised by Britain's 1763 peace treaty with France. Indeed, all the original
British colonial charter claims that could be interpreted as stretching to the
Pacific were in conflict with France's forced 1763 cession of the western
half of Louisiana province to Spain, which now said it owned virtually all of
North America west of the Mississippi except Canada.

In short, ownership of the western lands was a jurisdictional mess,
which the new nation would have to clear up as soon as possible in order to
stake out its boundaries and win international recognition of them. Settling
the states' internal territorial issues, however, would still leave open the
larger question of whether Britain or the United States had the more plausible claim to the western land, should the course of the war itself not resolve
the matter. Interestingly, each nation had a serious flaw in its contention.
How could the American states base any of their boundary claims on
seventeenth-century charters granted by the British crown, whose sovereign
authority over them they had just repudiated? The Americans' answer was
that if they succeeded in their revolution by dint of arms, they were the natural heirs to the territory spelled out in the crown charters. But then why
wouldn't they also be heirs to—and bound by—the subsequent rulings by
that same British crown, which had explicitly narrowed the boundaries of

the American colonies, ending their sea-to-sea claims, transferring the lands north of the Ohio to Quebec province, and confining the settlement of the thirteen insurgent colonies to the eastern side of the Appalachians? In purely legalistic terms, the American argument that the United States should be recognized as extending to the Mississippi—even if its armies had not conquered one square inch of territory west of the mountains—was obviously inconsistent. Even under so-called squatters' rights, the American case was thin since there were probably no more than a few thousand colonists settled in that whole territory.

The British, though, had a comparable problem, even though they could point to the peace treaty ending the French and Indian War as the basis for their imperial hold on the western lands. It was true they had reinforced old fortifications and built new ones along the perimeter of their domain and its principal waterways. But having won their great war against the French for undisputed title to the Ohio and Mississippi river basins, Britain had hesitated—as a conscious imperial policy—to encourage colonization of these backlands and, as a concomitant, bear the expense of administering and protecting the settlers in that remote, commercially unpromising region. Given the Americans' outrage over Parliament's imposition of taxes on them to help bear the defense costs, the crown had opted for the course of least resistance, applying a policy of studied neglect of the western lands, reserving them for the native peoples as a natural habitat, and letting the ornery colonies worry about protecting any of their people who chose to settle in an area forbidden to British subjects. The only trouble with such a solution was that it left a power vacuum—a sprawl of glorious real estate sat out there in ungoverned limbo, and while nominally under British jurisdiction, it was there for the taking, as land-ravenous American colonists and the habitually suspicious overseers of Spain's New World dominion recognized.

If the Continental Army had been large enough and adequately funded, Congress—a permanent, if not continuously sitting, body from 1776 onward—would likely have instructed Washington to thrust beyond the Appalachians and march as far as the Mississippi, certifying the states' collective charter claims as he went. Even if an American expeditionary force could hardly have exerted authority as an occupying power, such a foray might have gone far to substantiate Congress's claim to the western territory, but Washington had all he could do in the east to keep his army intact and harassing the far mightier foe. The British commanders holding the western forts saw the same military opportunity and hatched plans for swift strikes up the Ohio Valley, but they, too, lacked manpower and confined their efforts to sending war parties of their Indian allies against settlers who wandered west of the mountains.

The question of national jurisdiction over the western lands thus hung in abeyance as the fighting proceeded near the Atlantic coast. Meanwhile, the rebelling colonies tried to devise their Articles of Confederation, so that their new nation would have at least minimal guidelines to function as a sovereign entity without trampling on the cherished prerogatives of its thirteen constituent parts—no easy trick. Of all the issues Congress grappled with during this drawn-out process, none proved more nettlesome than trying to agree on who owned the western wilderness. The question came down to whether the individual states' prewar boundary claims under their colonial charters would be honored and the disputes over them reconciled once victory came, or whether the western lands ought to be treated as a single territorial commonwealth belonging jointly to the new nation.

Since Congress at that time operated on a one-state, one-vote basis, seven states held the balance of power with a full quorum on hand, and seven was the number of states with western land claims, which none of them wished to relinquish. The six so-called unlanded states (that is, those without territorial claims in the West) were thus unable to outvote the landed states on any question regarding titles and boundaries. But if the six banded together in favor of one side or the other in any jurisdictional dispute between two or among several of the landed states, then the unlanded six could exert decisive influence on the outcome.

Such a gang-up might well have been directed at Virginia, whose territorial claims under its 1609 charter amounted to roughly two-thirds of all the land between the Appalachians and the Mississippi. The landlocked states were understandably anxious over the prospect of Virginia in particular and the other states with western claims becoming still larger after the war and dwarfing them in size, population, and political and economic power. A lopsided union of such unequal members posed the threat of tyranny by the large over the small—and tyranny was what the fight to separate from Britain was all about. It was theorized, not altogether implausibly, by delegates in Congress from the smaller unlanded states that the larger ones, if extended farther westward, could more readily sell sizable portions of their territory and with the proceeds pay off their debts, reduce or eliminate taxes, and lure away residents from the small states, which would become still harder pressed to meet their financial obligations. Such concerns were no doubt heightened because Virginia, in drafting its new state constitution in 1776, reasserted its western land claims, pointedly citing the territory north and west of the Ohio River to which Massachusetts, Connecticut, and New York all laid at least partial claim.

Who could adjudicate such a dispute if the British crown was removed from the picture? The only plausible answer was Congress: there was no other authority, and it was a frail reed, indeed, at that point. When Thomas Jefferson rose in Congress during the summer of 1776 as the delegates considered taking up the western lands question, he declared, "I protest against the right of Congress to decide upon the right of Virginia"—and so the great issue of states' rights within a federal system was formally joined. Implicit in Jefferson's message was that if the rest of the states or a majority of them tried to wrest away any of what Virginia regarded as its sovereign territory, the Old Dominion would quit the federal compact—and without its largest member, the new nation would likely be aborted.

One state dared to challenge Virginia's position, and in doing so may have saved the United States from death in childbirth. At the time, though, it struck many as an obstructionist maneuver. Maryland had a population 42 percent the size of Virginia's, but if the latter's western claims were to be certified by Congress, its land area would become thirty-four times the size of its Chesapeake Bay neighbor. Rather than stressing its apprehension about possible future abuses of power by Virginia, Maryland made a more positive case by arguing that since the war for independence was being jointly waged by all thirteen states, spilling their blood together and pooling their resources in a common cause, the fairest arrangement would be for all the states with western claims to cede their unoccupied land to Congress for the greater good of the nation. That western territory would then be administered by the new federal government until portions of it became sufficiently settled to organize themselves into states that would be admitted to the federal union with the same rights and obligations as the original thirteen. Three other small, unlanded states, New Jersey, Rhode Island, and Delaware, sided with Maryland in urging cession of the western territory by the seven with such claims. But none of those seven would budge.

The absence of a formal compact truly binding the states seemed to mock the legitimacy of the American war effort. Thus, when the Articles of Confederation were completed by Congress on November 15, 1777, and presented to the states for their required unanimous ratification, the western lands issue was omitted by way of temporarily avoiding a crisis. Imperfect as the Articles were, state legislatures began to ratify them, so the United States could claim that its government, however limited in power, was up and running. But Maryland showed no inclination to ratify so long as Congress failed to confront the territorial issue.

FUELING MARYLAND'S RESISTANCE WAS A resourceful ally, an avowed enemy of Virginia's landed aristocracy with its inordinate power to shape the new nation. Before the Revolution, the syndicates of land speculators trying to stake out large proprietary holdings in the west had been forced to apply to the crown or its officers for royal grants, exempting them from the ban on new settlement under the Proclamation Act as well as from the jurisdiction of the colonial legislatures that jealously guarded their charter rights against incursions by outside interests. But none of the land companies had succeeded in winning the official sanction of the British government before the outbreak of the war. So they had no place else to turn now but to the newly organized state legislatures and to Congress.

Three companies in particular tried to win approval of their purchase applications, even though it was far from certain that the lands they sought to own and sell at a profit would wind up as part of the United States. The most persistent was the old group of Philadelphia merchants (still notably including Benjamin Franklin among its shareholders), which had been known successively as the Illinois, the Grand Ohio, and the Indiana Company and had come close to winning a crown charter for its proposed new colony of Vandalia, south of the Ohio and comprising a large portion of the modern state of West Virginia. But the war intervened, ending all efforts in London. The Vandalia consortium, turning its attention to soliciting Congress to sell it the land it had nearly been granted by the crown, stressed that the transaction would provide revenues badly needed for the war effort and running the new federated government. The syndicate did not hesitate to offer congressional delegates shares in the company at inside prices, just as it had tried to sway Britons in or close to the ministry and Parliament before the war. A second group of businessmen and politicians, from Pennsylvania, Maryland, and New Jersey, had formed the Illinois-Wabash Company, seeking to buy land north of the Ohio. A third group headed by a freebooting North Carolinian, Richard Henderson, had hired Daniel Boone to help carve out a large settlement from the wilderness of lush eastern Kentucky, which the Virginia legislature had designated as a new county soon after the war began, making it the first official American jurisdiction west of the Appalachians. Henderson called his project the Transylvania Company and let Congress know that his intention was, once enough settlers had purchased land there from him, to apply for recognition as the fourteenth state. All these companies' propositions to Congress shared two important characteristics: they would have removed large chunks of real estate from Virginia's sovereign jurisdiction, and virtually all the men connected with these land schemes were non-Virginians from the unlanded states, casting covetous eyes on the gorgeous Ohio Valley, the heart of Virginia's claimed western domain. Since Virginia's powerful aristocracy, centered in the Tidewater region and Albemarle County, included many who were themselves land speculators as well as planters, with a similar ambition to expand their holdings westward and no incentive to share the wealth with out-of-staters, they were highly resistant to the proposed cession of the state's western lands to the revenue-starved Congress, lest it sell them off speedily and haphazardly to speculators of small scruple.

The pressure on Congress to persuade the landed states to cede their western claims to the nation as a whole can be gauged by the stature of the leading backers of the land companies. These included three of Pennsylvania's signers of the Declaration of Independence—Franklin, James Wilson, and Robert Morris, who was a deep-plunging investor as well as the chief financial officer of the Revolutionary government and a war profiteer in the bargain. Foremost among the Maryland land speculators were two signers of the Declaration, Samuel Chase and Charles Carroll, and its first post-British governor, Thomas Johnson. The influence of the Pennsylvanians on Congress in pressing the land companies' hopes may be inferred from Franklin's July 1774 draft proposal for how the new American confederation would operate. It granted the national legislature power to create new colonies "when proper," implying it should have jurisdiction over the western lands. Fellow Philadelphian John Dickinson's more detailed 1776 version, much of which was incorporated in the finally adopted Articles of Confederation, would have given Congress the power to define state boundaries and to oversee the establishment of governments in newly created states. Speculators, officials with a stake in the land companies, and their hired agents put heavy pressure on the Maryland legislature to hold out against ratifying the Articles of Confederation and to instruct its delegates in Congress to keep pushing for cession of the western lands. By 1777 the landless states had begun to question the validity of Virginia's charter claims by contending that while all the colonies had general jurisdiction over the territory within their boundaries, actual title to all land ungranted by the crown had been inherited by the Congress of the sovereign United States—not by the states that succeeded the colonial governments—and it was Congress that had the power to hold, sell off, and administer all lands still in the crown's possession at the time the war began.

Virginia, sensing a conspiracy against it, was not about to be coerced. Its legislature outlawed the purchase of land from Indians within its boundaries unless the state assembly approved. Furthermore, no buyer of land purchased from a private party or group (that is, a land company) could take title to it without state inspection and approval of the deed claim. This was tantamount to declaring that only the state of Virginia could buy land from the Indians and sell it off, thus effectively putting speculators out of busi-

ness within its borders. When Maryland and other unlanded states introduced motions to give Congress the power to fix the western limits of the
landed states, Virginia beat them back and won approval for an amendment
to the Articles saying that "no state shall be deprived of territory for the benefit of the United States."

Virginia had more than self-interest in mind in fighting to keep its
claimed lands out of the hands of Congress. The land companies eager to
buy Virginia's western realty were not joint-stock ventures composed of
many small holders, like modern publicly held corporations; they were
small, exclusive groups—a handful of powerful partners, in most cases—
seeking proprietary grants similar to those originally given to William Penn,
Lord Baltimore, and the baronial organizers of Carolina. Such groups were
by their very nature undemocratic, holding final power to determine how the
vast tracts they controlled were to be merchandised and governed—a ves-
tige of feudalism that had no place in a democratic republic. Nor were such
speculative ventures conducive to rapid settlement and economic growth,
Virginia contended. The syndicates, according to their foes in the Old
Dominion, had no plans to develop the land themselves—only to hoard it
until the frontier moved farther west and their holdings could be sold for far
more than the wholesale bargain prices that Congress, under extreme pressure to raise revenues, was likely to accept.

As the polarizing issue dragged on, with Maryland playing David to Virginia's Goliath and refusing to allow the Articles of Confederation to go
into effect, there were stirrings of conscience and statesmanship among the
more farsighted Virginia patriots. Chief among them was the unorthodox
aristocrat Richard Henry Lee, a signer of the Declaration of Independence,
veteran member of Congress, and key ally of Jefferson and Patrick Henry.
Although a fervent supporter of states' rights over federal supremacy—so
much so that in 1787 he would vote against the Constitution in its final
form—Lee now stepped forward to urge his state to consider giving up its
claimed territory north of the Ohio River. Without such a politic concession,
formal confederation of the United States could probably not be achieved—
and if the states remained at loggerheads, further undermining America's
dire finances, the struggle for independence might soon have to be abandoned, to the delight of Great Britain. "Disunion among ourselves," Lee
wrote his colleagues, "and the precipice on which we stand with our paper
money are, I verily believe, the source of their [Britain's] hope." More than
altruism was behind this proposed sacrifice of territory. Lee and other Virginians, being realists in that premechanized age, doubted that a truly democratic government could be sustained by the state if it extended over tens of

millions of acres northwest of the Ohio. Jefferson's draft of a new state constitution, in anticipating the same logistical problem, had contemplated
establishing two or more future states from Virginia's western territory that
would become "free and independent of this colony [state] and all the
world."

But Virginia wanted to decide the question for itself, not under duress
from a Congress that was driven by less than noble considerations, like
Maryland's transparent envy of its much larger neighbor and the profit
motive of speculators using the small unlanded states as their stalking horse.
On the other hand, word spread that if Congress formulated a cession plan
that met Virginia's concerns and did not cater to the private syndicates, perhaps the door might be open for a compromise. In the meantime, the battle
was not going well for the Continental Army, the states were falling ever
deeper into debt and failing to fund the war effort, and Congress, as needy
as ever, was offered £10,000 by the Vandalia promoters to approve their
claims in western Virginia. The speculators sought to sap Virginia's resistance by attempting—but failing—to enlist Governor Patrick Henry to act
favorably on the land companies' application. More and more America's
destiny was linked to its most precious resource and who would control it.

THE UNWIELDY BRITISH ARMY was wearing itself out in pursuit of a fleet
foe that, fearing annihilation, refused to be cornered. But Congress understood that Washington's motley troops could pester and evade the redcoats
for only so long and probably could not outlast them in a war of attrition—
the empire had a great many more resources for the killing job. Nor could
the Continental troops, in all likelihood, ever confront the king's imperial
legions and gain a decisive victory without massive military assistance. So
America asked for it from the nation with the deepest grievance against the
British.

France had waged and lost four wars against Britain over the preceding
eighty years. Nothing would more delight the court at Versailles than to see
its cross-Channel nemesis lose the most valuable component of its relent-
lessly spreading empire. But as American colonists' discontent was rising
to a feverish level, an internal debate had divided the French court and its
ministry over how best to exploit Britain's colonial tempest without risking
renewed combat.

France's chief financial minister, the astute Anne-Robert-Jacques Turgot, a free market advocate and an acclaimed social reformer while serving
as a provincial administrator, argued that his country could not afford to

endanger its economic health by fresh foreign adventurism—specifically, by playing agent provocateur on the side of the American rebels. Let Britain foolishly embroil itself in a costly, never-ending struggle to suppress its colonies' revolt, Turgot urged, and let its wealth be steadily drained by maintaining a large army of overseas occupation, all without France needing to raise a finger. But Charles Gravier, the canny and normally cautious French foreign minister, held a contrary view. Elevated from a family of the petit aristocracy to the title of Comte de Vergennes as a reward for distinguished diplomatic service, he saw Britain's stranglehold on American trade as the linchpin of its accelerating national strength. The surest, soonest way to reverse British fortunes and thus restore France to the eminence it had enjoyed under the Sun King as Europe's ranking military power and most respected political arbiter, Vergennes contended, was to subsidize in secret the American uprising and promise the colonists diplomatic recognition at the earliest convenient moment.

The policy clash had to be resolved by twenty-two-year-old King Louis XVI, in the third year of what would prove to be the final reign of the old French monarchy. The corpulent young ruler, viewed by his detractors as a shy dullard, happier tinkering in his locksmith's shop than confronting complex affairs of state (and slurred as an incompetent lover by his willful Austrian wife, Marie-Antoinette), had several redeeming qualities. He was a better-read and far less extravagant autocrat than his predecessor (and grandfather), Louis XV, with at least an abstract interest in promoting social justice and a soupçon of appreciation for the humane sentiments of the Americans' democratic rhetoric. He also had a knack for choosing able ministers to run his realm—a skill that eluded Britain's blustery king.

Faced with a dispute between his two ablest councilors about how to deal with their British adversaries' woes across the Atlantic, the king sided with Vergennes, who advised him early in 1776 that "it is time to take revenge on [Britain] for the evil it has done since the beginning of the century to those who had the misfortune to be its neighbors or its rivals." In May, two months before the American colonists formally broke with their mother country, France clandestinely siphoned its first loan to Congress for arms and other military equipment, to be smuggled to the rebels via the West Indies. To extract more such assistance and enlist France's open alliance, Congress dispatched its most illustrious member to Paris that autumn.

For the chilly Atlantic crossing, Ben Franklin had worn a beaver cap that came down nearly to his spectacles and caused his straight gray hair to hang below it in an uneven fringe. Disembarking at Brittany, the lately denounced traitor to the British crown (endearing him to all Frenchmen) decided not to abandon his unstylish fur headgear, which at once became the emblem of his embattled frontier society. On his arrival in the French capital, Franklin also favored the simple garments of the Quakers, though he was not of their sect, as part of a studied pose that charmed his host nation. The old sage seemed the embodiment of the natural virtues of mankind uncorrupted by the deceits of civilization—the noble primitive so lauded by Enlightenment *philosophe* Jean-Jacques Rousseau. His poor spoken French only confirmed the impression. Yet the American ambassador's keen brain, gentle wit, barbed prose, and earthy insight reminded the French intelligentsia of its other favorite litterateur, Voltaire, that master of reason and irony, who would embrace Franklin at the Academy of Sciences to the delight of a crowd of onlookers. All of France was taken by this venerable figure who could amuse and flatter courtiers and commoners alike, all the while advertising his frail nation's dire needs along with its glowing promise. His benign countenance was reproduced everywhere—etched in engravings, embossed on crockery, profiled in cameo on snuffbox lids—and beaver hats became the rage of chic Paris. Franklin was a folk hero in a strange land, and the perfect collaborator in Vergennes's strategy for declawing the British lion.

So disarming was the American plenipotentiary that, before his work was done in France, he was able to extract from that kingdom some 45 million livres in gifts and loans (mostly the latter) to the newborn United States of America—roughly $225 million in early-twenty-first-century economic terms. Considering the small size of armies then, the unsophisticated state of weaponry, and the low cost of keeping a foot soldier in the field, such a sum represented a major contribution to the rebels' capacity to wage war.

What Franklin and the American cause needed as well to win the world's recognition as a sovereign state was a formal alliance with France. That, however, would be the equivalent of an open declaration of war against Britain—a step Vergennes was not prepared to propose to his king unless and until the Americans could demonstrate their fighting prowess and staying power against British military might. For the first year and a half of official warfare, Washington's troops succeeded only at belling the English cat and now and then yanking its tail. Then, toward the end of 1777, word reached Paris of the stunning surrender of Burgoyne's formidable army in the wilds of the Hudson Valley—and everything changed.

If France was deeply impressed by the outcome at Saratoga, Britain was still more so. Even though the loss of an army hardly meant the British war of suppression was doomed, King George's ministry under Lord North recognized that the likely cost of victory had just escalated and that if Franklin's mission in Paris, of which London was of course fully cognizant, should succeed and France enter into formal alliance with the Americans, the outcome of the conflict was now far less certain than the crown had anticipated. Reports were soon circulating in Paris that Britain might shortly extend an olive branch across the ocean. The very possibility played into Franklin's hands, for should the Americans, momentarily flush with victory, manage to negotiate a truly generous reconciliation that kept them subjects of the crown, France would have lost a singular opportunity to weaken its inveterate enemy. Franklin wasted few words in stressing to Vergennes that unless France was prepared to bind itself by treaty to the United States and overtly aid the Americans' fight for independence, his countrymen might feel they had little choice but to accept Britain's forgiving hand if proffered. For America to fight on without an ally of France's stature at its side, Congress might well conclude, would prove an intolerably bloody, expensive, and perhaps hopeless endeavor. Either way, whether the Americans rejoined the empire as dutiful subjects with new privileges or chose to fight on and were defeated, France would be the loser. And then Britain, increasingly enriched by America's great size, resources, fecundity, and the rapid population growth they afforded, would rule the global economy as no nation ever had, leaving France and the rest of Europe permanently diminished. Vergennes did not need much prodding; France was ready to deal in earnest.

Desperate as the United States was for help, it was wary, in leaguing itself with France, of inviting the same sort of intrusion on its civil affairs that Britain had lately imposed. Thus, the proposed treaty with France that John Adams had drawn up for Congress in 1776 had specified that there was to be no political connection between the two nations and that no uninvited French officials or soldiers were to be quartered on American soil. What America needed most from France was recognition of its sovereignty and money to operate the army. By 1778 it was clear that Washington could not repulse the British war machine without French troops and ships as well. Still, Congress was fearful that France might seize the opportunity, as the price for its active participation, to reestablish an imperial presence in North America that Britain had extinguished fifteen years earlier. Franklin thus applied his politesse, as the diplomatic talks began, to obtain France's agreement to, in the language of the treaty, "renounce for ever the possession . . . of any part of the continent of North America" that had ever belonged to Britain.

France, though, nursed its own fears about its prospective junior ally's territorial ambitions. Adam's treaty draft had indicated, and Congress fully concurred, that the boundaries of the newly independent United States should envelop all of Britain's North American holdings, including the trans-Appalachian lands, Canada, and the Floridas, well beyond the scope of the thirteen seaboard colonies. So large a country was not what Vergennes had had in mind in plotting the shrinkage of Britain's New World domain; he did not want France's archrival replaced in North America by an infant colossus—a Protestant, English-speaking one at that, with strong ancestral ties to Britain—which might readily rebuff French attempts at influence. An independent United States, even if a democratic republic, was acceptable to the French monarchy so long as it won free access to the lucrative American trade, which had been Britain's exclusive franchise from the first. The thirteen formerly British colonies also needed to be restricted in territory and resources so that they would remain dependent on France for their commercial and military security. This latter requirement meant that, from the French perspective, the United States ideally ought to be limited to an Atlantic seaboard existence hemmed in on the north and west by Britain, still in possession of Canada and the eastern half of the Mississippi Valley beyond the Appalachians, and on the south and far west by Spain, which might regain the Floridas from Britain if King Louis's uncle, Carlos III, entered the war under their Family Compact. Such an outcome, partitioning North America among three rivals, would allow France the chance to exert decisive influence in any disputes that arose and to reap rewards as a favored trading partner with the entire continent.

Accordingly, Vergennes and his ministry never endorsed the Americans' stated territorial goals. In agreeing to enter the war on their side, France approved treaty language that asserted, "The essential and direct End of the present defensive alliance is to maintain effectually the liberty, Sovereignty, and independence absolute and unlimited of the United States." Both parties agreed, furthermore, that neither would lay down its arms until that independence had been "formally or tacitly assured by the Treaty or Treaties that shall terminate the War," nor would either nation sign such a treaty with Britain without the consent of the other. Nothing was said about the size of the newly independent nation, but France agreed that any formerly British territory that the Americans managed to conquer could be confederated with the thirteen rebellious states. In return, France won a minor concession: America would approve of any French seizure of formerly British islands in the West Indies. What their treaty left hazy and unresolved—and would eventually cause serious friction between them—was the consequence if either party chose to pursue war aims beyond the declared essential one of American independence. If the two nations were bound to remain combatants until they mutually agreed to peace terms with Britain, wasn't each allowing the other to hold it hostage until its war goals—whatever they might turn out to be beyond a sovereign America—were realized?

Supremely confident of his bargaining acumen, Vergennes supposed—mistakenly, as events would prove—that since America needed France as an ally far more than the other way around, Franklin and his colleagues would not try to exploit the situation at the bargaining table by hinting to the British that the Franco-American alliance was impermanent and thus a highly negotiable item. The real prize for France, at any rate, was embodied in a companion Treaty of Amity and Commerce that the two countries consummated along with their military alliance in February 1778. In it the signatories agreed that neither would treat any third-party nation more favorably in matters of trade and navigation than they would each other, thereby ending the mercantilist monopoly that Britain had imposed on its American colonies since Parliament had passed the Navigation and Trade Acts more than a century earlier. Victory over the British might also restore France's trade opportunities in the West Indies, Africa, and India, where its defeat in the Seven Years' War had greatly reduced them, but it was the trade with America, as Franklin duly noted, that made the war a worthy, if perilous, risk for Louis XVI's realm.

Hearing that the American colonists had formally leagued with the scheming French, George III flew into a rage at Windsor Castle. His ministers calmed him long enough to win his assent to a conciliatory gesture toward the Americans in the hope of gaining at least a truce, if not a full settlement, before Congress had time to ratify the treaties tentatively agreed to with France. A top-level British mission blessed by Parliament set sail for the colonies bearing the peace proposal—essentially a renewal of the pre-war offer of home rule for America, with Congress functioning as the legislature for the united colonies but not granted full sovereign status. All the repressive crown acts that had become so obnoxious to the colonists, including any taxes not directly related to the regulation of overseas trade, would be dropped. As a sweetener, the British peacemakers promised future consideration of reciprocal political and commercial rights between the home isles and their American progeny.

But after the startling victory at Saratoga and with the French now committed to a military effort against Britain, America had passed the point of no return in its journey toward nationhood. The king's negotiators were sent home empty-handed, and France and the United States now began to press the fourth interested party in the geopolitics of the New World—imperial Spain—to join the contest against hobbled but still potent Britain.

· · ·

DWELLING IN THE LONG SHADOW of past grandeur, colonial New Spain remained spread over roughly two-thirds of the land of the Western Hemisphere. For Carlos III, the best of Spain's Bourbon rulers—a backhanded compliment, to be sure—to have indulged in still further territorial craving in the New World seemed preposterous on the face of it. But his empire's hold on its thinly populated northern sector was nominal, and to the east of the Mississippi it was confronted by an awakening British-American presence in the form of riverfront and lakeside forts, far-ranging traders, and a trickle of frontiersmen probing ever westward. While sullen over its reduced might since Britain's ascent, Spain was not so enfeebled that it failed to stir when the American Revolution presented an opportune moment to recapture some of its former loftiness. If the British could be vanquished and the victorious American republic—a repugnant concept, of course, to the entrenched Spanish autocracy—could be restrained under the joint supervision of the Bourbon powers, Madrid glimpsed rich possibilities. The Floridas could be reclaimed, for one thing, along with sole possession of the Gulf of Mexico's shoreline. For another, Britain's light grip on the eastern Mississippi Valley could be eased still further, allowing Spain to infiltrate that vast, verdant region and thereby solidify its shaky northern flank.

Unless such gains—and others that soon occurred to the Spanish ministers—were in the offing, King Carlos saw little point in renewed combat with Britain, especially if it fostered the creation of a democratic state in the New World, setting a flagrantly antiroyalist example for Spain's tightly repressed colonies. Carlos had won a measure of regard as a social reformer, mostly for having presided over the expulsion of the Jesuit order from his land and insisting on the subordination of the church to the crown in secular matters. But the king was in his sixties now, a short, unprepossessing figure with a florid face, large nose, bad teeth, and a hunched back, and famous for his frugality and piety. He was devoted to but two pursuits: hunting on a rotating basis near his four palaces, a pastime believed essential for the preservation of his faltering health, and the veneration of his nasty-tempered bigot of a wife, by then two decades in her grave. Aside from modest steps to stimulate his country's drowsy economy and ease the plight of its impoverished peasantry, the king deferred in most policy matters to his principal minister, the Conde de Floridablanca, a former lawyer who had won Carlos's pleasure by traveling to the Vatican and gaining the papacy's acceptance of Spain's decision to rid itself of the Jesuit scourge.

Floridablanca, no more enthusiastic than his king about promoting the independence of a republican United States, saw in Vergennes's plan for a concerted assault on Britain the chance to regain three prized possessions that the island kingdom had wrested from it—the rich Caribbean gem of Jamaica; Minorca, off Spain's southeast coast; and, especially, the two-and-a-half-mile-long peninsula of Gibraltar. This tiny appendage of the Spanish mainland, with its sheer rock palisade forming the northern side of the Pillars of Hercules and commanding a matchless view of the fourteen-mile-wide strait that separated Europe from Africa and the Atlantic from the Mediterranean, had been lost to the British in the War of the Spanish Succession in the early years of the century and turned into an impregnable fortress. Gibraltar's harbor may have been of limited utility to Spain, with its declining navy, but as a strategically sited base for British war and merchant ships, it had become an intolerable thorn in Spain's underbelly. Spanish pride, a notable contributor to its decline as a great power, demanded Gibraltar's return. So much so, in fact, that the quest became the centerpiece of the treaty Spain began to work out with France under the Family Compact, drawn up near the end of the Seven Years' War and pledging the Catholic neighbors to come to each other's aid diplomatically and militarily.

Spain's self-interest characteristically overcame dynastic fidelity, however, as Floridablanca chose, before allying his country with France, to try bluffing their mutual British enemy into making concessions as the price for preventing Spanish participation in the French-American military alliance. In return for Britain's handing back Gibraltar, Minorca, and the Floridas, Spain offered not only to refrain from joining the war but also to try brokering a peace accord between Britain and its thirteen colonies, perhaps freezing the battle lines where they were and thus denying the rebel states territorial integrity and control of vital port cities. Such a jigsawed nation could probably not long survive—an outcome agreeable to Spain—and would likely soon be begging to resume its colonial status. With scant regard for Spain's fighting prowess, Britain scoffed at such a proposal. King George, moreover, was said to be incensed by the nerve of any foreign government meddling in Britain's dealings with its own colonies.

Thus slapped by mighty Albion, Spain again took up France's entreaty to stand by its side in warring on Britain even if that step benefited America. That linkage was the troublesome part. Vergennes's ambassador to Madrid reported back to him that "this government singularly fears the prosperity and progress of the Americans"—a dread that caused "its excessive ill humor at our arrangements [treaties] with them." Vergennes did not mask his own ambivalence toward the Americans, whose alliance with France he feared might vanish with victory over Britain; gratitude was not a virtue he had often encountered in his diplomatic career. But the French foreign minister thought Spain overestimated the threat posed by the United States and sent back word to Madrid that there was no basis "for seeing in this new people a race of conquerors," adding his belief, often repeated to aides, that the American republic "will never be more than a feeble body, capable of little activity" and afflicted with the "inertia that is characteristic of all constitutional democracies." Since there were hardly any nation-sized constitutional democracies extant at the time—unless one stretched the definition to include Britain and Holland, neither of which could have been accused of inertia—Vergennes was probably as intent on calming his own qualms as assuaging Spanish anxiety over America's prospects.

In explaining to his new ambassador to the United States, Conrad-Alexandre Gérard de Rayneval, that he would not back down from France's pledge of support for a territorially viable and truly independent America by agreeing to Spain's proposal for the democratic state to be reduced in size and freedom from British rule, Vergennes emphasized that "we do not wish—far from it—that the new Republic should remain mistress of all that immense continent." Indeed, he was prepared to assure Britain that, if it reached a compromise settlement with the American colonies, France would strongly favor continued British possession of Canada (modern Quebec and Ontario provinces, more or less) and Nova Scotia, but not of Newfoundland unless the British fully restored France's right, taken away in 1763, to fish its teeming waters—a privilege that Vergennes thought the Americans were no longer entitled to after withdrawal from the empire.

On receiving mixed signals from Paris, Floridablanca decided that the feeble young American republic, even if it somehow contrived a victory, would never be capable of extracting satisfactory peace terms from an embittered Britain except with the joint, insistent backing of the Bourbon kingdoms. Thus, the United States would have to dance to whatever tune France and Spain chose to fiddle. But Spain's tune grated on France's ears. What it wanted in return for entering the war, Madrid told Paris, was not only recovery of Gibraltar, Minorca, and Florida from Britain but also American renunciation of claims to the territory between the Appalachians and the Mississippi, including all navigation rights on that river, the St. Lawrence, and the Great Lakes. The enormity of Spain's proposal was fulsomely captured a century afterward by George Bancroft, among the leading American historians of his day, who wrote indignantly,

The father of rivers gathers his waters from all the clouds that break between the Alleghanies [*sic*] and the furthest ranges of the Rocky mountains. His magnificent valley, lying in the best part of the temperate zone, salubrious and wonderfully fertile, is the chosen musterground of the most various elements of human culture brought together by men, summoned from all the civilized nations of the earth. . . . From the grandeur of destiny foretold by the possession of that river and the lands drained by its waters, the Bourbons of Spain, hoping to act in concert with Great Britain as well as France, would have excluded the United States totally and forever.

Appalled that Floridablanca's overt design was for Spain to fill the vacuum left by the reduction, if not the elimination, of both the British and American presence in the western lands, Vergennes was no more inclined to endorse such gross aggression by Spain than he had been to accept the American Congress's expansive boundary claims. All that France was prepared to pledge in signing the Convention of Aranjuez, the secret accord it finally reached with Spain in April 1779, was that it would keep fighting until Spain had rewon Gibraltar and Minorca from Britain. Nothing was said about binding Spain to the same commitment France had made to remain in combat until American independence became an accomplished fact. To further appease its Bourbon relative and neighbor, France agreed that Spain was free to extract any terms it could from the United States as its price for helping the Americans win the war.

In secretly obligating France to keep fighting Britain until it yielded Gibraltar—an objective in which the United States had no interest whatever—Vergennes arguably compromised the agreement he had made with America the year before. Because France was now committed, by interlocking treaties, to both American independence and the Spanish recovery of Gibraltar, the United States could not hope to win French approval of a bilateral settlement with Britain that did not also address Spain's grievance. Thus might the destiny of a whole continent have been held hostage by the possession of a towering rock of Old World limestone.

BY THE SPRING OF 1779, nearly three years after declaring American sovereignty and four years into active warfare, Congress still had no charter, no written accord parceling administrative powers among the individual states and their jointly created government. Even though the Articles of Confederation withheld the power of the purse and other political necessities from the central government, the proposed accord at least assigned Congress control of foreign affairs—including waging war and making peace in the name of the United States. Without the Articles ratified and in force, Congress could not demonstrate to the watching world America's seriousness of purpose and decent prospect for survival as a freestanding nation.

Yet the state of Maryland, still insisting that its economic viability would be gravely imperiled if Congress did not gain control of the western lands, continued to exercise its veto by refusing—alone among the states—to ratify the Articles. In May of that year Maryland's delegation to Congress renewed its cri de coeur that unowned American territory, "if wrested from the common enemy by the blood and treasure of the thirteen states, should be considered as a common property," subject to disposition as Congress directed. Maryland's principled stubbornness had turned to obstinacy that was threatening to strangle the country in its cradle. When Congress, hoping to curry favor with the land companies known to be the prime movers behind Maryland's diehard stand, agreed to consider several of the speculators' petitions for certification of their title claims to ungranted Virginia territory, the Old Dominion's legislature issued a fiery remonstrance asserting that any congressional taking of its sovereign turf would amount to handing the central government power sure to evolve into "an intolerable despotism."

Still, something had to give, or whatever Washington's troops might finally achieve on the battlefield would be lost in council chambers. Virginia, as the storm center of the intractable controversy and with the most to lose or gain from its outcome, now made two gestures of goodwill toward the federal union. Not only would it be receptive to a compromise plan so long as any state's cession of its western lands could not be exploited by land companies for private profit, but Virginia also agreed to contribute some of its territory north of the Ohio for distribution to war veterans from the smaller, landlocked states that had offered them land bounties in lieu of pay. It was progress of a sort, but the core issue of who owned the western lands remained unresolved.

BESIDES THE MENACE FROM CONGRESS, Virginia faced another worrisome issue in striving to protect its territorial integrity. Unless American soldiers could somehow reinforce the states' charter claims to their western lands, the United States might be hard pressed to win title to the region in the peace negotiations after the fighting ended. The British had been making it clear that they hoped to thwart any American intrusion into the enticing backlands. From their frontier forts they were busily mobilizing Indian raids meant to terrorize settlers in the Ohio Valley and thus divert elements of the Continental Army battling in the east. Plans were also afoot, spies for America learned, for a more sustained British-led strike—and perhaps more than one—through the vacant west, where even a relatively small force might have swept unimpeded across the virtually defenseless terrain and attacked the American rear with crippling effect. Something had to be done before it was too late.

But Virginia faced a dilemma no matter which way it turned. It could hardly order its militia to withdraw from Washington's scrambling forces in the primary war zone. But neither did it want to apply to Congress for military assistance by the Continental Army to blunt the British and Indian peril in western Virginia. Still, pacification efforts by the deployment of federal troops would have only reinforced the unlanded states' argument that jurisdiction over the region ought to belong to the national government, embodiment of their joint need and hope.

Virginia chose to operate on its own—and clandestinely at first, because it did not want to appear to Congress as if it were waging a separate war against the British just so it could hold on to its western claims. Its weapon was a covert expeditionary force, directly commissioned by Governor Patrick Henry and headed by an eager and highly capable frontier Indian fighter, George Rogers Clark. In his mid-twenties, a son of the Albemarle aristocracy that included the Jefferson family, Clark had served in a detachment of the state militia defending settlers in newly organized Kentucky County and later championed their rights in the Virginia Assembly. Promised generous land grants for himself and his volunteer followers, Clark assembled a band of sharpshooters and set out to check the British-inspired Indian terror campaign, even to win over the natives to the American side if possible, and disrupt British encampments on as wide a scale as possible. The importance of Governor Henry's sub rosa commission to Clark was stressed by an endorsement of it from Thomas Jefferson, shortly to succeed to the governorship, who wrote that the backlands expedition, if successful, would "have an important bearing ultimately in establishing our northwestern frontier." While the word "our" presumably referred to Virginia, it also necessarily enveloped Congress's earlier claim that the nation's boundaries rightly extended to the Mississippi.

Given the limited resources at his disposal—Clark never had more than a few hundred combatants under his command at any one time—it seemed a fanciful assignment. But he and his men were healthy, motivated, and swift, and Clark was gifted both as a tactician and as a recruiter of Indian braves and French farmers in the Illinois Country who had never been overly fond of the British. For more than two years beginning in mid-1778 Clark's raiders bedeviled their foes by seizing, through stealth, bluff, and good timing when keen marksmanship alone was not sufficient, British posts throughout the eastern Mississippi basin, among them Vincennes on the Wabash River and Kaskasia on the Illinois, and turning large sectors of the Old Northwest countryside against the crown. Their unpredictable and speedy movements—his troops dashed 200 miles over the flooded Illinois countryside in midwinter of 1779 to recapture Vincennes after the British had failed to garrison it adequately—kept the redcoats off balance and unable to mount a concerted drive across the Ohio.

For all his heroics, though, Clark never had enough men for a decisive assault on Detroit, the chief British base in the west country, or to sustain military control over that wide region. By war's end, his raiders were not in possession of a single British fort above the Ohio, and Clark himself was caught up in a nasty quarrel with Virginia officials who charged him with padding his expenses and refused to reimburse him in full. Based on military reality, then, British negotiators at the peace table in Paris after the fighting ended could justifiably contend that the Old Northwest above the Ohio River remained part of unconquered Canada, as defined by the prewar Quebec Act, and not a part of Virginia or therefore the United States. Still, Clark had undeniably scent-marked the western lands with an American aroma that foretold the coming tide of settlement.

Almost simultaneously with Clark's exploits, another young warrior, a Spanish aristocrat sometimes called "the Last Conquistador" by admiring countrymen, proved still more successful in advancing his nation's ambitions in territory within the boundaries that Congress had boldly staked out as belonging to the new United States. It helped that Bernard de Gálvez's uncle served as the king's minister in charge of Spain's New World empire and that his father was viceroy of New Spain (greater Mexico, which extended far north and west of the Rio Grande), ensuring his son access to a good deal more in the way of manpower and supplies than the resourceful Clark was ever provided.

It was not nepotism alone, though, that got Gálvez installed in New Orleans as intendant of the immense province of Louisiana before he turned thirty. He had fought well as a teenager in the Seven Years' War and then, as a captain in charge of a Mexican expedition against the Apaches, distinguished himself from centuries of Spanish commanders in the New World by treating his captives humanely. In charge of New Orleans, he further broke the mold of lackadaisical imperial administrators by encouraging commerce throughout the Louisiana territory, luring new residents there from all over the Spanish empire, shoring up the port city's defenses, and facilitating the upriver sale of arms and supplies to backwoods Americans, including George Rogers Clark, whose cause he favored.

Once Spain entered the war in 1779, Gálvez was ordered to assault British fortifications along the eastern bank of the lower Mississippi and the Florida Gulf Coast. Within a month, leading a patchwork of 1,500 Spanish soldiers and recruits of mixed French, Spanish, Indian, and black ancestry, he captured Baton Rouge and Natchez, seized British shipping on the river, ordered British subjects to leave the province, and put Spain in effective control of both banks of the Mississippi as far north as the Illinois Country, where Clark's raiders were on the prowl. Gálvez then directed his attention to the Gulf, where with the help of troops and warships dispatched from Havana he routed the outnumbered British defenders of Mobile and Pensacola and found himself named governor of West Florida as well as Louisiana. The indefatigable young commander thus lent muscle to Spain's previously hollow ambition to extend its imperial sway over America's southern tier at the expense of both Britain and the fledgling United States.

What Gálvez's triumphs portended for American peace negotiators became evident from his response to requests by Virginia governors Henry and Jefferson for Spain, as an ally in the war against Britain, to allow U.S. vessels unimpeded navigation rights on the Mississippi and to open New Orleans as a free port for shipments from America's frontier farmers. Since Spain was determined to restrict the boundaries of the new republic to the eastern side of the Appalachians and to compete with Britain for dominance in the Mississippi and Ohio valleys, Gálvez declined the eminent Virginians' request, explaining he had no authority to license such freedom of navigation. In so doing, he put Congress—and the world—on notice that Spain was set upon monopolizing the Gulf and Mississippi trade routes and blocking American settlers in the west from the only practical outlet to sell their produce in the world market. Spain may have been France's ally, but it was certainly not about to do the United States any large favors.

SPAIN HAD EXTENDED A SMALL LOAN to the United States at France's behest in the early days of the war, and Bernard de Gálvez's triumphs, like George Rogers Clark's, had served to prevent the British from launching a second front against the American colonies from the west or south. But after signing the secret pact with its Bourbon partner to join the war against Britain, Spain did not follow France's example in giving financial aid to the struggling republic. Nor did Spain grant diplomatic recognition of the Americans' self-declared sovereignty, a gesture that might have helped lift the flagging credit rating of the United States.

To help thaw the Spanish court's indifference—hostility, actually—to the American cause, Vergennes instructed his envoy in Philadelphia to beseech Congress to rein in its territorial expectations in the west, to forget about taking over Canada and the Floridas, and to drop its demand to continue fishing off Newfoundland. But when Congress drew up its instructions for future peace negotiators in 1779, it stubbornly and wishfully clung to the boundaries it had envisioned from the first. By virtue of the Treaty of 1763 and Gálvez's conquest of Florida, though, Spain held both banks of the Mississippi for its southernmost 200 miles, from the thirty-first parallel to the Gulf of Mexico, so it was able to obstruct or impose heavy duties on cargoes traveling in either direction—a geographical stranglehold that mocked America's claimed right to navigate freely the full length of the river. After Gálvez scored his lightning victories and extended Spanish control of both riverbanks well northward, into claimed American territory, Congress waffled. At one point it had offered to swap the American claim on the Floridas, assuming they were retaken from Britain during the war (as Gálvez shortly managed to do), for navigation rights on the whole river. At the least, Congress insisted on its full right of passage north of the thirty-first parallel, the claimed southern boundary of the United States, and asked Spain to let a new free port be opened in its territory near the river's outlet (or, more logically, allow New Orleans to serve the purpose). When Congress temporarily put the matter aside midway through the war, its revised set of peace instructions omitted any reference to navigation rights on the river, probably because asserting them was deemed both provocative and unnecessary. Since the United States, as presumptive heir to British territory, claimed it was bounded on the west by the Mississippi, its ships would naturally share the freedom to ply its waters with those of Spain, whose territory was bounded on the east by the river.

To try to put American relations with Spain on a more cordial footing and unsnarl the deadlock over river rights so the issue would not ignite a future clash of arms, the United States appointed its first envoy to Madrid. Even as Congress had sent its most illustrious member to Paris to win over the hearts, minds, and purse of France, so it selected another extraordinary member to beguile the court of King Carlos III into active participation in the war effort against their common enemy—a forlorn hope indeed.

When John Jay reached Madrid early in 1780 after a miserable journey, he was thirty-four years old, less than half Benjamin Franklin's age, and had scarcely a fraction of the fame and aura that had made the old charmer the toast of the French capital. But Jay was a formidable figure nonetheless. He had just completed his one-year term as president of Congress and had been, by any measure, the most successful occupant yet of that office. He was graced with good looks, savoir faire, family money, and impeccable social connections. The offspring of Huguenot merchants—his grandfather was driven out of France during Louis XIV's persecutions—Jay grew up in a prominent New York commercial family and married well. His wife's mother came from a landed Dutch patroon clan, the Van Cortlandts, and her politically eminent father was governor of New Jersey during the Revolution. Jay's upbringing in New Rochelle had been pious and austere, likely contributing to his contained, somewhat humorless manner. But he exhibited high character and a legalistic bent even as an eighteen-year-old in his final year at King's College (soon renamed Columbia). Charged with disobedience by the school authorities for refusing to identify classmates who had performed an act of vandalism that Jay had admitted witnessing, he pleaded in self-defense that the college rules did not require him to inform on his classmates. The technicality got him off with a suspension, and his high academic standing earned him readmission in time to deliver the commencement oration for his class.

Over the next five years he read law in the offices of leading New York practitioners and soon began to display the attributes that in time made him a virtuoso at his calling. Possessed of a nimble intelligence that quickly penetrated to the heart of the matter, Jay was also exacting over details when they counted and a tenacious negotiator, yet governed by "an amiable and conciliatory temper," according to the French chargé d'affaires at Philadelphia who so described him to Vergennes. On his admission to the bar Jay displayed such professional acumen that after only nine years of practice he was chosen chief justice of the New York State Supreme Court. Hardly a rabid revolutionary, he surprised associates by evolving into a leading supporter of the independence movement. As a delegate to the First Continental Congress in 1774, he objected to a motion to open each session with a prayer, explaining that the membership was so divided in its religious sentiments that any single invocation of divine guidance would likely offend some delegates. His motion failed to carry. As president of Congress five years later, he strongly endorsed the supremacy of the newly created federal authority over the divisive interests of the states and pressed the latter to meet their tax quotas by warning that otherwise the central government would perish from insolvency. With the blood of old Huguenot martyrs coursing through him, John Jay went to Spain as the American ambassador, harboring a deep suspicion of all things Catholic. He soon found his bias repaid in kind—and then some.

For two and a half years, he was treated with disdain, even contempt when the war news from America was glum. He was never granted a formal audience with King Carlos, whose court he earnestly pursued as it rotated among royal palaces, and his efforts to deal with the king's chief minister, the Conde de Floridablanca, infamous for his foul moods and bloated vanity, met with protracted delays and transparent excuses. His letters to the royal ministry often went unanswered while his own mail was routinely intercepted and read. When the letters of credit Congress had provided for operating the American mission were exhausted, along with Jay's private financial resources, he had to beg the Spanish government for a small loan; a serious commitment of its funds to aid the United States through its ordeal of liberation seemed a hopeless prospect. Reflective of his attitude, Floridablanca remarked privately that Jay had but two tiresome messages for him: "Spain, recognize our independence; Spain, give us money."

The only way Spain might consider obliging him, Jay was told, would be for Congress to drop its demand for navigation rights on the Mississippi. On the rare occasions he was granted an interview, Jay patiently explained to the cranky prime minister that a number of the American states bordered on the river and their future commercial prospects were tied to the shipping rights Congress was asserting. But the United States, he quickly added, would accede to any reasonable restrictions Spain might impose on river cargoes to minimize or eliminate contraband. Floridablanca, unyielding, claimed that control of the great river's traffic was a matter close to the king's heart. Translated from diplomatic double-talk, that meant Spain rated the Americans as a lot easier to push around than the militarily formidable British, whose treaty-based title to the eastern half of the Mississippi Valley, according to Floridablanca's way of thinking, did not have to be surrendered to the United States, even if it won the war. To grant Congress the navigation rights would have implied Spain's acceptance of America's claimed western boundary. Apprised by Jay of Madrid's ransom price—loss of Mississippi navigation rights in return for Spain's military aid and diplomatic recognition—Ben Franklin wrote back from Paris: "The very proposition can only give disgust at present. Poor as we are, yet, as I know we shall be rich, I would rather agree with them to buy at a great price the whole of their right on the Mississippi than sell a drop of its waters. A neighbor might as well ask me to sell my street door."

To bolster Jay's advocacy, Congress drew up a memorandum that reached him late in 1780 and expounded the case for the Mississippi as the U.S. western boundary. The first three reasons may have been subject to dismissive sneers by Floridablanca's ministry. (1) Sovereignty over the western lands had been exercised by the British crown in behalf of its American colonial subjects, but since the latter had chosen to overthrow their tyrannical ruler, that sovereignty reverted to the people themselves and their newly formed government. To an autocratic monarchy such as Spain, though, sovereignty was the king's entitlement, not a gift bestowed by his subjects, so the very thought of revolution against a royal regime was treasonous. (2) Americans had begun to exercise their charter rights to the western lands by settling in them, organizing governments there, and spilling blood in their defense, while Spain had no legitimate claim to the region east of the Mississippi. For Spain, though, the American states' invocation of ancient charter rights was laughable, since their own *conquistadores* had wandered across the whole southern tier of the modern United States, claiming everything in sight as the rightful possession of their Catholic king nearly a century before the first British settlers reached the Atlantic shore. And, at any rate, Gálvez's capture of British forts on the east bank of the Mississippi and along the Gulf had now established a Spanish toehold by conquest west of the Appalachians. (3) The Mississippi, Congress argued, was a "more natural, more distinguishable, and more precise" boundary for the new nation than any other and would be less likely to provoke international disputes. Yes, but from Madrid's perspective, such a boundary would have let the Americans leapfrog west from the Appalachians over the eastern half of the Mississippi basin, a 600-mile-wide no-man's-land, unpopulated except for at most 200,000 godless savages, and place the expansionist United States eyeball to eyeball with imperial Spanish territory. At any rate, America had no basis for claiming it had inherited the right to navigate the final 200-mile stretch of the Mississippi opening onto the Gulf of Mexico, since the western bank had been ceded to Spain as a consequence of the Treaty of 1763 and Gálvez had lately seized the eastern bank from the British.

A fourth argument raised by Congress ought to have struck Spain as more compelling. Unless Americans were allowed to navigate the length of the Mississippi, especially below the thirty-first parallel, where Spanish possession of both banks blocked passage to the Gulf and beyond, the river would be of slight commercial value to the new nation—or, for that matter, to Spain, if it could only manage to take an enlightened view of the situation. "In a very few years after peace shall take place," Congress's memo reasoned, "this country will certainly be overspread with inhabitants. . . . They will raise wheat, corn, beef, pork, tobacco, hemp, flax, and in the southern parts, rice and indigo, in great quantities," and they would be in steady need of foreign manufactured goods—all of which added up to a great deal of commercial river traffic that could redound to Spain's benefit. But if Spain persisted in denying American western settlers the Mississippi as a vital trade route, all their commerce would be forced northward, through Canada, to Britain's great advantage. Floridablanca, however, sensing American bravado and doubting the glowing destiny Congress predicted for its nation, held aloof.

THE LONG STALEMATE BETWEEN Virginia and Maryland over who ought rightfully to own the western lands if the United States prevailed over Britain began at long last to dissolve as a result of timely intervention by an unlikely savior.

Philip John Schuyler, a member of one of New York's wealthiest families, had given himself to public service as a soldier in the French and Indian War and a member of the New York colonial assembly. A strong advocate of American independence, he sat in the Second Continental Congress and was later commissioned a major general and placed in charge of the northern theater of operations. Though involved in the planning of the ultimately unsuccessful invasion of Canada, he fell ill and did not take an active part in it. But when one of his underlings later allowed Fort Ticonderoga to be retaken by the British without a shot being fired in its defense, Schuyler was charged with negligence and stripped of his command, thus losing the chance to redeem himself in the Saratoga campaign. A court-martial summoned at his request exonerated Schuyler, who then honorably retired from the military and returned to Congress late in 1779. It was there that he made his real contribution to the creation of the United States.

New York's was perhaps the most tenuous of the seven state claims to the backlands. New York officials contended that Virginia's sea-to-sea, west-by-northwest territorial outreach under its 1609 charter had been invalidated by the colony's 1624 charter, which failed to specify a western boundary, allowing New York to claim that Virginia did not legitimately extend past the Appalachians. The Old Northwest beyond the Ohio properly fell instead under the jurisdiction of colonial New York, because that territory had been put under the protection of the British crown as a result of a series of treaties with the six Iroquois nations—New York cited pacts executed in 1684, 1701, 1726, 1744, and 1754—whose lands were thus long considered an appendage of that colony and subject to its governmental oversight. This royally approved suzerainty over the Iroquois country and that of its allied tribes, which ran as far north as the forty-fifth parallel and deep into the northern sector of the Ohio Valley, was thus said to have been transferred to the state of New York now that crown authority over these lands had been canceled by the Declaration of Independence.

On his arrival in Philadelphia, Schuyler heard delegates from the other states and agents of the land companies seriously questioning the legitimacy of New York's claims and contending that the western lands at issue belonged either to the Indians or to the United States if it won the war. A consensus was forming, Schuyler was advised, behind the principle that land anywhere in the American colonies that the British crown had held the power to grant before the war but had not in fact bestowed should be considered the joint property of the United States and disposed of by Congress for the benefit of the whole confederation. But there was an escape route from this imminent confiscatory edict, Schuyler was pointedly advised—perhaps because he had been away from the intrigues of Congress for some years and was perceived to be a suggestible listener. He wrote back to the New York Assembly in late January 1780 that, as he divined the hardening lines of debate, if states "whose bounds were either indefinite or were pretended to extend to the South Seas [the Pacific] would consent to a reasonable western limitation that it would supersede the necessity of any intervention by Congress other than that of permanently establishing the bounds of each state." Otherwise, Congress was preparing to dictate each state's western boundary. In New York's case "a reasonable western limitation," according to the map Schuyler was shown, ran from the northwest corner of Pennsylvania due north to Lake Ontario—far less territory than the state was claiming but still leaving it with a substantial residue of unspoiled, highly saleable real estate. It had the great virtue of being a clean deal, which Schuyler hurried to Albany to promote before Congress could vote to encroach on New York's sovereignty.

Since Virginia and Connecticut claimed substantial parts of the same western lands on the basis of their earlier charter grants, New York's legislators decided to grab the half loaf dangled in front of them by operatives in Congress. On February 1, hoping to appear as selfless patriots, they passed "an act to facilitate the confederation and perpetual union among the United States of America" and surrendered their grants from the Indians by deeding them to the nation. It was the first pickle out of a very tight jar. Soon after, the war entered its southern phase, and the large landed states were preoccupied by the onslaught of British troops. By May the invaders had captured Charleston and its 5,400 defenders. It was not until October 10, after American forces were evening the score in the South, that Connecticut followed New York in yielding its western claims to Congress, which on that very day passed a resolution imploring the other five landed states to do likewise. In doing so, it promised that when federally supervised western lands had been sufficiently settled, they would be admitted to the Union as states in their own right and not treated—the way the thirteen original states had been—as permanent colonial appendages, subordinate to the central government.

Now the pressure mounted on Virginia to act unselfishly. Sensing momentum in their favor, the backers of the Vandalia project, the leading venture of the land speculators, hired Tom Paine to draft a pamphlet he titled "Public Good," passionately calling for Congress's takeover of the western lands. Joseph Jones, an open-minded Virginia delegate to Congress, wrote to Governor Jefferson and the politically powerful George Mason, leader of the Tidewater aristocracy, to suggest that the time was at hand for the state legislature to yield its land claims beyond the Ohio—and the two Virginia chieftains agreed with him. On the second day of the new year, the seventh and final one of the war, Virginia deeded to Congress its Old Northwest Territory, all the land it had been claiming above the Ohio River.

At the same time, though, Virginia was determined that its own selflessness should not serve to reward the arrant selfishness of the land speculators, and so the immense gift to the nation was hedged by several conditions. The donated land, the Virginia Assembly decreed, was to serve as "a common fund for the use and benefit" of the United States, present and future, and shared according to the "general charge and expenditure," and "for no other use or purpose whatever." And the state persisted in requiring, as Virginia's 1776 constitution had done, that all prior land purchases from the Indians by private individuals—usually arrived at under duress or some other equally dubious bargain—be voided. That meant most of the land companies' claims would be quashed. The other conditions Virginia laid down in gifting its land beyond the Ohio to Congress were less problematic. One prescribed that the ceded territory eventually be carved into states not smaller than 100 miles square (since too many state delegations in Congress would reduce Virginia's political clout in the federal government) or larger than 150 miles square (lest they become superstates and rival or dwarf their parent); a further condition called for reserving some of the trans-Ohio land to reward Virginia war veterans who served for no pay.

Virginia's conditional cession roused the speculators to call on Congress, in accepting the key cession, to make an exception for existing title claims by the land companies—the same ones that had incessantly lobbied Maryland not to ratify the Articles of Confederation until the landed states ceded their western claims. But now Virginia had turned the tables on its smaller neighbor, and for Maryland to continue holding out would have been to confess that its officials were up for purchase and willing to place the speculators' private interests above those of the nation. France's American envoy leaned heavily on Maryland's legislature to relent for its own financial well-being as well as that of Congress. Other states had some problems with the conditions Virginia had attached to its cession—indeed, it would take Congress three more years to thrash out a final compromise, and more than twenty years would pass before the last of the other landed states, Georgia, surrendered its western claims—but the essential sacrifice had been made.

Maryland authorities instructed their delegates in Congress to sign the Articles on March 1, 1781, in order "to convince our illustrious ally of an unalterable resolution" to support both American independence and the alliance with France and "to destroy forever any apprehension of our friends or hopes of our enemies, of this state being again united to Great Britain." The bells clanged throughout the day in Philadelphia to mark the formal adoption of the national charter, however inadequate for the task ahead, as the colors of all the states were unfurled, the cannons in the port discharged again and again, and fireworks lighted the night sky. The world had been put on notice now that the land the Americans were fighting for belonged first and foremost to their new country and not their separate states. Here was substantiation that theirs was a truly indissoluble union and no mere display of pyrotechnics sent skyward to scare away their overseas masters.

THE NEWS REACHING PARIS from America had been grim throughout much of 1780. British forces were storming through the southern states, where Loyalist sentiment was strongest, and small elements of the Continental Army and local irregulars were limited to guerrilla strikes to hinder the enemy's passage. Congress, on the edge of bankruptcy, was forced to devalue its paper currency to one-fortieth of its face amount, rousing howls from wounded creditors, especially in France, where holders of depreciated United States government paper felt that America, out of gratitude, ought to extend favored treatment to foreign lenders.

An exasperated Vergennes found his pro-American commitment increasingly challenged as misguided and spendthrift. Leading the criticism was Turgot's successor as the king's director general of finance, Jacques Necker, a rich and ambitious banker, who objected vocally that the war with Britain was dangerously swelling the nation's debt. Behind the foreign minister's back, Necker sent word to Lord North's ministry in London that France was receptive to a long-term truce with current military positions held "in a sovereign manner," that is, leaving a badly fragmented America to try to work out its salvation with the British crown. This was essentially what Spain had proposed to Britain a year earlier before entering the fray.

Just as he had then, George III, now sensing the tide of battle flowing his way and a sharp policy division within the French government, rejected the conciliatory gesture. If France was truly interested in advancing peace, Necker's deputy was told, his nation should quit subsidizing the American rebellion.

The episode laid bare Vergennes's vulnerable position. But while he continued to press the United States to submit to national boundaries substantially less expansive than Congress had repeatedly called for, the French foreign minister would not break under pressure and permit France to dishonor itself by violating its treaty pledge to the embattled new nation. Before he had been elevated to Comte de Vergennes, Charles Gravier had shown his mettle by withstanding criticism in French court circles for his notorious marriage to a woman deemed wholly unsuitable for a man in his position. As ambassador to the Ottoman Empire and a bachelor, he had carried on a seven-year affair with a physician's widow, an attractive woman of mixed Greek and French ancestry and from a social station well beneath his own. Compounding his display of bad taste, the couple had several out-of-wedlock children before being married, and Vergennes then committed the ultimate Parisian sin of unfashionableness by remaining entirely faithful to his wife. His domestic career may have made him the butt of tittle-tattle at the French court, but no one denied his fortitude or gift for diplomacy, which enabled him now to stymie his critics by trying to rally the rest of Europe against Britain and, in the process, salvage France's entanglement in the American cause.

While the monarchies on the continent were indifferent at best—and transparently hostile in the cases of Spain and Austria—to the democratic uprising of the American colonies, nearly all of them harbored an active and growing rancor toward Britain for its ascent to the apex of European power and the arrogance accompanying it. Of particular irritation was the bristling British policy toward international commerce. It was one thing for George III's navy to blockade France, preventing import of, for example, materials needed to build up the French fleet—after all, the two countries were at war. It was quite another, though, for Britain, with its naval preeminence, to insist that goods of any sort moving to and from its enemies on neutral-flag ships were fair game for seizure and disposal. Britain's victims called this high-seas robbery.

To check this scourge, Vergennes lent strong encouragement to Russia's energetic, German-born empress, Catherine II (the Great), who made known her nation's intention to defend its merchant fleet against further British bullying. By way of stirring other countries to do the same, Catherine proposed a League of Armed Neutrality to protect the sea passage of innocent cargoes on ships flying the flag of nonbelligerents, and with the help of France's adroit emissaries, nearly every nation in Europe was soon enlisted. Although subscribers to the league were in no rush to confront the British fleet, the very fact of its existence let Britain know it had isolated itself among the powers of the Old World.

Catherine, in tandem with the Austrian crown, then took the further step of proposing an all-Europe peace conference, to be held in Vienna, to force Britain's hand and work out a modus vivendi for all maritime nations. Also placed on the sponsors' proposed conference agenda was a prestige-seeking offer to broker a peace settlement between Britain and its rebel American colonies. Archroyalists to the core, the organizers of the projected conference declined to issue an invitation to the United States, that subversively self-proclaimed republic—although John Adams was standing by in Europe for just such an opportunity—and instead asked Vergennes to serve as protector of the Americans' interests. While the French minister was not averse to playing such a role, Adams made it clear to him that the United States was unwilling to have its fate settled for it by a council of distant Old World nations. Provided that the Americans were present at the peace table and thus recognized a priori as a sovereign state—a condition the British had flatly rejected—Congress signaled that it might entertain a truce along present battle lines, but only if Britain first removed its troops from American soil so that the pause could not serve either to strengthen the enemy ranks or further deplete the Continental Army.

The best the European powers could come up with by way of reconciling these conflicting demands was to invite spokesmen from all thirteen American states, as quasi-sovereign entities, to attend the conclave and represent their own interests—a transparent divide-and-conquer stratagem that ignored the pledge the states had made to one another, at the close of their Declaration of Independence, of "our lives, our fortunes and our sacred honor." Catherine's conference never assembled, the League of Armed Neutrality fired no shot, and the war went on.

ALTHOUGH FRANCE HAD SENT AN ARMY of 6,500 men to America in the summer of 1780 under the command of Jean-Baptiste-Donatien de Vimeur, Comte de Rochambeau, and a sizable fleet in support, its forces sat idle in Rhode Island while George Washington pondered how best to use the most potent weapon ever placed at his disposal. The British were decidedly on the march, from the coast of Maine, which they now occupied, to the southland, where they held the seaports and ravaged the countryside, though not without ceaseless harassment by the American resistance. As 1781 arrived, Washington wrote to Franklin of "the infinitely critical posture of our affairs," as mutinies swept through the Continental camps in Pennsylvania and New Jersey and Congress pleaded for more funds and supplies from abroad and for more fighting men from the states to sustain the seemingly endless ordeal.

By February, Congress had sent word to John Jay in Madrid that it would no longer insist on American navigation rights on the Mississippi through Spanish territory below the thirty-first parallel and free access to the Gulf—if Spain would only come to the assistance of the United States in its hour of maximum need. By May, British troops were scattering the Virginia Assembly and nearly managed to capture Governor Jefferson in his hometown of Charlottesville. By June, Congress was seriously considering the persistent advice of the French chargé d'affaires, Anne-César, Chevalier de La Luzerne, to cut back on its territorial claims and thus placate both its Bourbon allies. La Luzerne also strongly urged the delegates to replace the often caustic John Adams as America's sole peace negotiator in Paris, where its esteemed ambassador, Benjamin Franklin, was so much preferred.

Few questioned the intelligence and forthrightness of the short, stout New England attorney who had been a leading architect of the revolution and a mainstay in Congress. But Adams had thoroughly antagonized Vergennes, who found him outspoken to a fault, hopelessly nonobjective, and obviously jealous of the reverence that all of France paid to his senior colleague. Adams, while quick to concede Franklin's imaginative genius, found him at seventy-five to be indolent, devious, much too preoccupied with the pleasures of Parisian society, and fawning in his deference to the French court and its foreign minister. Rather than relying on the volatile Adams or the aged Franklin to deal forcefully with the British when and if the time came for hard bargaining over peace terms, La Luzerne called on Congress to repose its fullest confidence in Vergennes and to have no doubt that, as his remarks were reported in the official annals of Congress, "the King [of France] would most readily employ his good offices in support of the United States in all points relating to their prosperity."

Such blandishments by the French envoy flew in the face of Vergennes's secret pact with Madrid, which compromised American interests by yoking them to Spain's, and were at odds with the foreign minister's unstinting discouragement of expansive boundaries for the United States. Whether out of desperation, naïveté, or guile, Congress seemed to surrender to the French pressure. Having earlier directed Adams to proceed to Holland, Europe's banking capital, to seek financial aid and diplomatic recognition—and to arouse no further animosity among French officials—Congress created a five-man American peace commission, ostensibly to lend the panel better geographical balance and not leave the whole burden on the prickly New Englander's shoulders. Named as Adam's fellow commissioners were Franklin, John Jay, Thomas Jefferson, and another southerner, Henry Laurens, a South Carolina planter and Jay's immediate predecessor as president of Congress.

In mid-June Congress went still further to ingratiate itself with Vergennes and King Louis. It issued a final set of instructions to its peace commissioners that seemed to contain a pair of conflicting directives. "Since we think it unsafe at this distance," Congress asserted, "to tie you up by absolute and peremptory directions . . . [y]ou are therefore at liberty to secure the interest of the United States in such manner as circumstances may direct and the . . . disposition of the mediating powers may require." This sounded very much like a carte blanche delegation of authority. But then Congress added, in seemingly abject submission to its sole patron and hope for salvation, "For this purpose you are to make the most candid and confidential communications on all subjects to the ministers of our generous ally, the king of France, *to undertake nothing in the negotiations for peace or truce without their knowledge and concurrence; and ultimately to govern yourselves by their advice and opinion*" (italics added).

Such obsequious language, if obeyed to the letter, was a license for France to dictate the fate of the new nation—an act of subordination beneath the dignity of any self-respecting sovereign body. No less a member of that genuflecting Congress than James Madison would afterward confess that the wording of its instruction to the American peace team was a national humiliation. Surely Congress understood that the French monarchy, embroiled in Old World power struggles and political intrigue, could hardly be expected to share an identity of interest with an emergent democratic republic in the New World. Perhaps Congress, in a panic over the floundering revolution, had acted disingenously by wording its directive to flatter Versailles and assure the steadfastness of its indispensable ally, but never expected, or intended, the American peace commissioners to heed it literally. If so, no member of that Congress or any of the commissioners ever disclosed such a tacit and duplicitous understanding. Fortunately, the three commissioners who participated significantly in the peace talks* were

---

*Of the five men originally appointed as commissioners by Congress, Thomas Jefferson did not come to Paris because of his wife's terminal illness and Henry Laurens, a South Carolina planter-politician and leading member of Congress, was captured at sea by the British while en route to Paris in 1780 and held in the Tower of London as a prized prisoner of war until the last stages of the peace deliberations.

men of remarkable intelligence, courage, and vision who did not need to divine any cryptic intent on Congress's part in order to overlook the debasing passage in their instructions and act instead as they thought best for their country.

GEORGE WASHINGTON'S MAKESHIFT ARMY had managed to survive because of its commander's heroic willpower and its enemy's blundering irresolution. Lord North had none of William Pitt the Elder's verve for driving the British engines of war. His ministers dithered and bickered over their cautious, disjointed war strategy; his commanders in the field often worked at cross-purposes, and his king hovered with hectoring impatience as the imperial army kept failing to tree its prey. There had never been political unity in Parliament behind the colonial suppression, and the British public was tiring of its endless expense and bloodshed. The outcome seemed to hinge less on military prowess than on which side would lose heart first.

Suddenly, providence beamed on the Americans. The British had been expecting a joint assault on New York by the forces of Washington and Rochambeau, gathering northeast of the city, but the allies were far from sanguine that such an attack would succeed. When word reached their camps that a French fleet under the Comte de Grasse, with several thousand fresh troops aboard and a season to spare from their operations in the West Indies, had set sail for Chesapeake Bay, Washington saw his opportunity. Never before could he afford to gamble; now he had the resources to do so.

Choosing not to hamper Washington's forces as they crossed the Hudson north of New York in what was mistaken for an encircling movement southwestward, the British braced for a blow from the west. But Washington kept marching, as fast as his men could endure in the summer heat, for more than 400 miles while the British commanders' puzzlement grew. It did not occur to them that the allies' target was Lord Charles Cornwallis's southern army, which had lately wrought havoc in Virginia. Cornwallis had reluctantly parked his forces on Yorktown peninsula just above the narrow mouth of Chesapeake Bay, a site from which his men could be ferried to New York if needed to defend the city. By adroit seamanship de Grasse's fleet eluded the napping British navy in southern waters, arrived at the Chesapeake unimpeded, and deployed itself densely enough to plug entry into the bay by any trailing enemy vessels. Only a massive opposing force could have dislodged the French fleet—and there was none that could have been assembled in time for a rescue operation. When the allied army of 16,000 (9,000 American troops and 7,000 French, including the reinforcements de Grasse's fleet had brought) appeared before the narrow neck of the Yorktown peninsula, Cornwallis, his men outnumbered two to one, was hopelessly trapped. The British withstood a fierce bombardment and a first assault wave, then hoisted a bloodied white flag.

So humiliating did Lord Cornwallis find the defeat that he declined to appear at the surrender ceremonies on October 19, professing ill health and sending the deputy British commander, General Charles O'Hara, in his stead. In a shameful display of bitterness over succumbing to a colonial rabble, O'Hara attempted to surrender his sword to Rochambeau. But the French general, who had graciously deferred to Washington throughout their campaign and was perfectly attuned to the historic moment, directed O'Hara instead to the unconquerable American commander. With equal aplomb, Washington repaid both British generals' insulting breach of military etiquette by directing O'Hara to hand his sword to his own second-in-command, General Benjamin Lincoln. Then the surviving British force of 8,000 marched between the two long lines formed by the American and French armies and stacked their weapons in an adjacent field.

The British still had 10,000 soldiers in America and could have fought on—indeed, their mulish king, devastated by the prospect of losing his most prized colonial possession, vowed to carry on the fight or abdicate in shame. Washington, too, tasting the rare fruits of an immense triumph, wished to deliver a final crushing blow to the empire. He proposed to Rochambeau that their joint forces complete the expulsion of Britain from North America by marching on lightly defended Canada before it could be reinforced—and thus redeem America's misbegotten effort in Quebec at the beginning of the conflict. But the French commander declined to join in the project, which at any rate now seemed redundant. After Yorktown, the British military situation grew even gloomier. De Grasse's fleet followed up its daring intervention in the Chesapeake by returning to the West Indies and capturing a string of strategically located British islands. And Spain, having taken British forts along the Mississippi and Gulf Coast, added to its momentary resurgence by winning back Minorca in the nearby Mediterranean and intensifying its latest siege of Gibraltar, this time in tandem with French forces. Britain had been drained by the war, its national debt had soared, it had no allies in Europe, and Parliament had had quite enough.

A year-long war of words ensued, waged to determine how much of the territory the Americans had grandly claimed as theirs could be denied them by the leading powers of Europe. Once more, it looked to be an uneven contest; once more, appearances would prove deceiving.

CHAPTER 4

The kings outfoxed

1782–1783

THE DEFEAT AT YORKTOWN MAY HAVE effectively ended British hopes of retaining the rebels as subject colonies, but it did not leave the mother country inclined to reward the breakaway republic with a hearty "Well done, lads." The best the United States could hope for was the swift resignation of Lord North's discredited war cabinet and its replacement by a Whig coalition, whose most vocally conciliatory element was led by the brilliant but volatile enfant terrible, Charles James Fox.

Lord of the Admiralty and then the Treasury while still in his twenties, Fox had quit the North ministry when it opted for open war against the colonies. Now he was calling for an immediate grant of independence and liberal peace terms so that Britain might regain the friendship of its estranged brood—and the profits from the American trade, which had been accruing so handsomely before the outbreak of war. That way, Fox and his pro-American band reasoned, Britain could expeditiously detach its former colonies from their French protectors and settle accounts with the Bourbon kingdoms and their European sympathizers, thus compensating in part for the loss of America.

Others, led by King George, disagreed. It was one thing to swallow, painfully, the gross disobedience of the colonists because chastising them by armed force had failed. It was quite another to let the Americans make off now with great stretches of territory that they had not won on the battlefield. And why let them retain rights and resources they had enjoyed while subjects of the crown they had now repudiated? Why honor their claims, based on old royal charters, to the vast, empty lands beyond the Appalachians that the crown had never granted to colonial settlers? Why, by the same token, let them freely navigate the Mississippi and label it as their western boundary? Why let 10,000 New England fishermen still troll the cod-rich waters off Newfoundland and dry their catch on nearby British-owned shores? The masters of a proud but badly bruised empire were not likely to consent to such concessions, Benjamin Franklin in Paris and his colleagues in the Congress surmised, without the continued forceful presence at their side of Louis XVI and the court at Versailles.

While Parliament weighed its options over the winter of 1781–82, America's senior peacemaker tried to divine its mood from his hillside perch above the Seine, a spacious home in Passy, just across the river from the modern-day Palais de Chaillot, on loan to him from a French exporter (of, not coincidentally, supplies to the Continental Army). London was in no hurry to extend an olive branch in Ben Franklin's direction. But on March 22, 1782, he received an unlikely visitor, a minor British aristocrat of renown only for his dissipations, who was returning to England after wintering on the Riviera. His guest told him that they had a mutual acquaintance, the pro-American Earl of Shelburne, who retained a high regard for Franklin and would likely welcome a timely note of greeting from him, which the itinerant Briton would be glad to convey in person to his lordship.

Mindful that the prophetic Shelburne, out of the ministry for fourteen years and an avowed opponent of the war, was a presumptive candidate for any Whig cabinet that might soon replace North's, Franklin promptly drafted a message. It bore his classic velvet touch. He was addressing Shelburne, he wrote, because he held the earl's "talents and virtues" in high regard and observed approvingly "the new temper" in Britain for ending the war and reaching a general peace "which I wish to see before I die, and to which I shall with infinite pleasure contribute everything in my power." As a disarming grace note, the venerable diplomat added that the gooseberry bushes Shelburne had lately sent to their mutual Parisian acquaintance, Madame Helvétius, a wealthy widow of emancipated social views, whose salon Franklin frequented, had arrived in splendid condition. *Quel charme.*

And what perfect timing. Two days earlier and unknown to Franklin, Lord North had been overthrown, and the king was inclined to choose as first minister the Earl of Shelburne, a man of intelligence, culture, experience, and hauteur that suggested political ambition was beneath his dignity. Shelburne's other chief qualification in King George's eyes was that none among his party's leaders was less eager to yield independence to the American colonies or more hopeful—wishful, anyway—even after Yorktown that a grant of liberal home rule and some form of transatlantic confederation could yet prevent the final schism. But Shelburne, an independent thinker notorious for his indifference to party discipline, knew he had few ardent supporters among the factionalized Whigs and would be unlikely to assemble a cabinet broad-based enough to gain Parliament's sufferance. Instead he manfully urged the king to turn to the ailing moderate, Lord Rockingham, who had guided the ministry through its embarrassing repeal of the Stamp Act.

Rockingham agreed to serve only after extracting the king's reluctant pledge not to veto American independence if no alternative emerged. Shelburne was returned to the same cabinet post he had last held in 1768: Secretary of State for Domestic and Colonial Affairs. Because the boldly self-proclaimed United States was still considered as crown territory until otherwise designated by Parliament, determination of the colonists' fate now fell within Shelburne's purview. But since America was allied with France and France with Spain, and both were also at war with Britain, the pending peace negotiations also necessarily involved the Secretary of State for Foreign Affairs, Charles James Fox, the now thirty-two-year-old firebrand whom the king despised as an ardent American sympathizer and detractor of the crown. Fox, in turn, was known to harbor a deep dislike of Shelburne, who as a young lord in the service of Prime Minister Bute was given the thankless chore of advising Fox's father, then the royal paymaster for the military, that his services were no longer required due to charges of peculation, and although the huffy elder Fox was persuaded to go away quietly with a peerage to soothe him, his son never forgave the ministry's henchman.

If Fox's call for a prompt and unequivocal grant of independence were accepted as policy by the Rockingham cabinet, then the United States would qualify as a foreign sovereignty—and Fox's department alone would have jurisdiction over the peace terms. Shelburne, who favored withholding acknowledgment of America's sovereignty and employing it only as Britain's bargaining chip of last resort, acted quickly to avoid being maneuvered out of the negotiations.

Of the five American peace commissioners named by Congress, only one was positioned to begin negotiating in earnest. John Jay was still mired in Madrid, making little headway with the wary—and newly aggressive—Spaniards. John Adams was doing better in Holland, where he had to remain in order to work out the final wording of a treaty with the financially powerful Dutch republic to extend diplomatic recognition to the United States. Thomas Jefferson remained home in Virginia, a grieving widower now, and Henry Laurens was still held in London as a prisoner of war. That left old Ben Franklin, with whom—fortunately for them both—Lord Shel-

burne had been well acquainted in prewar days. To speak forthrightly with
the American sage, yet yield as little ground to him as possible, the British
minister sent no sly diplomat but a private subject of the crown, Richard
Oswald, a commoner friend of Shelburne, with a like-minded worldview,
extensive knowledge of American society, and no ulterior motive beyond
loyalty to his taskmaster.

By age (seventy-five), profession (wealthy merchant), and personality
(plainspoken Scotsman but so lively and well read, despite poor eyesight,
that historian Thomas Carlyle would describe him as "a man of great
knowledge and ready conversation"), Oswald seemed ideally suited to
engage in a fateful dialogue with Franklin. It would run, on and off, for eight
months. Having made his fortune as a supplier of equipment for British
troops, Oswald added to his wealth as a slave trader while attending to the
estates his wife had inherited in Jamaica and the Carolinas. "He is a pacifi-
cal man," Shelburne wrote in the letter of introduction that Oswald handed
to Franklin, "and conversant in those negotiations which are most interest-
ing to mankind. This has made me prefer him to any of our speculative
friends [those involved in the proposed American land settlement schemes
that Franklin had urged Shelburne to support in the 1760s] or to any person
of higher rank. He is fully apprized on my Mind, and you may give full
credit to every Thing he assures you of."

Oswald won Franklin's confidence almost at once with a confession so
candid as to seem unworldly. Britain, he opined, had become "foolishly
involved in four wars" simultaneously—in North America, the West Indies,
the Mediterranean, and India—and had strained its resources to the point
that reaching a general peace settlement had become "absolutely necessary." Lest the American luminary take his remark for indiscretion, Oswald
quickly added that, however war-weary Britain seemed, it would not, of
course, accept humiliating peace terms, that there was some sentiment in
Parliament to levy an emergency 25 percent war tax to fight on if necessary,
and that America, with its primary goal now in clear view, would be ill-
advised to yoke itself too tightly to France and Spain, which might foolishly
attempt to make excessive demands on the hard-pressed British ministry.

It was a well-targeted warning. France's majordomo in the peacemaking
process, the Comte de Vergennes, had the very opposite misgiving. He
feared that the Americans, ground down by the long war and swayed by the
still substantial segment of crown Loyalists among them—said to range
from one-tenth to one-third of the citizenry—would hurry back to nestle in
mother Britain's capacious bosom. Such a reunion, the French foreign minister wrote his envoy in Philadelphia, would "make us lose in large part the

fruit of the costly efforts that we are making to save America." When Franklin took Oswald to Versailles to meet Vergennes, the minister shortly advised the Scotsman that France would not take kindly to any effort to wean the United States from its benefactor or tolerate a separate British-American accord that failed to address French concerns as well.

Over the ten-day getting-acquainted phase of their exchanges, before informal talks turned into official negotiations, Franklin let Oswald know that just as he understood imperial Britain had hardly been brought to its knees by the war, neither was the United States prepared to settle for crumbs off the peace table or some sort of satellite sovereignty. When the Scotsman came to Passy for breakfast with Franklin and an hour of socializing before his return to London, his host framed a message for Shelburne and his ministry that he must have suspected would astonish his adversaries and throw them off balance. Franklin remarked that his countrymen were entitled to reparations for British war crimes, in particular the widespread destruction and looting of civilian property and the "scalping and burning parties," as he termed them, conducted by Britain's Indian allies.

The very mention of such a claim stole a march on the British. Throughout the peace talks their most persistent source of concern would turn out to be some form of compensation to the crown's American Loyalists, many of whom had lost their homes and other personal possessions, their businesses, and their civil rights, suffered punitive taxes and expulsion from public office, and, finally, were hounded from their communities altogether. Britain's honor would demand that the Tory victims of a fratricidal war be restored to their former standing. But Franklin was first to claim the higher moral ground. Then he very kindly suggested that nothing would better ensure "a durable peace and a sweet reconciliation" between the two countries than for Britain to make amends voluntarily—and he had in mind the ideal means to do so: Canada.

Ever since the British, with considerable assistance from their American colonists, had driven the French from North America, Franklin had been advocating a single, English-speaking domain occupying at least the eastern half of the continent. He had been much in favor of the doomed American military strike to gain control of Canada at the very start of the War for Independence. Now, speaking from rough notes, Franklin made his vision manifest to Oswald, who attentively heard out the Old Conjurer (as John Adams liked to describe him). There were at least three good reasons for the crown to cede Canada, all of it, to the United States, Franklin contended. First, it would save Britain the expensive headache of governing and defending so vast and frigid a wilderness, hardly worth the £50,000 or so of income from

fur trapping that the region produced each year. It was the same rationale
that had carried the day when the crown chose in the 1760s, in the face of
massive tax resistance by American colonists, to abandon the lands west of
the Appalachians to the natives and place the entire region off-limits to
white settlers. Nothing, though, could halt the westward flow of land-
hungry frontiersmen, as the British had discovered. If Canada was now to
remain in British hands, said Franklin, there would be constant tension and
endless disputes between American settlers and neighboring British subjects all along that immense stretch of boundary. This translated less subtly
as: Save yourselves a lot of lives, money, and anguish and just give us
Canada, or we pugnacious Americans will be compelled to take it off your
hands.

Franklin's other two arguments were only a bit less confrontational.
Canadian land, he pointed out, could be sold off to recompense America's
civilian victims of British war crimes. Then he added, with benevolence he
would shortly come to regret, that some sectors of Canada could be given
for settlement to, or sold for the benefit of, the 80,000 Loyalist refugees,
half of whom had fled the American colonies and taken refuge in Quebec
province or the Maritimes. Both of these functions could have been performed without a British handover of Canada, but Oswald was too polite to
nip Franklin's ploy in the bud. Finally, Shelburne's emissary was told,
unless the Americans won Canada along with independence, they would be
forced to preserve their close ties with France as a defensive measure—
presumably in case Britain someday chose to launch an invasion against the
United States from the Canadian provinces.

Did Franklin think that Shelburne, the king, and Parliament would
actually entertain the voluntary transfer of such a huge piece of imperial
real estate, the dimensions of which were unknown but indisputably colossal, to an adversary who (1) had failed to conquer the smallest part of it,
(2) surely did not require it for survival, and (3) had next to nothing in common with most of its occupants? Since he was too smart to believe his own
flummery, the more plausible explanation for this display of consummate
brass was that the canny Franklin was asking for the moon and stars at the
outset so that the true territorial ambitions of the United States would look
less monumental when unveiled. Franklin's chief obstacle in pushing Congress's mandate to gain the Mississippi as the nation's western boundary
was that no American soldiers and very few civilians could be found west of
the Appalachians by the war's end. Claiming he could not do justice to
Franklin's almost offhand, not to say laughable, Canadian proposition,
Oswald asked if he might please borrow the doctor's rough notes to convey

their essence more faithfully to Shelburne. Franklin, probably calculating that he had little to lose, reluctantly agreed.

Whatever the British cabinet's reaction, Franklin could not have been in any doubt about how Vergennes would have viewed his proposal that the boundaries of the infant United States should enclose Canada as well. To the French mindset the only thing more absurd than Franklin's suggestion would have been for Britain to succumb to his sweet talk and sophistry. Such a development would invite the resulting, monstrously oversized new-born to end its reliance on France and emerge overnight as a brash—and very likely unmanageable—player on the world stage, probably in close alliance with its mother country. That Franklin broached the idea without first clearing it with Vergennes was clear evidence that he had no intention of slavishly following Congress's instructions to the commissioners to act only in concert with the French court. If Canada could be had just for the asking, Franklin would have been guilty of negligence of duty not to ask for it. Besides, France was obliged by its treaty with the United States to honor any territorial gains the Americans might realize at Britain's expense, whether through conquest or at the peace table, even if France felt such self-aggrandizement by its young ally to be flagrant.

While Franklin awaited a more formal and detailed peace overture from London, he was cheered by news from Adams. The seven United Provinces of Holland had officially received the proud New Englander as America's minister plenipotentiary, the second nation to recognize the United States as a sovereign entity. It had been no inconsequential feat to persuade the small maritime country, even though it was on a quasi-war footing with the British over their protectionist policies and oppressive tactics on the high seas, to fall in on the side of the fragile American confederation. Redeemed for his earlier abrasive stint in Paris, Adams advised Franklin he would stay on in Amsterdam to seek a commercial treaty and badly needed financial aid from the Dutch banking community, the wealthiest in continental Europe.

With Adams not expected in Paris anytime soon and the British poised, however unhappily, to engage the Americans in peacemaking, the increasingly infirm Franklin felt the burden of solitary responsibility weighing heavily on him. Although—and because—his massive mind was still alert, he recognized the need for reinforcement of a high cerebral order. He found it languishing in Madrid, where John Jay had applied his abundant prowess as an advocate for two and a half years without extracting a single concession from the blinkered Spanish court. The usually imperturbable Franklin had had enough of the Spaniards' obduracy and let his irritation show as he wrote to his younger countryman that "the slight they have put on our offered friendship is very disreputable to us and, of course, hurtful to our affairs elsewhere. . . . [Spain] has taken four years to consider whether she should treat with us. Give her forty. And let us mind our own business." Lest Jay blame himself for the failure of his mission, Franklin summoned him to Paris with blunt reassurance: "Here you are greatly wanted."

WHATEVER REMNANT OF TENDER FEELINGS Britain may have still harbored for its fled colonies stayed well submerged as the Rockingham cabinet met late in April to frame its formal instructions to Richard Oswald. Franklin's rough notes that he had brought back from Paris, in effect asking for war reparations in the form of Canada, drew no comment from Lord Shelburne, who doubtlessly recognized the nervy request for what it was. During the ministry's deliberations, Shelburne's attitude prevailed over Fox's—there would be no quick recognition of American sovereignty, no ingratiating peace terms, no gift of Canada, no compensation for wartime losses of property by the insurgent colonists. If indeed American independence from Britain had to be ultimately conceded, the United States would have to be equally independent "of the whole world," Shelburne advised Oswald, "without any secret, tacit, or ostensible connection with France." The notion of using the sale of Canadian land to compensate the Loyalists for their losses was dismissed as a device to entice Britain to expend its own resources to succor the Tory victims rather than requiring America to do so. Furthermore, prewar debts to British creditors would have to be honored in full by citizens of the new nation, and if the United States expected to take title to New York City, Charleston, Savannah, and other choice pieces of American territory then held by British troops, it would have to pay tribute money for their removal.

But what of Congress's cherished territorial claims? Franklin had not brought them up in his preliminary talks with Oswald—and seeking Canada was admittedly Franklin's own idea, not part of the American peace commission's charge. Here the British cabinet grew a little vague. A nation composed of the thirteen insurgent colonies, the ministry ruled, could not exceed the boundaries set down by the Treaty of 1763, converting all of New France to undisputed British territory. But that treaty's language left undefined just how far west the established American colonies with "sea-to-sea" charters were understood to extend. The 1763 treaty with France set the Mississippi River as the western boundary of Britain's North American empire below the St. Lawrence River basin, but the crown's Proclamation Act of that same year banned, at least temporarily, further settlement by the colonists west of the Appalachians. Was that tantamount to the king's and Parliament's voiding the colonies' charter rights? Virginia in particular and the other "landed" colonies with expansive westward claims said no and went to war averring that King George no longer had the authority to grant, withhold, or control title to land in America. If not, then on what basis could the United States claim the Mississippi as its western boundary?

There were three plausible justifications, and the first two—by conquest or by established settlement, certified or otherwise—did not apply. The third, based on claimed inheritance of charter rights granted by the monarchy the colonists had now successfully disavowed, was arguable at best. Equally so was America's call for its northward extension. The Quebec Act of 1774 had advanced that province's southward boundary all the way to the Ohio River, effectively canceling Virginia's charter claim to the Old Northwest. But the British cabinet now made no reference to that act, seeming tacitly to withdraw to the boundaries of the 1763 peace treaty. Under that treaty, though, there was no clearly delineated boundary between "Canada," an amorphous entity, and the thirteen American colonies. The Proclamation Act had specified only the borders of the new crown province of Quebec, which encompassed much of the St. Lawrence basin running upstream from the estuary nearly 600 miles and then ran west in a line roughly parallel to the Ottawa River until it reached Lake Nipissing in the central sector of modern-day Ontario province. It was an immense swath of terrain, nearly 900 miles long and about 150 miles wide on average. Even so, most of what Franklin and other Americans had in mind in referring to Canada lay outside of Quebec province, as part of the undifferentiated land mass that the British had officially taken title to from France, including the large, temperate peninsula that makes up the southern sector of modern Ontario province and fronts on three of the Great Lakes.

The vagueness and confusion over boundaries had emboldened Franklin to propose the outlandishly simple solution of adding all of Canada, however delineated, to the American nation—historical justification be damned. But if Franklin had been seriously hoping for a generous concession of territory, he must have been disheartened when Oswald revealed to him the one boundary that the cabinet had instructed him to insist on. Instead of either the St. John or St. Croix River, which Congress had spoken of as forming the northeast boundary between the Massachusetts-owned province of Maine and royal Nova Scotia, the ministry now set the line at the Penobscot River, nearly 100 miles to the south along the coast, so some 6,000 square miles of claimed American territory would be chopped off for possible resettlement by the Loyalists. And if this stipulation was not enough to dim Franklin's hopes, the British ministry also expected that an independent United States, its commerce liberated from the Navigation Acts and thus free to traffic in the global market, would keep all its ports and waterways as free and open to Britain's merchant fleet as they had been before the war—that is, cargoes of British origin would be landed duty-free—even though no mention was made of extending reciprocal rights to American carriers entering British waters. Vessels under the United States flag, in other words, were to be stripped of the privileged status Americans had enjoyed in the colonial era while British ships would not be. For good measure, sweet-tempered Richard Oswald was told by Shelburne not to be submissive in his dealings with the famous and wily American negotiator.

Britain was equally determined to let France know that it ought not to cultivate any big ideas about what gains it might hope to realize at the bargaining table. Foreign Secretary Fox sent as his peace envoy to Versailles the callow son of George Grenville, architect of the Stamp Act that had stoked the fires of rebellion, and Thomas Grenville managed at once to get Vergennes's back up. If France expected Britain to grant independence to its client state—the ostensible casus belli—then King Louis should ask for no more, young Grenville declared, sounding as if Britain had won the war, and, instead, be prepared to make some concessions, like returning the islands in the West Indies that France had lately snatched.

Franklin, who was on hand for the meeting, set Grenville straight about Britain's power to bestow the glittering prize of independence. "We do not consider ourselves under any necessity," he said, to bargain for "a thing that is our own, which we have bought at the expense of much blood and treasure and which we are in the possession of." Vergennes weighed in with equal force, noting that since, in reality, America was already independent, Britain was not in fact yielding anything if it supposed France was entitled to no more than satisfaction over the outcome of the revolution. Then he delivered a stinging history lesson that went far to explain France's motive in joining the American war effort. Twenty years earlier, after the cross-Channel rivals had fought in North America primarily over the boundaries between their imperial claims, victorious Britain was not satisfied with a treaty that awarded it only the contested regions but demanded France's total expulsion from North America and denied it access to the Newfoundland fisheries and trading rights in Africa and India. Now it was payback time—beyond the vengeful pleasure France was deriving as facilitator of America's triumph.

Britain's defiant posture was soon braced by a shift in the empire's military fortunes. News reached London in the spring of 1782 that British forces and hirelings had captured Ceylon from the Dutch and beaten back a major uprising against the empire's growing commercial hegemony over much of the tumultuous Indian subcontinent. More pertinent to American concerns, a French fleet of thirty-five ships under Admiral de Grasse, whose timely action had been instrumental in the allies' land-sea success at Yorktown, had tried to extend his subsequent series of victories in the West Indies by heading for Jamaica to seize Britain's richest Caribbean outpost. Near Guadeloupe, they were intercepted by Admiral George Rodney's fleet in the "Battle of the Saints," as the French debacle was celebrated ever after in British naval annals. Rodney's forces inflicted 8,000 casualties, receiving only 1,000 of their own, before de Grasse surrendered and was carried off to London as a trophy of the French fleet's reversal. France's brief reign as master of the West Indies was over.

The British triumph further toughened the ministry's attitude toward making peace with the Americans. Despite Fox's urging of a prompt and liberal settlement, the cabinet majority remained slow to act; Parliament had not yet even empowered the ministry to explore formal arrangements for liberating the colonies. Shelburne, while keen for peace as he had been throughout the long, fierce dispute with the Americans, continued to assert that loss of the colonies would signal the decline of the British empire, so he held out, even with hopes fleeting, for a compromise short of full independence.

To soften resistance by the senior American peace commissioner, Fox and Shelburne had their surrogates pursue separate divide-and-conquer tactics. Oswald pointed out to Franklin that Britain would likely reach an accord with its former colonies a good deal more easily than with its historic enemies, France and Spain, and thus America ought not to hesitate at dealing directly and by itself with its mother country. To advance prospects for peace and recognition of an independent United States, Shelburne's man in Paris added, Congress needed to confront the ministry's deepening insistence that the Loyalists be justly compensated. But the more Oswald pressed this issue, the more Franklin resisted, arguing that if either side had a just claim for preparations, it was America, and at any rate Congress had no power under the federal compact licensing it, the Articles of Confederation, to order state and municipal authorities to remedy the Loyalists' losses. And why was the crown so concerned about the American Tories, Franklin wondered, when "it was by their misrepresentations and bad counsels she [Britain] had been drawn into this miserable war"?

At the same time, Fox's peace envoy to Versailles, Thomas Grenville, came with full authority, according to his papers, to treat with "France and

her [unnamed] allies"—the diplomatic way to avoid mentioning the United
States by name, which would have been equivalent to recognizing its sovereignty, or alluding to the thirteen British colonies, since France had no real
business intruding on an intrafamily quarrel. In effect, Grenville was signaling that Britain was prepared to work out peace terms with France as the
mature and presumably restraining partner in its alliance with the hotheaded
Americans. But Vergennes would not take the lure. He wrote to Franklin:
"They want to treat with us for you, [but] this the king will not agree to—he
thinks it not consistent with the dignity of your state. You will treat for yourselves, and every one of the powers at war with England will make its own
peace. All that is necessary to be observed for our common security is that
the treaties go hand in hand and are signed all on the same day."

It was a deft counterstroke. Vergennes was both reassuring Franklin that
France would not try to dictate peace terms to its junior ally and encouraging it to work out its own destiny with Britain—so long, that is, as Versailles
was kept fully au courant and approved the final settlement. That was, after
all, what Congress had instructed, and Vergennes did not want to loosen the
alliance at such a delicate moment by playing the domineering partner. Had
he been advised of Franklin's low-key bid for Canada to be included within
the negotiated boundaries of the new American republic, Vergennes would
surely have sounded less magnanimous in his communiqué.

The onset of the summer of 1782—a particularly soggy one in much of
France, as the rains played havoc with the grape crop—brought two important changes affecting the tortoiselike pace of the peace process. The first
was the arrival in Paris of John Jay during the final week of June. Jay was
delighted by the gracious reception the French accorded him after the icy
disdain he had endured in Madrid. Glad to find that Franklin was far from
succumbing to senility, Jay noted in a letter home that "his mind appears
more vigorous than that of any man of his age I have known." More pleasing still, the Spanish ambassador to France seemed eager to make up for
the slights Jay had been dealt by King Carlos and his court. Don Pedro
Pablo Abarca de Bolea, a politically astute nobleman from Aragon, known
by his title, Conde de Aranda, had headed the king's governing council
until maneuvered out of the way and sent to Paris by his jealous rival,
Floridablanca, the new first minister. Floridablanca thoroughly disagreed
with Aranda's belief that recognizing American independence and otherwise befriending the young republic would strengthen, not weaken, Spain's
neighboring New World empire. Treated cordially by Aranda, whose embassy was said to house the finest wine cellar and best-polished silverware
in Paris, Jay had reason to anticipate a thaw in the frigid diplomatic climate

between their two countries. Soon enough, though, Jay would discover the darker design behind the Spanish grandee's engaging manner.

Shortly after Jay had taken up residence in Paris, word arrived from London that the first minister, Lord Rockingham, had died after only three months as the head of government, and King George had turned to the only Whig minister whose attitude toward America he could stomach, the Earl of Shelburne. With just enough backing to form a coalition cabinet of moderates, Shelburne dismissed the troublesome Fox and his allies—"the leaders of sedition," the king had called them—from the ministry and took complete charge of the peace talks. It was just as well from the standpoint of the American commissioners. Oswald and the young Grenville had grown jealous of each other's separate but equal roles in the negotiations and often seemed to be at cross-purposes, muddying the whole business before it began in earnest. With Shelburne's ascent to Lord of the Treasury and first minister, Oswald was advanced to chief negotiator. Grenville's replacement from the foreign office, Alleyne Fitzherbert, a lackluster but sound careerist recently in charge of Britain's Belgian legation, served as spear-carrier, not pushing for a settlement with Vergennes until the American issues could be resolved.

For Franklin, Shelburne's arrival at the apex of Britain's government was a mixed blessing. The two men were well disposed to each other, shared much the same social and political thinking, and had reestablished rapport at a remove through Oswald's useful services. But Franklin also knew that the new prime minister could be rather a slippery customer with a reputation for sometimes speaking out of both sides of his mouth, as he began doing now about American independence. On one hand, he told the House of Lords, to sanction the sovereignty of the colonies would be "a dreadful blow to the greatness of this country"—one that he was not ready to suffer and, with the king, would rather Britain fight on "to obtain fair and reasonable terms of pacification." On the other hand, while opposed to the prompt grant of independence as Fox and his Whig ultras advocated, Shelburne had to concede the futility of trying to hold America within the empire. He understood that Britain's military was spread too thin worldwide to tolerate a continuous campaign of American pacification, which would soon bleed the royal treasury dry. Britain should now fashion an honorable, if not affectionate, peace accord, untangle America from France, and renew close commercial—and perhaps some sort of political—bonds with its former subjects. For Britain to walk this tightrope, though, would be a considerable feat. Shelburne had no personal following to speak of in Parliament, his ministry was divided and less than enthusiastic about his call for free trade and more democratic government, and if he was too conciliatory toward America, the hard-line aristocracy, dyed-in-the-wool mercantilists, and patriotic masses would demand his head.

In this volatile political environment, Franklin did not need to be instructed that if Shelburne failed, whoever replaced him as the head of government was certain to prove more vengeful and less enlightened about the usefulness of an independent America and how it could greatly benefit Britain's commerce. Within days of Shelburne's taking command of the government, Franklin drew up a list of what he called "hints" for articles to be included in a peace treaty and gave them to Oswald on July 9. No surviving documents indicate that Franklin had first shown his list to Jay, who was laid low with influenza at the time. The memorandum would likely have been less elliptical and more precise if the attorney had put his hand to it, but Franklin was still probing and almost certainly wanted to keep his bargaining position flexible. Since no whiff of flexibility had been forthcoming from London, Franklin divided his proposal into two categories of four items each so the British would be left in no doubt about America's priorities before they committed themselves to positions from which it would be politically disastrous to retreat.

The first part of his list Franklin headed with the single word "Necessary" and let it speak for itself. Leading the list was the acknowledgment of American independence, "full and complete in every sense," accompanied by the removal of British troops. There was no equivocating mention of a possible federal union or any other kind of formal connection between the two nations under the umbrella of the British empire, as Shelburne had wistfully envisioned. Franklin's second item was the need for settling the boundaries of the United States since no sovereign state could exist in limbo. But, whether out of fear of asking for too much or too little without some clue of Shelburne's receptivity, Franklin did not specify where the borders of the United States should be. True, Congress had indicated at various times during the course of the war that it considered the American republic to extend west to the Mississippi and ought to include the Floridas and parts of Canada as well. How much of that had been wishfulness and bravado in a dark time? Only with regard to the northern boundary did Franklin elaborate, in the third item on his list. Canada's borders, he said, ought to be confined "at least to what they were before that last Act of Parliament I think in 1774 [the Quebec Act], if not to a still more contracted State, on an ancient footing." Here he was insisting that Britain could not withhold from America the Old Northwest lands bounded on the south by the Ohio River, on the north by the Great Lakes, and running to the Mississippi—that is, the crown had arbitrarily and impermissibly encroached on

Virginia's charter rights to that territory by greatly distending the 1763 boundaries of Quebec province. The wording Franklin carefully chose here represented a retreat from his earlier, informal suggestion to Oswald that Britain would be better off ceding all of Canada to the United States. Now he was asking only that Canada revert to confined boundaries and hinting that they should be coterminous with those of Quebec as defined by the 1763 Proclamation Act. Fourth and last, Franklin said American fishermen had to be as free to harvest the waters off Newfoundland as they had been before the war, but made no mention—probably because he thought it was understood—of the need, in that age before refrigeration, to dry their catch on the nearest (that is, British-owned) shore. "I said nothing of it," Oswald noted to Shelburne.

The second part of his proposed settlement terms Franklin headed "Advisable," and here he thought a word or two of elaboration might prove useful. Conceding that he had no explicit instructions from Congress on the points that followed, he was offering them not as absolute demands but rather, according to Oswald's report to Shelburne, as measures "he would as a Friend recommend to be offer'd by England" in its own future interest and by way of speeding reconciliation. First, he returned to where he had begun his dialogue with Oswald in the spring by repeating his call for indemnification payments to American civilians who had been "ruined by Towns burnt and destroy'd" by British soldiers: Franklin suggested a pool of £500,000 to £600,000 to compensate "a multitude of poor Sufferers who would have no other Remedy" and would otherwise remain vengeful toward Britain. Helping them "would diffuse a universal calm and conciliation over the whole country." Franklin must have known it was a forlorn hope—Americans, after all, had rebelled against the crown's authority and should not have expected to escape injury or be reimbursed by their vanquished ex-rulers; their compensation was that the country was now theirs. But Franklin knew by now that Britain, as a matter of professed honor, was insisting that official acknowledgment of U.S. sovereignty hinged on the recovery of losses suffered by the king's faithful subjects in America—no more justifiable to Franklin than compensation from the crown to American patriots similarly victimized by the war. At the least, he was hoping the two grievances would be accepted as equivalents and cancel each other.

If that trade-off would not sit well with Shelburne and his ministry, Franklin's second "advisable" suggestion seemed conceived to infuriate them. It urged Parliament to concede "error in distressing those countries" (regions) where British soldiers had rampaged. To substantiate this grievance, Franklin showed Oswald copies of orders from the royal high command instructing troops to lay waste civilian areas, most recently wide swaths of countryside in the Carolinas. Indeed, the indignant Philadelphian charged, Britain had forfeited any right to intercede in behalf of the Loyalists by the scorched-earth conduct of its own army. Franklin could not for a moment have truly supposed that Britain would consider apologizing for whatever brutal measures were taken to suppress the American insurgency, but his recommendation served to underscore that neither side had clean hands when it came to war crimes, so the entire subject of compensation for the Loyalists was omitted from his proposed treaty articles. Plainly Franklin now regretted having mentioned earlier to Oswald that some portion of Canada, if ceded to the United States, might be set aside for, or sold for the benefit of, the Loyalists—an omission Oswald pointed out to London.

Franklin's third "advisable" item was far more reasonable on its face than the first two—reciprocal trade rights with Britain, exempting an independent America from the binding force of the Navigation Acts. The proposal, essentially the same commercial arrangement that the United States had made by treaty with France, was designed to match the new prime minister's well-known advocacy of free trade as a spur to British prosperity. But as always and everywhere, those with a vested interest in protectionist policies feared free-market competition. With Britain's manufacturers and merchant fleet dominant in the world market, sentiment was not strong for easing monopolistic practices as long as the empire could get away with them. And so long as Americans had more need to buy from the British than the other way around, why should Britain do any favors for a people who had just stormed out of the realm?

Finally, Franklin returned to his fixation that Canada was an integral part of America's natural domain and Britain would be the gainer by surrendering it, or nearly all of it, including Nova Scotia. Newfoundland was not mentioned, perhaps to leave the kingdom an imperial outpost in North America; just as likely, it was an oversight. Oswald had already advised him, after he had earlier brought Franklin's rough notes on the subject back to London, that Canada was not up for discussion, but to Franklin that was not a flat rejection. It was almost as if, having been frustrated before the war in his efforts to help speculative companies win crown approval of large new land grants to colonize the Ohio Valley, Franklin was now determined to come away with an exponentially larger mass of the continent as a crowning prize for his new nation.

WHILE THE MINISTRY WAS WEIGHING Franklin's proposed treaty articles, Oswald's commission as official plenipotentiary under the great seal of the realm reached Paris, enabling him to speak now with full authority for his nation. The wording of his commission, however, was offensive to John Jay and roused him from his sickbed.

Oswald, according to the crown's charge, was empowered to conclude a peace or truce with "certain Colonies in North America" and treat with any commissioners of "said Colonies or Plantations, or any of them, or any parts thereof." There was no mention of the United States of America, as if the very name stuck like a bone in Britain's throat. Jay, as punctilious a legal draftsman as the occasion required, pointed out that the accepted international convention in such official matters was to state the full and correct name of every participating nation or sovereign entity, just as signatories to private legal transactions were formally named. Oswald's commission provided only a geographical context and implied the continuing dependency of the former American colonies—a political status the United States did not accept. And by hinting that Britain might reach terms separately with the insurgent colonies/states or even parts thereof, the crown seemed to be disparaging the sanctity of the compact among them issued on July 4, 1776. None of this was an accident, so far as Jay was concerned; it was a calculated put-down.

Oswald was quick to assure the two American commissioners that if a treaty was consummated, it would, of course, acknowledge the independence of the United States. Still Jay objected. Reaching an accord might involve protracted discussions among the belligerents, and even if America were satisfied by the outcome, it could find itself enmeshed indefinitely in the intrigues of the European powers—and American independence was not to be postponed during the course of such machinations or for the convenience of any other nation. Vergennes, virtuoso of the diplomatic arts, dismissed Jay's concerns as hairsplitting and said the United States could hardly expect recognition of its independent status to precede the peace settlement. And wasn't Oswald's certified presence "a tacit concession of your independence"? Jay vaulted onto his high horse to joust with the French foreign minister: "To treat about this matter would be to suppose that our independence was incomplete until they pronounced it to be complete. But we hold it to be complete already."

If so, why did it matter that Oswald's commission failed to name the United States? And if it was already a truly independent entity prior to the signing of a treaty with Britain, what were its boundaries? To be sure, there was an element of disingenuousness in Jay's argument, but he had a point as well, and by standing on ceremony he hoped to convey young America's resolve to be treated like a grown-up at the bargaining table. Fellow attorney

John Adams wrote from Amsterdam that he agreed with Jay's position. Franklin, principle and expediency as always at war within him, thought it a distracting cavil. Time was not on their side, he told Jay; British troops were still doing damage in the South, Washington's army was evaporating, Congress was in a state of suspended animation, and Shelburne's tenure could be abbreviated. It was essential to accelerate the peacemaking, not burden it with nuances. Once he had a soupbone locked between his jaws, though, John Jay could be a very determined bulldog. His prideful objection was not withdrawn, and Oswald had to forward it to London, along with his impression that the new U.S. commissioner was usually well mannered, frank, and reasonable, but decidedly alienated to the crown.

This reading of Jay's character came as no surprise to Shelburne. The British secret service had previously sized up Jay's abilities as a leading young enemy statesman, reporting that he was courageous, indefatigable, articulate both in person and on paper, combative if aroused, and obstinate in standing his ground. Oddly enough, when the French took his measure as a mainstay in Congress, their envoys in Philadelphia found him a late-blooming patriot and anything but rabid. Because he had not been a passionate participant when the majority in Congress voted to demand the Mississippi as the nation's western boundary and access to the Newfoundland fisheries on the prewar basis, Jay was seen as a sensible chap, perhaps pliable, and strongly recommended by Vergennes's aides hovering about Congress for the sensitive diplomatic post in Madrid. The French had misread him, the Spanish badly underestimated him, but the British were already learning he was an adversary who might turn into an edgier obstacle to a reasonable settlement than the genially formidable Franklin.

Of more immediate concern to Franklin than his younger colleague's aptitude for quibbling were the rumors around Paris, said to stem from Thomas Grenville, lately relieved as the foreign office's peace emissary when Fox was dropped from the new cabinet. Shelburne, now in sole command of the peace talks and reputedly in sync with the king's thinking, was said to have no plans to acknowledge America's independence—certainly not anytime soon. The way Oswald's commission had been worded, ripe with effrontery, seemed to lend substance to the report. When Oswald himself inquired about it, Shelburne sought to reassure him, but in language that made clear his unhappiness over the prospect of a sovereign America. He wrote that "there never have been two Opinions since you were sent to Paris upon the most unequivocal Acknowledgement of American independency." Shelburne had made no secret of his deep concern over "the separation of countries united by blood, by principles, habits, and every tie short of territorial proximity," then had added: "But you very well know that I have given it up, decidedly though reluctantly; and the same motives which have made me perhaps the last to give up all hope of reunion make me the most anxious, if it is given up, that it shall be done so as to avoid all future risk of enmity."

And by way of evidencing his readiness to deal, Shelburne promised to send on a new commission for Oswald that he hoped would unruffle Jay's feathers and, more important, indicated the ministry would shortly address Franklin's proposed treaty provisions. The so-called advisable articles would not be taken up and "the necessary [ones] alone retained as the Ground of Discussion" in the hope that a peace accord might be "speedily concluded."

As a further gesture to mollify the anxious American commissioners lest they lean too heavily now on their French sponsors, Shelburne opened a second—and informal—line of communication with them in the person of a close friend of his, an avant-garde intellectual named Benjamin Vaughan, who, like many in his personal circle, admired certain American ideals. Vaughan, son of a Jamaican planter and a mother from Boston gentry, was among the best educated men of his time, having attended Cambridge (though he was denied a degree because he was a Unitarian), read law at the Temple in London, and studied medicine in Edinburgh. But now in his mid-thirties, Vaughan practiced neither law nor medicine, and while a sometime commentator on economic theory, he was mostly a dabbler, something of a plunger in stocks, a hanger-on in Shelburne's coterie (some considered him the earl's foremost spy), and enough of a family intimate to have been among the very few to attend his lordship's second wife on her deathbed. He had also cultivated Franklin in London before the war and, even though the American sage had become an official enemy of the realm, Vaughan published a volume of his collected writings in 1779. Since he was close to Jay's age, Vaughan would nicely complement the elderly Oswald, who had got on so well with Franklin. Not surprisingly, Oswald found the younger man an intruder on his turf and something of a busybody, of the sort that thrived in the salons of Paris.

Vaughan reinforced Shelburne's soothing letter to Oswald by advising Franklin that the ministry was indeed eager to reach a settlement with the United States. But he tried for a final time, at his lord and master's behest, to interest the American commissioners in some form—almost any form—of confederation between Britain and the insurgent colonies. Franklin told him to advise Shelburne, with all due respect, that it was past time to lay that wishful notion to rest. Vaughan would shortly prove a highly useful go-between, especially when Jay turned to him for help after Franklin took ill in late summer.

By then, though, Jay had formed a clear idea of just how things stood between the United States and the two Bourbon kingdoms also warring with Britain. Spanish ambassador Aranda met with Jay the first week of August, and while he was notably more gracious than his superior, the Conde de Floridablanca, had ever been to the American envoy, the two men were soon many leagues apart in their views of the new nation's geography. Aranda produced a map of North America and asked Jay to indicate his government's present position with regard to the western boundary of the United States. Without hesitating Jay traced a finger down the course of the Mississippi. Aranda recoiled, in no doubt feigned shock, contending that none of the lands west of the Appalachians had ever been part of the thirteen colonies, and proceeded to deliver a tendentious history lesson, which he soon committed to paper for the U.S. commissioners to study.

The western lands, Aranda expatiated, had generally been regarded as belonging to France prior to 1763, and after that date British-held Canada was understood to extend south to the Ohio—the Quebec Act eleven years later merely formalized the understanding and enclosed the region for administrative purposes. The Proclamation Act, moreover, served to void the seaboard colonies' charter claims to territory beyond the Appalachian ridgeline. And George Rogers Clark's raids commissioned by Virginia may have delivered some glancing blows but hardly rose to the level of an American conquest of the region. By contrast, Spain's recent victories in West Florida, along the eastern bank of the Mississippi, and in the Illinois Country—early in 1781 Spanish troops had seized Britain's Fort St. Joseph near the present Illinois-Indiana border—gave it at least as legitimate a claim as Congress's to jurisdiction over the western lands, or parts thereof, if Britain could be prevailed upon to relinquish some or all of them. And the Indians, Aranda added, surely had as good a claim as either the United States or Spain to the Mississippi and Ohio river basins. The Spanish government also disputed the Americans' claim that their southern border with Spain's lately reconquered province of West Florida extended along the thirty-first parallel from the southwestern corner of Georgia. Instead, Spain held that the northern border of West Florida was some 140 miles above where the United States said it was, running west along the thirty-third parallel and thus reducing claimed American territory by nearly 50,000 square miles.

Jay, no longer bewildered by the intransigence he had encountered in Madrid over Congress's claimed navigation rights on the Mississippi, asked Aranda to indicate what Spain would find an acceptable western boundary

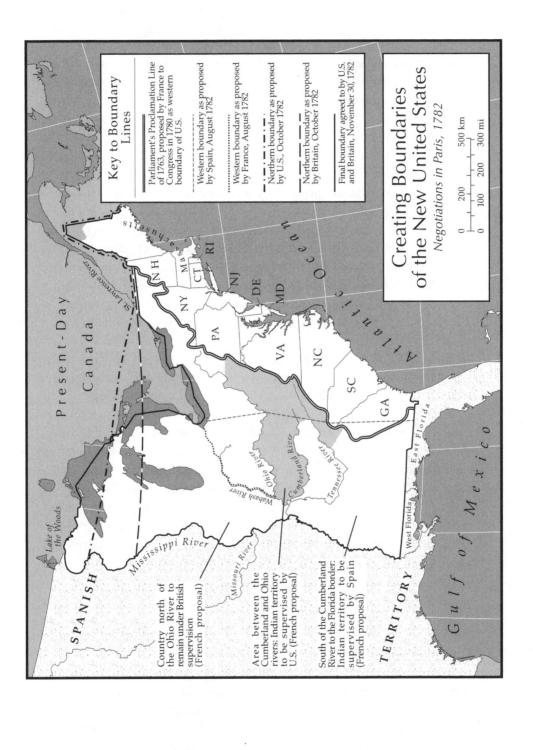

Creating Boundaries of the New United States

Negotiations in Paris, 1782

Key to Boundary Lines

Parliament's Proclamation Line of 1763, proposed by France to Congress in 1780 as western boundary of U.S.

Western boundary as proposed by Spain, August 1782

Western boundary as proposed by France, August 1782

Northern boundary as proposed by U.S., October 1782

Northern boundary as proposed by Britain, October 1782

Final boundary agreed to by U.S. and Britain, November 30, 1782

Present-Day Canada

St. Lawrence River

Lake of the Woods

Atlantic Ocean

NH
Massachusetts
RI
CT
NY
NJ
DE
MD
PA
VA
NC
SC
GA

Mississippi River

Missouri River

Ohio River

Wabash River

Cumberland River

Tennessee River

Country north of the Ohio River to remain under British supervision (French proposal)

Area between the Cumberland and Ohio rivers: Indian territory to be supervised by U.S. (French proposal)

South of the Cumberland River to the Florida border: Indian territory to be supervised by Spain (French proposal)

SPANISH TERRITORY

West Florida

East Florida

Gulf of Mexico

0   200   500 km
0   100   200   300 mi

for the United States. At their next session Aranda unfurled the map and disclosed a proposed red boundary line that began at the western end of Lake Erie and wriggled southward, bisecting the modern states of Ohio and Georgia and terminating in the Gulf of Mexico at Apalachee Bay, near present-day Tallahassee. The line was about midway between the Atlantic and the Mississippi and would have left Americans some 400 miles short of the great heartland river and without direct access to the three upper Great Lakes, Huron, Michigan, and Superior.

Jay was incensed that Spain, which had done next to nothing to assist the American war effort and became active against the British only late in the conflict for its own territorial aggrandizement, was now attempting to confine the United States to a largely landlocked interior. On August 10, he went to Versailles with Franklin to see Vergennes and protest the temerity of France's Bourbon partner. What the American commissioners did not know—and French diplomatic archives later revealed—was that Vergennes and his staff had been working closely with Aranda for several weeks to plot out a compromise boundary line that would suit the three European belligerents and give the United States some additional territory west of the mountains, though very much less than it aspired to. Jay derived no satisfaction that day from the French minister's reaction; quite the opposite.

Vergennes began by dismissing Jay's unrelenting objection to the lately arrived new version of Oswald's commission, which still referred to America as "colonies and plantations" but pledged that acknowledgment of United States independence would be made in the opening article of the treaty, no matter what the remainder of the document contained. France had long endured Britain's arrogance, Vergennes noted, in the form of its affected references in diplomatic documents to its monarch as king of England, Scotland, Wales, Ireland, *and France,* even though several centuries had elapsed since the British monarchy held actual control of any parcel of French soil. Therefore, Monsieur Jay should relax. As to Aranda's notion of a suitable western boundary for America, Vergennes listened to Jay's stressed recital without comment, then sent him off to parley with his first undersecretary and confidential agent, Joseph-Mathias Gérard de Rayneval, while the foreign minister and Franklin chatted less intensely.

Jay got an earful from Rayneval, who essentially parroted Aranda's views on the illegitimacy of America's western land claims. But to soothe Jay's palpable distress over the Bourbons' version of North American history and to appear the sympathetic arbitrator, Rayneval proposed that the western boundary suggested by Spain be moved modestly west and, in refinements that would be spelled out over the next several weeks, proposed that the remaining area of the Old Northwest beyond the American border and above the Ohio River be left to the disposal of the British; the rest of the land between the United States and the Mississippi from the Ohio south to the northern border of Florida would be declared Indian country and split in half, the northern sector under American protection and the southern sector under Spanish oversight.

Jay was left in no doubt that Rayneval's views perfectly reflected the policy position of the foreign minister—and thus the crown—of France. In their eyes, Jay intuited, North America remained an open arena for Old World powers to contend over. The French, he felt, had little interest in what the American Revolution was about, in its anticolonial impulse, in the dignity of its humanitarian ideals, in the national aspirations of the United States, or in its prospects to endure by ensuring that it had enough room to grow and prosper. No, France's only interest in supporting the American uprising had been to strike a blow at its despised enemy, and now that military success had been achieved, it was inclined to let America's zeal cool and now promote the reawakened imperial longings of its Bourbon family partner. This was hardly to say that France was now revealed to Jay as a treacherous double-crosser; the fact was that it had never pledged to do more than help America fight for its independence, and there was no sign it was being unfaithful to that mission. But as the descendant of Huguenots who had been persecuted by their countrymen, Jay now found confirmation for his instinctive distrust of the French. It had been a mistake, born of necessity, to repose full confidence in France's sentimental attachment to the future well-being of the United States. France's motives were neither more nor less altruistic than any other nation's, and so its policy toward the peace settlement, seemingly yoked to Spain's delusions of rejuvenated grandeur, had not been designed to accord with America's.

This assessment Jay now shared with Franklin as they returned to Passy from their fruitless engagement at Versailles. It was not a view the older statesman welcomed. Drawn from Jay's correspondence with intimates and Richard Morris's well-referenced but imaginary account in *The Peacemakers,* the heart of their sharp exchange went more or less like this:

JAY: Our hosts—this court—have put us on notice that we can ignore now only at our peril. We can rely on the French only to see that we are separated from England. But it's not in their interest that we should become a great and formidable people, and so they won't help us to become so.

FRANKLIN: I fear that's an unfair and unkind appraisal. They

are as eager as we to be done with the war and merely asking if we
might modify our ambitions so the British will more readily settle
with the contending powers. For them it is a question of our being
sensible—

JAY: By betraying our sacrifices, by denying our destiny. The
peace they favor would come at our expense.

FRANKLIN: Ungrateful words. We owe them better.

JAY: Gratitude, certainly—without France we would not be at this
point. But if we lean on her love of liberty, her affection for America,
or her outpouring of magnanimity, we'll be leaning on a broken reed
that will sooner or later pierce our hands. Our hands must be freed,
not bound to theirs.

FRANKLIN: If we can't rely on France to help us, whom can we
rely on?

JAY: On God—and ourselves. Monsieur Vergennes wishes to
control the peace process and withhold our independence until his
own and Spain's business with Britain may be resolved.

FRANKLIN: And so you would have us walk away from them—
and from our instructions from Congress?

JAY: I would do nothing at odds with our treaty commitment. But
if Congress's instructions conflict with America's honor and dignity,
I would break them—like this [*at which point, according to Jay
family legend, he removed the long clay pipe he was smoking and
hurled it into Franklin's fireplace*].

The upshot of this pivotal moment was a subtle shift in power and influence between the two leading American negotiators. Jay, respectful of his
senior colleague, did not fault him for undue past deference to Versailles, as
Adams did. Rather, Jay perceived that the hitherto invaluable ally of the
United States, with the fruits of victory to be plucked and parceled, now
posed as great a threat to the happy resolution of the conflict as its enemy.
And he would act accordingly.

That resolve, though, hardly meant Jay was prepared to fly into Britain's
arms in hopes of an embrace that would allow America to shed the French
alliance. Jay advised Oswald that the new version of his commission to
negotiate with the United States still failed to dignify his nation's existence
by properly identifying it. And Franklin remained steely in his resistance to
the Shelburne ministry's undiminished call for reparations for the Loyalists—without acknowledgment of a similar debt to American civilians for
their losses—and bristled because his elaborately rationalized entreaty for

the cession of Canada had been summarily eliminated from the bargaining agenda. There could be "no dependence on peace and good neighborhood," he hammered away at Oswald, so long as Canada stayed in British hands "as it touched [the American] states in so great a stretch of frontier." That amounted to excusing the unruly people of the United States for harboring an uncontainable urge to territorial expansion, which Britain might better accede to than open itself to interminable strife—an unexpectedly crude threat coming from a mellow old philosopher. But neither he nor his countrymen had got where they were by faintheartedness.

While reluctant to submit in the face of Britain's unbending posture, Jay was now emitting telltale signs of incipient Francophobia, or at least frank disenchantment with America's sole ally. When Oswald asked for some kind of assurance that the United States would sever its close bonds with France and not take up with any other foreign power, "Mr. Jay smiled and said they would take care of that," the Scotsman reported to Shelburne. And when pressed further for a promise that America would not stay in the war to help advance any exorbitant demands of the Bourbon kingdoms, Jay reportedly replied, "You have only to cut the knot [of colonial dependency] to get rid of those apprehensions." Oswald told London he was finding Jay to be more open and less stiff-necked than earlier, and more so actually than Franklin of late. This was cheering news at the ministry because Franklin's gout and a severe attack of kidney stones had reduced his vigor and mobility. From late August until well into October, crucial weeks in the peace talks, Jay advanced from adjutant to the commanding American presence in Paris.

THE EARL OF SHELBURNE SPENT the late summer at Bowood Park, his estate in Wiltshire, surrounded by his rare books and manicured gardens and weighing his options with an eye on the political calendar. Parliament was in recess, not due to sit again until November. Shelburne knew that he had to reach an accommodation with the obstinate and demanding Americans before then and present the treaty as a done deed to both houses for their ratification or face the prospect of constant hectoring by honorable members who denied the embarrassing reality that Britain could not quash the rebels and would demand retribution for slights to the majesty of the empire. The luxury of temporizing was over. It would be too costly to leave British troops in place indefinitely until the Americans might come to their senses and accept home rule and confederation on the model of Ireland. And for the ministry to order the forces home and leave the colonies in limbo as a self-declared sovereign state without internationally recognized boundaries would have made for a still larger mess, not put an end to it. No, Shelburne's realistic options for concluding hostilities came down to just two.

Signs were growing that the Franco-American alliance was fraying over the peace terms, now that independence was all but official. The British diplomatic team in Paris—Oswald, Fitzherbert, and Vaughan—were all urging Shelburne to recognize American independence promptly and end its reliance on France. The first minister's priority, though, was not to widen the gulf between discordant allies but to choose the course best for Britain. Why not, then, embrace the French and Spanish position and try to halt centuries of British strife with the two Catholic kingdoms? As a champion of free trade, he might try to sell Parliament on a treaty that would end Britain's isolation in Europe and expand its commerce in the bargain. The United States could be recognized as an Atlantic seaboard nation, hedged in by the Appalachians, and the interior of North America could be divided amicably among the European powers, who collectively would teach restraint to the Americans, who Franklin insisted be given the widest possible latitude to satisfy their frenzied land hunger. France could be readmitted, within clear confines, to the Asian and African trade if it agreed to make no further mischief for Britain, and even Gibraltar might be exchanged for prized Spanish possessions, such as Cuba and the Floridas.

Conversely, Shelburne asked himself, why shouldn't Britain smile upon its spirited offspring and grant the Americans generous terms in Paris? The empire had quite enough worrisome matters on its hands without having to look after the remote North American interior, with ruthless savages all about and oncharging settlers determined to stir them up. Far better—and less burdensome—to encourage the Americans to forge their own fate while the crown stood nearby and battened on the anticipated prosperity of the feisty young republic, with whose people Britain shared blood, language, laws, history, and customs. And then, if the republic should fail, the empire could pick up the pieces.

By late August the decision seemed clearer-cut. Shelburne neither cared for nor trusted the Bourbon monarchies, and their combined might, even with their Austrian relatives added, was not fearsome. France, bitter over its loss of primacy among the Old World powers, was not to be rewarded for wet-nursing the infant American state into being; reactionary Spain, its decay slowed momentarily, was not entitled to have its pretensions saluted. America had grit and big dreams that its rejected parent could not help admiring. Shelburne met with his cabinet on August 29 and agreed to accept Franklin's four "necessary" articles as the basis for a settlement. Under them an accord on all the boundaries still had to be thrashed out, but Shelburne's acceptance implied that the Quebec Act would be voided and the Old Northwest from the Ohio to the Great Lakes would become part of the United States, which would therefore extend to the Mississippi. Surprisingly, the ministry chose not to press its demand for the repayment of prewar debts to British creditors or reparations for the Loyalists—matters that Shelburne hoped could be worked out satisfactorily in a spirit of amicable compromise. On the face of it, Britain had opened the door wide to an expeditious agreement.

The Bourbon partners, likely anticipating the British ministry's disposition to reclaim the favorable opinion of the former colonists, now undertook several steps to discourage any such rapprochement. But they ran into a resolute John Jay, who acted—on his own and knowing that the ailing Franklin thought him rash to have abandoned faith in the French—to stymie them.

When Spanish ambassador Aranda renewed his argument that America had no just claim to the Mississippi as its western boundary and would be wise to settle for less, Jay lost patience with him. Congress had not authorized him to accept less, Jay replied, and at any rate he had no power to yield American sovereignty over the western lands. But the United States had no basis for claiming sovereignty over them, Aranda persisted—they belonged either to the independent Indian nations or to Britain. America had won them by defeating Britain, Jay parried, and the United States inherited colonial charter rights to them. If the issue were in dispute, moreover, the argument was properly between his country and the Indians. When Aranda looked skeptical about what sounded like disparagement of the Indian presence, Jay reminded him that Spain had once asserted similar territorial dominion over Mexico and Peru and that "His Catholic Majesty had . . . no doubt of his right to the sovereignty of those countries." Aranda might have rebutted that Spain had gained that sovereignty by bloodying the Indians of Mexico and Peru whereas the United States was using mere rhetoric to support its claim to the western lands. Jay, at any rate, gave no ground to Aranda, who then appealed to Vergennes to talk sense to the Americans.

The French foreign ministry mobilized to persuade the United States of the weakness of its bargaining position and to discourage Britain from satisfying America's expectations. Diplomatic correspondence and other internal documents reveal Vergennes's reasserted conviction that the American charter claims to the Mississippi boundary were "foolishness not meriting serious refutation" and that at any rate the United States had forfeited such claims when it traded colonial for sovereign status—the Americans could not have it both ways.

What France was seeking to impose on North America was balance-of-power equilibrium on the European model, so that the people of the United States, instinctively aggressive, would be penned up in a seaboard nation, needy of allies (France in particular), and restrained from spreading their revolutionary ideas to lure more and more European labor to emigrate and build an American dominion. Otherwise, how long would it be before the Americans tried to seize the St. Lawrence and its fertile basin, Newfoundland and its fisheries, all the Indians' western hunting grounds, the entire fur trade of the north country, and the mines and whatever other sources of wealth lay buried in the northern reaches of New Spain?

Accordingly, Rayneval presented Jay with an elaborate written plea for the United States to behave as an adult, conceding historical and political realities, and not as a bawling infant demanding instant gratification. If any doubt remained in Jay's mind about French designs to curb American ambition, it fled after he was handed a copy of a letter, intercepted by British agents, from the secretary of the French legation in Philadelphia, François Barbé-Marbois, who strongly urged his home office to contest America's claimed right to work the fisheries off Newfoundland. "Their pretension is not well founded," he wrote, because the privilege had been revoked by Parliament once the war began, because Britain alone held jurisdiction over those waters (and might now be prevailed upon to share them with France as a reward for restraining excessive American treaty demands), and because intensive use of the fisheries by New Englanders, serving as a training ground for sailors, would help transform a militarily feeble United States into a formidable maritime power.

The ultimate revelation for Jay came with the discovery that on September 7 Vergennes had sent off Rayneval incognito—and, of course, without notifying the American commissioners—to meet with Shelburne at Bowood. His chief purpose, Jay surmised, was to convince Britain's first minister that it was in the mutual interest of the Old World powers to cooperate in reining in the boundaries of the United States so they did not extend to the Mississippi, the Gulf of Mexico, and all of the Great Lakes.

Jay was not wrong in his guess, though Vergennes's subordinate was sent also to sound out Shelburne on settlement terms between their two countries and to push for British resilience in meeting Spain's needs. King Carlos, Rayneval confided, had his heart set on recovering Gibraltar and Shelburne's opposite number in Madrid, Floridablanca, was dedicated to making Spain "the complete mistress of the Gulf of Mexico." Shelburne had little interest in gratifying Spanish cravings, but he was attentive to Rayneval's assurance that France did not endorse the "unjust claims" of the United States and that King Louis would do everything in his power "to restrain the Americans within the bounds of justice and reason." At the same time, the French official, signaling that Versailles was not blind to Madrid's pomposity, indicated his foreign ministry did not support Aranda's scheme for introducing a Spanish presence east of the Mississippi in the region brashly claimed by America. According to Rayneval's report on his mission, Shelburne heard him out politely but was noncommittal, beyond agreeing that the American claims to the western lands on the basis of colonial charters were groundless.

To undercut Rayneval's mission to England, Jay enlisted Shelburne's personal representative in Paris, Benjamin Vaughan, to take a message to the prime minister, laying out a compelling case for him to ignore the siren song of the Bourbons. Jay did not ask Franklin to approve of his sending Vaughan to pitch for British magnanimity toward the United States. The reason may be readily inferred from Jay's letter at this time to his former law partner, Robert R. Livingston, newly installed by Congress as its secretary for foreign affairs. In spelling out his differences with Franklin over France's motives, Jay wrote that he believed the French were trying to delay British acknowledgment of American independence "to keep us under their direction . . . until not only their own and our objects are attained, but also until Spain shall be gratified in her demands to exclude everybody [else] from the Gulf." Vergennes had joined Spain to "dispute our extension to the Mississippi," and therefore, Jay felt, the U.S. commissioners ought to proceed with "prudence, circumspection, and if possible secrecy" in dealing with Britain. By contrast, he said, Franklin believed the French "mean nothing in their proceedings but what is friendly, fair and honorable [to us]. Facts and future events must determine which of us is mistaken."

Jay could hardly have had a more faithful conveyor of his message than the intensely pro-American Vaughan. The argument that Jay had crafted for Vaughan to present in his behalf to Shelburne was grounded in hard expediency, with none of Franklin's daring leaps into thin air. Jay's case may be paraphrased thus: O hail to thee, Britannia, mistress of the seven seas and marvel among the powers of the earth! But, alas, you now know you cannot conquer America except perhaps at a ruinous cost; ergo, it is in your best interest to treat with us at the peace table on an equal footing as an independent nation and by so designating us. Please do so, moreover, as soon as possible rather than playing into Bourbon hands by delaying and forcing us to remain a combatant under our treaty with France. And do not be gulled by French intrigue, proposing to you, inter alia, that Canada's border be extended to the Ohio River and thus sowing the seeds for a certain future war. Your empire has no need of, and will derive little foreseeable benefit from, owning endless tracts of wilderness in North America; accumulating distant real estate is not a prudent policy objective for a European commercial power. Imperial Britain's grand strategy is to secure a constant and growing flow of profitable trade, and who will be a more rewarding trading partner for you than your American progeny, provided you treat them kindly at this propitious moment of our arrival among the nations of the world?

Shelburne, already predisposed in this direction, was sufficiently taken with Vaughan's recitation of Jay's line of logic that he had a third version of Oswald's commission drawn up in time for Vaughan to take back to Paris with him. It stated that Oswald was officially authorized to treat with "the Thirteen United States of America"—British acknowledgment of its existence was now down in black and white—and although it was not accompanied by an edict from the king or Parliament countenancing its separation from the realm, that final act of authorization was definitely promised as the first article of the peace treaty. Jay had won his point, as British majesty bowed peevishly before American pride.

Gladdened by Shelburne's sign of good faith, Jay soon displayed a less militant face as he and Oswald now began to address the actual language of the provisional treaty. Jay, with his lawyerly craft, did the drafting for Oswald's consideration. As Shelburne's cabinet had agreed, His Britannic Majesty was to acknowledge unequivocally in the first article that the United States—and each state was named—was free, sovereign, and independent and that the British crown relinquished "all Claims to the Government Property & Territorial Rights of the same and every part thereof." Disposed of with equal ease was the signatories' joint pledge to end hostilities and to exchange prisoners of war. In the next sentence, King George agreed "with all convenient speed, and without causing any Destruction, or carrying away any Negroes or other Property of the American inhabitants," to withdraw all his armies, garrisons, and fleets from the United States "and from every Port, Place and Harbour within the same." Britain's failure to fulfill the last part of this pledge, by refusing to evacuate all crown forts in the west, in particular those fronting on the American side of the Great Lakes, would become a chronic irritant between the two nations for a generation, but at the time the treaty was drafted, total withdrawal seemed a cut-and-dried formality. The hard business at hand was to determine the "Territorial Rights" cited in the first article. How were the boundaries of the United States to be defined?

To brighten the appeal of the highly arguable American contention that by right the new nation should extend to the Mississippi, Jay made an inspired decision. Since British acceptance of that boundary would of course mean that navigation rights on the great inland waterway would be jointly controlled by the United States and Spain, Jay offered Britain coequal rights to use the river from its source to its mouth—and did so barely bothering to consult with his fellow commissioners and not at all with Congress, France, or, for a certainty, Spain. It was an unsolicited, unilateral concession, accompanied by a promise of access to all American rivers, lakes, and harbors, and intended to dramatize to Shelburne the great advantage that British commerce would enjoy by its right to deliver cargoes to and from virtually the entire eastern half of the North American continent via the St. Lawrence and Mississippi basins and the connective channel of the Great Lakes. In making his offer, to be sure, Jay added the request that American ships be granted reciprocal access to British waterways—thus reintroducing the third of Franklin's four "advisable" items on his July wish list, the part that Shelburne's cabinet had summarily ruled out of bounds—but he did not make the offer of Mississippi navigation rights contingent on reciprocity.

Whether eventually reciprocated or not, it was a shrewd stratagem. By exhibiting a willingness to invite the mother country to share in its progeny's destined growth and prosperity, the United States was hoping to soothe the sting of Britain's surrender of its inland empire beyond the Appalachians. If the offer by Jay served to invite Shelburne's cabinet to rethink allowing American vessels the same commercial rights they had enjoyed in the colonial period, so much the better. Best of all, perhaps, the offer was a thumb in Spain's eye. Madrid's New World deputies would have no right to deny vessels under the flag of the world's foremost naval power from plying their trade along the Mississippi—except for the final stretch in the Spanish-held delta area, blocking passage to the Gulf. But if Spain were to deny such access to British and/or American vessels through the river's mouth, British warships might easily shoot their way in and out, and a joint Anglo-American assault on New Orleans and West Florida was likely to ensue. Spain had been unwilling from the first to discuss sharing navigation rights to the river with the United States and continued to dismiss American claims to its eastern bank and all the land adjacent. Jay's move adroitly repaid Spain for its intransigence. Even its Bourbon partner could hardly object to the offer because France, under the 1778 commercial treaty with the United States, would be entitled to the same access to American waterways as Britain. Spain's dream of monopolizing the Mississippi–Gulf of Mexico trade route would become just that.

In drafting treaty terms agreeable to Oswald for forwarding to Shelburne and his cabinet, Jay did not waver in claiming the Mississippi for America's western boundary; otherwise, of course, his offer to share navigation rights to the river with Britain would have been pointless.* Establishing the northern boundary of the United States was a knottier issue.

The eastern end of it seemed easy enough, even though the British had earlier registered unhappiness with the traditional demarcation of the St. John River, which separated Nova Scotia from the Massachusetts-owned province of Maine. Jay's proposed line stuck by the St. John to its source, then went west along the ridgeline forming the southern extent of the St. Lawrence basin separating Quebec from northwestern Maine until it reached the Connecticut River at the forty-fifth parallel. From there the existing boundary headed due west along the parallel separating Quebec province from New Hampshire and New York state until it met the St. Lawrence River about sixty miles above Montreal. But then what?

Quebec's southern border, according to the 1763 Proclamation Act, ran northwesterly from the St. Lawrence in a straight line roughly paralleling the Ottawa River until it reached Lake Nipissing, some 250 miles into modern-day Ontario and about 40 miles above Lake Huron. That left most of the Canadian land mass, largely unknown to white men, outside the borders of Quebec, including the great southern Ontario peninsula, amounting to some 65,000 square miles—about the size of Missouri—of the most arable land in Canada, with full-length frontage on the northern shore of lakes Ontario, Erie, and Huron. Since Franklin's third "necessary" article had insisted that Canada's boundary should not extend south of what it had been as of 1763, the status of that big, fertile area between the southern border of Quebec and

---

*As a further symptom of his well-earned enmity to Spain, Jay shortly told Oswald that the United States would have no objection if Britain ferried some of its idle troops, then garrisoned at Charleston, to the Gulf to recapture Spanish-held Florida. The conquest would enhance Britain's commerce by providing deep-water ports along the Gulf, give its navy a strong base of operation for dominating the sea lanes to and from the West Indies, and allow Loyalist refugees to be compensated for their losses by starting anew with land grants from the crown in regained Florida.

Oswald was fascinated by the notion. To make it more appealing to the ministry, he asked Jay if the Americans would agree to extend the northern border of Florida three degrees north from the thirty-first parallel. That would have taken a large bite out of the proposed U.S. territory extending about 380 miles wide, from the western edge of Georgia to the Mississippi and more than 200 miles north to south. Jay agreed to it as an added inducement to Britain to drive Spain from the Floridas, provided the takeover occurred by the time the peace treaty was signed. The side deal, approved by Jay's fellow commissioners, was made in the form of a separate and very secret article to the main treaty. But since Britain was not in a frame of mind for new military adventures in North America, particularly an invasion of the marshy, buggy Florida peninsula and its Gulf Coast, nothing came of the scheme.

the Great Lakes was up in the air. Britain had never felt the need to draw a hard and fast boundary line separating the rest of Canada—that is, the areas surrounding Quebec—from the thirteen American colonies, although the Great Lakes seemed to provide a natural barrier. But then in 1774 Britain had jumped that barrier by declaring that Quebec province extended all the way south from the St. Lawrence–to–Lake Nipissing line to the Ohio River, a claim hotly opposed by Congress and explicitly ruled out by Franklin's July list of "necessary" British concessions.

Jay solved the dilemma by the simple expedient of designating the so-called Nipissing line (the southwestern boundary of Quebec) as the northern border of the United States in that region, and from Lake Nipissing the American-Canadian border would run west until it reached the source of the Mississippi, wherever that might be. The trouble with Jay's proposal, based on the assumption that the southern border of Canada was coterminous with the southern border of Quebec province, was that there was no foundation for the United States to claim the southwesterly angled prong of Ontario as belonging to America. There were no American settlers there, American soldiers had not set foot on that soil, and even Virginians did not claim that their 1609 colonial charter granted them title to territory north of the Great Lakes. But none of that had stopped Ben Franklin from repeatedly asking Britain to give up *all* of Canada (Quebec included) to the United States, which he said would otherwise forever covet it and cause the crown endless trouble over it. Jay displayed less blatant American avidity for Canadian soil, but the mere 42 million or so acres of it that he now asked for had the greatest agricultural potential of all the territory above the Great Lakes. That Franklin endorsed Jay's proposal for a far more modest bite out of Canada suggests the Old Conjurer had indeed been asking for the whole loaf as a means of ensuring that his countrymen would come away from the bargaining table with a smaller but far more delectable portion of North American real estate—namely, all the land between the Appalachians and the Mississippi, which Britain was by no means obligated, even as the vanquished party in the war, to turn over to the newly independent United States.

Jay, in his role of legal draftsman, added one final item to his provisional version of the treaty—the specific request, omitted in Franklin's fourth "necessary" article, that American fishermen would be able to dry their catch "at the accustomed places" on the Newfoundland and Nova Scotia shores. Vaughan drew up a letter to Shelburne in support of Jay's draft and noted the likely futility of denying American vessels full access to the Canadian fisheries. "We might as well think of making game laws for them," he wrote, and went on to endorse Jay's far more significant call for reciprocal free-trade rights, arguing that if the Navigation Acts were not revised to exempt the United States, it would be forced to turn elsewhere to trade on fair terms. Oswald sealed the treaty draft with his imprimatur, even though it lacked any provision for repayment of prewar debts to British creditors or reparations for the Loyalists, neither of which the cabinet's instructions of August 29 had required him to demand as requisite for an accord.

The treaty draft was sent to London the first week of October, and a few days later Franklin wrote to Livingston to advise Congress of their progress, adding that the commissioners were hopeful that Shelburne and his cabinet would approve, "but I have my doubts." On the same day that Franklin sent his advisory to Philadelphia, another statesman addressed a letter to a diplomatic operative in that same city. Had Franklin seen it, he would have had heightened cause for concern. Updating the Chevalier de La Luzerne, his envoy to Congress, Vergennes confided that the American negotiators were continuing to demand boundaries that he considered to be *"un pareil délire"* (madness), and to make matters worse, he was equally appalled by the Spanish clamor for a presence in the eastern Mississippi Valley. "Both parties," the foreign minister of France asserted, referring to the United States and Spain, "claim countries to which neither of them has a right." But he reserved his choicest scorn for the American negotiators, who, in his view, "do not shine by the soundness of their views. . . . [T]hey have all the presumption of ignorance." They were not ignorant, however, of Vergennes's efforts to foil them.

TEN DAYS BEFORE JAY'S TREATY draft reached London, the city was agog over the thrilling news that British forces at Gibraltar had shattered a combined Spanish-French land-sea assault on the craggy fortress. Intended as the coup de grâce of a three-year siege, the attack had been mounted by some 40,000 soldiers massed above the neck of the sandy peninsula, poised to pour across it and storm the British fortifications after an armada of forty-seven warships had pounded down their great stone ramparts. To enhance its firepower, the besieging fleet was led by ten specially designed and built gunships whose shoreward side was steeply pitched and shielded by a seven-foot-thick layer of green (thus less combustible) timber bolted with iron and covered with cork and raw hides so that enemy shot would bounce off harmlessly and slide into the sea.

The British defenders were well prepared for them. For one thing, they had improved their gunnery to a high degree of accuracy against targets sailing within 1,400 yards of shore; for another, they had moved grates from the heating system in the basement of the fortress close by the batteries so they could turn cannonballs red hot before firing them. When the Spanish and French task force sailed in close to the Rock in daylight, the better to reduce its defenses to rubble, the opening rounds from the defenders' batteries did indeed bounce off the angled sides of the gunboats facing the shore. But then came the red hots, which snagged on the sheathing of hides and quickly set the vessels ablaze. The resulting explosions rocked and tore apart the closely packed fleet. Some 2,000 attackers were lost on September 11—fewer than 100 of the British fell—and the toll would have been far worse if the defenders had not humanely fished many of the French and Spanish sailors out of the flame-mirrored drink. A small but lethal rescue convoy of British ships shortly sailed into the harbor, unmolested by the remnants of the joint Bourbon fleet, and restocked the fortress, which remained as defiant as ever.

Having spectacularly failed to remove the cancer gnawing at its underside, Spain now had to concede it could not win back Gibraltar except by bargaining for it in the course of the Paris peace process. But Britain quickly made clear that it had no intention of surrendering the rocky promontory, which it had just so fiercely defended, at any price—not for Florida, not for any or all of Spain's West Indies possessions, perhaps not even for all the rest of Iberia. The defeat at Gibraltar was hardly less galling for Vergennes. For the second time that year—the first had been de Grasse's intercepted assault on Jamaica the previous spring—French naval forces had been disastrously scuttled while trying to advance Spanish vanity by clashing with the British, and now the French foreign minister was fed up with Madrid's conceits. He wanted the war settled without further military, diplomatic, or financial setbacks for France.

The outcome at Gibraltar served to complicate America's ambitions as well. With news of the splendid victory still dancing in their heads, Shelburne and his cabinet now read Jay's draft for the peace treaty and were unhappy with the presumption of liberality it displayed—and Oswald had approved—toward their upstart ex-colonies. As the Spanish and French had lately learned (once again), no power on earth could push Great Britain around with impunity, and America, even if a blood relative, was no exception. The cabinet's August 29 instructions to Oswald appeared in hindsight to have been drawn up with excessive generosity in order to hasten America's separation from France. And as Shelburne had discovered firsthand from Rayneval's and Vaughan's visits with him, the United States and France were no longer operating in tandem—quite the opposite—so there was far less need, if any, to coddle the Americans. Jay was showing conciliatory tendencies, Franklin had at last backed away from his unseemly lust to possess all of Canada, and France and Spain favored a sharp diminution of the territory to be ceded to the United States. The confluence of all these factors allowed Shelburne to try to maximize his negotiating leverage even if his altered stance amounted to a disavowal of his ministry's earlier leanings. Not for nothing had Shelburne long been reputed to be a bit of a slippery article.

Always scornful of the so-called charter claims of the American states, Shelburne had nevertheless recognized that the new nation would want and need to grow by extending itself westward. Reconciled to losing the wilderness beyond the mountains that could little profit Britain for the time being, Shelburne sent new instructions to Oswald on October 17 that were intended to pressure the U.S. commissioners—if they wanted their precious land so badly—into yielding on the prewar debts to British merchants and the Loyalist reparations, as the honor of the kingdom now demanded. London was bristling with freshly chauvinist sentiment opposed to soft peace terms for the breakaway colonies. Commercial interests were baying in an ever louder chorus for American debtors to pay up. And a pro-Loyalist claque led by Franklin's Tory son, William, now transplanted to England, was arguing fervently to members of Parliament that colonists who had been faithful to the crown and victimized as a result deserved a kinder fate than abandonment.

Shelburne could no longer risk hoping that these issues would eventually be settled once independence was decreed and peace returned. He therefore chose to attack the American commissioners' insistence that Congress had no power to direct the states to extract such repayments from their citizens, who were sure to resist balm for British creditors and alms for despised Loyalists. So long as the Americans clung to that excuse—that its federated structure allowed the United States to dodge its financial responsibilities as a sovereign nation—Shelburne ruled that the boundaries America was asking for were quite unacceptable. Quebec's extension to the Ohio River under Parliament's 1774 act would remain in force, all the land beyond the Appalachians to which title had not already been granted would continue to be regarded as royal territory, and the St. John River could not serve as the northeastern boundary as proposed; it would have to be the Penobscot River, nearly 100 miles farther south, amputating eastern Maine. These vast lands being withheld from the Americans, Oswald was to hint broadly, would be set aside to resettle the Loyalists or to be sold off to pay them reparations. To underscore his aim, Shelburne told his chief negotiator not to relent regarding the boundaries unless the United States agreed to make "a just provision for the Refugees," meaning the displaced Loyalists. It was the principle of the thing; the land was disposable. To the American commissioners, Shelburne had cast himself as the proverbial dog in the manger.

As further evidence of Britain's newly toughened stance, Shelburne's cabinet refused to allow the drying of fish on British territory "on account of the danger of disputes"—perhaps meant to mock Franklin's combative justification for why Canada should be handed over to America. And by the bye, Britain would agree to accept Jay's kind offer of joint navigation rights on the Mississippi, but the American request for reciprocal trading rights would have to be set aside for future consideration. Finally, Congress was to be urged "as strongly as possible" to require the American people to pay their prewar debts to British subjects, and this obligation was not to be evaded by the use of grossly inflated Continental paper currency. Instead, Shelburne insisted that *"honest* Debts may be *honestly* paid in *honest* Money—no Congress Money"* (italics in original), meaning scarce British pound notes or specie had to be used.

Little more than a month remained before Parliament was due to reconvene, and Shelburne knew he needed to step up the pace of the negotiations in order to have a completed treaty ready for ratification by the end of November. Yet he also knew that he had to win substantive concessions from the Americans or be branded as a weak compromiser willing to accept peace terms that humiliated the proud nation. To show Jay and Franklin that he meant business, the first minister assigned a skilled and forceful subcabinet officer, Henry Strachey, undersecretary for the Home Department, to join Oswald, who was perceived in London as hardworking but too gentle and pliable in the Americans' hands. Strachey, who had been part of the diplomatic team that tried to negotiate a home-rule settlement with Congress shortly before the war broke out, was dispatched to Paris with a great bundle of books, maps, charters, and other documents intended to challenge the boundary claims of the U.S. commissioners.

Almost simultaneous with Strachey's appearance in Paris was the arrival of the third American commissioner on the continent—John Adams, fresh from Holland, where he had reached agreement for a commercial treaty similar to the trade alliance with France.* In view of the hardened British negotiating position, the American team should have welcomed the vigorous New England lawyer/patriot with open arms. But Adams was late in

---

*Jefferson remained grief-stricken in Virginia, while Laurens was still held captive in London.

coming to the party and, for all his success in Amsterdam, remained offensive to the French court and had made it no secret that he thought Franklin an old rascal, despite France's infatuation with him. Vergennes, though, was not a participant in the bargaining now, and Franklin had been forced by illness to yield the leading American role in the peace talks to Jay. Never wanting in self-confidence, Adams confided in his diary shortly after arriving, "I shall have a delicate, nice, critical part to act." He would play his part, but delicacy was not in John Adams's nature.

Up for the challenge, he took a bracing swim in the Seine and, while in no hurry to pay his respects to Vergennes (who learned of his arrival from the police) or the recuperating Franklin, Adams hastened to be briefed by Jay on where the peace talks stood. To his delight, he saw eye to eye with Jay on all issues, including the latter's assessment of the French as an immoral people and a faithless ally favoring Spain over the interests of the United States. The pair of them, bright as they were, failed to grasp what Franklin well understood—that France could work its wiles simultaneously in behalf of both America, the enemy of its historic enemy, and Spain, its Bourbon kin, that these dual purposes were not mutually exclusive, and that Vergennes was not double-crossing the United States but trying to perform a tricky balancing act in urging both his allies, even if not allied to each other, to rein in their ambitions. Adams recorded his keen approval of Jay's independence toward France and of "the principles, wisdom, and firmness with which Mr. Jay has conducted the negotiations in [Franklin's] sickness and my absence," adding he was determined to support Jay "to the utmost of my power." Jay, though, soon learned that in the admiring Adams, he had a loose cannon at his side.

A few nights after Adams and Strachey arrived in Paris, they dined at Jay's lodgings along with Oswald, and the four informally explored their differences. Among the topics were the American prewar debts to British creditors, which Franklin, though still infirm at Passy, had steadfastly opposed honoring on the ground that British armies had looted the shelves and warehouses of many an American merchant once the war began. To Adams, that was an argument better suited to repulsing British demands for reparations to Loyalists for damages suffered once the war was under way. Debts due from prior transactions were contractual obligations that lawyers, of all men, held sacred. Adams, without having consulted Jay, declared that neither he nor his countrymen were out to cheat anyone and that so far as he was concerned, the prewar debts ought to be paid. The startled British negotiators failed to hide their satisfaction with this sudden fissure in the solidarity of the American position.

That same evening Adams went to see Franklin at Passy. He disclosed but did not apologize for his spontaneously emitted opinion on the prewar debts and indicated bluntly, as he was wont, his total admiration for Jay's handling of the negotiations in their absence. The weakened but still very wise old fox was left in no doubt of his reduced position. Should the two lawyers, in their vigorous prime, conclude between them that, for all his incomparable service to America, Franklin was unduly deferential to France, implacably vindictive toward Britain, and at times less than fully lucid, they would speak for their country in the climactic hours of the peace talks.

HAVING UNEXPECTEDLY BREACHED the Americans' resistance when Adams displayed his moral fiber on the issue of prewar debts, Henry Strachey supposed he would soon put his adversaries to rout. He came loaded for bear to his first formal negotiating session at Jay's quarters, as his clerk carefully spread out the maps and documents the diplomat had brought along as evidence to shred the U.S. commissioners' territorial claims.

Strachey began by lecturing them on the history that he said belied their pretensions, very much as Aranda and Rayneval had. Then he went on to deny the relevance of colonial charter rights once the American states had rebelled, to call for the Illinois Country to be set aside for the resettlement and repayment of the Loyalists, and to endorse a western boundary of the sort that Spain and France had suggested. About half of the modern state of Ohio would be designated American territory and most of the rest of the area from the Appalachians to the Mississippi would become an Indian preserve jointly supervised by Britain, Spain, and the United States.

So much for British generosity, now that push was coming to shove. If Strachey's intention, under Shelburne's orders, was to soften up the Americans on the Loyalist issue by threats to demolish their dreams for an ample nation with room to grow, he was guilty of overkill. But if the Shelburne cabinet was serious about drastically compromising American claims to the western lands, then the irresistible force was about to collide with the unmovable object. In the high-stakes contest, the British were putting into play the one piece on the chessboard they knew mattered more to the Americans than all the rest except independence itself. But would Britain really risk the collapse of the peace talks by withholding the western lands unless the Americans agreed to wholesale extortion by paying off the Loyalists? If so, why had Strachey said nothing derogatory about the offer in Jay's treaty draft to share the navigation rights on the Mississippi? Britain, after all, already held those rights, so there would be no point in entertaining Jay's offer unless it was willing to cede the eastern Mississippi basin to the United States. Was Strachey's omission intentional or an oversight?

The commissioners chose not to try outguessing or outgambiting their powerful adversary; America's whole future teetered on a precipice. "If that line [leaving the United States border 400 miles shy of the Mississippi] is insisted upon," Jay replied forthrightly, "it is pointless to talk of peace. We will never yield on that point." Franklin, out of bed and back in the fray, wrote to Livingston, lamenting this sudden disagreeableness of the Shelburne ministry: "A little turn of fortune in their favor [the Gibraltar victory] sometimes turns their heads. I shall not think a speedy peace to be depended upon."

In view of the perilous turn in the peace talks, Franklin saw the necessity of casting aside any reservations he had about the soundness of his fellow commissioners—it was no time to put petty pride before country. In doing so, he hoped to erase any misapprehension Strachey may have been nursing about exploitable discord among the Americans, especially over how reliant on France they should remain in the face of British intransigence at the bargaining table. At their next confrontational session, after Jay had disputed one of Strachey's points, Franklin turned to his younger countryman and declared deferentially, "I am of your opinion—and will go on with these gentlemen in the business without consulting this [the French] court." Over the preceding weeks Jay had calculatedly risked challenging—and at times ignoring—the judgment of his eminent senior colleague in order to advance the American position as he saw fit. It was a lonely gamble against the divergent purposes of Europe's most artful power brokers, and at least in one sense he had prevailed. Franklin, Adams, and Jay, three of the smartest and ablest men ever to serve the people of the United States, acted in complete accord from that point forth.

While solidly behind Jay's unequivocal rejoinder to Strachey that the western boundary he had put forward, if a British ultimatum, would send the United States back to the battlefield, the American commissioners now made a good-faith concession by proposing a new northern border. It was hardly a major sacrifice, though. Instead of adopting the so-called Nipissing line that formed the southwestern boundary of Quebec province—thereby expropriating the temperate southern sector of modern Ontario from Canada and denying it access to three of the Great Lakes—the American team suggested a more southerly boundary. It bisected all of the lakes but Michigan and, when it touched the western shore of Lake Superior, angled northwesterly some 220 miles through a chain of interlocking lakes until it reached the northwest corner of Lake of the Woods a little below the forty-ninth parallel; then it was to run due west a short way until it reached the Mississippi near its presumed source.* The change, greatly simplifying the border by conforming it with the natural landscape, meant a loss to America of the 65,000 fertile square miles it had asked for—without justification—north of the lakes. But the 35,000 square miles it would acquire in the bargain, consisting largely of the northeastern prong of Minnesota, included the unknown Mesabi Range, one of the world's richest veins of iron ore and a resource of great future value to the nation.

In addition, the Americans gave a little ground on three other contentious issues in an effort to appear conciliatory. On the fisheries, Franklin first tried to shame their adversaries for even contesting the American request to continue farming the Newfoundland Banks. "Are you afraid there is not fish enough," he asked, "or that we should catch too many?" They ought not to object to such activity, he added, because "you know that we shall bring the greatest part of the money we get for the fish to Great Britain to pay for your manufactures." Still, the commissioners agreed to accept Britain's face-saving insistence that New England vessels could not dry their catch on the Newfoundland shore, but the American team would not rule out Nova Scotia, though less convenient Canadian territory for that purpose. On the prewar debts, Franklin and Jay went along with Adams's earlier impromptu concession and agreed that creditors of both nations "shall meet with no lawful Impediments to the Recovery of the full Value in Sterling Money of all bona fide Debts heretofore contracted." And on the Loyalist reparations the commissioners agreed to move the proposed Maine–Nova Scotia boundary west from the St. John River to the St. Croix River, a surrender of about forty miles of coastline and some 1,500 square miles, to be allocated, if Britain chose, to the Tory refugees. But there was no offer of direct compensation for their wartime losses. It was little more than a crumb but better than nothing.

In a week of heated discussions, Strachey had done well to budge the Americans on a number of points, particularly the prewar debts. Oswald would write of his colleague's performance, "He has enforced our pretensions by every argument that reason, justice, or humanity could suggest." But the Loyalist issue seemed unsolvable, even as the well-orchestrated outcry in London for amnesty and indemnity for the American Tories

---

*In fact, the source of the Mississippi is Lake Itasca in Minnesota, about 150 miles southeast of Lake of the Woods, but nobody knew that at the time. Thus, the boundary fixed by the treaty ended in limbo and was not corrected until well into the next century.

grew more vocal. The U.S. commissioners held their ground, though, and Franklin stood forth to press their argument.

It came down to two points: (1) Britain's intransigence would only force the United States to calculate the total value of the British troops' plunder and destruction throughout the war and demand reparations. Even though Franklin had raised the issue early in his first informal meeting with Oswald in April, the American negotiators had plainly erred by not pressing the matter more forcefully in the mistaken belief that the suffering of the patriots and Loyalists alike would be accepted by both sides as having canceled each other as negotiable issues. (2) The British ministry was attempting to wring blood from a turnip by insisting that Congress impose reparations on the federal union. Said Franklin: "We should be sorry if the absolute impossibility [of] our complying further with your proposition should induce Great Britain to continue the war for the sake of those who caused and prolonged it." He was trying his best to make the British understand that the Revolution had been as much a bitter fratricidal war, pitting family members (as in Franklin's own case), friends, and neighbors against one another, as a desperate struggle for independence from the crown.

Strachey left Paris on November 4 to report back to Shelburne, and for the three weeks he remained away, there was no sign of convergence from either camp. By disengaging until just before Parliament was due back in session, Shelburne was hopeful the Americans would blink, as they had on the prewar debts, rather than risk losing their last best chance for noble nationhood. But it was a misguided wish. Adams's November 11 letter to Livingston conveyed the resolve of the American triumvirate: "[T]here is every argument of national honor, dignity of the state, public and private Justice and Humanity, for us to insist upon a Compensation for all the Plate [silver and other booty], Negroes, Rice, Tobacco stole[n] and House[s] and Substance consumed, as there is for them to demand Compensation to the Tories, and this was so much the stronger in our favor as our Sufferers were innocent people, and theirs guilty ones." Adams wrote Livingston again a week later to allay any concern among the notables in Philadelphia, anxiously awaiting news on the peace talks, that their commissioners might have turned headstrong. With his usual bluff counsel Adams urged Congress to place its utmost confidence in the peacemakers' best judgment or "I really think it would be better to constitute the Count de Vergennes our sole minister, and give him full powers to make peace . . . than to continue any of us in the service under the instructions in being." John Jay was equally adamant on the reparations, telling Oswald during Strachey's absence that the United States would fight on for fifty years rather than satisfy "such cutthroats," meaning the Loyalists. Franklin was heard saying privately he would rather walk away from the peace table than give in to the Loyalists and urged Oswald to advise London that it would surely be cheaper for the British themselves to compensate their devoted Loyalists than to bear the expense of renewed warfare in America.

Vergennes was far from idle during this final interlude. While not precisely clueless on the course of the negotiations, the French foreign minister had been effectively held at arm's length by both sides and, unaware of the narrowing gap between them, fully expected to be called upon in the end to arbitrate their irreconcilable differences. He wrote La Luzerne in Philadelphia to stress anew to Congress that France would not fight on "to sustain the[ir] pretentious ambitions" and sent Rayneval back to Shelburne to reregister France's lack of sympathy with what he took for America's excessive demands. Having given as much ground as he thought he could without losing his ministry to an onslaught of his critics in Parliament, Shelburne tried to brace Oswald by writing him, "This country is not to be reduced to terms of humiliation, and certainly will not suffer them from America." The message was intended, of course, more for Franklin than Oswald. To give Strachey a bit more bargaining time on his return to Paris, the new session of Parliament was held off for an additional week, by which time the first minister expected the fate of the parley to be sealed, either for peace or for more war. "If the American commissioners think they will gain by the whole coming before Parliament," he added in his letter to Oswald, "I do not imagine that the refugees [displaced Loyalists] will have any objections." The only encouraging news coming out of London was that the American concession on repayment of prewar debts had served to divert the influential mercantile community from making common cause with the Loyalists and their fulminating backers who had won wide sympathy in Parliament.

Returning to Paris, Strachey told the American team that Shelburne's cabinet had accepted their proposed new northern boundary line running through the middle of the Great Lakes, but the ministry was unanimous in insisting on the restitution of all rights, estates, and property confiscated from the Loyalists. Jay asked him directly if this was an ultimatum. Strachey said no, but that if the issue were left unresolved another week until Parliament reconvened, every member would be howling for compensation and Shelburne's ministry left hanging on the outcome. To break their deadlock, the kindly Oswald asked the Americans whether Congress, even if powerless to make a grant of restitution, could not be directed by its commissioners to make an earnest recommendation to the states to act in relief of the Loyalists. Strachey was not satisfied by so vague a nostrum, and the Americans thought it pointless.

While a Loyalist solution continued to elude them, the two sides closed the gap that had remained on the fisheries question. Although the British had conceded on the main point, they had held out on some minor ones, forbidding the Americans to fish within three miles of shore and to dry their catch wherever they wished in Nova Scotia. They were to be given "the liberty" but not "the right" to troll the Canadian waters. This last nuance aroused New Englander Adams, who with righteous indignation observed that God Almighty had made the Grand Banks of Newfoundland as accessible to American as to British or French fishermen, so that "[i]f Heaven in the creation gave a right, it is ours at least as much as yours. If war and blood and treasure have a right [referring to the American colonists' participation in the French and Indian War], ours is as good as yours." His rhetorical flourish helped goad the two sides into splitting their differences. The Americans were permitted to fish the coast without restriction and to dry their catch on any unsettled stretch of the Nova Scotia coast they might lease for that purpose.

But the emotional wrangling over the Loyalists would not abate, and without agreement on that issue, the whole enterprise threatened to come to grief. To bring the British negotiators to their senses regarding the extent of the enmity in America toward the Loyalists, Franklin pointed out that even if His Majesty's forces had prevailed and put down the rebellion, it would have been no easier—in fact, it would have been all but impossible as a practical matter—for the victors and their appointed officials to extract reparations for the Loyalists. "And you will please recollect," he added, "that you have not conquered us."

It was Franklin whose indomitable convictions and commanding gravitas caused his antagonists to give way in the end. And this was fitting, for it was Franklin, the folk philosopher-king of a rambunctious people, who had long and prophetically called upon the crown to promote a great English-speaking dominion in the New World and not treat America as a mere colonial appendage fit only for harvesting—and the king, his ministers, and Parliament had spurned him. So America had been lost beyond their redeeming, and now Franklin, his prodigious memory less acute than it once was, drew from his pocket a paper containing a long list that he recited of the manner and instances of the devastation that the British forces had visited upon the Americans while vainly trying to suppress their demand for independence. The redcoats had torched Boston, Philadelphia, Charleston, and many other smaller communities. They had stolen food, supplies, and valuables by endless wagonloads and thousands of slaves. They had trampled crops, burned barns, torn up tobacco plantations, and destroyed their curing sheds. They had incited their client Indian nations to scalp women and children. Peace commissioner Henry Laurens of South Carolina, at last released from his harsh captivity in London (in exchange for vanquished British general Lord Cornwallis) and on hand for the culminating negotiations in Paris, added his firsthand knowledge of how Cornwallis's men had run rampant through the South in the last stages of the conflict. And Adams related how, at the outset of it, General Thomas Gage, upon seizing Boston, had promised residents seeking to flee the city with their possessions that they could do so if they first surrendered their arms—and after they had, Gage reneged, took their belongings, and had them carted off as the spoils of war.

Such recitations could not leave the British team unmoved. Plainly the misery and ruin of war had afflicted Americans of all political shades, and the anguish of victimized patriots and Loyalists alike could never be tidily quantified or compensated. War by definition was neither kind nor fair. Still, it was Britain that was being asked now to cede America sovereignty over an immense land, far larger than the threadbare Continental Army had won in battle, and it was British majesty that had to be sufficiently stroked for the kingdom to yield with dignity. It would not be shamed into submission, as Shelburne vowed. The moment was ripe for Oswald to renew his earlier suggestion, and both sides seized on it. The article they agreed upon read in part:

> It is agreed that the Congress shall earnestly recommend it to the Legislature of the respective States to provide for the Restitution of all Estates, Rights and Properties which have been confiscated belonging to real British Subjects; and also of the Estates, Rights and Properties of Persons . . . who have not borne Arms against the said United States. And that Persons of any other Description shall have the Liberty to go to any other Part or Parts of any of the thirteen United States and therein to remain twelve Months unmolested in their Endeavours to obtain the Restitution of such of their Rights Estates & Properties as may have been confiscated.

No further confiscations or prosecutions were to be directed against the Loyalists, any of them imprisoned were to be released, and Congress would further urge the states to reconsider any confiscatory laws still on their books so that they might be revised and made "perfectly consistent, not only with Justice and Equity, but with the Spirit of Conciliation which, on the Return of the Blessings of Peace should universally prevail."

The language was advisory and wishful, without binding force, but it conveyed a clear moral obligation on the victors' part to behave with charity, which was more than the Americans had been willing to concede before. The commissioners could well endure gagging on a little humble pie in view of the abundant fare the British were letting them take away from the peace table. Since none of the text had yet been shared with the French and it was still to be ratified by both Parliament and Congress, the negotiators designated their handiwork a "preliminary treaty," which, under the existing pact between the United States and France, would not be final until the French and British had also reached a peace agreement.

With their work on the verge of completion, the third member of the British team, Alleyne Fitzherbert of the ministry's foreign department, contracted a sudden case of cold feet. Wouldn't it be prudent, he asked, to dispatch the text of the treaty to London posthaste for the cabinet's approval? With less than a week remaining before Parliament was due to sit, Franklin was too wise in the ways of British politics not to see the pitfalls of such a course. The cabinet was sure to quibble over fine points and perhaps try to coerce further concessions, with the clock ticking ominously over all their shoulders. The American commission, moreover, had made its last concession. Franklin told their British counterparts that unless they were willing to sign the treaty the next day, his side would have to propose new language dealing with the repayment of prewar debts—the concession that Strachey was proudest of having extracted. The British team withdrew for a few minutes of private deliberation, then reappeared and agreed to reconvene the next day at Oswald's lodgings at the Grand Hotel Muscovite on rue des Petits Augustins to sign the agreement. By it, the Old World would christen the burly, restless infant arising from the cradle of the New World.

In his quarters that evening Henry Strachey recorded his private sentiments of the day's events. He would not care to wager, he wrote, whether his countrymen would applaud him or hang him and his colleagues for rescuing them from the interminable American war, but he tried to console himself, as he would his superiors: "If this was not as good a peace as was expected, I am confident that this is the best that could have been made." That he thought so was no small tribute to the stiff-necked posture of his adversaries, their senior member most of all. Even his querulous colleague, John Adams, wrote in his diary, "Dr. Franklin has behaved well and nobly, particularly this day." In a lifetime of wondrous achievements, this was Benjamin Franklin's truly monumental triumph, though rarely so credited by historians. It was Franklin's patient cultivation of the French court and foreign ministry that gained the United States the military resources to sustain the war and the critical diplomatic leverage to win a generous peace settlement. The grand prize was stunningly beyond anything rationally related to the outcome on the battlefield—a nation of nearly 900,000 square miles of the most fertile, well-watered, and scenic land on earth. It was four times the size of France.

For the ceremonial November 30 signing of the preliminary treaty, Franklin was said to have put on the same suit of figured Manchester velvet—authorities differ as to whether it was brown or blue—that he had worn in London nearly eight years earlier when hauled before a tribunal of Parliament for exposing the private correspondence of Loyalist Thomas Hutchinson, governor of Massachusetts, and thereby traitorously fueling rebellion. The harsh upbraiding cost Franklin his sinecure as postmaster for the American colonies. It cost Britain the American colonies.

FRANCE DID NOT ENTIRELY rejoice over the Americans' triumph, though it was a substantial French victory as well if measured by Vergennes's primary goal, a severe reduction of Britain's New World empire. But Vergennes chose to sulk, not only because his counsel to the Americans to compromise their demands had been defied but also because he now saw that the commissioners had outfoxed him by seizing on the Bourbon opposition to their outsized ambitions as a potent wand to beguile the British into granting them. "You will notice that the English buy the peace more than they make it," he wrote Rayneval in London, enclosing a copy of the treaty that Franklin had delivered to him after the fact. "Their concessions, in fact, exceed all that I should have thought possible." Vergennes shortly registered his sour mood by writing to Franklin and conceding that the Americans had done very well for themselves but had badly slighted their host nation in the process:

> You have achieved your preliminary articles without informing us, although the instructions from Congress stipulated that you do nothing without the participation of the King [of France]. . . . You are wise and discreet, Sir; you understand the proprieties; you have fulfilled your duties all your life. Do you think that you are satisfying those that connect you to the King? I do not wish to carry these reflections further; I commend them to your integrity.

As a slur on the old man's honor, it was both unkind and uncalled for, and reeked of hypocrisy. For one thing, Vergennes was entirely aware of the Americans' ambitions and had done his best to deride them as unjustifiable and an impediment to peace. Did he believe that men of the American peacemakers' intelligence and character would slavishly heed their instructions from a Congress that had issued them under extreme duress largely to placate their French patrons? Vergennes's complaint bore the hallmark of a monarchist bureaucrat without tolerance for civil disobedience as an honorable response to wanton authority. At any rate, it was Congress's place—not the French government's—to be offended if its negotiators in Paris had not strictly followed instructions. Besides, Vergennes had explicitly told Franklin that the Americans were free to negotiate their own treaty so long as it went hand in hand with France's settlement with Britain and was signed on the same day.

When Robert Livingston, foreign secretary for Congress, later groused that the peace commissioners had perhaps unjustly given France cause to complain by acting distrustfully toward their ally, his close friend John Jay set him straight. Vergennes's "plan for a treaty for America was far from being such as America would have preferred," Jay replied, "and as we disapproved of his model, we thought it imprudent to give him the opportunity for moulding our treaty by it." By discouraging the claims of the United States while advancing Spain's in preference, France "ceased to be entitled to the degree of confidence that Congress had prescribed." John Adams put it more bluntly to Livingston when the latter wondered why the commissioners had not reposed full confidence in the French to press the British in behalf of America's claims: "I have no such confidence, and never had. Seeing and hearing what I have seen and heard, I must have been an idiot to entertain such confidence."

Franklin had one more bit of wizardry to perform on Vergennes. Answering the foreign minister's rebuke, he chose not to confront him with countercharges of deviousness, which Vergennes richly deserved for the secret treaty he had made with Spain and all his efforts to undermine the American bargaining position with Britain. Instead, Franklin pointed out that there was nothing in the preliminary treaty with Britain "contrary to the interests of France" but promptly conceded his impropriety in not sharing the text with Vergennes. Tact, no doubt, prevented him from observing that it would have been a still graver breach of their friendship if he had shown the text to the foreign minister and then signed it in disregard of any or all of the minister's objections, as the Americans surely would have. Then, with the politesse that Adams mistook for abject bootlicking, Franklin assured Vergennes that his diplomatic faux pas did not stem from disrespect for King Louis. "No Prince was ever more belov'd and respected by his own people," Franklin wrote, laying it on thick, "than the King is by the People of the United States." In asking forgiveness, he hoped the achievement of the treaty, "so glorious to his reign, will not be ruined by a single indiscretion of ours."

Opportunistic to the end and nothing daunted, Franklin played his last card. "The English, I just now learn, flatter themselves they have already divided us [France and America]," he told Vergennes. "I hope this little Misunderstanding will therefore be kept a perfect secret and that they will find themselves totally mistaken." Then he asked France to lend the United States a final 6 million livres so it would not be utterly bereft of funds to tide it over while peace and normal commerce were being restored. Had he refused the nervy appeal, Vergennes feared the Americans might now side against France in its imminent peace talks with Britain. And, having championed the cause of the United States as no other European diplomat had, he could ill afford to turn away at its moment of crowning glory, as if his vengeful anti-British policy had been a mistake. The king agreed to the final loan.

France paid a steep price for its American alliance. At the peace table, Britain dished its ancient rival thin gruel—the restoration of limited trading rights on the coasts of Africa and India, license to fish the Newfoundland waters, permission to refortify its own Channel port of Dunkirk, and an exchange of some Caribbean islands. But the cost of the war, as Turgot had predicted, would prove financially ruinous to France. The kingdom's treasury slid heavily into debt, social reform was forgotten—none of the democratic precepts animating the American Revolution would penetrate the absolutist mindset of the *ancien régime*—and before the decade was out, the royal fleur-de-lis, emblematic of hereditary autocracy, would be trampled under and the tricolor of liberty and equality run up in bloody retribution.

Spain, without pretense of sympathy for America's aspirations and downright hostile toward its egalitarian ideals, did better than its Bourbon partner. King Carlos was allowed to keep his reconquests of Florida and Minorca, gained largely because Britain was preoccupied elsewhere. For the moment, then, Spain alone owned the Gulf Coast. But it had failed to prevent the seizure of the entire eastern Mississippi basin by the upstart Americans who had sought Spain's friendship and been rudely denied it. Spanish fears, far from groundless, of the expansionist tendencies of the buoyant new republic turned the strapping young neighbor, now formally hunkered just across the mighty Mississippi, into an enemy whose freewheeling ways would help doom Spain's empire in little more than a generation.

How did the neophyte Americans, whose margin of victory on the battlefield had been so narrow and heavily dependent on foreign assistance, emerge from the peacemaking process as the only big winner? In large part, surely, because of the skill of their negotiators, three extraordinarily gifted men, but especially Franklin, whose modest bearing masked the boldness of his moves. In fairness, Jay's blend of rectitude, wariness, and daring made him scarcely less valuable in the showdown clinches. The American peace-makers acted with consistency and resolve from the first, and in the end their mutual regard and unanimity of purpose made them unshakable on the issues that mattered most. Each was prepared to abandon the bargaining table if their hard-won new nation was not dealt with generously. What they emerged with was far more than equitable, because they understood the lim-itations and vulnerabilities of the European belligerents, whose supply lines were overextended, whose resources were becoming depleted, whose peo-ple were weary of imperial wars, and whose rulers were powerless finally to prevent the American phenomenon, consecrated in that apotheosis of insub-ordination called liberty, from blooming in the distant wilderness.

There was one other indispensable factor at work in favor of the United States—the Earl of Shelburne. Given the pigheaded vanities of the king and the political dissension in an age shy of statesmen, the British government was almost miraculously placed under the reins—and for just long enough—of an impolitic leader who understood the incongruities of his times. Some other, perhaps any other, prime minister might well have fought on, at George III's urging, or marched away petulantly and left the rebellious colonies in turmoil, hoping to pick up the pieces of empire if and when they tumbled into disarray. Shelburne, an odd blend of aristo-cratic sophisticate and dreamer of a better, fairer world, was also a practical man and an admirer (thanks in part to Franklin's tutelage) of American dynamism—so much so that he hated parting with it. Yet he fully fathomed the self-destructive nature of a diehard repression of the colonists' insur-gency and that the empire stood to gain far more by letting the Americans spread their wings and then, as their principal creditor, supplier, and—to the extent any sentiment remained on either side—benevolent progenitor, cash-ing in on their destined success.

In Parliament to defend the terms of the Treaty of Paris that his enemies had stridently denounced as humiliating to the kingdom, Shelburne coolly noted that the national debt was nearing £200 million, the army was badly undermanned, the navy was in poor repair, and all military supplies were short. Indeed, the American forces might easily have captured some or all of the Canadian provinces if they had had the will. The cost to the empire, moreover, of hanging on to the remote and economically unproductive western backlands, like that of trying to prevent New Englanders from fishing the waters off Newfoundland, would have been prohibitive and enlarged Britain only in spitefulness.

His listeners, though, were not really interested in such unexceptionable logic: they all knew America was a lost cause but could not resist slaying the messenger. It did not help that Shelburne's persistent calls for social and political reform—for a more democratic Parliament, for a civil service cleansed of corrupt practices, for abandonment of the monopolistic Navigation Acts in favor of free trade—alarmed the entrenched powers. For all the worthiness of his ideas and the courage he brought to his convictions, Shelburne had few friends among the leading men of the realm, and his character was found wanting. Horace Walpole wrote of him: "With unbounded ambition of governing mankind, he had never studied them." But Walpole was often waspishly unkind to those whose views he opposed. Shelburne was a poor politician not because he could not read others but because of the charmless transparency of his motives. He failed not out of excessive ambition but because he preferred being right to holding power for its own sake. Parliament narrowly, grudgingly approved his peace treaty in February 1783, then censured him and consigned him to history's graveyard of the unjustly forgotten.

For his troubles, the crown elevated William Petty Fitzmaurice from Earl of Shelburne to Marquis of Lansdowne. His foresight was soon confirmed. By 1790, its economy well revived, the United States was acquiring 90 percent of its imports from the mother country and was sending back half of its exports. One day in 1784 after he had been retired as first minister, Shelburne was paid a courtesy call by John Jay on his way home to America. The British lord, who could not help admiring the American attorney's conduct during the peace negotiations, asked his visitor whether he thought the United States would have resumed the war if Britain had not given up the western lands. "I believe so," said Jay, "and I certainly should have advised it."

Benjamin Franklin, on returning home to a hero's welcome in 1785 after his nine-year mission as ambassador to France, was pleased to learn that the value of his real estate holdings had risen threefold in his absence—especially satisfying news for a man who had met with no success as a wheeler-dealer trying to promote several gigantic land settlement schemes. Land was the great commodity and treasure of the new nation whose acreage he had done so much to extend. In addressing his neglected personal affairs, Franklin reviewed his last will and testament and, in the process, chose as one of the executors of his estate the younger colleague whom he might have resented for sharply disagreeing with him over French motives during the peace deliberations in Paris—John Jay. Nine days before his death at the age of eighty-four on April 17, 1790, Franklin wrote his last letter, addressed to Secretary of State Thomas Jefferson, who had visited him shortly before. In it he discussed in detail how he, his fellow commissioners, and their British counterparts had pored over a map in Paris in late autumn of 1782, trying to determine a boundary line between Maine and Nova Scotia. Those fateful proceedings remained in his mind until it thought no more.

CHAPTER 5

Owning the wilderness

1783–1800

THE MAGNITUDE OF THE AMERICAN people's diplomatic triumph in Paris, nearly as stunning as their military victory over
Great Britain, entitled them to a season of celebration. With independence at hand, their long years of sacrifice in a common cause were
rewarded by the heady satisfaction that comes from prevailing over desperate odds. But their exhilaration was fleeting, for peace had brought with it a
plague of jarring realities. The principal force binding them together in
opposition had been dissolved with the departure of the British troops, and
the din of protest that had been their defining anthem was stilled by success.
Americans were left with no commanding central authority to replace the
crown they had knocked awry with such relish. If their new nation was to
fulfill the hopes and justify the agony of its birth, they needed to learn—and
quickly—how to overcome the heated quarrels, discordant interests, and
fractious phobias that had nearly doomed their valiant uprising.

Without history to guide them, though, or the luxury of leisurely trial
and error, how were they to transform their barely clinging union into a
secure, stable, self-sufficient society? All the advantages of their superb natural setting would mean little if their centrifugal impulses could not be
tamed. Individualism and resourcefulness, to be sure, had served as wonder-
working hallmarks of frontier America, but unbridled liberty was a cousin
to easy virtue. Without a true sense of community, embodied by an enlightened, vigilant national government, the United States could not advance
from a colonial wilderness to a just, prosperous, and well-ordered civil society. Yet to empower their wobbly federation to issue and enforce directive
policies by rule of the legislative majority was also to risk curtailment of
their precious personal freedoms and throttling back on their unique dyna-

mism. Compounding this dilemma was their experience as British subjects, which left them distrustful of public officeholders who too often abused their powers and governed inequitably.

Fearing above all an oppressive central authority, Americans opted in the beginning for a dysfunctional one. As a wartime expedient, their Articles of Confederation had set up a phantom government deemed to be better than none at all. But it was not much better. The Continental Congress was impotent by design, save for its delegated authority to wage war. Beyond that it could do little, certainly nothing substantive to ensure financial stability or create a common national marketplace, urgently needed if Americans were to regain the prosperity they had enjoyed as colonists. Congress had no power to levy taxes or otherwise raise money for its operations; it could only beg the states to fund them. The government of the United States was a headless wonder, thrashing about for direction; it had no policies, only hopes. It had no executive, only a collection of delegates who assembled fitfully and often lacked a quorum. It had no national judiciary, no court of ultimate authority. Its army, after its indispensable leader bid his chief officers farewell over a famous luncheon at a tavern near the foot of Manhattan island, was reduced to a single regiment. America had no credit, only debts. Its aggregate pool of red ink exceeded $50 million, a stupendous sum for the time. Many individual citizens, too, were hurting economically after eight years of war and privation; debtors abounded, dreading imminent foreclosure or imprisonment and hoping for salvation in the form of inflated currency that might allow them to settle up with devalued paper. And the monarchies of Europe that had planted New World empires neither wished the United States well nor did it any favors, preferring that the rowdy experiment in what they saw as republican mobocracy should fail altogether.

No sooner had Parliament ratified the Paris peace treaty and fired Shelburne than, in an unsporting swivet, the ministry that followed his began to exact vengeance by denying the United States the trading rights they had formerly exercised as subjects of the British empire. No longer could American merchant ships put in duty-free at British docks; indeed, they could not land cargoes at any colonial ports, in particular in Canada or the British West Indies. Denial of the latter harbors was a singular hardship because the islands were a steady customer for American grain, fish, and lumber. American tobacco, rice, and naval stores could still be shipped to the Indies but only if carried there in British craft. A few months later, Britain slapped a prohibitive duty of 383 shillings per ton of whale oil brought to Britain under the United States flag, a grave wound to the American whaling industry and costing Massachusetts half its exports. And to rub retributive salt into the wound, British manufacturers were soon dumping cheap goods in the United States, a market hungry for them after wartime shortages, while the ministry was banning the export of machines, tools, and related items made from steel and iron—both measures intended to forestall the birth of infant American industries and thus perpetuate commercial dependence on the forsaken mother country.

To stymie America's territorial expansion as well as its economic growth, the crown created the new province of Upper Canada (coinciding approximately with modern Ontario), invited thousands more Loyalist refugees to settle there, and in order to secure the borders of what was left of British America, declined to evacuate His Royal Majesty's troops from eight forts along the shores of the Great Lakes and Lake Champlain—all on American soil and in violation of the Paris peace treaty, which mandated their removal "with all convenient speed." Behind this defiance, undertaken with confidence the demobilized United States military could do little to thwart it, was the crown's determination to sustain the British monopoly in the still lucrative fur trade, much of it derived from Indian trappers roaming the Old Northwest territory that Britain had handed over to the United States in the Paris peace settlement—much to the chagrin of Canadian fur traders and merchants. The longer American settlers could be kept out of the lands north of the Ohio, where beaver, fox, and bear abounded, the better for British commerce and the safer Canada would remain from its expansionist neighbors. Thus, on April 8, 1784, the cabinet advised Sir Frederick Haldimand, governor-general of British North America, that in view of the vague wording of the Paris treaty (what precisely did "all convenient speed" mean when indefinite delay was the operative policy?) the withdrawal of British troops from the American forts should be postponed "at least until we are enabled to secure the fur traders in the Interior Country [the Old Northwest] and withdraw their property." That translated into permanent entrenchment until further notice and active use of the forts to maintain ties with their Indian allies, who were told that American settlers above the Ohio were disturbing joint British and tribal hunting grounds and thus qualified as fair game for harassment, or worse.

Spain was no more obliging toward the rights the new republic hoped it had secured in Paris. The Spaniards lost no time in confirming their objection to the settlement terms Britain and America had reached without asking their approval. British rights to navigate the full length of the Mississippi, gained under the 1763 treaty closing out the French and Indian War, were not transferable to the victorious United States, Spain argued, in view of its recent recapture of West Florida, leaving it in possession of both banks of the river for its southernmost 200 miles. King Carlos III's court formally declared in July 1784 that the Mississippi was closed to American shipping.

Indeed, Spain continued to deny, as it had throughout the Paris negotiations, that the United States had any legitimate claim to the eastern Mississippi Valley. To emphasize the point, the Spaniards proceeded to bolster their fortifications at St. Louis, northern anchor of their hold on the river, and put up new forts at Memphis and Vicksburg—that is, on the side of the river America said it owned now by Britain's cession. They entered into protective treaties as well with several Indian nations, most notably the Cherokees and Creeks, among the most defiant native peoples on the continent, to ensure Spanish hegemony over the great plain that ran from the western slope of the Appalachian ridge to the Mississippi. In the United States, that area was considered the Georgia backlands and prime turf for settlement in the near future as rich coastal soil grew depleted from overfarming. To Spain, it was buffer territory, like its vast westward province of Louisiana, worth holding against any hostile Anglo-American intentions.

Ringed by European powers bent on containing its further expansion, the United States could theoretically have contested the issue. Neither Britain nor Spain had a large military presence in North America, and both were relying on Indian allies to bedevil the young republic and keep it in its place. But the new nation, deep in debt, longing for economic recovery, and hamstrung by its political incoherence, could not worry itself excessively over threats at its outer edges. Peace, however problematic, had confirmed Americans as a free people and owners of an immense territory they could grow into over time. They did not need to demonstrate at once that the land formally awarded them at Paris was theirs now by right of both conquest and settlement.

Yet neither could the new nation tarry in taking physical possession of its backlands, lest enemies seize them by default. More to the point, their newly certified but as yet unoccupied soil held the promise of economic deliverance for a hard-pressed people in the early hours of their national travail, even as the land—so rich, so spacious, so attainable—had nourished their whole colonial experience and provided cover and collateral in their long, hard campaign to gain independence. The land was their colossal collective treasure, an expansive resource that made them wealthy even when they had little money and no credit. The land, nearly a million square miles of it, *was* their money, their credit, and their future, and with the vibrancy and resilience of youth, they set out to envelop it in a hurry.

THE LAND RUSH BEGAN almost from the moment the boundaries of the United States were certified and its existence an internationally acknowledged fact.

During the war, the American population had declined by some 200,000 souls, as Loyalists fled the insurgent colonies, immigration dropped sharply, and family formation slowed in an age of pervasive uncertainty and travail. With peace, albeit well short of domestic tranquility, came a surge of growth as newcomers in unprecedented numbers were lured overseas to the land of liberty and the size of families rose in keeping with the needs of a flourishing frontier society. In just the seven years between the ratification of the Paris peace treaty marking the close of the Revolution and the first national census in 1790, the population of the United States increased 35 percent. And most of the new families needed land for their livelihood.

In a country where the population density was scarcely four per square mile, there was a good deal of space to spare. The lonesome piney woods of Maine were virgin land, the western side of New England was sparsely settled, Pennsylvania was half empty, New York north of the Mohawk River was yet a forested paradise where the native tribes were in slow retreat, and the splendid western uplands of Virginia and the Carolinas were only now beginning to welcome more than a trickle of young settlers. Beyond the Appalachians, virtually all was solitude. But change was in the air everywhere, as the Indians sensed and grieved. By 1785 an estimated 2,000 white families had forded the Ohio to take their chances in the Old Northwest, just ceded to Congress by Virginia and not yet legally open to settlement.

Demand for footholds in America's huge open territory was not limited, of course, to newcomers. Many who were established and prospering, or faltering and seeking greener pastures, were eager land-seekers as well. What distinguished farm families in the new nation from most in the Old World was the size of their holdings. American farms, considerably larger on average, afforded their tillers economies of scale that produced harvests well in excess of their own needs and allowed them to escape the impoverishing cycle of subsistence farming. Slave labor in the South, no more efficient than it was humane, was at least cheap and allowed plantation-size spreads to proliferate. Farms in the mid-Atlantic states of New York, New Jersey, and Pennsylvania, while smaller, were more carefully tended, and their rich soil yielded crops beyond the demands of their neighborhood and region. America the bountiful was destined to thrive from its agricultural abundance if, as, and when other nations availed themselves of it. Understandably, then, multitudes, whether ambitious immigrants, farmers and planters eager to extend their good fortune, or those down on their luck but hopeful of reversing it, were eager to lay their hands on as much land as they could afford—or even more.

A no less ardent interest in acquiring land was evident among many who never planned to work it. Land was the American investment of choice, the commonplace valuable everyone coveted in that preindustrial age, and the frenzy for buying into it prospectively swept the new nation. To dismiss all those caught up in the practice as speculators out for a killing was to demonize them as wild-eyed gamblers lusting after unearned increment. Opportunists they surely were, but more nearly in the sense of latter-day investors in shares of growth companies, that is, those purchased not on the strength of present earnings or dividend yields but in the expectation of their exponentially greater future prosperity. Few questioned that land values would only grow as America did, and the time to get in on the rewards was then and there. A lot of the best people—George Washington himself at times held as many as 70,000 acres—and some of the worst speculated in land, and little social stigma was attached to doing so.

Indeed, a not entirely specious argument could be made that it was as much an act of patriotism as self-interest to dabble in real estate. For the sooner land was bought, settled, and put to use, the more rapidly the United States would grow and prosper. If the land were just left in limbo, it would likely be stolen from the commonwealth by squatters, who paid nothing to help reduce national and state debts and often scorned their civic obligations, or encroached upon by foreigners set on obstructing the outward push of American settlement. So swift sale of unclaimed land by government officials was widely favored as a stimulus to business and national security.

There was an equally compelling downside to the argument that the American interior ought to be peopled as rapidly as possible. Precisely the same considerations that had led the overseers of the British empire to issue the Proclamation Act of 1763 temporarily barring settlement of the trans-Appalachian backlands applied with equal force to the United States twenty years later. If settlers were licensed to swoop down from the mountains or sail down the Ohio to carve out homesteads in indiscriminate profusion, forming widely dispersed communities that savored their idyllic isolation, the result was almost certain to be chaos. State and local authorities, rarely robust law enforcers even in established communities, could hardly ensure civil order in libertarian wilderness settings. Those living far from civilization would be nominal citizens, to be sure, but without access to markets and government services, they would have slight incentive to develop the industrious habits required for commercial farming or to shoulder the burdens of civic responsibility. Scattered frontiersmen, moreover, were easy prey for scalping parties of the natives they sometimes heedlessly riled.

The centrifugal force of migration raised other fears as well. Remote from populated regions and the notice of their countrymen, those moving west were more likely to lose their sense of national consciousness and, at times, allegiance to the federal union. Some political leaders worried that these distant settlers might drift away from the young republic and form self-proclaimed independent enclaves—or, worse still, be seduced into transferring their national loyalties to the British or Spanish empires, whose hovering officials hinted at respectful treatment. Men of commerce foresaw another potentially destabilizing force: lured west by cheap, fertile land, migrants abandoning the seaboard regions would leave them, it was feared, with a reduced labor supply, stagnating commerce, falling property values, and shrunken tax revenues.

Anxieties over such potential adverse consequences could not halt the westward flow of humanity. A vibrant, resourceful, impatient people could not be restrained by a loosely federated national government forbidding its subjects the right to roam and settle at will in dangerous country. If Congress and the states, famished as they were for income, had nevertheless chosen to withhold from the market their one merchandisable asset—the public lands—until a more timely season in the hope of gradual and less frenzied settlement, the process would likely have quickened anyway without government sanction. As it was, probably no less than half of the new settlers migrated as squatters, hoping to establish legal title by dint of possession and paying as little as possible for it when and if forced to someday. Thus, the states hurried to legitimize the inevitable by placing a sizable portion of their open lands—previously ungranted holdings of the crown or tracts confiscated from fled Loyalists—for sale at modest prices, averaging twenty-five to thirty cents an acre. Congress, however, awaiting final cession to it by the southern states with huge western land claims—a process that dragged on for nearly twenty years—could do no more than formulate fair marketing and administrative policies in advance of offering federal lands for sale. As a result, it was the older state public lands that got sold off in volume—an estimated 50 million acres between 1783 and the end of the century—while it was mostly squatters who homesteaded in the new federal territory. These intrepid poachers formed a thickening stream after the war, and by 1783 George Washington, who characterized them as "banditti" for stealing from the public domain, was sufficiently alarmed by the scale of the land-grabbing that he wrote about it to his fellow Virginian Richard Henry Lee, then president of Congress. Perhaps that august body, then more a chatty committee than an operative legislature, could not stem "the spirit of migration," the retired commander-in-chief observed, but he warned its members that if "you don't stop the road . . . it is yet in your power . . . to mark the way[;] a little while longer and you will be able to do neither."

Unwilling to wait for the new federal government to decide upon a public land policy, squatters also took up acreage illicitly because money of any sort was hard to come by. There was little hard currency in circulation, credit was difficult to obtain, and the economy in general was depressed by, among other factors, vengeful British trade policies. Paper currency and debt instruments, both federal and state, were greatly devalued because no one knew when or if government at any level would be able to meet its obligations in such a precarious economic climate. But this very condition worked to the advantage of speculators, financiers, and anyone with an inside track to legislators and their appointees who drew up the enabling statutes covering public land sales. These laws provided in most cases that public lands could be purchased with government paper at its full face value as opposed to specie or British pounds sterling. The redeemable worth, however, of government bonds and similar negotiable securities—such as veterans' certificates, issued as promissory notes for lifetime pensions at half the recipient's wartime pay, and land warrants given in lieu of pay for future title to public property—was highly uncertain. All these could be bought up at bargain prices, ranging from 10 percent to 25 percent of their nominal value. The supply of veterans' certificates and warrants swelled when many former soldiers, without work and lacking other resources, could not wait for the financially hard-pressed Congress and state legislatures to honor their pledges, and sold them for tuppence to survive. Those able to exploit the veterans' plight, often private bankers in collusion with government officials, were thus able to hoard cheap paper they could leverage to buy substantial quantities of public land at bargain prices. To compound their advantage in manipulating the feeble monetary and political systems, land speculators made payoffs in order to be advised when the most desirable public tracts were to be offered for sale. To get around statutory limits on any given individual's purchase allotment, shady operators used fictitious names or deceased persons as stand-ins for titleholders of record.

Not all these dirty tricksters were certifiably crooked, but the great postwar land rush smacked of the same cronyism and inside dealing that marked the rampant abuse of public office in the colonial era. It was not for nothing that George Washington, urging Congress to avoid the unsavory practices the states had promoted, wrote: "To suffer a wide extended Country to be over run with Land Jobbers, Speculators, Monopolisers or even with scatter'd settlers . . . is pregnant of disputes with the Savages and among ourselves . . . and for what? But to aggrandize a few avaricious Men to the prejudice of many, and the embarrassment of Government."

But the land program that Congress managed to piece together, while intended to meet Washington's caveat against insidious sprawl and more imaginative than any other initiative under the Articles of Confederation, had little positive effect.

VIRGINIA, AS THE LARGEST and most populous state, held the key to the federalizing of the western lands, which made up fully half the territory of the brand-new United States. In its 1781 conditional cession to Congress of the Old Northwest territory, crucial in the long-delayed ratification of the Articles of Confederation, Virginia had insisted that the transfer of its lands north of the Ohio be unencumbered by prior private claims of title, especially those extracted from the Indians. That meant Congress, in accepting the huge cession wilderness, would have to deny all land company claims in the Old Northwest—and probably, by extension, in every other state's ceded territory, regardless of the specific circumstances of the transactions. Congress balked at so sweeping a demand, and all cessions hung in abeyance.

Virginia's position was based largely on the prevalence of out-of-state speculators among the land syndicates and the often extortionate nature of their dealings with the Indians. The Old Dominion also persuasively contended that titles to all land within its borders that had not been granted or otherwise certified by the crown prior to the war now properly belonged to the commonwealth. Recognizing the merit of Virginia's arguments but still reluctant to approve a blanket prohibition on all purchases, past and future, by land speculators operating in western territories to be ceded by the states, Congress hit upon a simple expedient to end the deadlock. In reaffirming its earlier acceptance of Virginia's requirement that its ceded territory be used only as a "common fund" to benefit the entire nation—not for the profit or advantage of any special, private, or regional interests—Congress interpreted that language as tantamount to voiding all existing claims by speculators, so there was no need to specify them as malefactors. On March 1, 1784, the Virginians accepted that rationale.

The following day, Congress asked Thomas Jefferson to chair a committee to draw up a plan for how the newly ceded territory ought to be governed. Its members' guiding precept, embraced without dissent, was to avoid the course Great Britain had followed in treating its American colonies as permanent imperial territory. The colonies had the trappings of home rule but were in fact subservient to the crown and Parliament and obedient to their exploitive trade regulations. Jefferson's committee insisted that the United States, as it grew in area and population, must remain a representative democracy and not take on even the semblance of imperial

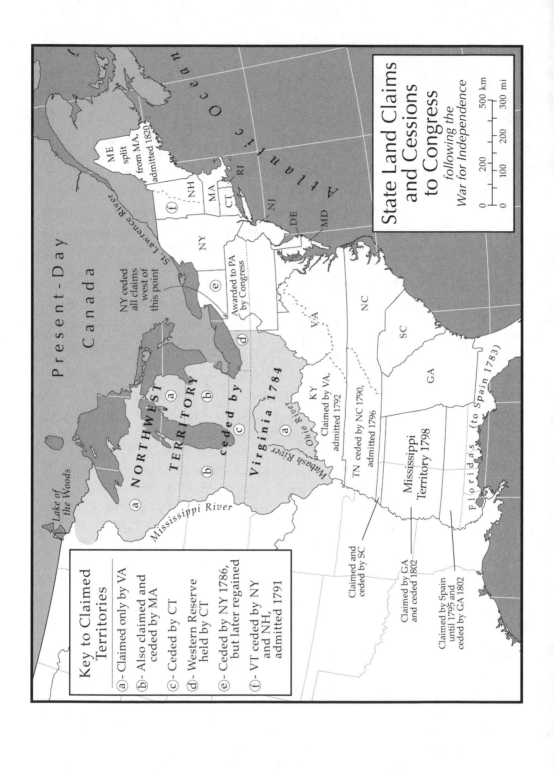

State Land Claims and Cessions to Congress
following the War for Independence

Key to Claimed Territories
- ⓐ - Claimed only by VA
- ⓑ - Also claimed and ceded by MA
- ⓒ - Ceded by CT
- ⓓ - Western Reserve held by CT
- ⓔ - Ceded by NY 1786, but later regained
- ⓕ - VT ceded by NY and NH, admitted 1791

Present-Day Canada

Atlantic Ocean

Lake of the Woods

St. Lawrence River

Mississippi River

NORTHWEST TERRITORY

Wabash River

Ohio River

Virginia 1784

ceded by

NY ceded all claims west of this point

Awarded to PA by Congress

ME split from MA, admitted 1820

NH
MA
CT
RI
NY
NJ
DE
MD
VA
KY Claimed by VA, admitted 1792
NC
TN ceded by NC 1790, admitted 1796
SC
GA
Mississippi Territory 1798
Floridas (to Spain 1783)

Claimed and ceded by SC

Claimed by GA and ceded 1802

Claimed by Spain until 1795 and ceded by GA 1802

0   100   200   300 mi
0   200   500 km

character. This, of course, was the very position Virginia had asserted in framing its original offer of cession (that is, its Old Northwest section would be subdivided into territories that, after they grew populous enough to stand on their own, would be admitted to the Union as states fully equal in rights and duties to the existing ones). An unexceptionable idea in retrospect, perhaps, but at the time it was a wholly new way of thinking about a nation's outlying settlements. In America these were not to remain tributary colonies forever but to become an integral part of the Union as soon as practicable. The plan stirred no controversy because most people understood that failure to grant political equality and full citizenship as promptly as possible to those living in the new territories would betray the principles of the American Revolution and could well have excited secessionist sentiments or even thoughts of defection to rival nations.

But how would Congress inculcate democratic habits and install a republican political framework in remote settings where self-reliance was the watchword, roads were rutted paths, and gathering a communal consensus was elusive? The answer offered by Jefferson's committee was to encourage the locals to organize themselves under federal guidelines. Jefferson's program, embodied in the Land Ordinance of 1784, was a leap of faith in America's future and ambitious beyond the committee's assignment. It projected a geographical grid encompassing not just Virginia's Old Northwest but all of the territory west of the Appalachians, including the western (Kentucky) section of Virginia below the Ohio River and the backlands of the three states south of Virginia that had not yet ceded their outlying holdings to Congress.

Jefferson's grid divided the whole region into fourteen future states of approximately equal size and rectangular except where rivers and lakes formed natural boundaries, and spelled out an orderly progression from wilderness to statehood. During a territory's larval stage, Congress would combat anarchy by imposing any strictures it felt "necessary for the preservation of peace and good order," but no means of enforcement were spelled out. Whenever the settlers in any given territory wished to organize themselves—no minimum number of residents was required—they had only to petition Congress for federal recognition, convene all the "free males of full age" in the territory who wished to attend, adopt a temporary constitution and basic laws modeled after those operating in any of the original thirteen states, and elect a legislature. When a territory's population reached 20,000, it could write an enduring constitution, form a permanent government, and choose a nonvoting delegate to Congress. And when the population reached the level of the least populous of the original thirteen states, the territory could apply to Congress for admission to the Union as a full-fledged state, provided it agreed unconditionally to remain a part of the United States, abide by the Articles of Confederation, assume its proportional share of the national debt, keep a republican form of government, and not interfere with Congress's disposition of public lands—that is, land ceded to it but that had not not yet been sold or settled—within the territory or try to tax them. Approval by two-thirds of the other states was required for admission.

Jefferson's original proposal to his fellow committeemen even suggested names for each of the fourteen western states-in-the-making. Two of them were patriotic (Washington and Saratoga), two were based on Indian names (Michigania and Illinoia), and the rest, reflecting Jefferson's love of the classics, bore such laughably unpicturesque names as Polypotamia, Metropotamia, Cherronesus, and Pelispia (the last to be given to the beautiful bluegrass land of Kentucky). The names were meant to make the whole conception more plausible and appealing, but they struck Jefferson's colleagues in Congress as too highfalutin for plainspoken Americans, and, at any rate, the territorial residents were thought likely to prefer choosing their own state names. Two other, far weightier proposals by Jefferson stemmed from his active social conscience: denying citizenship to any resident of a new state who claimed a hereditary title and prohibiting slavery in any territory or new state as of 1800. Congress was sympathetic toward the exclusion of titled aristocrats from the citizenry but felt that a statute devoted to territorial matters was not the proper vehicle for conveying it. The ban on slavery failed to pass only because of the absence due to illness of a single delegate from New Jersey.

The trickier part of the task undertaken by Jefferson's committee was to devise an orderly method to sell the public lands in the western cessions, thus providing Congress with badly needed revenues yet not making the process overly enticing to undesirable elements. If the method was too complex and the prices too high, the territory might attract few buyers and instead be overrun by squatters claiming their natural right to settle and farm whatever land they got to first—and daring any authority to dislodge them. But if the system was not sufficiently rigorous, speculators with their piles of devalued federal currency and government securities to invest might snatch up huge tracts, resell them for well under the government's going price (more than making up the difference from interest payments on the credit terms offered to buyers short of cash), or keep their large holdings off the market until the territory had grown enough to justify far higher land prices. This last strategy of stockpiling land purchases may have made good business sense but hardly served the national interest in rapid but orderly settlement of the west, stimulating commerce between regions, and heightened security against Indian reprisals.

Throughout prior American history, land was taken up in one of three ways: through crown grants and subsequent sell-offs by the titleholders thereof; through charter grants to a community of like-minded settlers forming a township, most often in New England; and through a helter-skelter practice most common in the South after the crown's authority was withdrawn. This last method, which Jefferson favored for inclusion in what became the Federal Land Act of 1785, called for purchasing a warrant for a tract of land of specified size but unspecified location in a given region, then going there to stake out the most desirable unoccupied site, and finding a county official—usually of low rank and minimal surveying skills—to map out the tract by use of the metes and bounds method (based in part on natural elements of the landscape). Finally the buyer took the certified drawing to the county court, where he hoped the claim would not be challenged during the period allotted for that purpose. If all went well, the claimant's title was said to be "perfected." But the process, which at its best was both speedy and unceremonious, was also often unruly and confrontational. In parts of Kentucky, for example, where squatting was epidemic, it was not unusual for six or more claimants to compete in court for title to the same tract or parts thereof. Jefferson's plan was to divide each territory into "hundreds"—surveyed townships ten miles square—under the direction of federal registrars and then to proceed in the southern fashion of selling warrants for land in any open part of the township where a buyer chose to locate his tract. New Englanders in Congress protested that such a method was chaotic, likely to promote disputes, and would result in a highly scattered pattern of settlement, making participatory government difficult and Indian attack more likely.

Congress made some sensible modifications to Jefferson's imaginative basic scheme. The ordinance called for the appointment of a chief United States Geographer, whose office would over time survey all the western lands, starting with the Northwest Territory. Each territory would be divided into a grid of six-mile-square townships (rather than Jefferson's ten-by-ten-mile units, considered too large for community cohesiveness), regardless of the ruggedness of the terrain or its degree of suitability for settlement. This concept was derived in spirit from the Age of Enlightenment's wishful belief in humankind's capacity to impose order and regularity on the wilds and obstacles of nature. Every township was then to be subdivided into thirty-six sections of 640 acres (one square mile) each and put up for auction one section at a time (but not in smaller tracts) by the federal Board of

Treasury, at a minimum price of one dollar per acre. One-third of the payment had to be made at the time of purchase, with the balance due in three
months. Five of the thirty-six sections were to be set aside for distribution to
war veterans still holding their land warrants, and one section in each township was to be reserved for educational purposes. The price was relatively
high, three or four times what public land was fetching in the established
states, but since the statute permitted payment in inflated federal paper at its
face amount rather than its true market value, the cost was far less than it
seemed—and, for their money, buyers would be ensured indisputable title to
their tracts, each surveyed, numbered, and officially registered.

It was a rational enough scheme but far from perfect. For one thing,
there was no limitation on how many sections any one buyer could accumulate, permitting speculators to assemble huge holdings. For another, the
smallest tract to be put up for auction—640 acres—would cost two to three
times the annual income of the average farmer at the time, and since the
government was making virtually no provision for credit, poor buyers
would be forced to deal with speculators who could offer them subdivided
smaller lot sizes and easier credit terms. Finally, the 1785 statute cut no
slack for squatters, who could not afford tracts of the size and cost mandated
by the federal law. The last thing Congress had in mind was to grant squatters preemptive rights—a government pardon, actually—confirming their
illicit possession of stolen public land if they would pay a fair or at least
minimal price for the title when confronted by law enforcement officers. To
offer leniency to squatters would only have encouraged the practice, Congress reasoned, and subsistence farmers of that ilk were thought to suffer
from poor work habits, worse manners, dubious patriotism, and little civic
spirit—not the sort to bring prosperity and stability to the new territories.

While certified property sales and uncertified land-grabbing were brisk
in the frontier sectors of the established states in the years just after the war,
neither the "banditti" nor more solid sorts of would-be settlers were flooding into the backlands, as many political leaders had feared. The Jeffersonian precepts of minimal government and maximum liberty as embodied in
the 1784 Land Ordinance, with its emphasis on self-rule and only the
vaguest provision for federal policing, was creating more anxiety than
eagerness over the prospect of migrating west. Potential settlers worried
that their lives, livelihoods, and property titles would be perpetually at peril
out where the rule of law barely existed, and those who had already gone
there to brave the wilderness were too scattered and preoccupied with survival to concern themselves with establishing social order.

Adding to such concerns, as Congress took up the task in 1786 of crafting a specific plan for organizing the Northwest Territory along the guide-lines set down in the 1784 Land Ordinance, was a fear of growing social rancor and political unrest in already settled parts of the nation. Most alarm-ing of these cases was the outbreak of civil disorder known as Shays's Rebellion, which raised doubts about the federal government's ability to relieve the causes of such unrest and maintain domestic tranquility. The issue was drawn by the failure of the Massachusetts legislature to address the increasingly desperate straits of the state's heavily indebted farmers, who had petitioned for more lenient foreclosure terms on their property and for the issuance of paper currency as a way of satisfying their creditors—money likely to sink quickly below its face value. When the lawmakers, influenced by commercial and creditor interests, adjourned without acting on the farmers' grievances, pitchfork-wielding legions of them rose to dis-rupt proceedings of state and county courts and threatened widespread vio-lence over the snowy winter of 1786–87. Civil war was averted only by a muster of 4,400 militiamen to quell the turmoil. The lesson was not lost on Congress (or on George Washington, who later as President would act deci-sively to end Pennsylvania's Whiskey Rebellion).

Jefferson was in Paris now as American ambassador, and his brand of libertarian politics suffered a setback at home as conservative leaders, favor-ing the protection of property no less than liberty, recognized that Congress would have to assert itself in ensuring law and order, personal safety, and durable land titles if settlers were to be coaxed to move west in serious num-bers. As a result, the Northwest Ordinance, passed by Congress in mid-1787 after a fifteen-month debate and admired by posterity for the extensive lib-erties it guaranteed in the territory, at the same time imposed terms of tem-porary federal oversight that were far more intrusive and antidemocratic than anything Jefferson and his congressional committee had envisioned in 1784. Congress held that the Old Northwest was to be treated as a single ter-ritory for administrative purposes and ruled by a governor appointed for a three-year term; to ensure his vested interest in the welfare of the region, he was required to reside and own at least 1,000 acres there (no humble yeo-man need apply). The governor was to be assisted by an executive secretary and three judges, all also appointed by Congress and required to own at least 500 acres in the territory. The five officials were to adopt and publish suit-able laws, drawn from those in the original states, and the governor would pick local magistrates and officers to lead the militia. Congress and its appointees, in short, and not the locals, would preside over the first phase of territorial development. Only when the region attained a population of 5,000 free males could it enjoy a measure of autonomous, democratic, rather than imposed, colonial-type rule. Residents could then elect representatives to a territorial legislature (only substantial citizens with at least 200 acres of property could be chosen), which in turn would select a legislative council serving as the upper house. But the governor, still appointed by Congress, would retain absolute veto power over all legislation and could summon or dismiss the lawmakers at will. Only when the population reached 60,000 free residents could the territory apply for admission to the Union with full statehood rights and duties.

The population requirement was actually a liberalizing feature of the new ordinance. Some in Congress, led by Jefferson's young acolyte and former law clerk, James Monroe, had feared that the minimum requisite for statehood as set by the 1784 Land Ordinance—the applying territory needed as many residents as the least populous of the original thirteen states—would force territories to wait for many years to qualify, and some might never. This likelihood was heightened by Congress's parceling the western lands into sixteen future states, not the fourteen that Jefferson had projected. It might have taken decades for these territories to attract as many residents as the least populated of the older seaboard states, although perhaps they would be easier to govern in the interim by virtue of their relatively small size. On the other hand—and it was a disturbing prospect to Monroe and his allies—if these smallish territories grew fast enough to qualify minimally for statehood, they would soon have disproportionate voting strength in Congress, to the potential detriment of the larger and more populous seaboard states. Thus, the Monroe camp prevailed in its effort to have the western lands divided into fewer, geographically larger future states.

Over time, nine new states would be carved from the backlands awarded to the United States by the Paris treaty. The Northwest Ordinance decreed that the former Virginia territory could be broken into no fewer than three nor more than five new states. Monroe's hunch that the evolutionary period for statehood might prove far more protracted than had first been supposed was borne out. Sixteen years would pass between the enactment of the ordinance and the admission to the Union of the first state sculpted from the Northwest Territory, Ohio, to attain 60,000 free residents; and even by that year, 1803, it had not quite equaled the least populous of the original states, Delaware.

Enacted in New York City by the old Congress, operating under the Articles of Confederation at the very time the Constitutional Convention, toiling in Philadelphia, was radically altering the whole structure of the United States government, the Northwest Ordinance was the proudest ornament in the nation's legislative history to that point. Its glow, though, owed less to the utility of the statute as a catalyst to western settlement than to its promised delivery of federally ensured rights and liberties to territorial residents. Among these were freedom of worship, habeas corpus, trial by jury, and proportional representation in the legislature as well as prohibitions against "cruel and unusual punishment" (wording borrowed by the new Congress three years later in the Bill of Rights), primogeniture, and, most notably, slavery. The ban on human bondage was uncontested by southerners who assumed that in consenting to its abolition north of the Ohio River, they would be permitted to impose the barbarism on future territories below the Ohio. The old Congress's action, one of its last, stood in contrast to the craven compromise by the framers of the new Constitution, who, resolved to avoid regional strife in order to achieve a federal compact that worked, did nothing to check America's most glaring social evil beyond banning the importation of slaves—but only after allowing the practice to be indulged for yet another twenty years.

As a package, the federal land ordinances of 1784, 1785, and 1787 set the high-water mark for the new nation's mostly dysfunctional central government. They had the clear purpose of systematizing and stimulating western settlement while trying to prevent confusion and corrupt practices by political and financial insiders and to discourage squatters and speculators, whose private gains were seen as inimical to the national interest.

THE OVERSIGHT CONGRESS HOPED TO apply to the federalized western territories was well intended but misguided and not a little oppressive as carried out in the Northwest Territory during the fifteen years after passage of the 1787 ordinance. The statute fed precisely those antidemocratic impulses that Jefferson had feared in the absence of representative government.

To serve as the first governor of the Northwest Territory, Congress chose a man who had been its own president, Arthur St. Clair. That he was retained in the gubernatorial post for fifteen years suggests that he was not only well connected but conscientious in enforcing both the spirit and the letter of the ordinance. Yet St. Clair, a former British and later Continental Army officer, large landowner, and successful politician, let power go to his head when placed in charge of the Northwest Territory. He sometimes denied the public's right of assembly, outlawed profanity, ordered the mandatory observance of the Sabbath, ignored the advice of his federally appointed judges, and was often AWOL. Returned to the rank of general to lead a force of 1,400 troops against aroused Indian bands stalking the Northwest Territory, he let his ill-disciplined soldiers be backed up to the Wabash River near modern-day Fort Wayne, Indiana, in November 1791 and lost 900 of them, dead and wounded—the worst defeat suffered at the hands of the natives in Anglo-American history. Widely regarded as imperious and paternalistic, St. Clair clung tenaciously to the governorship, thwarted rather than promoted the efforts of his territorial residents to attain statehood so that he might keep his fiefdom intact, and finally had to be pried from office by President Jefferson. His tenure was testament to the perils of tyranny when the first priority of government is the suppression of anarchy. For his efforts, St. Clair wound up owning 150,000 acres of frontier but was disgraced as an officer of Congress.

As a commercial enterprise, the federal land sales business was a slow starter. By 1800, only 100,000 acres had been auctioned off. By comparison, the state of Virginia sold or otherwise assigned title to 1.5 million acres of land in the western section of the commonwealth (the Northwest Territory included) in the single year of 1787. Why did the federal land enterprise stagger so badly in its early years?

One reason was that the law required all sectors of the national domain to be surveyed before they could be placed on auction, and an abjectly poor Congress had to delay the undertaking for years. When it finally began, the process proved far more arduous and time-consuming than anticipated. Then there was the fierce competition from the states. Why pay a dollar an acre for federal wilderness when you could buy a piece of Maine's piney woods from the Commonwealth of Massachusetts for half that price, or an acre of rich Pennsylvania soil for one-third as much, and New York was offering 5 million acres at twenty cents each? The Board of Treasury was empowered to offer only the most stringent terms of credit, and the 640-acre lot sizes were, as noted, beyond the resources of all but the wealthiest buyers. Since the climate was not suited to plantations, moreover, and slavery was barred by statute north of the Ohio, southern planters were not interested. Indians, kept aroused by the British military and fur traders still operating from forts on the Great Lakes, remained a serious menace. On top of that, prospective commercial farmers who might have bought in the Ohio and eastern Mississippi valleys knew they would not be able to ship their produce down the great river system so long as Spain refused to allow American vessels access to the New Orleans wharves and their cargoes to be transshipped to eastern and world markets. Finally, bids for federal land had to be entered at offices in settled eastern areas rather than nearer the frontier and the properties for sale—a serious inconvenience for many a would-be buyer. All these negative factors also helped doom the Ohio Company's grandiose settlement scheme.

Squatters meanwhile continued to infiltrate the backlands. Without officially approving of the practice but in view of stagnant federal land sales, Congress might well have acted as many of the state governments were doing by acknowledging the inevitable and granting squatters "preemption," the prior right of purchase, so they would be entitled to bid on land they had been occupying without title before it was offered for sale to the public. Advocates of such a liberalized policy contended that by helping needy, cash-poor farm families bootstrap themselves upward, the government would speed western settlement and the creation of internal commerce, keep frontier territory from falling into foreign hands or under foreign influence, and promote agrarian democracy with its social leveling instead of reserving the land just for the well-heeled. Historian Robert M. Robbins put it bluntly in his comment in the *Mississippi Valley Historical Review* that awarding squatters the right of preemption "was an expedient which a government was forced to adopt so as to make established law and order conform with the lawless and uncontrollable spirit of the American frontier."

That rationale failed to sway conservatives who insisted that squatting on public land, however dressed up, violated the sanctity of property rights at the foundation of any stable social order, rewarded irresponsible and law-defying conduct—it was, in fact, flat-out trespassing—and penalized the national treasury. But wouldn't the national treasury have benefited more by the assignment of law enforcement officers to require squatters to pay for the land they had been occupying even if what they could afford was well under the government's mandated minimum price? Why wasn't that preferable to letting a great deal of land sit idle out there or fall into the hands of conniving profiteers who had no intention of working the soil themselves? The rebuttal, of course, was that permitting preemption at less than the statutorily fixed minimum price would almost certainly have depressed the value of the federal lands and undermined the entire auction process. At any rate, Congress could not afford the manpower to hunt down squatters and make them pay a negotiated sum for the land or be forced from it through mass evictions.

Behind the seemingly self-defeating rigidity of the federal government's land policies lurked a darker reality. A deep ambivalence afflicted the nation's politicians and businessmen over the desirability of swift western settlement. They knew the tide could not be stemmed for long and that over time America would prosper increasingly as the backlands filled in, but no region—neither mercantile New England nor the agriculturally prosperous middle states nor the Tidewater South selling its tobacco and rice in world markets—was eager to sacrifice its present economic advantages and political power to a vast and quickly emerging rival sector beyond the Appalachians. Washington, Jefferson, and Hamilton among others feared as well that an overly rapid westward flight of population and trade would drive a wedge between the regions, promoting disunion, and soon plunge the nation into civil strife and conflict, if not open combat, with Spain and Britain. Washington, for one, strongly favored a go-slow policy that encouraged the private construction of roadways and canals linking the eastern markets with the near West. He himself joined a syndicate hoping to improve and quicken passage between the upper reaches of the Potomac River and the Ohio. Such incremental steps struck Washington as preferable to the federal government's stimulation of settlement farther west, where frontiersmen would naturally orient toward the Mississippi and thus rip, or badly strain, the fabric of national unity. The slaveholding South, though, saw the matter in a different light. The plantocracy was eager to extend its domain westward, where the fortunes of its families could be perpetuated and its progeny would gain enough economic and political power to dominate future, pro-slavery states.

The emerging regional conflict was brought into the open by the efforts of the formidable John Jay, wreathed in laurel from his diplomatic triumph in Paris and installed in 1785 by an appreciative Congress as its secretary for foreign affairs. One of Jay's primary tasks was to settle American differences with Spain, which had reluctantly conceded the existence of the United States but no other aspect of the Anglo-American peace treaty.

Frustrated by three years of dealing with disdainful Spanish ministers while he had been posted in Madrid and Paris, Jay was now in a more favorable position to negotiate with this obstinate adversary. Since the conduct of the nation's external affairs was one of the very few areas of jurisdiction that the states had surrendered to Congress, Jay as foreign secretary was perhaps the single most powerful officer in the American government. He had reason, moreover, to be hopeful that the envoy plenipotentiary whom Madrid had sent to deal with him, Don Diego de Gardoqui, would prove agreeable. Gardoqui's father had been a principal of a mercantile house that had served as the go-between for international operatives funneling military supplies to the American war effort, and Gardoqui himself had been Jay's unofficial contact with the Spanish court while he was being snubbed as an unaccredited visitor in Madrid.

The United States wanted Spain to acknowledge the thirty-first parallel as its southern boundary and the Mississippi as its western one, to let American vessels travel the length of the river, and to stop giving arms and comfort to the Creeks and other tribes that were raiding American settlements in western Georgia and resisting their advance into territory Spain claimed as its protectorate for the Indian nations. For a year Gardoqui spurned all these requests. But he registered some interest in a limited commercial treaty that would allow American ships to trade (except tobacco) on a mutual most-favored-nation basis with Spain's homeland and European islands—the Canaries and Balearics—though not with the far more important Spanish colonial markets in the Caribbean, Mexico, and South America. That was something, but not much.

Jay, from a family of prominent New York merchants and a close ally of Federalist commercial interests, found value in even a limited trade treaty with Spain, particularly when Britain was closing its markets to American shipping. So he told Gardoqui that if Spain would quit objecting to America's boundaries as defined by the Paris treaty, a fact of life that His Catholic Majesty and his court could not reverse, then the United States would agree to live for another generation—twenty-five or thirty years, say—with Spain's refusal to allow American cargoes to clear the Mississippi River. The limited commercial treaty was to be part of the bargain.

When the terms of the proposed treaty were revealed to Congress for ratification in 1786, incredulous critics damned Jay as the tool of the northeastern mercantile crowd and their political henchmen. Why would Jay have willingly yielded American freedom to navigate the full length of the heartland river forming the nation's western boundary—a right that Benjamin Franklin had considered priceless and that so many of his countrymen believed essential for development of the West? Why bother to placate an overextended, posturing imperial regime whose feeble military presence in North America could not long withstand the gathering momentum of the new republic? Jay, who was nobody's fool, thought the trade-off—Spain's acknowledgment of America's boundaries in exchange for retention of control over the lower Mississippi—a reasonable one because, as he told Congress, navigation of the river by American vessels was "not at present important" and by the time it would become so, Spain would have to concede the impracticality of resisting the wishes of the United States, for "they who make a lease admit the right of the leasor." America, in short, could afford to be patient, especially at a time when its people were still convalescing from their war for independence and had no military arm whatever for challenging the Spaniards.

It was a lame argument and a dubious bargain, and from the South's standpoint, both were unacceptable. The case against the Gardoqui treaty was deftly made by Charles Pinckney, a twenty-nine-year-old congressman from South Carolina, who said that anyone familiar with the western half of the United States knew that the Mississippi and its tributaries were "the mode of exporting their productions and of establishing a commercial intercourse with the rest of the world." If you were to give up the right to navigate it freely "even for a time, you check, perhaps destroy, the spirit of migration." Then Pinckney skewered Jay for arguing that "because we have not at present a government sufficiently energetic to assert a national right, it would be more honorable to relinquish it." The five southern states refused to ratify, and the treaty died.

It was a setback from which Jay never fully recovered, though he still had valuable service to render his nation. The episode helped explain why Congress was both eager to develop the vast western cessions made to it by the states and rid them of foreign impingement yet fearful what the costs of premature settlement might be in economic and political terms and human life.

WHILE FEDERAL LAND SALES languished in the West until America's three most critical postwar problems—the fragility of the national government, the status of the Mississippi River, and the lingering Indian menace—could be dealt with, confusion reigned over another, much smaller territory on the New England frontier. The issue there, too, had had everything to do with land-grabbing and the deep passions the practice stirred in the making of America. But in the case of Vermont, still in gestation when the thirteen colonies rebelled against Great Britain, the clash was over the legitimacy of land titles that caused a tug-of-war lasting twenty-seven years, starting in the pre-Revolutionary era. The accused tyrant in this miniature struggle for independence was the royal colony (and later proud state) of New York and its high-handed governors.

When New Hampshire, then a political ward under the jurisdiction of Massachusetts, was designated a separate colony in 1741, the crown named as its royal governor Harvard graduate Benning Wentworth, a prominent merchant of Portsmouth and member of the province's legislative council. Given the relatively small size of his colony and the fact that much of it was already settled, no governor was more adept or daring at making a killing in real estate from ungranted crown land. In Wentworth's behalf, it should be noted that he shared the loot—in the form of some 3 million acres of territory apparently beyond the governor's jurisdiction—with his fellow colonists, not just with relatives and cronies.

On taking office, with its unprincely annual stipend of £300, scarcely enough to keep the clapboards on his fifty-two-room mansion in decent repair, Wentworth asked London for permission to charge a small fee on his grants of crown land. Approval was given on the proviso that the grants be limited to the size of thirty-six-square-mile townships for the use of fifty or more families. The enterprising governor began examining maps and charters dealing with New Hampshire and its neighbors, in particular his own colony's western boundary, shared with New York and generally understood to be the Connecticut River, as fixed by the 1674 grant to James, Duke of York, from his brother, King Charles II. But Wentworth discerned that the 1674 charter, which also designated the river as New York's eastern boundary with New Hampshire's neighbors to the south, Massachusetts and Connecticut, conflicted with the earlier charters of those two colonies, which the river's north-south course roughly bisected. So that Connecticut would not be grotesquely amputated, the crown moved its border with New York some forty miles west, more or less parallel to and twenty miles east of the Hudson River. It later did the same for Massachusetts, so Wentworth concluded that the crown could not have intended New York's newly defined eastern boundary to take a violent jog to the east at the Massachusetts–New Hampshire line but to continue its northerly course paralleling the Hudson and eventually striking Lake Champlain—thus approximately doubling the area of New Hampshire, though nobody had bothered to point this out. When Wentworth was instructed by the crown in 1744 to take charge of Fort Dummer, lately recaptured from the French and located a little west of the Connecticut River near the present city of Brattleboro, he chose to interpret the order as confirmation that his colony's boundary with New York extended as far west as those of Massachusetts and Connecticut.

Accordingly, and apparently without bothering to check with any other royal official, Wentworth started issuing grants in the still sparsely settled areas on both sides of the serene Green Mountains west of the Connecticut River. Over time he gave out 138 patents for townships six miles square, as directed by the crown, but insisted on an unauthorized kickback of 500 of the best acres in each for his own possession. He further exceeded his power in making the so-called Wentworth Grants by awarding the land not just for planned communities as the crown had instructed but mostly to friends and family (for example, 350 acres in each of fifty-seven towns were reserved for Wentworth's brother-in-law) and to almost anyone able to meet his modest asking price of a halfpenny an acre.

For years nobody, least of all land-rich colonial New York, raised an objection to this unilateral annexation. But in 1763, as the flow of settlers admiring the beauty, fertility, and timber of the region—by then being referred to as Vermont, a Gallicized allusion to the Green Mountains— began to grow and many of the speculators who held Wentworth Grants began selling them for a plump profit, New York finally awoke and complained to the king's Privy Council. The following year the Council voided the Wentworth Grants, confirmed the Connecticut River as the boundary between New York and New Hampshire, and stripped the governor of his office. New York, which might have chosen to play the kindhearted neighbor by confirming the New Hampshire grants but requiring their titleholders to acknowledge New York's jurisdiction and meet all their obligations as residents of that colony, showed them not a whit of magnanimity. Instead, it demanded that the holders of the grants come forward within three months and pay a vindictive fee of a shilling per acre or face immediate eviction. One in five Vermont families complied, but 800 others appealed to the Privy Council for relief, arguing that they had purchased their titles in good faith, relying on contracts derived from crown authority, in the person of New Hampshire's royal governor, and ought not to be victimized ex post facto by New York.

Faced with a nasty intercolonial dispute, the crown might have prevented an explosive confrontation if it had done what New York would not do—confirmed both New York's jurisdiction and the New Hampshire grants, the latter on the ground that Wentworth's transgressions were not the titleholders' doing and that, at any rate, New York had for too long neglected to assert its rights in the matter. But the Council, not wishing to offend New York, the favorite crown colony and a Tory bastion amid the emerging American insurgency, temporized in a 1767 ruling that no new grants were to be made in the region nor should any colonial authority attempt to evict settlers presently cultivating the soil until the crown had time to render a definitive judgment. But no such judgment was ever forthcoming.

For the next twenty-two years New York, both as royal colony and American state, acted with towering contempt for the Vermonters, as the grantholders and their neighbors were now called. Colonial Governor Colden Cadwallader, in open defiance of the Privy Council's ruling, quickly awarded half a million acres of the Wentworth Grants to New York residents, many of them landed aristocrats and high officials, and ordered surveying parties into Vermont to lay out the property lines. When the surveyors were met with vocal protests and hindered in their assignment, Cadwallader authorized a round of "ejectment suits" in the summer of 1770, which proved a travesty of justice since several of the judges, operating under New York law, were themselves recipients of the new grants in Vermont (not to mention the lieutenant governor and the attorney general of the colony). Predictably, the judges declared the Wentworth Grant titles fraudulent and ordered their holders to pay the extortionate fee for New York's confirmation or surrender the land. It was then that one of the great rumpled folk heroes of American history, Ethan Allen, emerged as Robin Hood with a Yankee twang.

Quick of wit, tongue, and feet, the brash, bulky Connecticut native had planned to study for the ministry at Yale (but wound up an outspoken religious freethinker). After his father died young, Allen had to run the family farm to sustain his mother and seven siblings for a time. While later the operator and co-owner of the first iron mill in the state, he wandered north to hunt and fish in the pristine New Hampshire grants, fell under their charm, and stayed to become a shrewd real-estate speculator. His Onion River Land Company at one time controlled 64,000 acres in the bucolic Champlain Valley. When New York officials came after the Wentworth Grant owners, the latter appealed to Allen, a brainy, palavering hail-fellow-well-met type, to organize and lead their resistance. He carried on the fight for nearly twenty years, operating out of the Catamount Tavern in the heart of Bennington and constantly denouncing their New York tormentors as greedy, heartless, power-hungry oppressors.

A blend of political boss, propagandist (whose tracts in forceful if unrefined prose were well read), and guerrilla chief, Allen organized a vigilante corps of 200 or so rough-and-ready lads and louts—the self-styled Green Mountain Boys—to repulse New York deputies sent to dispossess the grant farmers and to taunt, kick, punch, whip, vandalize, and otherwise intimidate (but never fatally harm) those who dared to move in on the Vermonters' land. To flaunt his defiance, Allen, with a £100 price on his head, sometimes kidnapped New York officials and put them on mock trial to dramatize what he deemed the illegitimacy of their mission. Whenever Governor Colden and his successor, George Clinton, dispatched militiamen to march on Vermont to force the issue, Allen would cast his plucky band as the Sons of Liberty, like those in Massachusetts and elsewhere combating royal tyranny, and they invariably succeeded in outnumbering, outflanking, and outstaring the invaders until they retreated without firing a shot.

Although New York escalated the stakes by making more and more new grants in Vermont, Allen did not hesitate when the Revolution began to cast his lot with the American cause, which he analogized to his own war. He ingratiated himself and the Green Mountaineers with George Washington by swiftly seizing Fort Ticonderoga from the British even before the Continental troops took the field, thus securing the new nation's northeastern frontier. The big fort served as the jump-off point for the American attempt to capture Quebec province. When it failed, Allen later recklessly tried his own assault on Canada but was betrayed by spies and held in a British prison for three years until Washington arranged his exchange. Despite these and many other acts of patriotism during the war, Congress turned a cold shoulder when Vermont, by then a de facto polity on its own, requested admission to the United States as a freestanding sovereignty wholly separate from New York but equal to it (and every other state) in status.

Having effectively withstood their far larger neighbor, Allen and his followers now found themselves a society in limbo, for not only was New York unprepared to swallow its pride by acquiescing in any congressional certification of Vermont's defiance by admitting it to the Union, but the four big southern states were equally opposed to elevating the small northern region to statehood. Fearful that such recognition would only encourage the dismemberment of the large states by irresponsible and demagogic factions, the South also supposed that Vermont would side with the rest of New England and the middle states on sectional issues and, as an egalitarian society with strong antiaristocratic leanings, oppose the vested interests of the slaveholding planters. As James Madison later put it, the South's hostility toward Vermont in Congress boiled down to "the inexpedience of admitting so unimportant a state to an equal vote."

Unbowed, Vermont declared itself an independent republic in 1777, drew up a constitution more liberal than any already adopted by the American states (providing for universal manhood suffrage and outlawing slavery), established an efficient court system with a judicial code written in the vernacular, and eventually even issued its own copper coins. Needy of Vermont's military, financial, and agricultural resources but unwilling to risk New York's alienation in the midst of a war for survival, Congress sent a delegation to persuade Allen and his supporters to renounce independence if New York agreed to confirm the Wentworth Grants. But the renegade movement had advanced too far to be abandoned, and, at any rate, many in Vermont argued that the United States had no authority to intervene in internal state matters and lacked the power to overrule the New York courts if they should later undo a settlement of the grants fracas. Impatient with such effrontery, Congress urged, sotto voce, Vermont's three neighbors, New York, New Hampshire, and Massachusetts, to quash the breakaway movement by force, but the region was too remote, Vermont was too well armed, and no one wanted to wage a civil war on top of the endless one with Britain.

Spurned by Congress, Vermont began to flirt with Britain, which saw the uses of detaching the Green Mountain region from American territory (as it was shortly conceded to be by the Paris peace treaty, even if the United States continued to regard it as a pariah), and dignifying it as a new royal colony. The British offered a generous helping of self-rule and promised to confirm the Wentworth Grants, that nasty little matter the crown had never got around to resolving. Vermont, its sympathies with the United States but its survival dependent on British indulgence, danced along a tightrope for the remainder of the war in the hope Congress would relent rather than risk losing its loyal if insubordinate little ally.

Allen rallied his constituents to hold fast, raging that he would "fight, nay even run on the mountains and live on mouse meat" before bowing to New York or Congress. And Vermont could afford to wait. With its high principles, stable government, no war debt, and low taxes, the tiny republic was attracting many new settlers, and, as testament to their admiration for its conduct, twenty-five adjacent towns on the New York side of the disputed border and forty-three across the Connecticut River in New Hampshire asked the Vermont legislature to annex them. The flattered lawmakers obliged, theoretically doubling the size of their little republic. George Washington tried to broker a settlement by which Congress would admit Vermont if it would cancel the annexations, and Vermont complied, only to find Washington had been more wishful than politic in judging the temper of the congressional delegates.

Grumbles now grew among Vermonters that they were under the thumb of an entrenched autocratic regime, with Allen its permanent militia commander, his brother Ira in charge of the treasury, and their frontman, Thomas Chittenden, the perpetual governor. The Allens, moreover, again approached Britain to revisit the possibilities of an alliance with the crown as an autonomous satellite, an unpopular idea that smacked of collusion.

The real breakthrough came on the New York side. Admitting the hopelessness of trying to coerce Vermont into submission, elements in the New York legislature, led by Alexander Hamilton, champion of the refurbished federal government and spearhead of the drive to ratify the ingenious new Constitution undergirding it, overcame the pathologically obstructionist Governor Clinton. The United States needed highly solvent Vermont to help pay the federal government's bills and strengthen national security. And New York also needed Vermont as a good neighbor, with shared regional concerns, especially now that Virginia's progeny, Kentucky, was about to knock on Congress's door for admission as a new, slaveholding state. New York, furthermore, wanted its bustling port city to be designated the permanent capital of the United States, and a newly befriended Vermont was likely to cast its vote for that site over a more southerly one.

Prodded by Hamilton, the New York legislature finally withdrew its objections to statehood for Vermont—that meant, of course, the Wentworth Grants would at last be confirmed—and asked for $600,000 to compensate its losing title claimants. When Ira Allen and Governor Chittenden were caught sneaking through a private land deal that amounted to a theft of public property, the indomitable people of Vermont were ready for change. Their legislature sent the Allen clique packing, and with them any possible deal with Britain. In a final show of defiance, Vermont agreed to pay New York just $30,000 in tribute money.

In the first week of 1791, when Ethan Allen had been in his grave for more than a year, Congress admitted Vermont as the first new state. Three of the original states (Delaware, Georgia, and Rhode Island) had smaller populations than Vermont at the time of its admission, and four of them (Rhode Island, Delaware, New Jersey, and New Hampshire) were smaller in area than Vermont's 9,612 square miles. Only the last of the thirty-six states that have been admitted subsequently—the Hawaiian Islands, 168 years later—has less land than Vermont, diminutive but still noted for its nonconformist spirit.

THE WESTWARD MOVEMENT OF SETTLERS and speculators in the immediate postwar years was concentrated in the two-pronged penetration of the Virginia and North Carolina backlands beyond the Appalachians.

Virginia, having ceded its immense Old Northwest Territory to the nation and also set aside millions of acres for the use of the state's war veterans with bounty warrants, had sacrificed a great deal of potential revenue from the sale of its public lands. Now it was eager to sell what land remained below the Ohio and west to the Mississippi before it, too, got swallowed up. North Carolina, decidedly less patriotic, chose to sell off the public lands in its western sector before ceding the region to Congress. In both states the buying was frenetic, often gluttonous, and skewed by the preferential access to capital and inventory that financiers and politicians enjoyed—advantages that incited the unabashed conduct of squatters, who had no such recourse. The process was not fair, but it greatly accelerated the new nation's spread.

Because Virginia as the biggest state had issued the most land warrants, they were abundantly available at depreciated prices for speculators who knew where and how to get hold of them. Their purchasers included many a well-born son of the Tidewater plantation country who wanted to erect his own manorial home on the south bank of the Ohio. In Richmond, state assemblymen were busily helping themselves to disputed titles to Indian lands in the west country, and their partners and collaborators, Philadelphia speculators prominent among them, were able to accumulate holdings by the thousands of acres. In Virginia's lush Kentucky bluegrass country, beyond the mountains and oversight of state officials, county surveyors reigned supreme, marketing land allotments behind closed doors and accumulating sizable holdings of their own. Thomas Mitchell, for example, official surveyor for Fayette County, gathered up 300,000 acres of choice real estate for himself.

The more land that was bought up and settled in the western counties, the less eager the old Tidewater oligarchs were to pay for governing and protecting it. When the Virginia legislature chose to levy a tax of one shilling per twenty acres on estates of 1,400 acres or larger in the growing Kentucky countries to help cover the state's expenses for the westward expansion, the outlying residents were no happier than the commercial interests of Massachusetts had been when Britain imposed the Stamp Act two decades earlier. Such targeted taxation was among the grievances registered and sent to Richmond after the first convention of Kentucky residents was called in 1784 and separatist sentiment began to coalesce. Large and small landholders alike among the delegates recognized the evils of unbridled land-grabbing in the remote regions of the state and directed a noble plea to the Virginia authorities, holding it to be "subversive of the Fundamental Principles of free Republican Government to allow any individual or Company or Body of Men to possess such large tracts of Country in their own right as may at a future date give them undue influence, and it opens the door to speculation by which innumerable evils may ensue to the less opolent [*sic*] of the inhabitants." It was a telling indictment of the shameless land-hogging that Virginia officials ignored in their immediate backyard, even though they had fought hard to make sure, before agreeing to cede their Old Northwest Territory to Congress, that precisely the same sort of misconduct would not occur in that distant region.

By 1785, Virginia's political leadership, mindful of New York's useless intransigence toward Vermont, was preparing to cut Kentucky loose as a self-governing entity. But it was not a wholly charitable process. The parent state insisted, for one thing, on controlling the disposal of public lands within its offspring's borders after the separation. And in Kentucky, commercial interests were uneasy about their ability as a freestanding frontier society to deal with Spanish authorities who continued to deny American farmers transit of their produce all the way down the Mississippi. Political leadership was in turmoil in the roiling new region, Indian wars were an ongoing distraction, and the separatist movement found—or, rather, was seized upon by—its boldest advocate, James Wilkinson, an unscrupulous son of Maryland's landed gentry who had come to Louisville in his mid-twenties to make his mark. In no time he was conspiring to wrench Kentucky away not only from Virginia but from the rest of the United States as well.

A congenital schemer, Wilkinson spent much of his career serving ignobly as an American army officer, starting as a teenager in the Revolutionary War, during which he managed to betray every commander under whom he served, including Benedict Arnold, Horatio Gates, and George Washington. He nevertheless squirmed free of punishment, got appointed secretary of Congress's Board of War, and rose to the post of clothier-general, the Continental Army's chief supply officer, until he was fired for rendering defective accounts. After the war Wilkinson married into the Biddle family, lions of the Philadelphia business and social set, farmed for a time in idyllic Bucks County, and sat impatiently in the Pennsylvania legislature. Armed with letters of introduction from powerful friends, Wilkinson turned up in Louisville, where he passed himself off as a war hero and merchant prince with widespread connections. Soon he befriended the county surveyor, and with inside tips, a little cash, and a lot of ill-deserved credit, began speculating in land options for thousands of acres. Before long he was badmouthing Kentucky's foremost political and military leader, George Rogers Clark, a genuine war hero, and searching for his own opportunity to shine in the public arena. Wilkinson drew up and widely circulated several pamphlets demanding Kentucky's prompt separation from Virginia and, in a masterpiece of duplicity, appealed to his wartime acquaintance Arthur St. Clair, then president of Congress, urging ratification of Jay's treaty with Gardoqui, which would have damaged Kentucky's commercial future by denying American vessels access to the lower Mississippi for a generation. Once the public learned that Congress was giving serious attention to Jay's unfortunate proposal, Wilkinson loudly denounced it to Kentuckians as a prime reason for separating themselves from the ruling elite back east who were so indifferent to their fate.

Wilkinson was just warming up. Casting himself as the George Washington of a new western republic, he clandestinely approached Spanish officials in St. Louis and traveled to New Orleans to apply his con-artistry to Esteban Miró, governor of Louisiana province. If Miró would help finance his efforts and grant him and his business associates exclusive trading rights, exempting them from the ban on American navigation of the Mississippi, Wilkinson would use his position as a prominent separatist leader to pull Kentucky—as soon as Virginia freed it—away from the United States and turn it into an independent state allied with Spain. The Spaniard, mistaking treachery for statesmanship, went along. Over the next several years, Wilkinson played a dangerous game as a clandestine agent for Spain, taking a secret oath of loyalty to King Carlos, trying to wheedle a 600,000-acre grant for himself across the Mississippi in Spanish Louisiana, and applying for a lifetime pension. All the while he pushed for Kentucky's detachment from Virginia, talked up amity with Spain, and enjoyed the profits from tobacco and salt exports Miró was permitting him to make.

The winds of politics, though, were beyond one man's control. Virginia awaited the creation of the new Constitution before it would give up Kentucky for good, and Congress delayed taking up Kentucky's application for statehood until New York withdrew its opposition to Vermont's counterbalancing admission; meanwhile, Wilkinson strung along the Spanish governor in New Orleans. If one wished to be generous in assessing Wilkinson's role in the liberation of Kentucky and its admission to the Union in 1792 as the fifteenth state, the first west of the Appalachians, one could argue that his methods may have been perverse but his purpose was patriotic—to hoodwink Spain for his own advantage while urging Congress to ensure Kentucky's loyalty to the United States by speedily accepting it as an independent state.

Nothing about his subsequent career, however, confirms such Machiavellian subtlety. Wilkinson's political star waned, his land deals ended in financial failure, and he had to resume his career as a soldier in apparent good standing. Remarkably, the worse he performed, the higher he rose in rank, eventually replacing Anthony Wayne (after betraying him) as the top army commander during Washington's presidency and governor of territorial Louisiana under Jefferson. He gained these distinctions despite charges against him for, among other infractions, selling the army tainted food, shipping private merchandise through the military, conspiring with Aaron Burr to invade Mexico (and then denouncing Burr before Congress), and abysmally failing in his command during the American assault on Montreal in the War of 1812. When last heard from, Wilkinson was trying to hornswoggle the Mexican government into granting him a goodly chunk of Texas.

The settlement of North Carolina's western sector, which was about half as populous as Kentucky, and its creation as the state of Tennessee were far more unruly than the process in Virginia, which was by and large agreeable to its own dismemberment.

Like its northern neighbor, the Tarheel State began wholesaling its public lands as soon as the independence and boundaries of the United States were confirmed in Paris in 1783. Speculators swarmed to buy up the sweet woodlands, their avarice little tempered by the stubborn presence of the Cherokee and Creek nations, far more numerous and formidable than the Indian remnant in Kentucky. The native tribes, after all, had sided with the British during the Revolutionary War, and so they were officially enemies by the land grabbers' logic, and any treaty rights they had won earlier could be ignored in good conscience. To prevent the amassing of enormous individual holdings, North Carolina directed its county officials to distribute land warrants in 1,000-acre parcels and ration them to no more than five warrants per customer. While well intended, the directive was evaded with a wink and a nod, and many warrants wound up under title to fictitious buyers. William Blount, one of the most notorious North Carolina speculators and a leader of the western separatist movement that ensued, held forged warrants for 100,000 acres. In April 1784, after a discount sell-off of its western lands had allowed the state to reduce its war debts—and with little left to deed over to Congress for that same purpose—North Carolina ceded its 42,000 square miles of backlands to the United States.

The new settlers in the western sector grew panicky that the cession would leave them with no government at all—bad enough that North Carolina had neglected its frontier folk all along—and no protection against Indian attacks. Over the summer the westerners organized themselves, and by December, aware of the new federal land ordinance allowing residents in territories belonging to the United States (as theirs now did) to form their own governments with the future intention of joining the Union as states, declared themselves the "separate and distinct" state of Franklin and began to function as Vermont was doing, but without the need to defy their parent state. Or so they thought. What the Franklinites did not know, because of poor communications, was that some weeks earlier, the North Carolina legislature had had second thoughts about the cession of its western lands. Fearing that unless their state spanned from the Atlantic to the Mississippi, it would be economically and politically castrated and a pygmy half the size of Virginia, the lawmakers withdrew the gift to Congress. This placed Franklin in the same category as Vermont, demanding freedom from a mother who would not untie the cranky child from her apron strings.

Miffed that they had not been consulted about North Carolina's repeal of its western cession, the Franklinites resolved to operate as a sovereign entity and elected as their governor a fiery backwoodsman and longtime Indian fighter, John Sevier, who had distinguished himself as a militiaman battling the British during the war. Gifted at politics, land accumulation, and Indian-killing, Sevier went on a rampage against the Cherokees, ostensibly to reduce the threat they posed to his region, but the bitter frontier war he waged only intensified it. Among his atrocities was the massacre of Chero- kee chiefs who had joined his camp under a banner of truce for a peace pow- wow. His mad-dog distemper was precisely the sort of wanton conduct against the native Americans that the go-slow advocates of western settle- ment had hoped to avoid. Sevier now tried to enlist Georgia officials to join his troops in waylaying Indians (and to obtain a large spread of Georgia soil for himself in the bargain).

Faced with such a scourge leading the secessionist region, North Car- olina's governor, Evan Shelby, wisely opted to avoid military confrontation and hoped to win back Franklin's residents with patience and promises of a government more attuned to their needs. After three years of strained coexistence that somehow managed never to break into open civil war, Shelby gained a weapon that brought an end to the insurgency—the new Constitution of the United States. Its Article IV, Section 3 asserted that no new state "shall be formed or erected within the jurisdiction of any other State . . . without the consent of the Legislatures of the States concerned as well as of the Congress." Franklin's 1788 gubernatorial election was can- celed, and its secession became a dead letter.

The next year, though, North Carolina had third thoughts about ceding its western half to the newly energized and reorganized federal government. Having milked the backlands for revenue—by then only 300,000 acres of public lands remained unsold or unreserved for veterans' warrants in a region of more than 27 million acres—North Carolina now moved to reduce its share of the national debt, which was apportioned among the states according to their land mass. The legislature finally turned over to Congress the western half of the state, comprising now-defunct Franklin and the still farther western frontier lands backing up to the Mississippi whose residents had never thrown in with the secessionist Franklinites. Congress quickly accepted and designated the ceded area as the Southwest Territory, adminis- tered by a new law patterned after the Northwest Ordinance, which the new Congress had adopted from the old—with one glaring exception. Slavery was not prohibited in the Southwest Territory as it was north of the Ohio.

It took five years until the 450-mile-wide territory attained the required population of 60,000 free souls to qualify for statehood. Joining the Union in 1796 as the sixteenth state and named for the river that follows a serpen- tine north-south course through its western end, Tennessee elected John Sevier its first governor, a post he would occupy for eleven years. His prin- cipal antagonist for the remainder of his enduring career in public office was the younger, rising star of Tennessee politics, Andrew Jackson, with whom Sevier shared at least one passion: bloodthirsty contempt for Indians.

PROMINENT AMONG EUROPEAN STATESMEN who were certain the infant American republic would soon dissolve amid irreconcilable rancor and revert to its colonial status was Frederick the Great. Not altogether unhappily, the Prussian autocrat foresaw the ragamuffin states abandoning their fragile union one by one and abjectly beseeching their mother country's forgiveness.

After four postwar years of struggle and discord under a rickety confederation, the United States did indeed seem headed for just such a fate. But in checking their tangle-footed stumble toward oblivion, the American people cast aside their lingering phobias, animosities, and distrust of authoritarianism to design a new central government that would secure their national existence—and did so just in time. For Europe was about to be convulsed by the French Revolution and the long, bloody ordeal that followed, so the United States could hardly have depended on succor from abroad to rescue it from the follies of swelling factionalism.

The new Constitution was a glorious contrivance because it confronted so many of the disjunctive shortcomings of the inert old federal compact. This splendid if complex mechanism was understandable, flexible, broad-gauged, and sufficiently powered to govern a dynamic people in an expansive setting. Without its adaptive utility, the nation's rapid advancement, for all its natural blessings, might never have been realized. There was nothing sacred about its directive text or of literary note (its Preamble excepted). Its purpose, while ennobling, was wholly pragmatic, and by that standard it has not been surpassed since by any government.

The genius of the Constitution was the careful balance it struck between facilitating the processes of government and safeguarding the vulnerabilities of the citizenry. It equipped those chosen to operate the federated republic with enough tools, revenues, and authority to accomplish what the individual states had been unable to manage so long as all of them persisted in going their separate ways. The most pressing among these needs were providing adequately for mutual security and internal improvements to link the widely separated regions, a national marketplace with uniform rules of commerce and a single currency backed by the collective commonwealth, and a consistent foreign trade policy to meet the exigencies of global competition. At the same time, the ingenious new federal machinery came with a built-in set of checks, balances, trip wires, and alarm bells to prevent the whole engine from going haywire and causing widespread injury. It alleviated the fears of the small states that their rights and interests would be trampled on by the large states—and the large states' fear they would be held hostage by the obstructionist tactics of the small ones. Similarly, the Constitution spoke to the countervailing concerns of majorities and minorities, of creditors and debtors, of law enforcers and accused violators. It provided a broad array of individual rights, installed brakes on tyrannical tendencies of the central government, and imposed prohibitions on the states to protect all their citizens against impairment of their liberties. And it worked, if not flawlessly, from the beginning.

What the Constitution failed to address were the flagrantly inhumane practices of slavery and genocide that the American people imposed upon the non-Europeans in their midst. The slaveholding southerners who attended the constitutional convention made no bones about the expediency of their subjugation of the blacks. "We cannot do without our slaves," said one of the delegates from South Carolina. This was a bald-faced confession by the large planters that they could not have controlled so much of—and profited so richly from—the American soil if they had been forced to do the work themselves. Slave owner James Madison, who played so constructive a part in fashioning the set of compromises at the core of the Constitution, tried to explain, though he could not justify, its failure to face the slavery issue by contending that "great as the evil is, a dismemberment of the union would be worse." Slaves, at least, were valued as a living capital investment because the land they tended made their owners richer—and thus able and eager now to spread their vicious labor system westward. Native Americans, cited only once in passing by the Constitution, were simply a useless obstacle to be driven off and, eventually, removed. The framers of the hallowed federal charter produced a deeply racist document not for what it said or did to the nonwhites within the nation's boundaries but for what it conveniently—and not at all benignly—neglected to do.

The new government needed time to get its operations up and running, but some of its virtues were soon evident. The federal union assumed responsibility for all its own as well as the states' war debts, giving the national economy breathing room. Democracy was expanded and energized by the creation of a bicameral legislature with proportional representation in the lower house of Congress. And the first chief of state was a universally admired hero and peerless patriot who braced America's self-regard and fulfilled his duties judiciously.

Midway through George Washington's second term, the young country entered into three treaties that, taken together, announced to the world its growing strength and confidence and signaled a formidable future presence on the world stage. But Jay's Treaty, as the unpopular 1794 agreement with Great Britain was commonly called, as if to place the onus on its negotiator, also demonstrated that the United States was still a toddler when it tried to stand up to Europe's foremost military and commercial power.

Throughout the decade following the Paris peace accord, the British, still smarting from their monumental loss, exacted a degree of retribution by the curbs they imposed on American shipping. By their lights, there was nothing unsporting about treating the United States like any other maritime nation, now that it had rudely rejected the advantages of membership in the empire. By closing the British West Indies and other colonial harbors to American ships and laying heavy duties on American goods unloaded on Britain's shores, the crown and Parliament were not so much punishing their runaway colonies as dealing with them for what they were—a new commercial rival. Still, Britain's want of generosity toward the United States was unmistakable in view of the greatly favorable balance of trade it previously enjoyed with the American colonies. Some 90 percent of American imports came from Britain—its goods were better made, cheaper, more suitable, and more familiar than all competitors—which made America, consuming 15 percent of all Britain's exports, its leading global customer by the 1790s. America's economic dependency in the lopsided relationship was further evidenced by shipping fully half of its exports to Britain, where stiff duties enriched the crown's coffers.

The United States, eager to test its new musculature, puzzled over how to retaliate against Britain's oppressive trade policy. Applying reciprocally harsh rules was a theoretical option, but it would have been a senseless one. In the real world of supply and demand, America needed British goods far more than the other way around—at least until domestic manufacturing, ardently advocated by Secretary of the Treasury Alexander Hamilton, could take root in the mostly agrarian republic. As the nation struggled to escape the postwar economic doldrums, its trade handicap vis-à-vis Great Britain suddenly turned from oppressive to unbearable. The crisis was prompted by the outbreak of war between revolutionary France and royalist Britain, the latter fearing that the ferment of radical republicanism across the Channel would soon engulf Europe's stable social order. Accordingly, King George and his ministers resolved to bring Britain's naval supremacy to bear as heavily as possible on France and all who would encourage its roaring convulsions under the banner of universal brotherhood. In May of 1793 Orders in Council were dispatched by the crown to British naval commanders, directing them to intercept any merchant ships bound for France, whether from neutral nations or belligerents, and to confiscate their cargoes, including food as well as contraband supplies for making war. In short, Britain hoped to starve France into docility. No nation's vessels were as much affected by the British blockade as those of the United States, France's leading—and, due to the long trade route, most vulnerable—supplier. Within the first year of Britain's ironclad policy of interdiction, and in total disregard of President Washington's avowal of neutrality in the European conflict, the British navy seized some 250 American ships and their cargoes, treated their crews harshly, and impressed hundreds of sailors as deserters.

With comparable cheek, Britain was continuing to humiliate the United States by holding on to its forts on American soil in the Old Northwest Territory and on Lake Champlain. The British bases served, beyond protecting the Canadian border, to supply and provoke the Indians—with guns, liquor, and promises of protecting their endangered hunting grounds—in a campaign of terrorism against would-be American settlers, so that, as noted earlier, the region might still be harvested by native trappers and British fur traders. Britain justified its failure to abide by the 1783 Paris treaty, mandating the timely shutdown of British bases and withdrawal of enemy troops from U.S. territory, by arguing—not without cause—that the American states had lagged or been brazenly defiant in heeding the peace treaty's directive to Congress to urge the states' legislatures and courts to facilitate British creditors' recovery of their prewar debts and to compensate Loyalists for their confiscated property.

The boldest defiance of Congress's polite request to meet these expectations was carried out by the two biggest debtor states, Virginia and Maryland, whose planters were in heavy hock to London merchants. During the long war, as an expedient for claiming good-faith settlement of the debts and thus eliminating interest charges, the legislatures of the two states allowed debts to British creditors to be certified as discharged by payment in American paper currency, which dwindled to less than 10 percent of face value when exchanged for hard British currency; in the postwar period the evasive practice was not corrected. Nor was forgiveness soon forthcoming toward the Loyalists. In 1784, for example, New York disenfranchised Tory sympathizers who had in any way assisted Britain during the war or taken refuge out of state. By the late 1780s, however, the fires of rampant patriotism had been banked, some Loyalist properties were being returned, discriminatory laws set aside, and debts repaid, so Britain's firm grip on its lakefront forts could no longer be justified—or tolerated.

News arrived early in 1794 that convinced the American government it now had to check Britain's provocative policies if the United States was to hold up its head as a sovereign power. In the Old Northwest Territory, British troops were sent to occupy an old fort near modern-day Toledo at the western end of Lake Erie in order to discourage strikes against the Indians in the region by American expeditionary forces under General Anthony Wayne. In February, the ranking British official in Canada, Governor-General Guy Carleton, a skilled administrator and unregenerate hater of the United States, had told the seven Indian nations of Canada that aggressive conduct by American soldiers and settlers had invalidated the national boundaries drawn by the 1783 peace treaty; that he fully expected war would be resumed against the United States within the year; that, "if so, a new [boundary] Line must be drawn by the [native] Warriors," and that any Americans, their houses, and improvements on the Canadian side would be fair game for the braves; and that "[w]hat belongs to the Indians will of course be confirmed and secured to them." The British fleet, meanwhile, captured Martinique, a vital French trading post in the Caribbean, seized fifty American vessels anchored there, took their cargoes as war booty, imprisoned and mistreated their captains and crewmen, and put them on trial in portable kangaroo courts for aiding the enemy.

Congress and George Washington were being bullied beyond the point of forbearance. Representative James Madison spoke for the country when he said it was tired of being "kicked, cuffed, and plundered all over the ocean." But without a navy to fend off the British at sea or more than a token army to dismantle the British forts in the west, the United States could protest only by imposing a thirty-day embargo on all trade with its abusers and pressing London to address American grievances with a new treaty. Already warring with France, the British ministry sensed it was making an unnecessary enemy of America and agreed to receive Washington's envoy. The one chosen, taking reluctant leave after five years from his august but thus far undemanding position as Chief Justice of the United States, was John Jay, ideally suited for the delicate task. Jay ranked near the pinnacle of American statesmenship, and although his sterling reputation had been tarnished by dubious treatymaking with Spain eight years earlier, he was still well and widely enough respected to have been considered a likely successor to Washington if he had not chosen to serve a second term.

Viewed as a formidable adversary at the Paris peace table a dozen years before, Jay was greeted in London almost as warmly as Franklin had been in Paris during his extended wartime sojourn there. Jay's rooms at the Royal Hotel on Pall Mall, the most luxurious in the capital, were flooded with invitations to dinners, theater parties, and country weekends with the highest and mightiest of the realm, including H.R.H. George III, no longer apoplectic over the loss of America, and Lord Shelburne, who displayed his rare book collection at Bowood to his erstwhile collaborator at peacemaking. When he got down to business, though, Jay found himself pitted against a diplomat who was rather like himself, gracious, cool, and humorless, with a rapier of a mind. At the age of thirty-five, William Wyndham Grenville, son of the instigator of the disastrous Stamp Act, was in the third of his ten years as foreign minister in the cabinet headed by his first cousin, William Pitt the Younger. An expert on international commerce, as Jay was not, Grenville recognized the importance to the empire of the American trade. But he was far more concerned about the impact a French victory might have on Britain's global standing and, as a leader of the war party, favored unleashing the full might of the royal navy, however offensive to the United States.

Their exchanges were never less than cordial, but it was evident from the first that Grenville had all the weapons, military and economic. Jay, representing a government just five years old and without potent military capability, had only geography on his side. The American pressed his strongest case, Britain's illegal maintenance of the western forts, and parried the usual excuse that the American states had not met their treaty obligation to deal with the prewar debts and the Loyalists' confiscated property. Congress had in fact honored its treaty obligation to press the states to act, but as Jay and his colleagues in Paris had argued at the time, Congress could do no more than exercise moral suasion. At any rate, there had been some progress in both areas, however slow, and one could as well argue that Britain's continuing military presence on American soil justified the states' reluctance to press their citizens on the debts and Loyalists. Jay insisted the British withdrawal, long past due, had to be completed within one year. Knowing that the Pitt ministry was hardly likely to restore the free access to British harbors that American ships had enjoyed in colonial days, Jay pushed for the opening of the most important outlet for farm produce from the United States—the British West Indies. He also asked for a modification of the duties Britain was reaping from American imports, for a halt to interdiction of American shipping, for compensation for cargoes that British warships had already stolen from neutral American vessels, and for reconfirmation— in view of Governor-General Carleton's incendiary address to the Indians— of the boundary line between the United States and Canada.

Grenville's reply a few weeks later was more cheering than Jay had hoped, though well short of satisfying American concerns. And the foreign minister introduced a troubling counterdemand. Yes, British troops would evacuate the eight western forts they were still holding, but their departure would require two years (translation: we'll go, but in our own sweet time).

Jay would be further pleased to learn the king had already ordered his over-seers of Canada to quit heating up the Indians to waylay American settlers. And yes, American ships *not exceeding seventy tons* would be allowed to bring certain cargoes to the British West Indies, but excluding key staples such as sugar and cotton, which would still have to travel in British bottoms. The offer, while a welcome breakthrough, meant that only small American cargo ships—Jay had asked for access by those in the 100-ton class—would be allowed, but not larger craft that could reload in the Indies, endure the often turbulent swells of the Atlantic, and proceed to Europe and Africa, thus competing with British carriers. Yes, Britain would agree to compensate American merchants for their seized cargoes, provided proper documentation of the losses was presented for scrutiny by the British courts, but nothing was said about an end to intercepting American ships and manhandling their crews. On trade, Grenville suggested that there be no future increases on duties or tonnage charges (per-craft entry taxes based on ship size) levied by either nation—which sounded like an equitable enough offer. Because of the American imbalance of trade, though, the provision meant the United States would lose the ability to boost charges on British imports as a retaliatory device, one of the few economic weapons at its disposal.

Most troubling, though, was Grenville's surprise request for the United States to roll back its northwest boundary, which had been fixed by the 1783 treaty in the belief that the Mississippi River's source lay in Canada. More recent geographical evidence had disclosed that the river actually rose about 200 miles south of the originally supposed location, placing the source 150 miles or so inside the United States (though the precise spot remained unknown). This awkward discovery meant not only that there was no agreed-upon northwest corner boundary but also that Britain's right under the 1783 treaty to navigate the full length of the river—a concession of Jay's instigation that presupposed the Mississippi was navigable up into Canada—had been rendered meaningless. The only solution, Grenville said, was to redraw the boundary in a way requiring the United States to surrender a large wedge of territory in the northeast corner of modern Minnesota, amounting to some 35,500 square miles and providing British Canada with frontage on the Mississippi to satisfy the treaty's intention.

Grenville must have known that Jay would sooner have consented to swim the English Channel buck naked than yield an inch of American soil, so he did not argue when Jay dismissed the very idea as well as the smaller territorial concession the foreign minister then proposed. But he did extract from Jay the right for British goods to travel over American land to reach the Mississippi and other inland waterways and for British traders to deal with Indian hunters on the American side of the border. And Grenville would yield nothing more when Jay asked for both sides to agree neither to use nor to arm the Indians in case of war, not to build or station warships on the Great Lakes, and to define more tightly the contraband that the British navy could remove from neutral ships. Frustrated by trying to wear down the intractable Grenville and the futility of delivering idle threats to the dispassionate minister, Jay wrote to Washington in August, "It is very important that peace be preserved at all costs"—a far cry from his posture at the Paris peace table. But the circumstances were quite different, and caution was now Jay's guiding principle.

In the end he had to yield to Britain's naval supremacy and concede in writing its right to intercept American cargoes—a renunciation of the precept that "free ships make free goods," which the small-navy nations of Europe had tried to establish, in vain. But Jay did win Grenville's agreement that Britain would reimburse American merchants for future cargo seizures and join in the creation of an Anglo-American appeals commission to consider claims for goods that had been seized earlier if satisfaction was not first obtained in the British courts. The United States had to agree, however, that British creditors whose prewar debts had not yet been repaid could take their cases directly to the same appeals commission without first having to submit them to the hard scrutiny of American courts. "Further concessions on the part of Great Britain cannot, in my opinion, be attained," Jay wrote to Washington before signing the treaty in November. "If this treaty fails [to be ratified by the Senate], I despair of another."

Back in America, Jay was assailed for his efforts as a weak, traitorous anglophile. His political foes, led by James Monroe and James Madison, declared the treaty unworthy of acceptance by an independent nation, and effigies of Jay were hauled about in dung carts from Boston to Charleston. The loudest howls were raised by those who had neither read nor understood the treaty, which in fairness was probably as accommodating as America could have hoped for. Jay and his nation were treated with courtesy and accorded the dignity of a fully sovereign state, though as the clearly weaker party, not with parity.

Perhaps most important, Jay had settled the unfinished business of the Paris treaty: America's boundaries were confirmed, northwest corner gap and all, and Britain's intrusive redcoats were to be gone at last. The Senate, voting on partisan lines, ratified Jay's Treaty, 20–10, the bare two-thirds minimum that the Constitution required, and President Washington sat on it for four months, hoping the furor it had stirred would die down before he signed it. The mercantile elite of New York, grateful that war had been averted and a degree of civility restored to commerce with Britain, toasted Jay at the Tontine Coffee House as the "Steady Firm Patriot." And the people of his state had elected him their governor while he had been in London, defending the nation's honor.

JAY'S TREATY ENCOURAGED, if not compelled, a pair of agreements a year later that lowered the two principal barriers to swift settlement of the Mississippi Valley.

Congress's 1785 Land Act, which had pledged that the United States would take no territory from the native Americans without their permission, paid lip service to an ideal entirely at odds with the white race's history since arriving in the New World. The new American government, for all its exalted rhetoric about liberty and natural rights, dealt disingenuously with the native peoples from the first, starting with a 1778 agreement with the Delaware nation, which was promised its own state if it sided with the insurgent colonists against their British overlords. The Delaware abided by the pact—indeed, they signed eighteen subsequent treaties hoping that the Americans would one day fulfill their promises—but they never got their homeland and wound up scattered from Oklahoma to Canada. The vocal Indian rights advocate Vine Deloria Jr., in the 1988 edition of his book *Custer Died for Your Sins,* calculated that the U.S. government had entered into more than 400 treaties with the native Americans, dealing with them as foreigners and requiring them to surrender their ancestral homelands for exile to a guaranteed refuge—invariably of poorer land and far away—and had violated every one of these agreements.

This pattern began to unfold shortly after the War for Independence, when there was a flurry of treatymaking with the natives. In some cases, their chieftains were held virtual prisoner until they agreed to sign away their territorial claims, such as the 1784 Treaty of Stanwix, by which the Iroquois nations gave up their lands beyond the Niagara River. In other cases, only partial agreement was reached, such as the 1785 Treaty of Fort McIntosh, under which the Chippewa, Delaware, Ottawa, and Wyandot peoples gave up their claims to much of modern-day Ohio, but the Shawnee and Miami peoples would not comply and so continued to menace white intruders. In still other cases, native leaders followed the Americans in welshing on their deals, as did the formidable half-Scots chief of the Creeks, Alexander McGillivray, who forged a sometime confederation of southern tribes, waged a fierce frontier war in hopes of forcing the United States to establish an Indian protectorate, and finally signed a treaty in New York in 1790 that British persuasion and Spanish money soon led him to renounce. But in virtually every case, American settlers kept encroaching on Indian lands, either innocently heedless of or consciously defying tribal treaty rights. After all, the Indians had aided the British in the war and were now under foreign influence to harass American settlers—two splendid reasons for escalating the antipathy toward the natives that had persisted throughout the American colonial experience. After the war Congress allocated the bulk of its non-debt-service expenditures to quell Indian warfare—and failed miserably.

Early in his first administration, President Washington hoped to pacify the natives by promoting good-faith dealings with them. Under the so-called Intercourse Act of 1790, the government outlawed all private land purchases from Indian nations and tried to end unscrupulous trading practices with them. But Washington, a warrior-statesman, concluded that only a show of military force would ultimately convince the natives to lay aside their weapons. He sent out several expeditions to humble the western tribes, but the American troops, too few and poorly trained, were the ones humbled, and soon Congress had to empower the states to draft militiamen to cope with the frontier war. The issue was finally settled in August 1794 when Revolutionary War stalwart Anthony Wayne, called from retirement to provide competent command, led American soldiers against 2,000 Delaware and Miami braves beside the Maumee River in northwest Ohio in the storm-tossed Battle of Fallen Timbers. Wayne gained a crushing triumph that ended twenty years of frontier warfare.

The peace was sealed the following year, by which time the British had agreed under Jay's Treaty to close down their forts and stop provoking the Indians in the Northwest Territory. Thus abandoned by their paleface allies and decisively beaten in battle by the Americans, all twelve Indian nations of the region signed the Treaty of Greenville, under which, for a payoff of $20,000 up front and an annuity of $9,500, they ceded roughly the eastern half of the Old Northwest to the United States, surrendered another sixteen enclaves to the west including the villages at Detroit and Chicago, and pledged, sadly, "We do now, and will henceforth, acknowledge the fifteen United States of America to be our father. . . . [W]e must call them brothers no more." To which General Wayne replied, "I now adopt you all, in the name of the fifteen great Fires of America, as their children, and you are so accordingly."

But they remained alienated children, despised by their adoptive parents, who imposed their jurisdiction because they could and not out of compassion. The Indians, at least, honored the treaty to the letter. Within five years—by 1800—with the Indian menace lifted, some 45,000 Americans had settled in Ohio. Just three years later, Ohio's population qualified it to become the seventeenth state, and by 1810, more than 220,000 people resided there.

A comparable sea change—perhaps river change would be the more apt image—occurred when Spain, fearful that Jay's Treaty would presage a joint Anglo-American military attack to lift its fragile hold on the lower Mississippi and Gulf Coast, decided it had better end its diplomatic stalemate with the United States before it was too late. The step was made easier by two painful realities. For several years French troops, under their revolutionary tricolor banner, had been thrashing Spanish soldiers who had been sent north across the Pyrenees to discipline them, and now their Iberian homeland was threatened by France's army. Spain's Louisiana and Florida colonies, moreover, with their administrative nexus at New Orleans, had become an albatross with a 1,500-mile wingspan.

In accepting transfer of the western side of the Mississippi basin in 1763 from France, which saw no further point in trying to sustain a colonial presence in North America after the loss of Canada, Spain had never really expected to turn the province of Louisiana into a profitable venture. Its primary purpose had always been to serve as a buffer against future incursions by the pushy Anglo-American settlers, who needed to be kept as far as possible from Spain's still productive silver mines in Mexico and the Andes. New Spain's output of precious metals represented fully half the value of all goods shipped by the Spanish empire and provided one-third of the royal income, sustaining the government and propping up an otherwise listless economy. But this extracted mineral wealth served, as it had for more than two centuries, to keep Spain a lotusland of indolence, where enterprise was sapped by chronic inflation, ruinously driving up the costs of labor and materials for domestic manufacturers so they could not compete with cheap foreign goods. Spain produced too little of sufficient quality or utility to thrive in world markets, particularly in the New World, which should have been its best customer, comparable to the role that Britain's American colonies played for their motherland's exports. Spanish-made blankets cost twice as much as British ones at Mississippi trading posts, the creoles of New Orleans preferred mellow French wines to Spain's raw *rojas,* and the Creeks lamented that the guns the Spaniards gave them for nothing to bedevil American frontiersmen in the Georgia and Tennessee backlands had a nasty habit of splitting after being fired a few times. To compensate for their own failings, the Spaniards insisted on levying high duties on foreign goods that dominated the Mississippi trade, but given the shortage of officials to enforce their tariffs, smuggling was commonplace and denied the Spanish government the revenues it needed to maintain its costly occupation. If it had taxed less and let Americans bring their flatboats down the river valley, the colony would likely have paid its way instead of needing to be subsidized by a shipload of silver that arrived in New Orleans each month from Veracruz.

A hopeful change of policy followed the ascension of King Carlos IV in 1788. To attract more people and stimulate commercial activity in Louisiana, the colonial office liberalized immigration rules, gave generous land grants as bounties to foreigners, non-Catholics included, and tried to buy the loyalty of disaffected American frontiersmen such as James Wilkinson. New Orleans began to thrive as it never had before. But neither Spain's colonial government nor its resident nationals shared in the rising prosperity. Aggressive British and American traders did most of the business; the Spaniards simply lacked the entrepreneurial skills and temperament to exploit and service their huge buffer colony, so they wound up footing the bill to maintain a modicum of civil order—and got next to nothing in return.

There was no improvement with the arrival of François-Luis Hector, Baron de Carondelet, who, as governor of Louisiana and the Floridas, spoke no English and was hopelessly out of tune and tempo with bustling New Orleans. Fancying himself a warrior who could stem the advance of American settlers in the Mississippi Valley by force of arms, usually borne by Indian hirelings, Carondelet conspired with secessionist zealots, who were only too glad to relieve him of Spanish silver. He would send glowing reports to Madrid of illusory victories, along with pleas for more money and soldiers to beat back the steady infiltration from the United States.

This folly was finally confronted in Madrid after the Conde de Floridablanca, Spain's retrogressive chief minister, was replaced in 1792 by the brash, twenty-five-year-old Manuel de Godoy, whose precocious advancement probably owed less to his undeniable intelligence than his prowess in the boudoir of Queen Maria Luisa. Godoy realistically assessed Spain's growing woes. France's armies were pounding Spanish troops and those from other European powers as they spread their revolutionary zeal into the Lowlands and were readying to surge into Spain itself. King George's realm did not offer much comfort, either. The British monarchy, momentarily allied with Spain against the wild-eyed Jacobins, had nearly come to blows with it a few years earlier over proprietorship of the northern Pacific coast of North America, where a Spanish explorer had sighted a harbor in Nootka Sound on the west coast of Vancouver Island in 1774 and claimed the region for King Carlos III. But British Captain James Cook had come ashore there three years later, and in 1788 Britain authorized a trading post at the site. In a display of misplaced pride of the sort that had propelled Spain into one military disaster after another for 200 years, Spanish ships seized the Nootka settlement and carried off its British citizens to prison in Mexico. When Britain threatened swift and painful reprisal, Spain backed off and conceded British rights to explore and settle along the northern Pacific coast. And now not only were British warships terrorizing global sea lanes in their war to isolate France but Britain's foreign minister was negotiating with the Americans, whose shipping had been the prime target of the royal navy's seizures. If the talks in London led to an Anglo-American alliance, Godoy reasoned, the two English-speaking nations might assail Spain's overextended position in the New World, perhaps even its silver treasure in Mexico.

War-weary and anxious to reduce expenditures yet unwilling to retract its imperial reach, Spain under Godoy now chose discretion over valor and moved to make amends with the two nations most threatening its territorial integrity—France, lest its soldiers overrun the Iberian Peninsula, and the United States, lest its settlers turn the whole Mississippi Valley into a de facto annex of the new republic.

In the late summer of 1794, Spain's Council of State approved Godoy's initiative to reach an accord with America by finally acknowledging its boundaries as stated in the Paris peace treaty and permitting its cargo vessels to sail the lower stretch of the Mississippi from Natchez to the Gulf of Mexico. But so bumbling and conniving were Spain's envoys in Philadelphia that the offer to parley was not conveyed to the American government for the better part of a year. George Washington dispatched the urbane Thomas Pinckney, his ambassador at the Court of St. James's, to meet with Godoy. While it had served Spain's purposes fifteen years earlier to deal with the needy Americans' plenipotentiary, John Jay, as if he were a transmitter of the plague, the proverbial shoe was now on the other foot. In fact, Spain sought nothing more from the United States than assurances that its citizens would never violate His Catholic Majesty's empire.

Pinckney, whose family stood head and shoulders over most of South Carolina's low-country plantocracy, was no one to trifle with. He had been Oxford-educated, trained for the bar in London's Inner Temple, a soldier of valor in the southern campaign during the American Revolution, a former governor of his state, and its leading proponent of the new Constitution. Yet the negotiations with Godoy stretched on maddeningly and inexplicably. The reason became clear at the end of July when Pinckney learned that

Spain had broken faith with Britain—theirs had been a tentative romance at best—by making peace with its bellicose neighbor, republican France, now ruled by the five-man Directory, more moderate and acceptable than the radical Jacobins. By the Treaty of Basle, France agreed to withdraw its troops and end hostilities with Spain but insisted on a glittering trophy in recognition of its superior military strength—the return of the remaining portion of its former province, Louisiana, for example. France's reacquisition of the western Mississippi basin would signal a renewal of its national glory, now that its oblivious Bourbon dynasty and parasitic nobility had been violently purged. But Godoy, despite the dubious value of Louisiana, was not ready to hand it over and thereby kindle fresh French dreams of a New World empire next door to its own. Instead, Spain gave up its claim, dating from Columbus's first voyage, to Hispaniola, whose size (30,000 square miles) was surpassed only by Cuba, Spain's adjacent Caribbean bastion, among the West Indies. Then known as Santo Domingo, the loosely held colony had long been pirates' prey and its western side had been colonized by French sugar planters, who grew rich on slave labor.

The treaty with France, forfeiting the fruitless, anti-republican pact with Britain, now let Godoy attend to Spain's second most pressing adversary and make peace at last with the United States. Spain agreed to withdraw its troops forthwith from fortifications east of the Mississippi and north of the thirty-first parallel, ending all claims to that region. It further promised to restrain the Indians in Spanish territory from attacking nearby American settlers and ordered its warships to refrain from interfering with American cargo vessels in the arrogant British manner. More important still, Spain ended its objection to the free passage of American commerce down the full length of the Mississippi, thereby granting it access to world markets.

This vital concession, though, while assuaging western settlers who had long faulted the federal government for its puny response to Spain's blockage of the Mississippi lifeline, would matter little unless American vessels were free to off-load their cargoes in the port of New Orleans for sale and transfer to oceangoing ships. Without this "right of deposit," Pinckney told Godoy, the Spanish concession was "illusory, without utility and without effect." Godoy waved off the American envoy's concern with the vague assurance that some place would be found near the river's mouth for the exchange of merchandise. The answer did not satisfy Pinckney, but Godoy, as if peeved by the one-sidedness of the pact, would not yield. For nearly two months the negotiations languished.

Pinckney recognized, however, that Spain needed the treaty as much as America. For its own survival, the Spaniards had chosen to side with dangerously energized France even at the cost of alienating Britain, which, thanks to Jay's Treaty, was now on friendlier terms with the United States. If Spain refused to come to terms with America, Louisiana faced the distinct peril of attack from the sea by the British fleet and by land from freebooting Americans—with or without the sanction of Congress. Meeting this dual threat was beyond the resources and manpower Spain could continue to invest in its sprawling buffer province. Accordingly, on Saturday, October 24, 1795, Pinckney decided to call Godoy's bluff. The American envoy applied to the Spanish court for his passport and began packing his bags in earnest, ready to depart with the treaty unsigned.

Godoy folded the next day. A new clause was added to the pending pact, officially called the Treaty of San Lorenzo, that allowed American citizens "for the space of three years from this time to deposit their merchandize and effects in the Port of New Orleans, and to export them from thence without paying any other duty than a fair price for the hire of the stores." When the three years were up, the king of Spain could either renew the privilege so long as it had not proven inimical to the interests of his country or assign "an equivalent establishment" elsewhere on the banks of the Mississippi.

Congress unanimously ratified Pinckney's Treaty, and jubilation reigned, especially in the Mississippi and Ohio valleys, whose newly motivated farmers soon set about turning the American frontier into a land of abundance. With the departure of the last British and Spanish soldiers from United States soil, the boundaries of the nation finally seemed secure.

EVEN AS JAY'S TREATY and Wayne's victory at Fallen Timbers substantially eliminated the British and Indian menace in the Old Northwest, so Pinckney's settlement with Spain and new Indian treaties—spurred by fresh victories over the natives by southern militiamen—prompted an immediate rush to extend the settlement of the United States to the banks of the Mississippi below the Ohio. The confluence of ambition, avarice, and abusive political power that drove the swiftly expanding settlement of the American land was never more discernible than at the close of the eighteenth century in the Georgia backlands, comprising the modern states of Alabama and Mississippi. Known collectively as the Yazoo Grants, after the river that is a principal north-south conduit in the region before it empties into the Mississippi at Vicksburg, the episode illustrated both the venality and rewards of unbridled territoriality.

The highly manipulable legislature of Georgia, whose population was scarcely 100,000 at the time, decided early in 1795—on the eve of the pact with Spain to open the Mississippi and halt baiting the Indians—to sell off its western land claims before ceding them to the federal government, just as North Carolina had done. Given the uncertainties of the age, the remoteness of the terrain, and their need to raise funds to run the government, the Georgia lawmakers readily rationalized their sale of virtually all the state's western lands—nearly 35 million acres—in a single transaction with the Yazoo Land Company and three other speculative syndicates for a nominal 1.5 cents an acre. What could not be rationalized was that most of the investors benefiting from the bargain price were either New England speculators and out-of-state financiers and politicians, such as Philadelphia's Robert Morris and United States Supreme Court Justice James Wilson, or Georgia public officials, state and federal, including all but one member of the legislature, which voted unanimously for the virtual giveaway.

By that autumn, the gross nature of the scandal was evident, given the much enhanced value of the land thanks to Pinckney's Treaty. Produce from throughout the region, with its rich alluvial soil, was now within reach of world markets via the Mississippi as well as four smaller rivers that emptied into the Gulf through the narrow coastal band of Spanish West Florida. The Yazoo speculators were denounced as foes of agrarian republicanism, out to profiteer by reselling the land for a much higher price than the typical small farmer could afford—and probably in large tracts to already wealthy planters who would extend slavery westward. Georgia's outraged citizenry voted the corrupt lawmakers out of office, and the new reform legislature decided the next year to repeal the Yazoo Grants. The mostly well-heeled investors in the great land heist howled that the new legislature could not unilaterally abandon the contractual obligations entered into legally by the previous, repudiated legislature.

Because so many of the Yazoo plungers were non-Georgians, the issue qualified as interstate commerce, the province of the federal government, according to the new Constitution, so the grieving investors asked Congress and President John Adams to sort out the unholy mess. The easiest solution might have been for Congress to proclaim federal jurisdiction, even though Georgia had not yet ceded its claim to the backlands under its colonial charter. Then Congress and perhaps the federal courts could have tried to work out an equitable solution to the conflicting claims to the 54,000 square miles at stake. And there were many claims. The speculators hoped to be compensated for their lost investments. The Creek, Cherokee, Choctaw, and Chickasaw nations demanded that their treaty rights be honored. There were also settlers brandishing holdover grants from the French and Spanish crowns, squatters insisting on their preemptive rights, and the state of Georgia, which said the whole thing was strictly its own business and the United States should back off.

Anxious not to turn confusion into a conflagration, Congress bided its time until 5,000 residents of the Natchez district at the western edge of the Georgia backlands petitioned the federal government to create the Mississippi Territory in 1798. Only after Congress agreed not to recognize the Yazoo Grants—thus condoning the state legislature's right to rescind its predecessor's corrupt action—did Georgia consent, in 1802, to become the final state to cede its backlands to the nation. But Yazoo was still too hot a potato for easy handling. So intense was the pressure on Congress by the disputants and so convoluted were their conflicting claims that it took five years for the first newly federalized lands to be sold in the Mississippi Territory.

The Yazoo speculators may have been blatant in their cupidity (subtlety was rarely a necessity in the great American land-grab schemes), but in the end they were rewarded. The well-intended repeal of the original Yazoo sales by the reformist Georgia legislature was no match for the sanctity of contractual agreements, according to the United States Supreme Court's ultimate adjudication of the question in its landmark 1810 decision of *Fletcher v. Peck.* The Yazoo deal was binding, said the Justices, however strong the ensuing political sentiment to cancel it, and the investors were due compensation. Congress set aside $5 million—about ten times the total original purchase price (and worth some $800 million in early-twenty-first-century purchasing power)—for that purpose.

By 1800, two-thirds of the nation still lived within fifty miles of the Atlantic coast, but by then more than 7 percent of the 5.3 million Americans counted by the federal government's turn-of-the-century census had crossed the Appalachians and settled in the new frontier states of Kentucky and Tennessee and the Ohio and Mississippi territories. While barely 10,000 of them resided in the Georgia backlands, where the pending Yazoo imbroglio stunted new settlement, that infamous episode nonetheless emblemized the emphatically commercial impetus behind America's westward surge. The young republic may still have been largely wilderness, its sprawling limbs barely connected to its central body politic, yet most of that vast, raw emptiness was *owned* by somebody very soon after it became official territory of the new nation. Alexander Hamilton, probably the country's keenest student of its economic life, estimated that only one-sixteenth of America's land was occupied at the beginning of the nineteenth century, but title to the great bulk of it had been avidly bought up, optioned, stolen, or otherwise appropriated long in advance of its actually being needed for settlement.

Perhaps the simplest explanation of such territorial gluttony is that the burgeoning supply of capital for gainful investment had few more promising outlets in that day and age. Commercial activity was limited by a lack of credit facilities—there were hardly a dozen banks of any real size in the entire country, and they, along with the other machinery of capitalism, were generally mistrusted, especially by the powerful Virginia political oligarchy. "Banking establishments are more dangerous than standing armies," Jefferson once wrote. In that preindustrial age, moreover, there were few manufacturing ventures or other capital-intensive businesses to invest in, no stock exchange to serve as a marketplace for securities, and bonds issued by the now more financially secure federal government were in short supply. Indeed, the bulk of the nation's $80 million debt was held by foreign investors, and the states and their municipalities had not yet turned to debt funding to pay for large-scale public improvements. Only oceangoing commerce was a serious competitor to speculation in fertile American land, with its prospective abundance in harvests, as a magnet for capital investment. But international trade was proving highly risky as the Napoleonic wars began to wrack Europe and both British and French warships were regularly intercepting American merchant vessels.

Thus, the soil of the expansive new nation, as a fungible commodity, was in such heavy demand—even if mostly for future rather than immediate settlement—that, despite its already great size, vibrant America wanted to grow larger still. The territorial cravings of its incessantly go-getting people were transformed into a binding force that nourished an emergent nationalism, capable of overcoming regional and cultural distinctions. In the process, a strong, collective interest spread among land investors large and small, from stony New England to the sweet Cumberlands to the sweltering plantation country, all placing their bets on the prospective commonwealth of a much enlarged and far more populous nation.

For a perilous moment, though, they were forced to halt in their tracks and confront the possibility that the United States had already reached its farthest territorial extension. France, ignominiously expelled from North America in 1763, suddenly threatened to reappear as an imperial presence on that continental stage, this time as a military juggernaut commanded by an obsessive adventurer whose territorial hunger the world had not seen since Alexander the Great.

CHAPTER 6

For a nice little kingdom in Tuscany

1800–1803

I F THERE WERE LOGIC TO HISTORY, or we could look to ideological affinities as a reliable guide, the United States and France should have grown much closer during America's first ten years under its new Constitution, which coincided with the span between the overthrow of the French monarchy and the installation of a military dictatorship. The two republics struggled simultaneously to establish a just and secure social order while vowing devotion to universal liberty and equality. Yet instead of converging, their governments moved steadily apart and ended the century at sword point. Temperamental differences contributed to the schism, both peoples were quick to detect insults even when none was intended, and the resulting irritability threatened to erupt into all-out war.

The United States was probably more the victim than the cause of this nearly disastrous misunderstanding. Americans, while citizens of a much younger, less nuanced society, were longer acquainted with democratic ways and their requirement that partisanship yield eventually to compromise in order to advance the common welfare. The French insurrection, no simple expulsion of an oppressive foreign ruler but a fratricidal upheaval against a parasitic privileged class, was still more traumatic than the American War for Independence, as the adversaries proved less forgiving. French grievances were vented in alternating waves of liberation and repression that swept the overwrought masses toward the cauldron of anarchy. France became an inflamed society with a large and easily dislodged chip on its shoulder.

Most Americans, favorably disposed to the French people for backing their own earlier revolutionary cause, were sympathetic with the demolition of the self-indulgent Bourbon court at Versailles. But they looked on their sister republic with rising apprehension and then frank distaste as France passed into the clutches of Jacobin extremists driven by mindless vengeance and later into the looser but still sordid grip of the five-member Directory. To American eyes, French democracy seemed to regress from luminous to riotous to murderous to vacuous, and the Federalist administration of George Washington, partial to vested interests and wary of contagious civil unrest, acted to distance itself from France's orgy of promiscuous radicalism. Soon after the beheading of Louis XVI in 1793, the rabid, ironically dubbed Committee of Public Safety accelerated its purges, and the National Convention declared war on all of royalist, autocratic Europe, triggering widespread fear of chaos. Since most of the revenue to operate the United States government was derived from import duties—70 percent of the total from British goods—and the unfolding European conflict imperiled the free flow of all international commerce, Washington issued a proclamation of American neutrality and barred warships of the belligerent powers from putting in at American ports for supplies or repairs. This understandable effort to insulate the young republic from the ravages of what would prove to be a twenty-year European war failed to deter the British navy from waylaying American merchant ships and abusing their crews. Washington's insistence on neutrality also angered the French, who had supposed the United States, as a fellow republic and long-standing ally by treaty, would side with them in their crusade to free the masses everywhere from despots wearing crowns.

Things got worse with the arrival on American shores of revolutionary France's hardly diplomatic ambassador, "Citizen" Edmond Genet, who mocked Washington's profession of neutrality by conspiring to enlist vessels based in the United States to prey on British shipping and to organize an expeditionary force of soldiers of fortune to march on New Orleans and relieve Louisiana of its hated Spanish regime. The French did not take kindly to news of Genet's ouster as persona non grata and were still more resentful the following year of Jay's Treaty, which, though patently aimed at securing American shipping against British seizure and ridding United States territory of British garrisons hunkered in western forts, was perceived as hostile to France's interests. Under orders from the Directory, French ships began intercepting American merchant vessels, just as the British had done, and confiscating their cargoes—a clear violation of the 1778 Franco-American treaties of amity and commerce. When Washington recalled ardent Francophile James Monroe as the U.S. envoy to Paris for ineffectively defending Jay's Treaty against heated French outcries, France retaliated by refusing the credentials of Monroe's replacement, Charles Cotesworth Pinckney, and unilaterally severing diplomatic ties with America.

Elevation to the White House of Vice President John Adams, a confessed Francophobe who had served as the first U.S. ambassador to Britain, only made matters worse. Adams summoned Congress into special session and gave a fiery speech warning the French against treating the United States as "a degraded people, humiliated under a colonial spirit of fear." But France continued to bully American ships, and its militarism was growing; French troops were sweeping through the Lowlands now and into northern Italy. Adams prudently sent a high-ranking peace commission to Paris to try to correct the misunderstandings between the two nations and redraw their treaty ties. The Directory's adroit foreign minister, Charles-Maurice de Talleyrand-Périgord, was a political chameleon who had survived the Reign of Terror by taking refuge abroad. Talleyrand's price for access to the negotiating table in Paris, his aides told the American delegation, was an apology by President Adams for his intemperate speech, a loan to the financially beleaguered French government, and an under-the-table gratuity of about a quarter million dollars to be parceled among French officials, notably including Talleyrand, who was as self-indulgent in pursuing an aristocratic lifestyle as he was deft at statecraft. But by dabbling in this matter, labeled the XYZ Affair after the coded names the American commissioners gave to Talleyrand's henchmen, the foreign minister badly miscalculated. The United States became infuriated over being dealt precisely the sort of degrading treatment that Adams had warned against. The President retaliated by persuading Congress, which needed little goading, to fund a 10,000-man standing American army and construction of thirty-nine warships and, meanwhile, to order the pitiably tiny United States Navy to engage French vessels harassing American cargo carriers. In the undeclared naval war that ensued, more than eighty French ships were destroyed or disabled—a notable figure but well short of evening the score.

Having displayed his nation's moxie and naval skill yet recognizing it was heavily outgunned by Europe's seagoing powers, to the serious detriment of its transatlantic commerce, Adams split with the hawks in his own Federalist Party—a statesmanlike move that would cost him reelection—and accepted a French invitation to return to the peace table in Paris. This time, though, Talleyrand was under instructions from a new master, the conquering hero and lately designated First Consul of France, Napoleon Bonaparte, to come to terms with the United States. The thirty-one-year-old French ruler recognized that he had quite enough enemies to contend with in the Old World and that France could only benefit from renewed friendly ties with the growing New World power. In the United States he foresaw a rising maritime rival to its presently domineering mother country; America was unlikely to remain puny for long. In the waning months of the Adams administration, France joined the United States in signing the Convention of 1800, ending their sea war and reestablishing free and peaceable trade between them. Only itemized military equipment bound for enemy ports could be seized from the ships of either state by the other, and duties would be mutually levied on a most-favored-nation basis. A decade of hostility began to be reversed.

Almost as important, in hindsight, as what the 1800 treaty stated was what it omitted. It was a very limited agreement, and since the parties could not settle on how to address the cost of damages suffered during their naval conflict—particularly by American shippers—or what provisions of their 1778 military and diplomatic treaties ought to be renewed or modified, the two sides concluded that "the said [1778] treaties shall have no operation" pending future deliberations. Fair enough, perhaps, but the discarded earlier pacts had included one provision that ought not to have been sacrificed so readily by the American negotiators: France's unqualified renunciation of any future territorial rights or ambitions in North America.

If the voiding of this stricture was of concern to American leaders at the time, they did not say so. What concerned them was the need for a prompt end to French and American ships clashing with one another, thereby promoting only Britain's standing as global ruler of the waves. But by incontrovertible evidence, the subject of a renewed and substantial French presence in North America was very much on the minds of the First Consul of France and his foreign minister.

No SOONER HAD CHARLES GRAVIER, Comte de Vergennes, chief proponent of the 1778 treaty alliance with America, passed from the scene in the closing years of Louis XVI's reign than his successors in the foreign ministry began to speak aloud about someday reclaiming the old province of Louisiana—running from the Gulf of Mexico to Canada and from the Mississippi to the Rockies—as the core of a new French empire and a provider of food and timber for France's prosperous sugar islands in the Caribbean and the world trade beyond. It was hardly a nonsensical idea, considering that Spain had adopted policies that seemed designed to discourage the growth of Louisiana's population, agriculture, and commerce. As if to ensure that the colony would never amount to more than a buffer against possible future American or British assaults on their still productive silver mines in Mexico, the Spaniards had let Louisiana's lone sizable settlement, the port of New Orleans, deteriorate badly. Its shabby wooden houses lined streets full of holes, its bridges and levees were in disrepair, and its waterways were silted, stagnant, and putrid as its morals. What should have become a profitable center of commerce as the receiving depot for an enormous web of rivers linking the heartland of North America was instead being driven to ruin by hapless Spanish officials. Their laws were slackly enforced, their duties and fees for foreign shipping were exorbitant, customs inspectors helped themselves to a percentage of cargoes in transit, and the river pilots, whose services were essential to guide oceangoing vessels through the maze of delta channels, were famously negligent.

In French hands, though, as the would-be colonizers in Paris hypothesized, Louisiana could flourish with an infusion of efficiency, capital, and settlers who had become discontented in their homeland—in much the manner the British colonies had succeeded two centuries earlier. The pioneer French traders in North America, moreover, had got on well with the native peoples, far better than the British or Americans, and those harmonious relations could be readily renewed beyond the Mississippi. The reclaimed western portion of old Louisiana province would adjoin still heavily French-speaking Canada, which—who could say otherwise?—might eventually choose to reaffiliate with France. Such an eventuality, of course, would require some sort of sweeping, global accord with the British empire; perhaps in exchange, it would have to be granted a trade and colonizing monopoly in India and the rest of Asia, where Britain had long been running rings around French commercial efforts. Indeed, France was not doing at all well as a colonizer. Its only true success story was in the West Indies, where the sugar crop on Saint-Domingue and Guadeloupe was paying rich rewards to French investors.

Saint-Domingue, in particular, soon to play a fateful role in the expansion of the United States, was producing the kind of agricultural wealth that Spanish colonizers were too indolent and closed-minded to try to generate. Spanish planters had enjoyed some success colonizing the eastern side of the island they called Santo Domingo, but Spain's rulers had left the western side unprotected, allowing pirates to use it as a base for marauding in the Caribbean and French planters to settle, import African slaves in heavy numbers—as many as 30,000 a year—and grow enough sugar and coffee to supply the French demand and twice that amount for export to world markets. By the late 1780s, the Saint-Domingue commodities trade, carried in 700 shiploads a year, was valued at £11 million annually.

But the place was hardly a tropical paradise. At the onset of the French

Revolution, Saint-Domingue was one huge slave-labor camp, under a rigid caste system lorded over by 50,000 French planters and creole colonists. Beneath them were 50,000 mulattos who performed many of the administrative and commercial chores (and in some cases became planters in their own right), and half a million blacks, in the grip of a particularly brutal brand of enslavement. The French Revolution changed that. The mulattos petitioned the new republican government in Paris to lift the harsh colonial rule and sweetened their appeal by promising to contribute 20 percent of their possessions to the French state. Paris agreed, and the chain reaction that the decision set off on the island made the violence about to unfold back in France seem tame by comparison. The planters and creoles would not accept political parity with déclassé mulattos, and when civil war erupted, the long-suffering slave masses rose up with a vengeance as field hands hacked their masters to pieces with machetes. Panic enveloped the western side of the island, which the rampaging blacks now referred to by its native name of Haiti, and the rebellion there was soon out of control. Many of the French colonists fled for their lives—most to South Carolina and Louisiana—and the island's plantation economy lay in ashes.

A semblance of order was restored by the emergence of a daring native ex-slave and self-taught military leader in his early fifties, François Dominique Toussaint L'Ouverture, who assembled a well-disciplined cadre of 4,000 blacks, repulsed an invading Spanish force hoping to wrest control of the beleaguered colony, and found himself designated its military commander by the French republic. To calm the furies, the egalitarian-minded home government decreed an end to slavery, bringing a modicum of dignity to the black masses but hastening the impoverishment of the colonial economy. Toussaint, charismatic, wise, and stern, attracted a mass following, routed his rivals, and made himself the de facto ruler of all Haiti (the aboriginal Arawak Indian name for the island, meaning "land of high mountains"), even while paying lip service to French sovereignty over the territory. When Spain was obliged to surrender a colonial possession as part of the price for peace with France under the 1795 Treaty of Basle, it refused the French request for the return of Louisiana and instead gave up its nominal title to Santo Domingo. By then Toussaint held sway over the entire island.

Haiti, then, was a renegade state, and republican France controlled no colonies in the old imperial sense when the Directory appointed a foreign minister in 1797 who had captured Paris's attention by declaring that the way to end the national malaise and speed France's recovery of pride and prosperity was to establish a new, improved colonial system. Charles Talleyrand was an unlikely savior of the beleaguered republic; indeed, he had been fortunate to survive the Jacobin onslaught against the high aristocracy, into which he had been born. What perhaps made Talleyrand a survivor, again and again, was a childhood accident that left him lame for life and reviled as a misfit by his family. Like many a disfavored son of the nobility, he resigned himself to the priesthood, where his dubious piety and decidedly sensual habits did not prevent his appointment at age thirty-five as Bishop of Autun in the Loire district. A masterful diocesan politician and raconteur with a barbed tongue, he was chosen to serve as a church delegate to the States-General, the national assembly, in the closing years of the Bourbon regime. When the Revolution came, Talleyrand not only embraced it but became, for the time being, an ardent advocate of republicanism, co-authoring the "Declaration of the Rights of Man and Citizen," one of the sacred texts of the new democratic order. And he turned against the excesses of his church by helping the financially needy state confiscate ecclesiastic property and subordinate the clergy to civil authority—betrayals for which he was soon excommunicated. His talents earned Talleyrand important diplomatic missions to London, where he tried to convince the constitutional monarchy that it ought not to fear or oppose but rather befriend the new republic across the Channel. The execution of Louis XVI and the carnage wrought by the Committee of Public Safety rather undercut his position and left Talleyrand unwelcome in England and, as a defrocked cleric and unrepentant aristocrat, a promising candidate for the guillotine if he returned to godless France. He sailed to America with little to sustain him but his wits, charm, and letters of introduction from Lord Shelburne and the American ambassador to France, Gouverneur Morris, with whom he had shared a mistress.

Unlike Lafayette, another celebrated French aristocrat who went to the United States with high hopes, Talleyrand did not fall in love with the place. But it may be ventured that the twenty-five months he passed there helped form his impression of the fabulous wealth to be extracted from the immense and at times somewhat terrifying American landscape—and, as a result, his enthusiastic advocacy of renewed French colonization in the western part of the continent. His unbreakable hauteur left him disdainful of the vulgarities of American society, but Talleyrand admired its religious tolerance and openness to advancement and marveled, above all, at its unabashed materialism. In America, he wrote a friend, "everyone without exception is bent on making money. So money is the single universal cult; the amount one possesses is the measure of all distinctions." The best way to make money for someone in his circumstances, without capital but gifted with powers of persuasion, was as an agent for large real-estate speculators, earning commissions as a salesmen, particularly to fellow French émigrés. For all his manipulative aptitude and lifelong financial need to sustain hopelessly aristocratic tastes, Talleyrand was apparently an honest land dealer. He roamed from the Maine woods to Niagara Falls to the Ohio Valley, at times carefully skirting treacherous swamps or wielding an axe to chop a path through the forest in order to survey property he was delegated to peddle.

Eager to return to France at the earliest opportunity, Talleyrand carried home with him a fascination with the grandeur of the American wilderness—and what it could one day become. It was much on his mind when he was invited, as a newly elected (in absentia) member of the National Institute of Science and Art, to deliver several lectures that soon became the talk of Paris. The first, given in April 1797 and titled "Memorandum on Anglo-American Commercial Relations," was a sobering lesson on the profits of New World trade, in which France was sadly deficient, and made a strong impression on a large contingent from the French diplomatic corps who were in attendance. The follow-up lecture, corollary of the first, was entitled "Essay on the Advantages to Be Derived from Colonies Under Present Conditions." In it Talleyrand lamented the afflicted soul of his country and—as a tonic for its restless malcontents, the bankrupt, and those otherwise bereft—he prescribed a national colonial enterprise, "played out on landscapes equal to their dreams and desires." Mindful of the debacle of past French colonization, which he attributed to a "total lack of planning," Talleyrand urged a more ambitious program freed from state domination and licensed monopolies, a system "guaranteeing liberty and justice for all." Among likely sites for such a fresh overseas venture, he postulated, was Egypt, then the southernmost part of the Turks' Ottoman Empire, with a climate that made it ideal to replace the lost sugar and coffee plantations on Haiti. But also on his mind were any of several islands off the African coast and, of course, the large former French colony of Louisiana. Egypt was by far the closest to France, but it would have to be taken by force from the Muslims. African islands would presumably be easier pickings, but their climate might prove oppressive for transplanted Frenchmen. More alluring would be Louisiana, but Spain would have to be leaned on to give up that province, even wasted as it was.

The published version of the lectures was widely circulated—a copy found its way into the hands of General Bonaparte, then putting the Austrian occupiers of northern Italy to flight—and the Directory soon summoned Talleyrand to take charge of the foreign ministry. In that capacity, he naturally became acquainted with the forceful instrument of France's new expansionist impulse. In the course of their exchanges, Napoleon's imagination was arrested by Talleyrand's proposal that he lead his army up the Nile and turn its banks into one large colonial plantation. While that expedition was played out, the foreign minister brought his exquisite politesse and shameless guile to bear on the Spanish diplomatic corps in order to persuade King Carlos and his young first minister, Manuel de Godoy, to hand Louisiana back to France.

An up-from-the-ranks royal guardsman who seduced his way to power, the tough-minded Godoy had reluctantly concluded that hanging on to Louisiana just for defensive purposes was a losing exercise. By continuing to deny farmers in the American west use of the lower Mississippi to export their produce, Spain would succeed only in provoking an eventual war with the United States. Madrid could spare the governor of Louisiana and intendant at New Orleans scarcely 1,000 imperial soldiers, sprinkled among a dozen riverfront and Gulf Coast forts, and a small fleet of gunboats to patrol the colony's borders. These were hardly enough to put up even token resistance to land-hungry American invaders or to repulse a British task force out to avenge Spain's rupture of its two-year alliance with England in order to make peace with the French, threatening to overrun Castile. But Godoy was not ready in 1795 to give France the immense colony of Louisiana, despite all the headaches it was causing, as the price for curtailing its looming invasion of Spain; handing over its colonial title to Santo Domingo would be a large enough payoff. To hold back American settlers thirsting to cross the Mississippi, Godoy bowed to the inevitable. He accepted the borders of the United States as they had been established a dozen years earlier by the Paris peace treaty and granted American commercial vessels the right of deposit at New Orleans. But Spain's chief minister did not deceive himself about the enduring value of the arrangement. Hadn't the U.S. ambassador, Thomas Pinckney, in negotiating the 1795 Treaty of San Lorenzo, rejected Godoy's request for an American guarantee never to trammel on the territorial integrity of Spanish Louisiana? Did one require more telling evidence of America's future designs on the rolling plains beyond the Mississippi?

A year after coming to terms with France and the United States, Godoy had second thoughts about Louisiana. His civil and military authorities there, vowing to uphold the empire's honor, continued to clamor for more money and troops to keep the colony out of American hands. And despite Spain's having awarded American shippers the right of deposit at New Orleans, rampant smuggling seemed to be continuing unabated. To smuggle was cheaper and less obnoxious than to deal with extortionate Spanish customs agents, high docking and warehousing fees, picayune paperwork, cargo searches and theft, and other forms of harassment. So Godoy put out a feeler to the French diplomatic corps: Spain might be willing to hand over Louisiana to France if France would undertake—or force—Britain to return Gibraltar, that perennial canker in the Spanish underbelly, to King Carlos. As a territorial trade-off, Godoy's proposal seemed like a steal to the French envoy in Madrid, who signed on to the exchange. But the Directory failed to ratify the pact, realizing that France lacked both the military might and the diplomatic leverage to pressure the British into going along with the arrangement, especially since Spain had just abandoned its alliance with the Court of St. James's.

When Talleyrand took up France's pursuit of Louisiana the following year, he tried different tactics. First he contended that Spain should transfer title to the colony without expecting compensation, since once it was in France's hands, it would erect "a wall of brass [cannons] forever impenetrable to the combined efforts of England and America." Spain's relative position in the New World, moreover, would be strengthened if its neighbor and ally France reestablished a colonial presence in North America, thus adjusting the balance of power there between the English-speaking and non-English-speaking nations.

Such blandishments proved unavailing; Godoy knew he had a very large bargaining chip to dangle before the eyes of the now territorially acquisitive French. Thwarted for the moment, Talleyrand saw another possibility materializing as he approvingly watched Napoleon's army take control of the patchwork of duchies, principalities, papal states, and independent cities of northern Italy. Among them was the Duchy of Parma, whose ruler, Duke Luis, was the brother of Spain's Queen Maria Luisa, herself a native of Parma. The duchy had become a Bourbon family holding when Carlos IV's grandfather, Philip V, married into the Austrian Hapsburg dynasty, long in control of the region. But Duke Luis's subjects, like most under the Austrian yoke, were less than devoted to him—witness the welcome given Napoleon's conquering host, with an outpouring of food, horses, money, volunteer enlistees, and general ecstasy. Napoleon, valuing the duchy as a geographically strategic corridor, had secured Parma as a French protectorate but left Luis in place as its compliant head of state. Why not, Talleyrand's ministry proposed, assemble "an aggrandizement of territory" from the newly conquered states adjacent to Parma, designate the enlarged territory a kingdom, and place Duke Luis on its throne—or, better yet (since Napoleon loathed the duke), elevate his son, who was both nephew and son-in-law of Queen Maria Luisa, thus bringing new grandeur to the Spanish court—in exchange for Louisiana? The idea appealed to Spain's royal couple, but before any such swap could be formalized, France's revolutionary regime faced its terminal crisis.

During the five years the Directory had nominally presided over France, the country had been increasingly wracked by inflation, food shortages, idleness, conspiracies, political factionalism, blatant corruption, and such incivility that policy and personal disputes were more likely to be resolved by murder than by compromise. The country was desperate to end the chaos. Loath to find himself roughly discarded with the rest of the scandalous government, Talleyrand suffered no qualms over betraying the men who had elevated him to high office and helping bring down the Directory. That governing panel had been at best a pale remnant of republicanism, a political doctrine he had once embraced but now found a nuisance. What France badly needed now, Talleyrand concluded—and multitudes shared his submission to such a fate—was an enlightened and (if need be) ruthless autocrat, someone to end the political impasse, stifle the endless rancor, and impose domestic order and national purpose. Talleyrand saw but one candidate for the monumental task, only one widely admired figure untarnished by partisan intrigue, and the foreign minister had been courting Napoleon's favor since taking office and encouraging his feats of conquest. Now Talleyrand demonstrated his allegiance by helping engineer the coup d'état that placed the reins of power in the strongman's hands.

A CHILD OF THE LOW CORSICAN ARISTOCRACY, which put him at the opposite end of the blue-blood spectrum from Talleyrand, Napoleon Bonaparte had been educated exclusively at military academies, where he exhibited superior intellect, voracious reading habits, a serpent's tongue, and a solitary, driven character. As a young officer, he was zealous in the fulfillment of his assignments and made himself a master of artillery, which he grew adept at maneuvering at high speed for maximum utility. Apolitical when the Revolution broke out, he understood the necessity of pledging loyalty to republicanism. And in defending it mercilessly, the young officer rose like a fiery projectile across the military firmament. For turning cannonfire point-blank on a royalist mob gathered in the city square at Toulon and then demolishing its public buildings as an object lesson for all foes of the republic, he was made a general at twenty-five.

The taste of blood only excited his resolve, and Napoleon won fresh honors by slaughtering a civilian crowd protesting the policies of the recently installed Directory at its Paris headquarters near the Tuileries. This time, answering the rattle of occasional small-arms fire with his beloved cannons, he claimed 1,400 lives while ensuring the regime's survival. As a merciless defender of the state, he was promoted to major general, designated commander of the so-called army of the interior at twenty-six, and then sent off as head of the ad hoc army of Italy in a whirlwind two-year (1796–97) campaign. He defeated Austrian forces more numerous than his own in four straight battles, causing the Hapsburgs to yield hegemony over Italy's wealthiest area, and won—temporarily, at least—the hearts and minds of the liberated and long-oppressed locals, who were given republican governments with constitutions that Napoleon dictated. Indeed, the whole region, from Piedmont and Genoa across the Po Valley to Venice and southward halfway to Rome, as well as Switzerland, became a French protectorate. These conquests thrilled the Directory, struggling with anarchic conditions and flirting with imminent bankruptcy, not only because the victories distracted France from its woes and reawakened memories of its spent grandeur but also because Napoleon's army operated at a profit. The glittering loot that his soldiers systematically emptied out of great palazzos, state treasuries, and religious houses amply covered the costs of keeping the French forces in the field, and the considerable surplus was sent back to Paris to keep the government afloat.

The long Italian campaign, heralding a decade of nearly uninterrupted triumphs across the continent and beyond, revealed Napoleon's dread-inspiring gifts as a warrior and strategist. A serious student of military science, he was a tenacious gatherer of intelligence of many sorts, with a rare capacity to retain and process it. He read maps closely, used terrain to the advantage of his often outnumbered troops, knew how to divide his enemies' ranks and then, with the aid of efficient communication, move his own men with rapidity and strike when and where least expected. He saw to it that his soldiers were well armed, drilled, fed, and outfitted; their uniforms were designed to make their wearers appear larger and more formidable. And he kept their morale high by making promotions based on merit, not on birth, bribery, or bootlicking: he was a genuine democrat in that sense. He gave men of all ranks a material incentive as well by cutting them in on the plunder of war, even facilitating its shipment to their homes in France. He deepened his soldiers' loyalty by fraternizing with them while they were encamped and by displaying exemplary, though not reckless, courage on the battlefield. The iconic Man on Horseback, the little general had his mounts shot out from under him nineteen times (as close as anyone could keep track) and suffered several wounds, one of them the result of a bayoneting in his left thigh—an injury that never fully healed. Unsparing of himself, he was even more profligate in spending his soldiers' blood. In the course of his campaigns an estimated half a million French troops died. His dependence on speedy troop movement also made him a ferocious consumer of horseflesh. The animals, regularly ridden beyond normal endurance, were left to die where they dropped by the hundreds of thousands.

The better Napoleon served the Directory's purposes, the more leeway he was awarded abroad. He became a very loose cannon, indeed, hardly answerable to anyone in Paris, where his presence and prowess—as potential threats to civilian authority—were decidedly unwanted. Instead, the generalissimo was licensed, with Talleyrand prominent among the instigators, to fulfill the enduring dream of turning Egypt into a French sugar and cotton colony, then perhaps constructing a canal in the Sinai to the Red Sea. Such a feat would shave months off the sailing time to India and allow France to challenge Britain's dominance in the Asian trade.

In the late spring of 1798 Napoleon's expeditionary force, accompanied by an extraordinary entourage of scientists, historians, and artists (Jacques-Louis David, for one), swept across the Mediterranean, seized and sacked the stronghold of Malta en route, and parked the fleet off Alexandria, without interception by British warships. Barely pausing to get their land legs, the French force-marched up the Nile through terrible summer heat, sandstorms, and clouds of flies and encountered a waiting army of Mamluk Egyptians in the shadow of the pyramids. The defenders were no match for Napoleon's firepower and the ferocity of his cavalry; some 10,000 Egyptians were reportedly killed while the French, if their embedded corps of civilian onlookers is to be credited, lost only twenty-nine lives. The rout left Napoleon master of the former Land of the Pharaohs, where he proclaimed himself the defender of Islam, installed a suitably servile government to administer the Ottoman satrapy, and set to work stealing whatever riches, ancient or otherwise, his ships could haul back to France. All Paris sang his praises, gaped at the boatloads of exotica from the vanquished pre-Christian civilization, and spoke of their bantam warlord as Alexander reborn.

The party was cut short when Horatio Nelson's fleet caught up with the French vessels anchored off the Nile delta like so many sitting ducks and demolished them, leaving Napoleon's soldiers stranded in a strange land. Hoping to fight their way out of entrapment, they managed further brilliant victories over the Turks in the Holy Land but inevitably suffered from the British stranglehold on their supply line, the ravages of heat and disease, and the fury of local uprisings, some inspired by French atrocities.

After his first major battle defeat—at Acre, where the crusaders of yore had likewise failed to best the legions of Islam—Napoleon understood that his expedition was doomed. A skilled propagandist as well as a peerless warrior, he declared the Egyptian campaign a glorious victory, then abandoned the remnants of his army, and slipped back to Paris, where orchestrated acclaim awaited him. Home was the superhero who, like a providential force of nature, could end the political and economic disorder sundering France. In November 1799, at the age of thirty, Bonaparte was acclaimed chief of state with the title of First Consul, a historical reference to the republic of classical Rome. But aside from a few constitutional trappings, not much remained republican in Napoleonic France. The ten-year Revolution was over, and the consent of the governed was not asked by their savior in epaulets.

FOR A TERRORIST AND A WHOLESALE ROBBER—whatever more he was as well—Napoleon now proved to be almost as gifted at social reform as he was at waging war. Volatile, impatient, and egoistic on a titanic scale, he nonetheless moved with imagination, decisiveness, and hyperkinetic velocity to undo the malfeasance of the Directory and bind up the nation's hemorrhaging. His method was totalitarian, but his purpose was to rid French life of its residual feudalism and encrusted social privilege.

He demanded that careers in the civil and commercial fields, like those in the military, be open to all, with advancement by virtue of talent and perseverance. The legal code was modernized and standardized nationwide, and even within what amounted to a police state, the lawgiver ordered it to be applied equally to all citizens. Taxes were collected by professionals, not farmed out to locals who bid for the franchise. He staffed his ministries, bureaus, and departments with the best brains and most able administrators available, regardless of their past political affiliations. No one better typified the high level of intellect enlisted by the new order than one of the few ranking figures Napoleon chose to retain from the discredited Directory— Talleyrand, his avid patron and facilitator.

As Napoleon went about remaking France by his own lights, Talleyrand helped his master solidify France's spreading hegemony beyond its borders. The army had pushed the northeast frontier to the Rhine, and the French military presence and influence effectively dominated the small states of western Europe—Belgium, Holland, Switzerland, much of Italy—under protectorates acknowledged by a treaty with imperial Austria after Napoleon chased the Hapsburg troops out of Italy for a second time in 1800. East of the Rhine as well, France brokered a consolidation of the jigsawed petty German states and freestanding cities—there were fifty of the latter— many of whose rulers served at Napoleon's sufferance and vied for his favor. The foreign ministry also helped patch up the effects of the godless Revolution's quarrel with the papacy. In a concordat that would incidentally lead to Talleyrand's release from excommunication, Pope Pius VII acknowledged the legitimacy of post-monarchial France and the confiscation of church property in exchange for the reestablishment of Catholicism as the state religion and the Vatican's revived control of the clergy, though as civil servants paid by the state and ultimately under its thumb.

From central and eastern Europe the Prussians and Russians viewed this frenetic French activity with growing apprehension. Across the English Channel, Britain watched with ever heightening vigilance, its preeminent navy ready to hamper any new French initiatives it could from the sea. And next door over the Pyrenees, Spaniards viewed their energized neighbor and ally with mingled anxiety and pride; King Carlos was known to approve of the autocratic French ruler's commanding character and anti-republican policies. In view of Carlos's infatuation, Talleyrand now renewed his effort to separate Louisiana from imperial Spain.

The military debacle in Egypt may have dampened the foreign minister's yearning to rebuild France's colonial empire, but it did not extinguish it. Talleyrand's attention turned westward now, and with the benefit of his recent two-year stay in the United States he could play persuasive consultant to the First Consul as he scanned maps of North America, which was terra incognita for him. To succeed this time would require more coherent and muscular exertion than the nation had expended in creating the loose and ill-defined territory it had once called New France, that great arc of earth it claimed, running from the mouth of the St. Lawrence River to the Mississippi delta. It was too vast a stretch to control with a few French civilians and the same meager military resources and administrative machinery that Spain had invested in the region. The key to renewing the French presence in North America in a self-sustaining fashion without ruinous cost, as Napoleon saw it, was Haiti. If the black rebellion could be subdued and Toussaint, who was now fond of referring to himself as "the Napoleon of the Antilles," removed or persuaded to collaborate with French interests, the plantation economy could be restored in short order and serve as the profitable base for colonizing the North American mainland—that is, Louisiana—in the second phase of the undertaking. If Spain would agree to relinquish the province, France could use it to export food, timber, and other necessities from the Mississippi Valley in order to sustain Haiti's rebuilding process. Wealth generated in Haiti could, in turn, be invested in the wider settlement of Louisiana, and the yoked French colonies could carry on a lively commerce with the United States, Mexico, other Caribbean islands, and, of course, the rest of the world. The presence of French forces under Napoleon's driving direction and his top generals would protect the new colonial system against American or British challenges, likely to be mounted in reaction to France's resurrection as a North American power.

To bring this master plan to fruition but without disclosing it in advance, Talleyrand successfully executed treaties with the three other concerned nations. The first, discussed above, was the Convention of 1800, ending sea warfare with the United States and normalizing trade relations—and, by mutual agreement, to set aside the 1778 treaty, relieving France of its pledge not to seek or occupy territory in continental North America. The pact allowed the United States to breathe easier about the possibilities of engagement with ever more potent French forces under their superlative commander and audacious head of state. Just a few weeks after completing the new Franco-American treaty, Talleyrand directed his envoy in Madrid to proceed clandestinely with the retrocession of Louisiana, ceded to Spain thirty-seven years earlier.

Under the Treaty of San Ildefonso, reached at one of King Carlos's palaces in the mountains near Madrid and refined half a year later by the Convention of Aranjuez, Queen Maria Luisa's nephew/son-in-law Luis was to surrender sovereignty over his militarily useful (and lately inherited) Duchy of Parma, which would become a permanent French protectorate. In return, Luis was given the crown of the newly invented kingdom of Etruria, made up mostly of the Grand Duchy of Tuscany, the flower of Italy and seedbed of the Renaissance, and the contiguous principality of Piombino. The area of this instant kingdom was three times as large as Parma, and the forebears of its 1 million people included some of history's most illustrious artists, scientists, and philosophers as well as some of its most repellant scoundrels. Possession of this ripe plum as a new Bourbon holding, which included the cities of Florence, Siena, and Pisa, promised to bring fresh honor to the Spanish throne. To seal the bargain the French Republic pledged to seek the assent of the emperor of Austria "and that of other interested states so that His Highness the Infant Duke of Parma may be put into possession of the said territories without opposition." Translated from diplomatic double-talk, that meant Napoleon would place France's military might at the disposal of young King Luis in case any of the crowned heads of Europe acted by force of arms to challenge the legitimacy of his palpably synthetic state. As payment for this increment in territory and prestige, Spain contracted to hand over to France "six months after the entire execution of the above conditions . . . the province of Louisiana, with the same extent that it now has . . . and that it had when France [last] possessed it."

Talleyrand, the onetime American real-estate agent, had pulled off the biggest land deal in the history of the continent—of the world, actually— but it had not gone quite as ideally as he had hoped. His emissaries in Madrid had pressed Godoy to include both East and West Florida in the transaction, so that France could monopolize the Gulf's northern and eastern coastline through the deep-water harbors at Pensacola and Mobile and thus monitor the expected upsurge in maritime traffic (and harvest revenues derived therefrom). But Godoy resisted, arguing that Florida, unlike Louisiana, had never been a French colony and, moreover, the peninsula's long coastline served, along with nearby Cuba, as the portal protecting the main trade route between Spain's sprawling New World empire and the outside world.

Spain's refusal to yield the Floridas likely prompted Talleyrand's calculated response to Godoy's request that France agree, as a condition of the retrocession, never to sell or give Louisiana to a third party but to return it to Spain in the event the French, for whatever reason, ever wished to abandon the problematic colony. Plainly the Spaniards did not want to awaken one morning to find American or British soldiers and settlers licensed to press against the long frontiers of New Spain and New Mexico—a betrayal of the prime rationale for handing over Louisiana to Napoleon. That Godoy and his king were more willing to trust the newly militant and territorially ambitious French to be their New World neighbors was likely due to their shared Catholicism and a phobic suspicion of Protestant Britain and the land-hungry United States. At any rate, Talleyrand sent word to King Carlos and his councilors that Spain should have no fear and that France had no motive in reacquiring Louisiana beyond the satisfaction of regaining its former colony for the benefit and use of the French people—and by doing so in a vigorous and vigilant manner would serve Spain's defensive needs as well.

This fulsome reassurance was likely made in earnest, considering that Talleyrand was an ardent champion of renewed French colonization. But the French avowal of intent to retain title to Louisiana was not spelled out in the text of the Treaty of San Ildefonso or its supplementary agreement. Whether this omission was an innocent oversight, or had been intended simply to give France maximum maneuverability in light of future events, or signaled some darker purpose on Talleyrand's part, has never been clarified. All that is known is that Godoy did not convince his king to make the whole transaction contingent upon a French guarantee in writing of Spain's right of return in case France ever elected to dispose of Louisiana. Instead, Carlos took Talleyrand—and through him, Napoleon—at his word. Or perhaps, to be more charitable to the king, he dreaded what France might do if he had insisted on the right of return of Louisiana.

Because both parties to the retrocession of Louisiana had ample reason to fear that news of their arrangement might prompt Britain or the United States (or both in concert) to make a preemptive strike at New Orleans on the ground that French ownership of so huge a swath of North America would profoundly alter the geopolitics of the continent, Talleyrand and Godoy agreed that the Treaty of San Ildefonso should remain a state secret until the French were ready to take possession of the colony. A date could not be fixed in advance since Napoleon's armies were in need of reinforcement before any New World deployment could be undertaken—not to mention the still more critical necessity to expand and improve French naval forces. Accordingly, the treaty said France should take over "according to its convenience," assuming that it had previously fulfilled its part of the bargain.

Why did Spain agree to what, in modern eyes, would appear to have been a grossly unfair swap of territory? Why did it exchange an immense inland expanse of virgin soil in the heart of North America, much of it verdant, well watered, and accessible by a series of far-reaching rivers, with luminous potential to sustain population growth and a resulting accrual of wealth, for a small state—Tuscany was about 3 percent as large as Louisiana—in northern Italy?

However artfully the exchange can be, and was, rationalized, the retrocession of Louisiana was a painful admission of the failure of Spain's colonial policy in North America. It also testified to the larger failure of King Carlos III's relatively (for Spain) innovative efforts to revive his closed society's arrested economic development and to reverse its decline among the leading powers of Europe. With that acknowledgment in mind, the agreement struck at San Ildefonso made perfect sense for Spain. In giving back Louisiana, it was losing nothing it had paid for in the first place and was enticing its larger, richer, better-armed neighbor to take over the administration and defense of an unmanageably vast, costly, and underpopulated colony, good for nothing but farming, never Spain's forte. And for ridding itself of this bothersome wilderness, with scarcely 40,000 white residents and 25,000 blacks, mostly indentured, and one broken-down port city of louche repute, Spain's royal family would gain a new kingdom in one of the most charming and picturesque settings on earth, with a celebrated history, cultural distinction, and a population of a million, highly taxable residents. It seemed a better arrangement than hanging on to Louisiana, a boundless emptiness, until someone, probably the rowdy Americans, made off with it.

With France's once and future North American empire now a reclamation project in waiting, Talleyrand accelerated diplomatic efforts to end hostilities with Napoleon's European rivals, so that the would-be conqueror might have a free hand when he launched his ambitious colonial enterprise across the Atlantic. Most resolute of the nations determined to stymie the designs of radicalized, expansionist France was Great Britain, whose navy and merchant fleet constantly shadowed Napoleon's dreams of empire. The British, though, had become weary after a decade of combat against what it viewed as runaway French regimes: Britain's standard of living had suffered, its government was more fractured than usual, and so the ministry was receptive to peace feelers from Paris. It was time for an armistice—almost any interlude would do—in their age-old confrontation with France. Under the Treaty of Amiens, reached early in October 1801, Napoleon agreed to an honorable withdrawal of his tattered army marooned in Egypt, which was to be returned to Turkish rule; to retire from several lately occupied Neapolitan states, and to allow Portugal, which had been under joint Spanish and French domination for years, to enjoy independence again. Britain, in return, promised to give up some of its recent prizes of war, among them Trinidad, Minorca, and Malta, which its fleet had rescued from France's recent seizure after Napoleon had proceeded to ravage Egypt.

Thus, an edgy sort of stasis prevailed for the moment in Europe. Having worked out a new modus vivendi with the United States, Austria, Spain, Britain, and the Pope via Talleyrand's good offices, Napoleon devoted himself to refining the domestic changes he had mandated and strengthening both his civilian and military operations. His reforms had made it easier for his lurking state gendarmerie to stifle social unrest. The currency had been stabilized, tax evasion was no longer the national pastime, public finances were placed under far stricter scrutiny, government jobs and military commissions were not for sale as had been the custom, and universal male suffrage had been declared even if it was an empty entitlement under a system in which echelons of legislators served only as a claque for their supreme leader's wishes. By early 1802 the Man on Horseback sat poised before a prospering, stabilized, and united nation, the dominant cultural and military force in Europe, disdainful of its caste-ridden neighbors and promising to bring an enlightened if authoritarian new social order to the continent. That year his gratefully obedient countrymen made him First Consul for life.

Within weeks of settling final peace terms with Britain, Napoleon placed his brother-in-law, the highly regarded Charles Leclerc, in charge of a major expeditionary force that was to begin executing the new French colonizing venture across the Atlantic. Its first move was to hammer Toussaint L'Ouverture and his black brothers into submission, retake Haiti with as little cost as possible, and impose slavery anew in order to resurrect the once-booming plantation economy. As soon as the pacification of Haiti had progressed sufficiently, France and Spain would disclose the terms of their agreement at San Ildefonso, and Leclerc would send a portion of his forces to take control of New Orleans, a largely French-speaking community that was expected to greet the new owners of Louisiana with open arms. The operation would be carried out with the speed and efficiency characteristic of Napoleon's armies, and well before any American soldiers or British warships could stop them. And, at any rate, on what grounds could the French occupiers be challenged by Britain or the United States? Louisiana would belong to France now, signed, sealed, and delivered over by Spain. Soon reinforcements would flow into New Orleans unimpeded, and French soldiers and settlers would shortly fan out over the western half of the Mississippi Valley, up the churning Missouri, out along the Arkansas and Red rivers and the twin forks of the Platte, trading amicably with the native tribes and watching great herds of buffalo thunder by. Soon the settlement of New France would be under way, and all those rivers feeding the produce of the trans-Mississippi countryside down to New Orleans would make it the busiest port in the Western Hemisphere and one day the gatehouse for a fabulous flow of commerce between Europe, America, and—as some visionaries were projecting—the Orient after construction of a canal across the isthmus of Panama to link the two great oceans.

And, so long as Parisian chauvinists were dreaming, why should Louisiana's western boundary be fixed at the Rockies? The Spanish empire's northern perimeter was hopelessly overextended and indefensible, so why, over time, should its scattering of presidios and missions not give way to French settlers who braved the western mountains to reach the Pacific shores? *Vive la Nouvelle France!*

IT ALL MIGHT HAVE BEEN EASY to dismiss as a pipe dream if France had not lately given its soul to a power-intoxicated military genius still in his ascendancy. As it was, the only serious obstacles between him and the free-wheeling French colonization of the New World were a black former slave who fancied himself the heaven-sent emperor of Haiti and the newly elected third President of the United States, who came to the White House with the fierce conviction that he must be stingy about spending the power of his office. Neither man seemed a promising candidate to blunt the cutting force of France's saw-toothed field marshal. The black chieftain would die trying. The white President would succeed without a shot being fired and, ironically enough, in large part due to the heroic resistance of the Haitian blacks, whose race the American leader disdained.

Napoleon Bonaparte and Thomas Jefferson were polar opposites—physically, temperamentally, and philosophically. The Corsican was an autocrat and a war lover; he was short, dark-haired, moody, coarse, and impulsive, with a mind geared to the concrete and quantifiable. He wrote prosaically but could be a rousing orator when need be; his private speech was often tart and hortatory. And he dismissed republican democracy as an inconvenience because the wise state knew better than its people what was good for them. The American was a Virginia libertarian and a pacifist; he was tall, russet-haired, polished, and reflective, with an omnivorous mind equally at home pondering Newtonian physics or when it was best to plant the peas at Monticello or what ground cover to put down in his fallow fields (usually clover). He wrote artfully but spoke ineffectively in public, and his private conversation was typically low, confidential, and rambling. For him democracy was rooted in the soil, not the state, which he saw as a grave menace to the people's happiness.

The first President to take office in the brand-new White House, which stood in solitary elegance on a marshy field that was a sad setting for a national capital, Jefferson summarized his populist philosophy in the 1801 inaugural address. Calling his country "the world's best hope," he said Americans' well-being could be advanced by their government only if it was a wise and frugal one that "shall restrain them from injuring one another, which shall leave them otherwise free to regulate their own pursuits . . . and shall not take from the mouth of labor the bread it has earned. This is the sum of good government."

Consistent with this creed, Jefferson set to work with his highly able Secretary of the Treasury, Albert Gallatin, cutting to the bone the already lean budget of the federal government—the President set an example for frugality by forgoing a ceremonial coach and four to carry the head of state, traveling instead on foot or horseback—and canceling much of the military program that his predecessor had asked Congress to fund in the face of French belligerency. In view of the new agreement with France, Jefferson contended it made no sense for the United States to get into a naval arms race with Europe's larger, richer nations and that American ground forces could be maintained at lower cost and with greater logistical efficiency if the state militias would expand their efforts.

But the belt-tightening had scarcely begun when word reached the White House from Rufus King, the skilled U.S. ambassador to Britain, of rumors circulating in European capitals that Spain had secretly agreed to transfer Louisiana and the Floridas to France. From the clandestine nature of the arrangement, the President and his cabinet readily inferred that

France had in mind a far more ambitious plan to settle and develop the colony than any Spain had ever attempted. And backed by Napoleon's military might, such an undertaking could very well thwart any latent territorial hopes that America might be nursing west of the Mississippi.

Jefferson had long foreseen, and feared, Spain's abandonment of Louisiana. Writing a friend from Paris fifteen years earlier while serving as American ambassador, he cautioned, "We should take care not . . . to press too soon on the Spaniards. Those countries [lands west of the Mississippi] cannot be in better hands. My fear is that they are too feeble to hold them until our population can be sufficiently advanced to gain it from them piece by piece. The navigation of the Mississippi we must have."

While there was no immediate need to contemplate pushing the boundaries of the United States beyond those agreed to in the 1783 Paris peace treaty, Jefferson firmly believed America's orderly westward settlement depended on free commercial access for surplus harvests to world markets via the Mississippi. Such a view was by no means universal, especially among northeasterners, like John Jay, who that very year was reaching a peace accord with Spain that would have waived free American navigation of the river for another generation—a concession Congress refused to accept. The Americans' failure to prevail upon Spain to grant them full shipping rights on the Mississippi would inspire no fewer than five separate conspiracies by frustrated settlers and rascally freebooters between 1785 and 1796 aimed at breaking off sizable chunks of the western United States to form an independent confederation or a satellite state allied with the Spaniards across the river. Jefferson's 1786 letter from Paris was equally notable for revealing that the eventual trans-Mississippi expansion of the United States was very much in his thoughts long before he came to the presidency and that he supposed it far more likely to be realized—and at a much lower cost in blood—if the relatively harmless Spaniards temporarily maintained their scarecrow presence in the vast western Mississippi Valley.

Jefferson's political creed of maximum personal liberty and minimal government power had as its bedrock the widest possible ownership of the land, and the more land available to Americans, the better the prospects for their agrarian republic to prosper. Farming promoted individual responsibility and initiative, independence, and dedication to the prudently governed community, and every man had a natural right to enough land to make a livelihood from it for himself and his family. Jefferson had advanced this conviction for twenty-five years before it helped carry him to his nation's highest office. He had tried without success to persuade his fellow Virginians, when writing their state constitution, to ensure free farmland to any

resident of the commonwealth who could not afford to buy it. He had successfully drafted federal land ordinances to facilitate the sale of federally
owned public property in a fair fashion, not for the benefit of politically and
financially powerful insiders at giveaway prices. He had endorsed squatters'
rights and insisted that settlers in new territory ceded to the federal government have the same freedoms and protections as citizens of the established
states. Nothing better exemplified his enthusiasm for working republicanism than coaxing his fellow Virginians to reduce their sovereign borders and
allow settlers in Kentucky and above the Ohio in the Old Northwest section
of the state to govern themselves rather than become neglected wards of an
eastern landed oligarchy too far away to serve their needs.

The new Constitution, bringing the nation political and financial stablity,
had naturally accelerated western settlement. It also inevitably caused a
geographically based division of vested interests that gave birth to a new,
acrimonious party system: eastern Federalists, many anchored in the commercial community, favoring a strong central government, and dedicated to
defending their established social, economic, and political advantages, were
pitted against Jefferson's emerging Republicans, mostly farmers, large and
small, of the debtor class whose wealth was tied up in their land (and
slaves). As southern planters and poorer settlers moved the frontier west,
the political pendulum swung in that direction, and Jefferson's party quickly
mushroomed.

As Secretary of State in Washington's cabinet but disenchanted with its
prevailing Hamiltonian wing and its pro-business initiatives, Jefferson evidenced fresh interest in the prospects for an America that might one day
ford the Mississippi. Unofficially and with the connivance of the rambunctious French ambassador Edmond Genet, Jefferson arranged for the American Philosophical Society, of which he was a member, to sponsor a small
scientific expedition led by the well-regarded French botanist André Michaux, to travel as far up the Missouri River as possible, gauge the ruggedness of the Rockies, and perhaps even try to reach the incalculably distant
eastern shore of the Pacific Ocean. En route, the party was to record every
geographical detail and catalogue all the flora and fauna (including the
native peoples) it encountered—an invaluable fact-finding mission with
potentially great future consequences. Michaux unfortunately became so
distracted by his early findings that he never made it out of Kentucky, but
Jefferson's part in organizing the abortive trek foreshadowed by a decade
the celebrated expedition for the same purpose that as President he would
commission under his personal secretary, Meriwether Lewis. There was, in
short, a westward gleam in his eye as the master of Monticello weighed his
future political options.

What he saw was that as American settlers pressed ever closer to the Mississippi, Spain had been unable, or unwilling, to strengthen its position on the far shore. Louisiana remained an immense backwater colony, virtually empty of white settlers except in its southernmost sector and without any urban center except the underutilized port of New Orleans, off-limits to cargo from the United States. Even after the inexorable pressure by the steadily encroaching Americans forced Spain in 1795 to grant their flat-bottom barges the right of freight deposit at New Orleans, American farmers and shippers remained at the mercy of an officious foreign garrison, small in number, insufferable in manner, and tantalizingly vulnerable to seizure from abroad. More and more talk was heard among fiery westerners eager to rally their militias and march on New Orleans without waiting for federal authorization. And if such approval was sought and withheld, perhaps the aroused westerners would form a new sovereign entity composed of territory on both banks of the great river, which would be its most valuable asset.

Ambassador King's report to Jefferson from London, while wrong about the inclusion of the Floridas in the secret transfer of Louisiana to France, was correct in conveying Talleyrand's intention that the colony should become far more populous and commercially developed than it had been under Spain's languid custody. This was precisely what Jefferson had dreaded—that Spanish weakness might in the short run prove hurtful to America's expansionist hopes. His alarm was shared by the British, he learned from envoy King, who met in May 1801 with the crown's foreign secretary, Robert Jenkinton, Lord Hawkesbury, and heard expressions of unhappiness over the possibility of a French takeover of Louisiana—a defiant refutation, Hawkesbury said, of the outcome of the French and Indian War and the Treaty of 1763. And what was to stop Napoleon's troops, once bivouacked in New Orleans and surrounding Louisiana, from fanning out over the upper Mississippi Valley and threatening the Great Lakes region, Canada, and, for that matter, British mercantile mastery of the West Indies? When King let Hawkesbury know that, while content to let Spain hold on to Louisiana, his nation felt that the only acceptable country to take it off Spain's hands was the United States, the British foreign minister hinted broadly that his nation would support such a step. Their exchange fell short of a firm mutual commitment to fight Napoleon if he threatened to invade the Mississippi Valley, but the very possibility of a joint Anglo-American effort to repel a resurgent French presence on the North American mainland now became the sharpest arrow in Jefferson's slender quiver. It grew in importance when unwelcome word came from King in October that a French fleet carrying Leclerc's army was soon to sail for Haiti.

Neither the United States nor Great Britain could reasonably object to France's expedition to reclaim its richest colony, long in rebellion against colonial enslavement. Jefferson and his cabinet, moreover, could even rationalize that the return of firm white rule over what the French still called Saint-Domingue might actually benefit the United States. For one thing, it could reduce the piracy, much of it thought to be based on Haiti, that was feeding off the Caribbean maritime trade. Such a benefit would relieve the American government, which was already paying tribute money to fend off the Barbary buccaneers in Mediterranean waters. A restored plantation economy, moreover, might mean prosperity for America's western farmers, whose harvests could help feed Haiti's dense population. And the crushing of Haiti's slave rebellion would surely discourage any such notion from rooting in the minds of blacks in the nearby southern states. But Jefferson suspected that recapturing Haiti would take longer and prove bloodier than Napoleon was counting on in view of his soldiers' advantages in training and weaponry. Toussaint L'Ouverture, moreover, would be smart enough not to engage the French on open battlefields but to use the tangled landscape and oppressive climate to his advantage, even as George Washington had learned not to confront Britain's mightier armies but to keep harassing them into ineffectuality. Nor did Jefferson and Secretary of State Madison believe Napoleon had a fixed schedule for occupying Louisiana, even if he contemplated so bold a step.

While new to the presidency and determined not to overreact to news of the French menace, Jefferson knew the United States could not afford the luxury of waiting on events. Within the limited range of the federal executive branch's power as he strictly defined it, the President undertook three policy initiatives. The first was to strengthen the nation's defenses by putting its border garrisons, especially in the Mississippi Valley, on alert, encouraging new enlistments, supplying more firepower, speeding communications between the frontier and Washington, and urging state militias to be on standby status if emergency action was required. At the same time the administration initiated steps to hasten westward population growth, especially along the eastern side of the lower Mississippi Valley. Left empty, the border territory north and east of New Orleans might prove an irresistible lure to arriving French troops. Isolated American settlers in the frontier region might then feel abandoned by their distant federal government and grow more likely to defect to the French if they appeared in force. Accordingly, Jefferson pushed liberalized versions of his favorite land policies, including a lowered asking price for auctioned federal property, smaller and more affordable lot sizes, better credit terms spread over four years, and preemptive rights for squatters despite continuing opposition in Congress. More insidiously, the President urged territorial officials and others dealing with the Indians, especially in southerly regions, to encourage them to run up debts at government-regulated trading posts so that tribal chiefs most resistant to white settlers would be forced into selling their lands to federal purchasing agents. Such unkindness—some would say immorality—aside, the overriding purpose behind his hurry-up settlement program was summed up in a letter by Jefferson to onetime Virginian and Revolutionary stalwart Horatio Gates: "We shall have that country filled rapidly with yeomanry capable of defending it." A third presidential initiative was designed to deter Napoleon by diplomatic persuasion from pursuing an aggressive colonial program on the North American mainland. Jefferson decided to reopen official relations between the United States and France by dispatching a new American envoy to Paris, the first to serve there since the Directory refused Charles C. Pinckney's credentials five years earlier. The man he named was rather an odd choice for the challenging assignment.

Not that Robert R. Livingston lacked stature, which he possessed abundantly in more ways than one. A formidably tall, notably genial figure, Livingston was a man of superior intelligence, immense property holdings, and impeccable social and professional standing. But he had not been a very successful politician. Thanks to his great-grandfather, a singularly grasping English merchant who had settled near Albany and married into the Hudson Valley's Dutch patroon Van Rensselaer family, Livingston held title to some 200,000 acres, mostly in and near New York State's Dutchess County. After graduating from King's College (Columbia) a year behind his friend and future law partner, John Jay, Livingston joined the bar, grew active in the patriot cause, and served for ten years in the Continental Congress, part of the time as that body's first secretary for foreign affairs.

His connection with Jefferson while in Congress did not begin propitiously. Serving with him on the committee to draft the Declaration of Independence, Livingston parted company with the Virginian and did not support the Declaration, which he felt was premature. But once the war began, there was nothing halfhearted about his support of the American cause. As foreign secretary in 1782 and 1783, he had the temerity to wonder whether the eminent American peace commissioners had injudiciously snubbed France while negotiating the Paris treaty with Britain. He was a man willing to take a contrarian's position—a trait that likely hobbled his political advancement. His distinction as a lawyer and lofty social position had won him appointment in 1777 as Chancellor of New York, a title that he held for twenty-four years and made him the state's ranking jurist in matters of equity, with the power to issue remedies for grievances not involving criminal conduct. It was in this judicial capacity that Livingston had the honor in 1789—since the U.S. Supreme Court had yet to be appointed—to administer the first oath of office to an American President. But Livingston was not invited to join the Washington administration nor, to his disappointment, was he appointed to any federal post—an affront that helped drive him into Jefferson's political camp. As the Republican candidate for governor of New York in 1795, he lost to his formerly close friend, John Jay, and quit active politics, frustrated but hardly despondent. He was fifty-five when Jefferson asked him to go to Paris to try to tame Bonaparte.

The oddity of Livingston's selection arose from three handicaps: he had never been abroad, he spoke French poorly (though he could read it passably), and he was quite hard of hearing—something of a disadvantage in a calling where many exchanges took place in hushed tones and the overhead remark might have pregnant consequences. In contrast with the austerity that marked the White House during Jefferson's residence, Livingston traveled to France with pomp befitting the representative of the newly confident United States. He came with his wife, two daughters and their husbands, a staff of servants, an elegant carriage that had to be strapped to the quarterdeck during their ship's Atlantic crossing, and a small herd of livestock (sheep, pigs, chickens, a cow, and a calf) in case France ran out of them during his stay.

Livingston's initial assignment was to learn the details of the Louisiana retrocession and France's timetable for taking title—a top state secret, of course. Foreign minister Talleyrand, himself an aristocrat of matchless hauteur, relished toying with the novice American ambassador, whom he regarded, as he did all of Livingston's well-off countrymen, as nouveaux riches and hopelessly gauche. Talleyrand brushed aside Livingston's repeated inquiries with denials that Spain had signed over Louisiana to France—notwithstanding that the White House already had a copy of the executed Treaty of San Ildefonso. Many of the French minister's subtler blandishments were likely lost on the semi-deaf American, who, at any rate, had such confidence in his own unassailable social position that Talleyrand's snubs and evasions did not deter him.

THE STORMY WINTER WEATHER delayed the Atlantic crossing of the French fleet carrying Leclerc's army to reclaim Haiti, but news of its arrival in February 1802 drove up the anxiety level at the White House. The first reports said that between 15,000 and 20,000 invaders were already on the island and that a second wave of reinforcements was on the high seas. How long could Toussaint's defenders resist the best-trained and -equipped soldiers on earth? And how long would it be before those soldiers were diverted in strength to reclaim Louisiana as well?

No reassuring news had come from Livingston in Paris regarding the scale and timing of France's New World plans. The battle on Haiti was enough corroborative evidence, though, of the immediacy of the threat to the United States, and Jefferson decided his diplomatic approach needed a more urgent tone to win Napoleon's attention. Among the many highly placed French officials Jefferson had come to know during his years (1785–89) as American ambassador to Paris was the accomplished economist and diplomat in Vergennes's foreign service, Pierre S. Du Pont de Nemours. In the early years of the Revolution, Du Pont worked ably for the republican government, but when the Jacobins seized power, he went underground, emerging, as Talleyrand did, to work for the Directory—a discouraging experience that sent him off to America. When he learned that the quality of gunpowder manufactured in the United States was inferior and that an improved variety would both enhance the nation's security and earn him a nice profit, Du Pont and his son decided to build a factory for that purpose near Wilmington, Delaware. He was on his way to Paris to raise capital for his enterprise when Jefferson asked him to carry a verbal message to Napoleon and a new letter of instructions to Livingston. In the course of their interview the astute courier made a suggestion of historic importance.

The thrust of the message Jefferson wished Du Pont to deliver was that if Napoleon proceeded with his evident intention to occupy Louisiana, the act "will cost France, and not very long hence, a war which will annihilate her on the ocean"—not a very subtle way of suggesting that American officials had been discussing the matter with their British counterparts and were of one mind. At the same time and not wishing to sound too belligerent, Jefferson told Du Pont that it was his "sincere prayer" war could be avoided, and the best way was for the European powers to honor the present territorial arrangements in North America.

Du Pont was dubious that such words would register with France's young warlord, given the military weakness of the United States and Jefferson's transparent need to rely on the possible availability of the British navy as his nation's only credible threat to restrain French ambitions in Louisiana. Napoleon, moreover, had a paper in his pocket from the king of Spain officially deeding over the great North American colony. Instead of bravado, Du Pont proposed that Jefferson consider a less provocative strategy, one that came naturally to an economist. Rather than waving a wooden sword and telling Napoleon he would rue the day if he tried to colonize Louisiana—as he was well within his rights to do now—why not address the subject of gravest concern to the United States by offering to buy New Orleans from France, along with West Florida, the contiguous 160-mile-long strip of Gulf Coast immediately to its east? Such an acquisition would provide American farmers and plantation owners with urgently needed access to world markets for their produce, especially cotton, the burgeoning new staple of the lower South, by the Mississippi, without any further interference by foreign powers at New Orleans, and down the four smaller rivers that flowed through West Florida—the Alabama, Chattahoochee, Mobile, and Tombigbee—and emptied into the Gulf. Purchasing what it most prized, Du Pont pointed out, would surely cost the United States far less in the long run than going to war for it.

Jefferson promised to consider Du Pont's suggestion, but what he did not like about it was that it seemed to invite France to take over, unopposed, the entire western side of the Mississippi Valley, as if it were a matter of indifference to the United States. And it was not. For the time being, America had quite enough growing room east of the Mississippi, but its westward flow of settlement would likely change that before long—and when the time came, the French would certainly prove much harder to dislodge, whether by persuasion or duress, than the present loose Spanish grip on the territory. Thus, the President and Madison settled on incorporating Du Pont's idea into the new instructions they framed for Livingston, starting with a simple declarative: "The cession of Louisiana completely reverses all the political relations of the United States, and will form a new epoch in our political course." The main reason, the President's letter went on, was

> There is on the globe one single spot, the possessor of which is our natural and habitual enemy. It is New Orleans, through which the produce of three-eighths of our territory must pass to market, and from its fertility it will ere long yield more than half of our whole produce, and contain more than half of our inhabitants. France, placing herself in that door, assumes to us the attitude of defiance.

But then Jefferson glided neatly from foreign-held New Orleans as the prime source of American unhappiness to the far larger subject of all Louisiana. Because of its "feeble state," Spain could hold on to that vast colony "quietly for years . . . [and] it would be hardly felt by us" until a future accommodation could be worked out amicably. But in French possession, Louisiana was sure to become "a point of eternal friction with us"—the very argument Benjamin Franklin had brought up early in the 1782 negotiations to try to persuade Shelburne to yield all of Canada to the United States. Jefferson then blurred the issue still further by choosing not to distinguish between intolerable foreign ownership of New Orleans, located on the eastern (and mostly American) shore of the Mississippi, and foreign possession—be it Spain's or, after the retrocession, France's—of all the rest of Louisiana west of the great river, which nobody had ever said belonged to the United States by treaty, conquest, or natural right. "From the moment of French occupation of New Orleans," the President wrote, "we must marry ourselves to the British fleet and nation"—not a cheering expedient for a man who had fought British tyranny his entire political life.

Lest this courting of Britain be taken for a frank confession of total American military impotence, Jefferson added that the United States did not fear Napoleon's armies, whose theoretical strength was much greater than that of the American forces but would be much reduced in comparison when "exerted on our soil," as the British had discovered twenty years earlier. But since when was New Orleans or any part of Louisiana "our soil"? Without explicitly saying so, Jefferson was repeatedly implying to Livingston—and intended him to convey the same sentiment to Napoleon and Talleyrand—that Americans felt Louisiana was theirs, or should become so sooner or later. At any rate, the President went on, Livingston should point out what meager rewards France could expect from taking over Louisiana and how unnecessary it was to do so. In peacetime, American farmers and merchants could amply supply the needs of Haiti and other French holdings in the Caribbean, Jefferson contended—as if that were the only value France might derive from a colonial hinterland of nearly a million square miles—while in wartime, French shipping could be easily bottled up by the British fleet patrolling the mouth of the Mississippi. In short, the President was none too subtly insinuating that France had neither the will, skill, resources, nor motive to replicate in Louisiana the experience of Britain's American colonists. Napoleon, therefore, should give up the idea of owning Louisiana so that America could absorb it when ready. Short of that, the only compromise acceptable to the United States was for France to sell it New Orleans and West Florida (assuming the latter to be part of Louisiana, whose Spanish governor had administered it as a subdivision thereof).

Talleyrand, as a prime advocate of French colonization, gave the American arguments as conveyed by Livingston the polite brush-off. By June 1802, early reports from Haiti, where the resistance was fiercer than anticipated, were still encouraging enough for Napoleon to set in motion the next phase of his New World initiative. A second major task force of ships and troops was to be assembled for autumn departure, its mission to be given out as the reinforcement of the French troops pacifying Haiti, but in fact it would be devoted mainly to seizing New Orleans and planting the French tricolor firmly in the soil of Louisiana. Napoleon ordered plans to be drawn up for new fortifications at New Orleans and elsewhere on the Mississippi and, as a keen student of geography, asked for maps detailing the coastline from St. Augustine in East Florida all the way around the Gulf to the Mexican border—a sign that he was weighing a wide-scale attack to take control of the entire Gulf Coast north of Mexico if Spain persisted in not surrendering Florida to him.

Now in heat, Napoleon instructed his envoy in Madrid that the time had come for King Carlos to sign the order to his officials in Louisiana to yield the colony to their French counterparts, a formality the king and his ministers had been delaying for more than a year. Their excuse was that France had not yet fully honored its part of the bargain regarding the newly created kingdom of Etruria. French troops remained there in military control of Tuscany, leaving Luis, Queen Maria Luisa's nephew, merely a figurehead ruler. Nor had France succeeded, the Spanish court objected, in obtaining international diplomatic recognition of the new Bourbon kingdom. Such arguments were easily refuted. The French troops garrisoning Luis's domain were, arguably, on hand to fulfill France's pledge to repulse any foreign assault on the synthetic regime, and by the Treaty of San Ildefonso, France had promised only to seek "the assent of other interested states" for the creation of the new kingdom; Napoleon could hardly have been expected to impose it on the world. Accordingly, King Carlos was advised that further delaying tactics "will end with a thunderbolt." His ministers tried a final time for a formal commitment by France never to sell or transfer Louisiana to any other nation but Spain; they had to settle for Talleyrand's renewed promise that "France will never alienate it." In mid-October, King Carlos ordered Louisiana delivered to Napoleon.

The stage was all but set for France's occupation in force of New Orleans and its environs, with systematic colonization of the western Mississippi Valley in the offing, American unhappiness over the prospect notwithstanding. Napoleon had both the might and right to do so. But he had not been prepared for the ferocity of Haiti's defenders and the virulence of nature.

Using the hills and jungle for cover, Toussaint's forces waged a ceaseless guerrilla campaign against Leclerc's troops, who were untrained for tropical warfare and less than fully motivated to slaughter ex-slaves struggling for their freedom and against the reimposition of an oppressive colonial regime. Nor were the French immunized against the ravages of disease in that climate. Of the first 17,000 French troops sent ashore on Haiti, 5,000 were slain and a like number hospitalized for yellow fever. Reinforcements strengthened Leclerc's position, as did the use of psychological warfare to divide the Haitian leadership and turn Toussaint's ambitious underlings against him. Promised a prominent role in a postwar administration of the island, Toussaint was lured from cover in June for peace negotiations, then promptly betrayed, hustled onto a waiting prison ship, and carried off to France. Incarcerated in a cell high in the Jura Mountains, he died of exposure and malnutrition the following April. The treacherous treatment of Toussaint, far from cowing his soldiers, only stimulated their efforts, as did the disclosure that slavery would be reinstated when the combat ended. But it did not abate, nor did the yellow fever. In November, the disease claimed General Leclerc, grim testimony to the unfolding French disaster.

In Paris, Robert Livingston was not doing notably better than the French troops on Haiti. Talleyrand continued to give him the runaround even as preparations advanced for the occupation of Louisiana, and Napoleon was inaccessible except for short exchanges at occasional diplomatic receptions. Livingston bemoaned his difficulties in presenting the American case against French colonization to a government without a working legislature, whose ministers were powerless to formulate policies, and where, as he wrote, "[o]ne man is everything."

To spell out the American argument in detail to that one man, accomplished jurist Livingston composed what amounted to a fourteen-page legal brief that he titled "Is It Advantageous to France to Take Possession of Louisiana?" Twenty copies were distributed, with Talleyrand's approval, to top French officials, starting with Napoleon and including his brothers (and confidants), Joseph and Lucien Bonaparte, whose attention the American envoy had doggedly cultivated. As an economic risk, Livingston's paper argued, colonizing Louisiana was a miscalculation; the American market for French products throughout the Mississippi Valley would be minuscule. Westerners much preferred their harsh, homegrown whiskey to fine French wines, and other quality goods such as glassware and home furnishings making their way slowly and expensively upstream on the Mississippi could not compete with cheaper American goods being shipped down the Ohio. And why should France invest, as Spain would not, in the defense and administration of colossal Louisiana when it could apply its resources so much more usefully to consolidating its expanded hegemony in Europe and rebuilding its formerly prosperous holdings in the Caribbean? To proceed with colonizing Louisiana, moreover, was to ensure the constant harassment of British warships out to disrupt the new French mercantilism that could prosper only at Britain's expense. But if France stubbornly insisted on reclaiming Louisiana, it ought at least to heed the pleas of the Americans, who, as Livingston assured his readers, were "not a grasping people."

All the United States urgently needed at the moment, Livingston's paper emphasized, was New Orleans, "a small town built of wood" amid "barren sands and sunken marshes," with scarcely 7,000 permanent residents and little to recommend it beyond an exotic celebrity as a raunchy colonial outpost. Only an accident of history had caused New Orleans to be built on the eastern bank of the Mississippi: it was from that direction that French explorers and settlers first approached the site. In ceding or selling it to the United States, France could do itself a favor by then building a new port directly across the river at Fort Leon, on higher, drier, healthier, and more defensible ground, an altogether more suitable location. Beyond all that, Livingston's appeal asked, why should France "convert a natural and warm ally into a jealous and suspicious neighbor, and perhaps into . . . an open enemy?" This ultimate question, of course, collided with the American ambassador's claim that his countrymen were "not a grasping people"—if not, why should they be jealous and suspicious of their newly arriving French neighbors across the river? Indeed, the subtext of Livington's well-crafted brief, while useful in framing the practical aspects of the American case for the First Consul's steel-trap mind, was that France had no moral right to stand in the way of the future westward course of the United States, once it was ready to exceed the boundaries set for it twenty years earlier by the European powers.

Livingston was told the official French hierarchy had absorbed his memo—Joseph Bonaparte assured him Napoleon had read it carefully—and would think about it. But no further response was forthcoming. The amiable envoy was nothing if not persistent, even adopting unorthodox tactics that on at least one occasion flirted with the unsavory. Pointing out to Joseph Bonaparte that political power was ephemeral and that his brother might not always remain his country's hero, Livingston proposed that Napoleon transfer sovereignty of Louisiana to the United States, which in turn would assign ownership of it to the Bonapartes as a safe haven for the family and then buy back half of it for a tidy sum—$2 million was mentioned. It amounted to an attempted bribe of the absolute ruler of France. Joseph did not say no, but hearing no further from him, Livingston recognized his misstep—how could Thomas Jefferson, let alone Congress, approve such a transparent impropriety even if the First Consul had signaled interest in the byzantine arrangement?—and did not pursue it. But he did make a more modest and gracious effort to win Napoleon's favor by offering his sister Pauline—Mme Leclerc, who was said to be miserable in the tropical heat of Haiti while accompanying her husband during his campaign there—the summer use of Livingston's brother's townhouse in New York City (of which he was then the mayor) or of his own country estate. The gesture, if appreciated, was unavailing.

During the later frustrating months of 1802, Livingston tried to clarify whether West Florida, which the United States keenly wished to absorb, would belong to Spain or France once the retrocession of Louisiana was completed. Nobody, least of all Talleyrand, would tell him. On investigation Livingston learned why. The Treaty of San Ildefonso was ambiguous on the point. The text defined the territory of Louisiana as being of "the same extent that it now has in the hands of Spain and when France possessed it." But these were by no means identical. Livingston's research uncovered archival maps showing that when France was forced to give up Louisiana under the 1763 treaty ending the French and Indian War, it extended east along the Gulf for some 160 miles from the Mississippi to the Perdido River a little past Mobile, the border with Spanish Florida, and about 40 miles inland. As part of its spoils of victory, Britain then took over that stretch of the Gulf Coast, designating it West Florida, as well as the main Florida peninsula, which it called East Florida, and administered the two as separate colonies. But when Spain got the Floridas back twenty years later after capturing their key Gulf ports during the American War for Independence, East Florida was administered from the Spanish Caribbean base at Havana while West Florida was placed under the purview of the governor of Louisiana. That seemed to qualify West Florida as a subdivision of Louisiana and distinct from East Florida, which was indisputably excluded from the retrocession.

Partly because Livingston had let France know that Jefferson would accept, however unhappily, the retrocession of Louisiana so long as the United States was ceded or sold New Orleans *and* West Florida, Talleyrand's ministry also had a serious interest in the title question. The surest way to clear up the ambiguity would have been for Spain to surrender both Floridas to France, and so during the final months of the transfer discussions, the French foreign minister pressed Madrid to do so in exchange for the return of the Duchy of Parma to Luis's new kingdom of Etruria, increasing its area by about 25 percent.

While King Carlos and Godoy were considering the West Florida matter, Livingston was startled to be asked one day by Joseph Bonaparte which territory the United States might prefer to own, Louisiana or the Floridas. Livingston said his nation had no particular desire to own territory west of the Mississippi. But so long as the question had come up—and the Bonapartes understood that America's priority was New Orleans and West Florida—the creative ambassador floated a pet idea he had been pondering but never been authorized to pursue. Why should France go to the trouble and expense of administering all of Louisiana when so much of it, especially the northwestern sector of the Mississippi Valley, was wilderness uninhabited by whites and an incalculable number of native savages? Why not cede the upper part of the colony—north, say, of the Arkansas River, Livingston propositioned—to the United States, which would settle it over time and provide a substantial buffer between French Louisiana and Canada, owned by France's avowed enemy? Such a division, when future geographers finally settled on the boundaries of Louisiana, would have given the United States about 75 percent of the colony. Did Livingston assume that nobody in Talleyrand's ministry knew how to read a map? Even the crude ones of that era would have cast doubt on Livingston's earlier assurance to French officials that Americans were "not a grasping people."

Joseph Bonaparte's inquiry added urgency to Livingston's standing request to Secretary of State Madison to fix an offering price for New Orleans and West Florida in the event Talleyrand changed his tune and said France was now ready to negotiate with the United States. As a very large landowner and a prominent jurist used to adjudicating matters of equity, Livingston had a keen sense of American property values. But the commercial and strategic utility of the port of New Orleans and its adjacent Gulf Coast appendage, even though encompassing no more than perhaps 7,500 square miles, justified a premium price. Livingston thought $20 million about right—and a good deal less than a war with France would cost. Jefferson and Madison thought the figure too high. And since the question of who owned West Florida remained unresolved, Madison instructed Charles Pinckney, the American ambassador in Madrid, to make a suggestion to Spain no less outlandish than Livingston's for France to give America three-quarters of Louisiana. So long as Spain was ridding itself of the costly administrative burden of Louisiana by transferring it to France, Pinckney suggested, why not spare itself still further by ceding to the United States the small, neighboring colony of West Florida, which would have little or no further practical value to the Spaniards?

Pressed by both the French, who were at least offering a swap of territory, and the nervy Americans, who were offering nothing, to give up all or part of Florida, Spain sensed that the value of the colony could only rise with time and decided to gratify neither suitor. But even the calculating Godoy, if harder-headed than his monarch, failed to see that time was not on Spain's side. In mid-October, one day after King Carlos had signed over Louisiana, his lame-duck intendant at New Orleans added confusion and tinder to an already combustible situation by declaring—with monumental mistiming—that Americans had been badly abusing their right of deposit at New Orleans and that the port's shipping facilities were now closed to them.

The Spanish official had a point, but not much of one. The Treaty of San Lorenzo seven years earlier had promoted a heavy increase in Mississippi River commerce as Kentucky, Tennessee, and Ohio farmers sent their surplus crops down to New Orleans and the world market. The river traffic surged despite Spain's insistence on strict regulation of American produce by requiring Spanish export licenses, detailed cargo declarations, careful inspections, approved river pilots, and hefty warehousing fees, among other impediments. This policy seemed obstructive and punitive to Americans, who believed the 1795 treaty had granted them the free and easy right of cargo transfer at New Orleans without having to run a gauntlet of maddeningly officious colonial bureaucrats. And no Spanish bureaucrat was more maddeningly officious and harassing than Juan Ventura Morales, who, on becoming intendant at New Orleans in 1796, made no secret of his disapproval of the Americans' newly won right of deposit. With such a stickler in charge of the onerous export rituals, American shippers elected in growing numbers to avoid Morales's hassling inspectors, fees, paperwork, and the inordinate waste of time. Morales called the evasion mass smuggling and complained of it bitterly to Madrid.

In July 1802, nearly two years after they had agreed to give Louisiana back to France and three months before the final transfer order was signed, King Carlos and his ministers told Morales to terminate the American right of deposit at New Orleans. Precisely what they hoped to achieve thereby remains as unclear two centuries after the fact as it was at the time. Spanish government documents have disclosed only that Morales was directed to close the port to American cargo and to assert that he was doing so on his own authority in order to shield the Spanish court, at least for a while, from charges that it had blatantly violated American treaty rights. When Morales, gratified by his instructions, finally acted on October 16—without knowing, of course, that King Carlos had the day before signed the order transferring Louisiana to France—he claimed that the Treaty of San Lorenzo had given the United States the right of deposit at New Orleans for three years only and that thereafter the privilege would be extended there or at some nearby location only at the sufferance of the Spanish king. That meant, according to

Morales, that the privilege (it was not an American *right*) could be revoked at any time by the appropriate government officer, namely, himself, and that was what he was doing.

The intendant's action was plainly a violation of the 1795 treaty, which did not grant the king the unilateral and arbitrary right to end the arrangement. Both the Spanish governor of Louisiana and the Spanish ambassador to the United States, when he learned of the event in Washington the following month, denounced Morales for outrageously exceeding his authority and assured the Jefferson administration that Madrid would promptly reverse the foolhardy move. But meanwhile hundreds of flat-bottoms coming down the Ohio and Mississippi loaded with fall harvests were turned back at New Orleans, and westerners were infuriated. Kentucky newspapers demanded that the federal government act forcefully to punish the Spanish garrison at New Orleans for its gross effrontery or quit pretending it was truly dedicated to protecting the vital interests of all the American people. Washington was soon hearing reports that 3,000 western militiamen were ready and eager to march on lightly defended New Orleans whenever directed, or even if not.

Jefferson's cabinet, fearful of the imminent occupation of New Orleans by French troops yet prayerful that Napoleon might yet be persuaded by Livingston to sell the port city to the United States as a way of maintaining friendly terms, tried to unpuzzle Morales's action. It seemed almost too brazen to have been taken on his own authority. Had the President and his advisors known the truth—that Morales was in fact acting under covert directions from his king—their puzzlement would have been compounded. Why should Spain, on the eve of completing the Louisiana-for-Tuscany exchange, have jeopardized the transaction by giving the Americans the perfect provocation to storm into New Orleans and overrun the adjacent region in order to enforce—permanently, perhaps—their violated treaty rights to deposit cargo at the port? If American soldiers seized the hub and fortified it before Napoleon's forces could peaceably take control of the city and the surrounding colony, Spain would apparently have sacrificed the Treaty of San Ildefonso. Were the Spaniards, frustrated by the necessity to yield Louisiana, simply tossing a tantrum and hoping the American westerners were all talk and no action? Did Spain think it was doing France a favor by unilaterally canceling the American right of deposit on a pretext and thereby improving French commercial prospects? Talleyrand was known to believe that Spain's 1795 concession to the Americans would undercut France's new mercantilist program to monopolize the Mississippi Valley–Gulf of Mexico–Caribbean colonial trade routes. But why should

Spain have done France's dirty work for it? Or was Spain so deeply offended by the Americans' continual disrespect for Carlos's realm that it could not resist delivering a vengeful farewell blow against U.S. shipping and leaving the messy fallout for the incoming French forces to worry about?

There was also the possibility, of course—and the American government had to consider it—that Talleyrand's crafty hand was behind Morales's action. Spain's cancellation of the right of deposit had the effect of taking France off the hook for an action unfriendly to the United States but serving French commercial interests (that is, ownership of New Orleans unencumbered by any treaty concessions Spain had made to America). And if the Americans reacted impulsively by seizing New Orleans and interfering with France's takeover of Louisiana, Napoleon could then justify a full-fledged assault against them to enforce France's rights to the colony, which included the southernmost 200 miles of the Mississippi's eastern bank. Or, in a more Machiavellian vein, France might be playing the good cop/bad cop game. By quickly occupying New Orleans now and fully restoring (and perhaps even facilitating) the American right of deposit, the French would appear to be far more reasonable and cooperative neighbors than the Spaniards had ever been, thus at least partially disarming the Americans' sharp resentment over the Louisiana takeover. At the same time they would be conditioning the United States to accept the inevitability of living next door to an immense French colony: Americans would just have to resign themselves to a western boundary that ended at the Mississippi.

All of these scenarios ran the high risk of inciting U.S. military action before French troops could be landed in sufficient strength to secure Louisiana—which was precisely why France had insisted all along on the Treaty of San Ildefonso remaining a secret as long as possible. The last thing Talleyrand and Napoleon had wanted was to show their hand prematurely.

CHAPTER 7

Everything he does is rapid as lightning

1803

WHATEVER THE REAL EXPLANATION for the intendant Juan Morales's action at New Orleans—probably that Spain could not resist a parting blow at the incorrigible Americans—events in its wake quickly conspired to determine the fate of the immense province of Louisiana and, with it, the geopolitical configuration of the continent.

In Washington, President Jefferson and Secretary of State Madison took the position—because they had insufficient reason to believe otherwise and were anxious to calm irate westerners—that the closure at New Orleans was the misguided act of a zealous Spanish functionary and would be corrected as soon as Madrid was told about it. If Spain did not respond promptly, then appropriate measures would be taken, but meanwhile Jefferson did not call for any military deployment or buildup of troops, which would only stir up war sentiment in the country or the still greater peril, a preemptive French descent on New Orleans to beat Americans to the punch.

News from abroad gave the President grounds for hope that Napoleon might well be reconsidering the scale and timing of his colonial ambitions in the New World. Reports from the Caribbean indicated the French army in Haiti was continuing to suffer heavy casualties, likely delaying plans to divert a portion of the expeditionary force to take possession of Louisiana. The assembling of a new French fleet and fresh troops to bolster the effort on Haiti and in all likelihood occupy New Orleans seemed to have slowed, and with the arrival of winter weather the expeditionary force might be iced in until spring. The precarious peace between France and Britain, further-more, which had freed Napoleon to pursue his New World offensive without fear of opposition on the sea, was said to be near collapse. Napoleon refused to complete the evacuation of French troops from Egypt until Britain abandoned Malta, as per their Treaty of Amiens, but Britain was now refusing to leave the Mediterranean stronghold until France released Holland from its control. The rupture of peace between the two leading European powers, in the White House's view, would greatly increase the probability that the British navy would come to America's aid to check France's New World incursions. Spain, which had gained Louisiana in 1763 only with British approval, had now neglected to consult with it before returning the colony to Britain's archrival.

In the closing weeks of 1802 and early in 1803 Jefferson chose to temporize. In his annual message to Congress he said the unacceptable situation at New Orleans was being fully addressed, and asked for patience. What he could not disclose was the diplomatic effort that Livingston and Du Pont had been making in Paris to settle the New Orleans problem for good. The effort had proven fruitless so far, but circumstances were changing and to open the subject to congressional and public scrutiny could only decrease the chances of success. Nor could the President disclose the larger motives behind another pet project that he now asked Congress to fund—a journey of discovery by a small party headed by his twenty-nine-year-old personal secretary, Meriwether Lewis, a former army officer, to find the shortest overland route to the Pacific and learn as much as possible about the intervening terrain and everything that abounded there. It was almost precisely the same ill-fated undertaking Jefferson had organized ten years earlier under the French botanist Michaux, but now there was more urgency for such a fact-finding mission, with multifaceted implications for the nation's future. To win diplomatic clearance for the trip through what was inarguably foreign territory, the State Department had to tell other governments that the effort was strictly scientific, but since Jefferson doubted he had the constitutional power to authorize a venture for such a purpose, he told Congress confidentially that Lewis's party intended to collect information of potentially great value for America's commercial development and military needs. Plainly Jefferson did not have in mind a United States that ended at the Mississippi. Congress secretly appropriated $2,500 for the expedition; when it was undertaken, beginning in the spring of 1804, it would cost more than twenty times as much but pay incalculable dividends.

The President's apparent serenity in the face of the gathering storm at New Orleans did not sit well with his Federalist foes, normally not partial to western interests. Perhaps the most important of these critics was Alexander Hamilton, now out of office but still influential enough to have helped tip the deadlocked 1800 presidential election in Jefferson's favor. During the naval war with France in the latter part of the Adams presidency, Hamilton had been named inspector general of the provisional army Congress authorized to counter the French threat and in that capacity had drawn up plans for an American invasion of Louisiana and Florida. Now Hamilton denounced Jefferson's calming annual address to Congress as "a lullaby message," said the crisis at New Orleans could lead to "the early dismemberment of a large portion of the country," and called for the immediate seizure of New Orleans and West Florida, with negotiations to follow.

By February, with no Spanish correction of Morales's mischief at New Orleans (news of the cancellation order would not reach Washington until April), both parties in Congress were decrying Jefferson's seeming timidity. Federalist Senator James Ross of Pennsylvania won wide support for his proposal authorizing an outlay of $5 million and a gathering of 50,000 militiamen in the western areas to be placed under the President's command for the capture of New Orleans and adjacent territory in order to secure forever the American right of deposit. Jefferson's close ally in the Senate, Republican John Breckinridge of Kentucky, led the effort to tone down the Ross proposal's financial stipulation but called for 80,000 militiamen to be ready "at a moment's notice" if diplomatic efforts failed.

This display of resolve by Congress strengthened Jefferson's hand without forcing it into an overt act of war. But now the President saw that he dared not wait indefinitely and that a further initiative was required on the diplomatic front to energize Livingston's stalled mission in Paris. To act as his special envoy to France with negotiating powers coequal to Livingston's, Jefferson called on his ideally qualified political protégé, James Monroe, who had recently served as United States Senator for Virginia, American ambassador to France, and two terms as governor of Virginia, still the most populous state in the nation. Forthright, modest, and so passionately devoted to Jeffersonian principles of states' rights republicanism that he had voted against the adoption of the Constitution and Treasury Secretary Hamilton's innovations to strengthen the central government, Monroe had been a model public servant. At forty-four and in debt, he had just opened a private law practice in Richmond when Jefferson asked him to go to Paris with a firm American proposal to buy New Orleans and West Florida. The President's imploring message said that on the outcome of Monroe's mission "depends the future destinies of the republic," for unless the United States could purchase the land it needed for commercial security and settle the matter peaceably, "war cannot be distant."

Although a partisan figure who had been a vocal critic of the Washington administration, Monroe was well suited to his critical mission for two further reasons. A strong advocate of western interests, he owned land beyond the Appalachians and had vigorously protested John Jay's abortive Gardoqui Treaty, which would have surrendered American navigation rights to the Mississippi for thirty years—and so Monroe's appointment let fearful westerners know that Jefferson shared their concerns. And Monroe was well liked in Paris and known as having been highly sympathetic to the French republican cause, excesses and all; indeed, his partiality had contributed to his recall as ambassador in 1796. His continuing Francophilia was evidenced by his teenage daughter's attendance at a Parisian seminary school, where, at the time of Monroe's mission, she was a close friend of Napoleon's stepdaughter, the child of his wife, Josephine.

Not surprisingly, then, Monroe's appointment was quickly approved by Congress, firmly under the control of Jefferson's Republicans, along with an appropriation of $2 million for "any expense which may be incurred in relation to the intercourse between the United States and foreign nations." It was hardly an extravagant sum for such a considerable purchase—only one-tenth of the price Livingston had recommended offering. On the eve of Monroe's departure in early March, Jefferson and Madison saw no point in tying their envoy's hands so tightly. He was authorized to offer up to 50 million francs, or approximately $9.375 million, which included the $2 million Congress had already approved, for the purchase of New Orleans and any or all of the Floridas. Even so, the White House was not sanguine about Monroe's chances of success, and thus his instructions proposed a pair of fallback positions if the purchase of New Orleans could not be negotiated: a suitable alternative site to serve as an American port or, at the very least, an improved and guaranteed right of deposit at New Orleans once the French took it over. It was not exactly a ringing ultimatum Monroe was sent to deliver. The only weapon of intimidation he was able to bring to the bargaining table was an advance warning, well-circulated in Washington diplomatic circles so that it preceded Monroe's arrival in Paris, that the American envoy was to proceed directly to London in the event his proposal was rejected by Napoleon and to seek common cause with the British government.

Appreciative of Livingston's tireless if mostly unproductive efforts to that point, Madison corresponded with him ahead of Monroe's arrival to assure the proud but frustrated ambassador that he was not being superseded, just gaining a well-connected partner for the vitally important new effort to strike a deal with France. But Livingston's disappointment was palpable; he took Monroe's appointment as a vote of no confidence—and, in truth, Jefferson and Madison held Monroe in higher regard and thought him more politically astute. To be fair, Livingston had vigorously, if at times tiresomely and awkwardly, represented his nation's position and had managed, by harping on the issues, to extract a pair of important concessions from Talleyrand. First, if and when France occupied Louisiana, it would honor America's right of deposit at New Orleans; second, France would settle documented losses suffered by American shippers in the course of the 1798–1800 war at sea up to a total of 20 million francs (or $3.75 million). Without a credible military arsenal to brandish in support of his entreaties, however, Livingston had probably done as well as any American representative could have.

To his surprise, with Monroe en route, Livingston would now suddenly find all his efforts rewarded—and then some.

IN PARIS, Napoleon had been brooding.

From the beginning of 1803 developments had not been good. First had come the devastating report of his brother-in-law's death in the West Indies. The loss of a superior general was always sad, but this one was particularly demoralizing: it was not a heroic death on the battlefield that took the commander of the French forces on Haiti but a tropical disease. The more reinforcements he sent there, the higher the toll climbed, and it was becoming harder to recruit new troops eager to leap into that steaming cauldron and be cut down in ambush by the martyred Toussaint's avengers. Louisiana, meanwhile, sat there in limbo, awaiting its new French colonizers while the battle raged in the Caribbean. But there was no sign that the tide was turning in favor of France, and the once-abundant sugar, cocoa, and tobacco plantations on Haiti had been torn up, and what sense did it make to take possession of vast and empty Louisiana, which had scarcely one-tenth as large a population as Haiti and a fraction of its revenue potential for years to come? Haiti was to have been the heart of France's new colonial enterprise, and Haiti was a catastrophe.

Napoleon was further disheartened by reports from his able minister in Washington, Louis-André Pichon. The Americans, Pichon told him, would not sit still for the French seizure of New Orleans. Yes, they would accept, however grudgingly, France's occupation of the rest of Louisiana, but the United States simply had to have control over the entire eastern shore of the Mississippi and all territory to the east. That meant West Florida at once and, eventually, East Florida, which could be left to languish for the time being. Pichon passed on something else that James Madison had told him over a private dinner right after the turn of the year—a message that

Napoleon could not ignore. Even if France were able, after a gigantic investment of people, capital, and time, to turn Louisiana into a flourishing colony, the mother country would sooner or later lose it even as Britain had lost the thirteen American colonies. The distance from Europe, "[i]n spite of the affinities of custom and language," Pichon quoted Madison, made the independence of France's would-be New World colony inevitable, so why should Napoleon squander his resources on a forlorn hope?

By the first week in April, Napoleon had in hand a copy of the *New York Chronicle* describing the war preparations that the fevered American Congress had authorized. These seemed to confirm what Pichon had reported about the level of animosity toward Spain for shutting down New Orleans— an anger France was likely to inherit once it took over the port. But if he sold New Orleans to the United States as Livingston had been badgering him to do since coming to Paris, Louisiana would be a virtually landlocked wilderness and worth far less, if anything at all. And if he did not sell it to them, the Americans, perhaps in tandem with the British navy, would be at a large logistical advantage, should they choose to lay siege to the port city and then sweep west across the great river to take up what they seemed to believe nature had intended them to possess.

Why, then, antagonize the Americans when France's true enemy was, now and forever, the smug and insufferable British, with their choke hold on global commerce, acting as if they owned the seven seas and getting rich at the rest of the world's expense? They badly needed humbling, and here lay Napoleon's ultimate challenge—to storm Britain and take that haughty people in their island fastness, as William of Normandy had done seven centuries earlier, and Julius Caesar more than a millennium before that. Was Bonaparte not every bit their match in martial prowess? True, he had not yet beaten a first-class military machine—Austria's imperial troops and the Ottoman Turks were hardly legendary warriors in a class with, say, the Spartans or the Vikings—but he relished the thought of engaging Britain's power head-on to test his mettle to the utmost. He would do mankind a great favor by decapitating John Bull, mounting a mammoth cross-Channel assault, perhaps even with the help of the Americans. Sell them Louisiana— they were begging to buy small pieces of territory, so why not make them pay for all of what France now owned of their wilderness continent but could not readily exploit, and then use the money to build up its military might? Instead of laying waste to England at once, he might start by returning to Egypt, this time with a new and formidable fleet to secure his supply lines, and turn it into the colonial golden calf that Haiti was to have become and use that center of antiquity as a base to outflank the British, through

Araby, and sack their ruthless trading monopolies in India? How he detested them! Even now, as the ice thawed in the Dutch harbors where his expeditionary forces were gathered, the swarming British fleet had moved in to block passage of the French host through the Channel.

With all these fugitive thoughts racing around his brain, Napoleon sought the counsel of his closest aides, starting with his endlessly calculating foreign minister. To test him the First Consul said he was leery of retaining a vast possession such as Louisiana that might not be safely held and would likely cause sharp antagonism with the United States. He proposed to Talleyrand that it was far better to win the Americans to his side by selling them Louisiana for a good price, enlist them as allies, and turn them against the British to avenge France "if we do not succeed in avenging ourselves." To return Louisiana to Spain now, certainly, was not an option, since the Americans would almost surely overrun the all but defenseless province before long.

In circumspect but assured tones Talleyrand opposed Napoleon's proposed sale of Louisiana. Though he disdained Americans, by and large, as a coarse, materialistic people, he had enjoyed a love affair with the American land. During his exile he had seen much of its splendor, had bought and sold it, knew its incremental worth with a skilled financier's instinct. There was untold wealth that Louisiana could generate for France, its government, its rulers, its farmers and merchants, and in time its manufacturers—and, though he did not need to point it out to Napoleon, there were fortunes that well-positioned operators like himself could extract in the short run from generous land grants and preferential purchase prices. France stood to gain far more by tending the bird it now—almost—held in its hands than by thrashing about in the bush with the British. Napoleon heard much the same opinion from his two brothers and his faithful chief of staff, General Louis-Alexandre Berthier, who doubled as France's war minister.

Perhaps Napoleon was overreacting to the ongoing calamity in Haiti, which unhappily reminded him of the breakdown of his initially triumphal campaign to colonize Egypt. Louisiana, after all, was different—it was already his for the taking; all he had to do was hold it against a militarily puny, if clamorous, neighbor—and the British had no right to intervene, so long as they and the French were at peace.

In the midst of his fateful reflections, Napoleon received unsettling word from his secret police that British government agents had put out feelers to his brothers and his foreign minister—and reportedly a great deal of money—to dissuade the First Consul from resuming hostilities with Britain and to urge him instead to direct his zest for conquest to the New World. Whatever credit he gave to this report, Napoleon was well aware that his brothers and Talleyrand were not above lining their own pockets while doing the nation's business—not a mortal sin, perhaps, to a conqueror living off the gleanings of despotism, but the intelligence report from his furtive agents could only undermine the confidence he placed in their views on Louisiana. He turned now to two other councilors, starting with his financial minister, one of the ablest, longest-serving, and most incorruptible public officials in the annals of France—François Barbé-Marbois, who, in further contrast to Talleyrand, loved America and its ideals and had married the daughter of a prominent Pennsylvania politician.

Of bourgeois origins in Lorraine, Barbé-Marbois was blessed with a mind both quick and deep and had cultivated a love of literature during his boyhood tutelage by the Jesuits. In time he would become a prolific author, credited by the Bibliothèque Nationale with 108 titles, among them a history of Louisiana and its purchase, a primary source for accounts of the event (this one included). While a young diplomat under Vergennes's ministry, he was sent to Philadelphia as secretary to the French chargé d'affaires, dealt regularly with Robert Livingston, John Jay, and other leading statesmen, and grew to admire Americans as "natural" men in Rousseau's approving sense of the word. Posted to Saint-Domingue as its last French governor before the monarchy fell, he won few friends by his scrupulous honesty and efficient, impartial conduct of official business—a far cry from the conduct of his predecessors in charge of the oppressive colonial regime. His efforts to obtain humane treatment of the slaves still further infuriated the French colonials. Recalled to France, Barbé-Marbois found himself suspected of royalist sympathies by the Jacobins, even though all the evidence showed him to have been a thoroughly patriotic civil servant of his country. For his virtues, he was exiled to French Guiana until eventually recalled by Napoleon, who was in need of talented administrators. Napoleon elevated him to chief of the public treasury in 1801, a post he held for five years.

After returning from Mass on Easter Sunday, April 10, 1803, Napoleon sent for Barbé-Marbois to attend him at his palace in St. Cloud, a few miles west of Paris, where he liked to stroll the formal gardens and talk with underlings. Also present at the interview was Admiral Denis Decrès, minister in charge of the French navy and the colonies. The First Consul confided that much as he had wished to proceed with the colonization of Louisiana, he was wary of the British, who he said envied the colony and were well positioned to assault it from Canada as well as from the Gulf of Mexico. According to Barbé-Marbois's account, Napoleon went on:

I have not a moment to lose in putting it out of their [Britain's] reach. . . . I wish, if there is still time, to take from them any idea that they may have of ever possessing that colony. I think of ceding it to the United States. . . . They only ask of me one town in Louisiana, but I already consider the colony as entirely lost, and it appears to me that in the hands of this growing power, it will be more useful to the policy and even to the commerce of France, than if I should attempt to keep it.

The chief financial officer of France, according to his own version of the exchange, agreed. "We should not hesitate to make a sacrifice of that which is . . . slipping from us," Barbé-Marbois reasoned. Defending Louisiana from the formidable British navy and from the Americans coming overland, should they challenge the French occupation, would present a grave problem, the financial minister added, and then raised the same troubling point that James Madison had—even if the colonization succeeded, prosperity would carry with it the germ of independence. Already four times as large as France itself, French Louisiana might become within a few generations more populous and richer than the mother country and demand to be liberated from its colonial status. But such success, he noted with painful insight into France's national character, was unlikely because

[t]he French have attempted to form colonies in several parts of the continent of America. Their efforts have everywhere proved abortive. The English are patient and laborious, they do not fear the solitude and silence of newly settled countries. The Frenchman, lively and active, requires society; he is fond of conversing with his neighbors. He willingly enters on the experiment, but at the first disappointment, quits the spade or the axe for the chase.

Mindful of Barbé-Marbois's tenure as governor of Saint-Domingue, Napoleon pointed out that France had done rather well with its colonies in the West Indies. Only because slaves did all the work, his minister replied. Whites soon grew exhausted in the hot weather, with only enough energy to direct the work; in his view, "[t]he blacks and whites have both been the victim of this great fault"—and the same conditions applied in the settled portion of Louisiana. "But for what good purpose would you subject yourself to still greater embarrassment [after Haiti] in Louisiana? . . . Of all the scourges that have afflicted the human race, slavery is the most detestable." Far smarter to sell the colony and use the money to brace France's army and regime.

Barbé-Marbois's voice was a lonely one among Napoleon's close advisors. Invited to comment, Admiral Decrès differed sharply with the finance minister. So long as France stayed at peace with Britain, there was no reason for it not to take possession of the newly reacquired colony—to do less, he said, was "contrary to the honor of France." But the admiral was not just wallowing in chauvinism; he foresaw a glorious future for the western basin of the Mississippi, with its twenty rivers connecting even the farthest recesses of the colony to the mighty mainstream and carrying the bounty of the immense and fertile midcontinent to the world market via New Orleans. That port could become a thriving nexus of global commerce, particularly when a canal would one day be built to join the oceans, and Louisiana would doubtless far outstrip Haiti as France's richest colony. It was an appealing vision and gave Napoleon pause. He asked Barbé-Marbois to stay the night at St. Cloud while he pondered his decision a final time.

The conclusion he came to that evening, in the estimate of British historian Paul Johnson, was "Bonaparte's greatest single failure of imagination." Johnson, in his biographical profile of the warrior-statesman, argues:

> If Bonaparte had used France's legitimate rights to its American territory to explore and create an enormous dominion across the Atlantic, instead of trying to carve out an illegitimate empire in Europe, he would have enriched France instead of impoverishing her, provided scope for countless adventurous young Frenchmen instead of killing them in futile battles, and incidentally inflicted more damage on his British opponents than all his efforts in Europe. . . . But he knew nothing of America and desired to know nothing until it was too late. He feared the Atlantic as a great ocean.

Johnson's judgment is not rash. But the reasons he suggests for Napoleon's decision to abandon Louisiana are arguable. The First Consul's lack of knowledge about America would probably not have deterred him any more than unfamiliarity had discouraged him from seizing Egypt or would later stop him from invading Russia. He was a keen student of geography and had knowledgeable aides who had traveled to the New World, appreciated its charms, and knew its perils; Barbé-Marbois, for one, might have made an ideal governor of French Louisiana. And while Napoleon's experience as a warrior naturally left him far more at home fighting on land than on water, where he had to rely heavily on the judgment of others, he was hardly unaware that the French navy had distinguished itself across the Atlantic during the American War for Independence and had to its credit a number of victories in the Caribbean. Surely colonizing Louisiana would have necessitated strengthening France's fleet, but in view of the many other reforms he instigated, Napoleon might well have converted his nation, with its temperate climate and ample seacoasts facing north, south, and west, into a maritime power more closely competitive with Britain. There were more compelling reasons for the decision Napoleon reached on the evening of April 10, 1803.

To start with, he recognized that Haiti was a lost cause, and though he did not pull his dying army off the island at once, he resolved to invest no further resources there. Without Haiti to build on as the core of his projected New World empire, the process would no doubt have consumed incalculably more time, money, and imported manpower, yet might still have been well worth the investment. But without Haiti *and* New Orleans as the twin bases of the new colonial enterprise, the investment would have been still greater and more problematic. The Americans, moreover, were clearly itching to fight for the port, and if they did and won it, would they stop fighting at the eastern shore of the Mississippi? If so, for how long? They would have geography, to say nothing of the passions of youth and avarice, on their side, and possibly the British navy as well, poised to deal France a severe blow for its temerity in taking back Louisiana and reimposing itself as a major presence in North America without Britain's assent.

The only sensible way, then, for Napoleon to have exercised his right to colonize Louisiana would have been to come to terms with the United States—and in the process oblige the British to keep their distance. What terms would satisfy the aroused Americans long enough to tolerate a huge French colony taking hold and flourishing in their backyard, a hinterland they coveted and had assumed would one day become theirs by Spanish default? Guaranteeing the right of deposit at New Orleans and other sweet promises would no longer suffice. The blundering Spaniards had seen to that. No, France would have to concede to the United States *all* the territory between the eastern bank of the Mississippi and the Atlantic, starting with New Orleans, adding West Florida, which it could plausibly claim had been part of Louisiana when it was last under French rule, and—to clinch the deal—bullying Spain into surrendering East Florida as well to America, perhaps cushioning the blow by adding Parma to Tuscany, as earlier proposed, and several other small territorial and commercial inducements. In exchange, the United States would have to reconcile itself to a future without an endlessly expansive western frontier, and France could proceed to fortify its vast new trans-Mississippi dominion of Louisiana by way of driving home the reality.

But in the end, Napoleon probably understood both the history of North

America and his own temperament better than those who have retrospectively faulted his abandonment of Louisiana. Just as Barbé-Marbois had reminded him that the French were better slave drivers than colonizers, so Napoleon's own character did not lend itself to grand projects begun from scratch. He was not a patient builder, he was a conqueror, a speed demon, a dominator who paid for his war machine by plundering rich, established places and corrupt regimes. But there was nobody to conquer or dominate in Louisiana, and there was nothing there to steal but the land itself, so how would he pay for all the costs of constructing, governing, and defending a great colony 5,000 miles from Paris? Spain had declined to make more than a minimal investment there and lost it. France, of course, might have adopted Britain's policy toward its thirteen American colonies by letting Louisiana's new settlers and private investors foot the bill, but ultimately, as Madison and Barbé-Marbois reminded Napoleon, those settlers would similarly rebel.

"Irresolution and deliberation are no longer in season," the First Consul announced to his financial minister on Monday morning, April 11. "I renounce Louisiana," he said, his regret palpable, and agreed to give up not only New Orleans but the entire province. "To attempt obstinately to retain it would be folly." He then entrusted Barbé-Marbois to arrange the sale— not Talleyrand, who, disapproving of it, might scuttle it by driving too hard a bargain or, reluctantly complying with the decision, arrange a handsome commission for himself. Barbé-Marbois was told to begin negotiating at once with Livingston, even though special American envoy James Monroe had just arrived at Le Havre and could be expected in Paris in days. Napoleon may have surmised that Livingston, after all his diplomatic labors, was chagrined that the late-arriving statesman from Virginia would steal his thunder as the dealmaker of record and thus Livingston might be inclined to make a generous bargain that would be awkward to retract. Napoleon asked to be kept fully abreast of all developments.

In explaining his decision, he had told the finance minister, "I require money to make war on the richest nation in the world." Accordingly, Barbé-Marbois asked him at the end of their interview what price for Louisiana would please Napoleon. No less than 50 million francs, came the reply— which happened to be exactly the amount Monroe and Livingston had been instructed to bid for just New Orleans and West Florida.

KNOWING THAT NAPOLEON COULD be as impulsive as he was calculating, Barbé-Marbois waited two days before approaching the Americans about buying Louisiana, just to be certain that the chief of state was firmly decided to cut his losses in the New World. In the interim, Talleyrand, who had been advised that the finance minister was to handle the money end of the purchase agreement, chose to insinuate himself into the negotiations even before they had begun. Piqued at being cast aside as the primary deal-maker—not least because it was public knowledge that Congress had already appropriated $2 million for Monroe's mission to cover "expenses," presumably including gratuities (sometimes called bribes) to grease the open palms of French officials—Talleyrand invited Livingston to his impos-ing office in St.-Germain-des-Prés for a little chat that Monday afternoon.

Livingston, who had already received word from Monroe to expect him on Wednesday, April 13, supposed this would be his last chance for the breakthrough he had been assiduously pursuing on his own. If he could present Monroe with a virtual fait accompli, the feather would flutter in his cap, not Monroe's. So he tried once more to convince Talleyrand that the moment France resumed combat with Britain, American forces were likely to descend on New Orleans and the British navy was likely to blunt any planned French initiative in Louisiana; thus a peaceful settlement ought to be reached with the United States as soon as possible. The sniffish French foreign minister listened impassively, then with masterful nonchalance asked the American ambassador, who recounted the exchange to Secretary of State Madison, "whether we wished to have the whole of Louisiana." Coming from a man who had spent the prior eighteen months denying that France held title to the territory, the inquiry was doubly stunning.

At pains not to reveal his astonishment, the wary Livingston did not ask whether Talleyrand's question implied a change of heart by Napoleon or was merely a playful gambit. Instead he reminded the foreign minister that the United States was concerned only with New Orleans and next-door West Florida, but added that if France was now truly open to reducing its colonial holdings, America would gladly accept—as he had earlier sug-gested—cession of the Louisiana wilderness north of the Arkansas River. Talleyrand, though, was not in a gift-giving mood. He noted that the rest of Louisiana was more or less useless to France without New Orleans, which the United States had made abundantly clear was its sine qua non for contin-ued friendship, so what would America be willing to pay for the whole of it?

Since both men knew Monroe would almost certainly be carrying fresh instructions—and perhaps a sizable purse—with him, Talleyrand's probe sounded as if he were trying for a preemptive strike, hoping that Monroe would be compelled to support any offer his countryman might have made. Fully authorized to negotiate as a plenipotentiary, Livingston was tempted

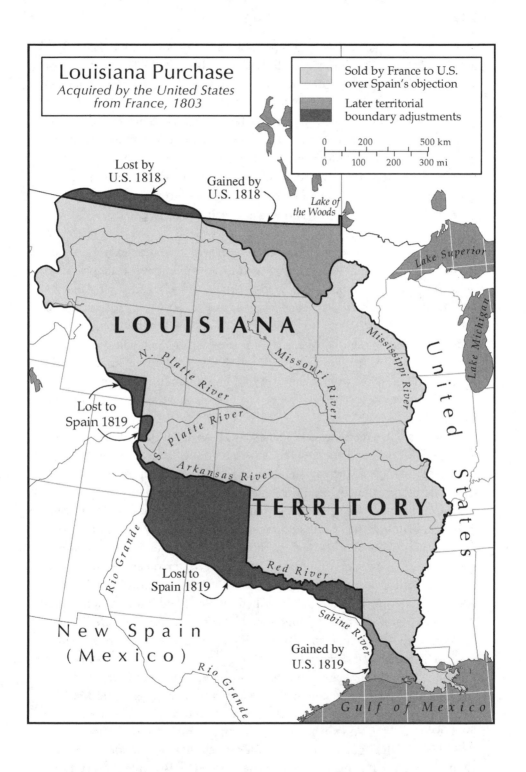

Louisiana Purchase
*Acquired by the United States
from France, 1803*

Sold by France to U.S.
over Spain's objection

Later territorial
boundary adjustments

0   200   500 km
0 100 200 300 mi

Lost by
U.S. 1818

Gained by
U.S. 1818

*Lake of
the Woods*

Lake Superior

Lake Michigan

LOUISIANA

N. Platte River

Missouri River

Mississippi River

United States

Lost to
Spain 1819

S. Platte River

Arkansas River

TERRITORY

Rio Grande

Lost to
Spain 1819

Red River

Sabine River

New Spain
(Mexico)

Rio Grande

Gained by
U.S. 1819

Gulf of Mexico

to engage the French minister and perhaps pull off a coup fast and cheap on his own, but now chose to risk as little as possible. He floated the figure of 20 million francs ($3.75 million), a sum equal to the pledge he had managed to pry from France in repayment to American shippers for their confiscated cargoes, and reminded Talleyrand that he considered their agreement on that score an integral part of any territorial transaction with France. The two payments—by America to France for Louisiana and by France for reparations to the Americans—would have theoretically canceled each other out, and the United States, though presumably obliged to recompense its own citizens for their lost cargoes, would walk away the huge gainer.

Understandably, Talleyrand was dismissive. He urged Livingston to reflect on the matter overnight and then meet with him the next day. When Livingston replied that he had best wait for Monroe's arrival if they were to get down to hard numbers, Talleyrand seemed to back off, saying that he had not been authorized to consummate such a sale—as indeed he had not—"but that the idea had struck him," as Livingston reported their conversation to Madison, and he was merely expressing his personal view. Thus covering his ploy to undercut Barbé-Marbois, the foreign minister held another brief session with Livingston on Tuesday and then dropped out of the picture so as not to be caught defying Napoleon's directive barring him as negotiator.

During all-day meetings on Wednesday at the Right Bank house Monroe was using for his headquarters, the American diplomatic team mulled over its strategy in view of the coy—and surprising—indication from Talleyrand that a far more extensive territorial package than the United States had in mind might now be for sale. That so much land could be had for the 50 million francs Monroe had been authorized to commit to for buying just New Orleans and West Florida seemed highly improbable; Napoleon would surely demand some lofty multiple of the figure Jefferson and Madison had specified, and that would be that. But with such a mercurial adversary across the table, who could tell? Nor had the President fixed in stone what the United States might be willing to pay if more territory was offered.

While the American team was winding up its deliberations over dinner, something rather odd occurred. Livingston glanced out the window nearest the dining table and caught sight of the chief financial minister of France, strolling in the rear garden. Invited to join their dinner party, Barbé-Marbois declined with thanks, saying he had no wish to intrude, but would return in an hour to join the Americans in their salon when they took coffee. In the course of socializing, the French minister stole a few private moments with Livingston to confide that he had been designated by Bonaparte to arrange a purchase of territory with the United States and invited the ambassador to meet with him at his office anytime before eleven that very evening for a preliminary exchange.

On its face, such a meeting, without the newly arrived special American envoy in attendance, was a breach of etiquette. But Barbé-Marbois may have just been hewing strictly to protocol, since Monroe had not yet formally presented his diplomatic credentials to Talleyrand and thus lacked official standing to join in a ministerial exchange. This was the reason, at any rate, Livingston gave to Monroe for cutting him out of the meeting later that evening. Barbé-Marbois might have waited, of course, until Monroe could be received by Talleyrand in the next day or two, but the finance minister was mindful of Napoleon's order to begin dealing promptly with Livingston and had perhaps delayed too long already—a fear soon corroborated by Livingston's disclosure to him that Talleyrand had met with him twice earlier in the week to discuss Louisiana informally. Since Barbé-Marbois was well acquainted with the American ambassador, he likely felt he could make headway faster with Livingston alone—or perhaps by dealing separately with the two Americans if they could be approached individually. For that evening, anyway, he succeeded, as Monroe, weary from his travels and coming down with a severe back ailment that would limit his activities for the next few weeks, bowed to Livingston's eagerness to accept Barbé-Marbois's invitation—on the proviso that the U.S. ambassador make no commitment of any sort until reporting back to Monroe the next day.

Soon after arriving at the Ministry of Finance, Livingston made it clear that if France was intent on toying with the United States, as Talleyrand's ambiguous remarks to him about buying all of Louisiana suggested, it would drive the Americans into Britain's camp—an arrangement that would not serve France's interest and might well end with New Orleans, if not all of Louisiana, in British hands. Once more, American diplomats were using the only effective weapon at their disposal, France's fear and loathing of its cross-Channel rival.

Barbé-Marbois, now apprised of Talleyrand's crafty game, tried to reassure Livingston by a straightforward approach aimed at a rapid resolution of the issue and thus fend off the foreign minister's sharp talons. In selectively recounting to Livingston his exchange on Sunday at St. Cloud, Barbé-Marbois stressed that Napoleon felt it would be most unfortunate if the United States and France went to war—a view in which the finance minister heartily concurred, prompting Napoleon to reply, as Barbé-Marbois quoted him, "Well, you have the charge of the treasury. Let them give you 100 millions [in francs] and pay their own claims [for the French navy's confiscation of American shipping], and take the whole country." The figure quoted was twice the number Napoleon had set as his lowest acceptable price, but his finance minister was, of course, charged with arranging the best possible terms, so anything extracted from the Americans over the minimum would enhance his standing. He also made it clear to Livingston that it had to be an all-or-nothing purchase; there was no possibility of parceling up the colony.

The price amounted to 120 million francs, since the United States was being asked to absorb the 20 million for the war claims that France had previously agreed to pay. That came to 140 percent more than Monroe had informed Livingston the White House had authorized them to commit. The sudden, solemn furrow across Livingston's brow told the Frenchman that he had overreached. Now he displayed his own aptitude for gameplaying by acknowledging the American envoy's grave look and saying he agreed that such a figure seemed extravagant for a young nation to pay—and that he had told Napoleon as much. In response, he said, Bonaparte suggested that the United States, which had nearly liquidated its Revolutionary War debt to France, could readily borrow the amount he had in mind.

Livingston sensed he was in a favorable bargaining situation because, as he had pointed out to Talleyrand and now reminded Barbé-Marbois, the United States did not have its heart set on gaining the immense Louisiana wilderness—at least not anytime soon. But he allowed that his nation would probably be willing to take the whole colony off France's hands for a reasonable and manageable sum. The finance minister, as eager as Livingston to reach rapid agreement on the price, pending formal settlement of all the details, asked what figure might be acceptable. Livingston parried by suggesting that, since Barbé-Marbois seemed to agree with him that Napoleon's price was wishfully high, perhaps "he would oblige me by telling me what he thought to be reasonable." As Livingston replayed the scene in writing for Madison, the French minister replied that "if we [the United States] should name 60 million and take on us the American claims to the amount of twenty [million] more," he would press Napoleon to accept.

In a trice, France had slashed its asking price by one-third. And while the 80-million-franc total was still 60 percent more than the amount the American negotiators had been authorized to bring to the bargaining table, that figure had been proposed to obtain only New Orleans and West Florida, an area that amounted to a tiny fraction of Louisiana. The terms were so numbingly attractive that Livingston must have been sorely tempted to shake the French finance minister's hand on the spot. And, in fact, after two weeks of posturing and pleading poverty, the Americans would meet the price Barbé-Marbois had set that night. But Livingston, like his French adversary, was charged with obtaining the best terms he could, and so he said that such a price was beyond the resources of the United States and, if agreed to by President Jefferson, would surely cost him reelection the following year for wanton spending on a trackless wilderness the nation did not, and might never, need.

It was well past midnight when the two men adjourned their deliberations, Livingston promising to share them with Monroe. In parting, Barbé-Marbois made two hard-selling points. "Consider the extent of the country," he said, by way of stressing France's generosity, "the exclusive navigation of the [Mississippi] River, and the importance of having no neighbor to dispute with you, no war to dread." In short, America would be foolhardy not to extend itself under the terms being offered. Barbé-Marbois, moreover, perfectly understood his overlord's volatile nature and urged the Americans not to tarry in their reply, remarking, "You know the temper of a young conqueror—everything he does is rapid as lightning."

Even before informing Monroe, Livingston dashed off a middle-of-the-night bulletin to Madison in Washington, which made clear that he thought the French proposition irresistible. "The field open to us is infinitely larger than our instructions contemplate," he acknowledged, but then counter-argued that if the United States accepted France's figure, "the whole sum may be raised by the sale of the territory west of the Mississippi. . . . We shall do all we can to cheapen the purchase but my present sentiment is that we shall buy."

Monroe quickly came around to Livingston's way of thinking. The undeniable virtues of the purchase that Barbé-Marbois had cited overrode the hard reality that the American negotiators would be far exceeding their instructions by dealing for such a huge increment of territory. Yet they could happily rationalize that the intrinsic value of the land was exponentially larger than its cost. The duties alone on the steadily rising volume of goods certain to be shipped through New Orleans would likely net at least $2 million a year, significantly reducing the principal and helping meet the carrying charges on the $15 million purchase package. And buying Louisiana would prove a lot less expensive and bloody than going to war over it. Given these advantages, the American diplomats had little trouble securing a loan from two leading private banks, one in London and the other in Holland, to cover the $11.25 million price of the land acquisition. The terms of 6 percent interest over eighteen years would bring the eventual total price of the real estate to $22.5 million, which came to a bit under four cents per acre.

Only two conditions that France insisted on would complicate the transaction. The first was timing. Since Napoleon was his nation's de facto government, his almost immediate signature on the treaty of purchase would commit France to the agreement. But he was not disposed to wait indefinitely for the American government to sign on, so the treaty called for Congress to ratify it by the end of October, six months hence. The second potential stumbling block was France's insistence that the heavily French-speaking residents of Louisiana "shall be incorporated into the Union of the United States and admitted as soon as possible according to the principles of the federal Constitution to the enjoyment of all th[o]se rights, advantages, and immunities of citizens of the United States." This requirement, expressing France's concern for the welfare of its cultural adherents overseas, seemed both just and modest enough to Livingston and Monroe, especially since the white population of Louisiana did not exceed 40,000, none of whom would have a say in the transfer of sovereignty over them to the Americans.

The final terms were approved without incident, and the two envoys from the United States were cordially greeted by the First Consul at his monthly diplomatic reception on Sunday, May 1, just three weeks after he had ordered the sale to be expedited. "Our affairs stand as settled, I think," Napoleon told the American team. He later remarked privately to his finance minister, "This accession of territory strengthens forever the power of the United States; and I have just given to England a maritime rival that will sooner or later humble their pride." Livingston, who had indefatigably stalked every French official who would hear him out on the matter, would celebrate by telling his fellow dealmakers that their transaction was "the noblest work of our whole lives" and predicting that "it will change vast solitudes into flourishing districts. From this day the United States take their place among the powers of the first rank."

For Barbé-Marbois, the americophile, the occasion was made even more joyful by the receipt of a bonus equal to $40,000 from an appreciative Napoleon.

NEWS OF THE LOUISIANA PURCHASE, which reached America toward the end of June, made for an especially jubilant Independence Day as geographers estimated that the new territory beyond the Mississippi would roughly double the size of the United States. France's able ambassador, Louis Pichon, whose reports to Paris had helped curtail Napoleon's projected colonial aspirations in North America, thought the acquisition the greatest event in the young country's history, and if some placed it a close second to the crafting of the Constitution, all but universal euphoria ruled the day. Even the Federalist press, which generally feasted on Jefferson's every imperfection, by and large found little to criticize.

To be sure, though, some concern was expressed over the ensuing weeks that the new territory would be too vast, distant, and difficult for the nation to pacify, absorb, and govern effectively and at a less than ruinous cost. The most strident criticism sprang from the New England Federalist press and some of the region's political leaders, led by noted orator and former United States Representative Fisher Ames of Dedham, Massachusetts, who summed up the opposition view with an epigram: "We are to give money of which we have too little for land of which we already have too much." Behind the raillery were two emotional incitements: first, the by now familiar antiexpansionist phobia that the abundance—indeed, superfluity—of cheap new western land would lure money and people from settled eastern areas, greatly reducing their wealth and political importance; and second, that the central government could not sustain national unity and the core values of republican democracy if American territory grew so great and the population mongrelized. All that space out there, claimed the naysayers, was sure to stimulate a new outbreak of economically wasteful land specu-lation, a fresh wave of socially irresponsible squatters, and a mass migration of slaveholders spreading their iniquitous institution across Louisiana's southern tier. Where many saw strength in heterogeneity, others agreed with Ames, who lamented the polyglot porridge of ethnicity in New Orleans and nearby Louisiana, calling it, with racist disdain, a "Gallo-Hispano-Indian omnium gatherum of savages and adventurers"—people largely Catholic and non-English-speaking, used to despotic rulers and ignorant of the demands of self-government, whose very foreignness would pollute the American polity. It was a sentiment that Jefferson himself somewhat shared.

Federalist extremists in New England, including the governor of Massa-chusetts, Caleb Strong, were so vexed by the purchase—some viewed it as a crude scheme for perpetuating the national dominance of the South's politi-cal establishment led by Virginia's Jefferson and Madison—that they called for the breakup of the federal union and creation of a northern confedera-tion. Most of those otherwise opposed to Jefferson agreed with the views of Federalist icon Alexander Hamilton. In an unsigned article in the *New York Evening Post,* he called the purchase "essential to the peace and prosperity of our Western country." But having risen momentarily above partisanship, Hamilton's generosity of spirit failed him. Once more chiding the Republi-can administration for having exhibited "feebleness and pusillanimity" in response to the Spanish treachery at New Orleans and the threatened French occupancy of Louisiana, he insisted, sounding like a peddler of sour grapes, that the spectacular purchase owed everything to the confluence of "unforeseen and unexpected circumstances, not to any wise or vigorous measures on the part of the American government."

This was a grudging and mistaken judgment. To be sure, Jefferson's triumph owed an immense debt to the incandescent Toussaint L'Ouverture and his black rebel cadres on Haiti for bloodying France's colonial dreams in the New World. So, too, was the President the beneficiary of Napoleon's highly volatile temperament. But Jefferson had anticipated that the French forces might get mired in Haiti's dank thickets and that Napoleon would— sooner rather than later—turn his attention from colonization back to conquest and resume warring with the British, and so he had played a waiting game. To have acted rashly and ordered the preemptive seizure of New Orleans might have momentarily gratified American passions and then shortly embroiled the nation in a long-term confrontation with Europe's most formidable army, a conflict that could have left the vast trans-Mississippi domain in French hands, perhaps forever. Instead of provoking a fiery young conqueror, Jefferson and Madison had acted with both moderation and resolve, appealing to sweet reason while clearly stating their absolute requirements through diplomatic channels. In emphasizing that the United States would not allow its vital needs to be trampled on now by the European powers, they were reminding the rulers of the Old World that the Americans had successfully defied them at their nation's birth. By seeking to deny the President the glory that their own intemperate policies would likely never have won, Hamilton and his ilk sounded like a pack of barking dogs in the manger.

Only one hazy area in the purchase agreement remained to be clarified—whether West Florida was or wasn't to be treated as part of Louisiana; the question was unmentioned in the text of the purchase treaty. All the land bordering both banks of the Mississippi was now to be under the flag of the United States except the western border of West Florida, which ran along the east shore of Lake Pontchartrain directly across from New Orleans, turned north to follow the Mississippi for fifty miles to Baton Rouge, and then continued another fifty or so miles until meeting the thirty-first parallel. Spanish gunboats still patrolled the lake and the riverfront—and if they were allowed to remain, obstructing the flow of commerce whenever it might suit them, American dominion over the full length of the river would still not have been achieved.

Spain adamantly denied not only that West Florida was part of Louisiana but also—and more important—that France had no legal right to sell Lou-

isiana to the United States. According to Madrid, Napoleon had still not fulfilled his obligations under the Treaty of San Ildefonso because his troops
remained encamped in Tuscany, now serving as a granary for the French
army, and he had not obtained diplomatic recognition for the kingdom of
Etruria from Britain, Russia, or any other European state, really, except
Austria. France, moreover, had promised not to sell Louisiana if it chose not
to keep the province but to give it back to Spain. Talleyrand and his envoys
had no difficulty in brushing aside these objections. Spain had formally
deeded Louisiana to France the previous October—and not at gunpoint; to
whine about it after the fact was not to lend legal standing to Spain's unhappiness. The retrocession of Louisiana, moreover, had been conditioned on
neither the removal of French troops from Tuscany nor the winning of general diplomatic recognition for Etruria; as noted earlier, France's pledge had
been only to solicit such formal acknowledgment. And in the end, realpolitik ruled the day: Spain was too weak to defy France, and if it now served
Napoleon's strategic design to renege on a verbal promise by Talleyrand not
to sell Louisiana to any third party, well, *tant pis.*

France's strength did not bolster American aspirations to control West
Florida as part of the Louisiana Purchase. Spain argued that, although it
had authorized its governors of Louisiana to administer West Florida, its
official status as a separate jurisdiction had never been altered, and thus it remained, as it had been under Britain's twenty-year rule, a colony apart from
Louisiana. James Madison, more hawkish than his commander-in-chief,
favored a bold stand against the intransigent Spaniards. As far as Madison
was concerned, based on Livingston's research in Paris, Louisiana when last
under French rule (as of 1763) had extended to the Perdido River, the eastern boundary of West Florida as designated by the British, and so, according
to the text of the Spanish retrocession to France in 1801, West Florida was
part of the Louisiana Purchase. Spain's claim to the contrary was based, in
the Secretary of State's opinion, on a flimsy technicality. Still, he asked Livingston to approach Talleyrand for clarification.

France had agreed, as part of the purchase, never to take possession of
any portion of the Floridas, but that was the extent of its involvement in the
West Florida issue. Talleyrand told Livingston, "I can give you no direction—you have made a noble bargain for yourselves, and I suppose you will
make the most of it." Madison, frustrated, privately excoriated Spain's stubbornness even though it dreaded "the growing power of [the United States]
and the direction of it against [Spain's] possessions within its reach. Can she
annihilate this power? Can she retard its growth? No." Why, Madison wondered, didn't the Spaniards smarten up and try a little friendship toward the

United States—a veiled assertion of American entitlement. Jefferson, however, having avoided war with France, was disinclined now to force the
West Florida issue with Spain. He assuaged Madison by telling him that
soon enough both Floridas "cannot fail to fall into our hands."

Jefferson was right again, but it took longer than he anticipated, and
West Florida would not exactly "fall" into American hands. All of Florida
soon drifted into limbo after France, with Spain on its side, renewed the war
against Britain. In 1805 off Cape Trafalgar on the southwest coast of Spain,
a combined French and Spanish fleet was routed by Nelson's two-pronged
attack, ending forever Napoleon's dream of a New World empire and permanently reducing Spain to a second-class power, if that. The Spanish
branch of the Bourbon monarchy crumbled in a civil war that allowed
Napoleon to seize control of Spain and place his brother Joseph on the
throne, igniting a rebellion that turned into the six-year Peninsular War.
French, British, Spanish, and Portuguese troops battled fruitlessly back and
forth and left Iberia in chaos. Thus preoccupied, the Spaniards were in no
position to challenge Madison's later decision, on succeeding to the presidency, to annex West Florida in two bites, the 4,000-square-mile western
half in 1810 and the rest in 1813. The seizure marked the first expansion of
the United States by military force. It would not be the last.

CONSIDERING THE MAGNITUDE OF THE EVENT, national debate over the
benefits and drawbacks of the Louisiana Purchase was scant—nothing like
the lively rhetorical jousting in newspapers and at town meetings and state
conventions that accompanied the ratification of the Constitution. It would
not be fanciful to suggest that the lone serious obstacle to automatic ratification of the purchase treaty by the Senate was the mind of Thomas Jefferson.

In the year and a half between his dispatching Robert Livingston to Paris
to discourage a French return to North America and receipt of the startling
news that Napoleon had offered the United States a discount purchase of all
of Louisiana, the President had shared with his cabinet a concern that the
Constitution did not explicitly empower the federal government to acquire
foreign territory or to incorporate it within the Union. New states could be
carved from old ones or from the territories ceded to Congress while it operated under the Articles of Confederation, but nothing else was constitutionally sanctioned, according to Jefferson's fundamentalist reading of the
sacred federal compact. This view, if literally adhered to, would have frozen
the nation's boundaries as established by the 1783 Treaty of Paris and forbidden expansion by purchase, treaty, or conquest. How, then, could the Jefferson administration legally justify the acquisition of any foreign territory?

Attorney General Levi Lincoln Sr. proposed avoiding the constitutional pitfall by appending or assigning any purchased territory to one or several of the existing states. But Treasury Secretary Gallatin dismissed the idea as transparent subterfuge, contending that if the President and Congress had no power to acquire foreign territory for inclusion within the nation's borders, on what basis could the individual states annex such territory? "What could, on this construction," Gallatin asked, "prevent the Senate and President, by treaty, annexing Cuba to Massachusetts or Bengal to Rhode Island?" Gallatin argued instead that he found no constitutional objection, as Jefferson did; the United States, like any other nation, had a natural right to conduct the basic functions of sovereign statehood, which included the organic process of growth. The Constitution addressed the matter by requiring Congress to approve treaties of purchase or declarations of war by a President it suspected of trying unjustifiably to extend the national domain. Since the territory that Livingston had been authorized to buy from France—New Orleans and West Florida—was relatively modest in size and its addition was intended to benefit the entire western and southern sections of the nation, such an acquisition could scarcely be considered a departure from the character, purpose, or dynamics of the federal system; it would only make the country function better as a whole. Jefferson had been content to leave the gnarly constitutional question unresolved for the time being.

The sheer size of the Louisiana Purchase forced the President to rethink the matter. And the more he thought about it, the more uneasy he grew. Doubling the size of the nation threatened to destabilize and fundamentally change the federal compact. How, as a practical matter, could the central government of a federated republic exercise control over such an immense hinterland without resorting to colonial (that is, antidemocratic and potentially oppressive) forms of rule? How would the nation deal with unknown multitudes of Indians as American settlers inevitably impinged on the native peoples? Was slavery to be extended across the Mississippi or outlawed as it had been above the Ohio River by the Northwest Ordinance? This was a profound question, since Congress was constitutionally empowered, if it chose, to ban the importation of slaves as of 1808, only five years hence. Nor did Jefferson feel he could blithely dodge the issue by claiming it was subsumed within the presidential treatymaking power, checked by a required two-thirds majority of the Senate to ratify. That argument seemed to grant constitutional latitude to any presidential action so long as it was wrapped within the sanctity of a treaty approved by a large Senate majority. Such an expedient, Jefferson wrote, would have rendered "the treaty-making power boundless, and if it is, we have no Constitution."

No legalistic shortcuts or devious tactics, then, could be resorted to for certifying the Louisiana Purchase, sure to effect a sweeping transformation of the country, with potentially profound consequences. The Union was a compact of sovereign states, and the states had to concur in so radical an alteration of its scale—it ought not to be imposed upon them by the central government, which, at any rate, was not explicitly licensed to undertake such action. At best, that power could be inferred, but as an avowed foe of fanning tyrannical tendencies by the federal government, Jefferson found it philosophically repugnant to read into the Constitution what it did not unmistakably declare. As he wrote his friend Senator John Breckinridge regarding the temptation for him to make an exception for such a remarkable stroke of good fortune as Napoleon's offered sale of Louisiana, "The Executive [that is, his administration], in seizing the fugitive occurrence, which so much advances the good of their country, have done an act beyond the Constitution." The only just solution, then, was to draw up an amendment to the Constitution legitimizing the purchase, and Jefferson, an adept legal craftsman, set to work writing two versions. Consistent with his scruples, neither version would have permanently enlarged the power of the presidency by sanctioning the acquisition of new territory; instead they were worded to certify the Louisiana Purchase as an exceptional transaction and, in effect, a fait accompli. The second version also provided full citizenship for the residents of Louisiana, as France had insisted upon in the treaty of sale, and reserved the portion of the new territory north of the Arkansas River for occupancy exclusively by the native tribes, without a time limit. Eventual white settlement of the area would require a future constitutional amendment.

Jefferson's solution suffered from two potentially serious problems. The first was timing. Congress was on summer recess and not due to reconvene until the beginning of November, after Napoleon's deadline for ratification had expired. Almost immediately upon receiving the text of the purchase treaty with its end-of-October cutoff, the President issued a call for Congress to reconvene two weeks early, allowing (barely) adequate time to debate the merits of the treaty and ratify it. Since Jefferson's Republican Party held a lopsided 25–9 majority in the Senate, with its strength concentrated in the southern and western regions that were most sympathetic with expansionist policies, the required two-thirds vote for ratification seemed likely. But the defection of just three Republican Senators could kill the amendment. The measure, furthermore, also required a two-thirds majority in the House of Representatives, where the loss of nine members of the 102–39 Republican majority would likewise do in the amendment. And if the congressional hurdles were cleared, the amendment still had to win approval by the legislatures or special conventions in three-quarters of the seventeen then existing states. That meant Jefferson could afford to lose only four states, and since New England, where anti-Jeffersonian Federalism and antiexpansionist feelings ran high, consisted of five states, the outcome looked chancy indeed. And even if the amendment sailed through Congress, the debates in the states would surely protract the process beyond Napoleon's deadline.

As confidants, with all due respect for Jefferson's high principles, tried to prevail upon him not to risk losing this glorious opportunity to double the nation's size, an urgent message arrived in early August from Livingston in Paris. Rumors were swirling that Napoleon, who just weeks after approving the Louisiana sale had himself crowned at Notre Dame as emperor of France for life, was now reproving himself for excessive generosity toward the United States. One whispered theory was that his new imperial standing—or call it (very softly) his megalomaniacal sense of grandeur—would suffer by the sacrifice of France's potentially superb North American colony. And Spain's ceaseless carping about the sale was not helping. Whatever the truth, Livingston registered his earnest prayer that nothing should delay the Senate's prompt ratification of the treaty, and without altering "a syllable of the terms"—foot-dragging in Washington or nitpicking the text would only further sour Napoleon, who might seize on any excuse to cancel the sale. Such was the emperor's mood that, at the suggestion of Barbé-Marbois, Monroe took the initiative of prevailing upon the two banking houses that had agreed to fund the Louisiana Purchase to advance the $2 million that Congress had already authorized for such a purpose as what he hoped would be a binding down payment on the deal. Livingston was leery of such appeasement because, once given over, how could the money be recovered if for any reason Napoleon changed his mind? And why would a despot who had stolen mountains of treasure from half of Europe hesitate to rob America as well? In the end, though, Livingston saw the risk as justified.

Livingston's alert left Jefferson between the proverbial rock and a hard place and plunged him into a painful reverie of soul-searching. He had either to forgo his cherished ideals in this instance or to face the possibility, if not the likelihood, of losing the epochal purchase—and with it, the nation's continental destiny. As he weighed his choices, three considerations drove him to an anguished abandonment of his ideological consistency.

Foremost of these compelling reasons was territorial and political security. Owning Louisiana would keep the Mississippi basin out of foreign hands forever. It would remove the need for and expense of a standing army. And it would ensure, for generations, the future growth of an agrarian republic through an infinite supply of farmland, with its bountiful produce readily accessible to world markets. Such an expanded American domain would prevent the older states from growing overcrowded, urbanized, and industrialized—conditions that Jefferson feared as conducive to dehumanizing habits and antidemocratic practices. At times in the past, he had opposed the extension of the United States beyond the Mississippi as incompatible with the effective practice of representative democracy; far-flung republics with a widely dispersed electorate were hard to sustain by their very nature. But now Jefferson rationalized an infinitely expansive America by borrowing an argument from Madison and asking, in an apologia to a friend, "[W]ho can limit the extent to which the federative principle may operate effectively? The larger our association, the less will it be shaken by local passions." More territory, in short, meant a safer nation and more stable polity.

It would also mean, the President knew, heightened economic opportunity, as vital to securing national unity as the Constitution had so far proven in promoting America's political cohesion. The swelling tide of new western settlers needed to earn a livelihood, and if the federal government did not promptly take control of the Mississippi Valley and protect commerce across the whole trans-Appalachian expanse, the Union was at dire risk of disintegrating into two or more nations. With Louisiana in hand, growing demand for America's farm produce could be satisfied, and national prosperity enhanced. Acquisition of Louisiana would also brighten the still more alluring vision, if not promise, of a colossal United States extending one day from ocean to ocean and providing a single, self-sustaining continental marketplace.

Beyond these twin blessings, the Louisiana Purchase provided, in Jefferson's view, a unique opportunity to resolve the endlessly rancorous collision of cultures between Americans of European extraction and the native peoples. He had long been a believer in the ultimate assimilation of the Indians into the nation's social mainstream and never abandoned his professed conviction that they were racially equal to whites but had just not yet advanced to as high a level of civilization: they were still savages, to be sure, but stout of heart and capable over time of refined behavior and intellectual attainment. First, though, they had to learn to act like whites. For all his insatiable reading habits, Jefferson was hardly a student of anthropology—indeed, a discipline not yet invented—so he faulted the Indians for what, by his lights, was a glaring omission in their value system, the concept of land as private property. Individually cultivating the soil as independent freeholders was an alien notion to the natives, who lived communally and farmed for subsistence, not as a commercial enterprise. Tending the land was women's work, and their meager crops were just a supplement to what their male hunters provided after ranging over the broad terrain they considered theirs by custom, not possession. Jefferson believed their tribal, nomadic existence doomed the natives to poor nutrition, improvident habits, and a generally low standard of living—a primitive state correctable by selling off most of their hunting grounds to white settlers and using the revenue to establish farms under individual ownership.

When the Indians rejected farming as the best way to attain all good things in life—individualism and independence were not the core creed of the Indian; they were Jefferson's—yet declined to sell off their sprawling, uncultivated domains cheerfully to white settlers for a pittance, Jefferson attributed their recalcitrance to weak character: "Endeavors to enlighten them . . . are combatted by the habits of their bodies, the prejudice of their minds, ignorance, pride, [and] a sanctimonious reverence for the customs of their ancestors." If this was the sentiment of one of the most enlightened men of his nation, blaming the Indians for inviting their own victimization, it is hardly surprising that intolerance and inhumanity toward the nonwhite races was the common American practice.

By 1803 Jefferson had concluded that acculturation of the Indians was a futile dream, and the kindest solution was to insist that they give up their tribal lands east of the Mississippi, making room for hardworking (read: deserving) white settlers, in exchange for settlements in the wide-open spaces of the Louisiana wilderness, where they could persist in their Stone Age benightedness. One of his abandoned constitutional amendments of that year formulated such a plan in some detail, and even after it was set aside, Jefferson urged this course on delegations from the Chickasaw, Choctaw, and Cherokee tribes who visited him during his second term in the White House. Over the next three decades, successor American Presidents and their subordinates would urge, threaten, bribe, trick, and ultimately compel Indian tribes—including the Cherokees, who were earnestly taking up the white man's ways—to surrender their lands for pennies an acre, if that, and move to foreign places beyond the Great Father of Rivers, the Mississippi, many dying en route, the rest with hearts and spirits broken on arrival. In his 1999 study on the subject, anthropologist Anthony F. C. Wallace concluded sorrowfully that "the federal policy of removal—involuntary or voluntary—as the solution for dealing with Indians who rejected 'civilization' or waged war on the United States was established by Thomas Jefferson."

Even assuming that the purchase of Louisiana, in the President's estimate, would serve a myriad of social purposes, at least a few contemporary commentators foresaw the price to be paid in pain and suffering for the prized acquisition. Wrote "Citizen" in the *Connecticut Courant* of August 24, 1803:

> Louisiana is to be a field of blood before it is a cultivated field, and indeed a field of blood while it is cultivated. The natives of the soil, a numerous race who have never injured us, and never will 'til encroached upon, must be driven out, and a still more numerous race from Africa must be violently brought in to toil and bleed under the lash. Is it for such an extension of human liberty and of human happiness that we are called upon for such actions?

At the critical moment in the late summer of 1803, Jefferson put to one side any such thoughts he may have had, along with the holy trinity of doctrines that formed his political creed—states' rights, strict construction of the text of the Constitution, and limited use of power by the federal executive, each a vital protection against tyranny and a shield for every citizen's political and personal independence. He understood the gift outright that fate, in the guise of the impulsive young emperor of France, had presented to him. For a relative token, the United States could purchase a limitless future, and the opportunity had to be seized. Accompanying problems, he faithfully believed, would be solved by the good sense, ingenuity, endurance, and benevolence of future generations of Americans. Having told close friends and advisors of his grave concern about acting extralegally, the President pocketed his proposed amendments and never publicly mentioned his misgivings about the constitutionality of the Louisiana Purchase—it was up to the Senate to ratify the treaty or not. He explained his decision in a letter seven years later, after he had left public office:

> A strict observance of the written laws is doubtless one of the duties of a good citizen, but it is not the *highest.* The laws of necessity, of self-preservation, of saving our country when in danger, are of a higher necessity. To lose our country by a scrupulous adherence to written law, would be to lose the law itself, with life, liberty, property and all those who are enjoying them with us; thus absurdly sacrificing the end to the means.

The Senate convened October 17 and, heeding Jefferson's plea for swift action and no cavils over a single word of the text, promptly ratified the

Louisiana Purchase. The House, called upon to pass a companion appropriations bill to cover the administrative costs for taking control of the new territory, registered its uneasiness over certain aspects of the acquisition, including the suitability for citizenship of their new countrymen, many of whom did not speak English and were used to despotic rule. Since the President himself shared this anxiety, the administration committed itself to a more gradual, less liberating transition from colonial oversight to American democracy with its full array of constitutionally assured civil rights. In the end, Congress presented no obstacle to the colossal real-estate deal. In November, Spain docilely lowered its flag in the central square at New Orleans, and the French tricolor rose in its place—but stayed for less than three weeks. On December 20, some 500 American soldiers and state militiamen under the command of the scoundrel general James Wilkinson (still secretly on the Spanish government's pension roll) marched into New Orleans from the north and took charge of a territory that, according to eventual measurements by the federal Department of Interior, amounted to 909,380 square miles—the largest land acquisition the United States, or probably any nation, has ever made.

The enormous addition, wedge-shaped on a map, was bounded on the east by the full length of the Mississippi, on the north by Canada, and on the west and southwest by the far rim of the Missouri River basin, the sources of the Arkansas and Red rivers, and finally the Sabine River, which forms the boundary between the modern states of Texas and Louisiana. Not quite sated by this massive accretion of land, Jefferson would later claim that under the purchase the United States also owned a large slab of southeast Texas, because the French explorer La Salle had established a colony at Matagorda Bay well down the Gulf Coast. But there seemed no point in pressing the claim. From the Louisiana Purchase thirteen American states would eventually be formed in part or whole, beginning with the 50,000-square-mile southernmost sector, which had been designated the Territory of New Orleans shortly after the American takeover. Most of the new immigrants to the territory were of Anglo-American descent, so fears soon faded that the ethnic, religious, and linguistic diversity of the region would produce a human bouillabaisse that was savory but politically indigestible by the rest of the nation. Just nine years after the purchase, the New Orleans Territory was admitted as the eighteenth state in the Union and renamed Louisiana. The remainder of the huge trans-Mississippi domain was thereafter called the Missouri Territory, among other names. It would take 104 years after the great wilderness was acquired until the last state carved from it, Oklahoma, was admitted by Congress.

Although the Louisiana Purchase, in the estimate of most historians, was the high point of Jefferson's two-term presidency, it was not among the three foremost achievements of his life that he chose to have carved into his gravestone. Perhaps, with becoming modesty, he attributed the monumental event less to his own acumen than to the whim of France's military overlord. But without the Jefferson administration's fixed purpose, unabrasive manner, and political resiliency, the outcome might have been very different— and the lingua franca of the United States far more Gallic.

Sadly, the two American statesmen who negotiated the purchase would squabble over which of them deserved more credit for the transaction. Monroe's presence added stature to the team, and his initiative in making sure the risky good-faith down payment on the purchase reached Paris well before the Senate could consider ratification may have kept Napoleon from weaseling out of the agreement. It was Livingston, though, who had done the heavy lifting and helped set the stage for the French dictator's decision to abandon his North American colonial ambitions and make the United States his beneficiary. Nevertheless, it was Monroe who would go on to enjoy a successful two-term presidency, while Livingston sank into political obscurity, shadowed by reports of impropriety on his part in the oversight of payments to the American victims of the French navy's confiscations.

Even so, Livingston made one further invaluable contribution to his nation's well-being. He provided financial backing and technical assistance to Robert Fulton, whom he encountered in France while the inventor had been trying to develop weaponry and underwater craft for Napoleon's needy navy. Livingston invited Fulton to build a steamboat to make regular trips on the Hudson River between New York City and Albany. In 1807, just four years after Livingston had completed his mission in Paris, Fulton's 133-foot steam-powered flatboat, the *Clermont,* named for Livingston's riverfront estate, made its first successful run. Five years later, the first steamboat came down the Mississippi to New Orleans; by 1830, steamboats were docking there at the rate of a thousand a year. The breakthrough in transportation technology was in full swing, hastening the settlement of the trackless wilderness Jefferson & Co. had snatched up.

CHAPTER 8

From motives of purest patriotism

1803–1823

FACING NO SERIOUS EXTERNAL MENACE to their newly expanded dominion—what President Jefferson now took to fondly calling "the empire of democracy"—Americans enjoyed boom times in the years just after the acquisition of Louisiana and full command of the Mississippi Valley. The thrilling success of the Lewis and Clark expedition (1804–6) began to define the immensity and promise of their westward expanse, someday perhaps encompassing the whole width of the continent, while eastward the nation's trade with Europe surged. Exports, due largely to the spread of the time-saving cotton gin, which filtered the stubborn seeds from the plant's blossom, rose fivefold from 1790 to 1807, and that year international commerce reached nearly a quarter of a billion dollars, a level the country would not record again for a generation.

Prosperity spurred family formation and immigration as the nation's population increased about 36 percent during the first decade of the nineteenth century. This sustained growth was accompanied by the inevitable breakdown of the largest landholdings in the older states, where colonial grants had fostered a maldistribution of property of feudal proportions. In a flurry of democratizing legislation during and after the Revolutionary era, most states had outlawed the Old World practices of primogeniture and entail, designed to keep great land baronies intact, and over several generations the effects of this seismic shift in inheritance statutes were telling. For example, New York patroon Stephen Van Rensselaer had inherited an estate of 700,000 Hudson Valley acres as a young man, but when he died at seventy-five in 1830, his immense manor was divided among his ten children. Within half a century, most of the Van Rensselaer land had been sold off to or otherwise passed into the hands of strangers.

This evolutionary process in the older states was too slow to accommodate the upsurge in the American population, so most newcomers and the
offspring of older families turned westward to establish their territorial
roots. Thus, by 1810 Ohio had nearly as many residents as Connecticut, and
more than 40,000 settlers had edged into the Indiana Territory, as the rest of
the Old Northwest was designated for the federal government's administrative purposes. Below the Ohio, where the nation's lately acquired access to
the whole length of the Mississippi had an immediate economic impact, the
population swelled even faster; Kentucky's reached 85 percent of Massachusetts's total, Tennessee's grew by 150 percent in the decade, and in
Georgia, where the Yazoo Grants mess was finally being worked out, westward settlement pushed the state total past 250,000, up 60 percent since
1800.

This relentless tide was slowed for a time by the final resistance of the
native peoples east of the Mississippi, rallying behind the remarkable
Shawnee warrior Tecumseh and his brother, called the Prophet, who had
urged the northwest tribes to put aside their ancestral quarrels and stand
together against further white advances. The Indians were exhorted to shun
the palefaces' easy handouts of alcohol and the treaties they were inveigled into signing under its influence. No individual tribe, Tecumseh argued,
could legitimately sell land that was the birthright of all the native nations.
While paying lip service to peaceful coexistence with American settlers, he
preached that only intimidation and bloodletting could stanch the white
overflow—a policy that British interests, operating from Canada and still
dominating the fur trade throughout the Great Lakes region, were understood to be encouraging covertly.

Tecumseh's tribal confederation was an intolerable obstacle in the eyes
of the new governor of the Indiana Territory (and future, if short-lived, ninth
President of the United States), William Henry Harrison. Assigned to oversee orderly, bloodless settlement of the northwestern frontier, Harrison discouraged squatters and promoted occupancy only through certified sales of
land that had been surrendered by the Indians to the federal government.
The young general, out to make a name for himself, pushed hard for tribal
treaties, using the carrot-and-stick technique with telling effect. Within the
first decade of the new century, he extracted treaties ceding some 50 million
acres of tribal land in modern-day Indiana and Illinois. Tecumseh's defiance
of these arrangements had a chilling effect on westward white settlement
until Harrison broke up a large encampment of allied warriors on Tippeca-
noe Creek near the Wabash River in late 1811—a costly victory that effectively scattered but did not eliminate Indian resistance on the frontier. In the

debris at the wrecked battle site Harrison's men found a large cache of guns and ammunition of distinctly British origin, solid evidence to American eyes—along with Tecumseh's flight to Canada and commission as a general in the royal forces—that Britain was actively conniving to slow white settlement above the Ohio and keep the region profitable for its fur traders.

For the most part, though, Americans got along with the British subjects to their north, a substantial number of whom had drifted across the border from the United States, less concerned about nationality than eager to settle on the rich soil of southern Ontario and the St. Lawrence Valley. The vagueness of the U.S.-Canadian border, especially on its western end, was not a serious issue during that innocent interlude; about 80 percent of the English-speaking residents of Upper Canada were born Americans. Still unresolved was the boundary at the northwest corner of the United States, which, due to geographical ignorance at the time of the Treaty of Paris, did not exist in reality. Distressed British authorities thought they had won navigable access to the Mississippi by means of the boundary line drawn due west from Lake of the Woods to the presumed source of the river. Because the river rose, as explorations had subsequently determined, more than 150 miles south of the lake, a gap persisted in the boundary line. An even larger question was raised by American acquisition of Louisiana, which was understood, while it had been a French and Spanish colony, to extend to the sources of the rivers feeding the Mississippi from the west. It was at best an imprecise boundary, and no one really knew how far north the Louisiana Purchase extended or where it might conflict with any of the land claimed for British America by the western explorations of the Scotsman Alexander Mackenzie in the 1790s.

Of more pressing concern to the American government were the southern and western borders of Louisiana, disputed by the neighboring Spaniards. Even in its imperial death throes, stiff-necked Spain kept bellowing that France had illegitimately conveyed Louisiana to the United States and that, while Spain lacked the legions to force cancellation of the sale, President Jefferson's claim that West Florida and a large part of Texas were included in the transaction was without any certifiable merit. As if confessing the thinness of his claim, Jefferson prevailed on Congress in 1805 to appropriate $2 million for the United States to purchase both East and West Florida, the latter of which bordered on the Mississippi.

Spain's firm rejection of the offer was especially maddening to Americans, who, just as they had long discredited the Indians for not cultivating the great wilderness tracts they claimed for their hunting grounds, scorned the Spaniards for failing to colonize the Floridas energetically and realize any of their great economic and military potential. The only Spanish settlements of any consequence were the shabby little port towns at Mobile Bay and Pensacola on the Gulf Coast and the old mission community of St. Augustine on the Atlantic coast of East Florida. The solitary Spanish military bastion in the Floridas was the twenty-foot-high, stone-walled fortress of St. Marks at the northwestern corner of the 450-mile-long peninsula. To defend the twin colonies and their 1,500 miles of low-lying coastline, Spain had posted fewer than 1,000 soldiers, closer to 500 now, as civil upheavals overtook the empire both at home and in its more southerly New World colonies early in the nineteenth century. The Floridas' scanty population was an amalgam of several thousand Seminoles, a branch of the Creek nation; British landholders left over from their empire's twenty-year occupation (1763–83); Americans enticed across the border with land grants for pledging allegiance to the king of Spain; bands of runaway American slaves seeking shelter on foreign soil; gangs of pirates who preyed on coastal shipping from their lair on Amelia Island just below the mouth of the St. Mary's River, forming the boundary with Georgia; and a small number of Spaniards and creoles who presided over the colonies.

Although deficient in human resources, commercial development, and terrain suited for traditional crops, the Floridas drew the covetous eyes of their American neighbors largely for geographical reasons. If the United States were to snatch the drowsing, sun-drenched colonies away from their passive caretaker, its southern border would no longer vanish into the thickets and swampy overgrowth along the thirty-first parallel. Instead it would conform to the natural configuration of the coastline, defining the northeast portal to the Gulf of Mexico and extending to within ninety miles of Cuba, the pearl of the Caribbean archipelago. Besides the commercial promise of their immense coastline, the unified Floridas would serve as a barrier protecting New Orleans, the Mississippi Valley, and the whole southern extent of the nation against stealthy assault from the sea. The waters off Florida, moreover, were the principal sea lane between the two halves of the United States, carrying western produce to the Atlantic states and the global markets beyond. How much safer this vital route would be if guarded by naval way stations in American hands. And southern planters could then ship their crops directly down the smaller rivers emptying into the Gulf without having to pay Spanish export duties or send them west to the Mississippi for the longer shipping route to East Coast ports and Europe.

American southerners, especially those from Georgia and Tennessee, nursed a pair of grudges against Spanish control of the Floridas that quickened their eagerness to remove them from foreign ownership. Spanish officials, they charged, were behaving much like British ones in Canada by encouraging Indian nations to resist American settlers pushing west. In the South, the Spaniards were accused of befriending and supplying the formidable Creek and Cherokee peoples and even allowing the Floridas to be used as staging grounds for raids, all designed to scare off white newcomers to the western portion of Georgia. These backlands had finally been ceded to Congress on the proviso that the federal government would eventually extinguish all Indian title claims as far as the Mississippi and sell the rich, damp land at low prices. With cotton mills in Britain and Rhode Island beginning to clamor for the new southern staple, the plantocracy was keen to broaden its dominion and intensify the use of its nearly 1.5 million slaves. The new plantations in the Deep South's coastal plain imposed a harsher form of slavery than in the older regions farther north. As a result, a growing number of blacks were fleeing across the border to asylum in the Floridas, which would not be available under U.S. control.

In blaming the Spaniards for inciting the Indians to war on white settlers, Americans were undoubtedly seeking scapegoats for their own transgressions. Few on the frontier made a genuine effort to understand the natives' culture or needs; most dealt with them harshly, deaf to the federal government's hollow call for fair treatment while its officers averted their eyes from the constant violation of the Indians' treaty rights. Such behavior naturally provoked reprisals, which, in turn, were seized upon by the ever-swelling ranks of white arrivals to demand the removal, if not the destruction, of the natives, whom they condemned as incorrigible savages and a vile impediment to civilization. How much easier for white America to heap scorn on the Spaniards for their alleged role in encouraging the Indians and runaway slaves—and to press harder still against their loosely held Gulf Coast colonies—than to admit that its own racially driven doctrines and conduct were the prime culprit.

By 1810 Spain was so distracted by the devastating Peninsular War at home and colonial insurgents on the march as far north as Mexico City and as far south as Buenos Aires that President Madison saw little risk in approving the successful assault by several hundred American civilians against the twenty-eight Spaniards holding the fort at Baton Rouge at the edge of West Florida. With congressional assent, Madison proclaimed the western half of the Spanish colony, from the Mississippi east to the Pearl River, to be U.S. territory, and annexed it to the District of New Orleans. Two years later, Congress designated the area as the eastern extension of Louisiana when it achieved statehood. By then it had become plain that only American self-restraint, in deference to Old World powers (Spain excepted), was preventing the United States from outright seizure of the rest of the Floridas.

Something beyond the passions of nationalistic pride and racism toward nonwhites sustained this expansionist impulse. One might have thought the nation's collective territorial appetite had been fully satisfied for the fore-seeable future by the Louisiana Purchase, extending beyond the wildest imaginings of most Americans. That their land hunger raged on seemed to defy rational explanation but for one salient factor: Americans were not effi-cient farmers—far from it. Their prodigious wastefulness was no doubt rooted in the sheer abundance of arable soil and its relative cheapness com-pared to the cost of labor to cultivate it. As a result, American farmers hack-ing a livelihood out of the wilderness typically cleared only as much cropland as they needed to survive and kept the rest in woodland for build-ing and fuel. Whether from inertia, ignorance, or fatigue, they were not dili-gent about rotating crops and manuring their fields, thus rapidly depleting the soil. Nor were they inclined to set aside enough cleared land for pasture or to plant grass seed for hay, forcing them to let their livestock forage in the wild and suffer the consequences. It did not help that farmers generally had too few tools—and poorly made ones at that—for performing their back-breaking chores and suffered the hardships of physical isolation when try-ing to buy supplies or sell their surplus harvests.

Jefferson's agrarian noblemen, the toilers in the American earth, thus saw no value in trying to maximize their productivity. Instead, they craved virgin soil, allowing them to prosper despite improvident habits, but it was played out all too soon. Unlike their Old World counterparts, who were forced to pamper their land and coax every last turnip from it or go hungry, the typical American farmer needed a large tract to survive; slave-driving plantation owners needed still vaster holdings to turn a profit from one-crop farming. Few of them, yeomen and large-scale farmers alike, ever had enough land for their perceived needs. Driven by their extravagant per capita consumption of the soil, they were always on the lookout for new and better fields. As the westward movement accelerated and new states and ter-ritories were added to the Union, the political potency of agrarian interests grew in proportion, resulting in a national policy of expansionism most evi-dent in the West and South. This territorial craving now provoked a danger-ous new encounter with Great Britain.

RENEWAL OF THE NAPOLEONIC WARS in 1803 had at first proved highly advantageous to the economy of the United States. Its trade with the combatants soared as Britain and France tried to starve and pauperize each other by intercepting cargoes bound to or from enemy ports even if on neutral carriers. Every major harbor in Europe was crowded with American vessels and produce, bringing high profits to the carrying trade and allowing seamen on ships flying the flag of the United States to enjoy a better livelihood—their pay rose from eight dollars a month to three times that amount—and better food and working conditions than crews of other nationalities. These benefits naturally attracted foreign sailors to sign on to American ships, especially tars from the British naval and maritime service who, in violation of their national law, gave up their citizenship and gladly filled out naturalization papers. An estimated 25 percent of the 70,000 or so crewmen in the American commercial fleet were ex-Britons. Locked in a grim war with France and its high-riding dictator, England's rulers did not take kindly to losing so many able-bodied seamen to America. The crackdown was not long in coming.

Under new Orders in Council, similar in kind to those inaugurated in the 1790s after the outbreak of war with the radicalized republic of France but now more rigorously applied, the royal navy began to hound American merchant ships, removing cargo bound for French ports and sailors charged with abandoning King George's service. Rationalized as a wartime necessity, this bullying practice (which Jay's Treaty, signed a decade earlier, had failed to curb) was a tacit declaration that Britain would pay the United States as much respect as its military prowess warranted—which was to say almost none at all. Even so, President Jefferson chose not to ask Congress for funds to build and man a navy capable of protecting American freedom on the seas, an undertaking he believed futile in the face of Britain's estimated 800 fighting ships. America's best—perhaps only—weapon, he thought, was economic pressure, and in 1806 Congress voted the Nonintercourse Act, barring all British imports, a tactic that had proven successful when employed by American colonists in the pre-Revolutionary years. It quickly proved a counterproductive measure, greatly reducing revenues from import duties, which provided most of the funds to operate the U.S. government.

The egregious nature of Britain's belligerency was dramatized in June 1807 when one of its warships hovering off the Virginia coast shelled the American frigate *Chesapeake* into submission, killing three sailors, wounding eighteen others, removing a handful of so-called British deserters, and leaving the crippled merchant ship to limp home to Norfolk. The unprovoked attack a stone's throw from the American shore goaded Jefferson and Congress into imposing an embargo on all American exports—to

France as well as Britain, because Napoleon had decreed that all ships in harbors under French control and carrying cargoes bound for Britain could be seized. Jefferson acted on the dubious theory that Europe's warring nations needed products from the United States so badly that they would soon be forced to restore the rights of neutral ships. This draconian measure at once awakened an outcry from the nation's commercial interests, concentrated in New England and New York, who denounced the policy as misguided and bound to hurt the United States far more than its antagonists by killing off the very trade it was intended to protect. Such wholesale interference with the disposition of property of American citizens, they added, was unconstitutional.

These fears and objections were well founded. The import ban further reduced government revenues while promoting heavy smuggling, and the embargo caused an 80 percent drop in exports within a year of its enactment, serious unemployment in the mercantile trade, and rampant inflation. The boom times were over; Jefferson left office with his luster dimmed and his misbegotten gestures of defiance toward the European powers repealed by Congress.

Faced with unabating British oppression on the high seas, the succeeding President, James Madison, soon heard a rising chorus of demands that he take military action, notwithstanding that the United States was practically devoid of armed forces while its chief antagonist was the superpower of the age. The clamor, louder the farther one traveled from the mercantile Northeast, which was opposed to war because it would badly disrupt commerce, grew more fevered with the 1810 congressional election. The results brought to the House of Representatives a flock of so-called War Hawks, mostly young, flag-waving, fist-raising firebrands from western and southern states who saw in Britain's punitive maritime policy a parallel to its connivance with the Indians to slow the westward push of American settlement. The press, feeding the political ferment (and vice versa), was full of reports, exaggerated if not apocryphal, of widespread mayhem visited on the settlers by tribal warriors under British patronage, rewarding them—it was said by way of example—for every American scalp collected along the frontier. The only way to repay Britain for such viciousness, ran the growing refrain, was to deprive it forcibly of the empire's principal remaining New World treasure, Canada—perhaps not all of it but at least some of it. The national Republican majority's endorsement of this enterprise was articulated, suitably enough, by its iconic spokesman, Thomas Jefferson, hardly a war lover, who condemned the British as inveterate enemies out to destroy the government of the United States. Their war on American shipping and endless intrigue with the Indians, said Jefferson, "prove the cession of Canada, the fulcrum for these Machiavellian levers, must be a sine qua non at a peace treaty."

The notion of ridding the North American mainland of its meddlesome and subversive British presence proved irresistible in part because it seemed so easily manageable. The population of the United States was twelve times larger than British America's, and the crown's military presence in scattered postings across more than 2,000 miles from Nova Scotia to Lake Superior was understood not to exceed 8,500 soldiers. Such thin deployment left the Canadian border open to easy violation in countless places. And if American troops managed to capture one or two key strongholds on the St. Lawrence, no British fleet could make its way upriver to rescue the Canadian heartland from the invaders. Such a mission, moreover, would be difficult for Britain to mount while it was struggling to overcome Napoleon's rampaging armies. So sanguine was the military outlook that Jefferson, suddenly eager for a military solution of the kind he had steadfastly rejected while in the White House, predicted in 1812, "The acquisition of Canada this year, as far as the neighborhood of Quebec, will be a mere matter of marching, and will give us experience for the attack on Halifax [hub of British North America's military operations] the next, and the final expulsion of England from the American continent."

Beyond avenging American humiliation at Britain's hands, two other justifications were commonly given for undertaking the conquest of Canada. One was the emerging creed of continentalism, the conviction that the United States was destined—indeed, entitled—to spread its dominion across the breadth of North America, perhaps even owning the entirety of it. The Canadian phase of the project was endorsed with evangelical ardor by a leading War Hawk, Kentucky's Representative (and future Vice President of the United States) Richard M. Johnson, noting, "The waters of the St. Lawrence and Mississippi interlock in a number of places, and the great Dispenser of Human Events intended those two rivers should belong to the same people." Either Johnson or the Dispenser got it wrong—the two rivers never quite interlock—but his figurative sentiment was what mattered to those beating the war drums.

In a more altruistic vein, the champions of American territorial aggrandizement insisted they were advocating not the conquest of Canada but its liberation. As early as 1805 Jefferson was saying in private, and apparently without need of corroboration, that Canada wanted to be a part of the United States. The doughty former Revolutionary War campaigner he appointed that year as the first governor of the Michigan Territory, William Hull, echoed Jefferson's conviction when, upon leading the first American assault on Canadian soil seven years later, he proclaimed the United States was offering the Canadians "the invaluable blessings of Civil, Political, and Religious Liberty," so that (like it or not) they could be "emancipated from Tyranny and oppression and restored to the dignified status of freedom."

Such rationales for an American takeover of Canada were open to persuasive rebuttal, suggesting that the true motive was something less ennobling. The Northeast's mercantile community and the remnant of Federalist Party spokesmen argued that invading Canada would play into the hands of Napoleon by distracting the British from their European war effort and almost surely inciting them to impose a blockade of American ports, with consequences still more devastating than those that had resulted from Jefferson's shutdown of shipping to and from the United States. And even if the invasion of Canada proved successful, wouldn't the infuriated British become more, not less, likely to deny the United States freedom of the seas and still more dogged in their pursuit of former royal seamen on American ships?

As to British incitement of the Indians along the American frontier, where was the hard evidence? British traders undoubtedly were supplying the natives with guns, but only for use in hunting, they claimed; at any rate, Americans also sold weapons to the Indians, not to mention alcohol, which could stir them to violence as well as drug them into submissiveness. But massacres of settlers were few and far between, and the native tribes, in the view of South Carolina's waspish and eloquent Congressman John Randolph, were more sinned against than sinning. The number of American settlers had greatly surpassed the surviving native population—by 1810, for example, there were an estimated 55,000 white males over twenty-one in Ohio alone and hardly 5,000 Indian warriors at large in the frontier regions, a ratio that should have been more than sufficient to deal with an occasional outburst of tribal vengeance. In the Federalist Randolph's view, it was purely propaganda concocted by Republican expansionists to blame Britain for stirring up what relatively little violence the Indians were guilty of; it was the American settlers themselves who supplied the tribesmen with all the grievances they needed by treating them as beasts of the forest deserving little better than to be hunted down and eliminated.

As to the great boon the United States would bestow on Canadians by liberating them from British tyranny, the only prominent evidence that such a gift would be welcome was a petition by a group of Montreal businessmen inviting American annexation. Few Canadians showed interest in embracing the mixed blessings of rowdy American democracy; most preferred the elitist privileges, commercial incentives, and officious orderliness that the royal British regime offered them for remaining loyal crown subjects. Finally, even if, as some argued, the Canadians could hardly be expected to appreciate what they were missing, what moral justification could the United States claim for seizing the territory of its inoffensive neighbors when the real objects of American wrath were the masters of the British empire on the far side of the Atlantic? A distinguished Massachusetts congressman, Josiah Quincy, came close to the mark when he branded the Canadian invasion "cruel, wanton, senseless, and wicked."

The patent disingenuousness of the pro-war faction emerges only when the War of 1812 is viewed not as a retributive crusade against British deviltry or as an act of deliverance in the name of democracy (very like the announced motive for the U.S. invasion and occupation of Iraq nearly two centuries later) but as an act of muggery, intended primarily for the territorial aggrandizement of a land-greedy people. The soil of the St. Lawrence Valley and the Great Lakes basin was as fertile as any on earth and had barely been violated by farm implements. The weather was temperate enough in southern Canada for a bountiful growing season, rainfall was plentiful, waterways were abundant and allowed relatively easy transportation of produce to foreign markets, and there was an immense supply of timber close at hand for building, fencing, and fuel. All of these advantages made the adjacent region of British America more alluring to western settlers than the remote trans-Mississippi plains that comprised so large a portion of the Louisiana Purchase. That far country was known to be drier and otherwise less hospitable to cultivation; trees were scarce, the sod of deeply rooted grasses was hard to turn with the crude farm tools of the age, and water transportation was much more problematic than over the splendid network of rivers constituting the eastern Mississippi Valley. Historian Louis M. Hacker, a leading proponent of this explanation for the war, which was hardly trumpeted at the time, stated his case bluntly more than a century later: "Land was necessary for the development of an agricultural society and the Ohio Valley turned to Canada for the replenishing of its supply."

The patriot's inclination to dismiss this argument as simplistic, or even subversive, collides with troublesome realities. How better than down-to-earth territorial greed to explain the apparent irony that the Northeast, the nation's engine of commerce and the region hit hardest by Britain's abusiveness toward the American oceangoing trade, was stoutly opposed to waging war while the agrarian, expansionist West and South, farthest removed from the British maritime depredations, were the most ardent in calling for the conquest of Canada? And if British abridgment of American freedom to trade as a neutral cargo carrier was its prime justification for going to war, why didn't the United States do so as well against France, which was an equally guilty, if less effective, offender? The most plausible answer is that France held no territory close by the United States that could be readily attacked and its soil seized under the pretext of a justifiable reprisal for Napoleon's harassment of American merchant vessels.

However speciously reasoned or cynically self-interested the outcries of the War Hawks and their allies, James Madison felt he could no longer resist them when his War Department reported in 1812 that the number of documented cases of sailors forcibly removed by the British from American merchant ships had reached 6,000. The war faction in his own party demanded military action as the price for backing his reelection to the White House that fall.

THE WAR OF 1812 was a masterpiece of miscalculation from the start. Madison, a brilliant student of politics but a pliable President, mismanaged almost every phase of the conflict, and his cabinet was of little help. Together they blinded themselves to the nation's total unpreparedness to go to war and, once in it, to fight it with conviction. Unlike the Revolutionary War, when the country's very existence was at stake, the 1812 aggression grew out of a perceived need to redeem America's sullied honor by helping itself to the tempting property of innocent neighbors. Subduing gentle Canada was a manifestation of expansionist ideology; it was not a cause, or even the coarse means to an exalted end, to inspire an outpouring of patriots ready to die for it.

Mindful that he had only a lilliputian army and a navy of, at most, twenty battle-worthy ships large and small, Madison prevailed on Congress to authorize armed forces of 36,700 recruits, about four times the total of British regulars defending Canada. But what ought to have been an overwhelming American advantage in manpower would never materialize. At no point during the two-and-a-half-year conflict were there more than 10,000 American regulars in the field. Madison's generals, mostly aging Revolutionary War veterans far from combat-ready, were forced to rely on state militiamen to do the heaviest fighting. In too many instances they balked at orders to cross the border and kill Canadians and would engage only when the enemy ventured onto the Americans' home turf.

Just how hopelessly unrealistic the War Department was in framing the American battle strategy may be inferred from Henry Adams's description of the assignment handed to William Hull in the opening phase of the war in

Canada. General Hull's chief credential to spearhead the assault appears to have been the virulent animosity he provoked among the Indians for having efficiently stripped away their lands while he was the territorial governor of Michigan. According to Adams, Hull was instructed by his government

> with a force which it knew did not at the outset exceed two thousand effectives, to march two hundred miles, constructing a road as he went; to garrison Detroit; to guard at least sixty miles of roads under the enemy's guns; to face a force in the field equal to his own, and another savage force [that is, of Indians] of unknown numbers in his rear; to sweep the Canadian peninsula [in southern Ontario] of British troops; to capture the fortress at Malden and the British fleet on Lake Erie—and to do all this without the aid of a man or a boat between Sandusky and Quebec.

Hull immediately proved to be a calamitous commander. After initially occupying a healthy swath of Canadian territory without meeting resistance, he failed to press his logistical advantage. Then he refused to engage at all—in part, he later explained in his defense, for fear of injuring noncombatants and damaging their property—and retreated to regroup, only in the end to surrender the American fort at Detroit without firing a shot. Hull's incompetence, unfortunately, was not an isolated case. Plagued by insufficient troops with inadequate training, indecisive and dilatory leadership, woeful disorganization, and frequent breaks in the chain of command, American forces could manage only an occasional display of military aptitude.

What had been forecast as an easy conquest soon degenerated into a see-saw contest as each side captured lakefront forts from the other and took temporary hold of the nearby territory. But neither belligerent ever penetrated very far into the other's land or took permanent possession of it. Since reinforcements were unavailable to the Canadian side until the big war in Europe wound down, the British troops sustained their effort on the strength of superior leadership. And if the American side had expected Canada's civilian population, a majority of them emigrants from the United States, to greet their invading former countrymen as liberators, it was shortly spared the delusion. Quite the opposite reaction set in as American soldiers preyed on the countryside, mindlessly despoiling homes, fields, and orchards. Perhaps they thought they would win over Canadian hearts and minds when in April 1813, in the war's most shameless display of American brutality, they overcame the 600-man garrison at Upper Canada's capital, York (later

renamed Toronto), and devoted four days to burning and looting the town—
an atrocity that would be famously avenged near the close of hostilities.
Even after William Henry Harrison scored one of the rare decisive victories
for the American side at the Battle of the Thames* above Lake Erie in the
autumn of 1813, taking 600 British prisoners and much equipment, the war
remained an exercise in protracted futility. Harrison was unable to follow up
his success with a breakthrough as Canada's defenders held the invaders in
check and at times sent them reeling back across the border.

Surprisingly, America's sailors fared far better than expected against the
vaunted British fleet. What few vessels the United States Navy sent into
ocean combat more often than not outgunned and outran British warships in
isolated encounters. A hastily built little inland fleet swept British craft from
the Great Lakes, and a gnatlike swarm of American privateers captured and
plundered hundreds of British merchant vessels on the open sea. In the end,
though, the United States could not long withstand the mighty royal navy as
it methodically imposed an ever wider and tighter blockade on American
seaports, causing severe shortages, soaring prices, and the virtual bankruptcy of the federal treasury, bereft of import duties.

On top of the dire civilian hardships and the War Department's failure to
gain the upper hand on the battlefield while the main body of British forces
was bogged down in Europe, regional dissension was poisoning the political atmosphere and further draining national morale. Many in the Northeast
denounced the war effort as pointless, some civic leaders called for constitutional reforms to exempt dissenting states from compulsory participation
in ill-considered national wars, and a secessionist movement grew apace in
New England and New York.

Disheartened by the blundering course of their military misadventures
and the deadlock on the Canadian border, Americans were cheered in midwar by news from the South, where it had been feared a British expeditionary force, with Spanish complicity, might land and sweep though the
thinly defended Mississippi Valley. Early in 1813, Congress backed Madison's request for American forces to seize the eastern half of West Florida
before it could be used by the British as a beachhead for a major campaign
aimed at New Orleans and control of the Mississippi. In April army units
under General James Wilkinson—that such an unsavory character was in
command of forces posted at New Orleans testified to the sorry state of the

---

*Upward of 1,000 Shawnees and other Indian warriors fought on the British side and
gave way to the American assault. Among the natives who fell at the Battle of the Thames
was their inspirational leader, Tecumseh, whose remains were mutilated by Kentucky riflemen, slicing strips of the skin from his thighs to use as razor strops, a grisly souvenir of the
fray.

American military—talked the Spanish commander of Fort Charlotte at Mobile harbor into surrendering his 150-man garrison and, with it, control of the strategic colony. It would prove the only enduring territorial conquest of the war by the United States, muting but not quite silencing Spain's insistence that it was the rightful owner of the territory. Soon after, word reached Washington of the exploits of a passionate militia leader, Andrew Jackson, a novice commander who, at the age of forty-six, had put aside his successful career as a Tennessee lawyer, politician, and land dealer to go on the warpath against the embedded Indian nations of the Deep South for allegedly abetting the Spanish cause.

A native of the North Carolina backcountry, born without rank or privilege, Jackson lost his parents at an early age and, as a teenage soldier in the Revolutionary War, endured imprisonment by the British and smallpox, which took his brother's life. Young Andy managed to gain enough schooling to read for the law and then headed west to make his mark, almost a caricature of the flinty frontiersman—bold, energetic, brimming with ambition, and beholden to no man.

But Jackson was no drifting backwoodsman. A mediocre lawyer but canny opportunist, he consorted with Tennessee's power brokers in politics and business to gain a leg up however he could. His arresting appearance helped: narrow eyes of a dazzling bright blue, a shaft of jaw, a full stiff crown of hair, ramrod posture that made him look taller than his sinewy six-foot-one frame, all imparting a granite will to his domineering manner. His uneven temperament, erupting volcanically at times and turning him into a foul-mouthed bully, made him a still more intimidating presence—not always a passport to advancement. In fact, his career was a mixed bag. Liked well enough to be chosen Tennessee's first member in the United States House of Representatives, where his modest performance served to win him promotion to the Senate, Jackson was too much a man of action to relish confinement in legislative chambers. Heading home to Nashville, he thrived as a state judge, cotton planter, and slaveowner but never notably distinguished himself.

Jackson's avocational interest in the state militia would now change all that. His natural bent for leadership and an easy comradery with the enlistees soon propelled him to the top command of Tennessee's military volunteers, whose principal task was to quell periodic clashes between settlers and Indians. His ambition as a part-time soldier was to rid the South of foreign elements threatening the peace, prosperity, and growth of the region: British arms dealers and traders, Spanish officials bent on inhibiting America's territorial and economic expansion, and, most of all, the native peoples. Jackson regarded them as incorrigibly wild creatures, ruled by what he called their "savage manners and customs" so long as they were allowed to roam unchecked over wide territory. Echoing Jefferson's contention and likewise casting himself as humane and paternalistic toward the Indians, Jackson called for their vast hunting grounds to be sharply reduced—for their own good, he said, since the shrinkage would compel them to become domesticated. He omitted, of course, that the Indians' territorial loss would be the white settlers' gain. His devoted soldiers may have nicknamed Jackson "Old Hickory" for his toughness, but it was not for nothing that the Indians would soon take to calling him "Sharp Knife." One of Jackson's leading biographers, Robert V. Remini, in evaluating his treatment of native Americans, remarked, "Fortunately, no one these days seriously indicts Jackson as a mad racist intent upon genocide." He may not have been a mad racist in his dealings with Indians, but he was certainly an industrious one. (The extent of his racism toward blacks may be inferred from his ownership of so many of them; at times he possessed no fewer than 150 slaves at his beloved Hermitage.)

The Creek Indians, concentrated in western Georgia and Alabama, close by the Tennessee border, had resisted growing pressure from white settlers, but some among them recognized the inevitability of their subjugation unless they adopted many of the white man's ways. These Creek assimilationists became locked in a civil war with tribal diehards who refused to abandon their culture and territory even if it meant dying for them. Their strife occasionally spilled over and claimed the lives of whites, sometimes accidentally in the crossfire, sometimes in reprisal for their trying to tame the holdouts. After a skirmish their side lost, a party of 800 angry native militants descended on Fort Mims in southern Alabama at the end of August 1813 and took the scalps of 250 whites and mixed-bloods. The assault was the Creeks' death knell.

Andrew Jackson, leading 2,500 militiamen from Tennessee and Georgia, was assigned to avenge the Fort Mims massacre. Inexperienced in battle and never a keen student of strategy, he learned as he went and excelled at inspiring loyalty and obedience among his men. Together, they overcame difficult terrain and low supplies, moved swiftly against an enemy practiced at stealth, and attacked with tigerish ferocity. Even on their native ground, the Creeks, armed mostly with red clubs and scalping knives, were no match for Jackson's soldiers, who soon perfected encirclement as a tactic to trap their prey and, with far deadlier weapons, slay them en masse. At Talladega his men killed 300 braves and lost only fifteen of their own. At Talluschatches they slew 186 and lost only five: "We shot them like dogs," recalled Davy Crockett, one of Jackson's militiamen. In the decisive battle at Horseshoe Bend, his forces cut off 1,000 Creeks camped on a peninsula, rumbled cannons to within 200 yards of the Indian dugouts, and between assaults blasted away for a day and a night; in the morning 550 Indian corpses lay on the killing field. Jackson was a virtuoso at exterminating native Americans.

His "Creek War," taking some 3,000 Indian lives, or about 15 percent of what was left of the Creek people, effectively ended their war-making capacity. The remainder were quick to surrender before "Sharp Knife" did them in as well or to take cover with their Seminole kinsmen in Florida. Though skeptical about entering into treaties with Indian tribes—who to his thinking were not sovereign nations as they claimed but subject to the same laws as all other Americans—he nevertheless imposed the Treaty of Fort Jackson in the summer of 1814, under which the Creeks, in expiation for the toll they had taken in white lives and property, were forced to renounce title to some 24 million acres, comprising 60 percent of the modern state of Alabama and 20 percent of present-day Georgia, more than half their domain. The rearranged map of the land remaining to them ringed the Creeks with white settlements separating them from their tribal neighbors, the Choctaws, Chickasaws, and Cherokees, in a transparent divide-and-conquer pattern. The treaty, accepted at gunpoint, allowed government-built roads and trading posts to impinge on Indian land, so almost at once passing soldiers, peddlers, squatters, and other white intruders were clawing away at the Creeks' shrunken homeland.

Jackson's punishment of the Creeks by decimation and confinement did not directly affect the course of the larger war with Britain. But his bloodletting solidified America's southern frontier and bound it more closely to the rest of the nation in two ways. By almost obliterating the threat of Indian reprisals for land-grabbing, Jackson advanced Jefferson's policy, first stated a decade earlier, of improving national security by promoting settlement of the southern Mississippi Valley. Beyond that, Jackson had denied the British use of the southern Indian tribes as guerrilla fighters or even, as in Canada, openly active allies in any contemplated military campaign in the region. For his conquests, achieved without direction or oversight by the War Department or anyone else, Jackson was awarded the rank of major general in the regular U.S. Army and given command of its southern operations. He was now in position to lead American forces in the concluding chapter of an inglorious war.

HAVING SQUANDERED ITS MILITARY ADVANTAGE in numbers, geography, and timing for more than two years and found itself mired in a stalemate, Madison's government learned to its dismay in late April 1814 that

Paris had fallen the month before to the British-led alliance. Napoleon was done for, and the full force of Britain's battle-hardened war machine would likely soon be directed against the empire's pesty foes in North America.

To teach their ex-colonists a painful lesson, the British high command hurried plans to send some 20,000 troops on a two-pronged sea-and-land expedition and bring a decisive end to the war. The northern arm of the British force was assigned a pair of objectives: first, to capture Massachu-setts's heavily wooded, lightly defended, and Tory-leaning province of Maine, Nova Scotia's immediate neighbor, opening an overland route from Montreal and Quebec to the warm-water port of Halifax, and second, to achieve what Burgoyne had notoriously failed to do in the War for Indepen-dence—drive a wedge from Canada down the Lake Champlain–Hudson River Valley corridor to the sea, shutting off commercially vital (and anti-war) New England and New York from the rest of the nation. The southern British assault force would deliver hard, destructive strikes at Atlantic coastal towns and try to disrupt governmental operations in Washington before sailing on to capture New Orleans and deny the Americans use of the Mississippi for exporting their western produce. If successful, Britain might even return Louisiana to Spain in exchange for permanent commercial priv-ileges on the great river to which Canadians had no direct access.

As the British attackers were weighing anchor, Madison learned that Britain's formidable foreign minister, Robert Stewart, known as Viscount Castlereagh, who had orchestrated the international alliance that brought down Napoleon, was prepared to welcome a United States peace commis-sion on neutral ground in order to end the bleeding in America. The Presi-dent, with his soldiers having gained little ground overall, his country's economy devastated by the effects of the unbreakable British blockade, his government on the edge of insolvency, and antiwar sentiment threatening to undo the federal union, lost little time in sending a five-man delegation to meet with Castlereagh's emissaries.

Convening at Ghent, Belgium's banking and textile center, in mid-August 1814, the American peace commission included, as it had at Paris in 1782, three of the nation's ablest public officials. Its nominal leader and sole professional diplomat, John Quincy Adams, had served while a teenager as his father's secretary at the Paris peace talks and grew up sharing many of his best and less winning traits. Father and son were both learned Har-vard alumni, keen lawyers, and courageous in defense of high principles. They were both also insistently puritanical, of a deeply suspicious nature, and deficient at times in the social graces—John Quincy called himself "a man of reserved, cold, austere, and forbidding manners." But behind his rumpled garments, high bald dome, rheumy eyes, and taut lips was a first-rate intellect, imaginative as well as analytical, that had served him well as an independent-minded U.S. Senator and American ambassador to Holland, Prussia, and, lately, Russia. Adams's senior colleague in the delegation was Albert Gallatin, the Swiss immigrant of aristocratic ancestry who fell in love with American republicanism. After succeeding as a Pennsylvania farmer, land speculator, and politician, he had turned in an extraordinary fourteen-year performance as Secretary of the Treasury under Jefferson and Madison. If not quite Adams's intellectual peer, Gallatin surpassed him in tact and worldliness, inviting his fellow commissioners to look to him as their de facto leader. The other member of the stellar triumvirate was Kentucky's thirty-seven-year-old politician par excellence, the eloquent and convivial Henry Clay, leader of the War Hawks in the House of Representatives, from which he had taken leave as the Speaker to join the peace talks to end the conflict he had done much to ignite. A cheerful wheeler-dealer and daring gambler, whom historian George Dangerfield described as "the airy master of men and events," Clay was a perfect foil to the dour Adams and pragmatic Gallatin and sustained his colleagues' often sagging spirits by labeling the tough British negotiating stance a bluff that should neither intimidate the American team nor drive it from the peace table in frustration.

Lord Castlereagh, a suave, handsome, amiable aristocrat who stood at the peak of his powers with the victorious outcome of the European war, was the first ranking British statesman since Shelburne to appreciate fully that Anglo-American amity could prove far more advantageous to his kingdom than antagonism. He saw as well that the British public, after twenty years of ceaseless warfare and accompanying economic privation, craved a period of repose. To prolong the conflict with the United States in the hope of highly uncertain and problematic territorial gains—and thereby hand the Americans a boxing about the ears for trying to snatch Canada from the empire—was surly policy, to his way of thinking.

Before embarking for the epochal Congress of Vienna, where the triumphant Continental powers planned to redraw the map of Napoleon-free Europe, Castlereagh concluded he would hold a stronger diplomatic hand if he could promise a speedy resolution to the war in America. A prospective peace there might well ease his dealings with Russia's semi-enlightened tsar, Alexander I, a rising force in the European power equation, now that Napoleon was seemingly out of the way. Behind this surmise was Russian sympathy with the demand by the United States for freedom of the seas, ostensibly the primary cause of the North American war, and for Britain to refrain from further interference with international shipping—a concession Castlereagh's government was not yet prepared to discuss.

The British foreign minister was convinced the surest way to bring the American negotiators to heel was to talk of peace, yield nothing, and simultaneously deliver hard military blows. He instructed his envoys at Ghent to demand a great deal at first, hoping the war-weary United States, fearful of worse bloodshed and major British victories ahead, would be willing to make highly unpleasant but unavoidable concessions. Thus, as the royal navy was ferrying the two large expeditionary forces to American shores during these opening talks, Castlereagh's peace team called for a major revision of the boundaries of the United States, providing direct British access to the Mississippi and Ohio rivers through the creation of a vast Indian territory, to serve as a buffer against future American attacks on Canada. For good measure, the British peacemakers added that by seeking to conquer Canada, the United States had forfeited its "liberty" to fish off the Newfoundland coast—as granted by the Paris treaty of 1783—and that Britain saw no reason to refrain from its self-protective policy of intercepting foreign shipping whenever it seemed warranted. But ending these abuses of maritime freedom, the American team replied at once under instructions from Secretary of State Monroe, was a requisite for any peace accord. And far from a willingness to yield an inch of American territory, they asked instead that Britain consider the handover of Canada, or at least Upper Canada, roughly the equivalent of the southern portion of modern Ontario province. The deliberations were not off to a promising start.

Ten days after the first session at Ghent, 4,000 British raiders swept inland from Chesapeake Bay, drove off a larger, haphazard assemblage of American irregulars defending the road to Washington, and then, without opposition, set the nation's capital ablaze, badly damaging most government buildings. It was an act of vengeance for the American destruction of York, the capital of Upper Canada, the year before and sent President Madison and his aides scurrying for the Virginia hills. A week later, at the beginning of September, a second British army debarked at the mouth of the Castine River and began marching on Bangor, Maine. It soon held the northeastern half of the province, including 100 miles of coastline, and was imposing an oath of allegiance to His Royal Majesty, durable George III, on the submissive residents. These humiliations were just the sort Castlereagh had hoped would swiftly bring America to its knees.

By the time news of the British expeditionary forces' opening victories reached Ghent, however, a series of events more encouraging to the American side had unfolded. They began with word of two pivotal peace pacts with the Indians—the Treaty of Fort Jackson with the Creeks, making the southern flank of the United States a far less tempting invasion route, and the almost simultaneous Treaty of Grenville with the remnants of the Tecumseh-led federation of Old Northwest tribes, the very ones for whom Castlereagh's negotiators were trying to obtain a vast British protectorate below the Great Lakes. The northern tribes had agreed not only to renounce their ties to the crown but also to declare war on their former patrons.

The reversal of the empire's fortunes grew more jarring by the week. In mid-September, a well-equipped, 11,000-man British invasion force (with 5,000 more troops held in reserve near Montreal) crossed the American border to take control of the Lake Champlain district in coordination with a sizable flotilla. But a far smaller squadron of American vessels, while drawing heavy fire, outmaneuvered the British fleet, scuttled its most lethal attack ship, and blocked any passage to the sturdy lakeside fort at Plattsburgh, New York, the intended target of a heavy naval bombardment. Denied artillery support from the lake, the British attackers were easily repulsed by the Plattsburgh defenders and retreated all the way to Canada. A similar fate awaited the British force that had torched Washington after it moved north for a sea-and-land assault on Baltimore. Its night-long cannonading failed to immobilize Fort McHenry, guarding Baltimore harbor (as famously celebrated in Francis Scott Key's "The Star-Spangled Banner"), where raking American crossfire pounded the attacking fleet. The land assault was no less decisively repelled, its commander killed, and the joint expedition sailed away badly scarred. A few days later the long British siege to dislodge the troops occupying Fort Erie on the Canadian side of the lake was broken by a daring 1,600-man raid on the siege batteries. Inflicting heavy losses, the Americans strengthened their grip on the Great Lakes. And in Maine the British were now meeting serious resistance. Everywhere Britain's initiatives were costing it dearly. Salvaging success now depended on the major attack at New Orleans.

As for the Americans, "[o]ur prospects are not more promising than they have been from the beginning," Adams wrote to Monroe. At the negotiating table, for months neither side gave any quarter. Yet as winter drew near and both teams kept repeating their fixed, irreconcilable positions—a mutual stalling tactic in anticipation of decisive news from New Orleans—the negotiators soberly recognized that the issue each side had assigned the highest urgency at the outset of the talks was no longer imperative for a settlement. The Americans saw that, with the end of the great war in Europe, the British, while unwilling to acknowledge past culpability, would no longer have the need or any excuse for continuing to intercept neutral vessels on the open seas and impress their runaway seamen. The British also had little further interest in demanding a broad protectorate zone for the turncoat Indian tribes of the Old Northwest and sought instead to demilitarize the Great Lakes region. As each side backed away from these confrontational issues, Castlereagh doubted it was worth risking another year or two of combat to win permanent territorial gains while Britain had so many other worries on its mind. Among them were the growing social unrest at home and endemic tensions on the continent, where absolutist regimes sought to restore political equilibrium by stifling democratic tendencies.

In an apparently serious concession, Castlereagh instructed his envoys at Ghent to seek a peace settlement on the basis of *uti possidetis,* whereby the combatants would retain the territory they currently controlled. Each side held Great Lakes forts on the other's soil, while British troops occupied nearly half of Maine and the Americans a sizable portion of the southern Ontario peninsula. But the United States commissioners saw no point in such trade-offs and chose to chance the outcome at New Orleans rather than give up an acre of American land. Based on the recent fighting, though, the British were disinclined to bet everything on a decisive victory on the Mississippi, and both sides embraced the only, and obvious, compromise at the very time the biggest battle of the war was being played out at New Orleans. The Treaty of Ghent, without saying so, declared the War of 1812 a draw and required each side to return any territory it had captured from the other during the hostilities. No boundary issues were directly addressed, but the parties agreed to convene a joint commission in the near future to establish a border between the United States and Canada west of Lake Superior. Nothing was said regarding U.S. fishing rights and abusive British maritime practices—a gain for each side—and the native tribes that were until lately the king's allies were left to their unkind fate under American sovereignty.

The treaty, sealed the day before Christmas 1814, would likely not have been altered if the signatories had awaited the results at New Orleans. But from the American side the battle was certainly not waged in vain.

THE ODDS WERE SURELY against the patchwork forces of the United States commanded by General Andrew Jackson, who had never engaged a professionally trained, well-armed, expertly led enemy, and—as was the case at New Orleans—one supported by the heavy guns of nearby warships. The British commander, Edward Pakenham, was a tested veteran of the Napoleonic Wars and happened to be the brother-in-law of the empire's hero of the age, the Duke of Wellington, then in Paris presiding over vanquished France.

The British would have had even more reason to expect a smashing triumph at New Orleans if they had been apprised of Jackson's initial movements after being notified by the War Department that a British assault from the Gulf of Mexico, likely targeted at New Orleans, was imminent and that 5,000 fresh recruits were being sent to help him defend the city. Instead of hastening there, Jackson chose to discourage the British from coming ashore anywhere else but through the mouth of the Mississippi. He sped to West Florida to bolster the American garrison at Mobile harbor and then, without authorization from Washington, expelled the small Spanish contingent defending Pensacola and replaced them with his own troops.

This prophylactic strategy might have proven disastrous if Jackson had not compensated by marching double-time to New Orleans, arriving a few weeks before the British convoy reached the delta. In short order he made a series of critical decisions that would materially affect the course of the monumental encounter. Aware that his troops were inexperienced and underequipped for waging a set battle against hardened veterans, Jackson reached out for all the help he could get in a hurry. A bit reluctantly, he accepted an offer of aid from one of the more unorthodox businessmen in New Orleans—Jean Lafitte, the thirty-four-year-old French blacksmith-turned-buccaneer whose band of cutthroats, many highly skilled at gunnery and close combat, was amply supplied with weapons and ammunition. Jackson also added eager volunteers from among the city's considerable number of free blacks and inspired their maximum effort by treating and paying them no differently than his white troops. To ensure full cooperation from the civilian community, he declared martial law, turning the city into one large armed camp and lending credibility to reports reaching British landing parties downriver that Jackson had assembled a host of 20,000 to defend the precious port.

Using gunboats and skirmishing units to hector the advance British elements, Jackson bought time to use his troops, guns, and the marshy terrain to best advantage. He installed his heavy cannons on both banks of the riverfront, taking pains to stabilize them on stacked cotton bales so that the impact of their firing would not cause them to sink into the spongy ground. For his main forces he established three parallel lines of defense several miles apart (the second and third lines serving as fallback positions if an orderly retreat was required) and all running perpendicular from the river to impassable cypress swamps on the east. The British, then, had no real choice—if the American gunboats and shoreline batteries kept their ships from passing—but to storm the defenders' position head-on. The front line, about five miles below New Orleans, was laid out along a millrace called Rodriguez Creek, a giant ten-foot-wide trench that Jackson fronted with a five-foot rampart, behind which he massed ferocious firepower from 5,000 Kentucky and Tennessee sharpshooters wielding accurate long rifles, and cannoneers ideally positioned to pour their salvos on the British ranks.

In a thunderous artillery exchange before the main battle on January 8, 1815, Jackson's accurate gunners shattered the exposed British batteries and left them unable to shell the defenders' ramparts. Pakenham's 5,500 troops were forced to advance wave after wave into a ceaseless barrage by American marksmen. At a distance of 200 yards, it was murderous. One British survivor recalled that the ramparts at Rodriguez Creek looked like "a row of fiery furnaces." By the time the redcoats stopped coming over the piled bodies of their comrades, the battlefield was redder still with the blood of 2,057 British dead, including General Pakenham, and many others wounded. Incredibly, Jackson lost only thirteen men. The losers lingered in the bayous below the city for a few weeks to salve their wounds and make their ships seaworthy, then sailed away. No uninvited British forces have since set foot on American soil.

If the War of 1812 displayed America's lack of will to mobilize its national resources in an uncertain cause and the perils of sectional divisiveness in a sprawling democracy, the conflict also demonstrated how fiercely the United States would resist when its own real estate, the core of the country's commonwealth, was seriously threatened. The victory at New Orleans served to elevate Andrew Jackson from a bloodthirsty freebooter to a national resource, a rough-hewn superhero and symbol of America's don't-mess-with-us spirit, and to instill in his countrymen the sense that they had nobly defended their honor against Britain's bullying provocations. A vocal minority among them, though, regretted that in the name of both self-preservation and self-fulfillment, the United States had itself resorted to bullying its peaceable northern neighbors for their mother country's transgressions, assailing Spanish soldiers left defenseless by their dysfunctional government, and destroying the native people who asked only to be left alone.

THE SECOND AMERICAN WAR with Great Britain, which ended so much more gloriously than it had begun, brought with it a new sense of national self-confidence and a return of good times economically. Cotton prices jumped in the restored world market, and sales of that even more basic commodity, land, grew at a frenzied pace as state-chartered banks doled out easy credit terms. Early in the postwar era President Madison and his successor in 1817, James Monroe, recognized the constricting nature of Jefferson's agrarian republicanism as the guiding ideology for the United States as it entered a transitional phase from postcolonial novice to emergent world power. The war, while wounding the American economy by denying it access to world commerce, had the salutary effect of jolting domestic industry to life and stimulating economic self-reliance. The government now helped fuel this new vibrancy by reinstating the United States Bank, solidifying the national currency, and imposing stiffer tariffs that shielded manufacturers from British dumping on a hungry American market.

Monroe, last of the remarkable dynasty of Virginia statesmen who arose during the Revolutionary era, had rather an antiquarian look about him: he wore the same sort of knee-length breeches and high, white-topped boots that the first President had favored and, like most other worthies of that fading age, powdered his hair and tied it behind his head; yet he lacked the brilliance, depth, and suppleness of Washington's three successors in the White House. But the fifth President had a flexible mind, and his considerable public service as an executive, legislator, and diplomat, while arming him well for political combat, had also made him aware of his limitations. As President, Monroe did not hesitate to surround himself with a brainy, regionally diverse cabinet advocating a variety of views. But after hearing out his counselors and making up his mind, he usually remained fixed in his purpose.

Riding a buoyant wave of national unity that a Boston newspaper dubbed the "Era of Good Feelings" during a presidential visit, Monroe proved a far more successful chief of state than Madison—and, it may be reasonably argued, Jefferson as well. Curiously, even as the nation focused on its internal development, Monroe proved most successful in dealing with foreign affairs, due largely to his unexpected choice for Secretary of State, ex-Federalist John Quincy Adams, whose frosty exterior and often contrarian views did not lessen the President's appreciation of his first-rate mind and sure political instincts. Adams, in abandoning his New England heritage of parochial antipathy toward westward expansion and the toll it supposedly exacted on the old Puritan society, understood the far greater stake all sectors of the country shared in an expanding commonwealth. A passionate convert to continentalism, he emphatically advocated America's transcendent entitlement to possess as much of North America as its people saw fit. Early in Monroe's first term, in an effort to clarify the nation's boundaries, Adams orchestrated concurrent negotiations with Britain, newly respectful of the United States and glad to enlist it as an ally as well as its prime trading partner, and with Spain, unflagging in its resentment that the United States was about to replace it as the ranking power in the New World.

Dealing with the British was the more urgent—and, as it proved, less difficult—matter. The 1812 war, launched with an unprovoked assault on their territory, had left Canadians far more conscious of an inchoate national identity, which, as loyal British subjects, they had not dwelled on earlier. Now, to avoid future territorial confrontations or innocent misunderstandings, it became essential to settle on a definitive boundary between the United States and British North America, extending across the entire northwestern quadrant of the continent, even though much of it was rugged, unmapped terrain of spectacular if forbidding beauty.

Four white nations had contended for dominion over the region and its aborigines, but their home territories were far distant and their probes of the remote area had been glancing and commercial rather than sustained attempts to settle and colonize. The Spaniards—largely on the strength of missions they established up the California coast a little beyond San Francisco Bay during the late eighteenth century, some probes farther north by their seafarers, and a few outposts in the New Mexican desert—made their usual absurdly broad claims to the entire western bulk of the continent. The Russians fished and hunted the northernmost sector of the coast, ranging from the Aleutian Islands down the deeply serrated shoreline of Alaska and modern British Columbia, even opening a trading post as far south as the Russian River in northern California. But the Russians had no interest in scaling the snow-wrapped mountain ranges close by the Pacific coast or planting inland settlements; they were there strictly for the fur and fish. The British, with better, farther-ranging ships and a sizable colonial presence in the eastern half of the continent's northern tier, sustained a broader but hardly definitive claim to the region, dating back to daredevil Francis Drake's landing near San Francisco Bay in 1578 and sailing the coastal waters as far north, probably, as Washington state. Drake named what he glimpsed New Albion and, heeding the custom of the age, claimed it all for his sovereign, Elizabeth I. Two centuries passed before another British mariner, Captain James Cook, on his third and final voyage of discovery, sailed that northern Pacific coast and sighted the Oregon shore but due to stormy weather missed the estuary of the great river that flowed into the sea nearby. Fourteen years later, in 1792, an American vessel on the trail of sea otter pelts for the China trade—the *Columbia,* under Captain Robert Gray—found that often treacherous estuary, sailed up the river, the longest (1,200 miles from its source in the Canadian Rockies) that empties into the Pacific along its entire eastern shore, named the broad stream for his ship, and claimed the Columbia basin for the United States. At nearly the same time as Gray's discovery, British Captain George Vancouver entered the Strait of Juan de Fuca, some 160 miles north of the Columbia estuary, and came upon a superb, 100-mile-long, deep-water sound that he named after his first mate, Peter Puget. But none of these shipboard sightings and territorial claims, a throwback to the age of imperial wishfulness, was accompanied or followed up by the planting of settlements.

The contest between Britain and America for sustainable title to the Northwest owed less to maritime probes than to overland treks from the east, starting in the 1790s when Alexander Mackenzie set out on behalf of the Montreal-based North West Company, fur traders, in quest of a western waterway from Hudson Bay to the Pacific. A thousand miles west of the bay and some 1,500 miles north of the Columbia basin, Mackenzie found a great river, later to bear his name, flowing from Slave Lake, but its 1,100-mile course took it north, not west, and it emptied into the icy Arctic Ocean, making it inaccessible as a trade route. On a second trip in 1793, well to the south and west, Mackenzie followed the 850-mile Fraser River and its tributaries—with arduous portages between—to the Strait of Georgia, separating the mainland from Vancouver Island not far above the forty-ninth parallel. Mackenzie's was the first overland expedition to reach the Pacific and, coupled with his earlier journey to the Arctic, formed the basis of Britain's claim to the northland.

The first serious American exploration of the region, several hundred miles below Mackenzie's wanderings and a dozen years later, was the Lewis and Clark expedition, aimed in part at learning whether the Missouri River, longest and most westerly of the Mississippi's tributaries, connected with the upper reaches of the Columbia, providing a passage over water to the west coast of the continent. If explorers at the time had had more than the most rudimentary understanding of the great barrier formed by the Rocky Mountains, they could have predicted that a Missouri-Columbia connection was a forlorn hope; the American pathfinders learned, to their peril and pain, that there was a 340-mile break between the two rivers, largely composed of what Meriwether Lewis called "tremendous mountains," far beyond any yet seen to the east. Yet their intrepid voyage of inland discovery persevered, reached the Columbia, and established a tiny stockaded camp at its mouth.

Five years later, not far from where Lewis and Clark came upon the Pacific, New York fur baron John Jacob Astor extended his commercial war against Britain's government-licensed Hudson's Bay and North West companies by building the first substantial coastal trading post in the region. Although Astoria, as its proprietor named the Pacific outpost, remained in his hands for only two years, it would serve as vital evidence in the evolving American claim of sovereignty over the region. Astor's far-ranging agents hustled up and down the Columbia basin purchasing furs from the natives and Russian hunters along the Pacific coast, then shipped them west to Canton and the eager China market and east to New York and Europe. In its first year, 1811, Astoria sent out an exploratory party far up the Columbia in the hope of finding an easier route to the east than Lewis and Clark had managed—between, not over, the most formidable of the Rockies and through less hostile Indian territory. The trailblazers succeeded by veering from the Columbia over the rugged but less than towering Blue Mountains, then heading southeast along the Snake River to the Wyoming plains and through the Continental Divide near the South Pass to the upper reaches of the Platte River, following it to the Missouri and eventually St. Louis. That route, later to be called the Oregon Trail, would have a fateful bearing on how the great northwest wilderness came to be apportioned between the United States and Britain.

So, too, would the rival route tracked at almost the same time by a Canadian party that discovered the Athabasca Pass through the Rockies near Jasper, Alberta, and a short trek to the northern reach of the Columbia. This course would strengthen the British presence along the Columbia basin after Astor, fearing that the outbreak of war with Britain would soon lead to the capture of his busy trading post at the mouth of the river, sold out to his Canadian rivals. As patriotic subjects of the crown, the new owners promptly renamed the post Fort George for their monarch, and in 1813, as Astor had anticipated, a British warship arrived there, discovered it was already the property of British colonials, and raised the Union Jack over the site. The outpost flourished under the aegis of the Hudson's Bay Company, which soon moved it from the coast to calmer waters ninety miles up the north bank of the Columbia, where its prosperous operations anchored the British government's claim of commercial and territorial dominion over the region. The United States, however, did not bow to this claim. On the contrary, it argued that the Treaty of Ghent had provided for the repatriation of all territories captured or claimed during the War of 1812—and that included, as John Quincy Adams would forcefully remind the British foreign ministry, the Columbia basin, which, he said, fell under American title because of Robert Gray's discovery, Astor's activities, and the Lewis and Clark expedition through the region.

As Secretary of State, Quincy Adams saw the big picture of his country's boundaries with great clarity. He understood how reaching an accord with Britain on the nation's northern border might be integrally connected to reconciling the southern and western boundaries of the Louisiana Territory with imperial Spain. His first priority was closing the unresolved "gap" between the westernmost point of Lake of the Woods and the now approximately known source of the Mississippi River 150 miles to the south. The feat could have been accomplished by the simple expedient of a straight line joining the two points. But it would have created more problems than it solved. For one thing, the Mississippi was not navigable at or near its source; the United States would have had to yield nearly half the modern state of Minnesota to satisfy what Britain claimed the Paris peace treaty had promised it. Such a surrender of American land was unthinkable, not merely for its own degrading sake but also for the impact it would have in determining the extended westward boundary with Canada as a result of the Louisiana Purchase. Dropping the border by 200 or so miles to the south to allow Canadians direct navigable access to the Mississippi and then running it west to the Pacific would have diminished the potential size of the United States by roughly 300,000 square miles.

In 1807 American and British diplomats had tentatively agreed on the obvious solution, one that made sense in light of the Mackenzie and Lewis and Clark expeditions: forget about navigation of the Mississippi from Canada and just extend the boundary from its previously accepted western terminus as of 1783—at the western edge of Lake of the Woods, approximately where it meets the forty-ninth parallel—all the way west along the parallel to the ocean. Such a boundary would have left the United States in full possession of the Columbia basin, to which it had a plausible claim, as well as a great deal of territory farther north to which it had no claim whatever—a generous concession by the British. But their unprovoked attack on the *Chesapeake* off the Virginia coast put an explosive end to the cordial Anglo-American negotiations, and the boundary question remained in limbo.

Ten years later, when Charles Bagot, Britain's new envoy to the United States, reopened talks on the northern boundary, his government appeared at first to be in a far less conciliatory mood. Britain's rights to the Pacific Northwest, Bagot contended, had begun with Drake's claim almost 240 years earlier and far antedated America's first appearance in the region in 1792, three years after Britain had forced Spain to renounce exclusive claim to the area in the Nootka Sound fracas. The young British diplomat's allusion to Drake's claim and reliance on territorial presumptions left over from the divine right of kings drew a chilly response from Adams. "You have a better claim from Sebastian Cabot or Sir Walter Raleigh," the Secretary of State said caustically, referring to the wolfish sea-to-sea proclamations of the first British captains to reach the North American coast. "No," Bagot countered in dead earnest, "that question is settled."

But Lord Castlereagh, a maestro of diplomacy, knew better and soon directed his posturing ambassador to relent. In the post-Napoleonic world, bygone pretensions gave way to power politics. Britain, which had pledged to pacify Europe through the Quadruple Alliance (with Russia, Prussia, and Austria) and keep France and Spain from further mischief-making under their restored Bourbon regimes, had scant interest in revisiting past quarrels with the United States, especially over the remote and sparsely settled northwest corner of the continent.

President Monroe and Secretary Adams, who shared Castlereagh's yearning for a painless solution to the boundary issue, had been in no hurry to press for a settlement and risk riling their late adversaries. More than three and a half years elapsed between the signing of the Treaty of Ghent and the arrival of an American navy sloop, the *Ontario,* at Fort George near the Columbia estuary. The ship's captain, James Biddle, calmly persuaded the British commander to lower the Union Jack in recognition of the treaty rights won at Ghent by the United States to its restored sovereignty over the Columbia basin. Biddle then led a small landing party half a mile or so away from the fort to a stout tree, nailed up a painted plaque that read, "Taken possession of and on the behalf of the United States of America," followed by his name, the date (August 1818), and the place (Columbia River), and sailed away without a shot being fired. Castlereagh, though, was left in no doubt, once negotiations began in London, that Monroe and Adams were out for every square inch of territory they could pry loose from British claims. With consummate brass, Adams wrote to his negotiator, ambassador Richard Rush, suggesting that since the United States had given Britain a free hand in its dealings with Europe, Asia, and Africa—as if Washington could have exercised any sway in such matters—His Britannic Majesty's government ought not to envy or challenge "our natural dominion of North America." Which sounded as if the Americans would sooner or later try to get their hooks back into Canada unless a firm boundary line could be agreed upon.

The best the two sides could manage was to get the job partially done.

Rush opened the London talks with the simplest possible proposal: run the northern border along the forty-ninth parallel from Lake of the Woods to the Pacific. But such a line would have denied British traders access to the Mississippi while awarding the United States the previously floating northern part of modern Minnesota and a comparably large piece of territory north and west of the Columbia River (including Puget Sound), which comprises much of the modern state of Washington, an area to which America had an even less plausible claim than Britain. Castlereagh understandably rejected the suggestion. His counterproposal was a bit more complex. Britain was prepared to yield on the Lake of the Woods–Mississippi "gap" problem in exchange for being ensured equal access to the Columbia basin and sole possession of the territory north and west of the river, prominently including Puget Sound with its superb potential for a deepwater port. Accordingly, Britain agreed to extend the border a thousand miles west from Lake of the Woods along the forty-ninth parallel until it reached the Columbia River, some 250 miles shy of the Pacific, and from there the boundary would follow the river as it wound southwest to the ocean. But Monroe and Adams had no interest in sharing the Columbia basin with Britain or ceding it exclusive possession of strategic Puget Sound and the region adjacent.

At this point Castlereagh's negotiators made an offer that sounded equitable but could well have stymied American aspirations in the Pacific Northwest. Britain would be given title to all territory north of the forty-ninth parallel, while the zone between the forty-ninth and forty-fifth parallels, which extended about fifty miles south of the lower (and widest part of the) Columbia, would be left open to occupancy by citizens of both nationalities, without prejudice to future territorial claims by their two governments. That translated into fixing the southern boundary of British America at or below the forty-ninth parallel and anticipating future bargaining over—and likely partition of—75,000 square miles comprising the heart of the Columbia basin. In eluding the British trap, Adams took the defiant position that the United States was unwilling to concede *any* British territorial claims in the Pacific Northwest and that by proposing the forty-ninth parallel to the Pacific as its northern boundary, the United States had retreated as far south as it intended to go. In view of the substantial British trading activity and absence of American settlements in the region, Adams's stance was, to say the least, highly combative.

At loggerheads, the two sides decided sensibly enough that it was not an area worth fighting over—not then, not yet—for all its beauty, temperate climate, wealth in timber and furs, and future potential as a portal to China and the rest of the Asian trade. For the present, it was an empty, innocent paradise, far too long and arduous a trek from the settled eastern half of the continent for imminent settlement, far too long a sea voyage to transport troops to for a war in the wilderness. So they agreed to a boundary extending west along the forty-ninth parallel from Lake of the Woods as far as the Rocky Mountains in western Montana—a significant, if relatively inconsequential, British concession that established the northwestern extent of the Louisiana Purchase. Then, the agreement continued, any Country that may be claimed by either Party on the North West Coast of America, Westward of the Stony [Rocky] Mountains, shall, together with the Harbors, Bays, and Creeks, and the Navigation of all Rivers within the same, be free and open, for the term of ten years . . . to the Vessels, Citizens, and Subjects of the Two Powers: it being well understood, that this Agreement is not to be construed to the Prejudice of any Claim, which either of the High Contracting Parties may have to any part of the said Country.

The "said Country," then, was to be no-man's-land—or everyman's land—with no established civil authority that its occupants, whatever their nation of origin, were bound to heed. Even more problematic, the text of the Anglo-American Convention of 1818, as the agreement was known, set the Rockies as the eastern edge of the territory in dispute and, by implication, the Pacific Ocean as its western limit, but it intentionally made no mention of a northern or southern boundary. To do so might well have embroiled the two sides in clashes with the Russians, whose trading posts clustered on the far northern end of the coast, and the Spaniards, who had never really renounced their vague claim to, essentially, everything in North America west of the Mississippi. To reduce the likeliest flash point of renewed hostilities along their new border, the negotiators in London also agreed to demilitarize the Great Lakes, the principal theater of combat during the lately concluded war.

On the commercial side, each party promised to outlaw the hiring of seamen born in the other's nation, although the British insisted on retaining the right to board American vessels, examine the papers of crewmen suspected of having renounced their British citizenship, and begin legal proceedings for repatriation—but not to remove them bodily and summarily from their ships. More favorable to the United States was the British grant of permanent permission to American fishermen to harvest the waters off the Canadian coast. Even a future war would not cause forfeiture of the privilege, and no reciprocal grant to British subjects to fish in American waters was asked or tendered. This civilized, partial meeting of the minds by two proud powers, one preeminent in the Old World, the other the rising star of the New World, was sealed on October 20, 1818. The timing could not have been more fortunate for Adams.

THE *STATUS QUO ANTE BELLUM* outcome at Ghent, the stinging defeat Jackson dealt the British at New Orleans, the settlement over the northern boundary, and the sensible reign of Lord Castlereagh as overseer of the crown's foreign policy all served now to free Monroe and Adams to deal more vigorously with Spain. Their priority was to remove the great peninsula of East Florida from nominal Spanish rule, largely to obtain its immense coastline from Pensacola on the Gulf to St. Augustine on the Atlantic, thus filling in the southeastern corner of the nation and making it more secure.

As a military undertaking, the task looked easy. East Florida was a marginal holding of an exhausted empire, quickly losing its prized colonies to the south; the United States could have seized it whenever it summoned the will and a few thousand troops to do so. But after the invasion of Canada, which had proven such a divisive fiasco, the country was unlikely to rally behind another unprovoked war of conquest. And it was at least possible that such an act of aggression might push the Quadruple Alliance to rescue Spain, with its historical and dynastic ties to the other monarchies of Europe, from impending disaster in the New World. But what if the United States could claim plausible excuses for pressuring Spain to yield East Florida, preferably by diplomacy but at gunpoint if necessary? Such justifications were not hard to fabricate.

More and more American squatters had been crossing the porous, unguarded border from Georgia, and land speculators were growing active in the Florida panhandle, especially around Pensacola, which a group of Tennessee investors, prominently including Andrew Jackson, foresaw as a vigorous Gulf port rival to New Orleans once the United States owned the region. This steadily heightening migration in the border area bred, as usual, demands by white interlopers to remove any Indians in their way—in this case the Seminoles, who were supposed to surrender their lands in southern Georgia and Alabama, according to the imposed Treaty of Fort Jackson. Some Seminoles did, finding haven in nearby Florida; some defiantly clung to their villages and hunting grounds, ready targets for relentless white settlers on both sides of the Florida border. Largely in self-defense and sometimes operating from camps in Spanish territory, Indian raiding parties bloodied American settlers in the vain hope of frightening them off. These attacks, along with the growing number of runaway slaves, who drew white pursuers after them into Spanish territory, were denounced by southerners as a ceaseless threat to public safety. Neither irritant, though, seemed to arouse the interest or concern of Spanish officials, who were too few to intervene and, at any rate, more inclined to harbor than expel the Indians and escaped slaves.

Concluding that East Florida could no longer be tolerated as an asylum for murderous Seminoles and an enticement for blacks who had thrown off their shackles, Monroe and Adams once more asked Spain to sell the great peninsula, useful only as an adjunct to Cuba, now the sole secure Spanish possession in the Americas. But King Ferdinand VII, restored to the throne after the havoc of the Napoleonic occupation, was an even worse monarch than his father—no small distinction. He had poor judgment and less self-confidence, leaving him prey to a hovering circle of sycophantic courtiers who convinced him that Spain's glory days as an absolutist power would return if only the realm stood up to its tormentors. Instead of embracing the mild democratic reforms that civil war had won for his subjects, Ferdinand snubbed the new national assembly. Instead of reaching out to his insurgent New World colonies and offering them privileges and a degree of self-rule, he solicited military aid from other European monarchs to quell the uprisings. And instead of recognizing that East Florida had ceased to be a tenable Spanish possession and accepting the 1817 offer by the United States to purchase it, the king said no.

Monroe required no further provocation. Parties of armed American civilians intent on stirring local settlers into insurrection against the passive Spanish authorities, along with officially sanctioned state militiamen and federal troopers, targeting Indians and refugees from slavery, now surged across the Florida border with impunity. One prized catch was a community of helpless black runaways hunkered in an abandoned Spanish post on the Apalachicola River near the eastern end of the panhandle; American soldiers blew up the place, killing 270. A village of Seminoles who refused to quit their land at Fowltown just on the Georgia side of the Florida border was destroyed in mid-November of 1817 by army units under General Edmund Gaines. In reprisal, a Seminole war party boarded a military supply vessel coming down the Apalachicola and scalped and otherwise mutilated forty-five American soldiers, their wives, and their children. After that, it was open season on any Seminoles who could be tracked down. Secretary of War John C. Calhoun instructed Gaines to "adopt the necessary measures to terminate" the problem, licensing him to intrude on foreign territory in pursuit of the Indians "unless they should shelter themselves under a Spanish post," in which case Gaines was to advise the War Department—presumably before rather than after violating the refuge. On December 26, ten days after issuing the order, Calhoun relieved Gaines, by all accounts a competent commander, and replaced him with the most celebrated soldier in the nation, the hero of New Orleans, and a past master at massacring Indians.

In placing Andrew Jackson in charge of the so-called Seminole War,

Monroe's cabinet could have been under few illusions about his abiding enmity for the native peoples. Earlier the government had directed him, perhaps with a wink, to carry out one of the terms of the Treaty of Ghent, obligating the United States "to return to such Tribes or Nations [with which it had been at war] all the possessions, rights, and privileges which they may have enjoyed or been entitled to in 1811 previous to such hostilities." That meant, beyond dispute, that the Creeks were fully entitled to the return of the 24 million or so acres taken from them, allegedly as war reparations, under the Treaty of Fort Jackson. But General Jackson did nothing of the sort. Indeed, his principal activity since his great victory at New Orleans had been evicting the Creeks and applying pressure to the other southeastern Indian nations to accept similar treaties of removal, sanitizing the region for white settlement.

If this open defiance of the Treaty of Ghent displeased his President, it is hard to understand why Monroe wrote to Jackson as he did, two days after Calhoun had sent off instructions to him to replace Gaines and take charge of dealing decisively with the Seminoles. His mission against them, President Monroe told Jackson in a letter sent December 28, 1817, "will bring you on a theater where you may possibly have other services to perform. Great interests are at issue. . . . This is not a time for repose . . . until our cause is carried through triumphantly." The President's letter did not explain what "great interests" were at issue, or what "our cause" was, or what conditions would constitute a triumphant outcome. Did he mean the liquidation of the Seminoles—not precisely an ennobling mission—or was he untethering his pet fighting cock and telling him to go directly for the Spaniard's jugular, driving them out of Florida? Surely Jackson could have been excused for making the latter assumption in light of his own frame of mind, as disclosed by the letter he sent to the President on January 6, 1818—just a week after Monroe wrote his letter, which the general had of course not yet received. Jackson's letter proposed that all of Florida be seized and "held as an indemnity for the outrages of Spain upon the property of our citizens; this done, it puts all opposition down, secures to our citizens complete indemnity, and saves us from a war with Spain. This can be done without implicating the government; let it be signaled to me through any channel [here he suggested Tennessee Congressman John Rhea, who carried the message to the White House] that the possession of the Floridas would be desirable . . . and in sixty days it will be accomplished."

Monroe would later claim that he was not shown Jackson's letter until a year after it had been sent. One can only wonder why an important message from the commander of his southern forces would have been withheld for a

year from the nation's commander-in-chief. And one can reasonably suspect Monroe of lying, because Jackson had stated all too boldly what the
President's letter had only cryptically hinted at. Monroe's wording, though,
perfectly accorded with Jackson's surmise that the conquest of Florida
could best be achieved "without implicating the government"—Monroe had
not specified in writing what glorious mission Jackson was to undertake
without "repose" and carry through "triumphantly." Jackson's letter was
also revelatory in framing what would later become the hard-core American
argument to justify seizure of East Florida. The Spaniards, Jackson charged,
had committed "outrages" against American property, presumably by facilitating, if not actively fomenting, Seminole raids and enticing fugitive
slaves to settle in Florida. That Americans might be at all responsible,
through cruel and abusive conduct, for the Indian attacks or the flight of the
slaves was not up for discussion. In fact, the only certifiable Spanish transgression had been failure to prevent Seminoles who had found a safe haven
in the Floridas from attacking American settlers on either side of the border—a policing action over a broad stretch of difficult terrain far beyond the
strength and resolve of Spain's little garrison.

Whether the Spanish sin was one of commission or omission was a
nuance of indifference to Jackson, who had his orders, and in their very
vagueness he found all the instruction he required. Mustering 5,000 army
regulars, Tennessee militiamen, and Indian allies in mid-March 1818, he
headed south into East Florida and laid waste any Seminole villages
encountered en route. It was a war in name only; there were no true battles,
because what few Seminoles remained in the area fled before the advance of
"Sharp Knife." Approaching St. Marks, the only formidable Spanish
fortress in Florida, Jackson revealed his justification for seizing the stronghold even if it was not harboring—as he later said had been reported to
him—hundreds of Seminoles. "The Spanish government," he contended in
a letter dated March 25 to Secretary of War Calhoun, "is bound by [the
Pinckney] treaty to keep the Indians at peace with us. They have acknowledged their incompetency to do this, and are consequently bound, by the
laws of nations, to yield us the facilities to reduce them [the Indians]." In
other words, Jackson's forces were within their rights not just to assume the
Spaniards' unfulfilled duty as peacekeepers by preventing Indian incursions
on American soil but also to enter Spanish territory and take over Spanish
military posts to achieve that purpose. As he informed Calhoun,

Under this consideration, should I be able, I shall take possession of
the garrison [at St. Marks] as a depot for my supplies, should it be

found in the hands of the Spaniards, they having supplied the Indians; but if in the hands of the Indians, I will possess it, for the benefit of the United States, as a necessary position for me to hold, to give peace and security to this frontier.

Consistent with his qualmless seizure of St. Marks was how rabidly Jackson dealt with two British subjects caught at the fort, perhaps because he had found no Seminoles there to slaughter. One captive was a kind, seventy-year-old Scottish trader who sympathized with the plight of the Seminoles and, in selling them supplies, had behaved so honestly that they entrusted him with acting as their spokesman in the region. The other Briton was an eccentric soldier of fortune, a former lieutenant in the Royal Marines who paraded about with a swagger stick, preaching the abolition of slavery and Indian resistance to American oppression. Jackson branded the pair as British spies and provocateurs and summoned a court-martial, which declined to credit the prisoners' explanation—that they were just trying to help the Seminoles survive, not to incite them to violence against Americans—and ordered their summary execution. Heedless of the convicted prisoners' pleas for mercy and of possible international repercussions for such dire treatment of third-nation citizens on foreign soil he had invaded, Jackson sent the pair to their deaths, one by hanging, the other by firing squad.

A few weeks later Jackson's forces moved west to Pensacola, the capital of East Florida, where he claimed—once again without corroborative evidence—that hundreds of Indians were being sheltered. His men vanquished the Spanish defenders in a fight lasting only a few minutes and costing the American forces five fatalities. Jackson ordered the Spanish commander to take the remnant of his garrison to Havana forthwith and then raised the Stars and Stripes over the ramparts of the fort. As a practical matter, none of Florida remained under Spanish authority. Upon hearing of Jackson's actions, the Spanish ambassador in Washington, Luis de Onís, denounced them as a heinous violation of international law "on the odious basis of violence and bloodshed" and demanded that the Monroe government reprimand Jackson, return the forts, and restore Spanish authority in Florida.

At the time of his protest, the conscientious Onís, by then a thirty-eight-year veteran in Spain's diplomatic service, the last nine of them in the United States, had been dickering with Secretary of State Adams for well over a year about the boundaries between American and Spanish territory. Their talks had gone slowly, but there had been some progress toward the close of 1817. The issue was no longer Florida, where the Spanish flag still

flew only at the sufferance of the United States government. The real trophy
of the treaty Adams sought to fashion with Onís was an agreement on the
sprawling, ill-defined southwestern boundary of the Louisiana Purchase—
no easy feat, since the Spanish envoy kept insisting, under instructions from
his foreign ministry, that the seventeenth-century French explorer La Salle
had usurped Spain's legitimate claim to the whole southern tier of North
America and that Napoleon had compounded the insult. Which was to say
that Spain simply would not recognize other nations' military might as a
legitimate tool of statecraft—conquest (by anyone but Spain) was lawlessness—and thus the claims of the United States to Florida and lands west
of the Mississippi were taken as an insult to Spanish honor and international law.

    As a negotiator, then, Luis de Onís was handicapped by serving a regime
whose abject weakness in defense of a once grand empire was transparent,
yet it remained in deep denial while still demanding to be regarded as a
vibrant player on the world stage. This hidebound mentality had left Spain a
chronic invalid among Europe's ranking states and something of a laughingstock. Its stature was not enhanced by King Ferdinand's latest display of
folly, the purchase of eight derelict warships from Tsar Alexander of Russia, who was only too glad to unload the leaky, antiquated craft on His
Catholic Majesty to serve as the nucleus of a Spanish armada intended to
quash the insurrections that had swept through his crumbling dominion in
the New World. Six of the rotted Russian vessels were deemed irreparable
upon arrival in Cadiz, one was taking on water by the time it reached the
Azores, and the sole survivor, on reaching South American waters, surrendered to a Chilean frigate without firing a shot. Yet Onís never wavered in
his loyalty to the Spanish throne, seemingly without regard for the deficiencies of whoever occupied it. The obtuse king and his nattering circle were
fortunate to retain such a gifted servant of the realm, the scion of a titled old
Salamancan family who had studied law and medicine, spoke five languages, and sent remarkably sound advice back to Madrid, pressing the
court to compromise over the status of its former colonies or lose them all.
But the foreign ministry gave Onís little room to maneuver.

    His opening proposal to Adams at the end of 1817 was to disregard the
status of Florida and fix the western boundary of the United States at the
Mermentau River, which drained into the Gulf of Mexico about 150 miles
west of New Orleans. Louisiana, by this time, had already been an American state for five years. From the source of the Mermentau, Onís's boundary
would have wandered north to the Missouri River along a course to be set
precisely by a neutral commission but that, at any rate, would have swung

well north of Texas and omitted a large southwestern chunk of what the United States believed was part of the Louisiana Purchase.

However irritating Onís's charade, Adams could not afford to respond scornfully—not if he hoped to settle the southwestern boundary question in a way that might dovetail with his simultaneous efforts to resolve the nation's northwestern border with Britain. Adams countered Onís's minimal offer with a two-part proposition of his own. First, Spain would cede the United States all its territory east of the Mississippi, meaning both West Florida, which America had already annexed over Spanish protests, and East Florida, which was no longer defensible (as Jackson's effortless conquest would shortly confirm). Second, the United States would drop its tenuous claim, first made by Jefferson, that the Louisiana Purchase included the Spanish province of Texas and extended northwest along the Rio Grande River—how far was never mentioned. Instead, Adams chose the Colorado River of Texas, which ran more or less diagonally from the northwest hill country 900 miles southeastward to the Gulf at Matagordo Bay, about 400 miles southwest of the Mississippi delta—a boundary that would have placed roughly half of modern Texas within the borders of the United States. From the source of the Colorado, Adams's boundary would have headed north to the Red River, followed its course to the base of the Rockies, and run along them to the sources of the Arkansas and Missouri rivers. Onís objected at once that the United States had no basis whatever for claiming any part of Texas, no matter that the colony was even less firmly in Spanish grasp than Florida. Texas had only 3,500 residents, a lot of them American newcomers—traders, speculators, squatters, drifters, smugglers, fugitives—and scarcely 1,000 Spanish soldiers to guard 300,000 square miles of wide-open country.

Within the week, though, Onís made what for him were two major concessions. Spain would cede the Floridas to the United States and start the western boundary a bit farther down the Gulf Coast, essentially acknowledging that the state of Louisiana now belonged to America. When Adams let Onís cool his heels for a few weeks without replying, the Spanish ambassador correctly concluded that his offer was far from satisfactory and feared, also correctly, that if Spain continued to stonewall, the Americans might take preemptive military action, overrunning Florida, Texas, perhaps even Mexico. So in the hope of buying time while his foreign ministry desperately tried to solicit the support of other European governments to prop up Spain's collapsing position in the Americas, Onís advised Adams that he had written to Madrid for further instructions. Madrid hungered especially for the backing of Britain, the one power that might be able to exert restraining influence on the United States and the rebel states to its south. It was an empty hope. Castlereagh let Madrid's London envoy know he would not consider helping Spain salvage its empire unless its rulers were prepared to undertake radical reforms of their rigid rules of trade, liberalize colonists' rights, banish slavery, and grant amnesty to all rebels. Privately the British foreign minister remarked that the Spanish regime was "perverse . . . and shortsighted."

In June, during the lull in the Adams-Onís exchange, word reached Washington that Jackson had toppled all remaining semblance of Spanish authority in Florida, drawing Onís's sharp protest. Adams could not ignore it and just bully the Spaniard into diplomatic submission as Jackson had done by military force. To do so carried the risk of provoking King Ferdinand into declaring war and perhaps even rousing the British—along with Europe's resurgent absolutist monarchies—to side with him. No, Adams had to engage Onís and his demand that Monroe disavow Jackson's Florida spree. Indeed, some in the cabinet disliked Jackson and his methods, suspecting him of lurking Bonapartism. The prevailing view among Monroe's councilors favored reprimanding the jut-jawed Tennessean for having exceeded his orders; his assigned mission had been to eliminate the Seminole menace, not to expel the Spaniards from Florida. The chief dissenter in the cabinet was John Quincy Adams, who noted in his diary entry of July 21 that to vilify national hero Jackson "must give offense to all his friends, encounter the shock of his popularity, and have the appearance of truckling to Spain." Adams told Monroe that for the government to condemn Jackson's excesses would only encourage Spanish intransigence. The preferable alternative was to elevate their very loose cannon to higher moral ground— and Monroe, no doubt mindful of his own complicity in Jackson's behavior, agreed.

Accordingly, Adams rebuffed Onís's demand for an apology and the return of Spanish Florida by turning the tables on him and asserting, in a letter sent on July 23, that Jackson had acted only in a self-defensive response to "the treacherous, unrelenting, and exterminating character of Indian hostilities"—a classic instance of the pot calling the kettle black. Those who most deserved upbraiding, Adams charged, were the delinquent Spanish officials who had failed to honor their nation's pledge to restrain the Indians and even given succor to the Seminoles, "a large party" of whom had been found within a mile of the Spanish fort at Pensacola. To gild this masterpiece of fabrication, Adams reminded the Spanish envoy that in contrast to the conduct of the native peoples, the policy of the United States toward the Indians had been "that of peace, friendship, and liberality." Luis de Onís's government had finally met its match in self-delusion.

. . .

WHILE STILL BRISTLING over Jackson's onslaught in Florida but afraid he might be unleashed for further forays into Spanish territory, Onís came to the bargaining table on July 11—Adams had not yet composed his unapologetic letter painting Jackson as staunch defender of American rights—and yielded ground. Onís said his country was prepared to move the border another 100 miles west to the Sabine River, then climbing toward the Missouri. The change would add a sizable crescent of territory to the Spanish concession, though still far short of what the Americans had asked for. It was a hopeful sign, however, and encouraged Adams to make a historic "suggestion," as he termed it in reply.

His earlier request for Spain to cede both Floridas did not need addressing now; Jackson had taken care of that. Since Florida was already de facto American territory, Spain's cession would be a formality, but one that Adams recognized as necessary if the United States was not to be perceived abroad as a rogue nation. What Adams proposed in the West, though, was a dramatic departure from the earlier American position that, as a result of the Louisiana Purchase, the western boundary of the United States extended along the base of the Rockies—but not beyond.

Adams indicated that in view of Spain's willingness to move the boundary a bit west to the Sabine, the United States might reciprocate by shifting its proposed starting point from where the Colorado River debauched into the Gulf to farther up the coast, yielding some of the Texas territory he had requested earlier. But in climbing northward in stepwise fashion to the Red, Arkansas, and Missouri rivers, the new boundary would encompass rather more of the Louisiana Territory than Onís had agreed to. And that was not the end of what Adams had in mind. When the boundary line reached the source of the Missouri, then commonly believed to be situated slightly north of the forty-fifth parallel (though it was later discovered to be farther north, in Montana), Adams proposed that it swing due west and keep going, beyond the Rockies, until it reached the Pacific at a point sixty or so miles south of the mouth of the Columbia River. If such a boundary line was agreed to, it would by no means ensure the immediate extension of the United States from coast to coast—that would still depend on the outcome of the negotiations with the British about to get under way in London to determine national sovereignty over the Columbia basin. But Adams reasoned that his hand would be strengthened vis-à-vis the British if Spain would agree to relinquish, or at least significantly reduce, its claim to territory in the Pacific Northwest. And the farther south Spain agreed to pull back, the wider the American corridor to the coast could grow, varying with the results of the northern boundary talks in London. Thus, Adams's new strategy for dealing with Onís, endorsed by President Monroe, was to bargain away most or even all of the American claim in Texas for the most generous (that is, southerly) transcontinental boundary that Spain would accept—if any—west of the Rockies.

But why not press Spain for more of Texas, so much closer to burgeoning Louisiana and the Missouri Territory? East Texas looked like promising cotton country, a natural extension of the South's plantation empire, population base, and political strength. The Columbia basin and the Oregon Country, as it was beginning to be called, were remote and could be contested with the British in due time. Adams, though, had his reasons. For one thing, Spain cared more about keeping Texas as a buffer for embattled Mexico than about the Pacific coast above California, where it had no settlements, so it would be more likely to yield its claim to the latter. For another thing, Texas would almost certainly be a lot easier for the United States to come by in the near future, given Spain's rapidly slipping hold on Latin America, than territory in the Northwest, which the powerful British coveted for inclusion in Canada. If Spain withdrew from the picture in the north, the United States was likely to emerge with far more terrain in any bargain eventually struck with Britain. Adams, a Massachusetts Puritan and avowed opponent of slavery, was also in no hurry to have Texas incorporated into the American union. The slaveholding South already had political power disproportionate to its white population, and adding the gigantic province of Texas as a state—or perhaps broken up into several states—would only enhance the plantocracy's sway over the nation's policies. Let more new states be formed farther west and north, Adams felt, in territory where climate and history were uncongenial to slavery, before welcoming Texas, a sure magnet for planters lusting for fresh fortunes from their bondsmen's labors.

On hearing Adams's bold proposal, Onís reflexively objected that the United States was trying to dispossess Spain of all its claims in the Northwest. That prompted Adams to scoff at the legitimacy of those claims and argue that the Americans, British, and Russians all had better grounds for making them. A few days later, to sweeten the air between them, Adams agreed—if Spain would consent to the transcontinental line—to drop his former proposal to begin the boundary at the mouth of the Colorado River on the Gulf Coast of Texas and retreat northeastward to the Trinity River, about midway toward the Sabine River, which Onís had proposed. A week later, Onís also had in hand Adams's letter strongly defending Jackson's seizure of Florida, and his mood darkened. He sent his superiors in Madrid

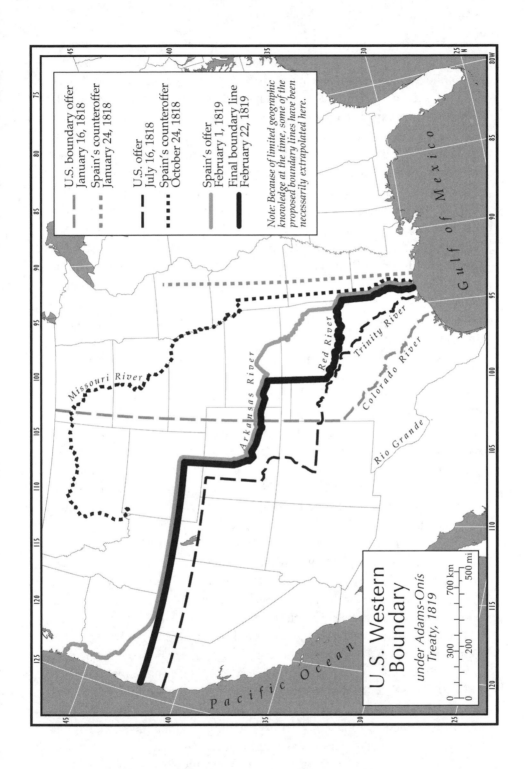

U.S. Western Boundary
under Adams-Onís Treaty, 1819

U.S. boundary offer
January 16, 1818

Spain's counteroffer
January 24, 1818

U.S. offer
July 16, 1818

Spain's counteroffer
October 24, 1818

Spain's offer
February 1, 1819

Final boundary line
February 22, 1819

Note: Because of limited geographic knowledge at the time, some of the proposed boundary lines have been necessarily extrapolated here.

Gulf of Mexico

Missouri River

Arkansas River

Red River

Trinity River

Colorado River

Rio Grande

Pacific Ocean

0   200   300 mi

0   500   700 km

a pessimistic assessment of the growing anti-Spanish sentiment in America, fed by demagoguery and rampant Jacobinism that advocated violent politics and policies. Was Adams's embrace of Jackson anything less? But if he were to walk away from the negotiating table now, Onís feared, he would hand the Americans just the excuse they were looking for to act unilaterally and seize more and more Spanish territory and perhaps extend diplomatic recognition to the new revolutionary governments in South America, further dooming any hope that Spain might yet reverse the democratic tide engulfing its empire. In such dire circumstances, Onís asked his ministry for a free hand to work out the best deal he could with the Americans before they chose to abandon diplomacy altogether.

King Ferdinand's council was not ready to capitulate to Adams; its members still hoped Britain and the crowned heads on the continent might rally behind Spain's cause—an escapist fantasy. Onís was directed not to entertain any American proposal until Monroe reprimanded Jackson and returned Florida to Spanish authorities. And if the United States recognized any of the revolutionary regimes in South America, Onís was to break off all exchanges with Adams. Toward the end of October, Onís, no doubt with misgivings, followed his orders and reverted to the position he had taken six months earlier: the boundary would begin not at the Sabine but at the point the Red River joined the Mississippi, about 125 miles above New Orleans, follow the Red to the ninety-fifth meridian, and then head north to the Missouri and its source—conceding the United States no more than one-third of the Louisiana Purchase. To make Spain's obstinacy more emphatic, the ambassador produced documents purporting to confirm his nation's rights to Florida and the Louisiana Territory, which France had allegedly sold without sanction.

Adams and Monroe were furious. Word was sent to London that the American government was indeed on the brink of recognizing the independence of at least one of Spain's rebel colonies, Monroe fully endorsed Jackson's efforts in Florida in the course of his annual address to Congress, and Adams made what he characterized as his final, take-it-or-leave-it offer to Onís. The boundary would run up the Sabine to the thirty-second parallel and then due north to the Red River (the present eastern boundary of Texas), follow the Red to its source in the Sangre de Cristo Mountains in what is now northern New Mexico, turn north again to the forty-first parallel (now the northern border of Colorado, so that about one-third of the state's area would have become American territory), and travel along the parallel to the Pacific. The new configuration would have left Spain with almost all of Texas but dropped its northern border to 350 miles below the Columbia

River, allowing the United States far more bargaining room in dealing with Britain on the northern boundary. Finally, Adams sent a letter dated November 28 to the American envoy in Madrid directing him to relieve the Spanish government of its delusion that the Monroe administration would ever castigate General Jackson.

His letter to Madrid, which respected Yale historian Samuel Flagg Bemis described as Adams's "greatest state paper," is worth dwelling upon because it is an instructive example of how rectitude may succumb to casuistry when good men decide they must ally themselves with bad acts. Professor Bemis's view of it aside, Adams's letter was a compendium of duplicity, hypocrisy, and mendacity amounting to a pious defense of Indian removal (if not outright genocide), slavery, and unilateral militarism in support of America's righteous expansionism. Embellishing the themes he had struck in his letter to Onís four months earlier in response to the ambassador's demand for an apology for Jackson's conduct, Adams claimed the United States had not been the aggressor in Florida but, rather, the victim of a conspiracy by wily Spaniards, meddlesome Britons, and savage Indians. Only after repeated warnings by the peace-loving Americans had met with "renewed outrages," visiting on them "all the horrors of savage war," did the armed forces of the United States attack "mingled hordes of lawless Indians and negroes." Since Spanish officers had egregiously failed to restrain the Seminoles and maintain the peace, American troops had no choice but to take over Spain's Florida forts to keep them out of the Indians' hands. The President had no intention of condemning Andrew Jackson for his actions, Adams wrote, "the motives for which were founded in the purest patriotism."

Even before Adams's letter reached Madrid, the Spanish court had at long last seen the light, and it was pallid indeed. Britain, the essential participant in any European coalition to subdue the uprisings throughout Spanish America, unmistakably signaled at a summit meeting of continental powers at Aix-la-Chapelle that it had no stomach for such a project. Nor was Britain likely to press the United States to ease diplomatic pressure on Spain in view of Lord Castlereagh's evident keenness to reach his own accommodation with the Americans. The foreign ministry had failed to demand an apology and compensation from the Monroe White House for Jackson's execution at St. Marks of the two British subjects accused of spying for the Indians; Castlereagh's staff had concluded that the pair were private persons acting provocatively on foreign soil and thus not entitled to their government's protection. Nor had Britain protested the foray by the American warship *Ontario* in August, politely forcing the removal of the Union Jack over

Fort George at the mouth of the Columbia River. And lately word had reached Madrid of the Anglo-American accord in November, amicably settling a long stretch of the northern boundary between the United States and Canada. Spain's new foreign minister and confidant of the king, the Marquis de Yrujo, untied Onís's hands and told him to make the best of things.

Early in January 1819 Onís returned to Adams's peace table, agreed to cede the Floridas, and for the first time accepted in principle the American proposal for a transcontinental southern boundary with Spain. But the line would begin its final westward run at the source of the Missouri and reach the Pacific by way of the Columbia—320 or so miles north of the forty-first parallel, which Adams had specified in his "final" offer. Adams said no. Meanwhile, Congress had investigated Jackson's behavior in Florida and now voted to exonerate him, leaving Onís to conclude that Monroe and Adams were licensed by their nation to pursue whatever belligerent measures they might choose for dealing with Spain. On receiving further instructions from Madrid to expedite a treaty with Adams before he might act to recognize any of the insurrectionist regimes in South America, Onís buckled. Early in February, after several more volleys on the zigzag route of the boundary, he finally settled, giving Adams almost everything he had asked for.

The critical changes were Spain's agreement to extend the boundary line west along the Red River from longitude 95 to 100—another 280 miles, ensuring that most of modern Oklahoma and Kansas would fall within the concession to the United States—before swinging north and climbing to the forty-second parallel, not to the forty-fifth as Onís had hoped, for the final extension to the Pacific. But Onís had managed to salvage some 25,000 square miles from the U.S. claim that the Louisiana Purchase extended to the source of the Red River as Adams, in his determination to gain a wider corridor from the Rockies to the Pacific, yielded the present-day Texas panhandle, northeast corner of New Mexico, and small portions of southern Kansas and Colorado to the Spaniards.

The net effect of these alterations was to add close to 250,000 square miles—beyond the widest claimed boundaries of the Louisiana Purchase—to the area Spain would no longer claim for its own. Twice in the closing stages of the talks, a weary Monroe was ready to accept the latest offer by Onís, only to defer to Adams, who thought the Spaniard could be squeezed for yet more territory. Adams, acting not unlike Jackson, had wanted to hold out and force Onís to accept the forty-first parallel, not the forty-second, as the final stretch of the transcontinental line, thus winning another 40,000 or so square miles for the United States to claim as its own without challenge by Spain. But in the end his brethren in the cabinet and congressional friends prevailed upon him to act mercifully and not appear to European onlookers as having ground Spain into the dust. All Onís asked in return was for the American government to place $5 million in escrow to cover claims by its citizens for property losses resulting from Jackson's Seminole War or the transfer of the Floridas to the United States. This sum, Onís stressed, was not a purchase price: selling off pieces of its once-glorious empire was beneath Spain's tattered dignity.

The so-called Adams-Onís Treaty, signed at Adams's request on February 22, 1819, eighty-seven years after the birth of George Washington, formally added unified Florida's 58,666 square miles to the United States. The territory developed slowly and would require another twenty-six years before qualifying as the twenty-seventh state in the Union. More important than confirming the American acquisition of Florida, the 1819 treaty and its companion pact signed a few months earlier in London induced Britain and Spain to approve generous northern and southern boundaries for the huge but hazily defined inland domain Jefferson had purchased from France fifteen years before. These concessions brought another massive bloc of territory, reaching all the way to the Pacific Ocean, within the perpetually outstretched grasp of the United States.

For John Quincy Adams, a driven visionary as well as a calculating tactician, the treaty with Spain was a spectacular diplomatic triumph, as he himself—for all his bouts of paranoia and insecurity—immodestly noted in his diary. "The acknowledgment of a definite line of boundary to the South Sea [the Pacific] is a great epoch in our history. . . . [T]he first proposal of it in this negotiation was my own." Adams was just a bit premature in his self-congratulation. Britain had not yet signed on to "a definite line of boundary" to the Pacific; that would not happen for twenty-six years, although the prospect of it seemed bright. And Spain, bludgeoned into submission by Adams, exacted a soupçon of consolation by refusing to ratify the agreement for nearly two years because of a rare, and in this case almost disastrous, blunder by the Secretary of State. Amid all the back-and-forthing over the boundary issue in the West, the normally punctilious Adams had failed to consider the ramifications of a brief provision proposed by Spain requiring the United States to honor titles to any land grants the Spanish crown had made prior to an 1818 cutoff date. Due diligence by the State Department would likely have revealed that shortly prior to the stated deadline King Ferdinand had doled out grants comprising close to half of East Florida to three of his aristocratic pals. Duped or not, Adams was mortified by his lack of vigilance and sank into a funk until the balky Spaniards figured out that sooner rather than later Monroe's government would begin treating Florida as official American territory whether or not the king fixed his seal to the treaty. The grotesquely generous royal grants, likely made only to spite the United States, were grudgingly rescinded. The President's first order of business thereafter was to appoint a territorial governor of Florida, and who was more deserving of the honor than the attack dog who had fetched it for him and his country? Andy Jackson held the post for eleven weeks before deciding he had more exciting things to do.

As the diplomatic drama of the twin pacts was played out behind closed doors, the spectacle of America being filled in east of the Mississippi was in full view. Soaring wheat and corn prices in the North and West paralleled the cotton boom in the South, luring more and more settlers from the East and Europe and hurrying the admission to the Union of one new state a year in the latter part of the decade: Indiana in 1816, Mississippi in 1817, Illinois in 1818, and Alabama in 1819, bringing the national total to twenty-two. Until then, the country had successfully postponed confronting its most grievous social pathology, thanks to the lateral pattern of its westward movement. Slavery had remained channeled in the states below the Ohio, while in the states and territories to the north, human bondage had been out- lawed. By 1820, when federal lands were reduced in price and offered for sale in lots as small as eighty acres, further accelerating western settlement, eleven states permitted slavery and eleven were free-soil. But in that year the precarious balance was imperiled by the application for statehood from Missouri, whose 66,000 residents already included 10,000 slaves. Their owners argued that the federal government had no business interfering with how they used their flesh-and-blood property.

When Louisiana, the first and southernmost of the states to be formed from the Louisiana Purchase, had applied for statehood eight years earlier, slavery had been long established along the bayous of the southern Missis- sippi, and the politically potent plantocracy and its commercial allies else- where had enough votes in Congress to fend off obstructive action by their conscience-stricken countrymen. Missouri, though, was a different matter. If it was admitted to the Union with a pro-slavery constitution, where would it end? Was the United States to achieve transcontinental dominion while continuing to condone its heinous original sin on a still broader scale?

For the first time, the future durability of the American federation was in serious doubt. A year's debate in Congress revealed the depths of passion that the slavery issue stirred. One solution, requiring Missouri to agree to the gradual elimination of slavery, was voted down and did not, at any rate, address the larger question. Another expedient, luckily, was at hand: Maine, the noncontiguous province of Massachusetts, with nearly five times the population of Missouri and an antislavery constitution in place, would be cut loose from its parent and admitted as a free-soil state to balance Missouri, which was accepted by Congress as a slave state. But as part of the historic compromise package, Congress ruled—with only a three-vote margin in the House—that slavery would be barred thereafter above Missouri's southern border (at the latitude of 36°30′) and, by implication, as far west as the nation might extend in the future.

Free-soil advocates were consoled by studying the map and seeing that the Missouri Compromise would outlaw the unconscionable custom in roughly 80 percent of the Louisiana Purchase territory as well as the Pacific Northwest region lately designated as land jointly and temporarily occupied with Britain. Southerners salved their militancy with the certainty that under the compromise Florida and Arkansas would one day soon be admitted to the Union as slave states. And Texas, in transition from Spanish to Mexican jurisdiction, would in time be annexed by the United States and form one or several more slave states, along with the Oklahoma region, confirmed as American territory under the Adams-Onís accord. Besides, future Congresses could always undo the 1820 agreement, if need be, to open more western land to slavery.

For the moment, then, the potential wildfires of sectionalism were banked. The surge in the nation's self-assurance and international standing during Monroe's two terms in the White House, for all the social, political, and economic turmoil that underlay the Era of Good Feelings, was bannered with more than a touch of hubris as the President prepared to deliver what would become his historic 1823 message to Congress. Not long before, the antidemocratic monarchies of the continent had once more approached Great Britain to consider King Ferdinand's persistent plea to launch a multinational crusade aimed at overthrowing the revolutionary regimes that had taken over Spain's former New World colonies. But the British stood steadfast against the repressive proposition and, despite the suicide the year before of their eminent, America-friendly foreign minister, Lord Castlereagh, invited the United States to join Great Britain in a declaration to all of mankind that the two English-speaking nations would not tolerate any future incursions in the New World by the Old World powers.

It was, of course, a flattering invitation to the United States by its parent and a frank acknowledgment of its coming of age as a serious presence on the world stage. Monroe was inclined to accept the overture and advised by his predecessors Jefferson and Madison to do so. But John Quincy Adams, ever the naysayer, disagreed and once more swayed Monroe to his view that the Americas were for Americans and those who would become such, and the United States ought to say so while standing on its own two legs, not as Great Britain's junior partner.

In Monroe's address, after promising that his nation would not challenge any existing colonial arrangements in the Western Hemisphere—apparently a pledge that the United States would never again invade Canada—he declared, in words drafted for him by Adams: "The American continents, by the free and independent condition which they have assumed and maintain, are henceforth not to be considered as subjects for future Colonization by any European Power." He added, with a clear hint of menace, that any such activity would be "viewed as the manifestation of an unfriendly disposition toward the United States." The Monroe Doctrine, as his cautionary message came to be known, failed to promise, however, that the United States itself would not attempt to dominate or interfere in the affairs of the other nations in its hemisphere—or anywhere else.

CHAPTER 9

Big Drunk wins the day

1821–1836

N O SOONER HAD THE UNITED STATES pressured imperial Spain into finally conceding the reality of the Louisiana Purchase—and, in the bargain, a corridor of American territory from the Rockies to the Pacific—than Spanish rule below the newly agreed-upon southwestern boundary evaporated. Mexico, for three centuries the glittering core of Spain's New World holdings, had made good its revolution, which began in 1810, gained independence in 1821, and now promised sweeping social reforms under a democratic government. Spain, a lingering convalescent from the Napoleonic Wars and struggling to reinvent a monarchy less autocratic in spirit, had been too weak to quell the uprisings throughout its American colonies and gave up the ghost of empire. What impact would the revolutionary change have on the United States and its expansive impulses?

Mexico was a neighbor of formidable proportions, nearly as large territorially and two-thirds as populous, but in almost every other way it contrasted starkly with the land and people to its immediate north. Its hot, arid climate was not conducive to agricultural abundance; much of its landscape was consumed by baking desert plains and rugged, barren mountain ranges, and it lacked the interlocking navigable waterways that facilitated transportation and encouraged commerce in the United States. The best land, under the dictates of colonial feudalism, was held by a thin upper crust of *haciendado* gentry and tended by a largely Indian peonage. Most farms were subsistence operations, inefficient and neglected as a commercial resource in a place where labor and capital were chiefly devoted to extracting mineral wealth from the dark recesses of the earth. The difficulty of the terrain, moreover, made it too costly to export much of anything except gold and silver, and commerce had long been restricted as a Spanish monopoly, resulting in a stagnant economy with little capital formation.

New Spain, as Mexico was designated, had no need to solicit the consent of the governed; it was ruled by an authoritarian elite of Spanish and creole officials, while the mestizo, pure-blood Indian, and black masses remained voiceless and, for the most part, landless. The American insistence on separation between church and state was not widespread in Catholic Mexico, where the two had a tight, symbiotic linkage. And, unlike the United States, where the people, wealth, and civil authority were widely dispersed, Mexico was run from its great metropolis of Mexico City on the high plateau forming the south-central sector of the nation, and most of its population was clustered in the southern half of the country. The regions in the far north—Santa Fe, capital of the province of New Mexico, was 1,500 miles and months of grueling travel from the national capital—were thinly settled and neglected by the central authorities.

Freshly independent Mexico, then, was not ideal turf for the blooming of agrarian republicanism. The success of its rebellion against Madrid was less a triumph of egalitarian ferment than a product of Spain's societal fatigue and belated recognition that its rigid brand of colonialism had grown irreversibly unprofitable. The Mexicans were released from bondage mostly by default and without need to forge a consensual revolutionary creed along broad democratic lines, as the American colonists had done, and to test it on the crucible of combat against their imperial tormentors. Mexico's revolution took the form of civil strife among warring factions—royalists, who were mostly creoles and feared that independence would breed instant social chaos; moderates, of largely mixed blood, who sought to rid themselves of suffocating Spanish rule; and radicals along with the apolitical Indian masses, spread across the countryside, who cried out for relief from systematic injustice and impoverishment. Their differences were never truly compromised, no fixed set of principles agreed upon as the victorious, formerly British American colonists managed to do at Philadelphia in 1787. As a consequence, postrevolutionary Mexico endured a grinding fifty-year struggle, often bloody and chronically destabilizing, between those favoring a strong central government under the colonial Spanish model (but more benign) and those devoted to a decentralized federal republic on the model of the United States, with authority dispersed over an immense, disconnected hinterland.

To ever-westering American frontier folk, Mexican territory at first loomed as a remote and uninviting destination for settlement; the fact that it did not even belong to the United States would have been of trifling concern to these unstoppable pioneers. But since the War of 1812 had demonstrated that territorial incursions northward, into the alluring temperate regions of Canada, would only invite military disaster, American expansionists began to cross the Mississippi in greater numbers and gaze southwestward with fresh eyes. The northern half of Mexico, much of it desert and rocky badlands unsuited for crops, had been left to languish by imperial Spain, guarded by a few token garrisons and thinly colonized except in the extreme north around Santa Fe, where some silver mines were still productive. Occasionally, Jesuit missions were founded to win over, or at least neutralize, the unwelcoming Indians. But the approach from the east by American settlers had caused Spain, in the closing years of its imperial rule, to fret about the vulnerability of Mexico's northeast frontier—and with good reason.

The province of Texas, a gigantic saucepan with a variegated surface tilting toward the Gulf of Mexico, was bounded on the east, under the 1819 Adams-Onís Treaty, by the Sabine River; on its long southeast coast by the Gulf; on the southwest, according to colonial records, by the Nueces River (although the broader Rio Grande 120 miles to the south was the more natural boundary); on the west by the Pecos River; and on the north by the Red River and the rest of the line set out in the Adams-Onís pact. This huge spread, while highly varied in topography, included some of the best land in Mexico. East Texas, tropically warm and humid much of the year, is endowed with rich soil nourished by half a dozen sizable rivers, each running several hundred miles or more southeasterly into the Gulf—ideal land for growing and transporting cotton and other staples, as the first American squatters discovered. The central region beyond the lush river valleys and bottomlands turned into a high plateau of flat, drier grasslands, well suited to cattle raising (and year-round pasturing that spared ranchers the need for winter feeding, required in the cooler American West). Farther west and north was the rolling, wooded hill country. Only in the south and southwest, where the land approached the Rio Grande, did Texas turn forbiddingly dry, scrubby, and mountainous. The whole of it, ill-defined on the northwest where it blended into New Mexico, comprised no less than 300,000 square miles and was occupied by fewer than 5,000 residents of even partly European ancestry and several times that many roaming Indians, including the fearsome Comanches, who constantly menaced the resident Spaniards and non-native travelers.

As Secretary of State, John Quincy Adams had renounced the American claim to Texas put forth by Thomas Jefferson, who had almost offhandedly contended, in an Olympian display of territorial hubris, that the western boundary of the Louisiana Purchase began not far above the Rio Grande. Recognizing the thinness of Jefferson's case, Adams conceded that Spain had an older and better claim to Texas, including existing settlements at San Antonio, the provincial capital, in the south-central region and Nacogdoches in the northeast. For his concession, Adams won the United States a far more generous western boundary, encompassing territory to which Spain had a claim about as flimsy as Jefferson's to Texas. Treaty or no treaty, though, imperial authorities feared that Texas, which had failed to attract settlers from Spain or the Mexican heartland because it was so remote, lacking in removable wealth, and infested with hostile Indians, would shortly be overrun by Americans, many of them disrespectful of unguarded international borders, as they had just brazenly shown in heisting Florida from Spanish control. Thus, officials in Mexico City and San Antonio were receptive to a proposition to colonize Texas that was put to them by wayfaring American businessman Moses Austin, originally from Connecticut, who had made and lost several fortunes as a frontier industrialist, most recently by mining and refining lead, the primary commercial metal of the age.

Austin's scheme called for the Spanish government to present him with a large land grant to which he would attract foreign settlers by giving them farmland free of charge, provided they agreed to work it and not hold it for speculation, became Spanish subjects, and accepted Catholicism as the one true faith. As a sweetener, the newcomers' colony would be exempt from import duties on the goods needed for their survival on the frontier. If the Austin colony took hold in Texas, imperial officials reasoned, it could bring prosperity and security to that hitherto forsaken region and attract other settlements that would serve as a barrier against rampant American intrusion. Austin was expected to enlist immigrants not just of Anglo-American extraction but also of French and Spanish ancestry, probably most of them living in neighboring Louisiana, as well as German and Swiss families from abroad—a truly multinational community that would also include native Mexicans coaxed north by the generous gifts of land. Austin's role as *empresario* (land agent/promoter) would be to enlist the immigrant families—300 were specified for the first phase of the operation—and then arrange to transport them, survey and register their tracts, import their supplies, export their produce, and generally maintain the peace. All of this was to be undertaken as private enterprise, without government resources or personnel, very much like the arrangements under which the British crown had authorized American colonial settlements by chartered grants to proprietary overseers, who, along with their settlers, were left to their own devices.

Upon completion of phase one, Austin's payoff, beyond a small fee from each transplanted family, was to be title to a large Texas tract.

Austin's vision was to prove the making of Texas. Just after winning Spanish approval of his project in 1821, though, he died, bequeathing his stake in it—along with considerable debt—to his twenty-seven-year-old son, Stephen, then a fledgling lawyer with little enthusiasm for frontier life in Texas. But he felt duty-bound by his father's deathbed wish that he see the undertaking to fruition. Besides, it was the only hope for settling the family debts. The problematic nature of Stephen Austin's inherited proprietorship was revealed to him almost at once by the untimely end of Spanish rule over Texas. It took him the better part of a year chasing after evasive officials of the newly installed Mexican government to confirm the grant made to his father by the ousted colonial authorities.

The younger Austin was an unlikely candidate to undertake the challenge of taming the Texas wilderness and the high-spirited risk takers willing to settle there. More a scholar and a poet by appearance, training, and temperament than a son of the soil, Stephen had been promised a Yale education before family financial reversals forced him to settle for attending Transylvania College in Kentucky, where he excelled in his studies. After helping with his father's troubled lead mines in Missouri, he chose to pursue the law under the tutelage of a successful New Orleans practitioner. Slight of build, with brown hair worn in ringlets and fair skin that burned too easily to withstand an outdoor existence, the well-mannered Austin was haunted by his father's failures, which left him cautious and diffident— hardly traits one looked for in a pioneer land developer. But he had an ingratiating manner and a decided gift for brokering political and cultural differences with the Mexican authorities. To win their trust, he promised to abide faithfully by whatever rules and regulations they imposed (including, as he knew from the first, a ban on slavery), to prevent the settlement of illegal immigrants on or near his grant lands, and to become a patriotic citizen of Mexico. "This solemn oath," he assured his benefactors, "cuts me off from all protection [by] or dependence on my former government."

Assuming the responsibilities of a de facto one-man governor of his settlement, Austin was awarded personal control of a vast domain—it would eventually amount to about 18,000 square miles, roughly twice the size of Massachusetts—between the Brazos and Colorado rivers about one-third of the way down the Texas Gulf Coast, with the right to build a port of entry to service his colony. There was no better situated or more fertile land in Texas. Austin wrote to a friend that it was "all first rate, plenty of timber, fine water, beautifully rolling . . . with the most luxuriant growth of grass I ever beheld." Fish, deer, and buffalo abounded. There was nothing at all baronial, however, about Austin's existence. He lived in a two-room log cabin, one room for sleeping, the other for his office. After arranging a loan from his legal mentor in New Orleans, he engaged the service of a schooner operating out of that humming port city and began pitching for settlers to transport to Texas.

Despite the hopes of Mexican authorities that Austin's colony would take on an international character, almost all of those he signed up to come to Texas were Americans. And many were Americans of a particular stripe, people who, like Austin's father, were failures seeking a fresh start in life or fugitives from their creditors, family obligations, or the reach of the law. Most came from the southern states of Georgia, Louisiana, Kentucky, and especially Tennessee, with its thin, stony soil that was unkind to farmers. Among the forces driving them across the Mississippi was the fallout from the Panic of 1819, which caused cotton prices to tumble, capital to erode, debtors to default, and thousands of farm families to lose their homes. Partly to relieve the widespread misery, Congress revised the federal land purchase rules in 1820, cutting the minimum price at auction by one-third—a boon to would-be buyers (though a blow to the value of existing holdings). But because the economic collapse had been triggered by a bursting credit bubble, Congress also required that buyers of federal land now pay the full purchase price at the time of sale. Thus, a typical transaction for the purchase of a quarter-section—160 acres, about the minimum needed to sustain a farming family—required between $200 and $300, more than many households could scrape together in hard times. As a result, a lot of families took to the road and headed west, where land could be bought cheap or just squatted on with little fear of early dispossession. Better yet, though the way was longer and farther from their roots, was to apply to Stephen Austin for a grant in Texas.

And what a grant it was, even at the cost of embracing Mexican citizenship and genuflecting to the Roman Church. In return, Austin deeded over to each of his new Texas settlers—virtually free of charge—nearly 1,000 acres for farming and grazing, with additional acreage for every member of their family and any slaves they brought with them. In 1825, the government consolidated the provinces of Texas and Coahuila, its more populous (and almost entirely Mexican) western neighbor, into one of the nineteen states created under Mexico's 1824 constitution. The new state government, given authority over its own immigration policy, permitted Austin to increase the size of a typical land grant to nearly 5,000 acres. This generosity was grounded on the theory that the more acreage put to use for farming and ranching, the more protection for the state's inhabitants against Indian raids and encroachments by squatters. The new constitution did not, however, permit slavery—and without slave labor, Austin knew his settlement's chances of early success would likely vanish. His settlers from the American South, though typically small to middle-sized cotton planters, were used to relying on their blacks to do the field work, a practice they would not consider abandoning in the hot, humid climate of eastern Texas. Austin felt he had no choice but to conspire with his settlers in circumventing the Mexican law through a variety of subterfuges. Prominent among these were the grantee's promise to phase out slavery over five to ten years and the transparently bogus claim that before coming to Texas their slaves had freely chosen to indenture themselves by signing on as "contract laborers" for an indefinite period and thus were not being subjected to involuntary servitude.

Austin's burdens were herculean and constant. While the Mexican constitution was a signal triumph for the more liberal *federalistas* favoring decentralized government and spared Texans from hovering government troops and customs officials, it had also yoked Austin's province to Coahuila, whose capital at Saltillo was 400 miles distant from his settlements. To protect their (and his own) interests, he honed his political skills, became fluent in Spanish, lobbied Mexican officials at San Antonio, Texas's provincial seat of government—a three-day ride from his headquarters at San Felipe on the Brazos River—and served in the state legislature when it was in session at Saltillo. There he labored to rationalize his colonists' continuing transgressions of the antislavery law and convince his fellow lawmakers that the Anglo-American settlers were otherwise law-abiding and productive citizens. When he was not on the road, Austin had his hands full contending with drought, crop failure, and resulting hunger that drove many a settler family back to the United States. Then there were the Comanche raiders, who regularly swooped down from the western plains to sack and bloody his colony, and the rowdies, bullies, and law-defilers among his own high-spirited, hard-drinking people, often too ornery to rein in, given the libertarian environment and glaring lack of peace officers.

For all his tribulations, Austin succeeded far better than any of the other twenty or so *empresarios* whom the Mexican government licensed to found settlements in East Texas. He readily fulfilled the first phase of his contract within two years—he was sure, in fact, that he could have enlisted five times the 300 families he settled in that time, so numerous were the applications to him for the generous handouts of lush Texas land. None of his competitors could match Austin's perseverance, promotional flair, and diplomatic skills. From the start his settlements were, and remained, the core of the burgeoning Anglo-American colony, whose residents seemed likely to outnumber the native Texans before long. For his initial efforts Austin was rewarded with title to roughly 200 square miles of verdant, rolling Texas countryside.

That Austin was making a go of his trying venture did not escape the notice of the newly elected President of the United States. Stung by criticism from southern and western political leaders that he had erred gravely as Secretary of State six years earlier in yielding American claims to Texas, John Quincy Adams studied reports of Austin's progress and the evident eagerness of Americans to settle beyond the Sabine River. Soon after moving into the White House, Adams undertook a new diplomatic initiative. Until then the United States had not pressed the young Mexican government to affirm the Adams-Onís agreement, reached in 1819 with Spanish authorities who no longer exercised power in North America. Perhaps Mexico would prove more pliable than Spain in yielding its remote, hard-to-defend northern provinces to the Americans' territorial ambitions.

Adams sent an envoy to Mexico City in 1825 to ask officials of the new republic to allow the boundary between the United States and Mexico to be moved southwestward about 350 miles along the Gulf Coast from the Sabine to the Rio Grande—just how far northwestward along the latter river's 1,900-mile length American sovereignty would extend was not specified. For handing over all of Texas and then some, Mexico was to be given a million dollars and a pledge of eternal friendship. This insulting proposition made no headway over three years of talks, so in 1828 Adams agreed to Mexico's offer to corroborate the 1819 boundary; Texas was to remain part of Mexico.

Adams's successor, Andrew Jackson, aware of the increasing flow of American immigrants, legal and otherwise, settling in Texas, renewed the American offer to purchase it and raised the ante to $5 million. For that price the United States would also relieve Mexico of the little-populated and useless area west of Texas as far as the Pacific Ocean if the Mexican government was so inclined. The offer was summarily refused; northern Mexico was not for sale. No evidence, it should be noted, has been unearthed to suggest that the American government, in the course of either the Adams or Jackson presidencies, actively connived with Austin or any other *empresario* to incite their settlers to pry Texas loose from the Mexican federation.

STEPHEN AUSTIN'S COLONY, despite a hopeful start, was soon stymied by two daunting problems. The first was of its own making.

The American immigrants' mandatory oath of allegiance to the Mexican government and its official religion was rarely more than transparent lip service. Although they were dispersed over a region running roughly 150 miles close by the Gulf coastline and extending almost as far inland, the new Texans formed an enclave unto themselves, hewing to their own language, culture, politics, and Protestant faith and energized by ambition and a frontier sense of self-reliance uncommon among the natives. Self-reliance, however, did not preclude slaveholding. Austin's settlers made no apology for their more or less open defiance of the Mexican prohibition of the practice beyond insisting it was an economic necessity, however unfortunate for their bondsmen. They shrank still less from their conviction that the Indians, an abiding nemesis throughout much of northern Mexico, could not be dealt with humanely; removal, preferably by extermination, was the only way to pacify the savages. Toward their Mexican hosts, the American immigrants acted with thinly veiled contempt, regarding them by and large as an indolent, dim-witted, untruthful, and mongrel people. That the 1824 constitution had placed the fate of Austin's and the other immigrant settlements under the control of "greasers," to use the favored American slur, galled the lately arrived Texans. Sentiment, more than a touch racist, soon gathered behind a proposal, delivered as unabrasively as possible by Austin to the Mexican state legislators at Saltillo, for culturally distinct Texas to be divorced from Coahuila province and granted self-rule. Austin devoted ten years to this pursuit with Mexican authorities—and got nowhere.

Their clannishness was by no means the only reason the Texans wanted as little as possible to do with Mexico. As the 1820s lengthened, the settlers came to the painful conclusion that the newly independent Mexicans, lacking experience in participatory democracy, did not know—and could not figure out—how to govern themselves. Many of the Spaniards and creoles who had run the colonial bureaucracy and commerce headed back to their ancestral Iberia as the revolution unfolded, leaving Mexico bereft of a citizenry trained to administer its affairs. Most in the wealthy and educated class had irresponsibly distanced themselves from politics and government, preferring to try to buy off or subvert any regime that seriously threatened their comforts and privileges by ardent advocacy of social justice. The colonial system, by its oppressive nature, had maintained some degree of domestic tranquility. Its place was taken by a swirl of clashing factions that left the baffled public uncertain of the will of the majority and unwilling to accept it as binding even when democratically expressed. Winning an election was no sacred license to govern, or not for long, anyway. Reformers and reactionaries, scorning the exigencies of practical politics, found no common ground; Congress squabbled endlessly, and statecraft was a phantom. The 1824 constitution, a response to the liberals' call for decentralized federal rule as practiced in the United States, succeeded only in making matters worse. While easing ironfisted control by Mexico City, it left the national government too feeble to check the military and the clergy, which grew more rapacious than they had been under crown oversight. To compound the problem, the newly strengthened state governments too often yielded to the domination of provincial satraps and cliques, prone to be despotic, corrupt, and wasteful.

On to this tumultuous stage marched a parade of *caudillos,* military chieftains idled after the long war for independence, many scarcely more than uniformed bandits, with little better to do now than shoot up the place. The generals and their cadres shifted their political allegiance as easily as they donned fresh uniforms; power rotated with dizzying frequency. The *caudillos,* servicing only their own vanity, soon bled the national treasury dry—and nobody stopped them.

If the American settlers of Texas understandably wanted as little as possible to do with the rest of Mexico and its civil, social, and economic dysfunction, some observant Mexicans were growing uneasy over the contrasting growth and success of the *empresario* colonies. To learn the size, strength, and attitudes prevailing in the long-neglected province bordering on the United States, Mexico in 1828 dispatched a team of official investigators led by one of the ablest men in the government, General Manuel de Mier y Terán, an authentic intellectual with credentials as a scientist and engineer.

Terán's team found the Mexican areas of Texas to be shabby and impoverished and the government in San Antonio incompetent. But the foreign settlements, especially Austin's, were thriving. Their farms and ranches were raising cotton, corn, mules, and beef, not only for subsistence and local consumption but as commercial operations exporting to New Orleans and beyond. Mingled with the investigators' admiration and envy was alarm over the growing number of illegal American immigrants boldly poaching on land within or close by the licensed settlements, including one community of fifty-eight families settled along the Trinity River, raising cattle and sugar. "Nature tells them that the land is theirs," Terán wrote in his commission's report, "because, in effect, everyone can appropriate what does not belong to anyone or what is not claimed by anyone. When the occasion arises, they will claim the irrefutable right of first possession"—a deft enough précis of the American squatter's creed since colonial times. A further source of irritation was the way Texans winked at the national ban on slavery. Among its most flagrant violators was James Groce, the wealthiest of Austin's grantees, whose plantation was served by a cotton gin, a grist mill, a steamboat, and 100 slaves. And the American immigration was only gathering momentum, prompting Terán to conclude that "these colonies, whose industriousness and economy receive such praise, will be the cause for the Mexican federation to lose Texas unless measures are taken soon."

Influenced by Terán's findings and recommendations and fearful that the loss of Texas would threaten the integrity and security of the troubled nation, Mexico acted to stunt the influx of Americans. Their colony's exemption from import duties, keeping the cost of goods low, was canceled. Immigrants were no longer permitted, under any pretext, to bring slaves with them on entering Mexico. Settlement by squatters was disallowed. Then, on April 6, 1830, the Mexican Congress gave still toothier notice that it did not intend to let the Anglo-Americans make off with the choicest sector of the country. A new law called a halt to all further American immigration, suspended unfulfilled *empresario* contracts, transferred the state of Coahuila y Texas's authority over immigrants to the federal government, ordered military posts to be installed in Texas, and proposed that a colony of at least 1,000 Mexicans be transplanted along the Trinity River to prevent further southward penetration by the Americans.

Predictably, the Texas settlers saw the crackdown as punishment for their success in taming a forsaken wilderness. The government answered that the American expatriates were simply not going to be treated as privileged citizens any longer. It was a faithful reprise of the debate that had turned to mutual rage when Britain decided that its national interest required an abrupt end to the permissive (that is, tax-free) self-rule that its American colonists had long enjoyed. The Mexicans, though, did not wait nearly so long to correct a risky policy that was backfiring. The trouble was, as in the transatlantic dispute with the British, that Mexico's concerted effort to clip the American settlers' wings turned previously peaceable colonists into active discontents. They were not like other Mexicans and did not want to become so.

The new anti-immigration laws threatened Austin with ruin. Although the government cut him some slack in its clampdown on new arrivals at his settlements because he had faithfully executed his contractual terms, Austin understood the implications of the new Mexican policy. Arguing that he was just defending the basic precepts of the 1824 constitution from which the government had strayed, Austin invested five anguished years in appealing to national officials to retract the stern 1830 rules and let Texas direct its own affairs as a separate state. He was simultaneously trying to keep a lid on simmering resentment among his American settlers, who now faced the glum prospect of being marooned in a land ruled by the caprice of a hostile, bumbling government in far-off Mexico City. Austin frankly shared their fear, writing a friend that "the Mexicans cannot sustain a republic. The present form must fall, and what is then to become of Texas? We are too weak to set up for ourselves, unless under the protection of our powerful neighbor."

THE NEARLY INEVITABLE COLLISION gathered force by small increments in a pattern strikingly similar to the events in Massachusetts culminating in the American Revolution. The Mexican government sent troops to enforce the newly required payment of import taxes. American sea captains and merchants resorted to smuggling and bribery to evade the imposts. The Mexicans seized ships and cargoes. The Texans formed gangs and posses to resist and intimidate; raiding parties stormed government jails to rescue alleged violators of the law. There were angry arguments and arrests over imported and runaway slaves, armed vigilantes confronted Mexican enforcers, shots were fired, militias were formed in Austin's colony, and Mexican troops tried to disarm the militiamen, who captured a government armory in the north.

By October 1832, the unrest led to a summoning of delegates from the immigrant settlements to air their grievances and consider sending spokesmen to Mexico City to ask the Mexican Congress to grant Texas separate statehood and restore its prior liberties. Austin, who chaired the convention though he knew it violated federal law against assemblies of protest, argued that such a step would be premature and likely treated as insurrectionist. His stature won a six-month delay; by the following spring, a new leader, thirty-eight years old and more charismatic than any of his predecessors, had taken charge of the Mexican government on a wave of popular sentiment.

The offspring of a landed creole family outside Veracruz, Antonio López de Santa Anna began his military career as a slender lieutenant of nineteen serving on the royalist side to subdue Mexico's freedom fighters. Like Napoleon, he was a political chameleon unvexed by idealism. A brave enough soldier, he rose swiftly more on his courtly manners and striking good looks—large brown eyes, dark curly hair, high forehead, and a plaintive countenance, said to greatly affect the men he commanded and the women he courted. He also benefited from a keen sense of timing and shameless lack of loyalty, switching to the revolutionary side when Mexican independence seemed inevitable, thereafter aligning himself with whichever *caudillo* was ascendant, then abandoning him before his doom was certain. All the while he was advancing in rank, popularity, and power.

Santa Anna's ascent was ensured in 1829 when he orchestrated a badly needed display of national purpose—the crushing of a 3,000-man expeditionary force sent by Ferdinand VII to reconquer Mexico. The hero of Tampico, site of the triumph over bedraggled Spanish invaders, bided his time as the nation's savior-in-waiting, his popularity rising in inverse ratio to that of warring, short-lived liberal and reactionary leaders without the skill or will to forge a popular consensus. A master at playing on the hopes, dreads, and pride of his sorely beset people, Santa Anna was called to the presidency by a majority of the state legislatures in March 1833—the first of eleven times Mexico would so empower him. He pledged an end to anarchy, a hatred of tyranny, and dedication to the principles of the 1824 Mexican constitution. That was enough for Stephen Austin to urge his fellow Texans to side with Santa Anna as the leader of "truly the liberal republican and constitutional party." What he turned out to be was a gifted poseur with seductive stage presence, a pretty package of vanity and treachery, and a dauntless acquirer of power without ever knowing how to use it to bind up his prostrate country.

A month after Santa Anna's election as president and de facto general-in-chief, impatient Texans reconvened and delegated Stephen Austin himself to register their concerns with the new government in Mexico City. Austin's partisans shared his hope that Texas could remain a loyal member of the Mexican federation if a more benevolent leadership granted it separate statehood. But that same April 1833 convention of representative Texans was marked by the emergence of a rival camp whose members, many of them newcomers with far less to lose than Austin's earlier settlers, saw the resolute *empresario* as an appeaser and his mission to the capital as a last-ditch effort to keep his colony under the Mexican flag. Regardless of the government's response to Austin's mission, the radical camp was bent on separate statehood for Texas and drew up a provisional constitution modeled—not by chance—after that of Massachusetts, seedbed of the American Revolution. Chairman of the drafting committee and the emergent contender for Austin's leadership mantle was a flamboyant, canny politician who had arrived in Texas only the year before, his career in cinders after a meteoric ascent.

Samuel Houston, though the same age as Stephen Austin, was his opposite physically and temperamentally—half a head taller, powerfully built, self-assured, and outgoing, with a brash stride, silver tongue, and abiding fondness for John Barleycorn. Left fatherless at thirteen, young Sam had rebelled when his five brothers insisted he join them laboring on the family's 400-acre eastern Tennessee farm. With little formal education, he clerked in a store, read enough to try his luck at teaching school, and drifted into the forest for a few years to learn the ways of the welcoming Cherokee people, who called him "the Raven," a symbol of good luck in their tribal lore. When the War of 1812 began, Houston joined Andrew Jackson's Tennessee militia; excelled as a platoon leader when Jackson assailed the Creeks, enemies of the Cherokee; and won an enduring reputation for his heroism in the climactic victory of the Creek War at Horseshoe Bend in March 1814. With an enemy arrow protruding from his thigh, Houston led his soldiers in a critical assault on the Creek encampment and did not falter until the breastworks were captured. The arrow was ripped out, along with a chunk of his flesh, but Houston rested just long enough—despite Jackson's ordering him to the rear—to head a second attack, this time coming within point-blank range of the defenders' guns and suffering a shattered right arm and shoulder. He was not expected to survive his wounds, but the Raven recovered. Jackson, admiring his courage, spirit, and good sense, took the younger man under his patronage, and Houston rode Jackson's coattails to power and fame.

A supple brain sped Houston's training in the law office of a prominent retired judge, and he soon hung out his own shingle, practicing successfully in the vicinity of Nashville, within easy reach of his guardian angel at the Hermitage. Before long the bluff, handsome bachelor was gathering steam as district prosecutor, a colonel in the Tennessee militia—on his way, with his reputation for bravery in combat, to becoming its state commander, the same title Jackson once held—and an ardent backer of his mentor's candidacy (as "the Nation's Hero and the People's Friend") for the White House. Elected to Congress unopposed, Houston served in Washington for two terms, during which he learned the craft of political horse trading but discovered, like Jackson, that legislative minutiae bored him; the executive branch of politics was more his wheeler-dealer style. Jackson's elevation to the White House encouraged Houston to seek the governorship, campaigning in a Cherokee hunting shirt, with fancy beadwork and a red sash, pumps with silver buckles, and a high beaver hat. The outlandish costume only added to his colorful character, and, winning handily, he pushed populist policies such as better roads, more schools, and lower prices for public land put up for auction.

All Sam Houston needed to win a second term in the governor's mansion—and perhaps grace his path to higher office—was a wife. He found one in a young beauty, the daughter of a prominent planter; their wedding, on the eve of the gubernatorial race, was the social event of the season. After just three months of evidently less than marital bliss, it all came undone.

Houston's bride fled to her parents' home without directing any charge of cruelty or infidelity at him. Indeed, no explanation was ever offered publicly by either husband or wife, though reports circulated that she had loved another and been forced into marrying the governor by her family's ambition for rank. Manfully, Houston never spoke ill of the flighty young lady, but the embarrassment forced him to abandon the gubernatorial race, then leave Tennessee altogether, fading into humiliated exile and one long, self-pitying alcoholic haze.

Houston found solace among his old friends, the Cherokees, in Arkansas, where some of them had been forced to settle by the federal government's heartless removal policy, pressed most ardently by the Indian tormentor in the White House. Houston did his best to ease the plight of the Cherokees and help them make peace with the Osage and other native peoples who had become their inhospitable neighbors. Too often, though, Houston got into brawls when liquored up—"Big Drunk" was the name the Osage gave him, and it would be tossed at him forever after by his detractors.

From his pit of despondency, Houston rallied and went east to confer with a New York financier who had invested in a Texas settlement contract with one of Austin's rival *empresarios* and faced heavy losses because of laws passed in 1830 by both the Mexican and the American congresses— the former halting further immigration from the United States, the latter permitting squatters to legitimize their trespasses on federal lands by paying $1.25 per acre for their tracts with the assurance that they could not be outbid (and thus dispossessed) at a public auction. Houston was engaged to sniff out the prospects of a Texas secession from Mexico—if that occurred and the United States annexed it, land values would soar. Before heading west, Houston stopped by the White House, where Jackson bucked him up and made him a confidential government agent (salary: $500) to explore a peace treaty with the Comanches, on the warpath along the Red River frontier, but did not—so far as surviving archives disclose—urge him to foment rebellion against Mexico among the Texans.

Like many who came there to escape their sorrows and find redemption, Sam Houston craved all the breathing room awaiting him under the starry skies of Texas and wasted no time settling in during the last months of 1832. The place suffered from a dearth of leaders, and his tainted celebrity and hard-drinking unconventionality suited his new neighbors just fine. He opened a law office, won a land grant from Stephen Austin, put out feelers for a peace powwow with the Comanches, and wrote to Jackson that he found Texas so pleasing that he intended to abide there, but promised never to forget the country of his birth. Mexico's governance of Texas was so lax, he added, that its separation, within or outside of the national federation, was likely.

Houston did his best to hurry the breakout. Elected a delegate to the Texans' second protest convention in March 1833, he gave the edgy assemblage a taste of his rousing oratory. "Can Mexico ever make laws for Texas?" he thundered, and then answered, "No . . . Mexico is acting in bad faith and trifling with the rights of the people. Plans formed without the assent of Texans are not binding upon Texas." Heads bobbed, and the delegates persuaded Stephen Austin to make the long trek to Mexico City to demand the return of their presumed rights—or else. Austin left in a few months, hopeful that Santa Anna's ascension would bolster his cause.

Austin's hopes, along with much of Mexico's, were misplaced. Santa Anna was less a working *presidente* than a dashing generalissimo on horseback, long on pomp and rhetoric, with little patience for reformulating public policy or supervising the gritty details of government, which he left to subordinates. He preferred to gallop about the country, exhibiting his personal magnetism, gathering the adoration of the masses, and choosing not to interfere with anticlerical reforms by the Mexican Congress, such as abolishing mandatory tithes and secularizing education at the university level. The state legislature for Coahuila y Texas was given more power over the immigrant settlements and Mexican troops were recalled from their posts there—surely a conciliatory sign from the federal authorities. But civil strife did not abate; the *centralistas,* anchored by reactionary bishops, military officers, and landed gentry, reasserted their concerns that the centrifugal dispersal of authority was creating anarchy. Order, not social justice, was their anthem. With full backing from the political right, Santa Anna abruptly shifted his course. Democracy, he declared in the spring of 1835, was not working in Mexico. "I threw up my cap for liberty, with great ardor and perfect sincerity," he related, "but very soon found the folly of it. A hundred years to come my people will not be fit for liberty. They do not know what it is, unenlightened as they are. . . . [D]espotism is the proper government for them."

And that is what he gave them. Assuming dictatorial powers, he dissolved Congress for being radical and ineffectual, then in short order voided most of its statutory reforms, shut down the nineteen state legislatures, reclassified the provincial bureaucracies as military districts answerable to the president, and set about silencing all protests over this chilling imposition of tyranny. Of particular note was Santa Anna's bloody suppression of rebellious elements in the state of Zacatecas, midway between Mexico City and San Antonio, where his soldiers cut down 2,000 civilians, including women and children.

Stephen Austin, sent to the capital to press for self-rule for Texas, encountered a riptide of intolerance for his province's deviationist clamor. Even before Santa Anna turned repressive, Austin could win no friends in Mexico City when he warned that Texas, despite his own efforts to restrain its hotheads, was likely to declare itself an independent state if the federal government refused to do so. He was told in response that he and his settlers were ingrates for having gladly accepted free land, minimal government interference, and virtual exemption from taxes and antislavery laws, and prospered as a result, yet now they were demanding to throw off Mexican rule. After six months of frustration Austin started back to Texas but was soon overtaken by soldiers, returned to Mexico City, and jailed for the next year and a half while Santa Anna was busy making liberty a fugitive. Though no formal charges were lodged against Austin, he was vilified for an intercepted letter he had addressed to friends at home, urging them to drum up support among Mexican officials in San Antonio for Texas state-hood, so the request would not seem to be purely American agitation. In Mexico City, that made him a conspirator.

Harshly treated during much of his imprisonment, the thoroughly disen-chanted Austin was released in August 1835 and urged to quash his settlers' complaints or they would feel the wrath of Mexico's patriots, who felt insulted by the Texans' demand for preferential status. Austin was greeted back home with sympathy for his ordeal but viewed as less than a martyr, for the faithful *empresario* had plainly been wishful in his contention that Texas might be permitted to thrive as an anomalous yellow rose within the Mexican rock garden. In his absence, Austin found, Texas had grown in numbers and militancy. Without his restraining hand—and in open defiance of the Mexican ban on immigration—the influx of American settlers, few with legal title to their land claims, had accelerated. Because record keeping was haphazard and squatters did not present themselves for registry, no accurate census could be taken, but historians have estimated the number of Texas immigrants from the United States by the mid-1830s to be no fewer than 15,000 and perhaps as many as twice that figure, not counting about 3,000 slaves; at any rate, they had far surpassed the province's Mexican population of about 4,000. Few of the Americans, Austin himself by now included, wanted any part of Santa Anna's suddenly and brutally autocratic Mexico, and many were spoiling for a chance to demonstrate their feelings.

They got their chance sooner than expected. In response to reports of proliferating units of militiamen throughout the American settlements and more frequent encounters between them and government officials, Santa Anna sent his brother-in-law, Martín Perfecto de Cos, and 500 soldiers to subdue the Texas protesters with any degree of force required. He was not to be swayed by the Texans' claims that they sought only the restoration of their rights—and all of Mexico's—as set forth in the 1824 constitution. Cos soon discovered he had ventured into a hornets' nest. Before he could reach the scene, Texas irregulars had forced the surrender of the Mexican garrison defending the customs post at Anáhuac off Galveston Bay. To prepare for Cos's looming assault, Austin was empowered to assemble volunteers from throughout the settlements and by the fall had as many as 900 men under arms, though scattered and poorly trained. As the base for his Texas operations, Cos had decided to fortify the capital at San Antonio and tore the roof off an old, rambling mission—once called San Antonio de Valero but later known as the Alamo—which served as the Mexican forces' stronghold.

As Cos's forces prepared their defenses throughout October, Texas militiamen drifted southwest, intending to pen in the Mexican troops before they could inflict damage on the American settlements near the Gulf Coast. With war imminent, a "consultation" of fifty-five delegates from thirteen Texas communities convened to determine whether the fighting already under way was designed to win their independence as a sovereign nation-state or to offer themselves up for annexation by the United States, which would surely condone the continued practice of slavery. There was no longer any talk of Texas remaining a separate Mexican state.

To the charge that Texans were ungrateful turncoats, the delegates raised essentially the same argument their ancestors had hurled back at the British crown for labeling rebel American colonists disloyal children—namely, that Texas had never truly been a part of Mexico, only a long-neglected wilderness that the American pioneers had sweated to develop without any aid or protection from the Mexican government. Austin, too much of a compromiser to be an effective military commander, was sent to Washington in quest of financial and military help for the defense of Texas. He was replaced as head of the army by the one experienced military man in their midst, General Sam Houston, his rank derived from having once been in charge of the Tennessee militia.

There was no real Texas army, of course, only bands of belligerents eager to repulse the "greasers," and Houston was more a figurehead at first than a commander, since his field forces, under officers of their own choice, balked at orders from on high. Houston saw no point in wasting his precious manpower by storming San Antonio—it was too far from the main American settlements to the northeast, too close to Mexico, too hard to defend,

and not where Texas would win or lose the war. But the volunteers cluster-
ing in that vicinity were restless, eager to fight, and, even untrained, better
shots than the Mexican conscripts, many of whom were newly freed convicts. So despite Houston's objections and a steady erosion in the ranks of
the Texas volunteers, enough of them remained to press a six-week siege
against Cos's reinforced garrison in San Antonio. After intense, street-by-
street fighting, the outnumbered Americans forced Cos to surrender in early
December. Mexican casualties were in the hundreds, the Texans' losses a
few dozen. Cos's troops had to give up their weapons but were allowed to
march back across the Rio Grande on their promise never to return.

Texas rejoiced, and many supposed the war had already been won. But
Sam Houston knew it had only begun, that Santa Anna would not give up
Texas without a real fight, and that the numbers would greatly favor his suc-
cess if he marshaled the forces at his nation's disposal.

FORTUNATELY FOR TEXAS, it was by no means all that Santa Anna had on
his mind. Mexico was big, proud, and poor; its government was in debt and
starved for revenues; its military ranks were composed largely of young
Indians, jailbirds, and others forcibly conscripted and obliged to live off the
land or from private handouts—and the heart of Texas beat at the northern
end of the country, a thousand miles from Mexico City over poor roads
through often rugged terrain. But to demonstrate his control over Mexico
and the inviolability of his nation, Santa Anna had to make an example of
Texas, which had clearly failed to grasp the lesson he had intended to teach
by the bloody subjugation of insurgent Zacatecas. The Texans, he asserted
now, were no better than "pirates and outlaws," undeserving of civility or
mercy. He set about assembling an expeditionary force large enough to
drive the American settlers perhaps all the way back across the Sabine,
where they had come from. And to prove his indispensability, the despot-in-
chief would lead the Mexican troops himself.

Sam Houston and the provisional governing council of Texas read intercepted messages disclosing Santa Anna's plan to gather, train, and march an
army of 10,000 north to San Antonio (though on arrival, its ranks totaled little more than half that number). Once the capital of Texas had been seized,
Santa Anna planned to divide his forces into a three-pronged offensive, his
left hurrying north to capture Nacogdoches, his right racing up the Gulf
Coast to secure the rebels' major port at Galveston Bay, and his main forces
driving into the midst of the American settlements. Houston had three
months at most to recruit and train an army—he figured 5,000 men could do

the job—before the tiger would be at the gate. He fell miserably short of that number. Despite repeated appeals to rally Texans to the defense of their liberty ("Patriotic millions will sympathize in our struggles") and to lure Americans across the Louisiana border to share in the noble fight against Mexican tyranny, Houston would never have as many as 1,000 men under his command in the same place at the same time.

Part of his problem was the sheer size of Texas, which served to filter the oncoming peril and make it seem distant and unreal. Then there was the small population base and the relentless physical demands of the agrarian culture, which forced most of the men to hang close by their fields and herds or risk losing them. More than sheer numbers, though, Houston needed soldiers of fighting caliber who would follow orders. His worst problem stemmed ironically from what should have proven the Texans' greatest advantage over the despotic Santa Anna—a libertarian mindset. Armies are not democratic institutions, but in Texas, where many men were kings of their own considerable spreads, civil authority was minimal to nonexistent, and no man's opinion was better than any other's; individualism reigned, and whoever attempted to impose a command strategy and the military discipline to carry it out was looking for trouble.

Sam Houston got plenty of it. He found the bulk of his volunteers to be "busy, noisy, second-rate men," contentious by habit, and his officers inclined to lead their men off on missions of their own devising. Houston never had the resources to hire professional soldiers or issue more than rudimentary equipment to the men who answered his call. Buckskin britches were what passed for a uniform in his army, and most of his men wore shoes or moccasins, not marching boots. It was not that Texas was poor— certainly not when compared to Mexico—but its wealth was mostly tied up in the land. Cash was scarce, taxes hard to pry from the countryside, and foreign credit (and the supplies it might provide) difficult to obtain. To woo conscripts Houston offered them land bounties, the same expedient form of reward the United States had relied on to pay its Revolutionary War soldiers. But in an immense territory like Texas, where so much land was practically free for the asking (or taking), the bounty system was a limited inducement.

Given an undermanned, ill-equipped, insubordinate, doggedly democratic army of amateur gunslingers, its ranks regularly thinned by desertion—the very problems that had afflicted George Washington while trying to combat a far more numerous and potent enemy—Houston had little choice but to adopt much the same cautious, defensive strategy that wore down George III's redcoats. Houston did not have enough soldiers to risk confronting Santa Anna's far larger host on the open battlefield or splitting up the meager Texas force to blunt the Mexicans' three-pronged attack. Instead, like Washington, he would use his home terrain to advantage, luring the enemy ever deeper into Texas, slowing their advance by forcing them to endure endless river crossings, buggy swamps, and steady sniper fire, all the while extending the Mexicans' supply lines and opening them to lateral assault. A tactical retreat would buy Houston time to gather his troop strength and pick the most advantageous place to pounce on the wearying enemy.

Accordingly, the Texas commander issued orders in January 1836 for his forward units not to wage an all-out defense of San Antonio, sure to be overwhelmed by Santa Anna's main force. Instead the Texans were told to pack up all the portable military gear in the provincial capital, destroy its fortifications, the Alamo in particular, and then fall back and wage guerrilla warfare to slow the enemy's advance. But a hard core of the defenders took Houston's order to be cowardly, vowed to wage so punishing a resistance that Santa Anna would abandon his offensive, and declared that even if they failed, they would rather die blazing away than surrender San Antonio to the Mexicans as Houston had told them to—without firing a shot. In view of the town's strategic uselessness, their defiance of Houston's orders amounted to suicidal bravado. The garrison of fewer than 200 men, inspired by the presence of legendary bear hunter (and three-term member of the United States Congress) Davy Crockett, chose to make its stand at the Alamo and appealed to other militia units in Texas for reinforcements. But Houston, with too few troops at his disposal, would not contribute to the folly; Texas needed not mutineers set on martyrdom but soldiers who would fight where they had a chance to prevail.

As advance units of Santa Anna's army crossed the Rio Grande late in February and closed in on San Antonio, fifty-nine delegates gathered at Washington-on-the-Brazos, 150 miles to the northeast, and reviled the Mexican president for tearing up his nation's constitution, replacing it with despotic one-man rule, and denying Texans their liberties. On March 2 the convention declared the province of Texas an independent republic. Then it went to work drawing up a new constitution, elected as interim president former Louisiana businessman David Burnet (who had once fought as a Venezuelan rebel against Spain), appointed a cabinet, and reconfirmed Sam Houston as commander of the Texas army. In the midst of these proceedings an urgent message arrived from the besieged Alamo garrison, begging the delegates and any other able-bodied Texans to come to their rescue. But Houston insisted the convention's work, about to be broadcast to the whole world, took precedence, and spurned the plea. Yet under the dire circumstances, he could hardly renew his earlier order to the men in San Antonio—with their wrenching battle cry of "Victory or death!"—to abandon the fight without giving the appearance of being a spineless commander-in-chief. A few days later, the fate of the Alamo diehards was reported. Massively outnumbered, the 187 Texas sharpshooters and cannoneers dropped 600 of the charging Mexicans before their fortress was overrun. True to his vengeful word, Santa Anna gave no quarter; he ordered all who had survived the assault to be shot on the spot and their bodies burned.

Two weeks later and sixty miles down the San Antonio River near Goliad, Santa Anna's strike force hurrying toward the Gulf Coast outflanked and then surrounded 430 Texas militiamen whose inexperienced commander had dawdled after receiving Houston's order to fall back. Caught in open country with no fortress for cover and running out of water and ammunition, the Texans surrendered in the hope that, like General Cos's troops surrendering at San Antonio four months earlier, they would be granted clemency and deported to New Orleans on the pledge of never returning to Texas. Instead, the 350 captives were marched to a jailhouse in Goliad and kept there a week while Santa Anna angrily reconfirmed his no-quarter policy to the reluctant field commander. Then the prisoners were marched back out to the countryside in a double column and on Palm Sunday, March 27, shot down like dogs and their bodies burned.

The twin tragedies left Texans quivering. "The day of just retribution ought not to be deferred," Sam Houston wrote the Texas cabinet. But he had at best 400 soldiers left to fend off their bloodthirsty Mexican stalker. His only recourse for the moment was retreat, and trailing along with him and his miserable soldiers came most of the civilian population, scurrying for their lives, their horses and oxen loaded with whatever household possessions they could salvage and clogging roads already mired by heavy spring rains. Houston's men lent a hand to keep panic from overtaking the sodden evacuees and left burning barns and fields in their wake to deny food to Santa Anna's pursuing forces. As the refugees fled northeastward, the Texas commander was decried on all sides for not making a stand against the steadily gaining Mexican forces and ridiculed as a besotted, used-up old warrior who had no stomach left for combat.

What Houston needed, with the survival of the republic in his hands, was soldiers: 3,000 would be enough to stop Santa Anna. He had hardly a quarter as many, though a steady trickle of recruits from the heart of the Texas settlements and the United States was helping. Houston's secret hope for salvation was his old mentor in Washington, in the final year of his term in the White House. Andrew Jackson had never been coy about his desire to bring Texas into the American union, along with as much territory to the west of it as Mexico might willingly yield. But he would not go to war for Texas since the feisty American colonists there seemed resolved to detach it from Mexico themselves. If the Texans, though, were driven back into Louisiana and many of them cut down in flight, the President and Congress would likely become infuriated, Houston calculated, and launch an American counterattack to conquer Texas and perhaps a lot more of Mexico.

Santa Anna quickened his pursuit now, knowing that Houston's meager forces would probably grow the deeper they fell back into the American communities and the closer they drew to the Louisiana border. Denied the bounty of their countryside by the retreating Texans, the Mexican army answered with its own scorched-earth destruction of everything in their path that the American settlers had built. For Santa Anna, the ethnic cleansing of Texas by driving the foreigners back across the Sabine held much appeal. It would save him the high cost and endless trouble of leaving forces behind to occupy and discipline the conquered province. But the Mexican president-on-horseback, with victory in his grasp, also knew his army was growing hungry and tired from its long trek and more vulnerable with every north-ward step it took. Rather than pausing to firm up his lines of communication and supply and consolidate his troops in a single, engulfing mass that might sweep the Americans to their doom, the impatient Santa Anna chose to make a swift, surgical strike aimed at capturing the newly installed officials of the Texas government and forcing them to disestablish the lately hatched republic. It was an even larger mistake than his bloodletting at the Alamo and Goliad, which had given outraged Texans their rallying cry.

SAM HOUSTON HAD YIELDED half of Texas to the invaders in six weeks, and the farther northeast his ragged little army of about 800 men retreated, the shriller the cries assailing him to stand and fight the Mexicans—or to stand aside for a commander who would. Just one victory would turn the tide of the war, went the clamor. President Burnet declared that the whole campaign had been a disgrace to the good name of Texas, and goaded his commander-in-chief: "The enemy are laughing you to scorn. . . . You must retreat no farther. The country expects you to fight. The salvation of the country depends on you doing so."

But Houston, sharing his soldiers' hardships in the field, had done well just to keep his forces intact, and he knew that if he engaged the Mexican army too soon, a single defeat would almost certainly bury the independent republic of Texas. Santa Anna, learning from spies and scouts how few troops Houston had, knew his own strength and felt he could take a bold gamble to end the war by decapitating the Texas insurgency. Burnet and his cabinet had kept moving as their pursuers approached, remaining just beyond reach. But as soon as Santa Anna heard that the Texas officials had taken refuge in the undefended hamlet of Harrisburg, he detached an elite corps of 750 cavalry and riflemen and led them there himself. It was unthinkable that Houston could or would drive his backpedaling troops, who were well to the northwest, to the rescue of his government. By the time the Mexicans arrived, however, the forewarned rebel leaders had slipped away aboard a steamboat headed for Galveston Bay—and Houston had somehow managed to show up in the neighborhood, positioning his troops for an encounter.

On being told that Santa Anna had deployed a force no larger than his own for a chase after the Texas officials, Houston had seen his chance. In two and a half days he marched his men fifty-five miles over roads turned to quagmire and positioned them on a wooded slope near the juncture of the San Jacinto River and its main tributary, Buffalo Bayou, about twenty miles north of the modern city of Houston. Summoning reinforcements to help him corner the little Texas army, Santa Anna, who was unfamiliar with the terrain, blundered by pitching camp on exposed ground scarcely a mile from Houston's position and leaving himself surrounded by water on both sides and to the rear, where a bridge was supposed to provide an escape route. The overconfident Santa Anna expected Houston's men to hang back in the woods and await the Mexican onslaught; he doubted the Texans would abandon their strong defensive position and risk being cut to pieces by the enemy's best cavalry. But Houston had ordered the bridge to the Mexicans' rear dismantled before they dug in. Now his men, who had been on the run so long, beseeched their commander to let them seize the initiative against a vulnerably encamped force of roughly equal size. With so much riding on the outcome, the Texas commander hesitated to give the attack order. After his scouts watched reinforcements arrive overnight at Santa Anna's camp, more than doubling the size of the Mexican force, Houston was subjected to a tongue-lashing by subordinates for delaying and knew the decisive moment was at hand.

Sun glints danced in the waters of the nearby San Jacinto River as April 21, 1836, dawned bright and clear. The Mexican camp was preoccupied with the new arrivals, who were dog-tired after their long, hurried march and in no shape to engage in battle. The Texans prepared for it as stealthily as possible just beyond the enemy's earshot. At three in the soft spring afternoon, while Santa Anna's men were drowsing in mid-siesta, Houston at last ordered his soldiers to advance, as noiselessly as possible. To their astonishment, they saw that the Mexicans had failed to post look-outs to guard the camp perimeter—an egregious, and in this case fatal, lapse of vigilance that was the responsibility of the commanding officer.

Undetected until too late, the Texans, with the mounted Sam Houston leading the charge, fell upon the startled Mexicans and stampeded them into a panicked retreat. In moments they found their escape route, the broken bridge, was gone and that they were helplessly trapped. The Texans, shouts of vengeance on their lips, blasted away furiously with their few cannons and then, using rifles, pistols, knives, and musket butts as clubs, staged their own slaughter. Houston, whose right tibia was shattered just above the ankle by an enemy bullet, made a halfhearted effort to stop the killing, but it went on for hours. The Mexican death toll reached 630; only two Texans died that day and twenty-three (including Houston) were wounded in the rout. The victors, at Houston's urging, finally curbed their fury by making prisoners of the 730 Mexican survivors instead of executing them all in the cold-blooded fashion that Santa Anna had ordered at the Alamo and Goliad.

Notably missing among the Mexican corpses and captives was *el presidente.* No one else was more to blame for the ignominious defeat at San Jacinto, but the vanquished commander was also his nation's indispensable chief of state, so he bolted from the battleground instead of valorously trying to rally his stunned soldiers and risking almost certain death in the melee or by firing squad. His higher duty, Santa Anna told himself, was to escape, rejoin the main body of his army, just a few days' march away, and lead a counterattack that would crush the momentarily jubilant Texans. He swam the river to safety, slipped into civilian garb, and was making good his getaway when Houston's outriders, hunting hard for the hated fugitive, picked him up on the road the next day but failed to recognize him in mufti. When delivered to the prisoners' compound at San Jacinto, the disguised president of Mexico was joyfully acclaimed by his men, and the game was up. His capture, more than the fighting itself, decided the war.

Sam Houston, the pain from his crippling wound eased a bit by savoring his now totally vindicated strategy of patience, acted with less charity than calculation as his archenemy was brought before him in chains. Many of Houston's men favored promptly shooting the Mexican chieftain as a murdering despot, but their commander knew the captive was likely to prove far more valuable as a hostage than a lifeless trophy. Even at gunpoint, though, Santa Anna was unlikely to sign an order for delivery to the generals of his nearby armies commanding them to surrender. For one thing, orders issued from captivity were universally understood to have been drawn up under extreme duress—and thus to be invalid. For another, why should the Mexican forces lay down their arms in ignominious submission when they still greatly outnumbered the Texans? A timely counterassault, even if it cost them their president and the lives of all the other prisoners at San Jacinto, would likely result in victory for Mexico and death for the republic of Texas.

Houston gambled that Santa Anna's generals would swallow a less shameful solution than capitulating without firing a shot. He made Santa Anna order the main body of the Mexican army to shoulder their firearms and withdraw unbeaten to below the Rio Grande, sparing the prisoners' lives and ensuring their own return home but, as a practical matter, conceding the successful secession of Texas. The council of Mexican generals was divided over how to respond, but in the end none of them dared to defy Santa Anna's orders, even though issued from captivity. Before his eventual release, the humbled Mexican dictator was obliged, as head of state, to sign a pair of treaties formally acknowledging the independence of the republic of Texas and promising to exert his influence on the Mexican Congress to ratify the agreement.

On his return to Mexico City, Santa Anna avoided disgrace by assuring his countrymen that he had submitted to the treaties only because he knew his government would never agree to them—and he disavowed them himself. He would not escape history's censure, though, for the bloody fiasco at San Jacinto or for saving his hide by directing his subordinates to quit the hard, nearly successful campaign to stifle the Texas insurgency.

The victor in that struggle was not embraced by his government. The provisional Texas president, David Burnet, carping at Houston's generalship right up until he won the short, ugly war, made no bones about his dislike and distrust of Sam Houston. Even with victory in hand, Burnet and his cabinet would not garland the triumphant Houston out of misplaced fear he might execute a Caesar-like coup and crown himself dictator. Worse, they jealously froze him out of their deliberations in the hope that when he left for New Orleans to have his infected leg properly tended to, he would stay away in permanent exile.

His petty, bickering enemies, though, were no match for Houston's expansive nature and restored heroic reputation. Big Drunk had morphed into the blazing Lone Star of Texas, lionized throughout the American press, very much as Jackson, his role model, had been hoisted to Olympus after winning the Battle of New Orleans thirty-one years earlier. Houston believed too fervently in Jacksonian democracy, of course, ever to have contemplated turning into a military autocrat. Yet his surging self-assurance overcame his reluctance to stand for high public office once again. Convinced that he was the best, if not only, man to unify the often brawling free spirits and disparate vested interests of the sovereign nation of Texas, the still hobbling hero of San Jacinto offered himself as a candidate for president of the republic in its first election of a permanent government. He received four times as many votes as his two rivals combined. One of them, Stephen Austin, dwelling deep in Houston's shadow, he named secretary of state, and the other was put in charge of the treasury as a gesture of magnanimity.

Austin's overwhelming defeat at the polls was the final rebuff for a man whose tireless if not entirely selfless labors had pumped life into Texas and sustained it for fifteen tumultuous years. No man had given more to it and had less to show. "I have no house, not a roof in all Texas, that I can call my own," he lamented in a letter to a friend. "I have no farm, no cotton plantation, no income, no money, no comforts. I have spent the prime of my life and worn out my constitution in trying to colonize this country." And though Houston had graciously honored him with the highest post in his cabinet, Austin died before the year was out, at age forty-three. He had never married; his only bride was Texas. Houston hailed him as "our founding father."

TEXANS' GRATITUDE TO SAM HOUSTON for saving the republic was understandable, but far more revealing of their state of mind at the birth of their nation were the results of a referendum held along with the general elections. So beset were they by their collective privations—a war-torn countryside, burned and looted homes, a scarcity of money, credit, and goods of every kind, a dysfunctional economy, a frail government deep in war debts, and a constant threat of Indian raids and reconquest by unforgiving Mexico—that they directed their new leaders to seek prompt annexation of Texas by the United States. The vote was 3,277 in favor to 91 opposed.

There was more reason than high anxiety for Texans to seek the comforting lap of their Uncle Sam. The United States had never been more robust than at the end of Andrew Jackson's presidency. Its prosperous economy had generated a favorable balance of trade, its national government was entirely free of debt, and its steady westward expansion was reflected by record federal land sales in 1836 of $24 million for about 20 million acres, roughly the size of South Carolina. The national genius for transforming land into wealth, moreover, flourished as never before. New technology was being rapidly applied to make the soil more productive, to fuel native industry, and to shorten travel time dramatically and thus overcome the daunting distances of the American landscape. The 1830s opened with the construction of the nation's first commercial railway line, a thirteen-mile stretch built by the Baltimore & Ohio. A web of iron arteries was soon being spun in all directions—and faster than anywhere else on the planet. The next few years saw the arrival of Cyrus McCormick's reaper, which did for the wheat fields of the Midwest what the cotton gin had done for the South; the use of anthracite coal deposits in Pennsylvania to improve iron-smelting productivity and open the way to the steel age; and the invention and prompt adaptation of the screw propeller to drive steamships far more efficiently than the paddle-wheel. For Texans, numbed by the trauma of war and shielded from its return by only a few hundred militiamen, exchanging their political independence for the security and likely rewards of membership in the American union seemed a small sacrifice. True, they had freed themselves, against all odds, from the inept Mexicans, but the Texans' prospects of sustaining that freedom from despotism—while still imposing it legally on their own slaves—would be immeasurably improved once their domain was declared official territory of the United States. That status would soon attract new settlers and investors as nothing else could and turn their outsized frontierland into a bonanza.

To make their petition to be annexed as enticing as possible to the American government the Texas Congress, in one of its first legislative measures, passed a boundary act at the end of 1836, proclaiming the republic to be much vaster than it had been approximately defined while still a province of Mexico. Taking their cue from Jefferson's feckless claim a third of a century earlier, the Texans said their territory was bounded on the south and west by the Rio Grande Valley all the way to the source of the nearly 2,000-mile-long river—and beyond it—to the forty-second parallel, the United States boundary under the Adams-Onís Treaty. That amounted to some 325,000 square miles, almost one-fifth the size of the existing United States, and included the eastern two-thirds of present-day New Mexico, indisputably a Mexican province, and its capital, Santa Fe, the largest Hispanic settlement between Texas and the Pacific coast. Since the American population was confined to an eastern crescent amounting to perhaps 10 percent of this claimed expanse, to call the Texas boundary act wishful and provocative was an understatement. For Houston, a canny gambler, it was a bargaining position; the more territory Texas offered to the United States, the greater the prize—and with American military force on call, the less likely Mexico would be to challenge the expansive claim.

To make itself still more attractive to Congress, the new republic began to offer free homesteads to all who were willing to settle there and cultivate the soil. This, too, was a gamble because Texas had already given away millions of acres of public land to its soldiers in the form of enlistment bounties and to public officials in lieu of pay. Offering more land as an enticement to newcomers, though, would presumably quicken the postwar rebuilding of Texas and stimulate productivity and purchasing power. The offer of free land was especially attractive to southern planters whose soil had been played out; their arrival contributed heavily to the tripling of the population of Texas, despite its many problems, during the nine-year life of the republic. All that free real estate, however, reduced the value of land scrip, the commonest form of Texas currency, and virtually eliminated the most promising source of government revenue—the sale of public land—for the financially strapped Texas authorities as they tried to pay off war debt, keep up a 2,500-man militia to ward off possible attacks by Mexico, and otherwise maintain a semblance of law and order in a land half again as large as France.

For all its great size and potential, Texas got the cold shoulder from the United States the first time it came knocking on the door for admission.

Several excuses were offered. Strict constructionists argued that the Constitution did not provide for the annexation of foreign nations. But the same sort of argument had been raised at the time of the Louisiana Purchase and was brushed aside by expansionists in the name of expediency: America simply could not afford to lose such a golden opportunity to achieve territorial security. And while the residents of Louisiana had had no say in their transfer to American jurisdiction, the people of Texas had voted overwhelmingly in favor of giving up their national sovereignty for the privilege of joining the United States. A second, hardly more persuasive argument against annexation was that it might ignite a war with the Mexicans, especially if they could enlist Britain, their chief creditor and trading partner, to join them or help finance the effort in order to brake the Americans' expansionist impulses. For if Texas were to become part of the United States, who would halt its march due west to the Pacific coast, where Britain still vaguely hoped to build a commercial base? Anglo-Mexican intervention, then, was not an entirely fanciful scenario. But military strategists at the time speculated that Mexico would likely need 20,000 troops to recapture the independent republic of Texas—an implausibly large force for the weak Mexican economy to sustain and for the government to mobilize, now that Santa Anna had been driven from power after his calamity at San Jacinto. And to go to war against the United States under

President Andrew Jackson might well cost Mexico a great deal more territory than Texas, possibly even its independence. The third argument against annexation, though, was compelling: such an initiative would likely threaten the nation's unity by reopening the explosive intersectional debate over the slavery question, largely quiescent for fifteen years.

Because of the climate, fecund soil, and generous scale of the landholdings, slave labor had been a prime factor in the colonization of Texas. But it did not escape the notice of the abolitionist movement, which sprang to life in New England in the early 1830s, that slaveholding Texans were thumbing their noses at Mexico's prohibition of the practice. The moral outrage of antislavery advocates only intensified over the prospect of Texas joining the Union, which was then equally divided between slave and free-soil states at thirteen each. Texas was so large, moreover, that, once annexed, it might eventually be divided into any number of smaller states, and since most of its claimed area fell below the 1820 Missouri Compromise line of 36°30′, all of them would surely become slave states, tilting the national balance of power toward the southern plantocracy.

Lending weight and fire to the antislavery sentiment against annexation was John Quincy Adams, who, having served as a magisterial Secretary of State and controversial one-term President, began a remarkable seventeen-year career in the House of Representatives in 1831. There he persisted like a beacon of righteousness cast upon the nation's more abominable tendencies. A dyed-in-the-wool expansionist, Adams was nevertheless hotly opposed to the spread of slavery, though he recognized as a practical matter the near impossibility of outlawing it where already established—essentially the view of the Whig Party, avowed opponents of annexing Texas. Adams's voice resonated across the free states of the North and West when he pointed out that if Texas was annexed and the United States forced into war as a result against Mexico and Britain, both of which had abolished slavery, Americans would find themselves fighting to extend and defend a repugnant practice against foes who were morally in the right.

Such an argument did not greatly move Adams's archenemy, slaveholder Andrew Jackson, who would dearly have liked to bring Texas into the Union as the crowning achievement of his activist presidency. But Jackson was committed to promoting the election of his loyal and able protégé, Vice President Martin Van Buren of New York, as his successor in the White House. Van Buren, like many northern Democrats—in tandem with the Whigs on this single issue—opposed the extension of slave territory, and Jackson feared he could not support the immediate annexation of Texas without inciting a coalition of Whigs, northern Democrats, and abolitionists to make Van Buren pay the price in the 1836 election. So Jackson sat on his hands with regard to Texas despite appeals for help from his friend Sam Houston.

On his last day in office at the beginning of March 1837, Jackson took the one action he could without compromising incoming President Van Buren. Failure by the United States to encourage Houston's frail republic, Jackson recognized, would drive Texas to seek aid and comfort from Britain, which had been avidly exploiting opportunities throughout Spain's former New World dominion by recognizing the new republics and counseling them on economic issues in return for favorable trade agreements. Houston, if rejected by the United States, might justifiably invite the British to extend their commercial empire to Texas and invest in its needy economy. Resolved not to let Texas slip within Britain's sphere of influence by default, Jackson appointed a chargé d'affaires to the Texas republic, granting it de facto diplomatic recognition on the eve of his departure from the White House. Mexico's ambassador promptly left Washington in protest.

Even if President Van Buren, once safely elected, had been inclined to reverse his stance on Texas annexation, a sudden downturn in the nation's economic fortunes cooled expansionist tendencies and left the sovereign status of Houston's republic in limbo. The Panic of 1837 had been unwittingly set in motion by President Jackson's order to withdraw federal funds from the self-serving Second Bank of the United States and distribute them among state-chartered "pet banks," which went on an easy-credit binge, allowing loan repayments in inflated paper currency, to the delight of eager land buyers and speculators. To check the easy-money frenzy Jackson directed that all future purchases of federal public lands be paid for in gold or silver specie or hard-currency notes, then in short supply. The resulting run by depositors and paper-currency holders caused 600 state banks to fail, federal land sales to plummet from $24 million in 1836 to $1 million in 1837, construction and other industrial activity fueled by credit to come to a standstill, and unemployment to reach record levels.

With investor confidence in the doldrums, the shaken nation was not giving much thought to Texas. In August 1837, Secretary of State John Forsyth told Houston's envoy that President Van Buren would not be submitting the Texas annexation request to Congress.

DENIAL OF THEIR PETITION to join the United States and the spillover impact of the severe American depression left Texans hurting during their first years as an independent nation. Sam Houston's heroic glow could not work miracles.

The uncertain political status of the country, its nearly bankrupt government, and the peril of a Mexican invasion stifled capital formation. With little specie and hard currency in circulation, Texas authorities had great difficulty collecting taxes and customs duties. To sustain any semblance of a working economy, Houston had to issue paper currency backed only by public lands. As more immigrants arrived from the United States, where they were required to pay hard cash up front to buy a farm from the government's inventory, they gladly took up the offer by Texas of free land, a splendid growth incentive but one that inevitably caused local currency to deflate and the value of older property to slump.

The surest way out of his quandary, Houston saw, was to reach an accommodation with the Mexican authorities. If they would just acknowledge the loss of Texas, confirming its independent status, the world, it was thought, would take note, foreign investment would flow, the economy would revive, taxes could be collected, the currency would stabilize, and the government, no longer pauperized, could provide public services beyond trying desperately to sustain a respectable militia. But even with British and French intermediaries pushing his case, Houston's peace overtures were refused. Wounded national pride made acceptance of the Texas secession a one-way ticket to oblivion for Mexican political leaders. Even the least astute among them recognized, moreover, that the slavery issue was likely to brand Texas as forbidden territory for inclusion in the American union for an indefinite period, leaving the infant republic in a precarious, if not entirely helpless, condition. Thus rebuffed by the United States and Mexico, Houston pitched Britain, the world's richest and most powerful nation, for help. The British, hopeful of keeping Texas out of the clutches of the United States and obtaining a ready, perhaps cheaper source of cotton as an alternative to American growers, were cordial enough but reluctant to pressure Mexico, a client state in thrall to British creditors, for fear of alienating it.

Houston's efforts were equally foiled by his fellow Texans. They disdained his attempts to make peace with the Indians. They clamored for a new war with the Mexicans for stubbornly refusing to admit they had lost the last one. Their populist sentiments stymied Houston's plans to set up a rudimentary banking system and to sell bonds in support of public services and basic infrastructure. Land titles were in turmoil; overlapping and fraudulent claims were rampant, and the court system was too feeble to untangle the mess. Adding to the chaos, the credit-starved economy could not provide enough work to occupy the steady influx of immigrants. Idleness invited dissipations—drinking, gambling, brawling—on a scale that made saloons the civic, commercial, and cultural hub of the community. The survival of the republic looked doubtful. Houston's principal (and perhaps only) success in his first term as president was, as it had been in his early months as commander of the vaporous Texas army, that his outgoing persona kept the country from falling to pieces altogether.

Constitutionally denied the right to succeed himself, Houston yielded the presidency in 1838 to his vice president, Mirabeau Buonaparte Lamar, a character whose delusional ambitions were as absurd as his name. That Texas survived him was testament to its inherent vigor.

A native of Georgia, where he worked as a newspaper editor and nurtured pretensions as a poet, Lamar won his Texas spurs on the battlefield at San Jacinto and strongly opposed annexation to the United States because he was sure it would mean the curtailment of Texans' liberties. He envisioned instead a two-fisted independent republic that would inflict fresh pain on Mexico as it extended its territorial sway to the Pacific. Dreaming of grandeur, he neglected the problems at hand, managed to triple the republic's debt, further devaluing its currency, and made frequent war on the Indians, who he believed had no rights and should be chased from the country—a policy that infuriated Houston but gratified most Texans. Lamar's idea of diplomacy was to send an envoy to Mexico City to buy recognition of Texas's independence for $5 million, earmarked for repayment to British bondholders who held the lion's share of the Mexican national debt. Britain championed the idea, but Mexico adamantly rejected it. To his credit, though—it was the only bright spot on his record—Lamar did manage to win diplomatic recognition for Texas from Britain, France, Holland, and Belgium and commercial treaties with them. This form of collective certification served to alert the American government that Texas was not a helpless young giant and might soon spin away from the gravitational pull of the United States.

Whatever chance Lamar may have had to advance his struggling nation's well-being was squandered by his obsession to punish Mexico for its obstinacy. Groundlessly confident that the 50,000 or so residents of New Mexico would welcome an expeditionary force of Texans as their liberators from Mexican tyranny, Lamar ignored his failure to obtain approval of the scheme from his Congress and organized—but did not accompany—what amounted to an outright invasion. Its dual purpose, Lamar reasoned, was to reinforce Texas's mightily overblown claim to the upper Rio Grande Valley, the heart of traditional New Mexico, and, by winning the allegiance of its inhabitants, persuade them to divert their trade over the Santa Fe Trail (between Independence, Missouri, and the New Mexican capital) to Texas. The venture, Lamar declared and expected to be believed, was an entirely friendly one, commercial in nature, not military, given how few soldiers there were in the 321-man expedition. But it was misbegotten from the start. Their destination, Santa Fe, was some 800 miles away, and they were unsure how to get there, unprepared for the broiling heat of summer, under-supplied for the ordeal, and unwelcomed by the New Mexicans. Their gov-ernor, while hardly a local favorite, had enough forces at his disposal to entrap the weary, wandering Texans, force their surrender before they set foot in Santa Fe, and send them on a cruel march to captivity in Mexico.

After that, Texas had enough sense to return Sam Houston to the presi-dency by a three-to-one vote in 1841, but its Congress was sufficiently infu-riated by the Santa Fe fiasco to retaliate by amending its boundary claims to include about half of all Mexico. Houston vetoed the act as "a legislative jest." His hope of normalizing relations with Mexico was dashed, though, when its soldiers twice crossed the Rio Grande in force in 1842 and cap-tured San Antonio as a payback for Lamar's Santa Fe expedition. Although the Mexicans withdrew in each instance after a few weeks—unmistakable evidence that their country was in no shape to reconquer its lost province— the aroused Texas Congress voted to declare war on Mexico, fund the fight with a huge new (and unsaleable) bond issue, and grant Houston almost limitless executive powers to take charge of the war effort. Again the sensi-ble Houston used his veto to spare his hotheaded countrymen the conse-quences of their folly. He busied himself instead trying to reduce Texas's debt by cutting jobs and slashing salaries, starting with his own, which he halved.

IN HIS MORE REFLECTIVE MOMENTS Sam Houston recognized that he had a choice to make: either reapproach the United States for annexation or form a strong alliance with Britain as its commercial satellite, at least until Texas became strong and populous enough to stand on its own. Then per-haps it might even expand westward at the expense of the hostile Mexican and indifferent American governments. Houston's adroit, if hardly subtle, statesmanship in playing off British and U.S. officials against one another was to prove the salvation of Texas.

By 1843 Houston was hinting broadly to the British chargé that if the combustible crisis between Texas and Mexico could be settled by a peace treaty through the crown's good offices, Texas would offer highly favor-able trade terms and make Galveston or some other Gulf port available as an ideal entrepôt for greatly expanded British commerce with Latin Amer-ica. He went on to confide that, in his view, the United States considered Texas as a mere appendage, to be reeled in at America's convenience, and that if Mexico could be persuaded to recognize Texas as independent, Houston's government would lose all interest in annexation. When the British envoy inquired whether Texas would consider ending slavery as the price of Britain's underwriting its independence, Houston backed off. But when British diplomacy succeeded in extracting an armistice agreement from Mexico, Houston expressed fulsome—and very public—gratitude.

Houston's guileful trolling in British waters was not kept secret from the new American President, John Tyler, who had ample reasons of his own now to revisit the annexation issue. An intelligent, personable Virginian who had served in both houses of Congress and as governor of his state, Tyler was a moderately conservative, anti-Jackson Democrat and states' rights advocate, chosen to lend intersectional balance to the Whigs' 1840 presidential ticket, headed by William Henry Harrison of Ohio. When General Harrison died after only a month in office, Tyler became the nation's first chief executive to reach that office under the Constitution's order of presidential succession. But he quickly parted company with the leaders of the majority Whig Party, who favored a high tariff and a reconfigured Bank of the United States. Although his cost-efficient administration was not lacking in accomplishments, among them modernizing the navy, opening formal trade relations with China, and settling an old, rankling dispute with Britain over the Maine border, nominal Democrat Tyler's vetoes of Whig fiscal measures led to the early resignation—except by Secretary of State Daniel Webster—of the entire Whig cabinet, which had been retained as a respectful gesture to Harrison's memory. Disowned by the Whigs and reviled as a turncoat by the Democrats, Tyler found himself a President without a party. Still, he badly wanted to be reelected.

When Webster, a fierce antislavery man, finally resigned, Tyler thought he saw an issue that he could embrace and might win him wide popular support: Texas. It was time to bring Houston's huge, gangling Lone Star Republic into the federal union, before Britain and other European powers could gain undue influence over it and block America's westward expansion. Texas, left on its own or in league with foreign states, might one day take possession of New Mexico and coastal California—a possibility that Tyler and his pro-annexation allies seized upon to win over or at least neutralize mercantile interests, especially in New England, seedbed of abolitionism.

In September 1843 Tyler instructed his new Secretary of State, Abel Upshur, to let Texas know that his administration looked with favor on a treaty of annexation. Because Upshur was a slaveholder from Virginia, Tyler was signaling his conviction that America's national interest would be

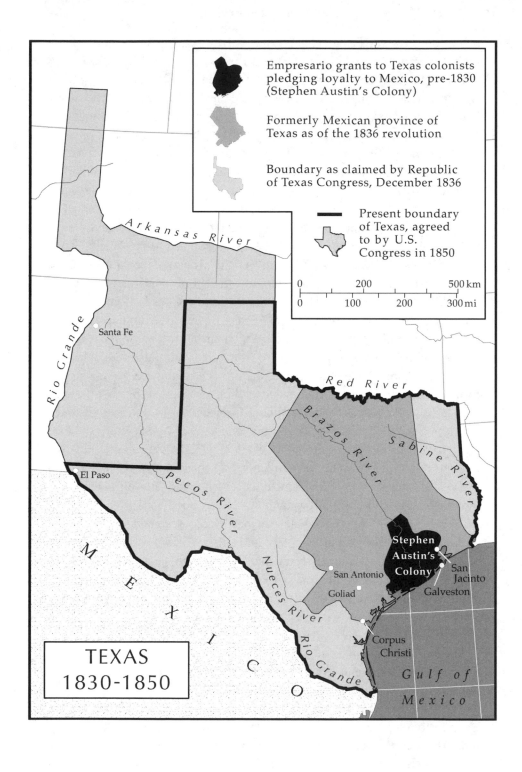

Empresario grants to Texas colonists pledging loyalty to Mexico, pre-1830 (Stephen Austin's Colony)

Formerly Mexican province of Texas as of the 1836 revolution

Boundary as claimed by Republic of Texas Congress, December 1836

Present boundary of Texas, agreed to by U.S. Congress in 1850

| 0 | | 200 | | 500 km |
| 0 | 100 | 200 | | 300 mi |

Arkansas River

Rio Grande

Santa Fe

Red River

Brazos River

Sabine River

Pecos River

El Paso

M E X I C O

Stephen Austin's Colony

San Antonio

Goliad

San Jacinto

Galveston

Nueces River

Rio Grande

Corpus Christi

Gulf of Mexico

TEXAS 1830-1850

better served by the acquisition of big Texas, the pathway to the commercially alluring West Coast, than by truckling to the deep regional division over slavery. The problem, Tyler's position implied, could be compromised away.

Houston played his cards coyly, even duplicitously at times, throughout the seven months of treaty negotiations (during which Upshur was accidentally killed by the explosion of an experimental cannon aboard the U.S.S. *Princeton*). On one hand, Houston was fearful that leaked word of the treaty talks would cool British efforts to broker a peace deal with Mexico, the key to sustaining an independent Texas, and might even excite the Mexicans enough to start a war. Accordingly, he sought Tyler's pledge of military support if needed and assurances that the Senate would ratify the annexation treaty. He got the first but not the second. On the other hand, the British envoy to Texas told his foreign secretary, Lord Aberdeen, that Houston had assured him "he would never consent to any treaty or other project of annexation to the United States" if Mexico would recognize Texan sovereignty.

It is impossible to know if Houston was simply trying to keep his options open or what his true feelings were. He said contradictory things at different times, revealing a deep inner conflict. In all likelihood, and despite his passionate love for and deep allegiance to the land of his birth, he may have believed in his heart that Texas, with so much space and other natural blessings, could realize a prouder destiny as a separate nation than as a part of the United States. He seemed to say as much in his farewell address as Texas president in December 1844, when the annexation issue was greatly in doubt: "If we remain an independent nation, our territory will be extensive—unlimited. The Pacific alone will bound the mighty march of our race and our empire." Did he mean it, or was he suffering from an advanced case of galloping Lamarism? Surely he had endured enough heartache to know how fragile his republic's prospects for survival were, considering the volatile and impractical character of his fellow Texans, who so often behaved like wayward children.

Evidence suggests that Houston indulged in such expansive pronouncements largely as a ploy to reassure Britain while arousing desire in the acquisitive American soul. In May 1845, when the issue was all but resolved, Houston lightheartedly told an audience in New Orleans that "if ladies are justified in making use of coquetry in securing their annexation to good and agreeable husbands, you must excuse me for making use of the same means to annex Texas to Uncle Sam." By this account, he was not so much duping Britain—a charge he denied when his remarks were published—as trying to keep two suitors on his string while his true love was clear all along. The likeliest explanation of his two-faced game was the one he confided to Andrew Jackson, who seemed confused by Houston's mixed signals as the treaty talks went on:

> [Y]ou will perceive that Texas is presented to the United States as a bride adorned for her espousal. But if, now so confident of the union, she should be rejected, her mortification would be indescribable. . . . Were she now to be spurned . . . it would then be left not only for the United States to expect that she would seek some other friend, but all Christendom would justify her in a course dictated by necessity and sanctioned by wisdom.

Houston's perhaps excusable double-dealing put Britain in a bind. The closer its diplomats came to coaxing the Mexican government, under the resilient Santa Anna's reins once more, to recognize Texas independence and work out a boundary agreement, the more they spurred annexationist sentiment in the United States. Most of all they aroused Tyler and his new Secretary of State, John C. Calhoun, freshly enlisted from the Senate, where he had been its iconic defender of states' rights and an unregenerate champion of slavery. To counter British designs to keep Texas independent, the American government offered to compensate Mexico financially if it would consent to annexation. Whether as a crass buyout or a gift of conscience money in acknowledgment that Mexico's grievance against the secessionist Texans was not altogether meritless, the American offer was refused. Santa Anna believed, not without cause, that antislavery activists in the United States could continue to foil any annexation treaty.

The secret terms of the treaty delivered to the Senate on April 12, 1844, called for Texas to become territory of the United States with the right to apply for statehood in the usual fashion and to control its own domestic institutions (which meant the practice of slavery would be left up to the Texans). The United States was to take title to all remaining public lands and military installations and equipment in Texas while agreeing to assume the republic's debts up to $10 million. The question of Texas's boundaries was left unaddressed; presumably the American government would deal with the matter when Mexico was ready to come to the negotiating table. Meanwhile, the United States promised to station troops on the Texas-Louisiana border and assign warships to duty in the Gulf to forestall Mexican military action as long as, and presumably after, the annexation treaty was being considered.

President Tyler's message to the Senate urging ratification stressed that (1) the Texans were Americans who had won their struggle for freedom from Mexico, (2) bringing them and the great land mass they controlled into the Union would be of economic benefit to all sections of the nation, and (3) annexation would prevent the United States from being encircled by European powers, especially Britain, which was conspiring to make Texas its satellite, force it to abolish slavery, and thereby undermine the economy of the American South. The last contention, and the most potent, had been heatedly and repeatedly denied by Lord Aberdeen, who insisted that Britain's only stake in opposing annexation was the protection of its own commercial interests. Secretary of State Calhoun, tone-deaf on the slavery issue, struck a defiant note in pushing for the extension of the practice into the Texas cotton fields. The blacks, he felt obliged to remind his erstwhile Senate colleagues, were an inferior breed and their enslavement was vital to maintaining peace in the South and prosperity nationally. In response, John Quincy Adams asserted: "The spirit of freedom and the spirit of slavery are drawing together for the deadly conflict of arms. The annexation of Texas to this union is the blast of the trumpet for a foreign, civil, servile, and Indian war." Were slavery to be abolished in Texas, Adams added, he would favor annexation at once.

President Tyler's hopes for the treaty—and riding with them any chance he might have had to be reelected as an independent—were jolted a few weeks after the Senate took up the question when the two leading candidates for the presidency, Henry Clay, the Whigs' founder and mainstay, and former Democratic President Van Buren, announced on the same day (though not by collusion, they insisted) that they opposed the annexation treaty. Clay's position was familiar to the public: his misgivings were based on constitutional grounds, the possible incendiary effects on Mexico, and the immorality of extending slavery beyond where it already existed. Van Buren, swamped in his 1840 bid for reelection largely because he was the handiest scapegoat for the hard times afflicting the American economy during most of his term, was still held in high regard in many quarters as a wise and enlightened administrator and retained the support of Andrew Jackson as the bridge between the northern and southern wings of the Democratic Party. But Van Buren drew a line at the Texas border when it came to tolerating the practice of slavery. For the present, he said, he could not support inviting Texas to join the Union (and thereby giving the slave states dominant power in Congress). Since his party drew its greatest strength from the South and West, citadels of expansionist feeling—and thus strongly in favor of annexing Texas—Van Buren's forthright stand on the containment of slavery cost him the Democratic nomination a month later at his party's convention in Baltimore.

But the former President gained a degree of consolation soon after.

When the Senate met on June 8 to weigh Tyler's Texas treaty, seven northern Democrats, Van Buren loyalists, vented their anger over the party's
refusing him the nomination because of the slavery issue and voted with
twenty-eight Whigs (fifteen of them southerners backing Clay) against ratification, which lost, 36–15. Sam Houston's Texas had been jilted at the altar
a second time.

DURING THE TWO-MONTH INTERVAL between the submission of the
annexation treaty and its rejection by the Senate, the Democrats made a pair
of decisions that would ensure congressional reversal of the vote against ratification and the admission of Texas to the Union the following year. They
devised a party platform that projected territorial expansion as a national
imperative and, in doing so, hinted at a quid pro quo benefit more appealing
to the antislavery camp than the dubious argument that accepting Texas as a
slave state was preferable to letting it fall captive to Britain's predatory
commercial empire. At the same time the Democrats chose an obscure presidential candidate who campaigned at full cry under the expansionist banner
and brought down Henry Clay, the most gifted politician of his time.

James Knox Polk, the son of a highly successful Tennessee businessman—his father was a land agent, bank director, steamboat operator, and
owner of a contract mail-delivery service—exhibited many outward signs
of an upbringing amid family wealth. He was well educated, well spoken,
well dressed, and well connected, all contributing to his rapid advancement
as a lawyer and politician, though he had neither a striking physical presence nor a notably engaging personality. A slender, nice-looking little man
with dark hair and a firm, square jaw, Polk had been sickly in his youth,
perhaps the source of the grimly serious expression he habitually wore.
Excelling in his studies at the University of North Carolina, he displayed a
keen, logical mind, but it was also a narrow and rigid one, not deep or curious or often troubled by doubt. His self-certainty made him a formidable
political operative, an intense partisan who knew his own mind so well that
he was rarely diverted from fulfilling his chosen mission.

After studying law with the retired chief justice of Kentucky, Polk was
awarded a prized post as clerk to the Tennessee Senate, where he sponged
up precocious knowledge of statehouse dealmaking and other aspects of
power politics. After a single term as a member of the lower house of the
state legislature, he spent fourteen years in the U.S. House of Representatives as an orthodox defender of Jeffersonian agrarian republicanism,
advocating states' rights, a low tariff, territorial expansion, and, most of all,

the policies and wishes of his senior Tennessean in the White House. His almost slavish devotion to Andrew Jackson's agenda boosted Polk to leadership of the House Democrats and the post of Speaker for two terms but also got him constantly heckled as a dogged, mirthless order taker. His acerbic House political rival John Quincy Adams sniped that he found in Polk "no elegance of language, no philosophy, no pathos, no felicitous impromptus." After Jackson left Washington, Polk served one more House term, then followed Old Hickory back to Tennessee and narrowly won the governorship in 1839. As a moderately progressive Democrat, whose party was blamed for the hard economic times, he lost an exceedingly close race for reelection in 1841 and failed to unseat the incumbent, again in a tight contest, two years later. As the presidential election year of 1844 dawned, James Polk was a political corpse.

His only hope for resuscitation was to be chosen as the running mate on the Democratic national ticket. But it was hard to imagine why any presidential candidate would have looked to him to bolster the national ticket when he was apparently incapable now of carrying his home state. Still, Polk had his share of admirers in high places and knew how to pull political strings. When ex-President Van Buren, front-runner to head the Democratic ticket, announced his opposition to the Texas annexation treaty, Jackson knew the New Yorker could not command enough support from southern and western delegates to gain the nomination and turned away from him in sorrow—and toward Polk. None of the more obvious candidates could garner the two-thirds majority of the convention delegates needed to be nominated, and Polk, cast in the role of Jackson's true heir, emerged as the compromise victor on the eighth ballot. The delighted Whigs sneered at the Democratic standard-bearer as a lackluster has-been and asked witheringly, "Who *is* James K. Polk?" They soon found out.

While negotiating the annexation treaty with Texas, Tyler's State Department had also been conferring with the British Foreign Office to arrange a mutually agreeable division of the Oregon Country, jointly held by the two nations since their 1818 agreement on the boundary between the United States and Canada. The pact had alluded to Oregon's borders as the crest of the Rockies on the east and the Pacific on the west, but no southern border was specified because Spain had a general claim to the northwest region of the continent until the Adams-Onís Treaty of the following year, cutting off Spanish territory at the forty-second parallel. No northern boundary was fixed for Oregon until the United States and Britain signed separate but congruent treaties with Russia in 1824–25, setting the line between the tsar's North American colony and the jointly held Anglo-

American region to the south at 54°40′ north latitude. Thus defined, the Oregon Country, including the southern half of modern British Columbia in Canada and the American states of Oregon, Washington, Idaho, and parts of Montana and Wyoming, was more than twice as large as Texas even under the indefensibly expansive claims of its Congress. As American pioneers began to make the torturous trek up the Oregon Trail in the early 1840s, both the British and U.S. governments hoped to avoid conflict by a timely division of the huge territory. The Americans had been willing to run the boundary along the forty-ninth parallel, the line agreed to east of the Rockies under the 1818 Anglo-American treaty. The British, however, arguing that there had been no American discoveries or settlements north of the Columbia, insisted on that river as the boundary, so the issue remained deadlocked for twenty-five years. And the new talks were not progressing. In view of Britain's working at cross-purposes with Tyler's efforts to bring Texas into the Union, the Democratic Party found a ripe target in the unyielding British position on Oregon—fresh evidence of a concerted policy, according to the Democrats' 1844 party platform, to block America's westward expansion.

After Polk's surprise nomination in Baltimore, his party approved a platform resolution that stirred little debate at the time but would soon reverberate across the nation. According to the language of the platform that Polk would now run on, America's "title to the whole Territory of Oregon is clear and unquestionable. . . . [N]o portion of the same ought to be ceded to England or any other power, and . . . the reoccupation of Oregon and the reannexation of Texas at the earliest practicable period, are great American measures."

Such an assertion was the purest political poppycock. How could Americans *re*occupy what they had never occupied in the first place north of the Columbia and all the way north to the 54°40′ line? The reference to the *re*annexation of Texas was an incendiary reminder that southern and western interests had never forgiven John Quincy Adams for his 1819 treaty, letting Spain retain Texas even though Jefferson had fancifully claimed it as part of the Louisiana Purchase. The murkiness of these allegedly "clear and unquestionable" territorial rights did not, however, detract from their demagogic utility. In seamlessly linking the two regions of expansionist aspirations, Polk and his party eased the stigma of slavery in Texas by claiming for the nation—without embarrassment—an even more immense territory, all of Oregon, which, located entirely north of the Missouri Compromise line, would implicitly become free soil. Eastern maritime interests pushing for bicoastal trade, land speculators with a practiced eye open for more inventory, and any would-be western settlers were entranced by Polk's gross outreach.

Unmoved by their rivals' expansionist posturing, the Whig-controlled Senate killed the Texas treaty a week later. President Tyler, with no political base or chance for reelection, nevertheless saw in the Democratic Party's platform and its nominee's flag-waving endorsement of it the opportunity to make the presidential election that fall a national referendum on the Texas question. In order to overcome the requirement of a two-thirds majority for Senate ratification, Tyler sent all the documents pertaining to the treaty to Capitol Hill a few days after its defeat and proposed that both houses of Congress, on the verge of adjourning for six months, recast the document later in the year as a joint resolution—needing only a simple majority in each chamber to win approval—inviting Texas into the Union. Tyler's move and Polk's candidacy, leaning heavily on his party's expansionist platform, made Texas the core issue of the campaign.

Foreign powers also took notice. Tyler's resubmission of the annexation proposal to Congress was soon answered by Santa Anna's vow that he would never consent to the dismemberment of his nation and a request to the Mexican Congress for funds to raise a 30,000-man army to recapture Texas. The American envoy in Mexico City heard that the British, under an ad hoc Anglo-Mexican military alliance, would intervene if the United States acted to annex Texas. The British envoy there chimed in that Mexico seemed determined to go to war over Texas. Such saber-rattling, far from discouraging American pro-annexation sentiment, seemed to feed it—so much so that the British ambassador in Washington advised his home office that the closer the Mexican quarrel with Texas came to being resolved in a way that secured its independence and borders, the more likely Congress was to vote for immediate annexation. The whole heated subject was put on the diplomatic back burner, pending the outcome of the U.S. presidential election, since victory by the Whigs' anti-annexationist Henry Clay would likely end the confrontation for the time being. Meanwhile the American press and campaign speechifying were glutted with chauvinist rhetoric flaunting the nation's righteous claim to a transcontinental dominion so that it might better cast liberty's light upon all peoples suffering under tyrannical rulers.

Polk, feeding fears of British interference with Americans' territorial entitlement, gained a narrow victory (by 38,000 ballots, a margin of 1.5 percent) in the popular vote but won decisively in the electoral count, 170–105, when two key Middle Atlantic states unexpectedly swung his way. A traditional low-tariff southerner, Polk had satisfied growing industrial interests

in Pennsylvania by saying he favored reasonable protection for native manufacturers but avoiding specifics. Clay, on the other hand, lost New York by
backing away from his clearly stated disapproval of annexation, a hedge
that probably cost him a decisive 5,000 votes cast instead for an abolitionist
splinter-party candidate. At forty-nine, James Polk was the youngest man to
be elected President of the United States to date. More telling of the national
mood than the coattail effects of Polk's unmagnetic personality was the
accompanying turnaround in the makeup of Congress. The Senate had
shifted from a 28–24 Whig majority to a 34–22 Democratic advantage,
while the House altered even more stunningly—from a 132–103 Whig
majority to a 142–81 margin for the Democrats in the new Congress, not
due to assemble until December 1845.

In his final message to Congress delivered a month after the 1844 ballot-
ing, President Tyler declared the election results to be an undeniable
endorsement by the American people of the annexation of Texas. He invited
the lawmakers to pass a joint resolution achieving that end at the earliest
moment possible in order to frustrate foreign intriguers opposed to further
extension of the boundaries of the United States. Seventeen different versions of such a resolution were submitted in short order, and the House took
the lead in winnowing them. In a striking departure from the old defeated
treaty, the emerging joint resolution called not for annexation of Texas as a
territory but for its immediate admission to statehood, thus binding it as an
integral part of the Union and not leaving it in an ambiguous status—and a
still tempting target for foreign encroachment. But there were thornier
issues that had to be grappled with.

Under the rejected treaty the United States was to have assumed the
debts of Texas up to $10 million, along with title to all its remaining public
land. Texas had wanted the federal government to take over its entire debt as
the price for receiving its public domain—essentially the same terms
granted to other states admitted to the Union. But many in Congress
objected to such an arrangement in the case of Texas. One reason was that
the republic had given away so much of its public land to reward its soldiers
and public officials. And nobody knew just how much land there was in
Texas since it had no fixed boundaries, only a broad, unilateral claim to
them. More troubling still, a great deal of Texas's public debt took the form
of land scrip and bonded debt based on land, long devalued but now likely to
rise dramatically if Texas became politically and economically secure as
part of the United States. Thus, the federal treasury would have wound up
footing a much costlier bill than the $10 million pledged to clear up the
Texas public debt while land speculators were making a killing at the
expense of U.S. taxpayers. The House resolution therefore provided that

Texas would retain all its public lands along with the responsibility for all its financial obligations.

To deal with the slavery issue, the House resolution provided that (1) new states "of convenient size, not exceeding four in number, in addition to said State of Texas" and with its approval, could be carved from the former republic and admitted to the Union, and (2) the practice of slavery would be permitted if the people so desired in "that portion of said territory lying south of thirty-six degrees thirty minutes north latitude, commonly known as the Missouri compromise line," but prohibited north of that demarcation. Since almost all of Texas, wherever its final boundaries were fixed, fell below the Missouri line, that meant it could be subdivided eventually into as many as five slave states. Such a provision would have been unacceptable to antislavery members of Congress if the huge Oregon Country had not been looming as imminent American free-soil territory, in accordance with the newly elected President's firmly stated goal. As to the borders of Texas, which had been left undefined under the defeated treaty, the House resolved that the formation of the new state or states would be "subject to the adjustment by this [American] government of all questions of boundary that may arise with other governments." In late January of 1845 the House version passed by a vote of 120–98.

The issue was more closely drawn in the lame-duck Senate, the same one that had so badly trounced the Tyler treaty. To gain a majority for the House's statehood resolution would require reversing the votes of the eight opposed Democratic Senators, led by Missouri's stentorian old warhorse, Thomas Hart Benton, nearing the end of his thirty-year career as the upper house's peerless curmudgeon. Earlier Benton, dubbed "the Thunderer" in the press and among the nation's most outspoken advocates of expansionism, had nonetheless insisted that a foreign nation like Texas could be annexed constitutionally only by a Senate-ratified treaty, and ought to be acquired only with Mexico's consent, or the United States was likely to inherit a war with the transaction. Noting the 1844 election returns, the Missouri legislature now pressured its senior Senator to drop his obstructionist tactics, especially his insistence that annexation be conditioned on Mexico's consent. Benton backed off but still promised to withhold his vote unless Texas was annexed by treaty, and he introduced a bill authorizing the President to appoint a five-man commission of leading citizens to negotiate new treaty terms with Texas authorities. During that process, Benton and his bloc of Senate adherents hoped that Mexico, with the obdurate Santa Anna again out of power, might reconcile itself to the loss of Texas if accompanied by a gift of tribute—that is, a payoff—for granting it generous boundaries.

Benton's solution, his foes argued, would be time-consuming and give the British, with the French at their side now as well, the chance to pressure Mexico into acknowledging Texas's independence and entice the republic into a favorable commercial alliance with the European powers. President-elect Polk and his allies in Congress greatly preferred the House resolution because it relieved the federal government from responsibility for Texas's debts while empowering it to determine Texas's ultimate boundaries instead of being roped into backing its grandiose claims. As a compromise that Polk helped work out behind the scenes, Benton yielded to a Senate resolution giving the President—presumably Polk himself, who was due to take office within a few weeks—the option either to transmit the terms of the House resolution to the Texas Congress for its acceptance or to appoint a commission of prominent Americans who would negotiate new terms with Texas officials. According to one of Benton's allies, Polk had "assured me if he had any discretion placed in his hands, he would exercise it in such a manner as to satisfy us"—a pledge, that is, to undertake direct negotiations with the Texans instead of handing them the terms dictated by Congress in its joint resolution.

This word from Polk was enough to swing Benton's bloc behind the thus amended House version, which was barely approved by the full Senate, 27–25. The House accepted the Senate's fix, and the joint resolution was adopted on February 28. Two days later, on his next-to-last day in the White House, John Tyler acted to redeem his checkered presidency by officially transmitting the congressional offer of statehood to Texas—the project that had been his consuming mission for a year and a half—instead of allowing his successor to choose between extending the offer as toughened by the joint resolution or launching fresh treaty talks. Polk could have objected, of course, when Tyler gave him the courtesy of approving his last-minute initiative, or he could simply have revoked Tyler's action the moment he took office, but neither course suited the incoming President. Tyler's seemingly impulsive step, which the two Presidents may well have planned together, spared Polk the necessity of honoring his pledge, made offstage prior to the Senate vote, to gratify the Benton camp by choosing, once in office, to open lengthy and unpredictable negotiations with Texas. When later charged with acting in bad faith toward Benton and his followers for not voiding Tyler's summary offer of statehood, Polk defended himself by saying his words had been misunderstood and he never promised to renegotiate. But there was much testimony to the contrary. "Clearly Polk deceived," his foremost biographer, Charles Sellers, concluded.

So eager was the new President to bring Texas into the Union that he put his diplomats and agents to work promising Sam Houston and other Texas officials that if their Congress promptly accepted statehood under the terms of the joint resolution from Washington, the federal funding spigot would be opened with reciprocal speed. Polk would pay for new fortifications and harbor facilities in Texas, for troops to drive the Comanches from the western plains and hill country, and for rewarding Mexico monetarily if it would agree to a liberal boundary. In keeping with Tyler's old pledge of military aid to forestall any attack on Texas during the annexation process, Polk ordered 3,000 American troops transferred to Corpus Christi, on the south bank of the Nueces, with instructions to repel any Mexican forces crossing the Rio Grande and occupying any of the disputed territory between the two rivers—no matter that Anson Jones, Houston's ally and successor as president, had not requested such assistance.

As the offer of American statehood was circulating among Texas officials, British diplomats in Mexico City knew that time was running out on their efforts to keep the republic from being swallowed up by the United States. With Santa Anna a fugitive now—reportedly rescued of late from a group of Indians who had been preparing to do away with him—the Mexican government at last capitulated to British entreaties to recognize Texas as an independent nation if it first rejected the American offer of statehood. If Mexico refused to seek a peaceful solution, the British had advised, they would not support, nor would France nor Spain, any military effort by the Mexicans to reclaim Texas. If Mexico yielded, Britain and its allies pledged to help arrange reasonable boundaries with the Texans. When advised that the belated Mexican acknowledgment was in the offing, President Jones told the British that the treaty of recognition from Mexico had to be on the table before—not after—the Texas Congress voted on the statehood offer from the United States. Jones wanted his fellow Texans to have a real choice between certified independence and American statehood. Near the end of May, the British delivered to Jones a treaty of peace and recognition signed by Mexican foreign minister Luis Cuevas.

But the offer came too late, Texas's financial and military vulnerability was too grave, and at heart—and in their basic attitudes—the Texans had always remained American. In late June the Texas Senate unanimously rejected the treaty offer from Mexico, and both houses of the Texas Congress voted unanimously to accept the joint resolution from the U.S. Congress. On July 4, 1845, a convention of delegates from across Texas ratified—with only one dissenting vote—the action by its Congress and began to draw up a constitution for American statehood.

Not everyone in the United States extended a welcoming hand to Texas. On February 28, the day Congress approved its joint resolution, one of those who voted against it, John Quincy Adams, described the event in his diary as "the heaviest calamity that ever befell myself and my country." Three days later, even as President Tyler was rushing the statehood offer on its way to Texas, Horace Greeley's *New York Tribune,* a clarion of righteous indignation, editorialized:

> Call it by what specious name we may, the lust of Dominion, the lust of Power, the lust of Avarice, the lust of holding our fellow men in Bondage, are the real incitements of all this zeal for Annexation. To grasp more and more of the face of the earth, has ever been a besetting sin of individuals and nations. Few men are satisfied with as much land as they can well cultivate, few nations have been satisfied to improve to the utmost their own, but must covet and seize what is justly their neighbor's.

The *Tribune,* by all available evidence, was decidedly in the minority. Grasping more and more of the face of the earth was anything but an unconscionable pursuit for most Americans, who, if asked at the time, would probably have added it to their sacred trinity of unalienable rights—life, liberty, and the pursuit of happiness. The acquisitive, combative spirit of the age was memorably encapsuled by a stylish, thirty-two-year-old New York editorialist, John Louis O'Sullivan. A few months after the *Tribune*'s killjoy remarks, O'Sullivan wrote in the midsummer issue of the *Democratic Review,* a party organ he had co-founded, denouncing other nations for "thwarting our policy and hampering our power, limiting our greatness and checking the fulfillment of our manifest destiny to overspread the continent allowed by Providence for the free development of our yearly multiplying millions." O'Sullivan elaborated on his high-flown (and not a little confrontational) paean to "manifest destiny" in the October 13, 1845, issue of his principal journal, the *New York Morning News:*

> It has been laid down and acted upon, that the solitudes of America are the property of the immigrant children of Europe and their offspring. . . . Public sentiment with us repudiates possession without use, and this sentiment is gradually acquiring the force of established law. . . . This national policy, necessity or destiny, we know to be just and beneficent, and we can, therefore, afford to scorn the invective and imputations of rival nations.

Such self-certitude, mistaking the blessings of Providence for a deserved reward, has evolved into an enduring fixture of the American mindset.

Congress approved the constitution of Texas on December 29 of that year and received it into the Union as the twenty-eighth state (Florida had been voted in nine months earlier) and by far the largest, although its formal boundaries were yet to be determined. One of the first two Senators sent to Washington by Texas was Sam Houston, who served usefully, honorably, and by and large soberly in that capacity for fourteen years. But in 1859 the Texas state legislature, by then in the grip of pro-slavery secessionists, removed him from his appointive Senate seat for opposing secession from the Union he had fought so hard and worked to resolutely to join. The people of Texas, resenting this dishonorable treatment, promptly elected him governor.

Abraham Lincoln's election in 1860 resulted in the summoning of a secessionist convention, whose legitimacy Governor Houston denied. When the gathering passed a new constitution requiring state officials to swear allegiance to the Confederacy, Houston spent a few sleepless nights and then announced, "In the name of the constitution of Texas, which has been trampled upon, I refuse to take this oath. In the name of my own conscience and manhood . . . I refuse to take this oath," and resigned. He died of pneumonia two years later, at seventy.

CHAPTER 10

Polking John Bull in the eye

1836–1847

NORTH OF TEXAS THE REMOVAL policies of Andrew Jackson and his immediate successors in the White House had shoved the eastern Indian tribes across the Mississippi, leaving behind only scattered remnants in the backwoods, and piled up the involuntary evacuees on the far edges of Arkansas and Missouri. The area between the Mississippi and Missouri rivers, all part of the Louisiana Purchase, was designated the Iowa Territory, where the native Americans, like their transplanted kin to the south, were not spared from encroachment by white settlers. Treaties were signed promising tribal sanctuaries, but they were slackly enforced or ignored altogether by the meager corps of federal troopers on the frontier. Homesteaders, squatters, speculators, and predatory politicians swept over the land like locusts, sometimes brandishing fake maps and title claims to justify their takings. By the time federal surveyors caught up with the migration in the late 1850s, tens of thousands had already settled in the western Mississippi and Missouri valleys, bringing with them diseases that ravaged the native people. The way west stood open with virtually no restraints except those imposed by nature.

For some pioneers the untimbered grasslands and semiarid climate of the plains were not alluring enough for them to tarry, and they looked still farther west, to the storied lands close by the Pacific coast. As early as 1830, when promotional pamphlets on the joys of the Oregon Country first appeared in Boston, word began to spread about the great beauty and fertility of the Far West, its towering forests and teeming fisheries, its clear, rushing streams for ready transportation and water power, and its unlimited commercial potential as a window on Asia and riches from international trade. Whether in pursuit of green or gold, most of these dauntless pilgrims looked not due west to California, which belonged to Catholic Mexico, but northwest to Oregon, the loosely defined territory between the Rockies and the seacoast, held jointly by treaty between the United States and Great Britain and open to occupancy by citizens of both nations. Since there was no functioning American governmental presence there, moreover, or established federal jurisdiction, Oregon was squatter heaven, where all the land was free to whoever managed to get there and claim it—and was prepared to defend it fiercely.

Hunters, traders, farm folk, missionaries, and mountain men trickled through the South Pass of the Rockies to settle the virginal Northwest throughout the 1830s, and their glowing letters back east, especially about the lush Willamette Valley stretching south from the Columbia River for nearly 300 miles, enticed more wayfarers, many of them victims of the nation's deep economic slump. By the early 1840s, the first wagon trains were heading up the Oregon Trail and enduring the nearly 2,000-mile travail. The radiant vision of a free and trackless Eden awaiting them compelled men to leave behind all familiar things and daily wager their lives and those of their dearest ones. The primal enticement for these doughty migrants was rendered without artifice in an unsigned, two-stanza verse, originating in a newspaper published in St. Louis, the jumping-off point for most of the Oregon trekkers, and widely reprinted at the time:

COME OUT TO THE WEST

Come forth from your cities, come out to the West;
Ye have hearts, ye have hands—leave to Nature the rest.
The prairie, the forest, the stream at command—
"The world is too crowded!"—pshaw! Come and take land.

Come travel the mountain, and paddle the stream;
The cabin shall smile, and the corn-patch shall gleam;
"A wife and six children?"—'tis wealth in your hand!
Your ox and your rifle—out West and take land!

Thus beckoned, intrepid frontiersmen, however desperate the economic circumstances propelling them westward, sallied forth with hopes and dreams as expansive as the landscape they had to traverse. Indeed, the very scale of the setting heightened the adventure. In the same month that New York City editor John O'Sullivan was coining the term "manifest destiny," the inspiriting mantra of the age for America's territorial boosterism, up the Hudson the *Albany Argus* was speculating editorially on why the outlook of those headed west seemed "so peculiarly colossal in their notion of things and the prospects of our nation" and answered:

> Does not this inspiration spring from their extraordinary country? Their mighty rivers, their vast sea-like lakes, their noble and bound-less prairies, and their magnificent forests afford objects which fill the mind to its utmost capacity and dilate the heart with greatness. To live in such a splendid country . . . expands a man's view of every-thing in this world. . . . These things fill their lives with great enter-prises, perilous risks and dazzling rewards.

The Oregon Country as configured by treaties the United States signed with Britain in 1818 and with Spain in 1819 extended nearly 800 miles at its widest along the forty-second parallel, forming its southern boundary, from the westward slope of the Continental Divide to the ocean, but its northward extent was left undefined for six years. The northwestern coast of North America from the Aleutian Islands chain south to the Columbia River had become an increasingly trolled international fishing and hunting ground over the preceding half century. Russian, British, and American vessels vied with one another and often employed the native people in pursuit of the whales, sea otters, and other marine life that abounded there. Fearful that the British and Americans were intruding on Russia's earlier established commercial ventures at the continent's northern extreme, Tsar Alexander I grandly (and unilaterally) proclaimed in 1821 that the coastline and all its islands from the Bering Strait, separating Asia from North America just below the sixty-fifth parallel, down to the fifty-first parallel—and for 100 miles out to sea—were henceforth reserved for the use of Russian subjects, in particular the Russian-American Company, a state-controlled enterprise centered at Sitka village.

This southward outreach by the Russian bear did not sit well with Great Britain, whose pathfinders and fur traders, both by sea and overland from the eastern Canadian provinces, had been actively roaming the northwestern sector of the continent. Nor did Secretary of State John Quincy Adams choose to recognize any Russian rights in continental North America, although the United States was powerless to dislodge the Russian fishing and trading posts on the far northern coastal islands. Tsar Alexander's proclamation thus had the immediate effect of forcing the American and British governments to define the northern extent of their jointly held Oregon territory and put a halt to Russian claims and ambitions below it. Adams said the United States, for its part, had no territorial ambitions beyond the fifty-first parallel, designated by the Russians as the southern limit of their commerce and settlement. But the British, anxious to gain as much Pacific coastline as they could below the chilly far northern waters, saw no reason to concede any of it to Alexander south of Sitka at the fifty-seventh parallel.

Adams, having won British agreement in 1818 to extend the northern border of the United States along the forty-ninth parallel from Lake of the Woods to the crest of the Rockies but no farther, used the Russian thrust of 1821 to renew his efforts to extend the American boundary to the Pacific. On the supposition that the farther up the coast the British managed to shove the Russians, the less southward London would try to push its boundary line with the Americans, Adams called for an Anglo-American agreement opposing Russian claims below the fifty-seventh parallel. In return, Adams asked that Britain agree to extend the northern boundary of the United States all the way west to the Pacific coast—along, say, the fifty-first parallel. When the British scoffed at such an idea as indefensible territorial gluttony, Adams fell back to the forty-ninth parallel, his goal from the start. The British, though, saw no basis for any U.S. claim farther north than the Columbia River, whose basin Americans had explored and mapped.

In 1824 Britain proposed extending the boundary line from the Rockies to where the river crossed the forty-ninth parallel some 200 miles short of the Pacific and following its course southwesterly to the ocean just north of the forty-sixth parallel. Adams, who had long envisioned the United States as a uniquely positioned global commercial power with busy harbors on the Atlantic, Gulf, and Pacific coasts, said no. And he had a good reason. By the early 1820s, both British and American mariners had come to recognize that the Columbia, a long, broad, and picturesque waterway, was nevertheless an unsuitable site for a major port accommodating oceangoing vessels. A massive, treacherous sandbar turned the river's estuary into a graveyard for hard-to-maneuver sailing ships of more than 400 tons. By far the safest and most generous potential harbor sites for international commerce on the Pacific coast were San Francisco Bay, owned by Mexico, and Puget Sound, the hundred-mile-long deepwater inlet off Juan de Fuca Strait, which runs inland for seventy-five miles just south of the forty-ninth parallel and separates the modern state of Washington from Vancouver Island. Both Britain and the United States coveted Puget Sound, lying in the very middle of their shared Oregon Country.

Given their impasse, the two English-speaking nations failed to present a united front to the Russians. Their separate treaties with the tsar signed in 1824 and 1825 agreed, however, that the southernmost projection of the compromise coastal boundary between Russian territory and the jointly occupied Anglo-American Oregon Country would be 54°40′ north latitude. The United States had no voice, though, in setting the much longer inland boundary between Russian and British North America. Seeking a cordon of territory to protect the southerly extension of their marine commerce, the Russians were awarded a strip of coastline that varied in width from sixty to seventy-five miles inland to the crest of the roughly parallel coastal mountain range, starting at the 54°40′ mark and running northwest nearly 500 miles to form the now familiar Alaskan panhandle. The boundary line met the 141st meridian north longitude just above the sixtieth parallel and followed the meridian 650 miles due north to the Arctic Ocean. Russian America, geographically identical with present-day Alaska and stretching 750 miles east-west from its newly designated border with British America to the Bering Strait, amounted to well over 500,000 square miles. At the time, nobody—certainly no white people—had an inkling about the spectacular scenic, wildlife, and mineral riches of that far and often frostbound land.

Big as Russian America was, the Oregon Country was nearly as large. The question of how this immense, eye-filling, lonesome territory should be apportioned between Britain and the United States did not seem particularly pressing in the mid-1820s. President Monroe, doubtful whether that distant terrain could ever be geographically and politically integrated with the American union—a view widely shared at the time—saw no urgency to reach a permanent settlement with Britain, especially if it might spark a military conflict.

As the ten-year joint occupancy arrangement neared its expiration date, President John Quincy Adams enlisted the former longtime Secretary of the Treasury, Albert Gallatin, to try to work out a formal partition of the Oregon Country. When the British renewed their offer to draw the boundary along the lower Columbia River, Gallatin objected that such a border would leave the United States without a usable port site on the Pacific oceanfront. Britain then offered to turn over to the United States the 6,500-square-mile, molar-shaped Olympic Peninsula, a mountainous rainforest that forms the western arm of modern Washington state. The ninety-mile-long northern edge of the peninsula, comprising the south bank of Juan de Fuca Strait, was said to be suitable for a safe port or naval base or both. But the offer would have left far more desirable Puget Sound in British hands, and any future American seaport or military base on the Olympic Peninsula would be surrounded by British territory and at the mercy of the potent royal navy. Gallatin declined the offer, and the parties agreed in 1827 to extend the joint occupancy pact indefinitely, with either nation free to withdraw from it upon one year's notice.

Time was on the Americans' side, but for the next dozen years, British commercial interests, exercised exclusively by the Hudson's Bay Company (called simply "the Bay" by contemporaries), thoroughly dominated the Oregon Country. In 1832, forsaking the rain-soaked strip of land between the Pacific shoreline and the Coastal Range, the Bay moved its operations from Fort George near the treacherous Columbia estuary ninety miles upriver to a site on the north bank, and built Fort Vancouver, close to where the Willamette River flowed into the larger waterway. It was an ideal spot from which to control trade throughout the Columbia basin, and the Bay took every opportunity to do so. Fort Vancouver swiftly grew into a stockaded, self-contained community with workshops, a sawmill, a shipyard, and a thousand residents, serving as the central supply depot for all of Oregon and the de facto capital of the region, with Parliament-approved jurisdiction over its British subjects. The Bay's Montreal-based director of North American operations, Sir George Simpson, favored letting American settlers straggling into Oregon fend for themselves. Company officials at Fort Vancouver, though, saw the newcomers, most of whom settled in the Willamette Valley below the Columbia, as prime customers and offered them emergency shelter, fair prices, and ready credit, vital to their survival.

For all its solidity, prospering Fort Vancouver was not a rooted community or a harbinger of systematic British colonization with an eye toward territorial dominion over the region; it was a company town, run by transients. The few permanent British settlers gravitated north of the Columbia over the Cowlitz Plains toward Puget Sound, but the terrain was not nearly as fertile as the Willamette Valley and attracted few farmers from Canada or Britain's home isles. To discourage American fur traders from encroachment north of the Columbia, the Bay urged its trappers to overhunt the region. The Bay's dominance of the Oregon Country was evident in the prominence of British place-names, such as Mount Hood (honoring the Lord of the Admiralty), Mount St. Helens (after the minister to Spain), and, of course, the Fraser River and Vancouver Island and the fort on the Columbia in tribute to those celebrated mariners.

The American presence, scattered for sixty miles along the Willamette's rich bottomlands and nearby timber stands, did not begin to coalesce into a loosely organized community until Methodist missionary parties arrived in the late 1830s. But Congress, hesitant to precipitate a collision with the Bay's quasi-official authority in the region, declined pleas by American set-

tlers to create some governmental presence there and left the pioneers to
fend for themselves. Their fields and flocks flourished well enough, even as
European demand for northwestern furs declined, causing the Bay to rethink
its regional strategy. So, too, did the United States government, which in
1838 dispatched an official, six-vessel expedition, with scientists, artists,
and surveyors aboard, to explore the South Pacific, Antarctica, and the
northern Pacific coastline. Upon dropping anchor near Fort Vancouver in
1841 (having lost one of the ships on the killer sandbar in the Columbia estuary), the little fleet's commander, Lieutenant Charles Wilkes, sent landing
parties to reconnoiter the fertile river basin. They found the region to be, as
Wilkes reported, a potential "storehouse of wealth in its forests, furs, and
fisheries," and he strongly recommended to his superiors in Washington that
they retain their claim to the forty-ninth parallel—and with it title to Puget
Sound—as the boundary if and when British and American diplomats
renewed efforts to divide the Oregon Country. What made Wilkes's advice
so boldly inimical to British aspirations in the region was that virtually no
Americans had settled north of the Columbia or anywhere near Puget
Sound.

By contrast, American migration quickened now in the Willamette Valley. In 1843, more than a thousand settlers came (with 5,000 head of cattle),
another 1,500 arrived the next year, and 3,000 more in 1845. Without guidance by federal officials, they formed a rudimentary government that won
the cooperation of the Hudson's Bay Company and Canadians, mostly of
French extraction, in the region. Since so few British settlers were arriving—India, Australia, and New Zealand were more alluring destinations for
colonists from the mother country—the southern portion of Oregon was
being transformed into de facto American territory, and the Bay prepared to
close up its headquarters on the Columbia and move it north. The stage was
set for a resolution of the disagreement that had kept Oregon in jurisdictional limbo for twenty-five years.

THE UNITED STATES WAS FORTUNATE that direction of the British foreign ministry had been placed for the third time in the hands of amiable
George Hamilton-Gordon, Lord Aberdeen, who had held the post under the
Duke of Wellington and in the earlier administration of Sir Robert Peel,
both staunch Tory prime ministers without any great love for America.
Calm, courteous, and the most favorably disposed toward the United States
among the members of Peel's hard-nosed cabinet, Aberdeen entered into
several years of diplomacy to settle outstanding issues with the Americans,

starting in 1841 not with Oregon but with the even longer-simmering dispute over the boundary between Maine and the British province of New Brunswick. At stake were 12,000 square miles of farmland and timber in the little-trafficked Aroostook Valley. To determine whether Britain or the United States owned them, Aberdeen sent Alexander Baring, Lord Ashburton, as his envoy to Washington to deal with Secretary of State Daniel Webster. Renowned for his eloquence, logic, and legal acumen, Webster was no subscriber to "manifest destiny," the expansionist slogan soon to be blazoned across the American firmament.

The northeast boundary fight had been nearly sixty years in the making. The peacemakers in Paris in 1782 had agreed that the northeastern line separating British and American territory would begin at the St. Croix River in Maine, follow the narrow waterway to its source, and then run due north to the crest of the highlands that divided rivers that flowed north to the St. Lawrence from those that ran south to the Atlantic Ocean. Unfortunately, no map precisely locating the St. Croix River was affixed to the treaty, and there were two small rivers in the vicinity, both of which the locals indiscriminately called the St. Croix. Furthermore, the due-north line from the source of one of them took only forty miles to strike the spine of the highlands, while the line from the other river's source covered 115 miles before it reached the irregular crest, and it was the latter that the Americans had insisted on as the Maine boundary. The British provincials of New Brunswick begged to differ, and when a band of their lumbermen entered the disputed territory in the midwinter of 1839 to begin logging operations, some 10,000 Maine militiamen mustered in subzero weather and threatened to bloody the interlopers. Only the restraining promise of the U.S. government to resolve the dispute at long last averted war.

A microscopic examination of old and current maps and supporting documentation did not yield a definitive answer, and Webster, no steely negotiator of the John Quincy Adams stripe, felt he had to compromise. Under the Webster-Ashburton Treaty of 1842, the United States turned over to Britain 3,207,680 acres, or roughly 5,000 square miles, somewhat less than half the area in question. Arch-expansionists labeled the Secretary of State a pushover at the bargaining table, even though the king of the Netherlands had earlier proposed a settlement equally dividing the contested territory.

Perhaps emboldened by their quasi-victory in the Maine boundary dispute, the British diplomatic office adopted an unyielding stance when the negotiations turned to the Oregon question. Webster renewed the U.S. proposal of the forty-ninth parallel as the boundary, denying Britain the southern tip of Vancouver Island, Juan de Fuca Strait, and Puget Sound. Lord Aberdeen, insisting there was no basis beyond land greed for the American position, held firm for a boundary along the lower Columbia, even though there were precious few British settlers living between the north bank of the river and the forty-ninth parallel. Singed by criticism that he had been soft in dealing with the Maine border issue, Webster now responded to British adamancy with a startling counterproposal. The United States would agree to the Columbia River boundary, provided that Britain (1) also ceded it the Olympic Peninsula, as offered nearly two decades earlier, and (2) succeeded in pressuring Mexico to cede the United States six degrees of latitude, thereby dropping the southwestern boundary between the two nations, set along the forty-second parallel under the Adams-Onís Treaty, some 450 miles to the thirty-sixth parallel and yielding San Francisco Bay to the Americans. The unspecified purchase price would be used, under Webster's formula, to pay off Mexico's many creditors in Britain and the United States. Such a settlement would have amounted to a net gain in American territory of nearly 250,000 square miles and won the nation the largest natural harbor on the entire Pacific coastline from the Bering Strait to Tierra del Fuego.

The prospective rewards of such an acquisition were palpable to the State Department, then on the verge of signing treaties to open five Chinese ports to American commerce. But why should Britain have settled for undisputed title to Puget Sound under Webster's terms when it could have applied its own considerable powers of economic and military suasion to coerce the Mexicans into selling it, not the Americans, San Francisco Bay and thereby all but guaranteeing the British empire commercial dominance over the Pacific trade?

Before that question could be answered, Webster stepped aside in 1843 as the last Whig in President Tyler's cabinet. His successor, another former Senate luminary, John Calhoun, postponed the Oregon talks and concentrated his diplomatic efforts on the annexation of Texas. Meanwhile, the Bay prepared to move its Oregon headquarters from Fort Vancouver 200 miles north to Fort Victoria on the southern tip of Vancouver Island, forty miles below the forty-ninth parallel, essentially conceding the lower Columbia basin to the Americans. The site of the Bay's new regional home would shortly prove a critical element in discussions to settle the dispute, but first the issue grew more heated and nearly brought the rivals to blows as their political leaders dug in their heels while subordinates in the diplomatic corps labored to head off a conflagration.

Below the top level, substantial progress was made in late 1843 between the British foreign secretary, Lord Aberdeen, and the gifted American minister to London, Edward Everett. A pillar of Boston's religious, intellectual, and political establishment, with close ties to the mercantile community, Everett had taught Greek literature at Harvard—of which he would become president after retiring from his diplomatic post—and lately served as governor of Massachusetts. Twenty years later, Everett, a captivating orator, would deliver the featured speech at ceremonies dedicating the military cemetery beside the battlefield at Gettysburg, although posterity has remembered only the much briefer address that day by the President of the United States.

One difficulty in determining an equitable division of the Oregon Country was that its southern boundary had never been agreed upon by Britain and the United States. In the Adams-Onís Treaty of 1819, Spain under American pressure had withdrawn all territorial claims north of the forty-second parallel. But that agreement did not cede to the United States any portion of the Pacific Northwest region between the Rockies and the ocean that the British and Americans had agreed in their 1818 treaty to hold and occupy jointly. Since both nations, under their 1824–25 treaties with Russia, had accepted the 54°40′ line as the northern boundary of their mutually held territory, the Oregon Country thus stretched from that line all the way south to the Mexican border (as inherited from Spain) along the forty-second parallel, where California began. That expanse encompassed roughly 470,000 square miles. Dividing it as the British wanted to along the lower Columbia River would have allotted the United States nearly 250,000 square miles with richer soil and a more temperate climate than the northern sector. Dividing Oregon as the United States proposed along the forty-ninth parallel to the Pacific would have added another 40,000 square miles to American territory, including the southern tip of Vancouver Island, and—more important—deprived Britain of invaluable potential port sites along Puget Sound and Juan de Fuca Strait.

In London, Everett softened American insistence on the forty-ninth parallel boundary by raising the possibility of granting the British free navigation of the Columbia River below that boundary and permission to establish trading posts along that waterway—a decorative fig leaf of marginal utility. Aberdeen replied that mighty Britain could hardly yield to previously rejected American demands unless they were accompanied by a more meaningful concession. Everett then broke the deadlock by proposing to seek President Tyler's agreement to extend the forty-ninth parallel not all the way to the Pacific but only to the eastern shore of the Strait of Georgia, separating the end of the North American mainland from 280-mile-long Vancouver Island. Thus, all of the island's 12,000 square miles would remain British territory, allowing the Hudson's Bay Company's new head-quarters to be built as planned on the Strait of Juan de Fuca at the southeast end of the island. This so-called Everett line, along with free navigation of the Columbia within American territory, might be acceptable to Prime Minister Peel, Aberdeen indicated.

The Everett-Aberdeen peace formula was soon shoved aside by a provocative display of chauvinist grandstanding in the United States and the predictable reaction to it in Britain. As his term in the White House neared its end, Tyler, an able chief executive, hoped to retain the presidency despite the loss of his political moorings. Since neither the Democrats, whom he had deserted to run on the Whig ticket in 1840, nor the Whigs, whose policies he rejected after succeeding to the presidency, would accept him, Tyler pinned his independent candidacy on the pursuit of territorial acquisitions likely to enhance his popularity with the electorate. He explored an annexation treaty with Texas through secret negotiations, as discussed earlier, but made quite public his expansive designs on Oregon.

In his annual message to Congress in early December 1843, Tyler reported that British obstinacy blocking a settlement along the forty-ninth parallel had prompted him to undertake a rigorous and unbiased study of the issue. As a result, he had concluded that the United States was entitled to the *whole* Oregon Country, and Britain, which wanted it only for commercial exploitation and not rooted settlement, was entitled to none of it. It was a thrilling overture to the expansionist Democrats, who would nonetheless spurn Tyler's hopes for their presidential nomination. But six months later they incorporated his disingenuous claim as a main plank of their platform at the party's national convention.

Tyler's claim of exclusive American entitlement to all of Oregon was a blatant insult to Britain, to the historical evidence, and to actual conditions throughout the region. It was one thing to seek, as part of a diplomatically arrived at compromise, title to the territory extending 200 miles north of the lower Columbia River to the forty-ninth parallel, even though there were no American settlers there and British commercial interests dominated. It was quite another thing to say the United States had a right to that territory—and altogether spurious to assert that it was legitimately entitled to seize the huge land mass from the forty-ninth parallel to the 54°40′ line—a region undiscovered, unconquered, and entirely unoccupied by American citizens. Repeated proposals by the United States to extend its northern boundary along the forty-ninth parallel from the Rockies to the Pacific at least had the virtues of geographical neatness and geopolitical logic. An asserted right to expand American dominion another 425 miles northward and deny the territory to Britain could be derived only from the confrontational precepts of the Monroe Doctrine, unilaterally banning European nations from establishing future colonies in the Western Hemisphere. The Anglo-American treaty for the joint occupancy of Oregon, however, antedated the Monroe Doctrine by five years, and, at any rate, the British imperial presence in North America was a good deal older than the United States of America. Finally, an American takeover of all of Oregon, if Tyler's provocative claim was realized, would leave Britain, the world's foremost naval and maritime power, without any territory whatever fronting on the Pacific coast—an intolerable prospect to policymakers in London.

Lord Aberdeen, with Everett's coaching, recognized Tyler's asserted territorial overreach as both a bargaining ploy and political exhibitionism and sent his new minister to Washington, Richard Pakenham, instructions to politely ignore the President's declaration that Oregon in its entirety belonged to the United States. Pakenham, a lively and adroit diplomat whose father had been a celebrated admiral and whose uncle had been the defeated (and slain) British commander at the Battle of New Orleans, was told to stick to the British position favoring the lower Columbia as the boundary. As a friendly gesture, he was further instructed to offer the United States the right to establish isolated ports on Puget Sound and Vancouver Island, but without any cession of adjacent territory. Aware that this small prize would hardly slake the Americans' territorial appetite, Aberdeen privately advised his envoy to explore the "Everett line" solution, which the Peel cabinet had not authorized but the affable foreign secretary thought he could sell to the ministry as the only practicable basis for settlement.

By the spring of 1844, Pakenham had to report home that the expansionist bacillus was grossly infecting the American polity. Congress was debating not only the newly disclosed text of the Tyler-Calhoun treaty to annex Texas, defying Mexico's angry opposition to such a step, but also a resolution to give Britain the required one year's notice that the United States intended to abandon their twenty-six-year-old pact for the joint occupancy of Oregon. The subtext of this notice was not subtle: we Americans are now emigrating to paradise-on-the-Pacific in such multitudes that we will shortly overwhelm the thin British presence there, so if you won't give us all or most of Oregon, we are going to move in anyway—and let nature run its course. Nor was this implicit threat embraced solely by the extremist school of manifest destiny persuasion. Democratic Senator James Buchanan, a political heavyweight in the swing state of Pennsylvania, who a year later would become Secretary of State, endorsed Tyler's claim that all of Oregon was rightfully America's. With such backing it was understandable how the

Democratic convention wound up in late May by choosing expansionist James Polk as its dark-horse presidential nominee, fully supporting the party platform's 54°40′ all-Oregon demand—one that the *Times* of London labeled "pure unredeemed bluster."

After Congress shied from voting to withdraw from the joint Oregon accord and the Senate heavily rejected the Texas annexation treaty in June, a cautioned Tyler began to heed Everett's advisory from London that vocal insistence on the 54°40′ boundary might push the British government into accepting the forty-ninth parallel as the lesser evil, provided the United States agreed not to extend the line through Vancouver Island—that is, the compromise Everett and Aberdeen had informally devised. Everett added, hoping to temper the President's oratory lest it inflame Britain's fighting spirit, that the White House ought not to continue stridently claiming all of Oregon "as to put ourselves in the wrong in receding from it."

As heated words over expansionist U.S. policy dominated the presidential campaign, Calhoun and Pakenham met six times in August and September to thrash out the Oregon issue but made little headway. Secretary of State Calhoun advised that the Senate, of which he was a past master, would never approve a treaty that set the Oregon boundary south of the forty-ninth parallel, so Pakenham ought to save his breath by dropping the Columbia River boundary proposal. On the other hand, Calhoun also hinted, his government might accede to the Everett line, but he would need to explore the sentiment in the Senate toward that idea when Congress reconvened in December.

The British prime minister, aroused by displays of American belligerency over Oregon and reports that Tyler's administration had begun strengthening the nation's naval forces, was disinclined to bend on the boundary issue. This rigid position was strongly encouraged by Peel's steely minister without portfolio, the Duke of Wellington, at seventy-five still the empire's hero and a hardliner in military matters. Yielding to American bluster, moreover, would have badly reduced Peel's standing with the British public at a time when growing poverty loomed as a threat to his ministry. Pakenham was told to give no ground but to sound out Calhoun on the possibility of submitting the Oregon problem to arbitration by a third power. Such an expedient would provide Peel with political cover if the ruling proved too generous to the Americans. But Calhoun and his successor, Buchanan, would steadfastly reject British proposals to have the deadlocked Oregon dispute settled by a supposedly disinterested outsider, asking rhetorically which of the crowned heads of Europe would qualify as a truly neutral arbitrator fairly disposed toward a democratic republic on the other side of the Atlantic.

Everything now hinged on the outcome of the American presidential election. A victory by the favorite, the antiexpansionist Whigs' Henry Clay, held the promise of a far more conciliatory U.S. government. But with Polk's narrow triumph, the sweeping Democratic takeover in Congress, and fevered expansionist sentiment in the air, Britain soon found its North American interests gravely menaced.

In the lame-duck Congress, having approved the Tyler-sponsored and Polk-backed joint resolution that offered statehood to Texas, the House of Representatives now let Britain know the mood of the American public by voting solidly in favor of a funding bill for new forts along the Oregon Trail to protect the swelling westward flow of settlers and for establishing a federal territorial government throughout Oregon to serve as a counterweight to the quasi-imperial authority of the Hudson's Bay Company. Duly alerted, Lord Aberdeen told American envoy Everett that any moves by the United States to take exclusive possession of, or unilaterally impose its jurisdiction over, territory north of the Columbia River would prompt a British military response. Tyler, wary of plunging the nation into war in his closing weeks as President, hastened to advise the Senate there was no need to concur in the House's aggressive action because negotiations over Oregon were progressing. In fact, they were not.

SOON AFTER MOVING INTO THE WHITE HOUSE, the usually unforthcoming James K. Polk confided to his Secretary of the Navy, George Bancroft, a popular historian and rare Democrat from Whiggish New England, that he had four principal goals in mind for his presidency. The third and fourth dealt with what he considered vital economic reforms—reducing the tariff and government dependency on it as a source of revenue, thereby promoting trade, and establishing an independent United States Treasury as a depository for federal funds, which could not be used for private gain as the first two United States Banks had done. Polk's first two priorities were territorial: to settle the Oregon question with Great Britain and to acquire California, which meant, if not in so many words, rounding out the United States as a coast-to-coast nation.

What made Polk's goals so remarkably ambitious was that he had given himself only four years to achieve them. Locked in a tight election race against spellbinder Henry Clay, Polk had calculated that to win he needed the all-out campaign support of his party's best-known and most dynamic leaders, including the very men from whom he had wrested the nomination. These defeated rivals might well have sat on their hands and muted their voices in the hope that the prim little Tennessean would be defeated—

a result boosting their own chances to become the Democratic standard-bearer in 1848. So Polk, though only forty-nine, pledged that he would be a one-term President and lured his former competitors to rally to his cause. And it worked.

His victory at the polls had already produced a signal achievement, one that Polk might otherwise have placed at the top of his to-do list—the acquisition of Texas, voted by Congress just four days before his inauguration. In truth, John Tyler deserved much of the credit for having pursued troubled Texas as a territorial prize in the face of strong antislavery opposition and widespread fears that Mexico might respond violently to such a move. But Tyler lacked backing in the Senate to bring off the transaction, and only Polk's victory—and sly tactics in tandem with the retiring Tyler—had reversed the outcome.

Polk's inaugural address in March 1845, delivered in a rainstorm to a sea of umbrellas, was notable for two themes. A known, unapologetic slaveholder, the new President sought to reconcile the fervent antislavery opposition to statehood for Texas by urging acceptance "on the broad principle which formed the basis and produced the adoption of our Constitution"—namely, states' rights. "Whatever is good or evil in the local institutions of Texas will remain her own," Polk contended, "whether annexed to the United States or not. None of the present states will be responsible for them any more than they are for the local institutions of each other." For the nation to have denied Texas admission solely because of its social customs would have been to adopt a policy under which "our forefathers would have been prevented from forming our present Union." Polk's rationale, not altogether without merit and faithful to his ideology, was also an artful pretense that nothing had altered in the national conscience over the fifty-six years since slavery had been constitutionally consecrated.

Polk might well have pointed to Oregon and told the nation that its pending inclusion, to an extent not yet determined, as a territory of the United States would serve to offset the admission of Texas and preserve the Union's fragile balance, however unsavory to some, between free-soil and slave states. Instead, Polk delivered a thunderbolt—the most memorable words in his inaugural address—in the form of a bristling anthem to America's rampant territorial yearning. Many of his listeners, he said, had witnessed within their lifetime how their countrymen, "increasing to many millions, have filled the eastern valley of the Mississippi, adventurously ascended the Missouri to its headsprings, and are already engaged in establishing the blessings of self-government" in river valleys flowing to the Pacific. The United States government had the duty, he said, while honoring its foreign treaties, to protect these hearty venturers "wherever they may be *upon our soil*" and to extend American laws to "the distant regions which they have selected for their homes" (italics added). Then, leaving no doubt about what he meant by "our soil," Polk invoked the words of the 1844 Democratic platform: "Our title to the country of Oregon is 'clear and unmistakable' "—but he did not say "all of Oregon" as the platform had and as the soon-to-be-unfurled outcry of "Fifty-four forty or fight!" would demand. California went unmentioned, but Polk now quietly authorized scouting parties and covert agents to assess conditions in that lightly held Mexican province, where insurrectionists were already reported active.

From the start, then, James Polk signaled his intention to surpass all his predecessors as an acquirer—one way or another—of new national territory. What had transformed him from a colorless, closemouthed party tactician to a daring, ruthless leader determined to fulfill his self-assigned continental mission?

Perhaps Polk understood that the power of the presidency had grown in keeping with the nation's boundaries and population and fully appreciated that his license to use it was short-lived. Perhaps he wanted to demonstrate that he deserved the nickname "Little Hickory," even though his frail health as a young man had kept him from seeking military glory of the sort that had lifted his dying patron, Andrew Jackson, to the zenith of national acclaim. Perhaps, if one favors a Freudian frame of reference, Polk's almost reckless aggressiveness in office—even Jackson was tame by comparison when it came to foreign adventurism—was symptomatic of a form of sublimated libido, stemming from the cruel effects of a chronic bladder ailment that surgeons tried to ease by removing urinary stones but in the process damaged his genital equipment and likely left him sterile and possibly impotent from late adolescence on.* Such theories of causation aside—and none may have validity—the world took notice that a resolute and defiant figure had assumed a leadership role in the New World and needed prompt curbing. The *Times* of London, bellwether of Toryism, called Polk's inaugural remarks "overbearing" and "aggressive," and Prime Minister Peel told Parliament that Britain, too, had "clear and unquestionable rights" in Oregon and "we are resolved—we are prepared—to maintain them."

Both sides had dug a diplomatic hole for themselves in the Oregon con-

---

*Polk and his devoted wife, Sarah, were childless—hardly definitive evidence of his (or her) reproductive powers but suggestive of frustrated biological urges. For a more detailed discussion of the subject, see John Seigenthaler's short 2003 biography, *James K. Polk,* p. 19.

frontation. Neither felt it could be the first to give ground for fear it would appear to have buckled under and, by its conciliatory stance, emboldened the other side to demand still further concessions. This mindset had led the British ministry to keep returning to third-party arbitration as a more politically sanitized method of settling the duel. Polk's approach was different. That he was posturing by reasserting the nation's "clear and unquestionable rights" to Oregon—and implying he meant *all* of Oregon even when not saying so—seemed obvious to his domestic foes; the Whig press called Polk's pugnacious inaugural speech "mere claptrap." But the President was also putting the Peel government on notice that so long as it refused to budge on the forty-ninth parallel as a fair boundary line, perhaps with a sweetener or two thrown in, the United States would behave just as unreasonably by insisting on its rights to the bulk, if not all, of Oregon.

Having cast himself as a tough guy, Polk was by no means unmindful of the advice he had been given by retiring Secretary of State Calhoun, after declining the President's offer to go to London as the American minister and instead returning to the Senate. The United States had no need to provoke Britain to the point of taking up arms in the Oregon dispute, Calhoun counseled, because "the whole territory must become ours by the natural progress of our population." Polk could then afford to be flexible until the British came to their senses. Lord Aberdeen similarly saw that time, logistics, and demographics were against Britain in Oregon, and so he had confided to U.S. envoy Everett that the American proposal of the forty-ninth parallel boundary, with the British retaining all of Vancouver Island, might be acceptable to the Peel cabinet, provided that it was (1) accompanied by the grant of free British navigation of the lower Columbia and (2) raised first by the United States. Polk, though, was wary of the continued British refusal to deal.

The President's wish to settle was detectable in the men he chose to carry on relations with Britain. For Secretary of State, Polk had selected James Buchanan of Pennsylvania, who had spent ten years each in the House and Senate, with a two-year tenure in between as the U.S. minister to Russia. There had been more bravado than conviction in Buchanan's early support for the "all of Oregon" position. He was no fire-eater but a cautious conciliator, so transparently ambitious to be elected President that he strove to offend no one and act the very model of a political pragmatist. It was his ambivalence on slavery, which he knew to be a moral iniquity but believed as a practical matter could not be abolished, that made the northerner Buchanan acceptable to Polk to hold the highest post in his cabinet. To succeed the estimable Everett as envoy to London, Polk chose independent-minded Louis McLane, who had held the same post as well as the two top cabinet jobs under Jackson. In accepting the London assignment, McLane made clear to Polk that he did not favor the 54°40′ position but recognized how intermittent allusion to it might have tactical value.

The surest indication that Polk's private attitude was less truculent than the flamboyant rhetoric of his inaugural address was the letter Buchanan wrote to McLane on July 12, 1845, detailing the steps the President had approved for ending the Oregon deadlock. Britain's Washington envoy, Richard Pakenham, was being advised that day that if the extension of the forty-ninth parallel to the Pacific was agreed to as the boundary between the two nations, the United States was prepared to allow Britain to establish a port and naval station on the southern tip of Vancouver Island, even though that portion of the island would fall within American territory. Aware of the earlier exchanges between Everett and Lord Aberdeen, Buchanan antici-pated that Pakenham, following protocol, would transmit the opening American offer to London, where it would likely be met with a counterpro-posal to adopt the so-called Everett line, running the boundary only as far as the edge of the mainland so that Britain would retain all of Vancouver Island, and to allow British vessels to navigate the Columbia through U.S. territory to the ocean. Polk did not favor the Columbia concession, but Buchanan's purpose now was to get the negotiations flowing. He added that since Oregon north of the forty-ninth parallel was suitable for neither agriculture nor otherwise sustaining a large population, it was not worth going to war over and incurring the world's ill opinion—an assessment that hinted at the apologia Polk would spin to calm anti-British, "all of Oregon" extremists who favored war over compromise.

At this sensitive juncture, Buchanan and Pakenham each made a grave error. To sustain the Polk government's hard-line tone even while throttling back on its collision course with stubborn British policymakers, the Secre-tary of State's memorandum to the British envoy fell short of a straight-forward settlement proposal, candidly conceding abandonment of the inflammatory 54°40′ stand. Rather, it came across as a gesture that smacked of condescension, reluctantly made only because Polk felt morally bound to respond, as Tyler and Calhoun had not, to the British request for the United States to state its terms for an Oregon agreement. The "all of Oregon" con-tention, Buchanan went on, hardly salving the wound, had been justified by the 1819 Adams-Onís Treaty under which Spain had vacated its claim to the Pacific coast above the forty-second parallel—a feckless argument that con-veniently overlooked British exploration of the region before Americans had appeared there, the absence of Americans north of the Columbia, and the 1790 Nootka Sound accord with Spain, under which Britain had won the right, never relinquished, to explore and settle the northern Pacific coast. Pakenham, a clever and seasoned diplomat, knew humbug when encountering it and saw red.

The British envoy, although fully briefed on Lord Aberdeen's receptivity to any feeler from Washington on the Everett line formula—or some variant thereof, as Buchanan, beneath the blarney, was offering—chose not to relay the proposal to his home office. No enthusiast of the United States and disdainful in particular of American politicians, whom he regarded as a dim-witted lot, Pakenham leaped at the chance to put the upstart Polk in his place and skewer his imperial ambitions. He abruptly rejected Buchanan's exploratory offer, challenged his abrasive misreading of history in the Pacific Northwest, and, without offering any new British terms in response, asked for a new, improved American proposal.

Polk, assuming that Pakenham had acted on standing instructions from London, felt he had been gulled by advisors calling for conciliation over Oregon. The infuriated President favored immediate withdrawal of the American proposal, which had been intended as a door-opener for serious negotiations, and formal adoption of the "all of Oregon" demand as the only way to bring the British down from their high horse. Buchanan, previously regarded as irresolute if not certifiably spineless, opposed such a swift, impulsive response. The extreme 54°40′ position, he argued to Polk, rather than punishing Britain by proposing to cut it off altogether from the Pacific coast, would likely goad it into wrathful military action, perhaps even into an alliance with Mexico, then snarling over the just approved annexation of Texas. Better to let Pakenham's abrupt and discourteous rebuke just sit unanswered for a while. Buchanan's argument was bolstered by the August 19 arrival of a letter from McLane, who, apprised of the opening conciliatory offer by the Polk administration, reassured the President that Aberdeen remained receptive to the Everett line/Vancouver Island idea but had to go slow in the face of resistance to it by the Hudson's Bay Company.

By late August Polk's patience had run out. Again Buchanan showed more gumption than was his custom. To withdraw the American offer in pique and instead insist upon a fabricated American right to all of remote and empty Oregon, as the President now ordered at a full meeting of his cabinet, would provoke a war with Britain that the people of the United States were unlikely to support, in Buchanan's view. Polk replied that the nation "would be prompt and ready to support the government" in the course he proposed to follow. Buchanan repeated his earlier caution that it would be unwise to provoke the British with the Mexican threat looming as well. Polk answered that "we should do our duty towards both Mexico and Great Britain . . . firmly maintain our rights, and leave the rest to God and country." The Secretary of State, risking a rupture of his ties with the President, answered that God would be hard pressed "in justifying a war for the country north of forty-nine degrees." But Polk, of course, had the last word. For his government to delay longer—it had already waited six weeks—in replying to Pakenham would convey "hesitancy and indecision." Buchanan was told to draw up a letter registering indignation over the British envoy's curt dismissal of the American proposal, which was withdrawn forthwith, now leaving it to London to broach an acceptable basis to end the crisis or—it went unsaid but was surely understood—face the consequences. Still, Buchanan had made his point; there was no explicit American demand for all of Oregon.

Aberdeen, a conciliator at heart, was not happy with the impulsive behavior of his envoy to Washington. Even the hard-shelled Peel agreed that Pakenham had been "needlessly harsh and peremptory" in rejecting the American intiative, which could have led to genuine bargaining and a swift settlement. Botched British diplomacy had given the Americans "a great advantage," and Pakenham, who would have been recalled if not for powerful connections and a superior record, was directed to advise Buchanan that he had erred in assuming the Peel ministry would not even wish to consider the American proposal, and so the British ambassador was withdrawing his earlier rejection of it in the hope the United States would likewise cancel its withdrawal of the offer. But Pakenham's crow-eating request was followed up not by any British counteroffer of terms but only by another call for arbitrating the dispute—a palliative, not a policy. The chastened Pakenham probed gingerly on his Washington rounds to learn precisely what terms would be acceptable to Polk, but the tight-lipped President would not tip his hand.

This sphinxlike posture was accompanied by signs in the American press, disconcerting to the Peel ministry in Whitehall, of a growing resolve to strike at the British presence in North America. The *Washington Union,* mouthpiece of the dominant Democratic Party, had renewed its drumbeat for the 54°40′ boundary, and other newspapers favored similarly punishing Britain for stonewalling on Oregon. Particularly troublesome was a series of five articles appearing that spring in the *National Intelligencer* by Lieutenant Matthew Maury, superintendent of the U.S. Navy's Department of Charts and Instruments and a well-respected writer on military strategy and organization. Maury advocated that, in the event of a new war with Britain, American forces ought to take permanent possession of Upper Canada's great Ontario peninsula, which denied the United States control of the commercially and militarily vital Great Lakes. Coming after a decade of incitements within Canada itself against British control and growing outcry for more home rule, such a provocative call to conquest in a prominent American periodical was doubly alarming to the Peel government. Even assuming the jingoist press did not speak for the Polk administration or the American people, it alerted the British government to likely difficulties ahead if it chose to go to war rather than to gratify what it judged to be Americans' insatiable territorial appetite. It was bad enough that Britain had failed to subdue their feeble revolutionary forces in seven years of fighting along the Atlantic coast and suffered a crushing defeat at New Orleans on the more distant Gulf of Mexico a generation later; how much harder and more costly it would be to wage a war now in the far western corner of North America—and to risk a full-scale invasion of Canada by the United States, already a nation of 20 million people, and not the hopelessly undermanned probes that American troops had attempted in 1775 and 1812.

Prime Minister Peel, though, was a stouthearted fellow and, with the still prouder Iron Duke of Wellington at his side, chose to test Polk's mettle. Instead of yielding to Aberdeen's recommended retreat from the proposed Columbia River boundary to the Everett line, Peel let it be known his government was ready to strengthen Britain's military presence in North America. But Polk would not back down, either. The only way to force Peel's hand, he was convinced, was to hold firm. The new Congress, its top-heavy Democratic majorities likely to comply with Polk's Oregon policies, was due to convene the first week of December, and the President used the autumn hiatus to firm up his strategy rather than await British initiatives that might never materialize. He found a potent ally in Tom Benton of Missouri, the pivotal figure in the Senate and one of its loudest proponents of westward growth. Benton had nursed no grudge against Polk for his slippery evasion of the promise he had apparently made to renegotiate the terms of Texas annexation more to the Senator's liking if his bloc of supporters came aboard. With Benton's blessing, the President decided to ask Congress to do what it had threatened but not actually voted to do earlier—cancel the Oregon joint occupancy treaty and establish American law throughout the region, even at the risk of escalating the conflict over the boundary issue.

The President, however, was not deaf to powerful voices calling for restraint. Eastern commercial interests and southern cotton growers saw scant benefit from a war over Oregon. Senator Benton, and even John Quincy Adams in the House, both passionate expansionists, backed Polk's hardline strategy, but that was quite a different matter from supporting the

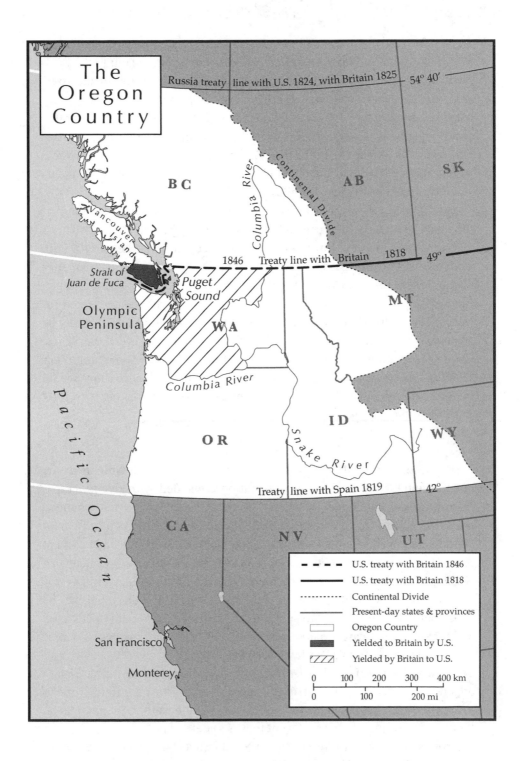

The Oregon Country

Russia treaty line with U.S. 1824, with Britain 1825   54° 40'

BC

Continental Divide

Columbia River

AB

SK

Vancouver Island

1846   Treaty line with Britain   1818   49°

Strait of Juan de Fuca

Puget Sound

MT

Olympic Peninsula

WA

Columbia River

OR

ID

Snake River

WY

Treaty line with Spain 1819   42°

Pacific Ocean

CA

NV

UT

San Francisco

Monterey

- - - - -   U.S. treaty with Britain 1846
──────   U.S. treaty with Britain 1818
·············   Continental Divide
──────   Present-day states & provinces
Oregon Country
Yielded to Britain by U.S.
Yielded by Britain to U.S.

0   100   200   300   400 km
0   100   200 mi

clamor for "all Oregon or fight" being raised by extremists. If the United States taunted Britain into an armed conflict, it was pointed out to the President, Peel and Parliament might just send a sizable portion of the royal navy to the California coast, land a powerful army, pay off the pauper Mexican government for the territory, and turn the coveted, undefended region—perhaps all the way up to the 54°40′ line—into an extension of British North America. Polk, like Peel, who had to face a conceivable American threat to all of Canada if the Oregon crisis got out of hand, understood that the adversaries were playing with fire.

At an October 10 cabinet meeting, the President indicated for the first time how he intended to proceed. While still insisting the next step had to be taken by Peel and doubtful it would prove acceptable if taken at all, Polk said he might nevertheless be willing to submit any reasonable British offer to the Senate for its *advice* only, not its *consent,* thus separating the two functions that the Constitution prescribed when a treaty was presented for ratification. If the Senate approved in the first instance, Polk could hardly be accused by the ultraexpansionists of failure to stand tall. And if the Senate voiced reservations, these could be relayed to London as something other than Polk's personal vehemence, in the hope that further concessions would be forthcoming to win the Senate's essential endorsement. Either way, Polk would be off the hook.

THE ESCALATION OF TENSION with Great Britain over Oregon in the opening months of the Polk administration coincided with rising antagonism between the United States and Mexico. The Mexicans felt wounded anew when Texas rejected their belated offer of recognition as a fully independent nation and negotiations over a boundary, choosing instead to accept American statehood. In both international situations the new President was willing to gamble—that he could bluff the British into relinquishing territory to which they had no lesser claim than the United States and that he could bully the Mexicans into surrendering territory they could not defend, and that in neither case would a war result, or at least not much of a war, if Americans now displayed sufficient resolve.

Polk got it half right. The British were rich and calculating and, though angered by the Americans' territorial aggressiveness, saw the futility of trying to forestall the inevitable. The Mexicans, poorer and more passionate, thought first of their honor and went to war to defend it.

Polk's policy toward Mexico was rooted in his—and many of his countrymen's—contempt for the unending dysfunction of its government and economy. After a quarter of a century as a free nation, Mexico's treasury was empty, its army unpaid and mutinous, its economy in hock to foreign creditors, its fundamental political quarrel between *federalistas* and *centralistas* no closer than ever to resolution, and its class warfare little abated. The Mexican presidency was a revolving door of preening, grasping despots, Santa Anna the most seductive of them, and a string of corrupt or powerless figures who kept replacing him and soon falling.

The latest to try running the republic was José Joaquín de Herrera, a moderate who won the presidency with the temporary support of warlord Mariano Paredes. His troops, the loss of Texas to American annexation, and the complicity of the wealthy class had forced Santa Anna from power at the end of 1844 and opened the way for Herrera. But he was soon confronted by Polk's endorsement, promptly on taking office, of the Rio Grande as the Texas (and now United States) boundary—left unspecified in Congress's annexation resolution—and the dispatch of Zachary Taylor's 1,500-man force to a camp set up at Corpus Christi on the south bank of the Nueces River about 120 miles above the Rio Grande. Mexico insisted that the Nueces, not the Rio Grande, had always been, dating from Spanish imperial days, the boundary between the province of Texas and its neighboring provinces to the south. No Texan troops, furthermore, had conquered or even occupied the territory between the two rivers to justify the secessionist province's claim to the area, so the presence of Taylor's troops just inside the so-called Nueces Strip was a blatant incursion into Mexican territory and drove the Mexican Congress to the brink of declaring war. President Herrera, more sensible than most of his predecessors, insisted that his Congress first figure out how to pay for an army capable of restoring the nation's honor. Then to evidence his grit, he ordered General Paredes to move his troops, said to number more than 5,000, to support the 3,000 Mexican soldiers already gathered near the Rio Grande and sent word via diplomatic channels—since Mexico had broken official ties with the United States right after the annexation of Texas—that his government refused to negotiate a boundary accord with Washington so long as its troops remained on Mexican soil.

In his heart, Polk was convinced that Mexico would not submit to a territorial settlement—and certainly not on the scale the President had in mind—until it had been thoroughly thrashed by American military might and faced up to its status as an inferior nation. All but daring the Mexicans to strike the first blow so he could be absolved of instigating war, Polk sent orders to Taylor to attack at once if Mexican forces so much as *attempted* to cross the Rio Grande and to his naval commander in the Pacific to take control of San Francisco Bay, the commercial diamond in the rough of the Mexican province of Alta California, at the first moment he was apprised that war had erupted. But Herrera held too few resources to risk a shootout. Paredes did not snap to the president's order to move his troops to the Rio Grande, preferring to linger close to Mexico City in order to execute a coup whenever he chose to depose Herrera. Lord Aberdeen, furthermore, relayed word that, in view of Mexico's failure—despite repeated urging from London—to recognize Texas independence in time to thwart the far broader territorial designs of the United States, Britain could lend no military support to stymie further American encroachment on Mexican land. By October, Herrera was willing to risk his shaky hold on power by sending word that his nation, though "deeply injured" by American actions, would receive a United States "commissioner . . . with full powers to settle the present dispute."

Polk obliged, dispatching John Slidell, a Spanish-speaking New Orleans lawyer who served in the House of Representatives, to negotiate in Mexico City. Herrera had specified that his government would receive "an envoy," but when Slidell presented his papers, they described him as a minister plenipotentiary. To recognize him as such in advance of negotiations would have been, according to Mexican officials, to accept Texas annexation as a fait accompli and the severed diplomatic relations between the two countries as fully restored—a concession that would have rubbed salt into the wounded dignity of a proud and stubborn people and stirred Mexican patriots to demand Herrara's ouster. Polk had no interest, though, in assuaging Mexican pride; his intent was to shatter it. Slidell's papers were not changed, and for the better part of four months, the duly designated American representative was left to cool his heels in Mexico without ever being officially received by its government.

It was just as well, considering the nature of Slidell's instructions. He had been told to offer $5 million in what amounted to conscience money for the loss of Texas, provided that (1) the funds were earmarked to settle claims by American citizens for property damage, confiscation, and loss of life suffered over the preceding twenty-five years of Mexican civil strife and (2) Mexico accepted the Rio Grande up to the thirty-second parallel (just north of El Paso) as its boundary with the United States. Furthermore, if Mexico would accept the declaration by the Texas Congress that its boundary extended north along the upper Rio Grande past Santa Fe, encompassing more than 80,000 square miles of the province of New Mexico—a claim the American government acknowledged was unsupported by actual settlement (or by anything else besides wishful thinking)—the United States would pay Mexico an additional $5 million. And if it would sell the rest of the territory between the Rio Grande and the Pacific Ocean (that is, the western third of New Mexico and the modern states of Arizona, Utah, Nevada, and California), bankrupt Mexico would receive another $20 million for what Slidell was told to characterize as nearly empty—if you didn't acknowledge the native tribes—and virtually worthless lands.

Had Herrera given Slidell the chance to present such an insolent offer and considered it for even a moment, he would have been tossed to the wolves at once. But Herrera's resistance failed to deter Paredes from discarding him anyway. The new Mexican president objected strongly to treating with the American envoy, and by the time Slidell returned to Washington in early May 1846, Taylor's troops had been ordered to advance to the north bank of the Rio Grande and position their cannons overlooking the town square in Matamoros on the Mexican side of the river. Paredes was hopeful that the United States would at any moment become embroiled in a war with Britain over Oregon and be unable to fight simultaneously on two fronts. Polk was still gambling he would have to fight on neither.

THE GAMBLE OVER OREGON WAS RISKIER, but Polk, in receipt of no conciliatory offer from London, persisted in believing that only by appearing immovable—and leaving the British in doubt as to whether he was bluffing or reckless enough to fight over a remote wilderness—could he force the Peel government to bargain fairly. Accordingly, he greeted the new Congress on December 2, 1845, with an expansive assertion of American rights in Oregon and a request that it promptly vote to put Britain on one year's notice, as required, that the United States was withdrawing from their joint occupancy of that huge region along the Pacific. It would not be a declaration of war, but it would amount to the next best thing.

Summoning officials and confidants to his deskside, the President made no secret of his strategy. Britain, he told one intimate, was "never known to do justice to any country with which she had a controversy, when that country was in an attitude of supplication." Polk put it still more bluntly to a friend, Tennessee Congressman James Black, who quoted him as saying that "the only way to treat John Bull was to look him straight in the eye. . . . [I]f Congress faltered or hesitated in their course, John Bull would immediately become more arrogant and grasping in his demands." Polk's confrontational words gave Wall Street the jitters. His foes denounced him as politically motivated and charged that his meretricious oratory was leading the nation into an unjustifiable war. His party's two leading Senators, Benton and Calhoun, who hated each other, agreed that in taking an ultraexpansionist position and calling for the abandonment of the joint occupancy treaty before settlement of the boundary question, the President was behaving in a most warlike way—which, of course, was true and exactly what Polk had in mind.

Western politicians were solidly with him. Southerners who strayed into the peace coalition led by South Carolina's Calhoun found themselves denounced as hypocrites by antislavery congressmen for having inveigled them to vote for Texas annexation in the spirit of maximizing the nation's dominion so long as slave territory was involved, but then pulling back from claiming all or most of Oregon because it would become free soil once it was added to the Union. The Whigs, sharply reduced in Congress and tempered in their views on expansion, found themselves pilloried as unpatriotic if they shrank from the contest with Britain. No American issue had become more divisive than whether manifest destiny was a legitimate, transcendent national faith or a hot-air excuse for indiscriminate land-grabbing.

In London, Polk's territorial adventurism was having its effect. Not that John Bull was particularly cowed by the threat of forcible American settlement of all Oregon and, with the end of the joint occupancy treaty, the region's metamorphosis into de facto U.S. territory. But gallant resistance to such American banditry was superseded by more pressing demands on the British ministry. Terrible crop failures had led to widespread hunger, and famine was beginning to ravage Ireland. Feeding the poor and preventing insurrection in the streets mattered more than costly empire-building. Instead, British public sentiment favored peaceably broadening the empire's commercial sphere of influence. Preferential trade treaties like those Whitehall diplomats had won throughout Latin America—the one with Mexico was a good example—made more sense than going to war to deny Americans more of Oregon than they could justly claim.

The hunger afflicting the nation's impoverished was attributable in no small way to Britain's Corn Laws, which for thirty years had protected domestic farmers by slapping a substantial tariff on grain imports, to the detriment of growers in the United States and Russia, and forcing up bread prices at home. Peel, who had grown less conservative with his years in public service—he had pushed through expanded civil rights for Catholics, a modified income tax, and controls on banking—saw no alternative now to the radical step of abolishing the Corn Laws. The change would be a boon to American grain farmers, whose crops Britain now badly needed to alleviate a national disaster. The Oregon dispute needed to be settled speedily, so long as Britain was not humiliated in the process.

Peel bowed to Aberdeen's counsel that adherence to the long-standing Columbia River boundary offer could no longer be sustained. With the consent of the Hudson's Bay Company, the prime minister indicated he would accept the Everett line formula, so long as the United States allowed British cargo to move freely down the Columbia below the forty-ninth parallel border. But Peel would not yield one additional inch of territory to Polk and waited for some overt sign that the President was not pathologically captivated by his "all of Oregon" pretensions. The shift in British policy could be detected in a January 3, 1846, editorial in the *Times,* the Peel government's closest ally among the London press, which reversed its longtime raillery against "the extravagant demands, reckless assertions, [and] disingenuous conduct" of land-coveting American statesmen and called on Polk to accept a boundary along the Everett line as an honorable solution to the crisis. Other papers hoped the repeal of the Corn Laws would induce Polk to arbitrate.

Arbitration was not what Polk had in mind, as Buchanan bluntly told Pakenham when the British envoy once more proposed it near the end of December. It was up to Britain to put a deal on the table, Polk insisted and his cabinet agreed, even while endorsing the President's earlier stated inclination to submit any reasonable offer to the Senate for its advice. But this receptivity—plainly Polk's line of retreat—was not yet disclosed to the British. Instead, Buchanan prevailed upon the President to let him make a subtle overture by explaining to Pakenham why there was no need for arbitration. In view of the close and enduring Anglo-American commercial ties, there were no two nations "who ought to be more able or willing to do each other justice without the interposition of any arbitrator." In other words, the Secretary of State was saying: make us an offer and we can work this thing out. But neither Pakenham nor his ministry took the hint or, if they did, was willing to act on it. Absent a British offer, Polk's cabinet now enlisted congressional leaders to authorize an expanded military budget for 1846, including the building of iron-sided ships better able to stand up against the royal navy.

The Alphonse/Gaston minuet over which nation would open the bargaining in earnest continued well into January as both sides watched to see how promptly Congress responded to Polk's call to withdraw from the joint occupancy treaty. Swift, decisive approval, suggesting the nation's resolve to take all or most of Oregon, would strengthen the President's hand; a narrow margin or rejection might tempt Peel to yield less ground. As the debate unfolded at the Capitol, British impatience with Polk's conduct was registered by Aberdeen at a January 29 meeting with U.S. ambassador McLane, who was informed that his government's repeated categorical refusals to enter into arbitration conveyed insincerity about reaching a peaceful settlement. As a result, Aberdeen said he was no longer able to restrain his fellow ministers from ordering the imminent departure of "thirty sail of the line," steamers, and other warships escorted by armaments carriers not only for the defense of British North America but "for offensive operations" as well. McLane shortly relayed the message, aimed at unsettling Polk, but added his suspicion that Aberdeen's war talk was required to placate Wellington and the militarists in Peel's coterie and did not reflect the government's true position. Indeed, the growing support in Parliament for repeal of the Corn Laws, McLane reported, was due partly to the hope that the measure, such a blessing for American farmers, would help restore friendly relations with the United States. Departure of the new British naval force, moreover, could be delayed indefinitely if only Polk declared his receptivity to a deal based on the Everett line.

In fact, Polk had sent just such a signal on the very day that Aberdeen told McLane about the Peel ministry's threatened naval initiative. The envoy was instructed to advise Aberdeen "cautiously and informally" of the possibility that Polk would seek the "previous advice" of the Senate about any new and reasonable British proposal before acting on it. Then, at last revealing the President's political escape hatch, Buchanan told McLane that Polk officially remained committed to the "all of Oregon" principle and was not disposed to veer from it *"unless the Senate should otherwise determine"* (italics added). Each side, then, had told the other it was ready to compromise, but both waited now for Congress to formally bury the joint occupancy of Oregon.

Whatever hope the Peel ministry had harbored that Americans might prove indifferent or fainthearted if their "Fifty-four forty or fight!" war cry were put to the test was dashed by the proceedings in the House. Among the most ardent of the spokesmen there for maximum American penetration of the Oregon Country was Representative John Quincy Adams, who had twice in his career—in 1818 as Secretary of State and nine years later as President—unsuccessfully urged Britain to accept the forty-ninth parallel boundary. Now Adams was after all of Oregon that the United States could get its hands on, in part no doubt because, as a fierce antislavery advocate, he wanted to acquire as much free soil as possible to offset the Texas annexation. But the crusty old statesman gave a different reason and, in doing so, came as close as anyone to putting a benign face on the manifest destiny doctrine and unbridled American expansionism. Neither discovery nor exploration justified title to territory, Adams contended; only possession and cultivation of it did. "We claim that country [Oregon] . . . to make the wilderness bloom as the rose, to establish laws, to increase, multiply, and subdue the earth, which we are commanded to do by the first behest of God Almighty." As if to document biblical support for his nation's seizure of all the world it could encompass, Adams then directed the clerk of the House to read the passage from Genesis in which the Lord commandeth mankind to "[b]e fruitful and multiply, replenish the earth, and subdue it." Then Adams heaped scorn on the British, who, he said, wanted Oregon merely "to keep it open for navigation, for hunters to hunt the wild beasts . . . for the buffaloes, braves, and savages of the desert."

Not surprisingly, then, with such a self-certifying motive ringing in their ears, House members voted on February 9 by a 163–54 margin to scrap the joint occupancy treaty. But they also let Polk and Peel know that their vote was no license for a military free-for-all. Nothing in their action, they declared, should be construed as interfering "with the right and discretion of the proper authorities of the two contracting parties to renew or pursue negotiations for an amicable settlement . . . respecting the Oregon territory."

Shortly after the gratifying House vote, Polk was in receipt of McLane's dispatch advising him that the British might soon send a heavily armed flotilla to Canada—news that was more compelling to him than his ambassador's reassurance that the Peel government was nonetheless eager to settle the Oregon issue bloodlessly. As the protracted Senate debate on ending the joint occupancy treaty unfolded, that body's leading advocate of concilia-tion, John Calhoun, urged the President to let the British government know that he would consider an offer of the Everett line boundary to be a reason-able one and direct it to the Senate for an advisory opinion. Polk, under sharp criticism on the Senate floor, agreed that the critical moment was at hand and directed Buchanan to send off the definitive signal. The Oregon Country would be divided at the forty-ninth parallel and Britain would keep all of Vancouver Island, but, Buchanan added, Polk would not grant British vessels free navigation of the Columbia within American territory. No for-eign ships, the President believed as a matter of principle, were entitled to the commercial and military advantages of open passage through the nation's inland waters. And if the Peel ministry persisted in its threat to send a large fleet of warships to North American waters, Buchanan further cau-tioned, it "would set this country ablaze."

Aberdeen and Peel chose to await the outcome of the Senate vote before accepting the invitation from Washington. Senators in the peace coalition strafed the President with charges very like those to be leveled against George W. Bush for leading the United States into war against Iraq early in the twenty-first century—namely, that Polk had practiced "a system of delusion . . . in order to affright, to irritate, to arouse the people of this country" to engage in war against Britain, with potentially dire consequences for American settlements along the Atlantic and Gulf coasts. It was a futile effort, though. Too many Whig Senators feared to oppose the President and face charges of appeasement. And even the holdouts Calhoun and Benton recognized that Polk had used the presidential pulpit to rally the expansionist forces and thereby dramatize American determination over Oregon. Unless Congress now backed Polk's request to vacate the joint occupancy treaty, Britain would not take the "all of Oregon" threat seriously and might refuse to bend on the forty-ninth parallel compromise.

Thus primed, the Senate voted 40–14 to break off the treaty, the joint congressional resolution was approved April 23, and Polk had made his point. A few days later, Buchanan advised London that any further adjustment of the Oregon dispute "must proceed from the British government." The President had scored a double victory. He had stared down the world's most powerful nation by forcing it to initiate the compromise settlement. And he had arranged to lay the responsibility for the deal on the Senate, so he could be acclaimed by moderates as a wisely flexible statesman and yet avoid a tarring by extremists for not having achieved the hopelessly unrealistic goal of winning the whole Oregon Country.

In the end, Peel understood that the Oregon issue far more deeply affected the people of the United States than those of Great Britain. American settlers were now flowing into the Columbia basin in unstoppable numbers, an American colony had lately been founded at the head of Puget Sound, a spontaneously established American government was exercising jurisdiction throughout the territory with the compliance of Bay officials, and—the most telling factor of all—the Americans could and likely would bring more force to bear in the arena of threatened conflict than the British could possibly have mustered. The time had come for John Bull to retract his horns.

One sticking point remained—open British navigation of the Columbia. Since the possibility of such a concession had been brought up by Edward Everett earlier in the Oregon talks, it now became "a point of honor," Aberdeen advised McLane, that such a right be granted in return for the British cession of all the territory between the lower Columbia and the forty-ninth parallel, where hardly 100 Americans resided. But McLane, who played a heroic role throughout the settlement struggle, made his final contribution by persuading the Peel government, just before sending off its proposal to Washington, not to ask for a blanket grant of free navigation rights on the river for all British subjects but instead to ask that they be limited to the Hudson's Bay Company and its customers.

Peel's proposal left England by steamer on May 19, more than three weeks after the outbreak of hostilities between the United States and Mexico along the Rio Grande—but ten days before the news reached London. Polk, poised to ask Congress for a declaration of war against Mexico but mindful of widespread opposition to a two-front war if the Oregon conflict remained, was thus forced to make a choice: either swallow the modified Columbia navigation provision or make a counterproposal to Britain that might well be declined, especially in view of the clash with Mexico now under way and its likely drain on American resources. Even a gifted manipulator like Polk saw he really had no choice. Despite a last-minute, non-sensical flip-flop by Buchanan, an early adherent of the 54°40′ cry and thereafter a strong advocate of conciliation, to demand more territory from the British, the President sent the Peel/Aberdeen treaty proposal to the Senate without any recommendation. On June 12 the upper chamber of Congress urged the President, by a 37–12 vote, to accept the British offer with no modifications. Polk accepted the advice, signed the treaty three days later, and the Senate ratified it, 41–14, three days after that. The Oregon treaty, ratified by Parliament immediately after its repeal of the Corn Laws, was the final measure put forward by the Peel ministry before it was voted out of office in the British tradition of firing prime ministers who had prevailed upon the nation to make painful but necessary compromises.

Thus, James Polk achieved the first item on his wish list, and the territory of the United States had grown by 286,541 square miles. By the time Oregon was officially organized as a federal territory in 1849, it was home to not quite 12,000 white residents. The following year the territorial legislature passed the Donation Land Claim Act, granting 640 free acres to every married couple that wanted them. So many did that by 1853 the northern sector of the region was detached and designated the separate Territory of Washington. By the end of the decade, when Oregon became the nation's thirty-third state, it numbered more than 50,000 residents. Washington and Idaho, the other two whole states to be carved from the Oregon Territory, would require another forty years before entering the Union. Although lovely Puget Sound would emerge as a busy seaport complex centered in Seattle, it would be surpassed in size and commercial importance by Vancouver, just thirty miles north of the forty-ninth parallel and the bustling capital of the gloriously scenic Canadian province of British Columbia, no part of which James Polk managed—and never really expected—to pry loose from John Bull.

CHAPTER II

The lost virtue of their better days

1846–1850

THE GREAT IRONY OF JAMES K. POLK'S career as territorial expansionist extraordinaire, the one-term President under whom the United States acquired more land than any other, is that he was personally the least expansive of men.

A slight, clenched, deeply suspicious individual, he was a classic stay-at-home, certainly when compared with the Founding Fathers and his predecessors in the White House. All had seen a good deal of America, and a number of them—Franklin, the Adamses, Jefferson, and Monroe—knew much of Europe. The determinedly insular Polk knew nothing beyond a narrow belt of the middle South and Washington, hardly a cosmopolitan place at the time; the farthest he ventured was an occasional trip to his Mississippi plantation. He never went to Europe, never saw the wildly beautiful western reaches of North America that he so coveted for his country. He never served in the military, never went in for fun and games, was rarely seen even to smile. His idea of a high old time was to take a brisk walk or horseback ride at dawn or dusk—and while President, he infrequently found time for even these escapes from his duties. He was so immersed in the minutiae of the nation's highest office that he almost never took a vacation or a whole day off—though he did go to a Presbyterian church some Sundays with his wife, Sarah. He did not read for pleasure or to broaden his frame of reference; as a result, he squinted xenophobically at the world and perceived political issues in stark black and white. To him, all Whigs were blackguards, fellow Democrats who challenged his policies were traitors, abolitionists were wicked, the British were predatory bullies, and the Mexicans, like other nonwhite peoples and races, were unworthy of and ill-equipped for democracy.

And yet James Polk, longtime Andrew Jackson stooge, party hatchet-man, and pedestrian thinker, in a feat of colossal and altogether unexpected imagination, came to power consumed by a grand vision of a continental nation that he intended to see realized within the single presidential term he had allotted himself. And no foreign power would be permitted to stand in the way of America's destined ascent to global greatness. If that meant war, then he would wage it, though he had no experience in military matters and scant respect for professional warriors. He nonetheless understood what war was, and knowing the strength of the British, he managed to avoid war with them over Oregon. Knowing the weakness of the Mexicans, he all but invited combat with them to gain the American Southwest. And when the war came with Mexico, he supposed that its fractious, woebegone people would thank him for liberating them from their long suffering at the hands of military tyrants, demonic clerics, corrupt bureaucrats, and a disdainful landed gentry. What Polk failed to understand was that the Mexicans' fierce pride in their nationhood was the binding element in their survival as a sovereign people.

The appropriation of Mexico's heartland and subjugation of its people were never Polk's purpose. Having all but ensured the inclusion of Texas within the Union by his election to the presidency and then stared down the British to gain all of Oregon that the nation could usefully digest, the President now dedicated himself to winning American dominion over the fragrant, primeval Shangri-la that formed the choicest stretch of the hemisphere's Pacific shoreline. California, with its dazzling, craggy 800-mile coast, long, lush central valley quilted between two soaring mountain ranges, and an ideal climate for growing fruits, grains, and vegetables of infinite variety, had languished in its virtually unspoiled state of nature since Spanish explorers had claimed it in 1542. The mostly Franciscan fathers who intruded on this paradise starting in 1769, by extending a chain of twenty-one missions and attached farms close to the coast, imposed a semi-feudal social order on the docile Indians and, in the name of saving their souls, reduced them to peons to tend the mission crops. European diseases did the rest of the damage.

The church's domination over California eased with the coming of the Mexican War of Independence and the republic's imposed secularization of the missions, aimed at fostering increased settlement and economic development in a region remote from the core of the nation. The ripest mission holdings were sold off to the few wealthy settlers of Spanish ancestry, but the Mexican government lacked the financial resources and personnel to superintend the far northern section of the country and encourage its colonization. Federal authority was loosely imposed, if at all, by a few hundred soldiers, many lately released convicts with still larcenous tendencies, and governors of often lax morals. Visitors were struck by the absence of commercial farming in so fertile a countryside, a veritable Garden of Eden with natural orchards abounding. Whether the lassitude or ignorance of the residents or the difficulty of transporting perishable goods was more responsible for such a colossal waste was debatable, but instead of overflowing croplands, the California economy was based on cattle, which needed little tending in a land of endless, perpetual pastures. The principal exports of the slumbering region were cowhides and tallow.

Pained by their loss of Texas after inviting American settlers to colonize that similarly underpopulated province, Mexican authorities were wary of admitting foreigners to California, except as a commercial necessity—and then only when they cooperated closely with government officials. Thus, in 1832, Thomas O. Larkin, a transplanted Bostonian, was allowed to open a highly lucrative import-export business out of picturesque Monterey, the busiest harbor on the California coast. Soon afterward failed Swiss businessman John A. Sutter was granted a 50,000-acre spread in the Sacramento Valley and turned it into a bustling, if financially overextended, commercial operation, the only inland hub in the province. For the most part, though, Mexican officialdom was invisible, and residents of mixed Spanish and Indian blood—*los californios*—enjoyed their relative autonomy until Santa Anna rolled back the 1824 federalist constitution and his centralist regime tried to assert dominion over outlying regions. The result was an 1836 rebellion against corrupt officers and tax collectors sent to California to hector the locals—much as the Texans found the national government's new outreach program to be oppressive, but in this case the rebels were Mexican citizens. The *californios* then established their own provincial authority, paying lip service and a modicum of taxes in tribute to the national government in return for virtual self-rule.

This pleasantly loose governance had one serious drawback: it could not stem the slowly growing encroachment of Americans, who by the early 1840s were picking their way through the Rockies, veering south off the Oregon Trail, and staking out farms in the Sacramento and San Joaquin valleys of the California interior, even though that often meant squatting on unpoliced Mexican soil. By 1845, California's population did not exceed 50,000—and may have been only half that size—with twice as many Indians as Mexicans and perhaps 1,500 foreigners, most of them Americans. It was a huge human vacuum. The dearth of civil authority in the final decade of California's Mexican era was evidenced by what historian Kevin Starr has described as "a confusion of revolution, counterrevolution, graft, spoliation, and social disintegration as Northern and Southern factions struggled for power in a series of internecine clashes" that even the most patient scholarly research cannot unravel.

This politically volatile and economically stagnant environment, it was plain to foreign observers, would not remain so for long. Because the constant woes destabilizing the national government left Mexico's landlocked military forces without sufficient manpower and resources to police far-off California, it was highly vulnerable to penetration by British maritime interests, which had gained commercial hegemony in the Oregon Country but been thwarted in their hope of winning similar trade advantages in Texas. The lure of a potentially vast and lucrative Asian trade had already caused a collision of British and French naval forces competing for mid-Pacific bases in Hawaii and Tahiti and drawn expressions of concern from the United States, fearful that the European powers might try to colonize coastal California before American settlers could arrive in sufficient numbers to ensure its eventual annexation. Presidents John Quincy Adams, Jackson, and Polk himself, through John Slidell's doomed peace mission to Mexico City at the end of 1845, had tried to buy all or part of California, arguing that the almost empty province was too removed from metropolitan Mexico ever to become an integral part of the nation. But the Mexicans had disdained all such direct overtures.

Their unwillingness to part with California, however, was betrayed by their inability to protect it from encroachment by foreigners. Overextended and underequipped to exercise hegemony, Mexico had all but invited the seizure of its paradise by the Pacific. The only question was when. Had the United States done nothing to hasten the process, California might have followed the pattern of Texas and Oregon, where free-flowing immigration led inevitably to American domination. But the path to the far side of the continent was long and torturous, and California was so prized that officials in Washington were anxious to speed the immigration process before Britain or an alliance of European powers, perhaps in league with the needy Mexican government, could provide the means to keep the seductive land out of American hands.

One highly useful agent in this effort by the United States was a daring young southern adventurer, John Charles Frémont, who began a series of explorations into the Far West in the early 1840s, undertaken like the Lewis and Clark expedition forty years before as an allegedly scientific foray into the wilderness but in fact a military and geopolitical reconnaissance to promote the extension of American settlement. Frémont, under the auspices of the U.S. Army's Topographical Corps and the patronage of his father-in-law, U.S. Senator Tom Benton, the most incessant champion of westward expansion in Congress, mapped the mountains, rivers, valleys, and best fort sites between the Rockies and the Pacific, eventually finding his way, after a reckless midwinter crossing of the Sierras, to John Sutter's compound near the Sacramento River. Most of the time, Frémont and his nervy band were trespassing on Mexican territory. His findings, invaluably enhanced by the companionship of Christopher "Kit" Carson, the most resourceful guide in the wild and perilous West, were recorded in a pair of travel books Frémont composed with the help of his wife, Jessie. These often lyrical, best-selling accounts, which established Frémont's dashing, nationally recognized persona as "the Pathfinder," served, like Harvard dropout Richard Henry Dana's paean to the allurements of California, *Two Years Before the Mast,* to entice Americans toward that coastal bower, which, in contrast to Oregon, belonged to another country. James Polk meant to remedy that technicality as soon as possible.

NEITHER THE DEMOCRATIC PARTY platform on which Polk ran in 1844 nor his inaugural address in March of the following year made any mention of American yearnings for California, but getting it was very much on the new President's mind. He confided as much during his first days in the White House to Secretary of the Navy George Bancroft, a former Harvard history professor. So long as the Oregon crisis with Britain remained unsettled, however, and Texas had not yet formally accepted Congress's offer of statehood, Polk's craving for California had to remain a clandestine passion; otherwise, the British were likely to be heard from, perhaps with a show of might by the royal navy cruising the Pacific coastal waters.

Unlike his Whig foes, Polk and his expansionist allies among the Democrats had little fear that the territory beyond the Rockies was too far away for inclusion in the already sprawling American republic. The arrival of the magnetic telegraph to speed communication and growing use of steam-powered transportation to shorten travel time fed the promise of a viable transcontinental union in the near, if not immediate, future. The Polk administration's spokesman in the press, the *Washington Union,* was less inhibited than the President about announcing his territorial ambitions. "The way to California will be open to us," the newspaper commented as the annexation of Texas was about to be realized. "Who will stay the march of our western people?"

The Mexicans and the British were the only plausible roadblocks, and Polk was more concerned about the latter. Reports had reached Washington from Monterey, where merchant Thomas Larkin was doubling as U.S. consul in California, that Britain was prepared to step in and aid the *californios* if they chose to renounce their nominal allegiance to the government in Mexico City. The *centralistas* had done nothing to provide them safety, education, or economic opportunity, and the government's scattered soldiers were mostly lazy, thieving rascals. Indeed, rumor had it that Santa Anna, before losing power in 1844, had approached British officials to sell them California by way of settling Mexico's $50 million debt to British bondholders. Since Britain had failed to bring Texas within its commercial orbit, there was reason to suppose London would press harder for economic influence, if not territorial control, over California, either in tandem with the Mexicans or directly with a breakaway independent regime. The prospect of California becoming, by choice or necessity, a British protectorate alarmed Larkin, who had envisioned instead the province's conversion into an independent republic of natives and foreigners enjoying equal status and evolving sooner rather than later into an American state, as Texas had done. Larkin's concern, as well as Washington's, was heightened by reliable reports circulating in Mexico City that the British consul and private British financiers were pursuing generous land grants in California by the Mexican government to English and Irish settlers who would serve as a barrier to American designs on the region. The plan was scuttled by, among others, the British foreign secretary, Lord Aberdeen, who several times rose in Parliament to deny that Britain had any intentions to fill the power vacuum in California. Certainly the British ministry had little confidence in any collaborative arrangement with the Mexican government, which had shown itself incapable of defending or commercially exploiting California. And why, after all the acrimony with the United States over Oregon, would the British invite renewed discord over California, where they had no historical claims or other grounds for intruding?

Aberdeen's disclaimers notwithstanding, Polk seized upon the potential British menace to play a more active, if still covert, hand in California. He summoned bold, glory-seeking Captain Frémont in that summer of 1845 and sent the Pathfinder on his most purposeful mission yet. Accompanied by 62 men, 200 pack animals, and 250 head of cattle—quite a formidable assemblage for a mere mapmaking expedition—Frémont was assigned to chart the least arduous routes for American settlers to reach the Pacific and, more important, according to his memoirs, was told "if needed, to foil England by carrying the war now imminent with Mexico into the territory of California." At about that same time the President sent instructions to Commodore John D. Sloat, commander of the U.S. Navy's seven-vessel Pacific

Squadron, to be on the alert for any authoritative report that war with Mexico had begun and, upon receiving it, to waste no time in seizing San Francisco Bay and any other California harbors his fleet could capture. They were to take pains to assure the locals that they were being liberated from Mexican tyranny.

Polk might not have been eager to go to war with Mexico, but he was so indifferent to the Mexican state of mind over the American takeover of Texas that he carried out a series of provocations making a clash of arms all but certain. If it came to it, Polk was confident, the Mexicans would prove no better at fighting a war than at running a government. Their soldiers were poorly trained and equipped, their officers incompetent and of shallow loyalty, they had a tiny and inept navy, and the Mexican authorities were at odds with the European powers over debts and other commercial issues, so none of them seemed likely to rush military aid to Mexico in the event of war with the United States. Polk thus supposed any conflict with Mexico would be short-lived and, as a highly desirable fringe benefit, would sanction the United States to retain title to any Mexican territory it conquered as a legitimate trophy under the international rules of war.

Polk's first anti-Mexican provocation was to supersede the joint congressional resolution granting statehood to Texas by announcing that his administration fully subscribed to the wildly expansive 1836 Texas Boundary Act, claiming for the newly independent republic far vaster territory than Texas had ever embraced under Spanish and Mexican rule. Congress had left open the boundary issue for settlement by future negotiations between the United States and Mexico. By way of reassuring Texas legislators and voters, then on the brink of deciding whether to accept statehood, that their rights would be best protected as full-fledged American citizens, Polk asserted that he would "not permit an invading army to occupy a foot of the soil East of [above] the Rio Grande."

Polk's pledge at once raised two serious issues. First, as designated by Mexico's 1824 constitution, the boundary between Texas and its neighboring states to the south, Tamaulipas and Nuevo León, was the Nueces River, which emptied into the Gulf of Mexico 120 miles north of the Rio Grande. Maps from the Spanish imperial era also failed to support the 1836 claim by the Texas Congress that its southwestern boundary was the Rio Grande. The barren Nueces Strip between the two rivers, extending inland about 300 miles and averaging 100 miles in width, with a small Mexican population and no American inhabitants, was never occupied by Texas soldiers during the rebellion from Mexico. On what basis, then, other than Texan bravado did Polk claim the Rio Grande as the American-Mexican border?

An equally pressing question was how far up the 1,900-mile course of the Rio Grande was Polk claiming the Texas (and thus American) boundary extended? The upper Rio Grande ran a little to the west of Santa Fe and continued into Colorado, so that Polk's open-ended endorsement of the old Texas Boundary Act, if taken literally, would have expropriated, among other territories, the larger part of modern New Mexico as well as the 30,000-square-mile Nueces Strip. Just in case the Mexicans took the new American President's words for bluster, in mid-June—a few weeks before Texas had officially chosen to become American territory—Polk ordered tough old Indian fighter Zachary Taylor to lead several thousand U.S. Army regulars across the Nueces to encamp "along the western frontier of Texas . . . on or near the Rio Grande del Norte . . . [at a site] best suited to repel invasion, and to protect what, in the event of annexation, will be our [south]western border." The War Department warned General Taylor not to attack any Mexican troops in the disputed territory, but after the Texas Congress had ratified annexation in mid-July and Mexico severed diplomatic relations with the United States, Washington grew less tentative and sent reinforcements to increase troop strength to 4,000 in Taylor's camp at Corpus Christi, just within the Nueces Strip. It was not a conciliatory act. In mid-October, Polk ratcheted up the border tension by ordering Taylor to shift his troops closer to the Rio Grande and to consider any movement in force by Mexican troops across that river—into what Mexico considered its own territory—to constitute "commencement of hostilities."

Not for nothing, then, did Whig newspapers charge Polk with "a taunting aggression" in unilaterally defining the new boundary with Mexico. Unhappy at being labeled a warmonger, the President hoped, without in the least backing down from the Rio Grande boundary claim, to reach an understanding with the newly chosen Mexican president, José Joaquín de Herrera, a moderate of sound judgment who did not indulge in outcries against American treachery. Through diplomatic channels Herrera was asked if his government would accept an American envoy with full powers to discuss all outstanding issues between the two countries. To Mexican officials that meant settling the boundary question—period. To Polk, the boundary was not open for discussion, but as a peace gesture, he and Secretary of State Buchanan instructed John Slidell, the envoy they chose for the mission to Mexico City, to place a price tag on Mexican acceptance of the Rio Grande border.

In 1841, after fifteen years of trying, the United States had won a judgment from an international tribunal led by the king of Prussia, awarding a bit over $2 million (out of $8.5 million claimed) to American citizens for property damage and losses suffered in the course of nonstop civil strife in Mexico dating back to the creation of the republic. Had their national character been even half as litigious as the Americans', the Mexicans might well have counterclaimed for reparations from the United States for its citizens' (and expatriates') seizure of the province of Texas and the collateral damage to the lives and property of Mexican citizens resulting from the insurrection, to which the American government had raised no objection. Instead, Mexico agreed to the compensation payments, provided they were spread over five years. But after two years, the pauper Mexican treasury suspended the payback. Slidell was now to tell Herrera's government that the United States was prepared to assume Mexico's debt to American citizens if it would accept a Rio Grande boundary running some 600 miles upriver to El Paso. And if Mexico was thus inclined to be cooperative, the United States would pay as much as $30 million—Slidell was told he might go even higher if necessary—for extending the boundary along the thirty-second parallel near El Paso all the way to the Pacific, thereby transforming the Mexican provinces of New Mexico and Alta California (comprising the modern states of California, Nevada, Utah, Arizona, and New Mexico and parts of Colorado and Wyoming) into United States territory. Such an adjustment, when added to acceptance of the annexation of Texas, would have reduced the total area of Mexico by about 40 percent.

Recognizing the unlikelihood that such a sweeping proposition would be welcomed, Buchanan urged Slidell to negotiate for any part of the desired territory the Mexicans might be willing to part with and to reduce the American offering price accordingly. Even a partial agreement, the State Department reasoned, would be far better than the constant friction that had marked Mexican-American relations during the nine-year life of the Texas republic. And Mexico would certainly benefit from whatever payment it would receive for surrendering the most remote, least populous part of its unmanageably extended territory, larger than any in Europe except Russia's.

What Polk and his people did not, or chose not to, understand was that for Mexicans, conveying parts of their country—at any price—to the grasping, offensive Americans was like selling their souls to the devil. If Herrera had considered the idea even briefly, Mexico's throng of militarists and ultranationalists would have had his head. Just how badly the United States had miscalculated Mexico's receptivity to a land deal became evident when Slidell, as noted earlier, presented diplomatic credentials that identified him not merely as a special envoy sent to solve the boundary problem but as a minister plenipotentiary. Receiving him with such a rank, Herrera objected, was tantamount to agreeing in advance to the reestablishment of diplomatic relations between the two countries when that very issue depended upon satisfactory settlement of the boundary question. Mexico's sovereign dignity precluded such an arrangement. Slidell was asked to have his papers adjusted to meet the Mexican objection.

Here now was Polk's second provocation. The United States had already taken Texas away from Mexico—the only question was how big a bite of Mexico that would amount to—and it could easily have displayed a little tact and patience by yielding to the Mexicans' wounded pride over what amounted to a mere diplomatic technicality. Polk and the State Department had probably not intended to show disrespect by commissioning Slidell as a minister of the highest rank—perhaps the very opposite was their purpose—but in declining to heed Herrera's request, they failed entirely to appreciate the pressure the Mexican president was under not to exhibit weakness in the face of American boldness. For Herrera just to agree to meet with Polk's emissary took courage. And even though the cautious Mexican president steadfastly refused to accept Slidell's unrevised credentials for the duration of the American envoy's visit to his country, Herrera was ousted from office at the end of the year by Mariano Paredes, the warlord-in-waiting, merely on the suspicion that he might have been contemplating a settlement with the Americans.

Even assuming the U.S. government had innocently offended Mexico's notion of diplomatic protocol, one may wonder what Polk could have lost by ordering Slidell's papers altered to accommodate the needs of the Mexican peace party. With each passing week it grew clearer that the President's stubbornness—he would have termed it steadfastness—was succeeding only in ensuring the failure of Slidell's mission. That all-but-certain outcome invites the surmise that Polk had never wanted the mission to succeed in the first place and that he knew very well that the offers Slidell had brought with him, had they been heard, would have been summarily rejected. If Polk had donned the mantle of peaceseeker just to disarm his critics, the Mexican refusal to receive Slidell served the President's purpose quite as well, allowing him to proclaim righteously that Mexico had insulted the United States by rescinding—and on the flimsiest of pretexts—its willingness to negotiate their differences. Then, citing the flagrant disrespect shown to his peace envoy as justification, the President sent orders to Taylor on January 13, 1846, to advance his forces entirely across the Nueces Strip and to establish a fort on the north bank of the Rio Grande—Polk's third provocation.

Three months later, with the guns of Taylor's newly erected Fort Brown, a few miles inland from the Gulf, staring down across the Rio Grande at the lively Mexican city of Matamoros, Polk ordered U.S. warships in the Gulf to blockade the mouth of the river. Within a week, President Paredes issued a denunciation of the United States for ten years of injuries to and attacks on the Mexican people and called it "an urgent necessity" for his 12,000 or so soldiers near the Rio Grande to dislodge Taylor's invading host. "From this day defensive war begins," he trumpeted. Two days later, on April 25, after Taylor had refused a Mexican ultimatum to abandon his position on the Rio Grande and his counterproposal for armistice talks was likewise spurned, a large Mexican force crossed the Rio Grande and ambushed a scouting party of sixty-three American soldiers about twenty-five miles upriver from Taylor's fort, killing eleven of them, wounding five, and taking the rest prisoner.

Polk had plainly dared the Mexicans to draw first blood, and now they had obliged him. It was a lure that cooler heads, such as those running the British empire, would have resisted. Mexico could have received Slidell and heard him out, tolerating his exalted title as simply a minor discourtesy. Mexico could have agreed to acknowledge, ten years after the fact, the loss of Texas and even to yield the only partly fertile Nueces Strip, if the United States would settle for a boundary that ran only partway up the Rio Grande and pledge not to claim or connive for more Mexican territory. But Mexico's national policies were ruled more by passion than logic—how else to explain the April 25 bloodletting along the Rio Grande that was sure to bring on a war likely to prove suicidal for Mexico? After all, Mexican forces had not managed to thrash Sam Houston's tiny, backpedaling Texas rabble a decade earlier; they could hardly now be expected to vanquish the far mightier, richer, and more populous United States of America. Some Mexican militarists, ill-informed and wishful, had been harboring the hope that the Oregon crisis would soon plunge the United States into war with the British, who would then naturally side with Mexico and lend it military assistance to block American expansionism. But the Oregon dispute was settled within weeks of the Mexican attack across the Rio Grande, giving Polk a free hand to pursue his military options without fear the British might take up Mexico's cause.

Some Americans saw in the peaceful Oregon settlement a strong recommendation for a less, not more, belligerent policy toward Mexico. The *Chicago Democrat* spoke for them in asking, "Why should we not compromise our difficulties with Mexico as well as Great Britain? . . . If it is wicked to go to war with England for disputed territory, it is not only wicked but cowardly to go to war with Mexico for the same reason." Polk, of course, pointed to the Slidell mission as a good-faith effort to reach an accord with Mexico and contended, in a war message to Congress sent the week after learning of the Rio Grande ambush, that the rebuff to the American peace envoy was but the latest evidence of the Mexicans' unwillingness to compromise. And there were other ongoing gestures of disrespect for the United States, the President asserted, such as Mexico's two-year arrearage in the payment of $2 million of adjudicated debts to American citizens who had suffered "long continued and unredressed grievances." Mexico, moreover, had made repeated threats to exact military vengeance for the annexation of Texas, requiring Polk, he later explained, to station Taylor's troops along the Rio Grande to defend American jurisdiction over the Nueces Strip—clearly the President's duty since Texas had officially become a state by then. And now, he said, stirring Congress's zeal for steely countermeasures, America's "cup of forebearance" had been drained because "after reiterated menaces, Mexico has passed the boundary of the United States, has invaded our territory and shed American blood upon the American soil. She has proclaimed that hostilities have commenced and that [our] two nations are now at war." The war existed "by the act of Mexico herself," Polk asserted, "not withstanding all our efforts to avoid it."

Which efforts were those? Endorsing Texas's unilaterally declared Rio Grande border and instructing Slidell that it was non-negotiable? Refusing to adjust Slidell's provocative diplomatic credentials? Occupying and fortifying the Nueces Strip and blockading the Rio Grande? Insisting that Mexico owed American citizens for property damage incurred during its civil wars but not conceding that the United States, now that Texas was part of it, owed anything to Mexican citizens for property losses sustained during the Texas rebellion? Polk, for all his disingenuous insistence to the contrary, was the more culpable party in the making of the war. He had not only provoked the Mexicans to strike first but, instead of downplaying the April ambush as an unfortunate border incident and responding to it in kind, had chosen to escalate the encounter into a full-scale war. As fixated as the Mexicans were on defending their national honor at all costs, Polk was still more arrantly swept up in his singleminded mission to extend the American dominion from sea to sea. Playing the wounded party with the greater grievances was his way to excuse the vehemence of his quest.

THE PRESIDENT WAS NOT UNOPPOSED in his Mexican pursuit, although the votes in Congress in favor of his request for $10 million and 50,000 volunteer soldiers to carry out the war were so lopsided—174 to 14 in the House and 40 to 2 in the Senate—that it almost seemed so. Northern Whigs and some southern ones who were antiexpansionist by conviction, abolitionists and others opposed to extending slavery in an expanded Union, and pacifists and those generally holding the United States to a higher moral standard than the Old World's monarchies all spoke out against Polk. He had indulged in distortions, half-truths, and outright falsehoods, they charged, in grossly overstating the American case for going to war against Mexico. Their most eloquent spokesman in Congress was Representative Joshua R. Giddings, an Ohio Whig, who would repeatedly assert that Polk had "without provocation . . . and without right" planted the American flag on foreign soil in a war of conquest against a weak sister republic, using military force "to violate every principle of international law and of moral justice." The President, Giddings contended, had committed a national crime, robbing Americans of "[t]he virtue of our better days."

But most Americans, believing their better days still lay ahead of them, rallied behind Polk's call to arms. Mass meetings of support assembled in major cities with the cry "Ho, for the halls of Montezuma!" vibrating in the air as thousands of volunteers flocked to the colors. All the previous wars of the American people had been fought, as their subsequent ones would be— in name, at least—to defend their liberties and those of others. Polk was able to propel them into their only war waged explicitly for territorial gain because of three reasons in particular.

By the latter half of the 1840s, Americans were feeling their oats. Their population was approaching 25 million, the hard times that had begun in the late 1830s were receding, industrialization was moving beyond its infancy, and technology was shrinking the great distances of America's hinterland. Migration to the free or dirt-cheap western lands looked more inviting now and lifted national prospects as a rising global power. The United States, moreover, had not fought a war for a generation, and the expansionist impulse captured in the catchphrase "manifest destiny" continued to heat up American patriotism—witness the "Fifty-four forty or fight!" outcry that had been stifled by the Oregon settlement and left many still spoiling for a bloody brawl. That overflow of testosterone afflicted some unlikely advocates of combat, including *Brooklyn Eagle* editor Walt Whitman, better known as the poet laureate of universal brotherhood but who now wrote, "Yes: Mexico must be thoroughly chastised" and that the time had come for the world to realize that "America knows how to crush . . . as well as how to expand."

Whitman's words reflected the third and least attractive of the elements spurring the nation to war on Mexico. Of that country's total population, only about one-sixth were white, more than half were Indian, and the balance were of mixed blood. White Americans, from colonial days on, had never shown their willingness to live at peace and on equal terms with those of other races, choosing instead to exterminate, enslave, marginalize, or otherwise abuse them, and justifying their actions by alleging their victims' natural inferiority. Their own compulsion to amass property and dominion went unmentioned. The Mexicans, of preponderantly swarthy cast, were a sitting target for virulent American racism. Their mixed blood made them a degraded people and explained, satisfactorily for many in the United States, the low Mexican character: they were portrayed as dumb, lazy, untrustworthy, and doomed to wither away, like the American Indians. And like the native tribes, the Mexicans made poor use of their land, letting idyllic California, for example, wither on the vine. James Polk was telling the Mexicans, not in quite so many words, that the United States could do wonders with California, so they had better sell it to the Americans or the United States would take it away.

America's racist attitude toward Mexico could not be written off as primarily the bias of the disadvantaged and ignorant classes. Assumptions of Anglo-Saxon supremacy were widely held, even by many of the nation's most accomplished figures, including opinion shapers in politics, the press, and academia. Typical were the views in a popular 1840 book, *Travels in the Great Western Prairies* by attorney T. J. Farnham, who called the Mexicans "a pusillanimous . . . race of men, and unfit to control the destinies of that beautiful country." Richard Henry Dana found the Mexican *californios* "an idle, thriftless people." Polk's Secretary of the Treasury, Robert J. Walker, erstwhile Senator from Mississippi, denounced the "barbarous tyranny . . . and superstitions of Mexico" and said it would be folly to tolerate the establishment of "this ignorant and fanatical colored population on the borders of the United States." Nor was this vile attitude merely a regional prejudice. Even Secretary of State Buchanan of Pennsylvania alluded to Mexicans as "an imbecile and indolent" race. What nation, then, were red-blooded, two-fisted American WASPs more entitled to beat up and take land away from than scrofulous Mexico?

The other side of that racist coin suggested a nobler motive for the American assault on Mexican territory—a moral crusade to lift neighbors from their degraded state, teach them how to sustain a truly democratic constitutional republic, with respect for the rule of law, and bring an end to military tyranny, religious intolerance, government by chicanery, and chronic factional dissension. Some Americans, with a straight face, endorsed this rationalization for the Mexican conflict even while acknowledging that no one had invited such an exercise in missionary zeal. Still, it was not an entirely ludicrous proposition, given that General Paredes, Mexico's militarist president at the outset of the war, was talking up the possibility of installing a monarchist government to stabilize his nation—an idea supported by reactionary church leaders and endorsed by influential European interests operating in Mexico City.

James Polk was not about to proclaim the improvement of the Mexican character or the purification of Mexican politics as his reasons for going to war—any more than he revealed publicly to Congress or the American people his real reason for doing so. But he left no doubt in the minds of his cabinet members and others in or close to his administration what he was up to.

Late in 1845, as the Mexican crisis heated up, Polk heard from U.S. consul Thomas Larkin in Monterey that British personnel were urging local authorities and commercial interests to cast off Mexican rule and establish California as an independent republic committed not to join the United States in return for Britain's protection. Larkin's report, which proved to be groundless, was sufficiently unsettling for the President to dispatch new and more pointed directives to his key players in the Far West. Commodore Robert F. Stockton, a vigorous expansionist from a politically and financially prominent New Jersey family, was ordered to sail his frigate from the Gulf of Mexico to Monterey, where he was to rendezvous with Pacific Squadron commander Sloat and tell him and Larkin to be of all possible assistance to rebel elements seeking to separate California from Mexican sovereignty. The American officials were to "render her all the kind offices in our power, as a sister Republic" but to emphasize that the United States would not stand idly by and let independent California slide under British domination. Secretary of State Buchanan added that if the inhabitants of California chose to join the United States, they "would be received as brethren, whenever this can be done without affording Mexico just cause of complaint." Polk also directed a young, Spanish-speaking army officer, Lieutenant Archibald H. Gillespie, disguised as a liquor merchant, to take the fastest route—by ship to Veracruz, overland across Mexico, and by ship again up the Pacific coast—to find Captain John Frémont, then traversing the Sierras on his way to reconnoiter eastern California. Which is to say that Frémont and his band of bearded mountain men, masquerading as a scientific expedition, were in fact American agitators in a foreign land. Gillespie's message from the President confirmed and strengthened the instructions Frémont had heard from Polk's lips the summer before: do whatever he could to secure California in the interests of the United States—none of Buchanan's niceties about not offending Mexico applied—and to push the *californios* toward secession and eventual American annexation.

The outbreak of hostilities with Mexico freed Polk from further beating around the bush. At a cabinet meeting in mid-May, right after Democratic loyalists stampeded his war bill through Congress, Secretary Buchanan made the astonishingly obtuse proposal that, in order to deter Britain and any other like-minded European power from intervening on the Mexican side, American embassies ought to circulate a memo worldwide, vowing that the United States harbored no territorial ambitions in Mexico and had gone to war with its southern neighbor for defensive purposes only. Polk, who supposed his expansionist mission was transparent to his inner circle, bristled. Such a disclaimer, an insult to the world's intelligence in view of the land-gobbling propensity of the United States, would have made the President an international laughingstock. To educate Buchanan in artful dissembling, Polk purveyed his standard cover story: territory was the only currency Mexico had at its disposal to repay its delinquent debt to American citizens, so it was surely fair game for U.S. forces to seize in combat. Then, in case Buchanan remained clueless, Polk said he would fight all the powers on the earth rather than make a pledge not to acquire Mexican territory if he could do so honorably. His definition of honor did not exclude bludgeoning a hopelessly mismatched adversary into submission.

If any doubt remained in Buchanan's or any other cabinet member's mind about his war aims, Polk ended it at the May 30 meeting at the White House when, according to his diary, "I declared my purpose to be to acquire for the United States California, New Mexico, and perhaps some others of the Northern Provinces of Mexico, whenever a peace was made. . . . [T]o secure that object military possession should with as little delay as possible be taken of all these Provinces." He added, hoping the Mexicans might greet their conquerors as deliverers from evil, that the conquest should be carried out "if possible with the consent of the inhabitants."

The inclusion of New Mexico on Polk's hit list was simple recognition that California, the glittering trophy that would make the United States a continental, two-ocean power, could not be left in detached limbo if and when it was pried loose from Mexican possession. Clearly, the intervening territory, from Texas—wherever its western boundary might finally be fixed—to the lower Colorado River, marking the de facto border between California and New Mexico, had to be annexed as well to make the United States a geographical whole. Comprising more than 275,000 square miles, two-thirds again as large as California, provincial New Mexico was, to American eyes, a big nothing. Mostly mountain and desert, arid and unforested, it had few people other than Indians and scant resources. Its only sizable settlement, the capital at Santa Fe, was a shabby trading center with a lively central plaza, but since it predated all other surviving European settlements in western North America, Polk had to have it.

To get California and New Mexico "with as little delay as possible," he had to overcome one not insignificant handicap: the United States did not have much of a standing army. And Polk was no enthusiast when it came to professional military men, favoring instead the American tradition of the citizen soldier who threw down his farm tools when the nation called, took up the gun, and routed any foe. Unfortunately, this arrangement, dependent on amateur volunteer forces, had not proven very effective during the War of 1812, and the U.S. Army in 1846 was still being run by aging veterans of that indecisive—indeed, nearly disastrous—conflict. Luckily, the army staff's highest-ranking officer, sixty-year-old Major General Winfield T. Scott, was regarded by all, starting with Scott himself, as the brightest military mind in the nation.

A six-foot-four package of energy and vanity, Scott towered over Polk physically and intellectually; the President took a strong dislike to him. To begin with, Scott was known to be a Whig, with presidential ambitions, and placing him in charge of field combat against Mexico would likely add to his heroic stature, which had its roots in his brilliant record as a young fighting officer in the 1812 war. It did not help that Scott was pompous, as obsessive as Polk about the details of his job, and fanatic in his insistence on military spit and polish; not for nothing did his subordinates call him "Old Fuss and Feathers" behind his back. Worst of all, Scott was not in the least deferential, lecturing the President to compensate for his nearly total ignorance about military matters. And Polk did not fully appreciate the main lesson Scott felt obliged to teach him: the United States could not fight and win a full-scale war over a huge theater of operations with a tossed-together army of amateurs. Men had to be trained and disciplined in weaponry and maneuvers in order to avoid blunders and heavy casualties, and that would take time. Polk, distrustful by nature, found him an insufferable perfectionist, but his qualifications for the top command could not be denied. After all, Scott had been a first-rate field officer, bravely contending with British forces along the Great Lakes, Canadians in the Aroostook Valley, and Seminoles in Florida; he had literally written the book on infantry tactics and turned the army, small as it still was, into a professional force partly by imposing standardized drill regulations.

While the President issued a call for 20,000 of the 50,000 volunteers Congress had authorized and Scott set about training them, Polk—who took his constitutionally mandated role as commander-in-chief literally—put in motion a military expedition to capture New Mexico with the nearest troops available for the job. Unfamiliar with the difficulties of the terrain in that remote region and in the dark about the number and battle-readiness of Mexican defenders of the vast province, the impatient Polk nonetheless directed Secretary of War William L. Marcy to create an "Army of the West" under Colonel Stephen W. Kearny, based at Fort Leavenworth on the Missouri frontier. Kearny was ordered to march over the Santa Fe Trail, seize New Mexico, and once it was secured, continue across the trackless desert to California and do what he could to subdue it as well.

To achieve this not inconsiderable objective, some 300 well-trained dragoons, or mounted soldiers, were available to Kearny, who was rated one of the soundest commanders in the army but had not been certified as a miracle worker. He was instructed to assemble recruits from his region, train them quickly, and head west with a force approximating 2,000. By July, the lilliputian Army of the West was on the trail, and it was hot out there. Hostile Indians and hungry wolves shadowed the progress of the hurriedly patched-together army, and water was scarce, but Kearny drove his men hard. The commandant at Santa Fe, who was also the governor of New Mexico, soon heard the Americans were coming and pleaded for reinforcements.

WHILE PREPARATIONS WERE AFOOT elsewhere for a far-ranging strike at Mexico's vulnerable northwestern provinces, Zachary Taylor's forces along the Rio Grande were charged with delivering a prompt reply to the April 25 Mexican ambush. But Taylor's men were outnumbered by Mexican troops who soon came pouring across the river above and below Fort Brown in a well-conceived pincer movement intended to cut off the Americans from their supply base at Point Isabel, about twenty-five miles to the northeast on the Gulf Coast. Low on ammunition and supplies, Taylor faced imminent disaster if he stayed in place, and he had failed to construct adequate defense works at Point Isabel to withstand a follow-up assault that could drive the American expeditionary force into the Gulf.

At sixty-two, Taylor was thought by some to be a used-up old warhorse, a longtime frontier Indian fighter who was Winfield Scott's polar opposite in most respects. Neither a heavy nor a quick thinker, lax about enforcing regulations—sanitary conditions in his camp were a nightmare and the sick list accordingly long—and tending toward shabbiness in his general's uniform, gruff, semiliterate "Old Rough and Ready" made an unimposing figure slouched with one leg slung over the pommel on his steed, Old Whitey. In his classic *The Year of Decision—1846,* Bernard De Voto offered this withering cameo of Taylor: "[H]e had no nerves, nothing recognizable as intelligence, he was afraid of nothing, and he was too unimaginative to know when he was being licked, which was fortunate since he did not know how to maneuver troops." An improviser rather than a battle planner, Taylor had basically a single tactic: attack, never retreat; he favored the bayonet over all weapons. His men loved his directness and gallantry and fought like blazes when he gave the signal.

Taylor's uncharacteristic signal just now, though, was to retreat—fast—before the Mexicans could cut off the main road back to Point Isabel. He left a small garrison to hold Fort Brown and was lucky that the Mexicans were slowed in crossing the river below the fort by a shortage of boats, allowing the bulk of Taylor's force to escape, bulk up the defenses at Point Isabel, and gather reinforcements, supplies, and artillery. After an ineffective bombardment of Fort Brown, the Mexicans chose not to launch an infantry attack that would surely have taken the citadel. Instead they concentrated their 4,000 or so troops on a broad, grassy plain called Palo Alto through which Taylor's 3,000 men would have to pass on their return to Fort Brown.

The May 8 battle that opened the war turned out to be anything but the hand-to-hand combat Taylor savored. His junior officers regretted that the grizzled commander had insisted on slowing the line of march with the supply train and artillery caissons instead of leaving them in the rear until the Mexican forces had been driven back across the Rio Grande. But it was the heavy American guns that carried the day, raking the colorfully arrayed Mexican ranks, in their bright shakos, saber sashes, and epaulets, while the enemy gunnery fell far short of Taylor's lines. Before long the American bombardment set the prairie grass ablaze, obscuring the battleground and sending the confused Mexicans into retreat. By the next day, however, they had regrouped, been reinforced, and fought off a frontal assault by the Americans at Resaca de la Palma. After meeting stiff initial resistance in the close, grisly combat that Taylor relished, his troops executed a flanking action through high chaparral that caused the Mexicans to falter while their commander, in his tent at the rear, failed to issue orders that might have prevented the rout. In the two-day battle, the American casualty toll was 120; the Mexicans, fleeing across the Rio Grande, had lost ten times as many. Within a few days, Taylor's men marched into Matamoros unopposed.

This opening triumph lulled American officials and the public into supposing that Mexican resistance would evaporate within a month or two and a peace accord would soon follow. Taylor's victories had the more salutary effect of convincing the European powers that the Mexicans had little chance to win the war and that foreign intervention to help them stave off the Americans would prove fruitless. Elated, Secretary of War Marcy sent word to Taylor "to prosecute the war with vigor, in the manner you deem most effective." That suited Taylor, who had no grand strategy and took his time building up his forces as more and more volunteers, thrilled by the news of the U.S. victories, flocked into his camp. The President urged Taylor to try to shorten the war by encouraging secessionist sentiment in Mexico's northern states. But the Mexican summer was hot, disease was rampant, and Taylor had no love of Polk, who reciprocated in kind, disliking him in large part because, like Scott, he was a Whig and fearing, with prescience, that public praise for the general's victories would enhance his stature as a war hero and boost his chances for the presidency. It was September before Taylor fought again.

By then, American military forces had gained control of California in a nearly bloodless conquest and proclaimed it U.S. territory. And they did so with a relative handful of men, never fielding as many as a thousand combatants in any of the encounters that marked the seemingly effortless takeover. The transition was achieved so painlessly—probably no more than a hundred Americans fell in the widespread campaign—because none of the forces opposed to them had the will, means, motive, or numbers to answer the shellburst of American encroachment.

There had been word the year before that the Mexican government was sending a 600-man contingent to reestablish active authority over rebellious California, but the effort fell apart before the group got anywhere near its destination. As a practical matter, Mexico had written off California as an autonomous province. But the *californios* themselves, left to their own resources, were not inclined to form a sovereign entity, as the Texans had done—that would have been disloyalty to their motherland, to which they still felt a cultural affinity even though it was incapable of nurturing them. Instead, the province continued to devolve into a patchwork of local satrapies whose chieftains declined to merge their jealously guarded domains into a civic union. And none of them had the money or charisma to enlist a large enough militia and supply it long enough to emerge as the undisputed leader of the province. Reports continued to circulate that the British would fill this void one way or another, for example, that the Mexican government would swap 50 million acres for colonizing if Britain would forgive Mexico's debts. President Paredes was said to have offered to mortgage all of California to Britain for financial aid to keep it out of the grasp of the United States. But there was never any firm evidence that the British were straying from Lord Aberdeen's repeated declarations of noninvolvement. All of which left the slumbering coastal colony open to American intrigue and usurpation. This prospect frankly appealed to some of the wealthiest natives, such as Mariano Vallejo, who owned 175,000 acres around Sonoma and reigned as unofficial regional vizier, and authorized immigrants like Sacramento Valley mogul John Sutter, who hoped American rule would be good for his—and everyone else's—business.

Thus, California beckoned as a very large, ripe plum for easy plucking by that vain, impulsive young glory-and-power-seeker, Captain John Frémont. He was as engaging in the drawing room as he was intrepid in leading his brotherhood of vagabond mounties, in the pay of the federal government, through some of the most rugged terrain on the continent into the golden land beside the far sea. By the spring of 1846, Frémont had made common cause with Sutter and, operating from a camp near the industrious Swiss's compound, ranged throughout northern California as far as the Oregon border, urging independence from Mexico upon American farmers, squatters, hunters, and drifters in the region as well as native *californios*. At times his gunslingers clashed with Mexican officials and military units that had begun rousting foreign illegals, but no pitched battles, only potshot skirmishing, ensued. Frémont's band was officially branded as foreign agitators and robbers after making off with horses that the local authorities had intended to use for rounding up alien troublemakers.

In May, after the war had begun but before word of it reached California, Lieutenant Gillespie, bearing letters from Frémont's wife and politically potent father-in-law and an oral message from the President, caught up with the Pathfinder near the Oregon border and gave him what he described in his memoirs as "the expected signal" from Washington. Frémont paraphrased Polk's directive thus: "The time has come. England must not get a foothold. We must be the first. Act discreetly, but positively." That very evening, three of Frémont's riders were butchered in their sleep by Indian raiders, and soon reports were rife throughout the Sacramento Valley that Mexican officials had put the Indians up to it as part of a concerted effort to terrorize and disperse foreign migrants. With heightened motivation and what he took to be a presidential command, Frémont began a more structured effort, seeking new enlistees, raising supplies, harassing Mexican authorities, and preaching insurrection. He allied his band with a group of local discontents who saw themselves as victims of Mexican persecution and took the name *los osos*—Spanish for "the bears"—after the neighborhood grizzlies whose fighting spirit they admired.

On the night of June 14, 1846, a mixed group of thirty-four riders composed of *osos* and some of Frémont's men, likely at his instigation but not under his personal command, clattered into the drowsy old garrison town of Sonoma and met no Mexican soldiers or other resisters. They quickly captured local baron Mariano Vallejo, who did not loudly object as the Americans proclaimed, with raffish solemnity, that the entire province was now the independent "California Republic." These words, along with a crude drawing of a grizzly—some wiseacres said it looked more like a pig—adorned the large red-and-white flag the rebels raised the next day in Sonoma's town square before issuing an earnest manifesto that promised freedom from Mexico's "military despotism." As a regular army officer, Frémont lingered in the background, unable to claim California for the United States until he had word that war with Mexico was under way. Soon his force of irregulars grew to several hundred, drawn by the secessionist proclamation, and moved to scare off what few Mexican soldiers remained in the countryside.

The U.S. Navy's Pacific Squadron under its hypercautious old commodore, John Sloat, arrived at Monterey in early July, by which time he had been apprised that the war with Mexico was officially on. But Sloat was wary of carrying out his standing orders to seize Monterey and other California harbors for fear that nearby British ships and their onboard forces might challenge any action he took. Before intervening he consulted with American consul Larkin on how best to conciliate the locals who had been unnerved by the Bear Flaggers' somewhat thuggish conduct north of San Francisco Bay. Sloat and Larkin together drew up a declaration aimed at coaxing the *californios* to end their lip-service allegiance to Mexico peaceably. It promised that under American authority they would enjoy full civil rights, low import duties, certified real-estate titles, and an end to corrupt government. The pledge satisfied the residents, who on July 7 welcomed ashore—or, at any rate, did not resist—a body of 225 U.S. sailors and marines from Sloat's fleet. As they raised the Stars and Stripes over the Monterey customhouse and the stucco homes and red-tile roofs of the pretty little town, American warships in the harbor loosed a twenty-gun salute signaling the transfer of sovereignty. The exercise was repeated a few days later by another of Sloat's ships putting in at the village of Yerba Buena at the head of the peninsula defining San Francisco Bay. On July 9 the Bear Flag came down in Sonoma and Old Glory replaced it; after a life cycle of twenty-five days, the California Republic was no more.

Frémont now took to signing his letters "Military Commander of United States Forces in California" and designated his men the California Battalion. While on a mission to salvage guns from an old Spanish fortress in the Bay Area during this period, the flamboyant, self-designated U.S. commander, still in buckskin, reportedly christened the four-mile-long, one-to-two-mile-wide strait between the Marin headlands and the San Francisco peninsula below them as "the Golden Gate," arguably the most spectacular harbor entryway in the world.

As Frémont's men headed south now, the Mexican military remnants fled before them, their ranks thinned to near invisibility by continuing desertions in the wake of the formal show of strength by the Americans. British naval personnel observed the peacefully unfolding conquest and, recognizing that their nation could reverse it only by a sizable deployment of ships, troops, money, and settlers, did nothing. On July 19, Frémont rode into Monterey, where the residents gawked at the already legendary Pathfinder and his leathery-faced brigade. Commodore Sloat was less awed. Since Frémont could produce no written instructions explicitly authorizing his forceful actions, Sloat treated him as little better than a brazen renegade and declined his request to muster in the California Battalion as official members of the U.S. military. But within days, Sloat turned over command of the Pacific Squadron to the younger and notably more aggressive Robert Stockton. He admired Frémont for his daring accomplishments, advanced him to the rank of major, swore in his men as legitimate American soldiers, and soon sent them south, where the more numerous Mexican population was thought likely to resist becoming involuntary citizens of the United States.

Loyalist Mexican authorities in southern California, it shortly became evident, could rouse little popular support and less money to field a counterinsurgency, and headed for Sonora and other nearby states in northern Mexico. In August, Stockton's marines and Frémont's hard-shell mounted force had combined to secure the coastal villages of San Diego, Los Angeles, and Santa Barbara, and informed their residents they were being blessedly liberated from abusive Mexican authorities. Stockton announced his further intention to move inland in pursuit of those "who, unless driven out, will with the aid of the hostile Indians keep this beautiful country in a constant state of revolution and blood."

The only blemish on this otherwise immaculate transition occurred in September after Archibald Gillespie, who had crossed the continent to deliver the President's inciting words to Frémont and stayed on to become his adjutant, was placed in charge of the fifty-man garrison left to oversee the Los Angeles region. Gillespie proved an inept peacekeeper. He issued draconian regulations in a misguided attempt to prevent an anti-American uprising, but the *californios* did not take kindly to a sundown curfew shuttering their shops, unannounced searches ransacking their homes for hidden weapons, and the outlawing of public assemblage by any group of people larger than one. The American military's restrictions were twice as oppressive as anything the Mexican authorities had ever imposed, and soon Gillespie had achieved the very thing he most wanted to prevent. Hundreds of natives, with burning resentment over the false promise of liberties the American invaders had made, rose up out of the darkness and sent Gillespie and his men scurrying for their lives, spared only when one of Stockton's ships came to their rescue.

Even as the American flag was being raised over most of California—the unfortunate insurrection centered in Los Angeles would take a bit longer to rectify—New Mexico was being likewise claimed by U.S. soldiers and without bloodshed.

While Colonel Stephen Kearny's 1,700-man Army of the West struggled over the Santa Fe Trail, enduring thirst and reduced rations, its train of pack mules halved by the cruel heat and rigors of the haul, the New Mexicans awaited their arrival with neither dread nor enthusiasm. Most of them had been long abused by the rotund, grasping governor, Manuel Armijo, his sheep-stealing soldiers, and the old-line gentry. American traders who lived in or frequented the market town—and were fond of calling Armijo "His Obesity"—brought a degree of leavening to the dusty old outpost of a faded empire, so few Mexicans there were eager to volunteer for the defense of the neglected province. Still, Armijo bestirred himself to raise a militia, which, according to reports carried to Kearny by scouts and defectors, amounted to several thousand men, to be positioned against the Americans in the hill country guarding the capital.

Kearny's army, fatigued by hard travel and sickness, was strung out behind him for many miles, and some of his dragoons, the spearhead of his forces, had been reduced to riding muleback. Aware that his troops were a tempting target for ambush as they neared Santa Fe and were in poor shape to challenge determined defenders, the American commander sent one of his subordinates ahead with a polite message to Armijo: the invaders were but the vanguard of a vast host following them on the trail and, since resistance was useless, Kearny was willing to discuss peace terms with the governor. Armijo replied cordially, proposing a time and place for their parley. As Kearny's column trudged up through the hills, half-expecting to be entrapped at every rocky pass, Armijo and his ninety-man personal entourage were heading south with all deliberate haste. New Mexico was abandoned to the Americans without a shot being fired to save it. Kearny's tired but relieved forces marched into Santa Fe on August 18 and assured the natives, "We come amongst you as friends—not enemies; as protectors—not conquerors."

If less than heroic, the conquest was all the sweeter because it was not purchased by blood, and it earned the dependable, straitlaced Kearny a generalship. After declaring New Mexico to be U.S. territory, he installed a temporary local government, left the bulk of his troops in the region to maintain law and order, and headed farther west to fulfill his instructions— to join in subduing California and taking charge of military operations if they were still going on. There was no trail, though, as there had been from Fort Leavenworth to Santa Fe, and he and a few hundred of his best dragoons set out on the 800-mile ride toward San Diego, proceeding mostly by dead reckoning over a vast terrain as bleak as the face of the moon.

By a stroke of good fortune, Kearny's party spied a thin plume of dust raised by Kit Carson and a couple of companions who were headed east to Washington with the momentous news that California was now a possession of the United States. The trio had left before the uprising against Gillespie's repressive regime at Los Angeles presented the American forces with a nasty bit of unfinished business. Supposing that his troops would prove redundant now in California, Kearny sent all but a hundred men back to Santa Fe to help pacify New Mexico and asked Carson to reverse directions and guide the general's reduced force to San Diego while his messenger colleagues continued on to Washington without him.

The fortuitous encounter with Carson no doubt shortened the desert passage for Kearny's column, but his loss of manpower nearly cost the general his life. As their party neared San Diego in late November, it was intercepted by about fifty Americans from Gillespie's command, which had regrouped with marines from Stockton's ships and was trying now to corral the Mexican holdouts in the country below Los Angeles. Alerted that he was in enemy-infested territory, Kearny neared the Indian village of San Pascual, about twenty miles northeast of San Diego, at the beginning of December as the weather turned rainy and bitter cold. His patrol detected a sizable encampment of Mexican troops on the outskirts of the village, but rather than making a surprise night attack, as some junior members of his staff urged, Kearny waited until dawn to advance through the brushy, unfamiliar terrain against a foe of unknown size and location. The Mexican mounted troops, whose expert lancers were also adept at wielding *reatas,* lassos for unhorsing enemy riders, had a clear numerical and logistical advantage over the Americans, strung out as they picked their way through the fog that enveloped the narrow ravine path. In the melee that followed, the Mexicans cut down Kearny's advance element with gunfire and spearpoint, then dragged some of the Americans from their saddles and skewered them on the ground. Before reinforcements could belatedly drive off the Mexican attackers, they had slain twenty-two and wounded another eighteen, including Kearny. The commander, who had been in the midst of the combat, slashing at the enemy lancers with his saber until he took wounds on the upper arm and the buttocks, escaped death only because two subordinates desperately turned back the lancers surrounding him. It was the worst carnage in the American conquest of California.

But the fiasco at San Pascual was also the final—and almost only—display of effective Mexican opposition during the coastal campaign. Kearny's recovered troops linked up with the main body of the Stockton-Gillespie force, a total of 600 men, retook Los Angeles early in January 1847, and pursued the smaller, poorly equipped, and disorganized band of Mexican diehards. The arrival from Monterey of Frémont's 430-man battalion trapped the last of the holdouts and forced them to surrender after wheedling lenient terms from the Pathfinder (by then a colonel), to the chagrin of the higher-ranking Stockton and Kearny. The three U.S. commanders soon became embroiled in a bitter and childish dispute over who was in charge of the American forces in California, and Kearny countermanded Stockton's appointment of the flamboyant Frémont as territorial governor. The feud was resolved only after a tedious court-martial proceeding in Washington against Frémont for defying Kearny's order to stand down. The obstreperous soldier of fortune was found guilty but with a recommendation for clemency to the President, who granted it, but Frémont's army career was eclipsed. While his reputation retained enough luster to win him the first presidential nomination by the new Republican Party in 1856, he lost the election decisively to Buchanan. His renewed military activity during the Civil War ended no more happily.

While California was being secured, Zachary Taylor solidified the American position in northern Mexico by his late September storming of Monterrey (not to be confused with the California port of the same name but spelled differently), about 250 miles south of San Antonio and the largest city in the region. It was defended by 10,000 Mexican troops against Taylor's force of about 6,500. The dogged American commander's frontal assault in a driving rain was skillfully supported by an attack on the enemy's rear under General William J. Worth, one of the spirited subcommanders Winfield Scott had sent to bolster Taylor's army. The stiff Mexican resistance, with snipers taking dead aim from many a rooftop, continued for three days. Finally, Worth's Texas dragoons, sending up wild outcries learned on the cattle range, pierced the fortress's defenses, and the main body of American attackers let loose with cannonfire down narrow streets, tunneled under houses to avoid sniper fire, and poked holes through adobe walls to toss grenades inside and inflict maximum damage. But by the time the defenders raised the white flag, they had killed or wounded 900 of Taylor's troops.

The bloody victory did not satisfy Polk, however. Instead of doggedly pursuing the retreating Mexican forces, Taylor paused to lick his wounds and granted the enemy an eight-week armistice, which prevented delivery of what the President hoped might be a knockout blow to bring the war to a quick resolution. But it was Polk himself who had ensured its continuation by taking a wishful gamble during the preceding summer.

WAR WAS THE MEANS TO AN END, not a fixation, for the President, and if his foes would just come to their senses and give the United States what it wanted of the territory that was wasted on the Mexicans, the killing could cease forthwith. Thus, Polk did not turn a deaf ear when a covert agent for Antonio López de Santa Anna turned up in Washington and offered a deal. The shopworn Mexican tyrant, an exile in Cuba, was eager to return to power, now that his people were running out of patience with reactionary President Paredes. If Santa Anna was allowed through the American blockade of his country, his spokesman indicated, he would again take up the *federalista* cause, restore Mexican liberties, and seek an honorable peace with the Americans for the benefit of his people. Santa Anna's idea of a territorial settlement, State Department officers learned during an interview with him in Havana, might include the Rio Grande border and the northern half of California, provided the United States paid enough tribute money.

But why should Polk have agreed to cooperate even for a moment with the mercurial Santa Anna, betrayer of his nation's noble 1824 constitution, butcher of Texas soldiers at the Alamo and prisoners at Goliad, master of duplicity, and virtuoso of corruption? Because, the President and his cabinet reasoned, Santa Anna as head of state could be no worse than the vile, stark-raving, Yankee-hating, war-loving despot then ruling in Mexico City—and perhaps Santa Anna had finally seen the errors of his past. In August he was allowed to slip back into Mexico. His allies and the liberal *puros* reconciled long enough to topple the hated Paredes, restore the 1824 constitution, and designate the allegedly reformed Santa Anna as president once more. Instead of seeking peace with the United States, however, he devoted himself to reversing his country's military fortunes.

The typical Mexican soldier had been undertrained—there was never enough time allotted for the task or enough able officers to oversee it—and badly equipped, often with cast-off British flintlock muskets that were hard to aim because they had to be shot from the hip to avoid the wicked recoil. Mexican troops were paid rarely, if at all, and called upon to march interminably under a harsh sun on minimal rations of beans and tortillas. But they had on occasion exhibited courage and resilience, reacted well when properly commanded, and were unwilling to surrender their native ground to the white predators from the north. Out of this raw clay Santa Anna dreamed of molding a reinvigorated army capable of punishing the invaders by forcing them to endure hostile climate and terrain and spend their blood and money until they had exhausted their voracious impulses. He had no other ambition, Santa Anna told his people, than to drive their hated enemy from Mexican soil. Then he turned over his presidential duties to a stand-in and headed north to San Luis Potosí to assemble his army. To pay for it he extracted loans secured by less desirable church property and lifted silver from the local mint. He planned to build a force of 20,000 that could overwhelm Taylor's army, dug in a few hundred miles away, across a forbidding desert.

Polk had several options at that moment. Over a thirteen-month span, the United States had grown enormously, by dint of arms and bareknuckled diplomacy. Texas was now a giant state, its final contours yet to be determined; the best part of the Oregon Country had been conceded by the British; and sunny California, with its promise of bountiful harvests and burgeoning coastal commerce, had been painlessly taken over, along with the infinite sandscape of adjacent New Mexico. The nation's territory had increased to a stupendous three million square miles, 40 percent of them added since December 29, 1845, when Congress formally admitted Texas to statehood. Surely this glorious continental expanse, most of it still virgin land, was all the space the American people would ever need. Why continue now to fight a war with feeble but mulishly defiant Mexico? Why not just declare victory and bring home Taylor's troops, even if the Mexicans refused to concede that their military prospects were hopeless? After all, their unwillingness to negotiate a treaty acknowledging that Texas was now the integrated possession of the United States had not deflected Congress from admitting the former Mexican province.

The problem with quitting the battlefield unilaterally and prematurely—without, that is, an official Mexican surrender—was the prospect of chronic border strife and civil unrest, if not active guerrilla warfare, in the newly conquered regions. Normalized diplomatic relations would stabilize social and economic conditions and stimulate trade. In Washington, there were several schools of thought about how to get the Mexicans to come around. One was to reinforce Taylor's army holding the northern tier of Mexico from the Rio Grande to about the twenty-sixth parallel and keep it there, requiring the local residents to supply it until Santa Anna, after a token show of valor, gained enough political strength to make peace with the United States as he had promised. A somewhat more aggressive approach called for seizing Tampico, Mexico's second largest port on the Gulf, and bringing American troops another 300 miles farther south, within ready striking distance of the Mexican heartland and its capital. Indeed, when Santa Anna failed to defend Tampico, choosing instead to bolster Veracruz, the principal Mexican port, U.S. naval forces grabbed it in mid-November as a supply depot for future operations while Taylor was extending his area of control to the north.

The third and most aggressive of the contemplated military options called for American forces to capture Veracruz and then advance 200 miles due west over Mexico's main highway artery, take its imposing capital, and thereby gain a swift and total victory. But such a direct strategy required enough trained troops to hammer their way into the rugged highlands leading to the Valley of Mexico, where the great capital city lay, all the while enduring killer weather and diseases (yellow fever in particular), well-positioned firepower in front of them and constant guerrilla activity to their rear, and ever-lengthening supply lines. A single setback along the way for U.S. forces, moreover, would snap their string of victories and dim their aura of invincibility, inspiring the stubborn Mexicans to hold out indefinitely and exact a growing toll on American lives, finances, and civilian as well as military morale.

Beyond strictly military considerations, the war—especially if protracted and extending American dominion over even more Mexican territory than already seized—raised two serious civil rights problems for the United States. The first was the question of what the nation would do with all the Mexicans that came with any additionally annexed territory. California and New Mexico had the great virtue of bringing much desirable land but very few alien people under the American flag. The *Richmond Times* revealed the racist syndrome likely to infect the body politic, should the nation try to amalgamate masses of its conquered neighbors as fellow citizens, by asking, "Are we prepared to place on a perfect equality with us, in social and political position, the half-breeds and mongrels of Mexico? The idea is revolting, and yet nothing less is to be expected."

Equally or even more troubling to many northerners was the prospect that the slave states, whose residents were far more active and enthusiastic participants in the war with Mexico than the rest of the nation, hoped to extend their region's sanction of human bondage into the newly acquired territories, the bulk of which lay below the 1820 Missouri Compromise line. Florida and Texas had just joined the Union as slave states, and if newly captured California and New Mexico, an area nearly twice as large as the new free-soil Oregon Territory, were also left open to slavery—to say nothing of any additional Mexican soil won by the United States—the South and its iniquitous practice would dominate American social, political, and economic life. Fear of that possibility flared into the open in August 1846 when a freshman Democrat from Pennsylvania, David Wilmot, introduced an amendment to a war-funding bill before the House of Representatives that would have forbidden slavery in any territory acquired from Mexico. Wilmot explained the purpose behind his proviso: "I make no war on the South or on slavery in the South. I have no squeamish sensitiveness upon the subject of slavery, nor morbid sympathy for the slave. I plead the cause of the rights of white freemen. I would preserve for free white labor a fair country . . . where the sons of soil, of my own race and own color, can live without the disgrace which the association with negro slavery brings upon free labor." In short, white workingmen were severely disadvantaged by residing in the same labor market with slaves.

While Wilmot's explanation took the ignoble form of demeaning the victims rather than the masters of the brutal custom, he managed to stir a furor over an issue that Polk's fervidly expansionist policy had tried to minimize. Pro-slavery advocates contended, on one hand, that much of the newly won Mexican territory was too arid to support the large-scale agriculture under which the plantation system thrived. On the other hand, they argued, any extension of slavery into the southwestern lands taken from Mexico would drain away the black bondsmen from the old South and actually reduce, not increase, the practice. Polk, a slavemaster, did not engage in such sophistry himself, insisting that the war had nothing to do with slavery because the 1820 Compromise had fixed the boundary for it at the 36°30' latitude—the southern boundary of Missouri—and left the question up to those living below that line to decide for themselves. All but lost sight of in the hot national debate was that the so-called grossly inferior Mexicans, from the creation of their republic, had outlawed the inhumane labor system that their supposed moral betters in the United States now threatened to impose on them. Wilmot's rider carried in the House by a vote of 83–64, but the Senate, where the slavocracy held sway, sat on the measure until Congress finally grappled with it in 1850, two years after the war had ended.

To speed its conclusion, Polk had chosen late in 1846 to follow the boldest of the military options before him. He reluctantly tapped his army's chief of staff, the insufferable but incomparable Winfield Scott, to lead as large an expeditionary force as was needed to strike from the Gulf at the Mexican heartland as soon as the winter weather lifted in 1847.

IN LATE FEBRUARY, while Scott was assembling his troops and supplies along the Gulf Coast in Louisiana, Texas, and Tampico for the amphibious invasion, Zachary Taylor was beating back an unexpected assault by Santa Anna's large new army. Aware that he could not sustain his troops indefinitely in a defensive posture, the Mexican commander drove a 16,000-man force north in a midwinter march across more than 200 miles of badlands in the hope of catching and crushing Taylor's army, reduced to about 5,000 men after Old Rough and Ready had been directed to send half his troops to Tampico to supplement Scott's gathering legions.

To repulse Santa Anna's far larger ranks, Taylor's men took up a strong defensive position near a hacienda called Buena Vista, where the main road wound through hills and ravines five miles below Saltillo, the capital of Coahuila, the state from which Texas had separated eleven years before. The American troops withstood two days of furious Mexican attacks that repeatedly bent but could not break their lines because Santa Anna failed to press his advantage by throwing the full brunt of his reserves into the melee. Had the offensive gone on for a third day, Taylor's forces would likely have yielded. The Mexican *jefe,* though, knowing that his hungry, exhausted, and badly shot up troops had given a good account of themselves but were incapable of continuing, left the field and led the long trek back to San Luis Potosí. By the time they got there, casualties, disease, and desertions had reduced the Mexican army by half.

There was soon more dispiriting news for Santa Anna. General Scott had arrived offshore at Veracruz by the ides of March and, after calling in vain on the city's 3,500 or so defenders to throw down their arms, leveled the full might of the American naval guns at the port city's fortifications and then at its nonmilitary sectors as well. Since the Mexicans had no ships of their own to interdict the U.S. Navy's Gulf task force, its barrage was scarcely challenged. After four days, much of the port had been demolished, and the remnants of its garrison surrendered. Scott, denounced for inflicting barbaric punishment on the civilian population, took pains to show civility toward the beaten occupants. He promised them fair treatment and his own troops stern rebuke if they abused the locals, carried a lighted candle in services at the cathedral to show he was a godly warrior, and then supervised the unloading of the supplies his 11,000-man army would need for the perilous drive on Mexico City. He began it quickly, hoping to beat the onset of the yellow fever season in the muggy coastal region. The offensive would require six months of fighting that grew more brutal the farther the Americans ascended into the highlands, following Mexico's most heavily trafficked turnpike. There was no easier way to reach the capital.

Scott, maneuvering his army as adroitly as possible through a hostile countryside, was constantly required to peel off some of his men to protect the lengthening American supply line back to Veracruz. His soldiers performed heroic feats, as at Cerro Gordo, where they scaled steep chasms, hoisted their heavy guns by ropes, stormed the heights in hand-to-hand combat, and turned the Mexicans' cannons against their own main units to gain a shattering victory. Frustrated by the enemy's stubborn resistance and hectoring guerrilla activity in the rear, American troops committed atrocious acts against the civilian population, and their vexed commander only infrequently took dire measures to curb them. Both sides understood they were locked in a savage war of national survival. The Mexicans, given their advantage in numbers and familiarity with the terrain and climate, ought to have repulsed the invaders. But Scott kept winning, often at a high cost, then pausing for resupplies and rest—weeks at a time when necessary—and resuming his inexorable advance while the increasingly erratic and disheartened Santa Anna never put enough men in the right spot at the right time to blunt the American onslaught. Improvising desperately as he gave ground, he was Mexico's gallant hero no longer.

Scott's slowly grinding success helped counteract the growing antiwar sentiment in the United States as the conflict entered its second year. Hopeful that the Mexicans would accept their fate before the ultimate humiliation of losing their capital city, Polk sent a peace negotiator to accompany Scott's forces and make his presence known to the Mexican government. The President was careful, though, not to repeat the mistake he had made a year and a half earlier when he invested Louisiana Congressman John Slidell with too exalted a diplomatic rank before sending him to Mexico City to seek a boundary settlement. In fact, Nicholas P. Trist, the man Polk now selected for the highly sensitive role of peace envoy, had virtually no political standing. A poor public speaker who had never run for office, Trist held the inconspicuous post of chief clerk in the State Department. Secretary Buchanan vouched for his competence.

Trist was no bureaucratic flunky, but at age forty-seven, he was surely an underachiever. It is doubtful that any American public servant ever had more celebrated and powerful political patrons in his formative years. A native Virginian, Trist attended West Point until he decided against a military career and dropped out, married Thomas Jefferson's granddaughter, Virginia Randolph, and began to study law under the great old man's guidance. During Jefferson's last years, Trist became his companion and confidant, taking frequent walks and rides with him, attending his bedside when the Sage of Monticello died on precisely the fiftieth anniversary of the Declaration of Independence he had drafted, and acting as administrator of his bankrupt estate. Trist also became an intimate of Jefferson's warm friend and neighbor, James Madison, for whom he performed duties in helping administer the University of Virginia.

Such connections might have helped establish Trist as a highly successful attorney and a comer in politics, but with an intellectual's disdain for the mundane he turned away from the law for an unsuccessful fling at running a local newspaper. Needing to make a living for his family, he used his pull to obtain a clerical job at the State Department. The work soon dissatisfied him, and Trist used his social ties and graces to wangle the position of President Andrew Jackson's personal secretary, residing in the White House and on call around the clock. His loyal service earned him the post of U.S. consul in Havana, a diplomatic dead end, where he lingered for eight years, absorbing Spanish culture and Latin American politics, but won no transfer to a choice assignment elsewhere. He had to settle for becoming chief clerk at State, the equivalent of a modern undersecretary. It was the resumé of a thoroughly dutiful civil servant, one most unlikely to defy his superiors.

Buchanan's instructions to Trist called for him to obtain Mexico's acknowledgment of the American annexation of Texas, with the Rio Grande boundary, and the conquest of California and New Mexico, for which the United States would pay $30 million or even more as both conscience money and a sop to Mexico's battered pride. As an afterthought, Trist was told to ask for two further Mexican concessions in the peace package. One was Baja California, an arid, largely desolate peninsula consisting for the most part of rugged, mile-high mountain ranges, but it would have added nearly 800 miles of Pacific coastline to the United States. The other, potentially far more important trophy of American military success that Trist was to seek was the right of transit for the United States government and its citizens across the isthmus of Tehuantepec in Mexico's far southern region, the country's narrowest point, where the Atlantic and Pacific oceans were only 125 miles apart. A canal and adjacent railroad built there would greatly shorten travel time between the east and west coasts of the hemisphere, promote the economic and political integration of the now continent-wide United States, and bring its eastern manufactured goods and the produce of the Mississippi Valley within reach of Asian markets. But neither Baja nor the Tehuantepec franchise was a dealbreaker, Trist was told; the rest was. If Mexico accepted a boundary line up the Rio Grande to El Paso and then west along the thirty-second parallel to the Pacific, some twenty-five miles below San Diego, American troops would withdraw from all the territory they were occupying below that line.

Trist began his mission by running into more difficulty with Winfield Scott, in whose company he was assigned to travel, than with any Mexican officials. For all his consorting with celebrated politicians and the polished manners it had ingrained, Trist had a complex, inward personality that at times emerged in oddly tactless, overbearing conduct. His elevation from glorified clerk to the nation's designated peacemaker puffed his ego to the point that he saw no need to act deferentially toward the nation's ranking military commander. Even before meeting Scott at the front, Trist sent him a letter of introduction intended for the Mexican foreign secretary and all but ordered the general, not yet fully apprised by Washington of Trist's commission, to see that it got forwarded promptly to Mexico City. Scott was instinctively distrustful of the diplomat, who he suspected was out to steal his thunder as the pacifier of Mexico, thereby reducing his postwar chances to win the presidency. The general was also aware that the Mexican Congress had lately passed a law forbidding government officials from negotiating peace terms with the Americans, so he declined to do Trist's bidding. Soon the envoy was writing to his wife that the smartest man in the U.S. Army was "an imbecile." The intercession of the British consul, a fuller State Department advisory to Scott, and a simple gesture of kindness by the general—sending Trist a jar of marmalade to cheer him during an illness—helped patch up their destructive feud.

Still, Trist's mission had to await some signal of receptivity from the Mexicans, whose forces seemed to grow more determined not to submit in humiliation the closer Scott's army drew to the capital. Yet the military hardliners around Santa Anna faced increasing challenges now—from conservatives who feared that prolonging a hopeless war would cause the confiscation of private property to pay for it, from secessionists in the north and moderates around the capital who were open to bartering territory for peace, and from liberals and radicals favoring a temporary American protectorate for all of Mexico while the country established a stable, truly democratic government. Santa Anna was unsure whether to risk a humbling peace—and his countrymen's scorn for making it—or to carry on a last-ditch fight in the hope of inflicting enough punishment on Scott's thinning ranks to force the Americans to settle for less Mexican territory. His ambivalence was detectable in an enigmatic message he sent to Scott suggesting that the nearer the American army came to Mexico City, the more it would frighten the foes of peace and free Santa Anna to come to terms with the invaders.

While some on his staff saw a trap in the Mexican commander's invitation, Scott acted to oblige his shaky rival by gearing up for an August drive against the capital and the 20,000 or so troops Santa Anna had scraped together to defend the region. Scott paused momentarily when Trist got word that a small gratuity—$10,000 was specified—paid to certain Mexican officials might get the peace talks going. It seemed a modest enough gamble, and such bribes were not wholly dishonorable; after all, American officials in the past had paid off Indian chiefs and Barbary pirates to cease their hostile activities. But when nothing came of the payoff, Scott moved ahead with his battle plan. His forces would skirt the two main roads into Mexico City from the east and avoid the lakes and marshes on that side of the capital, approaching it instead from the south. On the way, the Americans won back-to-back battles at two fiercely held sites, Contreras and Churubusco, when Scott turned the tide by sending reinforcements across a jagged lava bed under cover of darkness for a surprise assault at daybreak.

The harrowing American victories gave Santa Anna what he had asked for—Scott's forces were nearly at the gates of the capital, but it was not yet under siege. Now word came that the enemy would hear Trist's peace terms. The Mexican Congress, having reendorsed the 1824 constitution that vested the treatymaking power in the hands of the president, had disbanded in order to avoid the responsibility for countenancing a national disgrace. Santa Anna asked Scott for a two-week truce in late August so that Trist and Mexican peace commissioners could meet. Trist and Scott decided there were several good reasons to risk granting the request in the belief that Santa Anna would bargain in good faith and not just use the time to strengthen the capital's defenses. The peace commissioners Santa Anna chose were considered men of the highest prominence and rectitude and belonged to the party that had long opposed him. Furthermore, Trist was fully aware, as he would later explain in a historic letter to Buchanan, that Santa Anna was "the most unprincipled man whom [Mexico] holds" and one whom only a fool could otherwise have trusted. Nevertheless, the U.S. peacemaker still felt that the Mexican leader's professed wish for peace was in earnest "[f]or the same reason that a man who, when seen drowning, should be heard to express his desire for a plank, might, altho' he were the most notorious liar that ever existed . . . be believed to be sincere." And finally, Scott's weary men needed a rest.

The opening round of the peace talks was marked by Mexican posturing. Santa Anna's commissioners, as if to prove to him and the Americans alike that they were no easy marks, denounced Trist's terms as extortionate and said they would agree only to recognize the annexation of Texas with the Nueces River boundary and to permit the establishment of an American trading post at San Francisco Bay with a connecting road to Oregon; U.S. troops were to evacuate from all other Mexican territory they had seized. The settlement was to be conditioned upon adequate compensation for both territorial concessions, along with reparations for damage to Mexican property during the war and forgiveness of all of Mexico's prewar debts to American citizens. Also, all Mexican land grants made in Texas prior to the rebellion were to be honored.

These terms, as Trist observed, suggested that the faithful soldiers of Mexico had won, not lost, every battle in the war. Only when the two-week truce had nearly expired in early September did the Mexican commissioners relent and say they would discuss—informally and as individuals only, not with the official concerted voice of the nation—more realistic terms. Santa Anna had long been willing to yield California as indefensible, but he and his inner circle felt far differently about surrendering the Nueces Strip, because in their view Mexico's national honor and the whole basis for the war turned on exposing the illegitimacy of the American claim of the Rio Grande border. They were also set on retaining New Mexico, whose inhabitants had for so long been allegedly loyal Spanish subjects and Mexican citizens.

With California, the chief prize, already in his pocket, Trist agreed to three concessions. He withdrew the demand for Baja California, largely a bargaining chip, since American troops had never occupied the mountainous and mostly useless appendage. He accepted the Mexican contention that transit rights across the isthmus of Tehuantepec could not be granted to the United States because they had been sold five years earlier to private commercial interests and were currently held by a British banking house. And, in a departure from Buchanan's instructions, Trist tentatively accepted the Nueces instead of the Rio Grande boundary—he had long personally doubted the legitimacy of the Texas claim to the latter—but only on the proviso that Mexico give up New Mexico, which was ten times the size of the Nueces Strip. The Mexicans consented but asked that the southern boundary of New Mexico be set not along the thirty-second parallel, as Trist had required, but along the Gila River until it met the thirty-third parallel, which it would follow straight to the Pacific, about twenty miles above San Diego, so that Mexico could retain a land bridge at the head of the Gulf of California between the states of Sonora and Baja California. The Mexicans also tried to insert a prohibition on slavery in all territory ceded to the United States, just as the unsuccessful Wilmot Proviso called for, but Trist promptly rejected the idea outright.

When the deal was referred to Santa Anna as chief of state for his approval, however, it fell apart. The hardliners in his coterie, it was said, were adamantly opposed to such a sweeping cession of territory. The most Mexico would accept, the sheepish peace commissioners reported back to Trist, was acknowledging the loss of Texas to the Nueces and the sale of northern California down to the 36°30′ Missouri Compromise line, which ran just below Monterey, so that slavery would presumably be prohibited in the ceded territory. Although fully conscious that the Mexican offer was unacceptable to his government, Trist did not summarily dismiss it but sent back an inquiry to Washington as to whether the administration would consider relinquishing, as he had been prepared to, the Rio Grande boundary if the United States title to conquered California and New Mexico were confirmed by the eventual peace treaty.

The Mexican intransigence, meanwhile, had two immediate effects. Scott launched his attack on Mexico City, which Santa Anna had indeed better fortified during the two-week truce. And American public opinion, outraged along with President Polk by the refusal of the Santa Anna regime to face the reality of its nation's defeat, was tempted by the idea that so long as the beaten enemy preferred the war to go on, perhaps the United States ought to finish the job and conquer *all* of Mexico—even as ultraexpansionists had earlier called for the American takeover of all of Oregon. By extinguishing the Mexican nation and annexing it, the United States would end all further conflict with its mad-dog neighbor and come closer still to fulfilling its continental destiny. The *New York Globe* registered this emerging sentiment by asserting in mid-October: "Mexico must be made to *feel* this war. . . . It would almost seem that they, like the Israelites of old, had brought upon themselves *the vengeance of the Almighty* and we ourselves *had been raised up to overthrow* AND UTTERLY DESTROY THEM *as a separate and distinct nation.*" A more compassionate, if not precisely loving, rationale for the all-Mexico proposition was voiced by the *New York Sun:* "[O]ur victories will give liberty, safety, and prosperity to the vanquished. . . . [W]e offer them a position infinitely above any they have occupied since their history began." American energy, wealth, and education, it was suggested, would lift the low character of the Mexican people, while their ethnic cleansing would be accomplished by nature, the *Philadelphia Public Ledger* predicted: "Our Yankee young fellows and the pretty señoritas will do the rest of the annexation, and Mexico will soon be Anglo-Saxonized, and prepared for the confederacy."

Other Americans were unenthusiastic about the all-Mexico concept, especially antislavery advocates, who were skeptical of southerners' reassurances and fully expected them to migrate toward the newly acquired territories with their slaves in tow. Some of slavery's strongest champions were also outspokenly opposed to the absorption of more Mexican territory. John Calhoun contended that even if Mexico handed itself over in toto, it would prove impossible for the United States to rule 8 million people "so little qualified for free and popular government." Most of the nation simply wanted the war to be over and had little interest in turning the Mexicans into either a subject people or their fellow citizens, given their alien culture, language, religion, and disregard for the rule of law and the binding force of democratic rites.

While the all-Mexico debate was being aired across America, Scott made quick work of Mexico City. His supply of men and equipment was running low, so a protracted siege of the capital, with its 200,000 residents and perhaps 20,000 armed defenders, was impracticable and might have turned into a debacle. The key to the city gates, Scott decided, was the batteries on 200-foot-high Chapultepec (Aztec for "grasshopper hill"), where thirteen Mexican cannons looked down on the main southern approach road to the capital. Atop the hill, the site of royal residences since pre-Columbian days, stood a palatial complex that once served as the summer home of Spanish viceroys; now it housed a military academy and served as a symbol of Mexico's national identity. It had to be taken by the Americans.

A thousand fanatic defenders blocked their way, starting at a foundry near the base of Chapultepec, where it was reported—wrongly—that the Mexicans had been converting old church bells into cannons. Taking the factory was bloody business, and that was only the beginning. American guns pounded the strategic hill and its old palace for a day until it was clear that there would be no surrender and the heights would have to be stormed. Among the last and bravest of the defenders during the furious hand-to-hand combat were fifty teenage cadets who attended the military school on the site. Their patriotism made the lads into legends. One cadet raced to the palace roof to haul down the Mexican flag before the Americans could confiscate it, wrapped it around his body, and while either trying to make a heroic escape or seeking a martyr's end, was shot, fell, or jumped from the roof to his death. Other cadets also chose to leap off the heights rather than submit to the oncoming *yanquis*. The resistance at Chapultepec cost the Americans dearly and left Scott with hardly 6,000 men to assail Mexico City itself.

But he did not hesitate, sensing that much of the fight had gone out of the Mexican soldiers. Snipers took their toll on the American troops as they charged over the causeways and gateways into the city, but they kept on coming and driving the defenders down the streets before them. By the time they had taken control of half the capital, Santa Anna decided further resistance was futile and retreated with the remnants of his forces. The American flag waved over Mexico City on September 14. Scott had lost a quarter of his men in the late summer fighting in the Valley of Mexico. Santa Anna had lost his nation. He resigned the presidency, tried one last time to bloody his conquerors in October by falling on reinforcements moving up the highway to the capital from Veracruz—he was repulsed—and fled to Venezuela rather than answer the summons from a court of military inquiry for his disastrous leadership.

During the fighting in Mexico City, Nicholas Trist chose not to remain safely behind the lines. He rode into the capital on his own, nearly got caught in the crossfire, and at one point alerted the commander of an American cavalry unit of the location of a Mexican mounted unit he had spotted after climbing to the roof of the bishop's palace to view the battle. He later walked into the National Palace, the abandoned home of the Mexican government, and confiscated a pile of official papers he found on the foreign minister's desk. Then, without rancor or a great deal of hope that his labor would achieve anything, Trist composed—for the scrutiny of Mexican officials when the smoke cleared—a trenchant summary of the American position on the origins of the war and the differences between the two nations' negotiating positions. He wound up with an expression of personal esteem for "the eminent citizens of Mexico who had acted as her organ in the negotiations." It was a gesture of civility that would soon be reciprocated.

Pleased as he was by Scott's crowning, if costly, success, President Polk was angered by the Mexicans' continuing refusal to reach a peace accord on any terms except those insulting to the United States and the feats of its fighting men. When he received Nicholas Trist's report on his failed efforts, Polk concluded that the inexperienced negotiator was being played for a fool and ordered Buchanan to recall him at once. If Trist had subsequently signed a treaty, Buchanan told him, he was to bring it with him, but otherwise to cease forthwith lest he encourage the Mexican government—however it was now composed—in "delusive hopes and false impressions." A follow-up letter from Buchanan advised Trist of the President's "profound regret that you should have gone so far beyond . . . your instructions" by allowing the Mexican negotiators even to think that Washington might be flexible about the Rio Grande boundary. And in case the Mexicans doubted that Trist's dismissal signaled a pending tougher attitude by Polk, orders went out to Scott to suppress guerrilla warfare "with the utmost allowable severity" and to seize customs revenues and impose whatever other levies were needed for the upkeep of his forces during the occupation, however long it might last. Not coincidentally, looting by U.S. soldiers increased.

With Santa Anna gone and his army in dissolution, the national constitution invested the presiding justice of the Mexican Supreme Court, Manuel de la Peña y Peña, a cautious lawyer of pro-clerical leanings, as acting president. Having served as foreign minister in Herrera's government during the abortive Slidell mission, Peña y Peña knew that offering peace terms acceptable to the victors would be viewed by his countrymen, even while wallowing in the ashes of defeat, as a humiliation and probably cost him his office. Yet he also recognized that American power could now overrun his nation and end its sovereign existence if Mexico did not bargain in good faith—a courageous stand in view of the emotional state of his people. He moved what was left of the federal government to Querétaro, a town 125 miles northwest of Mexico City, and awaited a fresh feeler from the Americans.

Polk, for the moment, chose to let the Mexicans stew in their own apprehensive juices and sent word that any serious negotiating they might care to undertake could be conducted with General Scott until Trist's successor arrived. To emphasize his hardening stance, the President fanned the all-Mexico debate in his annual December message to Congress. What had begun as a defensive action was now openly embraced as a war of territorial conquest, justified, according to Polk, by four considerations, three of them transparent excuses and the fourth brutally honest but morally reprehensible. The United States was (1) entitled to seize, at the very least, California and New Mexico, said the President, because Mexico was incapable of ruling those provinces and (2) if left to their own devices, they would fall into the hands of or under the influence of other foreign powers, to the detriment of the United States. Besides, (3) Mexico had no other means to pay off its debts to American citizens. The truth was, Polk allowed more forthrightly, that (4) Americans had not fought the Mexican War for nothing and deserved their territorial reward. His tough talk, at a time when the nation was suffering from war fatigue and growing anxiety over the possible extension of slavery and absorption of millions of brown people, was aimed at forcing the Mexicans to admit defeat and act accordingly.

THE EMERGENCY MEXICAN GOVERNMENT under acting President Peña y Peña, surrounded by extremists who hated the Americans and said they could never be trusted to honor treaty terms, knew blind pride would not lead to his nation's salvation, so the interim chief of state summoned the scattered members of the Mexican Congress to confirm his appointment and nullify the statute making it treasonous to talk peace with the invaders. Then he turned over the presidency for a two-month interim to a former Santa Anna henchman, who named a cabinet of moderates, with Peña y Peña as

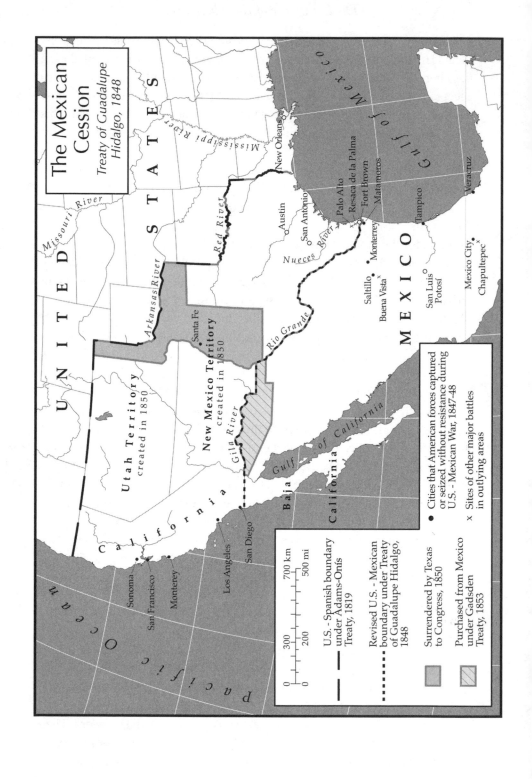

The Mexican Cession
Treaty of Guadalupe Hidalgo, 1848

UNITED STATES

Missouri River

Mississippi River

Red River

New Orleans

Arkansas River

Utah Territory
created in 1850

New Mexico Territory
created in 1850

Santa Fe

Gila River

California

Gulf of California

Baja California

Los Angeles

San Diego

Sonoma
San Francisco
Monterey

Pacific Ocean

Austin
San Antonio

Nueces River

Palo Alto
Resaca de la Palma
Fort Brown
Matamoros

Rio Grande

Saltillo
Buena Vista ×
Monterrey

San Luis
Potosí

Mexico City
Chapultepec ×

Tampico

Veracruz

Gulf of Mexico

MEXICO

700 km
500 mi

0   200   300
0   200   700

● Cities that American forces captured
    or seized without resistance during
    U.S. - Mexican War, 1847–48

× Sites of other major battles
    in outlying areas

U.S. - Spanish boundary
under Adams-Onís
Treaty, 1819

Revised U.S. - Mexican
boundary under Treaty
of Guadalupe Hidalgo,
1848

Surrendered by Texas
to Congress, 1850

Purchased from Mexico
under Gadsden
Treaty, 1853

foreign minister, and appointed a three-man peace commission composed of veteran legislators who had held key posts in earlier national governments. In extremis, Mexico was at last primed for serious peacemaking.

The news of Trist's dismissal, which reached Mexico City on November 16, was shattering not only to Trist himself but to the Mexican conciliators, who feared that Polk's appointment of a new negotiator likely to be less compassionate and reasonable would heat up the unreconciled militarists, bring down the precariously perched government, and cause resumption of the war. The peacemakers' golden opportunity was about to go up in smoke. Scott, who had grown close to Trist, wrote to Secretary of War Marcy that he doubted the Mexican negotiators would discuss peace terms with him, and Trist, though stunned that months of effort under trying conditions had resulted only in his curt dismissal, conscientiously urged Buchanan to make haste in replacing him. But those most familiar with Trist's astuteness, goodwill, and transparency—among them Scott, Peña y Peña, his peace commissioners, British consul Edward Thornton, members of the press, and foreign businessmen—all urged the fired negotiator to disregard his orders to return to Washington and instead proceed with the peacemaking. Most influential among those proposing that the longtime federal functionary consider such an unthinkable act of defiance, according to Trist's later testimony, was the *New Orleans Delta* war correspondent James Freamer. The two men had become friends through the mutually useful exchange of reliable information. "Make the treaty, sir!" Freamer told Trist. "It is now in your power to do your country a greater service than any living man can render her. I know your country. I know all classes of people there. They want peace, sir. They pant for it. . . . Instructions or no instructions, you are bound to do it."

Moved by such a supportive outpouring of confidence in him, Trist noted that his instructions from Buchanan did not revoke his earlier instructions or the American peace terms they contained. In recalling him, moreover, the Secretary of State had cautioned him not to risk danger in returning to Veracruz for the voyage home. Scott obligingly advised Trist that it might be some time before he could spare the troops needed to safeguard his trip to the Gulf through guerrilla-infested territory. Emboldened by the realization that his suspended status gave him sudden bargaining leverage he had not previously enjoyed, Trist turned to British officials at the beginning of December and asked them to relay a now-or-never message to the Mexicans: deal with me promptly or lose your last chance for a just peace.

In what amounted to an ultimatum, Trist told Mexico's peace commissioners they had to meet the minimal American territorial demands, the Rio

Grande boundary to El Paso and then due west to the Pacific, or he would go
home. Then, in a sixty-one-page memo to Buchanan on December 4,
explaining his insubordination, Trist tried to reassure his superiors that "I
am not acting stupidly or mischievously" and that he and Scott had not been
duped in agreeing to the two-week armistice with Santa Anna in the hope of
coming to terms with the faithless warlord. Trist might have pointed out—
but did not—that he had been no more gullible about the prospects of dealing with Santa Anna than Polk and Buchanan had been in facilitating the
general's return to power sixteen months earlier in the hope it would produce an early peace settlement. Instead, the nervy Trist registered disdain
for the President's assumption of infallibility regarding Mexican politics
and stressed the difficulties in dealing with a government "always destitute
of all semblance of stability . . . seldom anything but a soulless faction,
utterly devoid of sympathy with the people, & intent solely on haste in rob-
bing, ere it be ousted from its stolen base of political power, entirely ineffectual for the most ordinary purposes of government." He would persist in his
efforts, Trist said, based on three convictions: (1) "peace is still the desire of
my government"; (2) if the present opportunity for peace were not seized,
"all chance for making a treaty will be lost for an indefinite period" and the
war prolonged; and (3) the boundary he had proposed "is the utmost point to
which the Mexican government can by any possibility venture."

For all the internal logic of Trist's protracted apologia, the President
only saw red upon reading it. He confided to his diary that night that Trist
"has acted worse than any man in the public employ whom I have ever
known. His dispatch proves that he is destitute of honor or principle." But,
probably supposing that in the nearly six-week interval since Trist had sent
his memo he had tried to exploit his dismissal to bring the Mexicans to their
senses, Polk did not order General Scott to take the disobedient envoy into
custody.

And a good thing. For a maddening few weeks after Trist advised Washington of his insubordination, there was still no movement on the other side.
To placate hesitant Mexican officials who hoped that still further delay
would fan rising antiwar sentiment in the United States and lead to softer
settlement terms, the peace commissioners requested the withdrawal of
American troops and submission of the peace terms to international arbitration. The feint evaporated after Scott, with reinforcements arriving now,
revealed his intention to annex more Mexican territory and begin collecting
taxes to pay for the American occupation. Peña y Peña now instructed his
commissioners to come to terms with Trist. They accepted the Rio Grande
boundary to El Paso but said they could not agree to extending it straight
across the thirty-second parallel to the Pacific because that would remove

the northern extensions of the states of Sonora and Chihuahua—an action Mexico's federal government was constitutionally forbidden from taking. Instead they proposed running the boundary from the Rio Grande along the meandering Gila River, about a hundred miles on average north of the thirty-second parallel, until it reached the Colorado, the natural border between New Mexico (including modern Arizona) and California, and then west to the Pacific a little above San Diego—the traditional dividing line, the Mexicans claimed, between Alta and Baja California. Controlling the region around the mouth of the Colorado, they contended, would provide the essential land bridge connecting Sonora and Baja. The Mexicans also asked for the full $30 million that the United States had reportedly been willing to pay for California and New Mexico ever since Slidell's ill-fated mission, plus Washington's assumption of Mexico's debt for property damages to American citizens.

Nearly a month of haggling ensued. The lovely harbor site at San Diego proved the main sticking point. After first agreeing to give up San Diego, Trist uncovered documents in Mexico City that caused him to rescind the offer a few days later; the port town, investigation showed, had never really been included in Baja California. Trist was also assured by a brainy U.S. Army engineer, Captain Robert E. Lee, after studying maps of the region, that if the new boundary was drawn in a straight line but angled slightly southwestward from the intersection of the Gila and Colorado rivers to the ocean, San Diego would fall just within American territory and Mexico would be left with a land bridge extending seventy-five miles north to south around the head of the Gulf of California.

Despite grumbling by the Mexicans, the territorial deal was struck. The United States gave up the thirty-second parallel boundary for the Gila, sacrificing only a great deal of sand so that Mexico could claim a small, face-saving victory, while Trist got back San Diego. He also dug in his heels on the conscience money the United States would add to the peace package, offering only half of what his original instructions had authorized. A payment of $15 million—$3 million down and the rest in four annual installments—would make the treaty more acceptable to Washington, he told the Mexican negotiators, and to a nation that felt it had already paid a great deal in blood and money for the war. But Trist agreed that the United States would pay up to $3.25 million for Mexican damage to American property owners, including new claims to be reviewed by a government panel. The 100,000 or so Mexicans in the ceded territory would be allowed to remain there with full American citizenship rights and keep their property or move south of the new border and remain Mexicans.

To insulate the accord from charges that the Mexican peacemakers had

surrendered under the muzzles of American guns, the treaty-signing ceremony on February 2,1848, was held five miles north of Mexico City in
the suburb of Guadalupe Hidalgo, site of a celebrated shrine where the Virgin Mary was said to have been seen for the first time in the Western
Hemisphere.

Although obtained irregularly, the treaty results conformed closely with
Nicholas Trist's original instructions. The President, eager to bring American troops home, complete his hugely ambitious one-term agenda, and help
his Democratic Party retain the White House—without him in it—had no
choice but to embrace his fired envoy's handiwork and recommend it to the
Senate for ratification. The lone holdout in Polk's cabinet was the ever-
waffling Buchanan, who argued that the United States was entitled to a still
larger portion of dismembered Mexico. Aware that Buchanan was an all-
but-announced candidate to succeed him in the White House and that his
sudden territorial greed was an obvious bid for ultraexpansionist supporters,
the President chewed out his ranking cabinet member in front of his colleagues for entirely reversing the position he had espoused at the outset of
the war—that the United States should take an oath before the watching
world that it had no wish to annex even an inch of Mexican soil. In his message to the Senate favoring Trist's treaty, Polk dwelled on his cherished
prize of California, the lushest portion of Mexico: "In this vast region,
whose rich resources are soon to be developed by American energy and
enterprise, great must be the augmentation of our commerce, and with it
new and valuable markets for our manufacturers and agricultural products."

Most of his countrymen agreed, thankful for the end of the two-year war
that had taken 12,800 American lives, maimed many more, and cost the
nation $120 million. The Mexican dead were believed to total more than
50,000, and the devastation there was incalculable. The Senate approved the
Treaty of Guadalupe Hidalgo on March 10 by a vote of 38–14 with four
abstentions. Among the nays was the still vengeful Senator from Texas,
Sam Houston, who, like Buchanan, wanted more Mexican land, and Whig
leader Daniel Webster, who opposed extending the hegemony of the slavocracy. The Mexican Congress, whose members had to be nearly dragooned
back into session for the thankless task of certifying a treaty that unavoidably humiliated their nation, was moved by the report to its members by the
peace commissioners, who argued eloquently that the pact, while doubtless
a disgrace, nevertheless preserved Mexico's honor and sovereignty:

We have suffered the loss of our territory; but over the territory that
we still retain, our independence is clear and absolute, without ca-

veat of any kind. . . . [W]e have retained the rich mineral deposits of our mountain ranges, and the fruits of our temperate zones. . . . [W]e yet retain the coastlines of two oceans, from which we can maintain trade with Asia, Europe, and America; we are confident that if Mexico is not one day a prosperous nation, or a powerful one, it will not be for the lack of a substantial territory. We ask God that the harsh lesson that has been inflicted upon us will serve to unite us, so that we may repair the ancient vices that have divided our people.

While some argued that the Congress had no authorization to cede national territory to a foreign government and others were fearful that the withdrawal of American troops would return Mexico to a state of clamorous anarchy, the lawmakers decisively approved the treaty in May. By July the last of Scott's forces had sailed from Veracruz for home.

Nicholas Trist, whom the Mexican peace negotiators called "a person of noble dignity, a loyal and sincere friend of peace," even though he had been the instrument for codifying their shame, was not forgiven by James Polk for his transgression. That the State Department officer had had compelling reasons for not stepping aside as ordered—and had in the end achieved all that any diplomat could have under the circumstances—did not sway the President. Trist was denied further government employment, his salary and expenses were forfeited from the moment he received his recall notice, and he spent his final twenty-six years in obscurity, twenty of them as clerk-paymaster for the Baltimore & Ohio Railroad at $1,200 a year. His financial struggles were not relieved until three years before his death, when Senator Charles Sumner prevailed on Congress to honor the forgotten figure by awarding him $14,559 for his back salary and expenses (accrued interest included), and President Ulysses S. Grant, who had served with distinction as a young officer in the Mexican War and considered it an immortal undertaking, appointed Trist postmaster at Alexandria, Virginia, at twice his railroad pay.

The characteristic spitefulness Polk displayed toward Trist detracted from a presidency of monumental works. Polk had stabilized American currency, government finances, and the blooming national economy by creating an independent United States Treasury. He had spurred free trade and closer commercial ties with Britain by lowering tariffs. And he had presided over the acquisition of 768 million acres of national territory—Texas, by virtue of his election victory and some slick political double-talk; Oregon, by chauvinist bluster and standing tall to the British: and California and greater New Mexico, by contriving a war won for him by 90,000 doughty soldiers and able generals he did not like or trust. He used the power of the presidency even more willfully and productively than his revered mentor, Andrew Jackson, and perhaps more deviously than any of his predecessors. In his international dealings, he shamelessly overstated American rights and claims, letting partisanship beggar facts, and glibly cast Great Britain as the bogeyman in order to excuse his, and his countrymen's, territorial acquisitiveness. These deficiencies of character and principle, whether those of a scheming demagogue or an unflinching ideologue, allowed him to prey upon Americans' pretensions of national, moral, cultural, and racial superiority, to contrive a devastating war of conquest against their brown neighbors, and to blame the obscenity on their victims' shortcomings.

Yet even Polk's detractors conceded that the little man evidenced more courage than his often skewed convictions may have warranted, and few among his contemporaries—even the most righteous—wished his deeds undone. They had not made a pretty spectacle, any more than the elimination of the native tribes or the massive employment of slave labor had ennobled the self-certified American mission to master a vast wilderness and turn earth into heaven, or the closest thing to it. Like most successful politicians, Polk was a consummate pragmatist, yet like many of his countrymen, he eluded the charge of hypocrisy by seeming to believe so sincerely in his own devoutness.

The Mexican War, lasting much longer and costing the country far more than Polk had imagined, drained his slender physique and emotional stamina, leaving him fatigued and emaciated. He would succumb to cholera ten weeks after leaving office; he was only fifty-three.

IN THE LAST WEEK OF JANUARY 1848, while Nicholas Trist was working out final details of the peace treaty with Mexico, a thirty-eight-year-old former New Jerseyan named James Marshall was building a sawmill on the south fork of the American River, about 100 miles northeast of San Francisco, in partnership with John Sutter, whose fort and commercial compound stood a few leagues distant. A carpenter and sometime adventurer, Marshall had ridden for a while with Frémont's irregulars during the Bear Flag uprising. During excavations to deepen the millrace for the sawmill, Marshall and his laborers found gold—and California was never the same again.

Word sprinted down the Sacramento Valley to San Francisco, where the contagion of greed took hold that spring as an astonishing portion of the able-bodied male population in the region put aside their tools and mundane trades to head for the hills. Just whose hills they were was lost in the tumult. Landowners who had derived their holdings from the lately vanquished Mexican regime could not hope to be stoutly defended by the U.S. authorities, who had just taken over California as American territory. And although the gold country was now under the official jurisdiction of the federal government, which in theory could have required licenses for all who sought to stake a claim there and extract its mineral wealth, California's military commander, Colonel Richard Mason, understood that as a practical matter the rule of law had to yield to irrepressible human nature. "Upon considering the large extent of the country," Mason wrote of his policy decision that summer, "the character of the people engaged and the small, scattered force at my command, I resolved not to interfere but to permit all to work freely." Thus invited to help themselves, thousands more flooded in. The tide swelled still further after President Polk, in his farewell address to Congress that December, offered a self-congratulatory recitation of events in California and proclaimed, "The accounts of the abundance of gold in that territory are of such extraordinary character as would scarcely command belief were they not corroborated by the authentic reports of officers in the public service who have visited the mineral district." Squatters of all ages and backgrounds arrived the next year and, restrained only by vigilantism, overran, looted, and otherwise ruined Sutter's property and that of his neighbors, and turned the gold country into a brawling, bawdy mess. Many of those disappointed in their quest for a quick bonanza prospered instead by servicing the newcomers or harvesting the soil the old-fashioned way. By 1850 California had nearly 100,000 residents; by 1860, four times as many. A century later it became the most populous state in the Union, with an economy larger than that of all but half a dozen or so of the world's nations.

Spain had owned California for three centuries and let it drowse in the sun. Mexico had owned California for three decades and likewise left it fallow. Scarcely a week before California passed formally into the hands of the United States, gold was found there, sparking one of history's most spectacular examples of wealth creation. Was there ever a more manifest sign that Americans enjoyed providential favor and had been destined to possess the best part of the continent from sea to sea?

Most of the newcomers to California hailed from free-soil states and wanted no part of competition from slave labor. When they drew up a territorial constitution and sought congressional recognition, they outlawed slavery. But could they? The Wilmot Proviso, forbidding the practice in any territory taken from Mexico, had never won approval, but the issue it raised could no longer be ignored: what was the legal status of slavery in the

529,189 square miles that made up the Mexican cession? Did the Constitution's restraints on federal power over the states apply equally to territories? Southerners such as Calhoun argued that since Congress had no constitutional license to prohibit slavery in the states and deny its practitioners use of their living chattel, the federal legislature had no power to do so in their territories, which were the common possession of the states. Thus, the Missouri Compromise of 1820, which violated this principle, was held by Calhoun and others of his region to be unconstitutional. Daniel Webster artfully framed the opposing school of thought. The territories, while the joint possession of the Union, were not a part of it but a dependency, just as Britain's American colonies had been subsumed within the empire, and Congress had powers of territorial oversight beyond those it could exercise over the sovereign states. Slaves, moreover, argued the Webster camp—and the North generally—were not property in the legal sense but human beings held in involuntary servitude, so antislavery statutes covering the new territories did not deny slaveholders their property but only the right to indulge in the practice of inhumane bondage.

Resolving the issue was an agonizing challenge for a nation divided equally between free-soil and slave states—fifteen each. A clear majority of the population lived in the free-soil states, but the thirty United States Senators from slave states held the power to prevent the practice from being disallowed in the Mexican cession. Could the southern Senators refuse to grant California standing as a duly organized territory because its citizenry had promulgated a free-soil constitution? And would slavery be allowed in thinly settled New Mexico, which was likely to remain a territory for an indefinite period and shared a long border with slaveholding Texas? And where exactly *was* that border, which Texas claimed ran all the way to the source of the Rio Grande and included some 75,000 square miles of what New Mexico insisted it owned? The 1845 resolution by Congress granting Texas statehood assigned the federal government the power to work out the boundary issue with Mexico, as Polk had done by force of arms. But the Treaty of Guadalupe Hidalgo dealt only with the international border, which made all of New Mexico and Texas American soil without reference to the location of the border between them.

Within days of the Senate's ratification of the Mexican peace treaty in March 1848, the Texas legislature moved to reaffirm its own 1836 Boundary Act by chartering four new counties between the Pecos River and the Rio Grande, the largest of them to be called Santa Fe County and encompassing not only the capital of New Mexico but also several odd appendages that extended into modern Colorado, Kansas, and Wyoming. The New Mexicans protested that this land-grab, even if Polk had endorsed it to help win Texans' approval of annexation, had no legal, historical, or military basis, and they wanted nothing to do with the judges and district attorneys Texas was sending to enforce the law in its unilaterally created new counties, all of them presumably open to slavery. When the New Mexicans applied to Congress to establish their own territorial government, Texas officials complained that such an action would violate their state's rights under the joint congressional resolution for annexation—a spurious argument that nevertheless won Polk's backing. The New Mexicans tried again in mid-1849 and this time had a friendlier ear in the White House. Polk's successor, war hero Zachary Taylor, favored granting statehood to both California and New Mexico. The Texans began to mutter about sending troops to defend their claimed boundary while antislavery forces in Congress sought to check Texas's territorial greed. Plainly the boundary issue could not be settled in isolation, only as part of a larger package resolving the status of slavery throughout the entire Mexican cession.

After months of acrimonious and often brilliant debate in Congress, the great Compromise of 1850 was struck. California was admitted to the Union as a free-soil state. Texas was cut down from its claimed 379,000 square miles to 265,000, which still left it more than 100,000 square miles larger than California, the next biggest state. Most of the subtracted territory went back to New Mexico, where it came from. As compensation, Congress agreed that the federal government would pay off $10 million in debt incurred by the Republic of Texas and inherited by the Lone Star state. Old New Mexico was divided laterally, with the northern half designated the Utah Territory, the southern half the New Mexico Territory—and no restriction placed on slavery in either. But the dry climate and unsuitability of the soil for large-scale agriculture made the region most unpromising for plantation farming, and the largely ex-Mexican and Indian population there seemed certain to discourage the practice, if not forbid it altogether. As a sop to the sensibilities of free-soilers, slave auctions were disallowed in the nation's capital but not the practice of slavery itself, and southerners won a far meaner Fugitive Slave Law, requiring northerners to cooperate in the capture of runaway blacks. Ralph Waldo Emerson called it "a filthy law," and Harriet Beecher Stowe's 1852 melodrama, *Uncle Tom's Cabin,* a national sensation both in print and onstage, protested against the 1850 Compromise.

The United States, brazenly proud of its new territory, now gloriously extending from ocean to ocean, entered the final decade before confronting its fratricidal destiny.

CHAPTER 12

A wolf couldn't make a living on it

1850–1854

THE SCOPE, SUDDENNESS, AND DARING of the nation's territorial expansion between 1845 and 1850, creating a transcontinental empire scarcely three-quarters of a century after breaking away from Great Britain, were all the more stunning because the initiative met with so little sustained resistance from other countries and the native peoples. None could contend with the geographical advantages, self-justifying convictions, and dauntless drive of the Americans. Their keenest challenge now was the direct result of their spectacular success. They had encompassed a huge, sprawling wilderness not in a seamless evolutionary process over centuries but in a ceaseless series of incursions. How, then, was the raw, gangling country, dispersed over such vast and often forbidding terrain, to cohere as a single social and economic organism while holding fast to a republican form of government?

In truth, the United States, whose extremities took months to reach or communicate with, was a society united in name only. Distance, centrifugal force, and endemic antiauthoritarianism conspired to undermine democratic consensus and threatened to isolate the disconnected outer parts politically and commercially. The California gold discovery and its accompanying get-rich-quick adventurism compounded the problem even as they made it a certainty that the coastal region would not be left in idyllic solitude as it had been under Spanish and Mexican rule. The westward tide of settlement further swelled with refugees from hunger, poverty, and discrimination in Europe's latest round of revolutionary ferment and despotic reaction. Immigration rose from 114,000 in 1845 to 300,000 just four years later. The cross-country flow necessitated constant provisioning of settlers who were

more impatient and less self-sufficient than frontiersmen of earlier generations. They needed food, goods, mail service, military protection, and literature for the exchange of ideas if government was to operate with their
informed consent.

To link east and west and the regions in between, water routes would no
longer suffice: voyages from Atlantic ports to California around Cape Horn
took forever, and the overland trails even longer. The growing appeal of an
interoceanic canal across the isthmus of Tehuantepec, the narrowest part of
Mexico, had motivated President Polk in his failed effort to pursue the
project. For all its promise to slash travel time in half, though, Atlantic-
to-Pacific sea passage via the territory of a foreign nation would leave
American shipping in constant peril of interruption by hostile powers. A
surging national spirit demanded a coast-to-coast transportation lifeline
entirely within the borders of the United States, exercising its dominion
over newly seized soil in the far distant West. The age of the iron horse had
arrived, sooner and more urgently than anticipated.

The problem with railroads was that they were greedy consumers of capital, more so than any other technological marvels. Locomotives were complex, finicky machines, costly to build and operate; obtaining rights-of-way
and rooting rails and ties in a variegated countryside to span valleys, mountains, and rivers required a great deal of land, lumber, iron (later steel), and
labor. Weaving a great web of rails into a nationwide rapid transit system
would someday, no doubt, turn America into a commercial colossus to
match its physical dimensions. But in the mid-nineteenth century, it was
a mind-boggling conceit even for a young nation with limitless self-
confidence. What made the prospect of a transcontinental railroad still more
problematic was the prevailing political preachment, embedded deeply in
the majority Democratic Party's dogma, that the funding of "internal
improvements" by the federal government was a noxious infringement on
states' rights because it would surely invite congressional interference with
local prerogatives. Chief among these, it was well understood but rarely
mentioned, was slavery, the one custom the South regarded as constitutionally untouchable. The federal government, southern Democrats contended,
might provide engineering surveys and contracts to carry mail, but only the
sovereign states and local jurisdictions they chartered could contribute land
for rights-of-way and other direct subsidies to railway builders and operators. Thus, in the early 1840s railroads grew by small increments and along
separately owned short-line routes reaching out from urban hubs. All were
essentially private and local operations, especially in the South. As late as
1860, to travel the 600 miles between Charleston and Philadelphia by rail

required eight transfers. The huge costs and risks, leave aside the political problems, of creating a coast-to-coast trunk line railway before there were enough passengers and cargo to keep it solvent seemed to make such an undertaking visionary in the extreme—and, indeed, all but impossible without major federal intervention.

In January 1845, New York dry goods merchant and China trader Asa Whitney sent a petition to Congress that jolted national thinking about a railway girdling the continent. Anticipating imminent American acquisition of Pacific coastal territory, Whitney asked for a federal contract to build and run a railroad from a suitable terminus on the Great Lakes to the mouth of the Columbia River. Such an enterprise, he claimed with promotional flair, would "produce commercial, political, and material benefits, which must be seen and felt through all our vast Confederacy . . . [and] give us the entire control of the commerce of Europe with all of Asia, and increase our own far beyond the power of the imagination."

Whitney's plan was innovative, to say the least. He based all his calculations, he said, "upon the only possible means, the wilderness land, by which the work can be accomplished at all on any route." Just as Americans' land hunger had driven their government's voraciously expansionist policies, thereby creating an imperative need for swifter and safer transportation, so the land itself—the public portion of it that had not yet passed into private hands—would be utilized to build and finance the vital transcontinental link. Whitney wanted Congress to assign him a 60-mile-wide strip of territory to construct a 2,000-mile-long trunk line—some 120,000 square miles, about as large as modern New Mexico, to be used by their sale and settlement to pay for the railway. The construction itself would cost an average of $20,000 a linear mile, he estimated, and adding in equipment, repairs, and operational expenses, the whole project would cost $68.4 million over the twenty-five years it would likely take to complete the job—and that was with the government contributing all the land. To meet these titanic costs Whitney would sell off the land along the right-of-way on a kind of pay-as-you-go basis as settlements would arise, keeping pace with the construction, and the nearby access by rail would "open the wilderness to the husband-man . . . and take the products of the soil to all the markets of the world." To assure Congress that he was out to serve the public interest as well as fatten his own purse, Whitney offered to build his railway in ten-mile sections, allowing federal monitors to oversee the work as it progressed and the government to retain title to the railway and equipment as security until the satisfactory completion of the project. He also pledged cheap freight rates and low passenger fares and agreed to let federal accountants examine his books to determine if the proprietor was profiting unduly from his prodigious undertaking.

Five years of incessant lobbying won Whitney's bold scheme a great deal of attention and many supporters. By 1850, when the need for a railway to the Pacific had become undeniable, he had elicited the endorsement of no fewer than eighteen state legislatures. But his plan was also a lightning rod for skeptics. In 1846 a congressional committee on roads and canals came to the conclusion that "to construct a railroad of near 3,000 miles in length, across an uninhabited country, and passing over mountains the lowest pass through which is at an elevation of 7,500 feet above the level of the sea, is a project too gigantic, and, at least for the present, impracticable. A road of such length and through such a country . . . has never been attempted in any age, or in any nation." Whitney's detractors questioned not only the feasibility of the project but also the prudence, morality, and constitutionality of subsidizing a private individual, even one professing to be a public benefactor, by awarding him so much federal land, leeway to increase his rates and fares if necessary to cover his reported (and easily padded) costs, and power to sell stock and turn the whole venture into a giant land speculation. Even more worrisome, Whitney would gain a de facto perpetual monopoly since no competitor would enjoy his advantages.

Whitney's concept, adapted in modified form by later railroad moguls, immediately invited challengers proposing different and more politically motivated routes to the Pacific. At an 1845 Memphis convention of southern business leaders, James Gadsden, scion of a socially and once politically prominent Charleston family and president of the young South Carolina Railroad, fretted aloud about the increasing pace of railroad-building in the more populous North, where the growing volume of farm produce, lumber, and manufactured goods was starting to reach the marketplace over east-west rail lines, replacing north-south shipboard traffic on the Ohio and Mississippi rivers. A trunk line across the northern tier of states extending to the Pacific, as Asa Whitney had proposed, threatened to isolate the South from the nation's economic expansion and deny it ready access to the potential riches of the Asian trade.

Gadsden's concern was shared by other southern businessmen who feared that their region, if it continued to invest its energies and resources almost exclusively in a plantation economy and failed to diversify through industrial development, would sink ever deeper into vassalage to northern financiers and mercantile houses. At the least, said the more forward-looking among them, the South ought to build its own fleet of ships and become its own importer and exporter instead of relying on the Yankee carrying trade. And to stimulate regional business activity, individual southern states ought to charter new railroads within their borders and make state bank funds available to would-be train line operators, who could use surplus slave labor to prepare the roadbeds and lay the track. To his Memphis audience, Gadsden enthusiastically proposed that the South cooperate in creating a main railway route from Charleston to the Mississippi—Memphis itself would be an ideal terminus—with branch lines flowing into it from every southern state, and then a trunk line ought to be carried westward, across Texas and the southwestern desert beyond, still Mexican soil, to the Pacific coast, the window to Asian commerce. Gadsden, who had been a successful soldier and devoted military aide to Andrew Jackson but later failed as a Florida planter and political aspirant, crusaded for the next decade in behalf of a southern transcontinental railway. Although his pleas fell on deaf ears among the plantation aristocracy, he managed to attract enough backing from southern political leaders to become—for a season—a prime player on the national stage.

Between Whitney's proposed northern route and Gadsden's southern route, two powerful U.S. Senators championing midwestern business interests began pushing hard for more geographically central routes to the Pacific. Thomas Hart Benton, with his usual stentorian gusto, called for a line to be built and operated by the federal government—and paid for by the sale of public lands—from St. Louis or some other place in his heartland state due west to Monterey or San Francisco Bay. Many agreed, though, with Asa Whitney's objection that federal ownership of a trans-Mississippi railway to the Pacific, as Benton suggested, could be used "as a political engine" to give the national government excessive power. But Benton's loud advocacy of a central route, however it might be paid for, made it a formidable contender. Even more determined in his designs on a federally supported railway route west was the adroit Stephen A. Douglas, who had precociously mastered the Democratic Party machinery in Illinois, spent two terms as a congressman, and in 1847 entered the U.S. Senate at the age of thirty-four. There he was quickly named chairman of the committee on territories—and it was across territories as yet unorganized that a transcontinental railroad would have to be routed.

Douglas had moved his residence and power base to Chicago, now rivaling Cincinnati in size and commercial importance as connecting rail lines pushed west from Ohio into Indiana and Michigan. The Senator took an active hand in promoting both east-west and north-south routes of the Illinois Central Railroad and played a key role in obtaining federal land grants for rights-of-way by sponsoring breakthrough legislation for that purpose in 1850. To win the southern votes he needed, Douglas yoked the Illinois Central grant with one for land to be doled out for a route running from Cairo, Illinois, at the confluence of the Ohio and Mississippi, south through Tennessee, Mississippi, and Alabama to Mobile on the Gulf Coast. To calm southern opposition to federally supported internal improvements, Douglas's Land Grant Act specified that any government-owned lands set aside for building railroads had to be turned over to state or territorial governments, which would—without interference from Washington—oversee the transfer to private operators. Such enabling legislation served as a catalyst, in the wake of the huge territorial accession from the victory over Mexico, for a postwar railroad boom; total track mileage in the nation jumped from 8,800 in 1850 to 21,300 just four years later. As local rail lines were laid down across Illinois and its western neighbor, Iowa, Douglas spoke out strongly in behalf of a trunk line from Chicago to San Francisco, now the raucously growing Sodom-on-the-Pacific spawned by the Gold Rush.

The 1850 Compromise, which provided for organizing territorial governments in New Mexico and Utah, opened the way for Gadsden's proposed southern route to the Pacific, the whole length of which was now eligible for grants of federal land to serve as the right-of-way. Neither Douglas's route from Chicago nor Benton's from St. Louis could as yet qualify for such land grants because the great prairies west of Iowa and Missouri extending to the Rockies—called Nebraska and set aside for native and transplanted Indian nations—as yet held too few white settlers to become organized territories. The southern route also had other advantages. Angling southwesterly across Texas to El Paso and then almost due west along the thirty-second parallel to San Diego, such a route would be cheaper and hundreds of miles shorter than a central or northern path—partly because it could avoid surmounting or zigzagging through passes in the Rocky, Sierra, and Cascade mountain ranges and partly due to the southeastward bend of the Calfornia coast. A further compelling argument for the southern route was that it would allow swift deployment of American armed forces to guard the newly won border with disconsolate and possibly vengeful Mexico.

Given such advantages, the South might have altered its destiny by acting with resolve to construct a coast-to-coast transportation system across the bottom tier of the nation. And in the opening years of the 1850s, the possibility was further enhanced by a marked upturn in cotton prices, bringing renewed prosperity to the region, and by the return to the White House of a Democratic President with distinctly pro-southern leanings.

WHEN HARD TIMES ROCKED the plantation economy in the late 1830s and throughout most of the 1840s, the South chose not to view the downturn as an omen of a still graver calamity if it did not mend its improvident ways. Instead of correcting careless agricultural practices by, for example, rotating and diversifying their crops and investing seriously in the use of fertilizers to renew their depleted soil, planters prayed that cotton prices would recover. Meanwhile, to compensate for their falling per-acre income, they abandoned worn-out fields, bought up new lands to the west, and put their slaves to work boosting production—thereby further glutting the world market. When the good times did return in the early 1850s, as planters reaped profits of 30 to 35 percent on their annual operations and per capita income in the South surged 50 percent between 1840 and 1860, few people in the region saw any reason to alter their farming methods, adopt other ways of doing business, or question the social system that distinguished them from the rest of the nation. Quite the opposite, in fact; their economic recovery was taken as vindication of their customs and the superiority of their wholesomely—and exclusively—agrarian way of life.

The result was a regional economy that remained badly skewed. The South existed for its exports, consisting of a very few agricultural staples, of which cotton was of course absolute king. The southern states had little incentive to exchange goods within their region, and because its consumers were widely dispersed, its home market remained small and lethargic. There seemed no need for an extensive transportation network—for investing private capital in railroads or levying taxes for building roads and canals and dredging rivers and other navigational improvements. Better to invest their gains in new lands and the upkeep of slaves, who were becoming ever more valuable commodities on the open market. Faced with a choice between preserving its distinctiveness as an agrarian society dependent on slave labor and outside creditors or striving for self-sufficiency by commercial and industrial development, the South opted for inertia. Planters, large and small, scorned the North's style of go-getting as gross, grinding materialism. Owning slaves, their most prized possessions, provided white southerners, lordly and humble alike, with an exalted sense of self that they had no desire to cast aside.

The relatively small band of southern businessmen who, like James Gadsden, thought the region could have it both ways—diversifying enough so it could afford to sustain its unique lifestyle—found themselves up against encrusted attitudes and raging paranoia. Rising antislavery feeling in the North and the specter of forced submission to the onslaught of industrialization fueled secessionist leanings and a reconsecration of the states' rights creed. A modicum of local railroad-building with the help of revenues from federal land grants to the states did no violence to the South's insular psyche. But efforts to coordinate a region-wide rail network led to endless bickering among communities competing for the most desired routes, pitting Baltimore against Richmond, Charleston against Savannah, New Orleans against Mobile, and the Mississippi River–front cities of St. Louis, Memphis, and Vicksburg against one another, and there was insufficient leadership to overcome such petty divisiveness in the interest of the South's overall well-being.

As backers of the proposed northern and central rail routes to the Pacific lobbied all the harder, southern interest in the transcontinental venture waned despite the presidential election of Democrat Franklin Pierce, an avowed supporter of the slavocracy's political rights. Among Pierce's early acts was his appointment of James Gadsden as minister to Mexico, assigned to settle a boundary dispute of critical importance to the southern railroad route he had long pushed.

A competent but colorless attorney, Pierce had been a big fish in the small pond of New Hampshire politics. After serving as speaker of his state assembly, two terms as a congressman, and one as a U.S. Senator of no distinction, Pierce went home to a lucrative legal practice, took a star turn as an officer in the Mexican War to validate his expansionist beliefs, and returned to obscurity. With the Whigs in disarray after the divisive 1850 Compromise on the slavery issue, which cost moderate Millard Fillmore renomination for President, the Democratic convention of 1852 went through forty-eight futile ballots to find a nominee behind whom the northern and southern wings of the party could unite—and finally dredged up Franklin Pierce, whose principal credential was that he had no enemies.

His margin of victory over Whig candidate Winfield Scott was narrow in the popular vote but overwhelming in the Electoral College, an outcome Pierce chose to regard as a mandate to resume Polk's belligerent foreign policy. His inaugural address, otherwise notable only for being delivered entirely from memory, promised an administration that "will not be controlled by any timid forebodings of evil from expansion" and called for American acquisition "of certain possessions, not within our jurisdiction, eminently important for our protection"—but none was specified. In fact, Pierce had only a vague agenda; his first priority was to stifle intersectional tensions over the slavery issue by hewing closely to the 1850 Compromise and to end the wrangling within his own party by choosing cabinet members with disparate views who would govern by consensus. A political anomaly from antislavery, antiexpansionist New England, Pierce picked two other northerners for his inner circle: as Secretary of State, former New York governor and Senator William Marcy, who had been Polk's Secretary of War;

and as Attorney General, Massachusetts brahmin Caleb Cushing. Marcy, by far the ablest politician in Pierce's cabinet, had to devote his efforts to foreign affairs rather than domestic issues. Cushing was no less sympathetic than the President to southern concerns, as was the rest of the cabinet. It was not an administration reflective of the American political spectrum or conducive to achieving intersectional harmony.

Among those closest to Pierce, an indecisive chief executive prone to adopt the views of the last advisor he consulted, was his charismatic Secretary of War, wealthy Mississippi planter Jefferson Davis. Tall, handsome, brilliant, and wreathed in hubris, West Point graduate Davis had earned his nimbus as war hero when the regiment he commanded, the Mississippi Rifles, was thrown into the breach at a critical moment in the Battle of Buena Vista and shredded the ranks of the on-charging Mexicans with blistering, well-directed firepower. A term in the Senate sharpened Davis's oratorical gifts, which ranged from deft sarcasm to the pulverizing directness of a sledgehammer, but he returned to plantation life and only reluctantly accepted Pierce's plea to join his cabinet. A closet secessionist, Davis doubted the slavery issue could ever be settled amicably, but since Pierce was dedicated to that proposition and deferential to southern concerns, the Mississippian could serve the President without sacrificing any of his regional biases.

Convinced that the South without access to trade outlets on the Pacific was doomed to subservience to the North's growing economic base, Davis backed Gadsden's southern railroad route and had no qualms about pushing it as a military measure made necessary by continuing Mexican enmity. Nor did he consider the project sacrilegious to the South's long-standing opposition to federal involvement in internal improvements—in this case, through public land grants to the affected states and territories—so long as the nation's security and unity were advanced in the process. As the Pierce administration took office, Congress funded and Davis was placed in charge of a survey by U.S. Army engineers to select the most practical railway route to California. The Secretary of War was quick to harness the whole federal military apparatus at his disposal to find in favor of the route across Texas and the southern portion of New Mexico, where the nation's border was militarily most vulnerable. To further facilitate the selection of the southern route, Davis urged Pierce to designate Gadsden, who had been deposed as head of the South Carolina Railroad for devoting himself more avidly to the transcontinental project than the pursuit of profits for his company, as envoy to Mexico to resolve several rankling quarrels between the two nations.

The most pressing of them grew out of the terms of the Guadalupe Hidalgo treaty ending the Mexican conflict. That pact had called for a joint boundary commission made up of a surveyor and commissioner from each country to mark off the border line after taking scientific readings at the site. The task, begun at the western end of the boundary in mid-1849, at first presented no special problems for the American commissioner, John Bartlett of Rhode Island, and his Mexican counterpart, Pedro García Condé. When they traveled to El Paso late the following year to start laying out the boundary from the Rio Grande westward, trouble arose. The Guadalupe treaty, referring to the map affixed to it, said the boundary turned west from the river at a point eight miles north of El Paso. But the map, which placed El Paso at 32°15′ north latitude, was an 1847 copy of a twenty-five-year-old map that was crude to begin with. The astronomical readings taken by the joint commission's surveyors showed that El Paso was in fact half a degree, or about thirty-six miles, farther south and about 100 miles farther west than the map indicated. Which was to prevail—the errant map appended to the treaty, the text of which had not specified the latitude or longitude for that sector of the boundary but only its position relative to El Paso, or the now scientifically verified actuality? The area of dispute involved only a few thousand square miles and had only 3,000 or so inhabitants, but if the inaccurate map was allowed to govern, the United States stood to lose the Mesilla Valley, adjacent to the Rio Grande and opening to a strip of flat desert running about fifty miles from north to south and 200 miles or so to the west. This desolate stretch had just one virtue: it formed a natural funnel between the southernmost peaks of the rugged Rockies, making it the ideal—in truth, the only practicable—pathway for the southern rail route to the Pacific.

After arguing for four months, Bartlett and García Condé compromised. The treaty map would prevail with regard to El Paso, so the Mesilla Valley would revert to Mexico, but the boundary would be extended 120 miles farther west than the treaty map had shown before it swung north toward the Gila River, thereby providing the United States with a net gain in square mileage and possession of the Santa Rita de Cobra Mountains, reputedly the site of rich copper deposits and possibly still workable gold and silver mines. Bartlett's colleague, Lieutenant A. B. Gray, a U.S. Army surveyor from Texas, declined to go along with the compromise, however, and southern Democrats in Congress, favoring the Texas–New Mexico rail route, also balked at surrendering the Mesilla Valley. When President Fillmore, a New York Whig with no special fondness for the southern route, approved the Bartlett–García Condé settlement, Senate Democrats argued that the administration had no right to depart from the Guadalupe treaty language placing the boundary just past El Paso—wherever it was really located—and thus encompassing the Mesilla Valley. To put teeth into their objection, southerners in the Senate blocked further funding of the boundary survey, and for the final year of Fillmore's term, the issue was stalemated in Washington. Meanwhile, the Mexican government, back in the hands of militarists, insisted the deal struck by the two boundary commissioners was valid and ordered the repatriation of both Anglo-Texan and Mexican ranchers in the Mesilla Valley, over which the state of Chihuahua now asserted jurisdiction. Mexican troops prepared to enforce Chihuahua's authority. An ugly collision loomed.

A second rancorous issue arising from the Guadalupe treaty was the commitment by the United States in Article XI of the pact to protect Mexican citizens from Indian raids originating on the American side of the border. The then Secretary of State, Buchanan, had insisted his government had both the will and the ability to carry out the pledge, but five years of experience had shown otherwise. Comanche, Apache, and other tribal warriors had been punishing Spanish, Mexican, and American intruders into their stark homeland wilderness for three centuries and been given no incentive to let up their murderous marauding and pillaging, horse stealing in particular. The U.S. Army had posted nearly 8,000 of its total of 11,000 soldiers along the southwestern boundary, but they could not halt the 75,000 or so native nomads in the region from attacking swiftly and taking refuge among the hills, buttes, and arroyos in a landscape where one's enemies could be spotted twenty or thirty miles away.

By 1853, the United States had spent $12 million trying to tame the Indian raiders, to little avail. General Winfield Scott thought an expenditure five times that size was required to do the job. The Mexican government, in view of the ongoing terrorism unleashed against its citizenry from American soil, branded the treaty pledge a farce and presented Washington with a fat bill for the loss of life, limb, and property. The State Department commiserated over the losses but pointed out the peace treaty did not obligate the American people to pay reparations to Mexico for savage attacks by the Indians; the United States was required only to try to protect its neighbors as vigilantly as it did its own citizens. Mexican officials, always in dire need of cash, countered that they would forgive the American failure and allow Article XI to be stricken from the treaty, provided the United States paid $12 million in damages—a real bargain, Mexico argued, since the actual value of Indian depredations was closer to $40 million. Fillmore offered only $2 million to get out of the bind, so the unhappy Mexican envoy kept piling up the debt claims on Secretary of State John M. Clayton's desk.

A third overhanging problem with Mexico that greeted President Pierce stemmed from Nicholas Trist's failure in the course of the peace negotiations to secure the right to build and operate an interocean canal or railroad (or both) across the 125-mile-wide, north-south Tehuantepec isthmus— a privilege that Santa Anna had sold to a Mexican promoter in 1842, along with a land grant 300 miles wide for colonization. The right was resold five years later to a British bank "without any limitations whatever"—an alarming thought to American officials, who dreaded the idea of Britain, in defiance of the Monroe Doctrine, planting a new colony in the strategic midst of the Western Hemisphere and thereby obtaining a choke hold on by far the shortest passageway between the world's two great oceans.

Although America's need for a rapid interoceanic connection had grown more pressing, the great problems and costs involved dimmed any immediate prospect of building a transcontinental railway. Interest was thus rekindled in the Tehuantepec project, a far less daunting challenge. Financiers in New Orleans, fearful that the Mississippi's heavy downriver traffic would be siphoned off by a northern cross-country rail route, were particularly intrigued. Takeover of the rights for the Tehuantepec enterprise was far more easily arranged than American officials had dreamed. Early in 1849 the Hargous brothers, whose family conducted a busy import-export trade between New York and Veracruz, bought the Tehuantepec franchise for a token amount—reportedly as little as $25,000—apparently including the generous land grant for settlements surrounding the projected canal. But what good was a paper license to undertake such a monumentally expensive project without a pledge by the Mexican government to safeguard the construction and operation of the canal? And, in view of the dubious trustworthiness of such a pledge by Mexico, the full backing of the U.S. government and military in case of trouble was also essential.

The Hargous firm, confident that it was pursuing the American national interest as well as its own self-enrichment, applied to the Senate and State Department to work out a joint guarantee of its Tehuantepec franchise with the Mexican government. Secretary of State Clayton was receptive. He offered a treaty protective of Mexico's rights in the isthmus and promising that the Hargous group or any successor proprietor of a Tehuantepec canal would grant Mexican citizens preferential freight rates—at least 20 percent less than what Americans paid. In return, the United States would be permitted to introduce military force if needed to protect the canal and American citizens would be ensured most-favored-nation cargo fees.

While the status of the Hargous franchise was being weighed, Clayton moved to counteract the volatility of the Mexican government, unstable as ever, and to remove the ongoing danger that Britain or a consortium of its subjects would strike an accord with Mexico or very possibly neighboring Nicaragua to build and control a canal across the isthmus. Half a loaf, Clayton and Fillmore concluded, would be better than none. The result was a treaty Clayton drew up with British emissary Sir Henry Bulwer under which their two countries, rather than remaining competitors for proprietary canal rights and the commercial dominance that might flow from them, agreed to guarantee the neutrality of any isthmus canal and pledged that neither nation would seek to occupy the adjacent territory or install fortifications or establish colonies in the region.

The Clayton-Bulwer Treaty greatly reduced Mexico's ability to play off American and British interests against each other in the canal arena. But since the Mexicans wanted the canal built and badly needed all the revenues it would yield, they swallowed most of the treaty terms Clayton had proposed to secure the Hargous franchise—except for denial of American military intervention without Mexican approval. The Senate ratified the arrangement early in 1851, but the Mexican Congress refused to endorse the treaty and, by implication, the validity of the Hargous firm's purchase of rights originally granted nine years earlier to a Mexican national. Remembering the outcome of their government's old colonization program in Texas, where Americans had been invited to settle and wound up walking off with the province, the Mexican legislators said enough was enough. The Hargous firm, even without a supporting treaty between the two governments, acted as if its contract was still legally binding. With money partly raised in New Orleans, where the locals expected much of the cargo bound for canal passage to flow through their port facilities, Hargous operatives began making land deals within the original grant region in open defiance of the Mexican Congress. The enraged legislators soon officially annulled the entire arrangement. Claiming losses of $5 million, the Hargous interests asked the State Department to intercede, but President Fillmore declined to risk a diplomatic or military confrontation with Mexico to enforce a contractual arrangement made by a private company that ought to have been diligent enough to obtain indemnity provisions.

Rumors soon swirled that the Hargous people might act extralegally and even forcibly to seize the isthmus; Washington also heard reports that Mexico was selling the canal rights to British developers. It was all scuttlebutt. But the Mexicans, still eager for the canal to be built yet fearful the American government might use the cancellation of the Hargous grant as the pretext for sending a military expedition to occupy the isthmus, decided to gamble. They sold the canal franchise to a New York developer, A. G. Sloo and Associates, for $600,000, but this time no land grant was provided for

American colonization—which might have helped defray construction costs—and no armed intervention by U.S. troops would be tolerated. The Sloo firm displayed early initiative. It capitalized itself at $10 million, contracted with a British company to build a railroad across the isthmus as part of the canal project, and in March 1853, as the Pierce administration was taking office, asked for an exclusive government contract to carry the U.S. mail between New York and San Francisco via the Tehuantepec isthmus, promising delivery at least fifteen days faster than any other route.

These displays of purposefulness could not long cloak reality: Sloo was more manipulative than moneyed. To pay the Mexican government the purchase price, the firm had to borrow from a British banking house. But Sloo and Associates soon defaulted on the loan, and the British bank promptly resold the Tehuantepec franchise back to Hargous, which thus held both the original but now voided grant and the Sloo firm's new, more circumscribed one. This turn of events was not what Mexico had had in mind. The canal's prospects were so muddled that the intervening hand of the American government seemed the only recourse for straightening them out. The new Pierce administration, though, soon made clear that it preferred a transcontinental railroad along a southerly route to an interoceanic canal across a resentful neighbor's territory.

A WELL-INTENTIONED YANKEE lacking leadership skills, Franklin Pierce served as a cat's-paw for expansionists pushing the United States (notwithstanding its recent addition of the northern 40 percent of Mexico) toward new worlds to conquer. There was Cuba, for example, though Spain had made clear it would not sell the Pearl of the Antilles for any price. Then there were the Hawaiian Islands or other Pacific way stations of potentially high utility for the expected surge in the Asian trade. Also Baja California, since the United States could someday probably use—for an as yet undetermined purpose—another 800 miles of coastline, albeit rock-bound, arid, and connected to nothing. Far more useful would have been a single harbor on the eastern shore of the Gulf of California, which would have necessitated relieving Mexico of a thick slab of the state of Sonora. And there was the possibility of helping itself to more Mexican territory in order to create a natural boundary between the two countries rather than an arbitrary and artificial one along a line of sand—a broad expanse of desert, say, or, better yet, the Sierra Madre mountain range, costing Mexico healthy chunks of Chihuahua, Coahuila, and Sonora.

Franklin Pierce, trying to morph himself into James Polk, would indulge in such territorial daydreams and even talked the talk, but he had little stomach for confrontational policies, let alone mortal combat. Still, he had to clear the air with Mexico if his presidency was to succeed, so soon after taking office he heeded Jefferson Davis's advice and assigned James Gadsden, a novice at diplomacy but a stalwart at pushing southern causes, to settle the disputes over the American-Mexican boundary, reparations for Indian attacks, and the status of the isthmus canal.

Gadsden, for all his advantages—impeccable family pedigree, Yale education, Andrew Jackson as his military patron, John Calhoun and Jeff Davis as his political patrons—had never made much of himself or of the railroad he had run for ten years. A secessionist sympathizer, he had lately lobbied the California legislature to permit slave labor in the southern part of the state. His talents for the assignment as minister to Mexico were questioned by Gadsden's fellow southern nationalist, former South Carolina governor (and future U.S. Senator) James H. Hammond, who predicted privately that the new ambassador would "add one more failure to his list, which embraced every undertaking of his useless life . . . [He] has been bolstered up from all quarters and put forward and yet never does anything."

Davis's glowing endorsement was enough, though, to offset reports of Gadsden's ineffectuality. But just to play it safe, Secretary of State Marcy's instructions to Gadsden were very specific: (1) settle the boundary dispute in any way that included the Mesilla Valley within American territory so that the United States could run the southern railway route over that level terrain—there was no other pressing reason to revise the border spelled out in the Guadalupe treaty; (2) tell the Mexicans that the U.S. Army had done its best to stem Indian attacks from the American side of the border, that there was no requirement in Article XI of the treaty for the United States to indemnify Mexican citizens for losses suffered at the tribal raiders' hands, and that the Mexican government had the primary responsibility to protect its own people; and (3) inform Mexico that it should cooperate with the American citizens who had contracted in good faith to build the Tenhuantepec canal. Gadsden, however, had grander ambitions.

The postwar political struggle centered in Mexico City showed that little had changed and no lessons had been learned. After the occupying American troops had departed, fragile coalitions broke apart, reformers and reactionaries chased each other out of office in an unbreakable cycle, the Mexican national treasury was $17 million in debt, and the average lifespan of the government's finance ministers was about two months. In these dire, anarchic circumstances, the Mexican people did what they had repeatedly done for two decades—dusted off their fallen hero, Antonio López de Santa

Anna, and made him president. Proven disaster though he was, Santa Anna was still perceived as an authentic patriot and second to none in his enmity for the United States. Reanointed chief of state at almost the same time the Pierce administration took power, Santa Anna soon demonstrated that he, too, had learned nothing from his own and his countrymen's past misfortunes. Just as he had done nearly twenty years earlier, he tore up the 1824 constitution, disbanded the Congress, and replaced it with a twenty-one-member council of advisors, all chosen by the president himself and headed by a bishop. Mexico's unsinkable warlord had again chosen despotism over democracy as the only cure for a perpetually dysfunctional government. He was willing to receive the new American envoy for only one reason—an urgent need of money to bail out the national treasury and raise an army that could put muscle behind his tyrannical policies and guard Mexico's northern border against new *yanqui* seizures.

Gadsden met with the Mexican dictator toward the end of August and, exceeding his instructions, tried to become a hero. He suggested to Santa Anna that the security of both their nations would be improved if the open border between them was replaced by a wider natural barrier such as the Sierra Madres. But the Mexican leader had not returned to power to dismantle his country further. The only items he would discuss were the disputed southern boundary of New Mexico and the bill he presented to Gadsden for the cumulative, ever worsening damages that Mexican citizens had suffered from Indian attacks across the American border. Told that the United States had no obligation to the Indians' victims beyond trying to restrain the attackers, as its soldiers had done to the best of their ability, Santa Anna proposed that the matter be resolved by a neutral international tribunal. Although the State Department considered the Mexican claim for reparations to be extortionate, Gadsden saw that unless he was prepared to yield some ground on the Indian issue, he might be staring at a stone wall when it came to revising the boundary for the benefit of his precious southerly railroad route. But he was also astute enough to perceive how tenuous Santa Anna's hold on power was and that the key to a successful negotiation was how much money Mexico could pry from the United States—whether it was for an expanse of largely worthless desert or for the damage done by the Indians was beside the point. Gadsden sent a message to Secretary Marcy to that effect, suggesting that for the right amount Santa Anna might part with a lot more Mexican territory than he was letting on. And since he might not be in power for long, the moment was ripe for a prompt, bold cash offer.

Marcy, with Pierce's blessing, sent a special messenger bearing a map and revised instructions to Gadsden to offer Santa Anna a choice among six possible parcels of territory the United States wanted to purchase, with the price stipulated for each. And it was to be a package deal: the payment would cover any newly ceded land as well as all claims against the American government for Indian damages; Article XI, moreover, would be stripped from the Guadalupe treaty, freeing the United States from its duty to safeguard Mexicans from future Indian attacks. For the top payment of $50 million, Mexico would have to surrender Baja California and a large portion of its northwestern states; for the smallest price tag, $15 million, Mexico would have to yield about 38,000 square miles of sand so the Americans' southern railroad could avoid being routed through the Rockies.

His domestic needs aside, Santa Anna was piqued by what he and his diplomatic aides took as Gadsden's antagonistic manner. The diplomat from Charleston was likely less than subtle in revealing his contempt for Santa Anna's autocratic regime; he strongly recommended that the Mexican accept the largest of the territorial packages the United States had offered to buy because "the spirit of the age"—that is, the yearning for democracy and economic opportunity—would soon drive the northern Mexican states to secede and apply for acceptance by the American republic. Such comments marked Gadsden, in Mexican eyes, as a true disciple of James Polk, disdainful to the point where fellow Americans in Mexico City had to be enlisted to urge their ambassador to tone it down if he hoped to strike a deal with the proud Mexican potentate.

Further souring Santa Anna on a conciliatory agreement was the mischief-making of a twenty-nine-year-old American semi-mystic, William Walker, a freebooter looking for a cause. In the company of about fifty fellow adventurers, Walker landed in Baja California, declared the virtually empty peninsula independent of Mexican rule and himself its president, and, so long as he was there, proclaimed the annexation of the neighboring state of Sonora. Whether viewed as an American agent provocateur in the manner of John Frémont or just plain loco, Walker was an embarrassment to Gadsden's efforts. Even though the envoy gave every assurance that Walker's party had not been sanctioned by the American government, which soon took a hand in removing the wayward gang and pressing criminal charges against it, Santa Anna concluded that one way or another, the United States was determined to annex much more, if not all, of Mexico. He appealed to Britain to restrain the Americans' raging territorial appetite and put out word that he would resign from the presidency if a foreign prince of sufficient majesty could be enticed to set up a throne in Mexico and bring order to the land. But the British, having lately secured through the Clayton-Bulwer Treaty their primary vested interest in Mexican territory—a shared role with the United States in safeguarding any canal through the isthmus—had no further motive for heeding Santa Anna's plea. Nor was any European royal eager to ascend a newly carpentered throne to reign over the roiling Mexican polity. The generalissimo saw that he had better strike a deal with the egregious Gadsden before it was too late.

Santa Anna agreed to yield the smallest territorial package among those the United States had proposed. For $15 million, the boundary between the two countries was altered from the Guadalupe treaty to run from the Gulf up the middle of the Rio Grande to 31°47′ north latitude, just above El Paso, and turn due west for a hundred miles, enclosing the Mesilla Valley as U.S. territory, then south for thirty miles, west for 230 miles, and finally angling northwest for 240 miles until it reached the Colorado River at a point twenty miles below its juncture with the Gila River. The angled westernmost sector still allowed Mexico to retain a land bridge, though a narrower one, linking Sonora and Baja above the Gulf of California. The United States agreed to assume up to $5 million of claims by its citizens against the Mexican state, prominently including the Hargous firm's demand for losses due to the annulment of the original Tehuantepec canal grant. Mexico agreed to give the United States the right of transit across the isthmus for its mail, its citizens and their merchandise, and its soldiers and their armaments, but Mexican sovereignty over the region was not thereby compromised. And the United States was spared from future duty to restrain Indians rampaging into Mexico. Gadsden had won his railroad route but not much more. Santa Anna had lost some desert but won a bundle of sound American currency.

THE OUTCOME DISAPPOINTED the President. But where Polk might have torn Gadsden's draft treaty into pieces and ordered the cavalry to march on Sonora, Franklin Pierce acceded to the cooler heads around him who counseled acceptance of the Gadsden Purchase and its side agreements. Pierce, though, did insist on striking from the treaty the language that obliged the nation to make good on the likes of the Hargous claims against Mexico. That country's annulment of the license the firm had purchased to build the canal and colonize the region was not the U.S. government's business, nor would it come to blows with the Mexicans over it.

The nation's reaction, once the treaty was sent to the Senate for ratification and its terms were leaked to the press, was mixed. The North's growing antislavery legions were at best unenthusiastic; a southern transcontinental railway route would only strengthen the slavocracy's hand economically, and the newly acquired 38,000 square miles of Mexican territory, though infertile, might contribute enough added bulk, as the *New York Herald* contended, to allow two or more slave states to be created south of the Missouri Compromise line, thereby offsetting California's 1850 entry into the Union as a free-soil state. California's Senators opposed the Gadsden deal because it did not gulp down a lot more of Mexico, starting with Baja California. Clearheaded citizens complained that the price agreed to was pretty steep for a region that superscout Kit Carson, who knew it as well as anyone, described as "so utterly desolate, desert, and God-forsaken . . . that a wolf could not make a living upon it." Ohio Congressman Joshua Giddings, the Whigs' best orator, said the United States, for all that money, was buying only "rocks, volcanic mountains, [and] precipitous bluffs."

In fairness, the United States was paying up not just for title to a small Sahara but to indemnify itself against exposure to damage claims arising from the now defunct Article XI of the previous treaty with Mexico. More to the point, Gadsden's package would allow American commerce potential use of not one but two much faster southerly routes linking the Atlantic and Pacific coasts: a cross-country railroad through Texas and New Mexico, the shortest and cheapest of the projected routes, as U.S. Army engineers would soon conclude, and a canal through Tehuantepec. And if the United States did not embrace the new treaty and protect its transit rights in the isthmus, foreign powers or proprietors might step in. Even so, some skeptics questioned the morality of handing Santa Anna a lot of money to help prop up his antidemocratic rule. The Senate, furthermore, was lobbied vigorously to insert in the treaty a strong pledge of protection by both governments for the Sloo franchise. Southern lawmakers in particular were susceptible to the argument that American possession, whether by the government or private entrepreneurs, of transit rights across the isthmus provided a realistic, time- and cost-saving alternative to any coast-to-coast railway route. And the Sloo franchise, no less than the Hargous grant, which the Senate had earlier agreed to defend by a treaty the Mexican Congress rejected, was worthless—and its holders were unlikely ever to break ground for the canal—unless American military force could be called upon to safeguard the project if required.

Gadsden's treaty reached the Senate in the first part of February 1854, but its members did not address it seriously for weeks while they grappled with a bill that had at its core the same goal as the proposed new acquisition from Mexico—a transcontinental rail route to be funded in significant part by federal land grants. Though the ramifications of the Kansas-Nebraska Act reached far more directly into the slavery question than Gadsden's purchase, the fates of both were closely connected.

Given the huge costs of labor and material likely to be required, most people familiar with the proposed transcontinental railroad assumed that the nation could afford only one route, at least for the foreseeable future. And because the terminus cities, other major stops on the trunk line, and new communities that might spring to life as the tracks advanced westward were thought likely to prosper as a result, regional competition intensified over which route Congress would finally select. In 1853 federal land grants to Missouri and Arkansas for railroad-building seemed to strengthen the advocates of the southerly route through Texas and New Mexico, but would-be financial backers and elected officials continued to squabble over where the eastern terminus of the new trans-Mississippi line ought to be. St. Louis, Memphis, Vicksburg, and Little Rock were prominent contenders, but concerted action awaited settlement of the boundary dispute with Mexico over the Mesilla Valley. That same year, vigorous activity by northern rail magnates posed an imminent threat to southern hopes. Eleven smaller railroads combined to form the New York Central; trackage from Michigan reached Chicago, connecting the East and Midwest; and beyond the Great Lakes a web of iron rails was being feverishly spun across Illinois and Iowa—all of which pointed to likely congressional backing of a New York–Chicago–San Francisco route. But such a line would have to be built across the wide, unorganized Nebraska Territory, still reserved by law for the Indians and closed to other settlers and travelers.

Near the end of 1853, as James Gadsden was wrapping up his land deal with Santa Anna and materially advancing the prospects of the southern route, Senator Augustus Dodge of Iowa introduced a bill to organize the Nebraska Territory into a single jurisdiction 400 miles north to south and stretching westward nearly 500 miles from the Missouri River to the foothills of the Rockies. The resident Indians would just have to be shoved aside, again—north to the Dakotas and south into Oklahoma, where other tribes were already concentrated. If the native Americans behaved themselves and did not harass the white settlers who were rudely dispossessing them, they were promised military protection and annual cash payments.

Southern Senators killed Dodge's proposal. Since all of the Nebraska Territory lay north of the Missouri Compromise line, to license it as a federal jurisdiction would presage its early entry into the Union as a large free-soil state, further reducing southern political power already diluted by California's sudden attainment of statehood under the 1850 Compromise. And once Nebraska was organized, its territorial government would be eligible to apply for federal land grants for constructing the northerly transcontinental railway from Chicago—anathema to southern commercial and political interests.

For "Little Giant" Stephen Douglas, the ambitious Illinois Senator who had spent ten years pushing federal land grants for railroads and preparing the way for a northern route to the Pacific, the swift demise of Senator Dodge's bill to organize Nebraska presented him with a strategic opening. An unsuccessful contender for the presidency in 1852, Douglas hoped to narrow the growing gap between the northern and southern wings of the Democratic Party, thereby advancing his own political fortunes, with a bill to organize the Nebraska Territory in the same way Congress had dealt in 1850 with the New Mexico and Utah territories—by allowing its settlers to decide for themselves through "popular sovereignty" whether slavery could be practiced within their borders. Since the Utah Territory (including the modern state of Nevada) lay north of the Missouri Compromise line, Douglas's proposal was not without a precedent.

Unburdened by strong antislavery sentiments and doubtful that the practice would thrive in the Nebraska region—an expedient assumption—Douglas did not scruple over offering southern Senators added cause to back his bill. He proposed that the Nebraska Territory be split into two separate entities, Nebraska to the north and Kansas to the south. Because of the expected immigration pattern, Nebraska settlers were likely to be small farmers from the North and East with antislavery convictions and no desire to compete with the plantation system; settlers in Kansas, more likely to emigrate from southern states, might well vote to sanction slavery. To make sure Kansas would have that opportunity and to reduce federal power over settlers with regard to slaveholding in any future organized territories, southern Senators insisted that the Kansas-Nebraska Act explicitly supersede the Missouri Compromise by wiping away its fixed boundary between free and slave soil. Furious antislavery proponents railed against Douglas's pact with the devil, but they were outnumbered by moderate northerners who wanted the coast-to-coast railroad to run through their precincts and by the solid South embracing the possibility of additional slave states and renewed political parity in the Senate.

Douglas got his bill through Congress, but not without an important concession inimical to those pressing the northern railroad route. Southern Senators felt Douglas had not done enough for them simply by allowing the possible extension of slavery into new territories. There was no certainty under his bill, they argued, that either Kansas or Nebraska would become a slave state—indeed, the latter seemed a highly improbable candidate—and, at any rate, organizing Nebraska, the likely pathway for the northerly railway route from Chicago to the Pacific, without also ratifying Gadsden's purchase would all but eliminate a southern railway and ensure Douglas's route. So with passage of the Kansas-Nebraska Act imminent, the Senate took up the Gadsden treaty, which attracted a majority but fell short of the two-thirds needed to ratify.

Repeated efforts were made to amend the treaty, some seeking additional territory, such as a port on the Gulf of California, some asking for less desert land and a lower purchase price. Particularly persistent were Senators seeking treaty protection for the Sloo franchise holders by the American and Mexican governments—an extension of federal power that President Pierce heartily opposed. On April 17, the Senate voted 27 to 18 in favor of the treaty; a switch of just three votes would have ratified it. To remedy the shortfall, Jefferson Davis and leading southern Senators prevailed upon Pierce to relent on the Sloo issue. Without naming the present holders of the isthmus franchise, a clause was inserted in the treaty obligating the Mexican government "to protect with its whole power the prosecution, preservation, and security of the work [the canal]" and allowing the United States to act in like fashion "when it may feel sanctioned and warranted by the public or international law." To mollify antislavery Senators and those fervently against subsidizing Santa Anna's despotism by paying him millions for worthless desert, the treaty reduced the territory to be acquired by 9,000 square miles and the price from $15 million to $10 million. In that form, it passed by a 33–12 vote, leaving seventeen Senators' votes unrecorded— a sign of their moral ambivalence toward the treaty and, in some cases, revulsion over the proslavery features of Douglas's Kansas-Nebraska deal.

Gadsden took his somewhat shriveled treaty back to Santa Anna, half-hoping he would refuse to sign it. But the Mexican strongman wanted to end the feuding with the United States, and since it was immaterial to him whether the American railway to the Pacific was routed along the nation's southerly latitudes or by way of the North Pole, he considered even the $10 million price delightfully rich for the territory involved. He signed the treaty and soon after squandered its $7 million down payment, pocketing 10 percent of it for property damage he claimed to have suffered personally over the years at the hands of the Americans. Gadsden, to his credit, stayed on in Mexico as the American ambassador, working clandestinely and at times openly with rebel elements opposed to Santa Anna's autocratic regime. Despite the repeated demands of the Mexican government for his recall, Gadsden remained at his post in Mexico City for two years, outlasting Santa Anna, who was forced to resign—once again—in August 1855. By the time Gadsden arrived home in the last months of Pierce's presidency, Mexico's government reformers were locked anew in their endless struggle with the military and the clergy.

Douglas's legerdemain won Senate passage of his 1855 bill for federal backing of a railway to the Pacific routed through either Iowa or Missouri (so long as the latter connected with Illinois at Cairo), but it failed by a single vote to pass in the House. His Kansas-Nebraska Act soon unleashed the frenzied wrath of many who had never before joined in antislavery agitation, and the sad spectacle of Kansas turned into a bloody cockpit of free-soilers battling slaveholders for control of their territory spawned a new northern political party, the Republicans. The polarizing effects of the Kansas-Nebraska Act blocked agreement on a Pacific rail route for the few years remaining in the antebellum period. But the railroad-building boom, with state aid supplementing private enterprise, accelerated in the North and West, where most of the nation's 30,000 miles of track were located as of 1860. In the South, railroad activity failed to keep pace. What southerners wanted were more plantations and bumper cotton harvests. All the efforts by northern appeasers and supplicants of the South such as Douglas, Pierce, and Buchanan served chiefly to stoke the slavocracy's intransigence as well as the moral outrage and religious fervor driving the antislavery crusaders.

When civil war came, the Confederate States of America found themselves fatally handicapped by a transportation system inadequate for the movement of troops and supplies. Not until 1880 was a main train line, the Southern Pacific, laid across the Mesilla Valley to connect with California. The northern through route had been opened eleven years earlier. The one sizable community to have been established over the ensuing century and a half in the area comprising the Gadsden Purchase is Tucson, Arizona. Mostly the region remains sand, bought for fifty-four cents an acre.

CHAPTER 13

The great white elephant sale

1854–1867

ABOUT TEN O'CLOCK ON THE EVENING of April 14, 1865, in the nation's capital—at very nearly the same moment that the deranged actor John Wilkes Booth entered the presidential box at Ford's Theater and put a bullet in the back of Abraham Lincoln's head—another member of Booth's conspiratorial gang appeared, with similarly murderous intent, at the front door of Secretary of State William H. Seward's home on Lafayette Square, close by the White House, and rang the bell.

Seward, convalescing from a serious carriage accident that had left him with a broken jaw and injured shoulder, was nearly asleep in a third-floor bedroom, attended by his devoted daughter, Fanny, and a male military nurse. His wife, Frances, and their sons, Frederick, an aide to his father at the State Department, and Augustus, an army man, were also at home along with several servants. The would-be assassin, an ex-Confederate soldier who had fought at Antietam and in several other major battles, been wounded and captured at Gettysburg, and later escaped from a prison hospital in Baltimore, was Lewis Paine. Two of his brothers had been killed in the fighting. Paine had been sent by Booth's gang of conspirators to slay the sixty-four-year-old Secretary of State not because he had played a key role in the military defeat of the Confederacy but probably due to his fervent antislavery oratory prior to the war, which had made him the best-known member of Lincoln's cabinet.

Paine told the nineteen-year-old black servant who answered the doorbell that he had brought medicine from Seward's doctor and been ordered to deliver it in person and instruct the patient how to take it. The servant said that strangers were not permitted upstairs, but Paine insisted, pushed past him, and headed up the staircase. There he encountered Fred Seward, in his undergarments, who intercepted the intruder, said he would take responsibility for safe delivery of the medicine, and, still not suspecting the worst, barred the assassin's path. Paine drew a large pistol from inside his light overcoat, aimed it at Fred, and pulled the trigger. When it failed to fire, Paine lunged at him and viciously brought the gun barrel down twice on Fred's head, fracturing his skull and leaving him in a coma that would last a month. The commotion drew the male nurse from Seward's sickroom. The assailant produced a Bowie knife with a ten-inch blade, slashed the nurse across the forehead, and shoved past the wounded attendant into Seward's dimly lit bedroom. He saw the Secretary of State lying in bed on the side farther from the door, reached across—flailing madly now, as Seward did his enfeebled best to evade him—and struck twice, one blow opening a deep gash in the invalid's cheek, the other grievously wounding his neck and barely missing his jugular. Only heroic intervention by the wounded nurse and the loud sounds of other approaching members of the household prevented Paine from finishing Seward off. The attacker fled on horseback but was captured a few days later at the boardinghouse where the Booth gang had stayed.

Although he lost a good deal of blood from his wounds, Seward received prompt medical treatment and, after six more painful weeks of recuperation, returned to his post under the new President, Andrew Johnson. Three weeks later, the ordeal took the life of Seward's strong-willed but emotionally fragile wife; soon thereafter, Lewis Paine and three other fellow conspirators were hanged. As the martyred survivor of the same plot that had slain the Great Emancipator, Seward now emerged as the principal advisor to President Johnson and chief cabinet supporter of his conciliatory policy toward the eleven vanquished Confederate states—a stance that both men took to be in the spirit of Lincoln's second inaugural promise, delivered the month before his assassination, to bind up the nation's wounds "with malice toward none, with charity for all."

That alliance was to cost Seward his high standing as an outspoken political reformer and champion of the rights of the downtrodden, be they Irish immigrants, enslaved blacks, or abused native peoples. In 1860, the shrewd, suave, and articulate Senator from (and former governor of) New York had been the leading candidate for the Republican presidential nomination. But his strong—and often impolitic—humanitarian views brought him too many enemies, and Seward had to settle for the top post in the cabinet of a man he considered much his inferior in grace and intellect. Seward came to admire Lincoln's finer qualities, but his own conduct in office, while competent and dutiful, did not entirely cloak his grudge toward the President, who never fully trusted him. Johnson, a courageous, intelligent, but somewhat intemperate Tennessean with little of Lincoln's profound understanding of human nature, badly needed Seward's support. But in lending it, Seward had enraged the radical wing of the Republican Party, which dominated Congress and believed the southern states ought to be reduced to the status of territories on parole and not welcomed back into the Union until each had demonstrated contrition by extending liberty and justice to all its citizens, freed slaves included. Largely to restore his reputation as a statesman and deflect the rebuke he had been dealt in the embittered public discourse over the reconstruction of the South, Seward turned his efforts to the last great territorial acquisition by the United States. His contemporary critics called it folly, even at two cents an acre; posterity has ruled otherwise.

The truth was that no one else in the federal government had any interest in the project. Russian America, as Alaska was still called in 1867, was hardly an irresistible piece of real estate. Dimly perceived as a remote, forbidding wasteland, unsuitable for growing anything but timber, too cold for civilized people to live in, economically worthless except for its coastal fisheries, its interior inaccessible behind great walls of glazed, towering, wind-whipped mountains, the place was simply beyond the imagining of most Americans. In the wake of the terrible fratricidal struggle that had wrenched apart their glorious republic and the expansive dominion it had so rapidly accumulated, Russia's North American colony seemed no more than a glossy, unnecessary bauble, of neither commercial nor strategic value to a nation groaning under a war debt of a nearly unthinkable $3 billion. But William Henry Seward was a visionary politician who knew that on a small planet in a vast universe, land is a finite commodity and none of it is without value.

AFTER 126 YEARS AS RUSSIA'S most distant possession, the northwesternmost extremity of the New World had long since become an albatross. Enveloped in constant coastal fog, it had been come upon by sea captain Vitus Bering in 1741 sailing under commission by Peter the Great, in whose name the Danish mariner claimed it. Aside from a narrow coastal strip warmed by the Japanese current, the Pacific Ocean's counterpart of the Atlantic's Gulf Stream, and its multitude of nearby islands, the topography of the far land made it impenetrable to the Russians—and the natives were none too friendly. Still, the Russians were the first white people to probe the region, and they were struck by the spectacular abundance of fish and the swarming sea otters, a species indigenous to the north Pacific, with remarkably fine and soft fur that was soon greatly prized in China as well as St. Petersburg. But even the Russians, used to long rages of wintry weather, found the climate unsuitable for colonial settlement. They used their North American possession only as a hunting ground and employed the natives to do most of the dirty work.

Late in the eighteenth century the Russians saw their New World territory encroached on by merchant vessels and an occasional warship from Spain, Britain, and the United States, all with their own claims to the northern Pacific coastal waters. To solidify his nation's hegemony over the region, Tsar Paul I in 1799 chartered the Russian-American Company (RAC) as a profit-seeking monopoly with quasi-governmental authority to administer the commercial operations and any territory where they were quartered. The RAC was created in the image of Britain's Hudson's Bay Company, with exclusive trading rights and delegated civil authority over vast stretches of wilderness but no expectation it would establish permanent settlements for immigrants. Profitable in its early stages, the Russian venture was based on brutal exploitation of the Aleuts and other native peoples, whose hunting waters they plundered, movements they restricted, chieftains they humiliated, and lives they shortened by fatal contact with Europeans' microbes. To resolve conflicting claims over the coastal hunting grounds, the Russians reached diplomatic accords with the other contending powers, so that by 1825 they were acknowledged masters of the territory above 54°40' north latitude and west of the 141st meridian.

Soon thereafter, the sea otter population began to decline, and with it the RAC's profits. Meanwhile American vessels appeared in growing numbers to harvest the "whale pasture" off Kodiak Island just below the coast of Russian America, sometimes straying from international waters too close to shore and ever more frequently putting in at coastal harbors for supplies or repairs. The Russians protested such incursions but in vain; it took nearly a year for a message from the RAC's main depot at Sitka to reach St. Petersburg, and another year to get a reply. By the 1840s some 300 American whalers were trolling close by, overwhelming the Russian presence, while on the mainland to the south, Britain and the United States were clashing over how to partition the Oregon Country. The Russian hold on the northwest corner of the continent grew more precarious and less rewarding with each passing year. By the time the Crimean War began in 1854, as Britain, France, and Austria sought to check the spread of Russian power into the Balkans and Ottoman Turkey, the military vulnerability of Russian America was all too apparent. It was just too far away and costly to defend, and a small flotilla of British warships with a few hundred troops on board could have seized the territory anytime they chose. To head off that possibility, Russian America was declared neutral territory, unusable for military purposes by any of the combatants—an arrangement Britain agreed to only because of the likelihood Russia would otherwise have sold the immense territory to the United States, leaving British North America only a few hundred miles of Pacific coastline and threatening the takeover of British Columbia.

On the eve of the Crimean War, another solution to Russia's problematic commercial colony in North America was broached by the governor-general of eastern Siberia, who in 1853 sent a letter to Tsar Nicholas I and suggested ceding Russian America to the United States. The Americans had lately, by diplomacy or at gunpoint, taken possession of the Pacific coast from San Diego to the Strait of Juan de Fuca and seemed certain to continue their push northward. It seemed smarter to sell them Russian America and instead devote Russia's resources to colonizing and commercially developing its contiguous expansion across the northern tier of East Asia. The idea grew more appealing after the Russians' defeat in the Crimean War thwarted their aspirations in eastern Europe. By 1857, the Grand Duke Constantine, brother of the new tsar, Alexander II, and commander of his navy, was advising imperial circles in St. Petersburg that "Russia must endeavor . . . to become stronger in her center, in those fundamentally Russian regions which constitute her main power in population and in faith." He pressed the tsar's foreign minister, Prince Alexander Gorchakov, to consider shutting down the RAC, by then surviving on a government subsidy, and added, "We would do well to take advantage of the excess of money at the present time in the treasury of the United States and sell them our North American colonies."

The proposals were viewed with favor by Alexander, who had ascended to the throne in 1855 at the age of thirty-seven and was proving to be an enlightened reformer, at least for a tsar. In his first half dozen years as ruler, he acted to liberalize the autocracy by granting a degree of local self-rule and modernizing the legal system along Western lines. More surprisingly, he acted to ease the plight of the peasant masses and decreed freedom from feudal bondage for 23 million serfs. In keeping with these progressive changes, Russia negotiated a series of agreements with China between 1854 and 1860, establishing commercial relations with Peking and gaining undisputed title to the lower valley of the great Amur River, the 1,800-mile-long boundary between the two empires that emptied into the Sea of Japan. The newly established military post at the nearby seaport of Vladivostok, serving as colossal Eurasian Russia's eastern terminus, made the North American colony seem a still more useless overreach.

To supplement its reduced revenues, the Russian-American Company experimented with coal mining and logging, but like an earlier attempt at farming on the northern coast of California, slack management doomed the efforts. Its dividends and stock prices plummeting, the RAC was saved from bankruptcy only by the indulgence of the imperial treasury. Even the discovery of gold in 1861 in the Fraser Valley near British territory did not brighten Russian America's prospects; indeed, St. Petersburg feared that the whole region would soon be overrun with American and other foreign squatters, just as California had been a dozen years before, taking de facto possession of claimed Russian territory. The tsarist regime had three choices: defend Russian America before it was grabbed away, surrender it, or sell it. The last option was chosen, and there was no debate about who the buyer should be; timing was the only question.

AMONG THE FIRST OFFICIALS in the United States to propose the acquisition of Russian America was President Polk's gifted, hard-driving Secretary of the Treasury, Pennsylvania-born Robert J. Walker. A lawyer and land speculator who moved to Mississippi as a young man, he took the side of squatters and poor farmers, arguing for low land prices and preemption laws during nine years as a U.S. Senator, and freed his slaves. But Walker was second to none in his vehemence as a territorial expansionist. He pushed hard in the Senate to bring Texas into the Union, advocated the annexation of all of Mexico, and in 1845 urged Polk to go after Russian America rather than restricting his northwestward reach to the 54°40′ line. It was a reach too far even for Polk. Twenty-two years later, Walker would play a useful— and well paid—role in bringing the idea to fruition.

A yet more determined proponent of the purchase made his first public pitch for it in 1846. "Our population is destined to roll its resistless waves to the icy waters of the North and to encounter oriental civilization on the shores of the Pacific," prophesied William Henry Seward, lately the governor of New York and soon to enter the U.S. Senate. In another speech that same year, he told listeners in St. Paul, Minnesota, that as he looked still farther to the northwest,

> I see the Russian, as he busily occupies himself in establishing seaports and towns and fortifications on the verge of this continent, as

the outposts of St. Petersburg; and I can say, "Go on and build your outposts all along the coast, up even to the Arctic Ocean; they will yet become the outposts of my own country—monuments of the civilization of the United States in the Northwest.

That the Russian was not in fact so occupying himself did not stand in the way of Seward's rhetorical flourishes. The point was the Russian was there and, under Seward's reading of manifest destiny, would have to give way. It was no passing fancy of his; in 1852, soon after coming to the Senate, he proposed a naval survey of the northern Pacific and the Bering Strait.

No American brought up the subject with the Russians until 1854, when Senator William M. Gwin of California, a hustling lawyer pal of Robert Walker from their Mississippi days, got wind of a report floating around San Francisco that Russia might sell its North American possession to the United States or to private American investors in order to discourage its Crimean War foe, the British, from grabbing the unprotected colony. Like most newcomers to California, Gwin had been drawn there by the Gold Rush and hoped to cash in on the excitement financially as well as politically. The San Francisco business community had sent him to Washington to look after its interests, including potentially lucrative commerce in ice, furs, fish, and lumber with the Russian colony. Its Aleutian Islands, moreover, would provide a natural way station for transpacific cargoes en route to China and Japan, with whom the United States had reached trade agreements in 1844 and 1855 respectively.

When Senator Gwin approached Edouard de Stoeckl, a leading member of the Russian legation in Washington, to inquire if the colony was on the market, the diplomat denied the report. In fact, the rumor was based on a Russian brainstorm: if a strictly fictitious sale of the RAC's assets—which, as a practical matter, would have been tantamount to selling the whole place—could be arranged with a San Francisco–based consortium and word of the pending deal put out, that might be enough to foil any potential attack by the British, who were not inclined to incite the Americans to take up arms against them. Secretary of State William Marcy had declined to play along with the scheme, in part because he was sure the British would see the ruse for what it was. Stoeckl himself thought the idea harebrained for a different reason. Russia's North American holdings, he wrote to his superiors in St. Petersburg, "arouse a passionate desire among Americans. They are dangerous neighbors, and we must avoid giving them the least pretext."

Over the next five years that desire grew still more ardent with the rapid development of commerce in California. In 1859 the ebullient Senator

Gwin, by then entwined with San Francisco's new-money crowd pushing for a steamship route and telegraph line to be extended to Asia along the Pacific rim and routed through Russian America, won President Buchanan's permission to explore the purchase idea anew but on a strictly unofficial basis. At a moment when the sectional quarrel over slavery was approaching a boil, Buchanan knew the South would not take kindly to a scheme to add a very large expanse of free soil to American territory. But if the United States did nothing, it might wake up one mornig and find that Russia had sold its North American colony, with so many promising harbor sites, to Britain, giving it a Pacific coastal presence to rival the Americans' and enhancing its primacy among the world's maritime powers.

By the time Gwin renewed his dealmaking efforts with Stoeckl, the Russian had been advanced to head of the legation. After eighteen years in Washington, his polished manners, fluent English, and new wife—a woman from Springfield, Massachusetts, who he advised the tsar was "an American Protestant, without property . . . [but] stately as a queen"—had helped make Edouard de Stoeckl a popular and well-regarded figure in the capital. And while he scorned the crass territorial greed of the United States and considered most American politicians to be transparent finaglers, Stoeckl genuinely liked his host nation and its energetic people. Though not an aristocrat, the Russian minister passed himself off as one by adding the title "Baron" and inserting a suggestive "de" between his first and last names to gain gravitas in his dealings with the tediously egalitarian Americans.

The Baron was cautious but not dismissive when Senator Gwin came to call and quite directly pointed out that Russia's North American holdings were too far away to be of much use to the tsar and his people. "We are nearby and can get more profit from them," said Gwin, adding that the President had hinted to him the government might pay as much as $5 million for Russian America if domestic tensions over slavery eased enough for him to propose such a step to Congress. Stoeckl indicated he thought the price mentioned not unreasonable and relayed the feeler to his foreign minister, Prince Gorchakov, along with his endorsement of such a transaction. The envoy agreed with Gwin's argument, which dovetailed with the established position of Grand Duke Constantine and others in the regime that Russia would be best off applying its resources to the development of its newly expanded dominions in East Asia and not fritter them away on the hopeless enterprise in the most remote corner of North America.

Stoeckl's report of Gwin's fresh inquiry stirred fresh thoughts in St. Petersburg. Constantine urged his brother to give serious consideration to the idea, even though, in the wake of Russia's humbling loss in the Crimean conflict, the tsar was not eager to further diminish his imperial glory by giving up the nation's only overseas colony. Constantine's position emboldened one of his top admirals, Andrei A. Popov, commander of the Russian Pacific fleet, to address a crackling memorandum to Gorchakov that denounced the Russian-American Company for its greed, inept administration, and brutality toward the natives. The RAC had brought no benefits whatever to Russian commerce, Rear Admiral Popov railed, and what's more, the company was vastly overcharging customers in the motherland for sea otter furs. The solution, for Popov, was to sell it to the Americans, whose

> doctrine of manifest destiny is entering more and more into the veins of the people, and new generations are sucking it in with their mother's milk, and inhaling it with every breath of air they inhale. There are twenty millions of Americans [thirty million, actually, according to the 1860 U.S. Census], every one of them a free man and filled with the idea that America is for Americans. They have taken California [and] Oregon, and sooner or later will get [Russian America]. It is inevitable.

But the Russian foreign minister feared that selling off the territory was not to his nation's advantage just then. Queen Victoria's government had lately designated British Columbia a crown province and might take unkindly to the tsar's handing over Russian America to the United States and thus placing Britain's new colony in a territorial vise. Besides, $5 million would not be enough balm to soothe Russia's wounded pride.

Stoeckl passed the word back to Gwin, and the Senator supposed that the money was all that mattered to St. Petersburg. If it were up to him and his California cronies, he said, the American offer would be fattened, "but I was not so sure," as he had to concede, in later recounting the exchange, "of the consent of the other states of the Union who have no direct interest there." The subject was put on hold, pending American political developments. With Buchanan's presidential goose cooked by the torch he carried for southern sensibilities, the fate of Russian America would have to await the arrival of the new President in 1861—one who perhaps would narrow the gaping sectional rift. The wisest course for Russia, Gorchakov decided, was to reconsider the issue at the beginning of 1862, when the RAC's charter was due to expire. Meanwhile, the government sent two inspectors, one each from the naval and financial ministries, to survey the situation in Russian America. Their report in 1861 found the operation an incurable wreck,

placed the value of the RAC's hard assets at $4.4 million, and said the time
had come to grant the native Indians the same freedom the tsar had lately
decreed for Russia's serfs. Given such findings, the RAC's charter was not
renewed, and Gorchakov was open for a deal. But by then the United States
was deep in a massive civil conflict and the possession of Russian America
not even a fleeting thought.

Still, events during and at the close of the Civil War served to advance
the transfer of the Russian territory. By far the most conducive factor was
the oft-repeated expression of Russian support for the Union's cause. While
most other European powers hoped the war would lead to the breakup of the
obstreperous young republic that had so quickly metamorphosed into the
titan of the New World, Russia, the territorial titan of the Old World, rallied
behind Abraham Lincoln's struggle to keep his nation whole. The two countries, for all their social and political differences, had enjoyed cordial relations since their 1824 treaty defining the parameters of Russian America,
and the United States had studiously avoided siding with its English-
speaking parent during the Crimean War. A growing force—and menace,
their enemies said—in Europe since Napoleon's defeat, the Russians had
long since ended their alliance of convenience with Britain and now had to
contend as well with emergent German and Italian states, resurgent French
militarism, and the receding but still annoying Austrian autocracy. Faced by
this host of adversaries, Russia looked hopefully for an ally in the United
States, which had shown the potential by its surprisingly strong naval performance in the War of 1812 to become a seafaring power able one day to
challenge British supremacy over the waves.

Accordingly, while Britain was siding with the Confederacy—letting it
build war vessels in its shipyards, among other forms of open encouragement of the rebellion—and France under Napoleon III was providing financial aid to the South, Alexander II was sending Lincoln a magnanimous
letter of support that Seward asked Stoeckl to translate aloud for the President. In the middle of the war the tsar ordered his brother to send two
squadrons of six Russian warships each to visit leading ports on both American seacoasts. The 1863 naval courtesy calls at New York and San Francisco were welcomed by the press and public as a warm gesture of Russian
friendship during the nation's terrible ordeal and, of course, as a message to
the British not to consider direct naval intervention. It mattered little to the
embattled North that the antiquated Russian ships were no match for anything Her Majesty's Royal Navy might send against them or that the real
reason for the visit by the tsar's fleet was less altruistic. Despite the reform-
minded Alexander's grant of limited self-rule to his Polish subjects, they

had just revolted against Russian control and were punished with stern suppression. This reaction drew a sharp diplomatic rebuke from Britain, France, and Austria—which the United States did not join in—and the Russians feared that the British navy might actively intervene at any moment on the Polish side by assaulting or at the least bottling up the Russian fleet in the Baltic or Black seas. A dozen of the tsar's best vessels were ordered to take refuge in American waters on the supposition they would be perceived as protectors against, not fugitives from, Britain's mighty floating arsenal.

Already favorably disposed to Russia and to relieving the tsar of his useless and unprofitable North American colony, Secretary of State Seward was given an added reason at the war's end to pursue acquisition of the territory. Shortly after the peace terms had been reached at Appomattox Court House but before news of the event had spread to distant parts, a Confederate raider, the *Shenandoah,* built in a British shipyard and prowling in northern Pacific waters near Russian America, attacked and sank or disabled dozens of American whalers—a fate, Seward told himself, that need never again befall ships under the U.S. flag in those waters if the tsar's colony, with many potential sites for naval bases, passed into American hands.

With the Civil War over, that possibility was now fully acceptable to Russian leaders. The tsar, whose own recent escape from an assassin's hand had won him a resolution of kindly wishes from the American Congress, made a point of greeting visitors from the United States, including one of its leading literary lights, young Mark Twain. The mayor of Moscow allowed that his countrymen favored Americans over all other foreigners. And Grand Duke Constantine pressed Gorchakov to act by writing the foreign minister, "[I]t cannot be said that cession to the United States of these remote [North American] colonies, which have no essential ties with Russia and which we cannot defend in case of need, would not satisfy the need of foresight and common sense." To make sure that Gorchakov would no longer stymie the transaction, Constantine went directly to his brother and argued that (1) to allow the RAC to remain in business "by artificial means and monetary contributions from the [imperial] treasury" was madness, (2) the time had come for the nation to devote itself seriously to settling and defending its Amur River domain in the Far East, where "the future belongs to Russia," and (3) the United States needed Russian America to round out its holdings on the Pacific coast. And since Russia needed the friendship of the United States, it was essential to eliminate any source of friction that "could cause disagreement between the two great powers."

That clinched it. At a meeting of the high Russian council in St. Petersburg on December 16, 1866, the tsar ruled that his retiring minister to the

United States, Edouard de Stoeckl, then slated to take up duties as envoy to the Hague, should return to Washington and actively pursue the sale of Russian America. The Baron was given just two guidelines: the price could not be less than $5 million and the first step in the negotiations had to appear to be taken by the Americans. To invite such an intiative, Gorchakov told a ranking official from the Western Union Company, which was then hoping to string a telegraph line across Siberia to the Russian capital, that his government was ready to give up its presence in North America. On returning to the United States, Stoeckl urged well-placed American friends to pass the word to Seward. But once again, the timing seemed off, for in the early months of 1867, any proposal for the annexation of new U.S. territory, regardless of its merits, that the Secretary of State might put forward with the blessing of the President was almost certain to be flatly rejected by Congress, many of whose members were out to drive Andrew Johnson from office, not to enshrine him.

ALTHOUGH JOHNSON AND SEWARD were both accomplished politicians and avowed champions of the downtrodden, they were very different kinds of men. Like Lincoln, Johnson was of poor-white stock, self-taught (he did not learn to write until he was nineteen), and quick of mind and tongue, despite a certain crudity of expression. And like Lincoln, he was neat, courteous, hardworking, and thrifty, operating a successful tailor shop in Greenville, Tennessee, until he turned to politics as a Jacksonian Democrat. Unlike Lincoln, though, Johnson was a perennial holder of public office. His reputation for honesty and courage helped him rise from alderman to mayor to state legislator to congressman (for ten years) to governor of Tennessee to U.S. Senator, all the while pushing measures to protect small farmers, artisans, and laborers against the abuses of the landed gentry who dominated southern politics. Typical of his populism was an ardent avowal of the Homestead Laws, aiding settlers without means to obtain and operate small farms. No tool of the slavocracy, he did not resign his Senate seat when Tennessee voted to secede in 1861—the only southern Senator to remain in the upper chamber and declare his loyalty to the Union. Lincoln named him military governor of Tennessee, and largely through his efforts, marked by frequent clashes with occupying officers, helped the state become the first in the Confederacy to disavow secession, abolish slavery, and win readmission to the Union. To help lead a nation in need of binding up its wounds, Johnson, a states' rights southerner, a Democrat, and an unswerving Union loyalist, was a logical running mate for Lincoln in 1864.

Inheriting the presidency at a grave moment in American history, Johnson pursued the postwar policy of reconciliation that Lincoln had laid out, but, reviled as a traitor to his region by many from the South, he proved to be too quick with the carrot and too chary with the stick. Johnson's Reconstruction program granted wholesale amnesty to secessionists who took a simple oath of loyalty to the Union, quickly restored provisional civil government—barring from office only ranking leaders of the rebellion—and accepted at face value pledges of obedience by the southern states (except Mississippi) to the Thirteenth Amendment, outlawing slavery, which the free-soil states adopted at the end of 1865. But the South was far from contrite, in the eyes of many northerners, and fully expected to regain a large measure of its former political power after the congressional elections of 1866. In short order, the emancipated slaves learned they were free in name only. Denied civil rights, education, economic opportunity, and respect as human beings, the ex-slaves were still subjected to the South's infamous black codes, reducing them to a subservient class and without recourse against the resentful abuses of their former masters.

To compound the freedmen's misfortune, the new President, whatever his other virtues, had never risen above the racist convictions of his region. While opposed to slavery, he did not believe that black Americans were entitled to the same citizenship rights and privileges as whites—and he was unwilling to demand that the South so honor its freedmen. But the Republican Party, especially the radical wing now running it, sharply objected, and it had the votes to override Johnson's resistance and jam the principle of civil equality for all down the throats of intransigent southerners, at gunpoint if necessary. Plus there would be no grace period for a soft transition to a separate-but-equal parity. Congress passed a sweeping civil rights act to enforce the Thirteenth Amendment and mandate full citizenship for blacks, the right to vote included. When Johnson vetoed it, Congress not only overrode him but passed the Fourteenth Amendment to enshrine the act and insulate it from future reactionary majorities. Then it passed, again over Johnson's veto, a radical program of reconstruction that revoked civil rule in the South, replaced it with five military districts, and refused to seat southerners elected in 1866 until their states had voted to accept the Fourteenth Amendment.

William H. Seward (his friends and family called him Henry) was, on the face of it, an unlikely ally of Andrew Johnson in his generously forgiving attitude toward the beaten but unbowed (and defiantly white supremacist) South. Seward was an advanced social thinker throughout his career, though unlike Johnson, he was a child of privilege, a bright, outgoing little redhead, whose father was a highly successful merchant (also a doctor, judge, and land speculator) and social leader in Auburn, New York, thirty miles below Lake Ontario. Young Seward earned a Phi Beta Kappa key in his junior year at Union College, from which he graduated at nineteen, joined the bar two years later, quickly built a legal practice in his hometown, and became a popular member of the state legislature. There and later as governor and a two-term U.S. Senator, he shared Andrew Johnson's passion to help the disadvantaged, promoting education and health care for blacks, Indians, and, in particular, Irish immigrants, who were a growing part of his New York political base. In the Senate, he was a leading voice among the antislavery members, denouncing the Compromise of 1850, the Kansas-Nebraska Act, and the *Dred Scott* decision and asserting that slavery violated "a higher law than the Constitution."

Despite his lofty moral stance, Seward was hardly blind to the exigencies of practical politics and spoke out as an incessant booster of national expansion and commercial development. He called for vigorous federal backing of internal improvements and ocean surveys, government subsidies for shipping lines and a transcontinental railway, liberalized immigration policies, and cheap prices for public lands—all measures serving to stimulate the national economy. A firm subscriber to the manifest destiny doctrine, Seward believed that Britain's and Russia's North American colonies were an anachronism and ought to be included within an ever-greater United States, but unlike arch-expansionists such as James Polk and Robert Walker, he strongly opposed acquiring territory by conquest. Seward's detractors, among whom the *New York Tribune*'s Horace Greeley, a Republican kingpin, was the most vocal, found him too glib and egotistical, prone to be flippant—friends attributed it to his dry wit—and his purity of heart detectably adulterated by ambition.

One reason for this final cavil was that the higher Seward rose on the political ladder, the more he seemed to trim his sails and veer from radicalism. With his eyes on the presidency in 1860, he distanced himself from abolitionism by a call for gradual emancipation with compensation for slaveowners. In the crisis set off by Lincoln's election, Seward worked to wean the states of the upper South away from those deep in the cotton kingdom and proposed a national constitutional convention to try to thrash out the grievances between the sections—by then a wistful dream. As the war drew to a close, he fully endorsed Lincoln's moderate approach to rehabilitating the rebel states and thought the radical Republicans' insistence on immediate equality among the races both vindictive and unrealistic; thus, he sided with Johnson's less dire approach, even if it meant consigning blacks to a degraded caste while a more enlightened social order emerged in the South. For this, Seward, who helped draft some of Johnson's vetoes of the jarring civil rights legislation, was cast as a traitor to the noble cause he had long espoused. "Americans like their heroes to be unambiguous," wrote one of his biographers, John M. Taylor, "and William H. Seward steadfastly refused to oblige them."

Having abandoned the high ground to seek a path through the thicket of wrath enveloping Washington, Seward now tried to salvage his own reputation as well as the tortured Johnson presidency by looking outward, beyond the lingering domestic rancor and toward the nation's longer-term strategic needs. The one he identified seemed unlikely to be infected by the sectional conflict. The nation needed harbors away from the mainland to serve as convenient bases for U.S. naval squadrons engaging hostile craft. Assaults such as the *Shenandoah*'s against unarmed U.S. merchant vessels at the close of the Civil War had to be prevented, as did blockades of American ports and incursions on sea lanes serving as American lifelines to world commerce. These overseas bases, furthermore, could function as coaling stations for American cargo ships in an age when steam power was replacing wind and sail. Seward concentrated on four locations.

EVEN BEFORE THE CIVIL WAR ENDED, the Secretary of State had learned that Denmark was willing to part with its Virgin Islands, then known as the Danish West Indies. At the western end of the Lesser Antilles, the three small islands, with a total area of just 133 square miles and equidistant (about 750 sailing miles either way) from the southern tip of Florida and the isthmus of Panama, were well located for both military and commercial purposes. For the Danes they were too costly and remote to bother with any longer. Visiting them in January 1866, Seward found the islands charming and suited for the practical ends he had in mind, and recommended their purchase to the President and the cabinet. Caught up in the battle with Congress over how to deal with the South, they were apathetic toward Seward's proposal. Yet they did not oppose it; the transaction, to benefit the nation's security and trade, might serve the salutary purpose of diverting attention from the Reconstruction crisis and gaining consensual support for at least one administration initiative. Seward was authorized to offer $5 million for the islands. The Danes wanted four times as much and also required a plebiscite of the islands' residents to approve the transfer of ownership. Seward did not press the issue and for the moment turned to other possibilities.

One was the purchase of a naval base at Samana Bay on the northeast coast of the Dominican Republic, about 200 miles closer to the U.S. mainland than the Virgins. The black warlords who ruled the island nation were up for the idea, but the chronic military revolutions that rocked the country made it too unstable to deal with in the normal diplomatic manner. With the door opened, Seward left the project in abeyance, hoping the Dominican political upheavals would subside. Easier to arrange was American annexation of the Midway Islands. The atoll, consisting of just two square miles and located 1,200 miles northwest of Hawaii, had been claimed by an American naval commander in 1859. Midway offered three advantages: the atoll was empty, free, and almost at dead center of the Pacific. Since the United States, Britain, and France had all tried earlier, with varying intensity, to get hold of the Hawaiian Islands as their Pacific bastion, only to run into objections from their international rivals, who insisted that the island kingdom remain independent and open to all ships, hoisting the American flag over Midway was a small consolation prize. Congress declared it a territory in August 1867. The public took little notice—nor would the rest of the world until the U.S. Navy won a pivotal battle off Midway seventy-five years later. By mid-1867, though, Seward had struck a territorial bonanza he was in a hurry to mine.

Accelerated American settlement along the Pacific coast had prompted growing complaints by U.S. merchants that trading with Russian America was a one-way street. Under the 1824 treaty with Russia, its ships and citizens were free to conduct business on United States territory, but Americans had been given no reciprocal rights. The nearly defunct Russian-American Company had sold ice, furs, fish, and lumber to San Francisco buyers, but now American entrepreneurs wanted to make their own arrangements and through the embassy in St. Petersburg had tried to obtain commercial leases for harvesting the resources of the Russian territory. Incursions for that purpose had been going on illegally for some time, to the impotent RAC's annoyance. Lately the Territory of Washington's legislature had petitioned Seward's department to seek permission for its residents to fish in Russian waters and buy supplies and cure their catch along the colony's shore. Seward was studying the matter when he heard in March 1867 that Stoeckl had returned from St. Petersburg, prepared to sell his nation's North American white elephant.

Was there any point, though, in trying to negotiate the purchase at a moment when the bad blood between Congress and Andrew Johnson—and, by extension, Seward—was at full flow? The radical Republican majority had just passed the intentionally disrespectful Tenure of Office Act, denying the President power to dismiss, without congressional sanction, any officials, including his own cabinet members, whom he had appointed and Congress had confirmed. Meant to tie Johnson's hands, the act was of dubious constitutionality but would become the basis, after he tried to fire Secretary of War Edwin Stanton for rank insubordination five months later, on which Congress sought to remove Johnson from office. As Seward pondered the dilemma, two powerful considerations seemed to justify the high risk of proceeding.

In a nation with so vast an emptiness to explore and settle but still two years shy of boasting its first transcontinental railway linkup, few Americans knew a blessed thing about Russian America. Those who did were aware only that it was far, far away, much colder than the United States, and not even contiguous to it. Given the country's pressing postwar worries as well as all the opportunities in the offing, what did the United States need with a trackless, frozen wasteland fit only for walruses and polar bears to frolic in?

But Seward knew there were good answers to that question, starting with the immensity of the region and its geographical reach. Russian America occupied 570,000 square miles—twice the size of Texas and one-fifth as large as the entire United States—and extended 2,500 miles from its eastern boundary with British America to Attu, the farthest west of the Aleutian chain of islands dangling like stepping-stones across the northern Pacific to within 2,000 miles of Tokyo. Because its jagged coast was indented by so many bays and inlets and it had so many islands within its territorial waters, the shoreline of Russian America was longer than that of the entire United States. Nor was that coast icebound. Warmed by the Japanese current, a lot of it was habitable year-round, and its promising harbor sites for American shipping were significantly closer to Asian ports, thanks to the curvature of the earth's surface, than San Francisco was. By stopping in midvoyage for coal, thought to be plentiful in some of Russian America's coastal areas, transpacific vessels could both save time and carry more cargo in their holds. The scanty population of this sprawling northland had several advantages for the nation that purchased it. The fewer the natives, the less problematic the task of pacifying and integrating them into their new country after swarms of white settlers came. And with so little of the territory occupied, there was a huge supply of public land available for sale to help meet the newcomers' needs for commercial opportunity and government services.

The fact that the Russians had not made a go of their North American colony did not mean it was a barren place. Traffic in furs may have fallen,

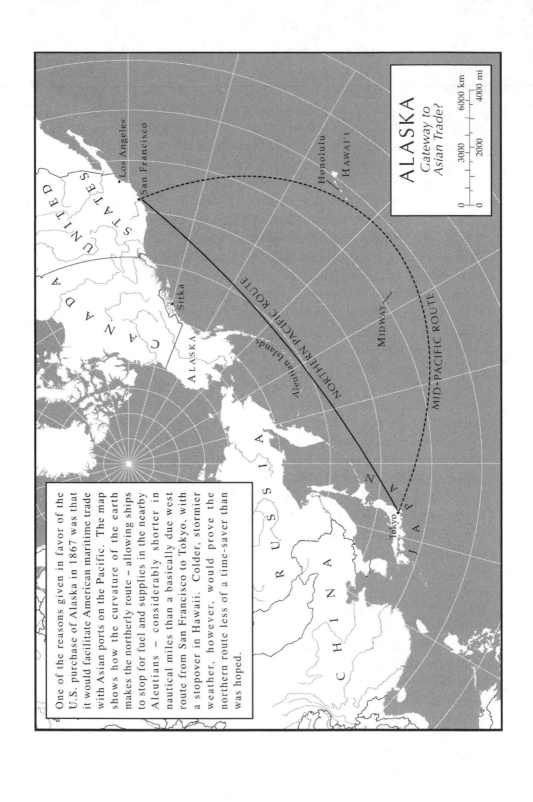

ALASKA
Gateway to Asian Trade?

One of the reasons given in favor of the U.S. purchase of Alaska in 1867 was that it would facilitate American maritime trade with Asian ports on the Pacific. The map shows how the curvature of the earth makes the northerly route – allowing ships to stop for fuel and supplies in the nearby Aleutians – considerably shorter in nautical miles than a basically due west route from San Francisco to Tokyo, with a stopover in Hawaii. Colder, stormier weather, however, would prove the northern route less of a time-saver than was hoped.

NORTHERN PACIFIC ROUTE

MID-PACIFIC ROUTE

UNITED STATES

CANADA

RUSSIA

CHINA

JAPAN

ALASKA

Aleutian Islands

Los Angeles
San Francisco
Sitka
Honolulu
HAWAI'I
MIDWAY
Tokyo

0   3000   6000 km
0   2000   4000 mi

but the fisheries were known still to be incalculably rich in salmon, herring, halibut, and cod, and the largest herds of whales in the world made the nearby waters their nursery. Farming there was impossible in the conventional fashion, but the land nourished millions of acres of virgin forest, towering stands of fir, spruce, and pine available for harvesting, and beneath the surface copper, coal, and other valuable minerals were said to exist in abundance. And beyond the challenging climate and obstacles to accessibility that left them as yet barely glimpsed by whites, there stretched some of the most stunning pristine landscapes on earth, including the longest and steepest fjords outside of Norway and the tallest mountains on the continent. Here was a territory twenty times larger than the Gadsden Purchase and exponentially more promising for commercial exploitation. If the United States could buy it from Russia for what it had paid Mexico for a desert just to run a railroad across (or perhaps get it for even less), Seward knew it would be a greater bargain than the Louisiana Purchase.

The other compelling reason for Seward to pursue the prize was the emergence at that very moment of a new and formidable neighbor to the north—a nation now and no longer a mere mélange of unassimilable British colonies afraid to wean themselves from their mother country. Two years earlier, in 1865, the *Times* of London had held that there could be no objection by Britons to the absorption of their North American colonies by the United States, provided it was done "freely and spontaneously" and not by coercion. But such a consummation of American dreams under a self-ordained manifest destiny to rule the continent was not at all the will of most British subjects residing in bilingual Canada and the four smaller Maritime Provinces to the east. Nor had it been since anti-American sentiment was firmly planted during the War of 1812. Yet many in the United States, including some of its more astute leaders, were so steeped in expansionist hubris that they could not conceive why their northern neighbors would rather fashion a nationality of their own, also with ocean-to-ocean boundaries but with cultural, military, and economic affinities to Britain, than be swallowed up by the exuberant, disorderly American republic.

By the spring of 1867, the reality had hit home, and Washington was unable to reverse it. The yearning for home rule had inspired rebellious outcries and acts in British America during the 1830s, and Parliament responded with the Union Act of 1840, fusing previously separate Upper and Lower Canada under a unitary legislature but, for administrative purposes, still partitioned as East and West Canada; the Maritimes were each to maintain their own legislatures, with little if any coordination among the five colonial governments. Their overriding allegiance to Britain was increasingly strained in the 1840s by Parliament's repeal of the Corn Laws and new free-trade policies that substantially eroded British mercantilism and the advantages it had brought to the loyal provinces in North America. Without such economic advantages on which they had come to depend, the Canadians and Maritimers were forced to become more self-reliant. Reduced British patronage and governance led to a less oligarchic society, evidenced by the diminished hold of the old seigneurial land tenure system and recognition that civility, or at least a muted enmity, had to prevail between the English- and French-speaking sectors if domestic tranquility and prosperity were ever to be achieved.

The contours of a confederated nation, in place of a collection of semi-autonomous provinces, were emerging by the late 1850s, in part as a response to the aggressive expansion and swift settlement of the American West. Parliament designated British Columbia a full-fledged province to help keep it out of American clutches, reaching northward from San Francisco and Puget Sound to establish commercial ties to the region. The expiration in 1859 of the Hudson's Bay Company monopoly over Rupert's Land and the British Northwest Territory—which had given the private enterprise quasi-independent authority over the whole expanse between the Canadas and Russian America—signaled yet another rite of passage for the fast-slipping British hold on North America. What would become of that great wilderness hinterland? Was Parliament to subdivide the empire's North American frontier into new colonies and act as their administrative incubator? London, though, was set on cutting the crown's colonial expenditures and reducing the arena of possible conflict with the United States, which had turned into a far stronger military power after mobilizing for civil war. Canada's provincial legislature had asked Parliament to cede it jurisdiction over the western lands rather than letting the colonial office run them as imperial possessions. But the Canadian legislature, unfortunately, had turned into rather a muck-up. As a gesture of bicultural tolerance, largely French-speaking East Canada had been awarded equal representation with more populous West Canada, necessitating delicately balanced coalitions and endless negotiations to get any legislation passed—a system all but guaranteed to create permanent political deadlock and civil tension.

To break this impasse—and forge a nation of their own—Canadian and Maritime leaders thrashed out a fresh approach, genuine confederation, approved by Parliament's landmark British North America Act of 1867. Under it, virtual autonomy was ceded to the new Dominion of Canada, consisting of four provinces proportionately represented in a House of Commons—Ontario (formerly West Canada) with eighty-two members, Quebec (the old East Canada) with sixty-seven members, and two of the Maritimes, Nova Scotia with nineteen members and New Brunswick with fifteen. The latter two were expected to serve as a force for compromise in Commons and a check on Ontario's numerical advantage. The other two Maritimes, Newfoundland (including mainland Labrador) and Prince Edward Island, professing to see no advantage in confederation and fearing their larger neighbors would overpower them, held aloof for the time being. The provincial legislatures were to provide local services, but unlike the American federal system, with its relatively weak central government—a system that seemed to have invited the South's secession—the Canadians assigned all powers not explicitly delegated to the provinces to the new federal government in Ottawa, chosen as the dominion capital largely because of its location very close to the Ontario-Quebec boundary. The British Parliament, moreover, deeded its Canadian counterpart authority to settle up with the Hudson's Bay Company for its lapsed title to the still empty western territory, thus greatly expanding the dominion's frontier region and hastening its early settlement.

As a result, Canada's national shape would be defined with breathtaking speed. Manitoba, Ontario's western neighbor, was recognized as a province in 1870, Prince Edward Island joined the dominion the following year, and British Columbia came in two years after that, turning Canada into an ocean-to-ocean realm and dashing whatever delusions American expansionists might still have harbored about someday coaxing several or perhaps all of the provinces to join the United States.

As this process was unfolding in 1867, Secretary of State Seward could not have failed to see the likelihood that the imminently continent-wide Dominion of Canada would want to become the new owner of adjacent Russian America if and when St. Petersburg was ready to sell. It would give Canada the whole northern tier of the continent and a great deal longer Pacific coastline, which would be denied it if the Russians sold to the Americans instead. Seward lost no time, then, in inviting Stoeckl to the State Department's new offices on Fourteenth Street when the Russian ambassador returned to Washington that March.

SEWARD WAS SURE he had to act secretly as well as quickly. Secrecy was important because news of his dealings might incite the Canadians, perhaps with British financial support, to enter a bidding war with the United States for possession of Russian America or stir Andrew Johnson's enemies to unite in spiteful opposition to the transaction before it could even be formulated. And speed was necessary because Congress was due to adjourn at the end of the month, and the Senate might be persuaded, if the acquisition was presented as an indisputable bargain, in the national interest and beyond caterwauls of partisanship, to ratify the treaty of purchase. If the decision was held over until Congress reconvened late in the year, the opposition would have time to build up its case, however specious, against the acquisition.

The first exchange with Stoeckl went well. It helped that the two men knew and liked each other. The envoy opened the serious talk by regretting recent "incursions" in Russian America by citizens of the United States— which Seward diplomatically conceded were unacceptable but perhaps to be expected if the tsar's government steadfastly refused to grant commercial licenses to foreign nationals. Stoeckl said that was St. Petersburg's fixed policy, causing Seward to bring up the petition he had in hand from the Washington territorial legislature for license to fish in Russian waters. That too, alas, was an impossibility, the envoy replied. In that event, asked Seward, cued in advance as to how their exchange should proceed, would the tsar agree to sell the United States his North American colony? The inquiry, put without fanfare, satisfied one of the two conditions Stoeckl was told had to be honored—the Americans must initiate the transaction. The practiced Russian envoy allowed that such a transaction might well be to the mutual interest of both their nations. Since Congress was nearing adjournment, Seward said he would seek the President's approval of the purchase without delay; only then could the two diplomats discuss a price.

Confronted by a Congress in open rebellion against him, Johnson knew the odds were long against winning the lawmakers' backing of any measure, even a nonpartisan one such as this, simply because it emanated from the White House. The prospect of acquiring Russian America did not excite the President, but at least the subject would divert the national dialogue for a time from his torrid feud with the radical Republicans. He told Seward to carry on as he thought best.

Johnson was "not inclined to the transaction," Seward told Stoeckl at their next meeting on the subject, but the President was willing to be guided by Seward's judgment. Seward added that he now had to elicit the support of the cabinet but left no doubt in the Russian's mind about his own enthusiasm for the purchase. Well connected in Washington, Stoeckl offered to ease the way for congressional approval by sounding out some of the Senate and House members he felt closest to and pointing out the virtues of the deal for both countries. Seward recoiled at the suggestion, insisting that their exchanges remain confidential because if word got out, the Johnson-haters would pounce on the proposal and kill it in utero. Far better to hand the Senate a finished package with a fair price tag attached and let its attractiveness be all the harder to deny.

A bit offended that his services had been spurned, Stoeckl nonetheless accepted Seward's recommendation that they try to settle quickly on a price, since there were no boundary issues or other complications to resolve. Seward opened with a bid of $5 million, the same amount Senator Gwin had mentioned to the Russian minister seven years earlier—and the lowest figure the latter had been authorized to accept. But Edouard de Stoeckl wanted to please his tsar and, not incidentally, make sure he would be rewarded with the bonus of 25,000 gold rubles (roughly $18,000) the foreign ministry had promised him for a job well done. His blank expression told Seward the offer would not do. "We might even go to $5.5 million," the Secretary hastily upped the ante, "but no higher." It was a gambit, and they both knew it. The Russian said he had more like $10 million in mind. If he had to go higher, Seward thought he might extract a fringe benefit. Would Stoeckl's ministry be willing, as a courtesy, to lean gently on the Danish government and urge it to accept reasonable terms for selling their expendable Virgin Islands to the United States? The request struck Stoeckl as inappropriate, even repellent—America could jolly well do its own negotiating—but he agreed to pass on the request so long as Seward seemed willing to sweeten his offer. In reporting the progress of their talks to St. Petersburg, the ambassador said he was hopeful that Seward might go as high as $6 million or even half a million more, so it might be best for Stoeckl to stall answering Seward's plea for Russian diplomatic intervention in the matter of the Danish West Indies—perhaps the Russian envoy to Copenhagen could be said to be off on another assignment temporarily.

Although surprised by the suddenness of Seward's secret dealmaking with the Russians, the cabinet raised no objections to the purchase and, with the President's agreement, authorized him to bid no more than $7 million. He offered Stoeckl $6.5 million at their next session but said the Russians would have to include the Russian-American Company's warehouses at Sitka and elsewhere along with its other fixed assets. That would cost the United States another $500,000, the Russian countered. Keenly aware time was running out before Congress was due to adjourn, Seward chose not to haggle; $7 million it was.

But they were not quite done. Stoeckl had to reapproach Seward with a request by St. Petersburg that, in taking title to the territory, the United States agree to honor the RAC's contract to supply ice to a substantial customer in San Francisco—and, by the by, if the $7 million payment could be made in London, the exchange rate would be rather more favorable to the

Russians. Now it was Seward's turn to dig in his heels. The transfer of funds had to be made in Washington—no other way was as secure or certifiable—and the RAC's ice contract was not an American problem; the transfer of territory had to be free of all encumbrances or it was no deal. But having made those terms absolute, Seward did not want to get the Russians' back up over minor matters. On his own and confident the cabinet would still find the purchase price a bargain, he offered an extra $200,000 to cover the Russians' loss on the currency conversion.

Stoeckl wired the text of the treaty to St. Petersburg on March 25 over the eight-month-old transatlantic cable at a cost of nearly $9,000, explaining, "I send this telegram at the request of Seward who pays for it and said that it was not without great opposition in the cabinet because of the sum agreed on, and for the affair to succeed it will be necessary to make haste" due to the imminent adjournment of Congress. "This whole affair has been managed," the envoy added, "in the go-ahead way of the Americans."

Late on Friday, March 29, Stoeckl received a favorable reply from St. Petersburg. Since Seward's home on Lafayette Square was only a five-minute walk from where the ambassador was temporarily lodging, he came to the Secretary of State's front door and delivered the good news in person. Seward, who had been playing whist with his family, was so delighted that when Stoeckl proposed to come by his office the next day to draw up and execute the treaty, Seward in his American go-ahead way asked, "Why wait until tomorrow—let's make the treaty tonight." His 25,000-ruble reward no doubt in mind, the Russian was obliging but pointed out it would be difficult to assemble their staff clerks and aides at such a late hour. A minor inconvenience, Seward said, reminding the Russian that the Senate was in session the next day but likely to adjourn then or very soon thereafter. Messengers were dispatched to round up the supporting personnel, who were to assemble at the State Department by midnight.

It was at that moment that Seward came face-to-face with the problem his secret diplomacy had created. He had been unable to do any advance missionary work to prepare even those Senators who still held him in some regard to look with favor on the purchase of Russian America. The proposition would be sprung cold on the upper chamber the next morning in the hope that it was so obviously advantageous to American national interests that it would sail through the ratification process, even if that meant dignifying—at least momentarily—Johnson's reviled conduct of his office. But there was one member of the Senate whom Seward could not risk keeping in the dark a moment longer.

In his sixteenth year in the upper chamber of Congress and sixth as chairman of its committee on foreign relations, Charles Sumner of Massachusetts was likely the most brilliant—and certainly the most scholarly—man in the Senate. A Harvard-educated attorney who had taught the law and written legal texts and other books, Sumner was also the Senate's finest orator, ranging easily from the lyrical to the vituperative, and so aggressive in pressing his moral precepts that he had almost got himself killed for it eleven years earlier while sitting at his Senate desk. In a two-day philippic denouncing the slavocracy for what he characterized as its rape of Kansas free-soilers, Sumner chose to heap scorn on South Carolina's Senator Andrew Butler—who was not present to defend himself—as the personification of his region's villainy. Two days later Sumner was so brutally caned by Butler's nephew, a member of the House, that he did not resume his Senate duties for three years. But when he did, he became an instant hero of the young Republican Party, with its strong antislavery commitment. After the Civil War he was perhaps the most respected member of the Senate and, by insisting on the political subjugation of the South until it acknowledged universal human equality, became leader of the radical Republican camp along with Representative Thaddeus Stevens of Pennsylvania. If Sumner opposed the treaty with Russia, it would be dead in the water.

Seward sent his son, Fred, now an undersecretary in the State Department, to the Senator's home with an urgent request that he hasten to Lafayette Square "to discuss a matter of public business." The two men, after all, had long been political allies and outspoken enemies of slavery; their disagreement now about how to deal with the South for its past sins and present aversion to reform its ways ought not to prevent Sumner from rising above partisanship to advance the well-being of their country through the acquisition of huge Russian America. The Senator was out for the evening when Fred Seward called, and by the time Sumner read the message left for him and hurried to Lafayette Square, Secretary Seward had gone to his office. But Fred and Stoeckl were there to brief Sumner on the treaty and show him a map of the proposed territorial transfer. Sumner listened closely and studied the map but said nothing. The Russian appealed to him for his support, imploring, "You will not fail us." The eminent politician declined to commit himself.

Hustling to the State Department a little before midnight, Stoeckl joined Seward and their experts on the verbiage of diplomacy. While the treaty language was being fine-combed, the Russian tried for one last-minute alteration in the agreement that the tsar had asked for: an earlier date of payment than the ten months Seward had specified because he knew the House could not pass the necessary funding bill until after the Senate had ratified it—

and the congressmen would not sit around in session awaiting the outcome of the Senate debate. They were not scheduled to reconvene until December and would then need some more time to consider the matter, Seward explained to Stoeckl, saying he hoped the tsar would understand that they were all prisoners of an immutable legislative calendar. There could be no doubt, however, Seward stressed, that the House would authorize the payment if the Senate ratified the treaty—the honor of the United States demanded it. Stoeckl relented.

They signed at four in the morning of March 30. A few hours after sunrise Seward took the text to the White House, where the President granted his immediate approval and attached a brief message urging the Senate to ratify the greatly advantageous treaty. He also issued a call for the Senators to gather for a special session on the following Monday to consider the matter. The treaty reached the Senate floor at 10 a.m. and was read aloud in executive session. The revelation was startling; it drew its share of smiles and derisive catcalls directed at Johnson, and at Seward for toadying to him. Sumner, miffed at Seward for keeping him in the dark until the very eve of disclosure to the rest of the Senate, had mixed feelings about the huge purchase. Would it be the precursor of a still broader, diversionary campaign of territorial acquisition by the administration? Sumner refused to be stampeded and moved to have the treaty referred to his committee for careful consideration, beginning on the following Monday. However his committee voted was likely to foretell the full Senate tally.

THAT SAME SATURDAY EVENING, Seward had Sumner, some of his Senate colleagues, and a few cabinet members to dinner at his home. It was the opening round in a week-long whirlwind assault by friendly persuasion, part recreational and the greater part educational. Night after night, the Secretary played host—with ebullience, wit, passion, good food, superb wines sent over from the State Department's cellar, and the best Cuban cigars (of which Seward smoked up to a dozen a day)—to Senators and carefully selected associates to sing the praises of Russian America.

It was true that the temperature often fell to −40 degrees Fahrenheit along Russia's Arctic Ocean coast in North America, but most of its colony's shoreline was not on the Arctic—it was a habitable, strategically useful, and resource-rich territory, Seward told them all, and he directed his departmental staff to digest all the data and studies about the Russian colony that had been assembled over the previous several weeks. Some of it was solicited, such as reports from three leading scholars at the Smithsonian Institution about the colony's history, geography, flora and fauna, ethnography, and economic potential. Among the material was a detailed new description of the rugged interior of the mainland and its central waterway, the Yukon River, by a team of explorers for Western Union who had just returned to Washington from a two-year quest to map the best route for a telegraph line connecting with Asia across the fifty-five-mile-wide Bering Strait. Some of the documents were in foreign languages, hastily translated for Seward's use. Some of it took the form of letters he had obtained from military officers past and present with firsthand knowledge of the Far West and a favorable opinion of the potential utility of Russian America for the nation's defense. Some of the letters had been solicited with Charles Sumner in mind as their most influential reader, such as the one from his friend Louis Agassiz, the great Harvard naturalist, who wrote with a nice touch of candid bigotry, "To me the fact that there is as yet hardly any population [in Russian America] would have great weight, as this secures the settlement to our race." This compendious assortment was synthesized in a State Department white paper the first week in April, rushed into the hands of every Senator, and disseminated to the press.

Seward had correctly gauged that he could not rely upon appeals to realpolitik—arguing that the treaty would further friendly relations with Russia and serve as a countermeasure to the emerging confederation of Canada—to overcome the two most likely obstacles to ratification by the Senate: ignorance about the remote Russian colony and enmity toward Andrew Johnson. The latter was more problematic. The Civil War had cost the Union 360,000 dead, twice the South's total, 280,000 wounded, and $4 billion, three-quarters of it still owing. Seward's only hope was that Congress, whose members now came only from the North and border states, had not grown so vindictive toward the recalcitrant South and so enraged by the President's permissiveness toward it that the legislators were incapable of objectively weighing the case for buying Russian America.

The immediate reaction by the press to the announcement of the treaty was more one of bewilderment based on ignorance than hostility to the Johnson administration, although the latter was pointedly manifested. Four of the seven leading New York newspapers embraced or leaned toward the treaty. Seward's longtime enemy, Horace Greeley, offered perhaps the most barbed criticism in the *Tribune,* calling the proposal a "hideously expensive and tax-burdensome folly" and the territory a "useless continent of ice, . . . rocks, and Esquimaux" that he dubbed "Walrussia." James Gordon Bennett's expansionist *Herald* approved the deal, not least of all because it boxed in the new Canadian dominion, but agreed with the *Tribune* that the territory was "an ice house, a worthless desert, with which to enable the Secretary of State to cover up the mortification and defeats he has suffered with the shipwrecked South Policy of Andrew Johnson." But the Democratic *Post* backed Seward, as did his two staunchest supporters, the *Commercial Advertiser*, just bought by his old crony and political confidant Thurlow Weed, and Henry Raymond's *New York Times*. The latter faulted the *Tribune* for lacking any sense of American destiny, jeering at the acquisition of "Walrussia," and crusading against Seward as a traitor to his party's ideals when he had, rather, been "quietly pursuing great objects of permanent and paramount interest to his country." The Boston papers, which one might have predicted would oppose the purchase on the ground that the teeming fisheries off Russian America posed a threat to New England's historic fishing industry, were uniformly approving. The *Herald* demolished the claim that the purchase price was too dear by stating simply, "[T]here can be but one opinion—it is dog cheap." The arithmetic worked out to 1.973 cents per acre. At the other end of the country, the California press was also enthusiastic. In between, opinions varied. Among the leading periodicals, *Harper's Weekly* sneered that the climate was so bracing that the cows in the Far North sat cross-legged on the frozen turf, giving ice cream instead of milk. *Frank Leslie's Illustrated Newspaper*, perhaps the most widely circulated sheet in the country, said it was all very well for the United States to express its gratitude to Russia for its support in wartime, "but really to ask to pay $7 million for exhausted hunting grounds and an Arctic climate, no matter how extensive, with the seigniorial rights over 80,000 semi-savages who must be made American citizens, is imposing too much on our good nature."

There was, then, no swelling chorus of assent, no ringing endorsement, but rather a divided opinion, tilting toward acceptance of the treaty. Ratification, though, required a two-thirds majority by a body most unfriendly to its sponsorship. Only Charles Sumner had the stature to sway it.

His position evolved over the course of a single week. When his seven-member foreign relations commitee gathered behind closed doors on Monday, April 1, there was likely some banter about who the April Fool might be, and one committeeman was widely reported to have said he would vote in favor of purchasing the frigid desert on the proviso that Seward agreed to move there. Sumner encountered enough initial opposition from his panel and in discussions with other members of the Senate that he met with Seward and Stoeckl and reported that the votes for ratification were simply not there, and he urged the Russian minister to withdraw from the treaty—an infelicitous proposal, to say the least, since the tsar's officials had acted in good faith and it would have been dishonorable for them to abandon the agreement when it was the American administration's unpopularity that was causing the problem. Seward instead pressed Sumner to review the merits of the treaty and, if they prevailed in his mind, to speak out in favor.

When his committee met again on Wednesday, Sumner still had his reservations, among them a fear that the purchase price would cut into the funds needed to sustain the Reconstruction of the South under the North's military surveillance. He recorded his oscillating sentiments in a letter written to a friend two weeks later: "The Russian treaty tried me severely; abstractedly I am against further accessions of territory, unless by the free choice of the inhabitants. But this question was perplexed by considerations of politics and comity and the engagements already entered into by the government. I hesitated to take the responsibility of defeating it."

By Friday, despite concerns about the undue haste of the treaty proceedings, Sumner had sponged up enough intelligence about Russian America and been subjected to warm letters of endorsement from well-informed people, particularly Professor Agassiz, who probably knew more about the environment of North America than any man alive, that he was no longer straddling the fence. When his committee met on Monday, April 8, to vote on the treaty, the chairman and three colleagues were in favor, two opposed, and one did not register an opinion. The vote portended a very close outcome when the treaty was transmitted to the entire Senate later that morning. At 1 p.m., Sumner took the rostrum as the first speaker in support of the treaty. By the time he finished his three-hour recitation, the issue had effectively been resolved.

A fawning admirer of his, D. A. Harsha, author of *Eminent Orators and Statesmen,* wrote of Sumner in 1856, the year his speech on Kansas nearly got him caned to death, "In public address his manner is captivating; his gestures are graceful, animated, and often vehement, and every motion is made with suitable dignity. . . . There is something very seductive and thrilling in the full, rich, bass voice, and his melodious tones have repeatedly enchanted huge and brilliant assemblies. . . . When excited in debate, his eye brightens and becomes almost radiant with what is passing within." Safe to say, this Massachusetts Demosthenes commanded the Senate's attention for a goodly portion of his remarks, which, as edited, filled forty-eight crammed, double-column pages in the *Congressional Globe.* The sheer sweep of his presentation seemed to exhaust human knowledge of his subject. It was studiously informative but did not, as it were, gild the glacier by pretending Russian America was the Garden of Eden: "Perhaps no region of equal extent on the globe, unless we except the interior of Africa, or possibly Greenland, is as little known. . . . The immense country is without form and without light, without activity and without progress. . . . Its life is solitary and feeble. Its settlements are only encampments or lodges."

This terra incognita was peopled, he said, by no more than 2,500 Russians and creoles, 8,000 or so natives within the Russian colony, and between 40,000 and 50,000 Indians, Eskimos, and other indigenous groups—which came to about ten square miles per inhabitant. This great vacancy, he suggested in invoking Agassiz's letter to him, ensured scant opposition to the white race's proliferation there. But its present sparseness of settlement did not mean that the place was lacking in natural resources or economic promise—quite the opposite. After discussing the history of the colony and the negotiations for its purchase, Sumner sang the glories of the immense country with Whitmanesque lyricism: its thronged fish catchable everywhere along the coast, its "superb pines fit for the masts of our largest vessels," its berries "in constant abundance," its sea otters' fur that was the softest and warmest on earth, its walruses—are you listening, Horace Greeley?—with ivory tusks weighing up to several pounds each and hides "excellent for carriage braces." You could all but taste the tang of the sea, sniff the fragrance of the spruce, and feel your lungs fill with the clear air as the Senator waxed on.

His socioeconomic points were still more telling to his listeners. He cited British sources commending the great promise of the China trade and pointed out the shorter travel time from San Francisco to Hong Kong via the northerly route, the scarcity of American harbor sites above San Francisco, and how it could be alleviated by buying title to the many bays and inlets along the coast of Russian America, warmed by the transpacific thermal stream originating in the equatorial waters off Asia. There were populist considerations as well, said Sumner, revealing his own expansionist mindset: "With an increased size on the map there is an increased consciousness of strength, and the citizen throbs anew as he traces the extending line [of the nation]." And Russian America, he added, might not be the end of it. Obtaining the colony would not only rid North America of another monarchy but also be "a visible step [toward] the occupation of the whole . . . continent." Lest he be taken for a jingoist, Sumner added the caveat that "[t]his treaty must not be a precedent for a system of indiscriminate and costly annexation." And lest he be mistaken for an extreme expansionist, he contended that establishing a republican form of government in Russian America would be a far nobler purpose for buying it than the mere extension of American territory. A further reason, he asserted, was to repay a valued friend: "The Rebellion [by the South], which tempted so many other Powers into its embrace, could not draw Russia from her habitual good will . . . nor was any rebel agent ever received, entertained, or encouraged at St. Petersburg."

Toward the close of his glorious cascade of rhetoric, Sumner observed that if the treaty passed, as he fervently hoped, Russian America would need to be renamed. He proposed as most fitting the Aleutian Islanders' word for the mainland, which translated more poetically as "the great land"— Alaska. The suggestion sounded right and was taken up at once.

After Sumner's stupendous performance, a motion to delay the Senate vote for ratification was defeated, 29–12. Victory seemed certain. The next day, though, disclosed some lingering ambivalence. The motion to approve Seward's treaty carried, 27–12; it was just one vote over the minimal margin. When a further motion was offered to make the vote unanimous, there were only two holdouts; thirty-seven said yea. So persuasive was the case to buy Alaska, as mounted by Sumner and orchestrated by Seward, that even Greeley's *Tribune* came around, conceding that newly offered data gave Alaska "a more attractive aspect" and calling it "the American Norway."

Victory seemingly in hand but mindful of the combustible political climate in the capital, Seward took the precaution of arranging for the transfer of Alaska to American hands before the purchase payment was due. Stoeckl was assured by Seward that the House's approval of the funding bill was just a constitutional formality, and two key House members, Thaddeus Stevens, chairman of the appropriations committee (and most radical of the radical Republicans), and Nathaniel Banks, chairman of the foreign relations committee, similarly promised the Russian diplomat that the lower chamber would comply. Russia, ready to rid itself now of the burdensome colony and trusting the American pledge of payment, lowered the tsar's double-eagle standard over the barracks at Sitka that October as the 500-man garrison obediently saluted, and the Stars and Stripes replaced it, much to Seward's gratification. American possession of Alaska was a fait accompli—and one that the House of Representatives would hardly dare reverse and thereby dishonor the nation.

That same month, Seward scored what he hoped would be a further triumph. After months of secret dickering, he had overcome Denmark's insistence on a high selling price for its colony in the West Indies and won an agreement to buy two of the Virgin Islands—St. Thomas and St. John—for $7.5 million, pending the islanders' approval by plebiscite. Seward planned to submit the treaty to the Senate at its December session. But unlike the Alaskan negotiations, word of the proposed Virgin Islands purchase reached the press before it was presented to Congress, and just as Seward had once explained his penchant for secret diplomacy to Lincoln's secretary (and a future Secretary of State), John Hay, when the public is let in on it, "obstacles spring up in an hour." The price for the Virgin Islands seemed high, especially compared to the "dog cheap" acquisition of Alaska, the country was already heavily in debt, and the islands were offshore territory as well as too small and unsuited for eventual statehood. Was Seward trying to turn the United States into a colonial power? Greeley charged the Secretary of State with a mania "for outlandish possessions." And House members now began to grumble that they had never been consulted about the Alaska deal and that American occupation of the territory as ordered by the Johnson administration was high-handed and disrespectful of the House's prerogative to appropriate the purchase money.

At the same time, the radical Republicans' quarrel with the President over Reconstruction policy intensified as Johnson tried to rid himself of the mutinous Secretary of War, Stanton. The latter, maintaining that Congress had the ultimate power to direct the military occupation of the South, barricaded himself in his office and insisted the recent Tenure of Office Act protected cabinet members from being fired without congressional consent. Reconvening in November, the House vented its animus toward Johnson and annoyance with Seward's acquisitive activities abroad, pursued as if nothing were amiss on the domestic side, by effectively killing the Virgin Islands treaty before it reached the Senate. By a vote of 93 to 43, the House resolved "[t]hat in the present financial condition of the country, any further purchases of territory are inexpedient, and this House will hold itself under no obligation to vote money to pay for any such purpose unless there is greater present necessity for the same than now exists." It was a signal that the House might yet balk over the Alaska funding bill, even though most supporters of the resolution clipping Seward's wings said it would not apply to that already ratified treaty. Johnson felt he had no choice but to transmit the proposed Virgin Islands treaty to the Senate, which, cognizant of the House's antipathy and despite an overwhelming vote in favor of the sale by the islands' residents, never acted on the ratification request.

Johnson's foes in the House, where only a simple majority was needed to authorize the Alaska payment, were now handed a new monkeywrench with which to bollix up consummation of the deal. Learning the terms of the Alaskan treaty, the widow of an American arms dealer, Benjamin Perkins, surfaced to claim that her late husband had entered into an oral contract with the Russian government during the Crimean War to purchase 154 tons of gunpowder and 35,000 guns, but by the time they were to be delivered in

1856, the war was over and the Russians had refused to pay. Perkins, charging that he had made the deal with Stoeckl and a go-between who said he was attached to the Russian legation, had taken his claim to the New York Supreme Court. When that tribunal ruled against him, he accepted $200 for his promise to drop the case. His wife, though, had made no such promise; in financial straits after her husband's death and with a family to raise, and with all that American money about to be handed to the Russians for Alaska, the widow Perkins asked to be compensated with some of it.

Hoping to embarrass the Russians and put Seward on the spot, a phalanx of lawyers, lobbyists, journalists, and righteous House members went to the widow's defense and demanded that she be paid $500,000 of the money earmarked for the Alaska purchase. Seward had considered her plea, but there was no written proof of the arms contract, and Stoeckl said he had no memory of any such arrangement and that the now deceased legation aide who was said to have been in on it was a discredited spy. Seward was no more inclined to renegotiate the Alaska sale price than Russian foreign minister Gorchakov, who said he would not even review the Perkins matter until the United States had tendered payment in full.

The House was in no hurry, though, to accommodate the Russians. Its leaders put off consideration of the treaty-funding bill while the drama to impeach and convict Andrew Johnson was played out during the early months of 1868. In March, Republican House leaders advised that the funding measure would be held up for two more months to await the outcome of the impeachment trial before the Senate. The delay meant that the United States would miss the April 20 deadline to pay for Alaska under the terms of the treaty. Stoeckl, while edgy and unhappy, advised St. Petersburg to remain patient with the Americans because, as he later explained, "I could not refuse them this sign of confidence." But as the trial, a protracted display of partisan vindictiveness, dragged on, Stoeckl himself lost patience and mused to Gorchakov that perhaps Russia should try to shame the Americans into paying by offering to donate Alaska to them free of charge if they kept withholding their overdue debt. "I find it imprudent," the foreign minister replied, "to expose American cupidity to this temptation."

Johnson escaped removal from the presidency by a single vote, as eight Republican Senators crossed the battle line and opted for acquittal. By the time the House grumpily took up the Alaska funding bill, the Johnson-haters were at full cry. The foreign relations committee narrowly approved the bill on May 18, but the vitriolic minority report left the issue in some doubt. The report declared that Alaska was "of no value to the United States . . . [has] no capacity as agricultural country . . . no value as mineral

country . . . its timber [is] generally of poor quality and growing on inaccessible mountains," its fur trade "will speedily come to an end," its fisheries
likewise of dubious value. The right "to govern a nation [Alaska] of savages
in a climate unfit for the habitation of civilized men" was "not worthy of
purchase." The findings reeked of vengeance.

Fearing the worst, Edouard de Stoeckl, who knew his way around Washington as well as any American pol, got the friendly Riggs Bank to advance
him $200,000 secured by the American government against the purchase
price in order to influence House members. His principal lobbyist was former Secretary of the Treasury and expansion enthusiast Robert Walker,
whose ten-year tenure in the Senate gave him lifetime privileges to congressional chambers and the House floor. Down on his luck financially, Walker
gladly accepted the Russian envoy's payment of $26,000 and pushed the
Alaskan cause without letup.

When the bill reached the House floor for debate, its proponents delivered on their promise to push it through. Former House Speaker (and
ex-governor of Massachusetts) Nathaniel Banks, who had served as a
courageous if not always successful Civil War general, led the charge with a
ninety-minute speech that was nearly as effective as the one by his Bay
State colleague, Charles Sumner, before the Senate. Calling Alaska "a
drawbridge between America and Asia," Banks assailed the doubters by
noting that "whenever and wherever we have extended our possessions we
have encountered these identical objections—the country is worthless, we
do not want it—and Government has no right to buy it." Attesting to the
value of the purchase, he stated that the fishing grounds off the New England coast, encompassing some 84,000 square miles, yielded about
$34 million in revenues annually, and the fisheries off Alaska, covering
almost 250,000 square miles, promised a catch far more abundant—enough
to pay for the purchase many times over. If the United States did not want
Alaska, Britain and/or Canada would surely pay the Russians' price. "We
have in our grasp the control of the Pacific Ocean," Banks admonished the
House, and if America yielded it to European states, "the power of the
future is theirs and not ours, and its progress is after their spirit and idea and
not ours."

Cadaverous Thad Stevens, approaching his grave with still raging hatred
of Andrew Johnson, tugged himself upright after Banks had spoken and
asserted that, spleen aside, the House was constitutionally bound to vote the
money for Alaska and that, its detractors aside, the place "is not half so barren as their brains are" and would one day become a national glory. Added
California's Representative William Higby, "When the American people
get hold of a country there is something about them that quickens, vitalizes,

and energizes it. Let American enterprise go there, and as if by electricity all that country will waken into life and possess value."

The funding bill passed 113 to 43; 41 of the nays had voted to impeach Johnson. The money paid lobbyist Walker had been well spent.

In a malodorous aftermath to the Alaskan purchase, Washington churned with rumors that Stoeckl, the counterfeit baron, had used his $200,000 slush fund not just to sway the opinion of congressmen while the appropriation bill was pending but actually to buy the votes of key lawmakers. An inquiry by the House committee on public expenditures failed to elicit information from the Russian legation about how the ambassador dispersed the money, although the foreign ministry registered approval of his lobbying efforts, and Walker and officials of the *Daily Morning Chronicle* in Washington admitted being employed to influence the outcome.

No incriminating disclosures turned up until scholars examining Andrew Johnson's personal papers decades after his death found a memorandum in his own hand that described a drive in the country that the President took in September 1868 with his Secretary of State. During a stop the two men made for refreshments—a euphemism, more than likely, for some swigs from a liquor bottle, since both men were known to be serious tipplers—Seward allegedly revealed that Stoeckl had told him that the largest part of the $200,000 had been used to bribe House members, including Banks and Stevens. Another source for this charge was John Bigelow, a former U.S. ambassador to France and good friend of Seward, who allegedly told him the same basic story, although some of the details differed, in particular Bigelow's recollection that ten additional House members were paid $10,000 each.

It was a sordid tale, but one that invites more than a little skepticism. Alcohol might have skewed Johnson's memory of the details, and he might well have wanted to blacken the reputation of Thad Stevens, his bête noire in the House. And why would Stoeckl have risked bribing Banks and Stevens, both of whom had indicated their strong support of the funding bill early in the game? It is hard to believe, too, that Stoeckl would have confided his dark scheme to Seward—or that Seward, even if a bit in his cups, would have relayed his knowledge of it to Johnson. When officially confronted by congressional investigators, Seward stonewalled, testifing, "I know nothing whatever of the use the Russian minister made of the fund."

AFTER LEAVING OFFICE, Seward visited Alaska in 1869, three years before his death, and assured an audience at Sitka that Congress would shortly authorize a civil government for the region, which was designated a

U.S. military and customs district but not a territory. "It must do this," Seward said, "because our political system rejects alike anarchy and executive absolutism."

The architect and facilitator of the Alaska purchase was not around to witness how shamelessly his government neglected the vast northland over the course of the next four presidential terms. Congress did nothing whatever to encourage the settlement or economic development of Alaska— there were no land laws, no political rights, no roads, no forum for residents to address their common needs; you could not legally buy land, build a cabin, take timber, stake a mining claim, get married, or have your civil grievances addressed by a court—there was no court. The only authority was the commander of the tiny army garrison at Sitka. The principal pastime was quaffing "hoochenoo," as the Indians called the potent local brew of fermented sugar and molasses; drunkenness was rampant among soldiers and civilians alike, and tensions were high between them and the natives, who were not infrequently abused. A few customs officials, paid intermittently, were charged with policing an endless, mist-laden coastline and a 1,200-mile border with Canada; smuggling was epidemic. And the U.S. mail came just once a month. Things got so bad when the army left after ten years that the neglected residents had to call for help from the British navy in 1879 until an American relief vessel was shamed into appearing.

It was a total betrayal of the promise by Seward and Sumner of republican government under the democratic process. Despite constant pleas to Washington, Congress did not respond until 1884, when it made Alaska a territory, appointed some judges and law enforcement officials, and allowed mining operations on government-leased land. But there were still no enabling laws for local government, no provision for raising taxes, and no juries, because you had to pay taxes to qualify as a juror. The total territorial budget for government operations in 1887, twenty years after the purchase, came to $25,000 plus a pittance for schools. There were no real towns until the discovery of gold in the Klondike region ten years later. Alaska was not given its own legislature until 1912, finally leading to compulsory public schools and some medical services for the natives. By 1917 only 9 percent of Alaska's coastal waterways had been charted. The population in 1920 was about 55,000, no higher than it had been when Alaska was bought. Surveyed public lands were sold to homesteaders for the first time in 1934.

One simple reason for such criminal indifference was the remoteness of the place—a classic instance of out of sight, out of mind. In an age when the nation's population was rising 20 to 25 percent every decade and industrial production, farm output, and internal improvements were growing even faster, federal lawmakers assigned the lowest priority to what many of them regarded as a bad bargain, a pointless appendage way out there in frigid limbo, and by doing nothing for it, kept it that way. A more insidious reason Alaska languished was that a number of private operators were exploiting the place extralegally, taking away fish and timber and running canneries, mines, and logging mills free of government regulation or oversight— a privilege they paid for, often in cahoots with federal and state officials who had a proprietary interest in the status quo. Even as unhappy Alaskans appealed to Congress for help, economic exploiters lobbied harder for the government to keep hands off and save its money for better uses. The extent of such corrupt practices may be inferred from one example of federally regulated commerce permitted in those pioneering years—the Pribilof Islands off the Alaska Peninsula were made a reservation for hunting seals, limited to 100,000 skins a year, and put up for rent. The hunting contract was awarded to a San Francisco firm, even though it was the lowest bidder.

The third and meanest of the causes for the nation's towering indifference to Alaska during its first generation as American land was the ethnic composition of the people. With immigration discouraged by social and political conditions kept intentionally primitive, the stagnant population remained more than 80 percent Indian, Eskimo, or other native groups— and the whole history of the United States to that time, starting with its colonial period, was steeped in hostility, indeed scarcely disguised genocidal impulses, toward nonwhites. Keeping native Alaskans, generally categorized as savages, as far from civilization as possible suited a nation unready to confront its unregenerate racism.

Only when Alaska was imperiled militarily did the rest of the United States begin to pay serious attention to it. U.S. Army visionary Billy Mitchell, who well before the onset of World War II had preached the imperative need for American military air power, pointed to the strategic value of Alaska, but when Japanese troops seized the outlying Aleutian Islands of Attu and Kiska in 1942, there was no air base or army garrison in the whole territory. The only pieces of American soil to be captured during the war were retaken the following year after fierce fighting that at last won for Alaska a place in the public's consciousness as a part of the United States. After the war, air transportation flourished to and from the "lower forty-eight," as Alaskans called the rest of the country, and their integration into the national mainstream began, though not without misgivings by many residents who craved their isolation from the din and hustle of modernity.

The economic potential of the northland that Seward, Sumner, and others had foretold began to gush forth in 1968, a century after Congress paid the bill for Alaska and nine years after it entered the Union as the forty-ninth state. The largest fossil fuel reservoir in North America, with an estimated recoverable 10 billion barrels of oil and 27 trillion cubic feet of natural gas, was found on the north slope of the Brooks Range close to Prudhoe Bay on the Arctic. When the $7.7 billion, 800-mile Alaskan pipeline went onstream in 1977, petroleum at once became the state's leading industry. The threat that such mammoth commercial undertakings pose to the still largely virginal environment was dramatized a dozen years later when the supertanker *Exxon Valdez* spilled 10 million gallons of crude oil into Prince William Sound off Alaska's southern coast, inflicting severe damage to the fragile ecosystem. Conservationists, business interests, and politicians being tugged by both groups have since debated the conflicting demands of nature and an energy-hungry population in deciding whether to permit offshore drilling for a still greater hoard of oil believed to lie beneath the Beaufort Sea east of Prudhoe Bay. In the early years of the twenty-first century, Alaska remains, however endangered, the last American frontier.

CHAPTER 14

Treachery in the tropics

1869–1902

FEW WOULD HAVE PREDICTED, in view of the breathtaking territorial expansion of the United States over the preceding quarter century, that the purchase of Alaska would prove to be its final major and
enduring land acquisition. The nation would not make any further additions,
even minor ones, to its geographical dominion for another thirty-one years.
And when it did so, the areas involved were more a collection of miniatures,
mostly scattered islands in the sun, gathered up for their strategic value,
commercial and military, rather than great expanses of earth to fulfill the
dream of an imperative continental destiny.

Although a war hero, Dixie-dominator Ulysses S. Grant, the first chief
executive to serve two full terms in the White House since Andrew Jackson,
presided over a people weary of war and still struggling with sectional
strife. New military adventures to gain territory that the country did not
truly need were an unappealing prospect. But that reality did not preclude
diplomatic initiatives, perhaps with a little menace behind them. Grant
focused on the Caribbean, where European powers still held sway and the
United States could use an offshore naval station for safeguarding its coasts
against unfriendly approaches, rescuing ships in distress, and ensuring maritime freedom throughout the Western Hemisphere.

As they scanned the heavily trafficked waters to their southeast, Americans had long eyed the largest and closest of the West Indies as the choicest
object of their longing. "I have ever looked upon Cuba as the most interest-
ing addition which could be made to our present system of states," Thomas
Jefferson disclosed, but buying mammoth Louisiana sated his territorial
appetite. When Spain was forcibly unburdened of its New World empire

two decades into the nineteenth century, American fears grew that the British or French might grab Cuba, with its lush sugar and tobacco plantations, and gain a commanding position between the eastern United States and the sprawling market of young Hispanic nations to the south. Secretary of State John Quincy Adams had given voice to this concern in 1823, the year the Monroe Doctrine was issued to fend off just such new colonial incursions in the Americas, by remarking that for him Cuba held "an importance in the sum of our national interests . . . with which that of no other foreign territory can be compared, and little inferior to that which binds the different members of the union together." But buying Cuba or trying to wrest Spain's sole remaining New World possession from its ever-weaker grasp would have aroused the antislavery forces then emerging in earnest in the northern states. As Adams said and many northerners feared, the great island, once under the Stars and Stripes, would almost surely have followed the ways of the South's plantation culture and served as a precedent for the slavocracy's limitless outreach. Andrew Jackson, an unabashed slaveholder, offered to buy Cuba, but when refused, would not resort to the contemptuous force he had earlier directed against Spain in relieving it of Florida.

It was left to Jackson's fellow Tennessean, James Polk, to make the first serious bid for Cuba. Word reached his White House that some of the island's richest planters were ready to put up all or much of the purchase price in order to gain the economic and political stability that U.S. jurisdiction would bring. Their chief concern was the preservation of slavery, already outlawed in the rest of Latin America and by most of Europe. In Polk's view, fertile Cuba would not only open vast new markets in tropical products for U.S. traders but also serve as a kind of hybrid Gibraltar/Malta of the American Mediterranean, outflanking Britain's Caribbean bases and denying it the future ability to prey unhindered on U.S. shipping and the coastal trade. "I am decidedly in favor of purchasing Cuba & making it one of the States," Polk wrote in his diary in 1848, still savoring the territorial fruits of his triumph over Mexico, and instructed his envoy in Madrid to offer $50 million for the island and go twice as high if necessary. Hostile to the United States from its creation, Spain told Polk's emissary with relish that it would rather see the entire island sink to the bottom of the sea than sell Cuba to the Americans. Franklin Pierce, the New Englander who gained the presidency by doing the South's bidding, renewed the offer to buy the prosperous island, by then the world's largest supplier of sugar. While hopeful of extending their dominion to the island, American planters feared that Cuban blacks, if not soon emancipated by Spain, would shortly revolt as their brothers had in Haiti and the Dominican Republic and serve as a dreaded example of incitement for slaves in the United States.

When the Spaniards had the nerve to reject Pierce's 1854 bid—he had authorized a top price of $130 million, a good deal more than the total the nation had paid for all its other acquisitions—the American ambassadors to Spain, Britain, and France, all slavery-tolerant Democrats like Pierce, gathered in a secret fist-waving conclave at Ostend on the Belgian coast and drew up a manifesto insisting that "the Union can never enjoy repose, nor possess reliable security, as long as Cuba is not embraced within its boundaries," and if the island's owner remained intransigent, "then, by every law, human and divine, we shall be justified in wresting it away from Spain." Public disclosure of this petulant axe-grinding was both an embarrassment and a confession of American frustration. James Buchanan, who as envoy to Britain had been a party to the Ostend intrigue, asked Congress in his 1860 presidential message to appropriate funds to buy Cuba—a sure symptom of his cluelessness about the prospects for adding slave territory to the Union on the brink of its dissolution over the issue.

As President, Ulysses Grant did not renew the quest for Cuba, knowing that Spain was unlikely to part with it at any price and that the British would surely object—and probably go to war—if the United States tried taking the island by force. Nor did he choose to reopen William Seward's treaty with Denmark to acquire the Virgin Islands. A better prize, Grant thought, was the nearly all-black Dominican Republic, not quite half as large as Cuba but in the grip of proprietors apparently willing to sell it. Successive revolutions had wrecked the island republic's economy and driven the surviving warlord, Buenaventura Báez, to appeal for U.S. protection from his domestic enemies and neighboring Haiti. Grant, hoping to win a naval base in return, sent three warships to prop up the dictator's regime and was rewarded by Báez's offer to annex his whole country to the United States for certain considerations. As an added inducement, he exhibited the results of a plebiscite purportedly registering his countrymen's approval of such an arrangement. Arguing that one or another European power would likely make a deal for— or step in to take control of—the shattered Dominican Republic if the United States fumbled its chance to gain a Caribbean stronghold, Grant sent a draft treaty to the Senate that would have turned the larger part of the island of Hispaniola into American territory. But the proposal had a strong whiff of corruption about it on both ends. Reports swirled that New York land speculators were pushing Grant, that financiers were bidding for trade and other concessions, that Báez and his crew were soliciting payoffs or kickbacks and selling out the long-suffering Dominican people. Grant's use of naval force to secure the tottering island regime and beat off any foes of the transfer to U.S. jurisdiction was sharply criticized by, among others, Charles Sumner, who told the Senate that the transaction was a naked power grab for an impoverished, defenseless black nation and rumbled, "I protest . . . in the name of justice outraged by violence, in the name of humanity insulted, in the name of the weak trodden down." When the Senate failed to ratify, the President, for whom ensnaring the island had become an obsession, tried to ram the annexation through by congressional resolution but got beaten in the House.

Expansion, Grant now understood, was not on the nation's mind as it turned to the far more pressing task of postwar recovery—how to rehabilitate the South, still militantly negrophobic if no longer secessionist—and the business of harvesting the fruits of continentalism in the scarcely developed and still largely unexplored West. The latter process was accelerated by a pair of actions Abraham Lincoln undertook while the outcome of the Civil War was still in doubt. On May 20, 1862, he signed the Homestead Act, awarding 160 acres of free federal land to any U.S. citizen over twenty-one who agreed to farm it for five years. As a result, some 600,000 new farms, spread over tens of millions of acres, were begun in the 1860s, and vastly more land was out there beckoning. Six weeks later, the President signed the first of a series of measures granting federal financial aid and land—twenty miles wide on each side of the track—to whoever would build a transcontinental railroad after the war. Several years were required to get the plans and funding in place, but construction began just a few months after peace returned and was completed in under four years. On July 29, 1870, the first through train from California reached the Hudson River terminal in New York harbor after a run of six and a half days, a trip that by sea or wagon train still required six or more months. In less than a century the United States had amassed a coast-to-coast domain in which unimaginable distances and daunting physical obstacles were overcome by the ingenuity and energy of a people set on making their land whole.

The consequences were immediate. By its second year of operation, freight carried over the Central Pacific line had leaped more than sixfold; within three years American cargo shipped to China doubled. Over the next two decades, the United States put down by far the world's most extensive railway network, causing once thunderous herds of buffalo to be stilled and the thin remnant of Indian tribes to be penned into barren wastelands, while indefatigable whites turned the western wilderness into a pulsing landscape of green and golden grain fields, cattle and sheep ranches, logging camps, and mines thickly veined with silver, copper, and iron ore. The nation's overflowing bounty, much of it directed east now on rolling stock, poured into the global marketplace. New England turned into a textile-manufacturing center rivaling England, Pittsburgh into the steelmaking capital of the New World, and nearby a revolutionary source of heat, light, and energy for transportation—petroleum—was discovered and became the basis for a major new industry. By 1880 U.S. grain exports were ten times higher than two decades earlier and the largest in the world. American manufactured goods tripled over that same span, thanks to the nation's abundance of natural resources and time-saving transportation facilities that allowed economies and a scale of production impossible in Europe. Suddenly the precocious United States had surged to global leadership in industrial output.

This remarkable feat, in the immediate wake of the dreadful human toll taken by the Civil War, required new hands to perform the labor, and they were forthcoming, largely from Europe—with a small fraction from China who proved essential in constructing the hardest and most dangerous stretches of the transcontinental railroad. Under the nation's unrestricted immigration practices, the number of newcomers from abroad rose from 80,000 in the midwar year of 1863 to 420,000 ten years later. By the mid-1880s, the United States was more populous than any other industrialized nation except Russia.

With so much frenetic energy applied to creating a society of unprecedented and widespread prosperity, Americans paid dwindling attention to fulfillment of their so-called manifest destiny, the self-assigned mission to possess their entire continent. Territorial aggrandizement on that scale had become a practical impossibility not only because the United States was otherwise occupied but also because its two immediate neighbors had evolved into far more coherent and formidable entities during the final three decades of the nineteenth century. Canada, now out of the British nest but still the beneficiary of its commercial kindness, enjoyed able political leadership that helped it emerge as a transcontinental dominion, however thinly peopled and loosely connected. Mexico, too, had been remade under the whip hand of the ruthless but effective Porfirio Díaz. At first a democratic reformer, Díaz hoarded power by co-opting traditional military and clerical opposition to a strong federal government, embracing policies skewed toward the landed class, and enticing foreign capital to build roads, railways, and public works Mexico desperately needed to provide employment and bring the nation into the modern age. His crackdown on banditry and harsh imposition of law and order brought unprecedented domestic peace but at a grave loss of liberty—a trade-off many Mexicans reluctantly tolerated until the inequities of the oligarchic Díaz regime drove the landless peasantry to rise up and demand a share of social justice. While neither Canada nor Mexico could rival the United States in wealth, drive, or na-

tional coherence, both had become capable of fierce resistance if Americans
had made further claims on their territory.

AS THE FAR-FLUNG AMERICAN nation grew rich by developing its internal empire, its surplus productivity was directed largely to the European and
Latin American markets; the Pacific trade was slow to develop. British and
Dutch merchants had been plying East Asian waters for two centuries
before U.S. vessels began to compete, and the predicted advantages of the
shorter north Pacific route that American craft could follow after the purchase of Alaska had proven wishful. The northerly route was colder and
often stormier, and the Aleutians were short on food, water, and coal for
reprovisioning. China, moreover, even with its trade door pried open, was
none too eager to buy American wares—only to sell its porcelain, silks,
spices, and tea to the U.S. market. But one place in the Pacific where Americans were prospering was Hawaii, a kingdom of eight islands spread across
a 400-mile archipelago 2,200 miles southwest of California.

Yankee clippers began to appear in the Pacific in growing numbers in the
1820s and were soon calling at ports all along the ocean's rim running coun-
terclockwise from Valparaíso, Chile, to Monterey, California, to Sitka in
Russian America, then across to Kamchatka, Canton, Tahiti, and Australia,
hoping to sell furs, hides, tallow, lumber, whale oil, and whatever they
picked up on the way before returning to New England. At the hub of this
great Pacific wheel was Hawaii, where prevailing trade winds and currents,
a glorious climate, and fertile soil made it the most convenient and appealing way station for ships of all nations. The welcoming natives, who had
settled the islands a millennium or so before Europeans found them, traced
their origins to India, where their progenitors had set sail eastward and, via
Indonesia, reached what came to be called the Polynesian Triangle of mid-
Pacific islands. Hawaii was the farthest north of them. English explorer
James Cook estimated the native population at 300,000 in 1778 when he
came upon the serene paradise of broad beaches, soaring mountains, emer-
ald valleys, and luxuriant forests, all bathed by cooling sea breezes. Three-
quarters of a century later, after the so-called civilized world had infected
them with its lethal germs, there were only 75,000 natives left in the idyllic,
6,400-square-mile kingdom. By then it had fallen under the spell of all too
purposeful U.S. sailors, missionaries, and merchants.

Yankee whalers, first appearing in Hawaiian waters before Americans
had settled on the Pacific coast, frequented the islands in ever-growing numbers until the early 1850s when, on any given day, there might be 150 whal-

ing ships and two dozen cargo vessels berthed at Hawaii or one of its sister islands. Resupplying them had become a major source of revenue for the natives. Given the charms of the place, almost every ship would lose one or two crew members to it as the foreign population slowly incubated. A still more invasive element was the Congregationalist missionaries who arrived in the 1840s. The trusting Polynesians greeted the American proselytizers as public benefactors. They learned the native language, converted it into a Roman alphabet, and translated the Bible into it, all by way of propagating the superiority of the Christian faith to the ancient gods of the Hawaiians, the magic and taboos taught by their *kahunas,* and the degrading sensuality of the hula dance. Soon Christianity was embraced as the nominal state religion, the natives were asking to have their children taught English, Americans were acting as political advisors to the king and his retinue, and the first Hawaiian constitution was based on the U.S. model. Missionary families were treated as a privileged caste, allowed to buy real estate at a bargain price, and exempted from property taxes. In time all foreign whites, collectively and not altogether fondly referred to as *haoles* by the natives, were permitted to buy land from the crown, and more than a few accumulated sizable holdings, enlarged still further by intermarriage with leading Hawaiian families. The missionaries' progeny turned to profit-seeking, not soul-saving, activities, of which sugar plantations and mercantile houses were the most common. Native farmers, lacking the resources, know-how, and drive of the *haoles,* often had to borrow ahead on their crops, and when poor yields put them in the hole, they lost their fields to foreclosure and transfer mostly to American hands.

For a time British and French interests challenged the Americans' emerging hegemony in Hawaii. Their trading ships made frequent calls, and in the 1840s their naval forces threatened Hawaiian sovereignty at gunpoint. Loud objections from American officials and residents helped keep the islands independent under an informal agreement among the three concerned foreign governments. But the Gold Rush and California statehood, bringing a surge in commerce between the islands and the mainland, led to growing American influence and talk of turning Hawaii into a U.S. protectorate to deflect further European incursions. Although British and French agents were quick to remind the natives of the virulence of American racism toward nonwhites, the Hawaiian king fretted more—and forty years prematurely, as it happened—that the *haoles* might steal the islands away if Washington did not intercede. The natives were thus open to a treaty of annexation, offered under President Pierce's imprimatur, with the promise of eventual statehood and preservation of the royal family in tribute to the indigenous culture. The British and French objected strenuously, however, to this arrangement as a usurpation of Hawaii's status as an open, independent, and neutral refuge for all seafarers. The treaty never reached the Senate, but Hawaii had nonetheless evolved into a de facto American protectorate.

When the whaling industry declined in the mid-1860s, sugarcane became the primary fuel driving the islands' economy. Grown on sixty plantations owned mostly by Americans, many of them absentee proprietors like the Spreckels family of San Francisco—the most powerful of the lot—the sugar crop was sold primarily to U.S. processors (of which the Spreckels refinery was the largest). British merchants, ranging the Pacific from Vancouver Island to Australia, were also active buyers and proposed to increase their stake in the sugar business by importing field workers from India to supplement the shrinking supply of natives willing to sweat for demanding American overseers. The French, too, did not want to be left out. These designing foreigners drove the small but potent American community— their number did not exceed a few thousand residents—to press the U.S. government to protect the islands for both commercial and military reasons. Closer ties between the two nations meant tightening American control of the sugar, mercantile, and carrying trades while enhancing the prospect of gaining the splendid harbor at Pearl Bay on the most populous Hawaiian island, Oahu, for a mid-Pacific U.S. naval station.

The *haoles* finally succeeded in convincing Washington to lift import duties on Hawaiian products by agreeing in 1875 to a reciprocal free-trade treaty, allowing sugar and rice from the islands to be sold in the United States, which imported 90 percent of its sugar, at a cheaper price than any other foreign growers could afford to charge. In return, Hawaii agreed not to sell or lease any part of the kingdom to a foreign government other than the United States. The deal helped to encourage a new wave of American capital investment in the islands—particularly in the expansion and upgrading of the sugar plantations (the Spreckels family now owned six of them) and chartering of U.S.-owned banks (the Spreckels family establishment predictably prominent among them). The resulting surge in the Hawaiian economy led to a renewal of the free-trade treaty in 1887, this time granting the American government the right to build a naval base at Pearl Harbor— a concession extracted from the weak and profligate king, David Kalakaua. Between 1877 and 1898, the value of Hawaiian sugar exported to the United States rose sixteenfold. The lion's share of the newly generated wealth stayed in American paws; Hawaii more and more resembled a colony from which U.S. entrepreneurs, holding much of the islands' public and private debt, extracted goodly profits, rents, and interest. Here was the new form of American expansionism at work—no longer territorial, in the sense of obtaining sovereignty over others' real estate, but economic in form, aimed at wielding pervasive power over—and, where possible, control of—commerce in foreign parts.

The cultural fiber of native Hawaiian society, compliant with—however resentful of—the disproportionate *haole* influence over the islands' life, was further softened by the demographic shock that accompanied the expanding sugar harvest. Chinese immigrants came to undertake the strenuous field work and were soon followed by a far larger influx of Japanese workers idled by the depression then ravaging farms in their homeland. Japan's rulers arranged contracts amounting to indentured servitude for its immigrant laborers, who had to work twenty-six days a month under a merciless sun for minimal food, cramped housing, and about three cents an hour in pay. Still, it was better than what they had left, and they were a hardy breed who became the backbone of the plantation workforce. Those Japanese who survived their three-to-five-year term of peonage often stayed in the islands and went on to better things. In the two decades following the Hawaiian free-trade treaty with the United States, some 100,000 mostly Asian farm-workers came to the islands, far surpassing those of Polynesian stock. By 1900 the Asian immigrants made up nearly half of the islands' population; 37 percent of the total were Japanese. Their government pressed Hawaii's to grant citizenship rights to the immigrant workers, but the king and the legislature in Honolulu resisted, with the concurrence of the *haole* elite, who feared that a genuine democracy would soon boost property taxes and otherwise curtail the baronial Americans' privileged status. Racial friction intensified over widening economic, political, and social inequities.

Feeling themselves to be an increasingly endangered species among the foreigners threatening to engulf them, the Hawaiians rallied behind their king, Kalakaua, to strengthen their prerogatives of government. But the king was a weak reed, whose extravagant habits (champagne was his choice among the potables he liberally indulged in) led him into blatantly corrupt practices. Almost everything under the crown's control was for sale or otherwise tainted by irregularities. Importers could save on customs duties by having their purchases shipped directly to the palace, lepers could avoid exile to Molokai, bank charters could be expedited, the opium trade monopoly could be obtained—all for a suitable consideration. But roads, harbor facilities, and other public improvements needed to service a growing economy were notoriously neglected. Even so, the Hawaiian government managed to fall into debt while the insouciant Kalakaua indulged his pleasures and pursued the feckless notion of expanding his kingdom by annexing other Polynesian island groups. This fantasy failed to materialize, but no strong native politicians arose to check the king's louche conduct: he was, after all, at least *theirs*.

In late 1886 white business interests, unhappy over the destabilizing effects of Kalakaua's wanton ways and fearful that growing native resentment might imperil their license to make a commercial killing, organized the Hawaiian League, with a sprinkling of civic leaders and others of mixed blood among their members. Its aim was to reinforce *haole* supremacy by eventually toppling the monarchy and replacing it with a republic, which, like Texas, could soon become a part of the United States. To advance their intrigue, the league members infiltrated the Honolulu Rifles, a quasi-official militia that stockpiled weapons and ammunition at an armory in the islands' capital. The following year, as the vital reciprocal trade treaty came up for renewal with Washington, the American cabal called a protest rally that drew 2,500 startled citizens to the armory, who then helped themselves to enough weapons to look as if they meant business, and marched to the Iolani Palace to confront the badly frightened king. He readily accepted their demands for a new cabinet arrangement to police his conduct, a pledge not to interfere with government operations or abuse them for his private gain, and acquiescence in what the royal claque would later call the "Bayonet Constitution," reducing the king to little more than a figurehead. Any crown act or decree would now have to be approved by a cabinet member, the royal power to veto legislation could be overridden by two-thirds of the lawmakers, and members of the upper branch of the legislature, the House of Nobles, were no longer to be chosen by the king but popularly elected.

These imposed reforms attained legitimacy less by force of *haole* arms than by wide acknowledgment that something had to be done to bring responsible government to the islands. But the Hawaiian League's actions hardly merited cheers as a glorious revolution aimed at supplanting a tinhorn monarchy with a vibrant and truly representative democracy. The new constitution required voters to own property worth at least $3,000 or to earn $600 a year—a high standard for many islanders and one that meant the *haoles* would retain disproportionate electoral power. To drive home this advantage, all Asians other than those of Polynesian blood were denied the right to vote. It was classic American disdain toward nonwhites, and it foretold a still more decisive degradation of the native islanders six years later.

THE HAWAIIAN ECONOMY WAS SENT reeling suddenly in 1890 by congressional enactment of the so-called McKinley tariff, which had the effect of nullifying the extension three years earlier of the reciprocal treaty allowing sugar from the islands to be imported duty-free. The McKinley Act, while generally raising tariffs, scrapped duties on all U.S. sugar imports and wiped out the advantage Hawaiian growers had enjoyed for fourteen years. At the same time, Congress aided American growers by giving them a two-cents-per-pound subsidy. Angry Hawaiians, and not just the sugar barons, vengefully called for cancellation of the concession to build an American naval base at Pearl Harbor—a self-defeating reaction that would have denied the island economy millions in construction outlays and commercial activity. An alternative response, as Hawaiian sugar sales to the U.S. plunged, was a renewed effort to interest Washington in annexing the islands. Their sugar growers would thus be eligible for the two-cent bounty the government had begun to pay American growers. Since the Hawaiian harvest had lately reached 300 million pounds, that would have amounted to a $5 million gift to island planters—and since they would still have the advantage of cheap Japanese contract labor, they would prosper anew, and the trickle-down effect would be felt all over Hawaii.

Yet not all the sugar barons, despite the punishing effect of the McKinley tariff on their property values, favored annexation, even assuming the United States would welcome a mostly nonwhite territory into the Union. Their most powerful member, German-born Claus Spreckels, who had come to America as a teenager and made his fortune as a California sugar refiner, doubted that annexation would prove a quick fix for Hawaii's troubles. He predicted that Congress would soon kill the sugar subsidy (he was right) and that U.S. jurisdiction over the islands would also spell an early end to the cozy arrangement keeping Japanese laborers under contract to American planters in virtual bondage (right again). The more pressing reason many growers and their allies hesitated to push annexation was the prospect that U.S. laws, with their broadened citizenship rights, would have to be extended to all residents of Hawaii, thus reducing oligarchic control over the islands by American business interests. Spreckels was probably being candid when he remarked, "We [big sugar planters] would much prefer that Hawaii would remain a kingdom, and then we should know that our business would not be interfered with."

Not all *haoles,* of course, worshipped the dollar and laissez-faire dogma to the exclusion of the overall well-being of the islands. Like most American settlers from colonial days forward, they had come there to take hold of, tame, and extract wealth from the land, using whatever labor was available. Yet many remained mindful of the missionary calling that had drawn their forebears to the islands to guide, comfort, and uplift the wayward and benighted natives. Even so, the copper-skinned islanders' meek submission to the uninvited benevolence of their pale soul-savers had implanted in the missionaries' progeny a perceived birthright of privilege and power. But the faltering sugar market, resurgent nativism, and the spreading sea of Asian faces whose eyes mutely protested their subjugation left many in the American community uneasy and looking homeward for strengthened backing. Only annexation would safeguard their status, lock in their property rights, and improve the general welfare, all of which, since the death of King Kalakaua in 1891, appeared threatened by his formidable successor, Queen Liliuokalani.

A woman of large girth and larger spirit, the queen was far better cultivated and stronger-willed than her brother, whom she faulted for having spinelessly surrendered the power of the royal household—and she meant to restore it forthwith. Charming when she chose to be, a gifted musician and songwriter, well traveled and well spoken (her English was fluent and precise), and free of delusions that her people's past had been altogether blissful, the queen nonetheless made no secret of her resentment over the kingdom's domination by foreigners and dependency on the United States. Hoping to nullify the effects of the 1887 Bayonet Constitution, she was determined to be far more than a rubber-stamp monarch. Her agenda was to restore native culture, correct her government's improvident finances, and prevent construction of a U.S. naval base that would reinforce the disagreeable perception of Hawaii as an American colony.

This unhidden agenda put Liliuokalani on a collision course with the *haole* elite, who had had their fill of a wasteful, indolent monarchy they wanted relegated to ceremonial irrelevance. The queen did little to allay the non-natives' anxiety by choosing inept cabinet ministers to counsel her and failing to address administrative inefficiency and the problems a laggard economy was inflicting. Her dubious judgment and suggestibility were evidenced, her critics said, by the airy schemes she favored to increase government revenues—for example, a public lottery, promoted by a German spiritualist who read occult messages in playing cards, and an auction for exclusive rights to the opium import trade, which her brother had tried to manipulate. The legislature, with *haoles* overrepresented, began casting no-confidence votes against the queen's cabinet, forcing her to alter its makeup without ever improving quality; the result was a revolving-door regime.

Chief among the royal party's detractors was the U.S. envoy to Hawaii, John L. Stevens, who had arrived in 1889 at the age of sixty-nine to take up his final diplomatic posting. An old friend of Secretary of State James G. Blaine, and fellow Down-Easter, Stevens had been trained as a Universalist minister and a journalist before turning to diplomacy. He was an ardent expansionist at a time when the United States seemed to have forsaken its territorial acquisitiveness, and he was keenly aware that Blaine, as early as 1881, during his previous tenure running the State Department, had called for "drawing the lines of intimate relationship between us and the Hawaiian Islands so as to make them practically a part of the American system without derogation of their absolute independence." Understandably, Stevens felt his job was not to let Hawaii stray from its ordained role as an American dependency and, toward that end, urged Washington to apply freer trade policies toward the islands, proceed with the naval base at Pearl Harbor, and facilitate an undersea telegraph cable from California to Honolulu. His impatience with Queen Lili's royal pretensions, her failure to confront social problems seriously, and the constant squabbling between her and the legislature drove him at times to highly undiplomatic displays of rudeness toward the monarch. She, in turn, distrusted him and suspected—correctly— that he was plotting annexation. The queen, Stevens advised Blaine, "is surrounded by some of the worst elements in the country, persons of native and foreign [non-American] birth, and seeks a cabinet made up entirely of her tools." His intentions were clear, and on January 14, 1893, Liliuokalani presented him and most of the American business, cultural, social, and religious leaders with the opportunity they had been waiting for.

That day, making good on a vow she had taken upon ascending the throne, the queen told her cabinet she wished to promulgate a new constitution, restoring most of the crown's pre-1887 rights, and asked her ministers' approval. But they were divided over the wisdom and necessity of an autocratic initiative that seemed certain to provoke rancor in the *haole* community. Word of the cabinet confrontation quickly reached the ever-vigilant membership of the Hawaiian League, where all agreed the critical moment was at hand. The quixotic queen had to be unhorsed for the good of her subjects and the welfare of the whole island nation. A thirteen-member "Committee of Public Safety," modeled on the American Revolution's ad hoc patriot councils, was organized by thirty-five-year-old attorney Lorrin Thurston, a skillful propagandist and great-grandson of a prominent missionary. Their plan was to declare Hawaii an independent republic, force the queen's abdication, and apply at once to President Benjamin Harrison and his State Department for a treaty of annexation to the United States. To serve as their public leader the committee prevailed upon perhaps the most prominent jurist in the islands, Sanford Ballard Dole, a tall, lean, long-bearded, Hawaiian-speaking son of missionary parents, who was well regarded for his fairmindedness by both the *haole* and native communities. Dole and Thurston apprised American ambassador Stevens of their intentions and requested that he direct the commander of the destroyer U.S.S. *Boston,* on call in Honolulu, to ready the contingent of marines on board for imminent intervention ashore.

The following day, as they had done six years earlier, the *haole* vigilantes summoned a mass meeting of the public at the Honolulu Rifles' armory and declared their litany of grievances against the decadent monarchy—they were more on the order of misfeasance and nonfeasance than of malfeasance—culminating in the queen's haughty disregard for constitutional procedures, and they asked her to step aside. They did not bother to remind their listeners that the Bayonet Constitution imposed on the queen's brother in 1887 had likewise been an exercise in extralegality. A rival gathering of crown loyalists at Palace Square drew a far smaller audience, circumstantial evidence that Lili was not mindlessly venerated by her native subjects. They did not, at any rate, arise from the streets to join her modest palace guard and the Honolulu constabulary to confront the American insurgents. That night, John Stevens, piously professing that he was not taking sides in the power struggle, directed 162 blue-jacketed marines to debark from the *Boston* in full battle gear, bearing two cannons, a pair of Gatling guns, and a field hospital, in order "to protect American lives and property." But the troops, a mightier force than any that could have been assembled from the queen's loyalists in a timely fashion, bivouacked close by the government building and Iolani Palace, located on the opposite side of the city from the main American quarter. The message was unmistakable. No overnight violence was reported.

As the members of the so-called public safety committee marched toward the government headquarters the next morning to take command of administrative operations, they stopped by to receive the blessing of the allegedly neutral Stevens. The U.S. envoy told them, according to Judge Dole's later account, "I think you have a great opportunity." And they took it, bloodlessly; only a single shot of protest was heard several blocks away from the scene of the coup. With well-equipped U.S. marines at the ready but out of immediate sight, the minimal security staff at the government building stepped aside, and the American insurgents swept in to occupy the new locus of Hawaiian power. Once inside, they proclaimed the kingdom defunct, the islands a constitutional republic, and themselves its provisional government. Documents to that effect were delivered to the queen, who, fearful for her safety if she challenged the revolutionary council, yielded to what she termed "the superior force of the United States," pending what she hoped—not in vain—would be a full investigation by officials sent from Washington.

At no time had the rebels said they were acting in the name or under the auspices of the United States. Envoy Stevens, nonetheless, acted as if the uprising had been fully sanctioned by his government. Without waiting for a signal of approval from the President he extended diplomatic recognition to the new regime, even though it was unelected and unrepresentative of the Hawaiian people. Two weeks later he declared the islands a U.S. protectorate and ordered Old Glory to be raised over the government building. Meanwhile, American marines patrolled what, for the moment, had become a police state in order to quell any signs of counterinsurgency.

A five-man commission from the new *haole*-led republic left for Washington within days of the putsch and quickly reached agreement with the Harrison administration on an annexation treaty. The President, who had to be talked out of insisting on a plebiscite throughout the islands—as Liliuokalani had requested—to certify the legitimacy of the provisional government, sent the treaty to the Senate with only three weeks remaining before he left office. The nation did not seem greatly concerned one way or the other about acquiring a far-offshore possession. Alaska, after all, was not geographically adjacent to U.S. territory. But there were those who worried that annexing Hawaii was a more extreme case of untethered expansionism: If the country could stretch well over 2,000 miles across the ocean to add to its sovereign domain, was there to be no limit to its potential outreach? Most of the Hawaiians, moreover, were people of color—not a favored admixture to the prevailing racist mindset in white America. It was argued in rebuttal that the natives and the far larger population of Asian immigrants were securely under the thumb of the American oligarchs who dominated the islands' economy and culture and that, as a practical matter, Hawaii had been a satellite of the United States for over a generation. The Senate, however, chose to await the second coming of Grover Cleveland before deliberating.

The only President to be returned to the White House after having been voted out of it, Cleveland was a stubbornly independent-minded apostle of clean government. He had eluded the snares of political hackdom as mayor of Buffalo and gained national prominence while governor of New York as an advocate of social justice without turning populist panderer. And the Hawaiian revolution frankly troubled him on moral grounds. He questioned whether the nation should legitimize a coup by a group of elite American expatriates who, in cahoots with the misbehaving U.S. ambassador, may well have stolen the place from the cowed natives. Democrat Cleveland, faulting Republican Harrison for rushing to judgment on the annexation pact, withdrew the treaty from the Senate and called on former Georgia Congressman James H. Blount, who had chaired the House foreign relations committee, to go to Hawaii to investigate.

The queen's loyalists were soon relieved of their suspicion that Special Commissioner Blount had come to whitewash the revolutionaries' conduct. His first act on arrival was to order the American flag taken down from government headquarters and the marines to return to their ship. Indeed, Blount gave signs that he was not only bending over backward to avoid siding with Judge Dole's provisional republic but was actually determined to undo their power play. In the course of his four-month investigation, Blount failed to interview the insurgent leaders or any of the *Boston*'s officers. His report to the President and Congress was a blistering two-volume *j'accuse,* in which he attributed the political strife and disgruntlement in Hawaii to control of the islands' resources and commerce by white immigrants and the resulting imposed subservience of the natives and other nonwhites—in short, it was very like feudalism. Blount painted the uprising as a fraudulent exercise by an undemocratic junta, without a mandate from anyone, and envoy Stevens as a co-conspirator for deploying U.S. troops to back the rebellion. His conclusion was that most Hawaiians, whatever their degree of allegiance to the monarchy, opposed annexation to the United States—a view that the leaders of the newly declared republic were unwilling to contest by putting the issue to a popular, and truly democratic, vote. Cleveland refused to resubmit the treaty and withstood the considerable pounding he took in Congress and the press for insisting that the United States behave like a democracy and not an imperialist bully like the European powers then carving up Africa and China's coast.

Hawaii then fell under the dictates of the American oligarchs, who formally inaugurated their nominally republican government on July 4, 1894. Surrounding themselves with a vigilant militia, they railroaded through a constitution that restricted voting and officeholding rights and continued to deny the natives and Asians fair representation. No thought was given to restoring the monarchy, even on a radically reformed basis—a possibility that the deposed queen squelched by reportedly saying she would rather behead the *haole* rebels than grant them amnesty. Crown lands were parceled up for sale on a preferential basis to old and new American residents.

However autocratic its rule, President Dole's regime improved Hawaii's public works and services and operated a school system as good as any in the United States. And all the while it lobbied Washington—and across America—for Hawaii to be annexed in the national interest.

HAWAII'S FATE WOULD BE RESOLVED not by moral or ethnic considerations but by concerns over U.S. military and economic policy that surfaced during the nation's four-year confrontation with Spain at the close of the century. The Hawaiian settlement hinged on the perception that the American navy was the vehicle by which the country would arrive at the vanguard of global power and prestige in an age when the leading European states were acting out their imperial ambitions.

The peerless apostle of this proposition was the previously uncelebrated Captain Alfred Thayer Mahan, who, upon completing his term as president of the U.S. Naval War College at Providence in 1890, brought out his seminal book, *The Influence of Sea Power upon History, 1660–1783,* and followed it two years later with a study of naval inadequacies and their effect on revolutionary and Napoleonic France. Mahan's work gained instant attention well beyond American military circles, particularly in foreign war ministries, where it became required reading.

Noting the U.S. evolution from an agricultural economy to an industrial one with a productive capacity outstripping domestic demand, Mahan argued that the resulting need for purveyors of American goods to penetrate overseas markets required enhanced naval capability, because in an increasingly competitive global arena "neither the sanctions of international law nor the justice of a cause can be depended upon for a fair settlement of differences." It was the naval version of social Darwinism. Mahan pitched persuasively not only for a bigger, better navy but for strategically dispersed overseas naval stations to service mightier military and commercial U.S. fleets.

Heeding this premise, President Benjamin Harrison's administration (1889–93) adopted what its Secretary of the Navy termed a "battleship strategy," allowing American squadrons led by big-gunned dreadnoughts to roam far from home to protect expanding U.S. trade and investments abroad while better safeguarding the nation's home ports. What the United States needed, then, to bulk up its prosperity was not new, extensive increments of territory but naval bases of the sort proposed for Pearl Harbor.

Harrison's successor, Grover Cleveland (redux), adopted a more defensive naval policy. Determinedly antiexpansionist and sometimes demeaned as isolationist, Cleveland believed the nation could best advance and protect its interests by firm, clear warnings against threatened foreign aggression. That translated into support for a naval buildup as a defensive necessity but not for certifying hijacked Hawaii as American territory, despite all its potential utility. The U.S. military establishment solidly disagreed, envisioning a bright commercial future in the Pacific even though the "China trade" accounted for little more than 1 percent of all American exports. Cleveland's withdrawal of the annexation treaty would serve only to discourage growth in trade with Asia. In magazine and newspaper articles at the time, Captain Mahan challenged the Cleveland policy by asserting the United States could never become a Pacific power without owning Hawaii and that such island bases were imperative if American business in Asia was ever to amount to much. If Hawaii was left out there unclaimed, some other country—Britain, most logically, because of the islands' perfect position astride the route between Canada and Australia—might well strike a deal to take them over as a colony or protectorate, and where would that leave the United States? The answer seemed to be, in deference to the President's principled stand, that so long as he held office and opposed annexing the Hawaiian Islands, no other nation would be allowed to move in on them.

Though a reluctant international dabbler, Cleveland was not averse to engaging in brinkmanship when a controversy arose close to home. Invoking the Monroe Doctrine, he warned off Britain in an 1895 stare-down over 23,000 square miles of mineral-rich jungle along the disputed border between British Guiana and Venezuela. The United States had no territorial stake in the matter but chose to put its prestige on the line as defender of the Western Hemisphere against the bullying tendencies of European powers. Cleveland won that contest by threatening to side militarily with a weak, corrupt Latin American republic if Britain refused to arbitrate—and in the end it did so and won most of the disputed territory. Yet that same year Cleveland took what at first seemed an oddly unsympathetic attitude toward other Latin American neighbors up against an Old World tormentor and longtime U.S. antagonist.

The agrarian Cuban underclass and its urban liberal compatriots, inspired by poet-essayist José Martí, would no longer tolerate abusive Spanish rule of their island and rebelled early in 1895 with the help of money and arms raised by refugees from Cuba centered in New York but active across the country. Spain's homeland government, beset by the nation's latest outbreak of political turmoil, chose to use the colonial uprising as a way to rally the nation behind it and sent heavy reinforcements to its island garrison to put down the insurgents rather than offer substantive reforms to allay their grievances. The bitter clash soon destabilized the island's economy, in which American investors held a $50 million stake. Anxious to prevent anarchy and unmoved at first by the rebels' cause, Cleveland did nothing to discourage the Spanish campaign of suppression and even tried to pinch off the flow of weapons and supplies being smuggled onto the island from the United States. But soon the Spaniards' inability to quell the rebellion drove Madrid to assign its ultimate enforcer, General Valeriano Weyler, to the task. Dubbed "the Butcher" for his indelicate methods in crushing an earlier, ten-year guerrilla war in Cuba, Weyler showed that he had not forgotten his trade. Warning that no reforms would be considered until order was restored, he sanctioned almost daily atrocities by his troops and reintroduced mass starvation as a weapon through a systematic roundup of the peasantry, which he supposed—correctly—was sympathetic to the revolution. He herded whole villages into concentration camps with hideous living conditions, a brutal measure that effectively destroyed the morale of its victims but also further infuriated those still at liberty. The ultimate cost of this antirevolutionary vendetta was estimated to be at least 100,000 Cuban lives—and may have actually reached four times higher out of a population of 1.6 million.

As the savage civil war reduced the dominant island in the West Indies to a horrid killing ground close by their shore, Americans paid heed, even though they themselves were then beset by wrenching domestic troubles. Their nation had grown into an industrial powerhouse, but the boom-or-bust cycles of capitalism had spawned a polarizing class struggle and loosed an outcry for humanitarian reforms, among them better wages and shorter hours, safer working conditions, easier credit, a brake on the competition-crushing might of giant corporate trusts, an end to urban slums, and more public transportation. Still, after thirty years of self-absorption, America's better angels drew the people's eyes toward the appalling spectacle of Cuba on the rack, with two-thirds of its mostly black and brown population in poverty and ignorance and under assault by Spanish soldiers with a ferocity that the press—and not just the sensation-mongering "yellow journals" of Hearst and Pulitzer—began waving in their faces day after day. American entrepreneurs who traded with Cuba, more hardheaded than sentimental, complained that the hostilities were ruining their business and destroying property indiscriminately. In his farewell address to Congress in December 1896, President Cleveland had to concede that the Cuban rebellion was beyond Spain's control, that the conflict was damaging American interests, and that its continuation could not be tolerated much longer. Deepening nationwide compassion for the rebels' plight sparked early calls for active military intervention on their side. Even isolationist newspapers demanded Spain be booted out of the hemisphere for keeps.

The 1896 elections, inaugurating sixteen years of Republican control of the White House and both houses of Congress, crystallized the new spirit infusing U.S. foreign policy. Fully subscribing to Mahan's doctrine of naval assertiveness, Republican leadership favored displaying the nation's hemispheric dominance by establishing bases in the Caribbean, blunting further attempted incursions by European powers (such as the British border clash with Venezuela), building an American-controlled canal across the isthmus at either Nicaragua or Panama, and extending U.S. commercial reach for Asian markets by acquiring island stepping-stones across the Pacific, starting with Hawaii. This policy was articulated by a cadre of younger, well-placed Republican intellectuals, many with Harvard degrees, some holding public office, others behind the scenes, and almost all devoted to the Mahan gospel. Perhaps their most vigorous—and at times almost fanatic—spokesman was the brahmin Henry Cabot Lodge of Massachusetts, who, as a freshman U.S. Senator, had written in the March 1895 *Forum* magazine that the United States ought to defy Britain in its "strong places" in the West Indies, where they posed "a standing menace to our Atlantic seaboard. . . . We should have among those islands at least one strong naval station, and when the Nicaraguan canal is built, the island of Cuba . . . will become to us a necessity." His anthem, catching the fancy of many as an acceptable rationale for a revised form of American expansionism, was "Commerce follows the flag." But Lodge's fervor turned to zealotry when he added, in what sounded like an appeal to reawaken old-style territorial lust, "The great nations are rapidly absorbing for their future expansion and their present defense all the waste places of the earth."

Such snobby belligerence was not shared—or ever couched in those terms, anyway—by the new President, William McKinley, a cautious, godly Ohioan who emerged from a small-city legal practice to become the embodiment of Republican orthodoxy, in particular its passion for protectionist tariffs. Short on magnetism, McKinley excelled at keeping his own counsel while providing a presentable, dutiful front for Ohio tycoon (coal, iron, banking, shipping, media) and power broker Marcus A. Hanna, who funded his career. After seven terms in Congress, where he won the chairmanship of the House Ways and Means Committee by mastering more of the arcane details of the tariff issue than anyone else, McKinley lost his seat in the 1890 Democratic sweep. But Hanna rescued his career by guiding him to two respectable two-year terms as governor of Ohio, grooming him to step forth in 1896 as the steady counterweight to the fiery, thirty-six-year-old Democratic presidential nominee, William Jennings Bryan. The Nebraskan Bryan thrilled the country as a spellbinding populist crusader, calling for the return of "free silver" to help the "toiling masses" pay their debts with currency inflated by government purchases of silver pegged at an artificially high value to gold. In contrast, the lackluster McKinley stayed close to home, said little beyond vowing his devotion to a sound dollar, and won 52 percent of the vote in a land where the haves outvoted, if not outnumbered, the have-nots.

Once in the White House, McKinley exhibited little yen for a shootout with Spain over Cuba, so long coveted by American expansionists. The new President's core constituency, the northern business community, was traditionally opposed to war—always a risky proposition, destabilizing, inflationary, and disruptive of commerce. And under its emergent policy of economic rather than territorial expansionism, the United States did not need, or really want, to own nonwhite, Spanish-speaking, Catholic Cuba, with its long antidemocratic heritage. If Spain would just grant independence or self-rule to the Cubans, American business could readily expand its commercial role on the island, eliminating the need to annex it as captive territory. McKinley was careful to take no incendiary action that might whip up war frenzy over Cuba in a nation that had not engaged in military combat for more than thirty years and seemed to have forgotten its horrors. But Hawaii was quite a different matter.

In keeping with the 1896 Republican platform, calling for an end to Cleveland's freeze on the annexation treaty, McKinley favored confirming Hawaii as a U.S. territory. The islands had only one-seventh of Cuba's land mass and not even one-tenth of its population, and they were already under political and economic domination by transplanted American immigrants. True, most Hawaiians were nonwhite, but the natives were docile and largely English-speaking, and the Asian immigrants were an inferior caste, denied a political voice, and might well opt for repatriation if so urged. The presence of so many Japanese workers, who made up Hawaii's largest ethnic bloc, also helped underscore another reason for the United States to act promptly on annexation. Equipped with modern weaponry and obsessive military discipline, Japan had lately emerged as a Pacific power by routing China in an 1894–95 war and capturing Taiwan and the strategic Liaotung Peninsula as well as asserting hegemony over Korea. It was by no means unthinkable that the land and sea forces of the Rising Sun might soon push their imperial perimeter eastward to enclose Hawaii, where so many of its nationals had immigrated.

Three months after taking office, McKinley resubmitted the dormant annexation treaty with the full backing of the Dole regime in Honolulu. But there were still enough Democrats in the Senate respectful of Grover Cleveland's opposition to imposing U.S. rule on the islanders to deny his successor the two-thirds majority needed to ratify. Back on the shelf went Hawaii.

The setback came as a particular disappointment to one of the President's strategically placed underlings. At thirty-nine, Theodore Roosevelt displayed a radiant and paradoxical nature that could irritate as well as stimulate his associates, but there was no denying his verve and talents. On one hand, he was an omnivorous intellectual, informed by a book-a-day reading habit, and a prolific author whose style exhibited more exuberance than grace. In the 1880s, while still in his twenties, Roosevelt turned out a book a year, starting with *The Naval War of 1812* and including more famously his three-volume *The Winning of the West*. On the other hand, he was an irrepressible man of action who had overcome frail health in his youth to become a passionate advocate of physical prowess. He made himself into a boxer, a hunter, a horseman, and a rancher who loved the challenge of combat and could write, "All the great masterful races have been fighting races. . . . No triumph of peace is quite so great as the supreme triumphs of war. Diplomacy is utterly useless when there is no force behind it. . . . It is through strife, or the readiness for strife, that a nation must win greatness."

The offspring of wealth and elite social standing derived from a Manhattan mercantile fortune, Teddy Roosevelt declined to pursue a career in the law or on Wall Street in favor of the grubbier precincts of politics and the singular reward of public service—power. He apprenticed as a New York state assemblyman with a reformist bent, favoring labor relief measures and other liberal causes; as a member of the U.S. Civil Service Commission, pushing clean-government practices; and as president of the New York City board of police commissioners, where he tried—without great success—to root out corruption and sloth. His progressive impulses made Roosevelt a dangerous and irksome boat-rocker to New York party elders, who got him out of their hair by prevailing upon Hanna and, through him, McKinley to bring the jaunty fellow to Washington with his flashing eyeglasses, gleaming teeth, purposeful stride, and flair for publicity. He joined the new administration at the subcabinet level as Assistant Secretary of the Navy; it was thought he could not spread his wings in that pigeonhole.

Eager for the fray, Roosevelt wrote his good friend in the Senate, Henry Cabot Lodge, a few months before McKinley entered the White House in March of 1897, "I hope he [the President] will take a strong stand both about Hawaii and Cuba." Roosevelt's boss, Navy Secretary John Long, was a model of tact and passivity, and his first assistant lost no time in filling the power void. Roosevelt, a naval historian himself and frequent correspondent with Alfred Mahan, whose views he fully subscribed to, on more than one occasion exceeded his authority or issued orders without Long's prior approval, as he managed to accelerate the buildup of the U.S. fleet and bring more vigorous leadership to its top level of command. After six months on the job, he was recommending—as he indiscreetly confided to Lodge—that if the Cuban situation led to war, the navy's Pacific Squadron "should blockade and, if possible, take Manila," capital of Spain's other principal colony, the Philippine Islands.

What made this proposal remarkable was that the large archipelago (115,000 square miles spread over 400 islands), only 500 miles southeast of Hong Kong, was undergoing a revolution against Spanish rule very like, if not quite as brutal as, the one in Cuba, yet very few Americans knew a thing about it or, for that matter, even where the Philippines were. But here was the top deputy to the man in charge of the U.S. Navy plotting to capture a harbor halfway around the world from Washington simply because the nation had a quarrel with its owner over an entirely different matter—and, more to the point, because American ships could manage the feat. It was Roosevelt who engineered the appointment of resourceful, spirited Commodore George Dewey to command the Pacific Fleet. And it was Roosevelt who, as Acting Secretary on February 25, 1898, when Long was away from the office and ten days after the battleship U.S.S. *Maine* blew up in Havana harbor, sent Dewey the fateful cable ordering him to collect his squadron at Hong Kong and to "[k]eep full of coal. In the event of war [with] Spain, your duty will be to see that the Spanish squadron does not leave the Asiatic coast, and then offensive operations in Philippine Islands."

DESPITE MADRID'S PLEDGE to pacify rebellious Cuba with an army now approximating 200,000, the carnage and devastation only grew. In big cities and small towns, Americans rallied to denounce the infamy of the endless war as Spain rebuffed U.S. pressure to grant Cuba self-government and allow Washington to mediate the peace settlement. State Department diplomats were advised that the United States should butt out of other nations' internal quarrels and, if it really wanted peace, bar its citizens from further funding and arming the rebels. That sort of brush-off fueled the passion of frustrated American jingoists who spied a safe enemy in Spain, nasty but puny, and filled the air with shouts of moral indignation—*"Cuba libre!"*—beyond party lines. The British might be disporting their imperial power elsewhere in the world, in South Africa, India, Australia, Malaya, and the China coast, and Japan might be the new scourge of the Far Pacific, but the Western Hemisphere was the domain of the United States, and Spain had to be taught as much.

The more futile the Spanish effort to smash the rebels, the more brutal the repression grew, as the American press reported daily on its front pages. Riots in Havana in January 1898, protesting Spanish officers' refusal to accept orders from Madrid to appease the rebels by promising reforms, were put down with so much violence that McKinley sent the three-year-old steel battleship *Maine* to pay a "courtesy call" to the Cuban capital. Its purpose, everyone knew, was to protect American citizens and property. The big ship had been anchored in Havana harbor for three weeks when, on the evening of February 15, a shattering explosion below the waterline sent it quickly to the bottom, dooming 260 American sailors. Whether the explosion was caused by a submerged mine pre-planted at the ship's mooring by Spanish divers or resulted from spontaneous combustion in one of the *Maine*'s coal bins, unwisely located right next to the ammunition magazine—the two leading theories—has never been conclusively determined despite exhaustive and repeated investigation.

The American public, conditioned by the press to think the worst of Spain, had no doubt the *Maine* disaster was an act of intolerable sabotage. McKinley, after nearly a year of enigmatic temporizing in the hope the Cuban war would be resolved without intervention by the American government, knew he could not accept Spanish denials of culpability in the *Maine* affair so long as Madrid remained intransigent over reaching an accord with the rebels. The combustible tension was further heightened when a letter by the Spanish envoy in Washington was intercepted and leaked to the press. The letter, terming the President of the United States "weak" and a "bidder for the admiration of the crowd," also disclosed that Spain's hints it might make concessions to the rebels if they put down their arms were strictly for diplomatic effect. Although the offending ambassador was promptly yanked from his post and apologies tendered, McKinley now sent a clear signal to Madrid that his patience had come to an end. The U.S. Treasury was overflowing with tax revenues, thanks to the robust national recovery from the Panic of 1893, and Congress had no qualms about acceding at once to the President's request for a $50 million standby war chest. It was an immense sum, considering that no U.S. territory was directly affected by the Cuban crisis, and all the more daunting to the hand-to-mouth Spanish government.

Having thus arrested Madrid's attention, McKinley made a final effort at the end of March to let the Spaniards know they had to settle the Cuban war then and there or the United States would settle it for them. But his diplomatic language did not put it quite so curtly. Spain was told it had to meet three conditions: end the fighting and shut down the concentration camps, grant the Cubans self-rule, and allow the United States to serve as arbitrator of the peace process. Madrid, after trying without success to enlist the Vatican and other European powers to restrain the Americans, made some conciliatory noises. Yes, it would agree to an armistice and close the slave-labor camps, and maybe it would work out some form of self-rule with the Cuban people, but nothing was said about allowing Washington to have the final word on the peace terms.

The Spanish response was too grudging, too waffling, and too late. McKinley could no doubt have continued the diplomatic fandango or tightened the screws by delivering an ultimatum that American armed forces would be unleashed against Spain if it did not abandon the fight in Cuba by a given deadline. Had he done so, however, it is doubtful the outcome would have been much different. Surviving documents suggest the Spaniards felt, as usual and like their colonial progeny, the Mexicans, that it was more honorable to fight in a hopeless cause than to face up to the reality of their weakness. The President decided he could no longer withstand the tide of jingoist fervor sweeping across the nation, enveloping Congress, and pounding hard against the White House door. Even the usually dovish business community had swung around in favor of quick and decisive American intervention in Cuba rather than allowing the barbarous war of attrition to drag on and on at Spain's sufferance. By all accounts, McKinley was a reluctant combatant, pushed by the nation into warring with Spain instead of leading it, as Polk had done against Mexico half a century earlier—or defying the popular will, as Cleveland had done in rejecting Hawaii as stolen goods. There was the distinct possibility, moreover, that Congress would have declared war on Spain even if the President had not asked it to.

He did so on April 11, seeking the lawmakers' authorization to apply whatever military force was needed to drive the Spaniards out of Cuba, and signed the joint congressional resolution to that effect nine days later. But to assure the world that the American mission was pure in heart and dedicated to the humanitarian purpose of gaining freedom for long-suffering victims of Spanish tyranny, Congress inserted a pledge known as the Teller Amendment (after its author, New York Republican Senator Henry M. Teller), which vowed that the United States would not assume "sovereignty, jurisdiction, or control" over Cuba "except for the pacification thereof, and asserts its determination when that is completed to leave the government and control of the island to its people." Americans, presumably, would derive their reward for this adventure in altruism by demonstrating to the world that they were indeed the irresistible champions of liberty and justice in the Western Hemisphere. Nothing was said, though, in the Teller Amendment about any other piece of Spanish territory beside Cuba that might fall into U.S. hands in the course of the fighting.

This omission, events would very shortly suggest, was no oversight. When American forces struck their first blow hardly a week after war was declared, it landed nowhere in embattled Cuba—the stated *casus belli*—but 10,000 miles away. U.S. war planners had decided that Spanish territory was fair game wherever it was vulnerable and whenever American firepower was ready to be delivered. It was ready, thanks in no small part to

Theodore Roosevelt's anticipation, in Hong Kong, where George Dewey's squadron of seven warships had been alerted to steam 600 miles to Manila Bay and destroy the Spanish fleet watching over the Philippine Islands. The American flotilla arrived at dawn on May 1, defied the stunned artillerymen at the batteries rimming the reputedly well-fortified harbor, and sank the Spaniards' whole eleven-ship force in what amounted to an exercise in target practice. Some 300 Spanish sailors were killed and 400 wounded; none of Dewey's ships was seriously damaged, though one sailor was lost. If this opening foray was intended to shock and awe the enemy and the watching world, it succeeded. Overnight the United States had become a Pacific power and international presence.

Hearing the news of Dewey's spectacular victory and convinced that their nation's cause was righteous, young Americans rushed jubilantly to join the expeditionary force presumably about to liberate the Cubans from hated Spain. Nobody had yet said anything about likewise freeing the Filipinos. A million men applied to the U.S. Army and Navy, 200,000 were accepted, and mobilization quickly began. But Winfield Scott was no longer around to preach the necessity of careful training and close drilling; as a result, 16,000 American troops were sent into combat near Santiago, at the southwest end of the Cuban coast, with scarcely six weeks of training. Among those itching to get into the fight was Lieutenant Colonel Theodore Roosevelt of the New York State National Guard, whose three years of drilling got him invited to take command of the First U.S. Volunteer Cavalry, the self-styled "Rough Riders," a colorful assortment of he-man equestrians ranging from Ivy League polo players to retired Indian fighters. In a rare show of modesty, Roosevelt recognized that his limited experience did not qualify him to lead the unit, so he accepted the post of second in command. His subordinate role did not restrain him from a gallant but foolhardy display of heroics in leading the dismounted riders on a furious charge up heavily defended Kettle Hill in the siege of the San Juan Heights close to Santiago. His survival guaranteed his ascent to political Olympus. Returning home to cheers and dashing off a book about his and his comrades' exploits, Roosevelt promptly got himself elected governor of New York, to the consternation of state Republican bigwigs, and two years later, his voter appeal undeniable, was chosen as running mate of the bland incumbent President.

John Hay, U.S. ambassador to the Court of St. James's and Secretary of State after Roosevelt inherited the White House, famously labeled the conflict with Spain "a splendid little war." But it was even less splendid than most. The enemy did not put up much of a fight, so the United States wound up looking rather like a muscular young lout waylaying an Old World dowager. The war's only virtue was that it lasted just 113 days before Spain, with most of its navy underwater and its troops in Cuba marooned by an American blockade, surrendered ingloriously. At the time, U.S. forces held only part of the eastern tip of Cuba, all of next-door Puerto Rico, and a few of the outskirts of Manila, in tandem with Filipino rebels. American losses due to combat came to 385; another 2,000 were victims of tropical diseases.

Having formally renounced any intention to annex Cuba, American leaders did not feel so bound by their scruples that they avoided eyeing other delectable helpings of Spanish territory as suitable trophies of their triumph. The largest and most tempting were the Philippines. But they were a good deal more than a morsel: their 400 inhabited islands had three times the land mass and five times the population of Cuba, and they were nearly 7,000 miles from California. Their proximity to the China coast and other Far Eastern markets, though, helped McKinley decide they would make an ideal place for a naval base and trading depot, probably at Manila, for the convenience of U.S. commerce. Toward securing what his Secretary of War, William Day, called "a hitching post" in the Philippines, McKinley ordered troops transported from the West Coast to rendezvous with Dewey's fleet and, supported by his big guns, to rid the Manila region of its Spanish garrison.

While the American expeditionary force was steaming across the Pacific, the aggressive Dewey had been busy plotting the invasion of the Philippines as a joint effort by U.S. troops coming ashore from Manila Bay and Filipino guerrillas assailing the Spanish defenders from the countryside. The rebels were inactive under a truce that had sent their handsome, spirited young leader, Emilio Aguinaldo, into exile in Hong Kong. It was there, while his squadron had been berthed awaiting word that the war with Spain was under way, that Dewey enlisted Aguinaldo to return to his home islands, reignite the Filipino revolution by joining the American siege of Manila, and thus hasten Spain's surrender of the whole archipelago. Apprised of the noble American mission to liberate Cuba from Spanish rule and hand control of the island back to the natives, Aguinaldo had every reason to believe that U.S. forces would act identically in helping free the Philippines—perhaps after a brief protective occupation to ensure their transition to independence. This was not just a wishful expectation by a naive rebel chieftain, because, as Mark Twain would remind U.S. readers in the February 1901 issue of the *North American Review*, "[W]e had been so friendly to them [the Filipino rebels], and heartened them up in so many ways! We had lent them guns and ammunition; advised with them; exchanged pleasant courtesies with them . . . praised their courage, praised their gallantry, praised their mercifulness, praised their fine and honorable conduct . . . officially proclaiming that our land and naval forces came to give them their freedom and displace the bad Spanish Government."

The American troops came as promised, Aguinaldo was spirited ashore to resume command of the quiescent Filipino rebellion, and the encirclement of Spanish-held Manila resulted in its early surrender. But instead of facilitating the handover of power to Aguinaldo's forces, the U.S. command barred them from entering Manila while armed, and then more American reinforcements arrived, and then some more, while in the United States, the public was delighted by the news that Spain had been driven out of the Philippines as well as the Caribbean, and the business community was weighing how best to utilize the nation's large new outpost close to the Asian market. Aguinaldo, bereft of hope his country would soon be returned to its patriots' hands, readied for war against their treacherous liberators from Spanish despotism.

WHILE U.S. NAVY TROOP CARRIERS were traversing the Pacific to join what was billed as the liberation of the Philippines, some of them paused en route to gather a few stepping-stones across the great ocean. On June 20, 1898, the U.S.S. *Charleston,* a cruiser out of San Francisco with 500 soldiers aboard, dropped anchor at the port of San Luis d'Apra on the 212-square-mile, Spanish-held island of Guam in the Marianas, about 1,500 miles east of their final destination.

The *Charleston* lobbed a few warning shells toward the little old fort in the harbor and drew in response two small rowboats of Spanish sailors from the sixty-man garrison. Their handsomely uniformed commanding officer apologized for not returning the Americans' gunnery salute but explained that just at the moment his fort was out of ammunition and no supply ship, or any other vessel, had visited for the past two months. The *Charleston*'s commander brought the courteous Spaniard up to date, then disarmed him and the rest of his unsuspecting contingent, imprisoned them on the ship, and raised the cruiser's ensign over the fort. Guam has remained American territory ever since, except for a three-year occupation by Japanese forces during World War II. One-third of it is used as a U.S. air and naval base.

On July 4 another U.S. naval ship put in at tiny (2.5 square miles), empty Wake Island, halfway between Midway and Guam, and claimed it as American territory. It, too, has remained so except for the Japanese takeover in the Second World War after a courageous resistance. In that same period the United States added, by diplomatic means, another, more extensive coaling station in the South Pacific. The volcanic island group of Samoa, 3,000 miles west of Hawaii, had long been an object of contention among the white military powers, but in 1899 British, German, and American negotiators worked out a trade-off permitting U.S. occupation of seventy-seven square miles of tropical beauty, ceded to Washington by native chiefs in 1900. McKinley did not bother to dignify the ceremonial gesture by submitting the cession to the Senate as a treaty of annexation, and U.S. sovereignty was not formally certified by Congress until 1929. The navy operated a major base at the American Samoan capital of Pago Pago during World War II; today the islanders thrive on tourism and their sizable export of canned tuna.

By far the largest permanent U.S. territorial acquisition resulting from the Spanish-American War occurred in late August 1898, a week after the fighting ended on Cuba. Puerto Rico, about 1,000 miles southeast of Miami and 500 miles due east of Cuba but much smaller (3,425 square miles), made an attractive prize. A mountainous but fertile island with a mild climate and a number of coastal sites suited for a naval base and supply station, it was held by 18,000 troops, half of them regulars in the Spanish army, the rest an assorted militia who had no artillery and no seriously armed vessels to fend off the 15,000 American invaders. The well-deployed gringos converged from beachheads on opposite shores of the rectangular island, and the Spaniards salvaged their honor by firing a few shots. Then they gave up, and the militia deserted en masse.

Unlike the Cuban rebels, the Puerto Ricans were not entirely pleased by the Americans' arrival. They had been granted a representative in the Spanish parliament twenty years earlier and just lately awarded a degree of self-rule by Madrid. Since Washington badly wanted a naval base in the Caribbean, but, according to the Teller Amendment, all of newly freed Cuba had to be preserved for the Cubans, there was no pretense that Puerto Rico as well would be handed back to the natives to rule as an independent entity. To assuage that island's residents, the conquerors began a gradual transition to home rule after two years of U.S. occupation. Under the 1917 designation by Congress, the island became an organized territory, and its residents won most of the rights of American citizens, although their governor was still chosen by the federal government.

Absentee ownership of its numerous sugar plantations, dependency on that single crop, and urban crowding all had a depressing effect on the Puerto Rican economy, which came to life only with the upswing in military activity during World War II. Soon after, the islanders were empowered to elect their own governor, who succeeded in attracting manufacturers and other businesses from the mainland, drawn by the pleasant climate and even more agreeable absence of federal corporate taxes. In 1952, when no offshore or noncontiguous U.S. territory had yet been made a state of the Union and lingering anti-Hispanic sentiment made it still more unlikely that Puerto Rico would soon—if ever—be granted statehood, 80 percent of its voters in a special plebiscite approved congressional designation of the island as a "commonwealth," an anomalous status conveying complete political autonomy and almost full U.S. citizenship rights and duties. The sole exception, in a reversal of the historical American objection to taxation without representation, denied Puerto Ricans the right to vote for federal officials so long as they remained exempt from the federal income tax, an immunity under the island's territorial status. It was a trade-off that seemed to satisfy most residents. While some sentiment for an independent Puerto Rico endures, that aspiration has receded to a fringe movement. Statehood is a more popular cause, but in four referenda held over the second half of the twentieth century, Puerto Ricans voted decisively to retain their special commonwealth status.

THE OUTBREAK OF WAR WITH SPAIN and the immediate satisfying sensation of a huge and unexpected victory at distant Manila Bay at once renewed American interest in the suspended status of the Hawaiian Islands. The *New York Herald* expressed the widely held opinion that "the United States government must have a base of supplies in the Pacific Ocean"—and Hawaii was the obvious place for it. Just days after news of Dewey's startling victory reached the White House, President McKinley was emboldened to dust off the annexation treaty that the Senate had failed to ratify a year earlier and sent it back to Capitol Hill. This time, though, in order to avoid the possibility of a second rejection, he borrowed President Tyler's tactic of fifty-four years earlier when reviving the annexation of Texas after it had been trounced the year before in the Senate: McKinley resubmitted the Hawaiian annexation measure not as a treaty but in the form of a joint congressional resolution, requiring only a simple majority in each house.

Curmudgeonly House Speaker Thomas Reed, an avid antiexpansionist, tried to bottle up the proposal in committee, but the McKinley administration twisted some arms to get the bill a fair hearing, and it carried in mid-June by a solid 209–91 margin. The Senate took up the measure with the outcome still in doubt, but in the course of its deliberations news was flashed to the capital that the remnants of the Spanish Atlantic fleet had tried to escape the American blockade ringing the harbor at Santiago and been utterly destroyed on July 3. With no hope now of their supply lines being restored, and with reinvigorated rebel forces on the warpath, the Spaniards on the big island faced imminent catastrophe, as American troops now moved in to seize Santiago. Madrid would shortly, mercifully, capitulate. Buoyed by the happy war news, the Senate voted 42–21 to annex Hawaii— McKinley would have won ratification, just barely, if he had posed the issue in the form of a treaty—and the President signed the bill the next day.

That summer, as military transport ships stopped off at Honolulu, U.S. soldiers on their way to occupy the Philippines were warmly welcomed by Hawaiians, treated to festive luaus on the lawn of Iolani Palace, and sent off to war with prayers of Godspeed. On August 12 the American flag was raised over Liliuokalani's palace in a ceremony watched by most Asian residents with little regret for the fallen monarchy but without optimism that the arrival of U.S. jurisdiction would materially improve their status. Native Hawaiians, with lingering memories of royal corruption and chronic misrule, seemed more reconciled than resentful as their islands were officially transformed into American territory. No great outcry was raised when Sanford Dole's title was changed from president of the undemocratic republic of Hawaii to first governor of the U.S. Territory of Hawaii, a post he held for five years—testament to the caliber of his administration of the islands— after which he was appointed the first federal district judge for the territory.

American rule brought changes and improvements. Congress assumed Hawaii's public debt, the economy strengthened, the evil contract labor system was dismantled as a form of indentured servitude, and a new pineapple industry flourished on plantations that were once idle royal property. But there was no rush to grace Hawaii with statehood, any more than Alaska, although the islands basked in far more favor with vacation-goers and the War Department as Pearl Harbor grew into the largest U.S. military base west of the American mainland. When finally admitted to the Union in 1959, Hawaii had a lower proportion of Caucasians—18 percent—than any of the previous forty-nine states at the time of their admission; those of native Hawaiian blood comprised a slightly higher percentage, while those of Asian origin made up 60 percent of the population. In the ensuing half century, marked by the surging number of Hispanic and Asian immigrants, the rest of the nation has grown notably less *haole* and more polyethnic.

In 1993 Congress passed a resolution of apology to the people of Hawaii for the part played a century earlier by American troops and the U.S. envoy in the forcible seizure of their islands. In the interim, few Hawaiians had called for the restoration of their independence.

AFTER ACQUIRING HAWAII, President McKinley had to decide what to do with the far larger and more populous Pacific island group—the Philippines, with an area as large as Italy's and a population approaching 9 million—that

American soldiers were occupying that summer. With victory over Spain in hand and the nation eager to be rewarded for its conquest of a third-rate power, the administration faced several choices in determining the fate of the Filipinos. The most aggressive of these was annexation, bandied about Washington prominently by Senator Lodge, who wrote privately that "we must on no account let the islands go. . . . [T]heir value to this country is almost beyond imagination." Just installing a naval base in the Philippines as a "hitching post" and forgetting about the rest of the archipelago— McKinley's second option—would not satisfy the rampant Lodge and the legions who were like-minded.

Emilio Aguinaldo, though, had issued a rousing declaration of independence in June, and his provisional government had drawn up a constitution along genuinely democratic lines. Were the Filipinos just to be shoved aside as the native Hawaiians had been in 1893—not to mention the American Indian nations, the Spaniards in Florida, or the Mexicans in Texas, New Mexico, and California? All their territories, at least, had been amalgamated into the United States; there seemed no likelihood whatever that the Filipinos, given the traditional American bias against nonwhites as racially inferior and hopelessly primitive aliens, would ever become U.S. citizens. Still, the United States was a democratic federated republic, not a colonial empire, and had never held unwilling foreigners under permanent custody. Taking possession of the Philippines, moreover, and retaining them by force might well arouse sharp objections by other powers now highly active in the Far East. McKinley, who Teddy Roosevelt once said in private had no more backbone than a chocolate éclair, studied the national press for a clue about which way the wind was blowing and discerned a trend. According to a poll of leading newspaper editors taken by the *Literary Digest,* eighty-four endorsed outright annexation, seventeen preferred a protectorate, sixty-six favored just building a naval base there, three wanted to sell the islands, and nobody endorsed the Cuban solution, that is, letting the liberated Filipinos have their independence.

The President's decision, if one credits the account of it he gave to a delegation of visiting Methodist clergymen the following year, owed less to realpolitik than divine intervention. He had walked the White House floor night after night, weighing the Philippines dilemma, and "I went down on my knees and prayed [to] Almighty God for light and guidance," and the Lord caused him to conclude that "we could not give them back to Spain— that would be cowardly and dishonorable." Nor could they be turned over to any other foreign power or commercial rival—"that would be bad business and discreditable." And worst of all, "we could not leave them to themselves—they were unfit for self-government—and they would soon have anarchy and misrule . . . worse than Spain's." So there was no choice left to the United States but to take over all the islands "and to educate the Filipinos, and uplift and Christianize them, and by God's grace do the very best we could by them as our fellow-men for whom Christ also died." A less transcendent view of McKinley's decision to order the military conquest of the Philippines was offered by Mark Twain: "What we wanted, in the interest of Progress and Civilization, was the Archipelago, unencumbered by patriots struggling for independence."

McKinley's new, heaven-inspired U.S. colonial policy was embodied in the Paris peace treaty drawn up in December. It provided that Spain, hitting bottom after a three-century decline from the zenith of its imperial glory, would evacuate its forces from Cuba, cede Puerto Rico and Guam to the United States, and sell the Philippines to the Americans for $20 million and their vow "not to exploit [the Filipinos] but to develop, to educate and to train [them] in the science of self-government," preventing what Theodore Roosevelt would later call "murderous anarchy." Neither of the signatories solicited the Filipinos' opinion of the transaction. The Senate ratified the treaty by a one-vote margin.

Even granting the sincerity of McKinley's justifications for it, the takeover of a gigantic archipelago on the far side of the Pacific was a morally indefensible departure from the nation's historical conduct and even its most expansive ideology. Would the manifest destiny of the United States now be amended to prescribe acquisition of the entire Far East?

The seizure of the Philippines rapidly degenerated into a national nightmare, but as in similar debacles in Asia over the ensuing hundred or so years, U.S. policymakers were loath to concede their gross miscalculations. The result, beginning in 1899, was a grisly three-and-a-half-year guerrilla war that incited bestial, take-no-prisoners conduct by both American troops and Filipino resistance fighters. To the latter the invaders were no more welcome than the Spaniards had been in savagely abusing the Cuban rebels—and their conduct at times no less brutal. Aguinaldo denounced the "violent and aggressive seizure" of his homeland "by a nation which has arrogated to itself the title of champion of oppressed nations."

The pacification process in the Philippines, employing 125,000 U.S. troops, would cost the country twenty times the $20 million it paid for the franchise and a much heavier human toll—4,200 dead and 2,800 wounded—than the war with Spain. Members of the recently formed Anti-Imperialist League and other Americans who opposed the undeclared war as a betrayal of national ideals and lamented its atrocious cost in Filipino lives, estimated to be no fewer than 200,000, were routinely branded traitors by those who took refuge in McKinley's assurances that the U.S. purpose was none other than to teach the virtues of democracy, literacy, Protestantism, and the work ethic—"the mission of our race," progressive Senator Albert Beveridge of Indiana called it, as "trustees under God of the civilization of the world." British author (and Anglo-Saxon supremacist) Rudyard Kipling bestowed literary sanction on the bloody crusade in his poem "The White Man's Burden," subtitled "The United States and the Philippines," applauding the capture of "Your new-caught, sullen peoples / Half devil and half child." McKinley, a man of few public utterances, put it more succinctly with an aphorism of blinding sophistry: "Duty determines destiny." But it was Mark Twain, the best-loved American writer of his time and a masterful ironist, whose pen skewered all the racist rot and left the most telling indictment of the Philippines madness:

> There have been lies; yes, but they were told in a good cause. We have been treacherous; but that was only in order that real good might come out of apparent evil. True, we have crushed a deceived and confiding people; we have turned against the weak and the friendless who trusted us; we have stamped out a just and intelligent and well-ordered republic . . . we have bought a Shadow from an enemy that hadn't it to sell; we have robbed a trusting friend of his land and his liberty; we have invited our clean young men to shoulder a discredited musket and do bandit's work . . . we have debauched America's honor and blackened her face before the world; but each detail was for the best.

Having invested so heavily, if misguidedly, in subjugating the Philippines, a majority of the nation was in no hurry to abandon them. Instead, the country began to enjoy the fruits of its conquest through rising free trade with the islands as Filipinos became dependent on American goods, which were also conveniently marketed from the archipelago to other Asian nations. Not until the Taft and Wilson administrations (1909–21) did Filipinos win full civilian government and substantial self-rule as an unorganized U.S. territory. Three less-than-enlightened Republican Presidents, however, reversed this democratizing trend until a Democratic Congress voted in 1934 to grant the islands commonwealth status and a pledge of independence after a demeaning ten-year probationary period to develop political stability. Having endured another savage invasion and far less benign occupation by the Japanese during the Second World War, the Philippines finally gained their full independence on July 4, 1946. The United States was granted the long-term right to operate military bases in the archipelago, which was all William McKinley had had in mind before being engulfed by imperialist mania and enlightened by the word of God.

ALTHOUGH THE UNITED STATES had told the world its rescue of the Cuban people was based solely on philanthropic and humanitarian grounds, some postwar domestic commentators carped that the Teller Amendment pledge had been a sentimental mistake. Cuba was simply too valuable economically and militarily to American interests to be cast adrift; its people, like the Filipinos, simply could not be trusted to control their own destiny and maintain a stable government without close U.S. oversight. But a promise was a promise, and McKinley could not abscond with Cuban territory without being cast as an international war criminal. If Cuban sovereignty could not be openly violated, though, the United States did not feel at all constrained about turning the independent island nation into a client state and de facto commercial colony.

American troops did not relinquish their hold on Cuba for three and a half years after the formal end of the war. The transitional period was marked by the occupiers' largely constructive activities as U.S. federal manpower and money helped repair the war-ravaged island and greatly improve health conditions, especially by reducing the yellow fever peril. Private American capital, secure in the knowledge that U.S. soldiers were patrolling the country and keeping it tranquil, flowed heavily into Cuba during the early postwar years. U.S. investors bought up and revitalized Cuban sugar and tobacco plantations, banks, hotels, cigar factories, iron and copper mines, streetcar systems, and railroads that were extended into the countryside to open up millions of acres for cultivation. By late 1903 the American investment in Cuba had surpassed $100 million and helped resurrect the island's economic base. Such absentee ownership, exploitative and detached by nature, set the pattern for twentieth-century U.S. economic expansionism by means of private capital investment that, the misbegotten Philippines experience aside, replaced the territorial form of national aggrandizement.

To safeguard this growing offshore investment, stateside businessmen and government policymakers resolved to maintain a close vigil over the political, financial, and military affairs of the island nation the United States had liberated and midwifed into being. When Cuban patriots were invited to write their own constitution in 1901, McKinley could not resist forwarding a list of "hints" to their convention for what he deemed suitable provisions, even though the draft of the document already included liberal commercial and political concessions to the United States. The Cubans balked, but the White House and Congress insisted on the American right and responsibility to intervene as Washington saw fit in order to preserve Cuba's independence and maintain a government "adequate for the protection of life, property, and individual liberty." More intrusive still, Cuba was to be denied the right to make treaties with foreign governments without U.S. sanction. These degrading directives took the form of an ultimatum: either the Cubans had to submit to them or American troops would remain on their soil indefinitely. Given Hobson's choice, Cuba saluted and got its island back, even at the cost of becoming a weak dependency on eternal parole pending good behavior in American eyes.

The construction of the Panama Canal and issuing of the so-called Roosevelt Corollary (see Chapter 15) intensified U.S. surveillance of the Carribean, and the Cubans soon learned that uninvited American intervention was not an idle threat. When turmoil overtook the island after fraudulent elections in 1905 and the ouster of a pro-U.S. government, American troops reoccupied Cuba and remained for three years. They came back in 1912 to put down another violent disturbance, and the island thereafter gravitated toward more autocratic regimes that, though often riddled with corruption, took pains to protect U.S. citizens and their financial interests.

The American right to intervene when it chose was revoked in 1934 as the island fell under the heel of a military despot, Fulgencio Batista, who for twenty-five years kept Cuba a safe haven for U.S. investors while ruling its masses with a heavy hand. The price for Washington's tolerance of right-wing autocracy was the rise of a *yanqui*-bashing Marxist, Fidel Castro, who confiscated American property and brought egalitarian reforms in health care and education to his people, but for decades has acted to quash their liberties and mire them in privation.

CHAPTER 15

The so-called mandate of mankind

1903–1999

THE BATTLESHIP *MAINE* HAD BEEN submerged in its shallow grave in Havana harbor for a month when U.S. Navy strategists decided, in anticipation of imminent hostilities with Spain over the Cuban crisis, that their Atlantic squadron close by Caribbean waters needed reinforcement. The navy's most powerful weapon—and probably the deadliest warship afloat anywhere—was the five-year-old, 12,000-ton U.S.S. *Oregon.* The battlewagon, its steel sides sixteen inches thick at the waterline, was armed with four 13-inch guns, eight 8-inchers, and four 6-inchers, all of them capable of piercing the armor of most ships then in service within a range of two miles; it also carried twenty rapid-fire guns, two Gatling machine guns, and six torpedo tubes. The only problem was that the *Oregon* was berthed at the moment more than 12,000 miles from Cuba by sea, in its home port of San Francisco, where it was intended to protect the nation's Pacific shore and deal with problems on that ocean.

But the signal went out to the *Oregon*'s 486-man crew to rev its big twin-screw, triple-expansion engines and proceed posthaste to the Caribbean. No ship that size, requiring so much coal, had ever before covered such a distance as speedily as the *Oregon* now did. Even so, the voyage took sixty-seven days, and the bristling behemoth arrived barely in time to help put the finishing touches on the Spanish fleet trying to flee the U.S. blockade of Santiago harbor.

If the long-projected canal across the isthmus of Central America had been in operation, the *Oregon* could have made the trip in one-third the time and given U.S. forces the full firepower of its mightiest craft going into the war. The lesson was now crystal clear to American military strategists, especially in view of the nation's emergence from the war with Spain as the owner of the Hawaiian and Philippine islands: if the United States was to function as a two-ocean power, it absolutely had to own and operate an isthmian canal. There were pressing commercial reasons, too, for undertaking the stupendous labor that had been begun and abandoned several times already. While northern, central, and southern transcontinental railroad lines now crossed the United States, manufacturers, farmers, and ranchers were forced to pay all-the-traffic-can-bear freight rates to the carrier who monopolized the rail route in their region. Shipping via an isthmian canal would offer a competing mode of transportation, forcing down rail rates and, equally important, making the export of industrial goods from the East Coast and farm products from New Orleans to Asian markets an economically more realistic proposition.

With these benefits in mind, the State Department pressed none too gently on the new Cuban government to grant the United States a long-term lease on a forty-two-square-mile site at Guantánamo Bay, at the southeast tip of the island, for a major naval base, ideally positioned to guard the canal that U.S. Army engineers were about to construct across the Panamanian jungle. But getting hold of the land for that purpose—without seizing it outright—had taken some doing.

A passageway in the form of a canal constructed through the fifty-mile-wide midpoint of the Western Hemisphere had been envisioned ever since Balboa came upon the site in 1513. But four centuries were to pass before technology, geopolitics, commercial demand, and American wealth could bring it into existence. Until the eighteenth century nearly all of Spain's trade with its west coast colonies in South America—most valuably silver from Andean mines—was carried across the S-shaped isthmus at Panama, its narrowest sector, but then the region reverted to jungle except for two small coastal colonies of creoles and mestizos at opposite ends of the route. By the early nineteenth century, Thomas Jefferson foresaw an isthmian canal as vital to creation of a transcontinental American empire, and arch-expansionist Henry Clay pushed the idea as a key to westward settlement. The opening of the Erie Canal in 1825 gave the dream substance.

A few years earlier, as part of the mass uprising by Spain's New World colonies, little Panama (about 30,000 square miles, smaller than the state of Indiana) had declared independence but soon chose to confederate with Bolívar's Gran Colombia republic. Cut off from the rest of the nation by stark mountains and impenetrable jungle, the isthmian province was separated as well by a different mindset. Because Panama's unique geography invited the free movement of people, goods, and ideas, it never succumbed to the shuttered, feudal, church-haunted culture long afflicting the rest of Spanish America, so it was never happy about the union with Colombia. Four times in forty years it broke away, only to return after Colombia, recognizing the potentially great strategic and economic value of the province, granted Panama privileges of self-rule and free trade denied to the rest of the sleepy nation. Panama, though, suffered from internal dissension between its elite class of landed whites and merchants in the port cities and the masses of rural poor and underemployed urban blacks and mixed-bloods. The national government in Bogotá dispatched soldiers to quell the chronic and often violent unrest in Panama over the second half of the nineteenth century and succeeded only in winning deep resentment for intruding on the isthmians.

Despite the volatile social conditions there, Americans took a closer look at Panama along with nearby Nicaragua, wider across but more tranquil politically, as soon as the United States had won sovereign title to Oregon and California, where gold was luring tens of thousands. Set on carving a shortcut to the Pacific coast, the federal government crafted a pair of treaties aimed at establishing the U.S. claim to a passageway across the isthmus, a lifeline it could not allow any other nation to block. The first, won by Benjamin Bidlack, the American chargé to New Granada (as Colombia was then called), and ratified by the Senate in 1848, was curiously—and perhaps purposely—ambiguous. The Bidlack Treaty guaranteed U.S. citizens and cargoes "the right of way or transit across the Isthmus of Panama . . . upon any modes of communication that now exist, or that may be hereafter constructed." But that wording left open to question whether Americans, either through their government or by acting privately, were licensed to build and use a highway, railway, or canal across Panama, or were merely ensured access to any such passageway that might be built by anybody in the boundless future. The clear quid pro quo the United States had to agree to for its isthmian rights under the Bidlack accord were an American guarantee of (1) "the perfect neutrality of the isthmus . . . with the view that the free transit from one to the other sea may not be interrupted or embarrassed in any future time" and (2) the "rights of sovereignty and property which New Granada has and possesses over the said territory."

Its right of passage across, and role as protector of, the Panamanian part of the isthmus thus solidified, the United States moved to avoid a collision with Great Britain over transoceanic hegemony in the region. As would-be proprietors of an isthmian canal to enhance their already vast worldwide commerce, the British had been busily putting down territorial markers on both the Caribbean and Pacific coasts of Nicaragua, where they projected a

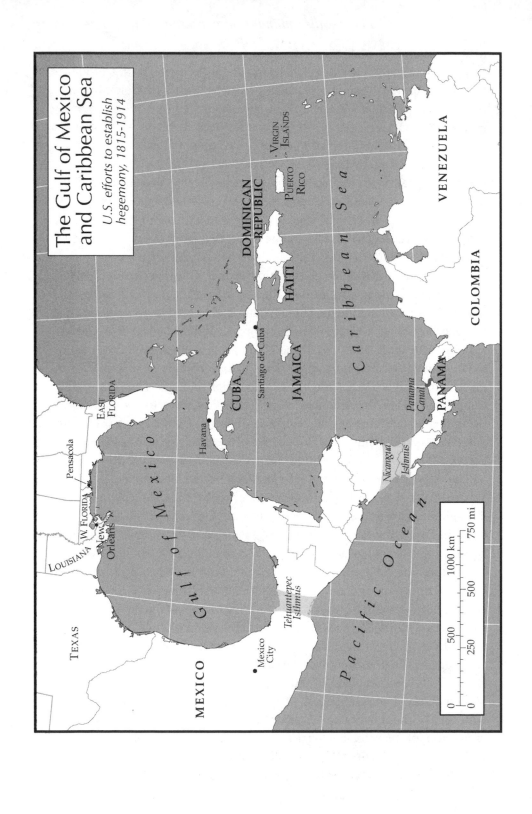

The Gulf of Mexico
and Caribbean Sea

*U.S. efforts to establish
hegemony, 1815-1914*

VENEZUELA

COLOMBIA

VIRGIN
ISLANDS

DOMINICAN
REPUBLIC

PUERTO
RICO

HAITI

Caribbean Sea

Santiago de Cuba

JAMAICA

CUBA

Panama
Canal

PANAMA

EAST
FLORIDA

Havana

Pensacola

W. FLORIDA

Nicaragua
Isthmus

New
Orleans

Gulf of Mexico

LOUISIANA

Pacific Ocean

TEXAS

Tehuantepec
Isthmus

MEXICO

Mexico
City

1000 km

750 mi

500

500

250

0

0

maritime channel up the San Juan River and across forty-five-mile-wide Lake Nicaragua with a final stretch of excavated canal to reach the Pacific. It seemed a plausible plan, outflanking a possible future American effort in Panama, but the last thing either nation needed was dueling canals in Central America. Secretary of State John M. Clayton and the British envoy to Washington, Sir Henry Bulwer, reached an accord in 1850 forbidding either of their countries from assuming dominion over any part of Central America or holding sole possession of a canal there; instead, they would exercise joint control over such a passageway and guarantee that it would be open to all nations.

The Bidlack and Clayton-Bulwer treaties encouraged New York financiers to obtain Colombia's permission to construct the forty-eight-mile Panama Railroad across the isthmus. The $8 million project, completed in 1855, took six years to build through the rain forest, as the heat and mosquito-borne diseases of the tropics claimed the lives of 2,000 workers. Allowing riders who could afford the $25 one-way ticket to cross the isthmus in just three hours instead of enduring a three-day trip on muleback through the jungle, the railroad proved highly profitable. It attracted 40,000 passengers a year, most from the eastern states and bound for California, roused the slumbering economy of the province, and made the locals who supervised its operation among the most important men in Panama. The little railway thrived until the completion of the transcontinental railroad in the United States in 1869. That same year, the Suez Canal opened, shaving 5,800 miles from the London-to-India sea route and diverting European interest from the Central American isthmus as a shortcut to Asian markets. Extension of the U.S. rail system, the anguish and disruptions of the Civil War and Reconstruction eras, and the subsequent surge in industrialization and urbanization all served to cool American interest in an isthmus canal. Nevertheless, seven engineering expeditions were sent to the region by the Grant administration, and all concurred that Nicaragua would be a more felicitous site than Panama for a future canal.

A spirited dissenter from the demotion of Panama as a canal site was the renowned impresario of the Suez Canal, Ferdinand de Lesseps, who obtained a concession from the Colombian government to create a passageway across the isthmus. Officials in Bogotá were only too happy to license the Frenchman's project since U.S. engineers were leaning heavily toward Nicaragua as the preferable canal site and, at any rate, the Bidlack Treaty had not bestowed exclusive rights on the United States to build the canal, only the assurance that its citizens and their property would be allowed the right of transit—and de Lesseps pointedly declared that passage through his canal would be open to vessels of all nations. In 1881, when the charismatic French promoter was seventy-six, his Compagnie Universelle du Canal Interocéanique began operations after buying up the Panama Railroad to transport the massive equipment and labor force from the two terminal ports of Colón and Panama City to the work sites. But channeling a waterway through the swampy Panamanian jungle, where torrential rains caused frequent mud and rock slides and the hum of deadly insects was never distant, presented formidable problems. De Lesseps, who was a diplomat by training, not an engineer, had badly underestimated the difficulties of the task. In opting for a sea-level canal, as he had built across the Suez desert, instead of a tiered system of locks to lift ships up the elevated terrain along the route, his engineering scheme entailed much more excavation, and the earth-moving expenditures mounted dizzyingly. So did the death toll, which reached nearly 17,000 by the time the enterprise was abandoned in 1889—a $260 million disaster, resulting in bankruptcy, national disgrace for France, and criminal charges against the de Lesseps management for negligence and corruption.

As the French canal debacle played out, a smaller American effort under a former U.S. Navy engineer began in Nicaragua, but after three years and $4 million, it, too, collapsed. The conviction grew in Washington that if a canal was ever to be built successfully, the scale of the project would be so large and the cost so high that it could only be undertaken by the federal government. By the early 1890s, spurred by Alfred Mahan's endorsement of a U.S.-owned isthmian canal as vital if the nation was to become a two-ocean naval power, support for the idea revived. With the French out of the picture, now was the time to promote American security, trade, and moral and cultural values worldwide by accomplishing the immense public work, to the nation's glory. But the Panic of 1893 brought hard times and temporarily soured enthusiasm for such a costly and problematic venture.

FROM THE ASHES OF THE de Lesseps fiasco, French investors in and survivors of the defunct enterprise launched a salvage operation in 1894 by buying up the failed firm's assets, which included the 40 percent completed excavation, a mountain of expensive equipment, and several thousand buildings, and obtaining a ten-year renewal from the Colombian government for the right to finish the canal. The plan was to find a buyer who was prepared to carry the project to fruition; the buyout price would be distributed among the stockholders of both the original and new canal companies as a consolation prize. The rescue mission, known as the New Panama

Canal Company, was blessed with a singleminded missionary among its investors—Philippe Bunau-Varilla, whose professional training, energy, and self-confidence had won him promotion to interim chief engineer of the original canal construction while still in his twenties. Relieved of his position when a senior engineer became available, Bunau-Varilla never lost his passionate belief in the canal, even after succeeding as a private contractor in Panama and returning to Paris to oversee railroad-building in the Belgian Congo and flood control projects in Romania. Nobody would play a more useful role in the eventual creation of the Panama Canal than this slight, high-domed Frenchman who invested $440,000 of his own money in the New Company and set out to restore the honor of his nation and his inspiration, Ferdinand de Lesseps.

Because private financiers had been badly burned by the extravagant mismanagement of the original company, Bunau-Varilla approached the Russian and British governments to fund the revived project and gain the prestige and commercial advantages that he argued would accrue to the nation that completed and ran the canal. Turned down in St. Petersburg and London, he concluded that the only promising customer for the New Company's assets was the government of the United States. That prospect, however, was clouded by the strong preference for a Nicaraguan canal route by southern congressional Democrats, of whom the formidable Senator John Tyler Morgan of Alabama was the ringleader. A canal in Nicaragua, some 300 miles northwest of the Panama site, would provide better "access to the eastern Asiatic countries for our cotton," Morgan contended, and was preferred by his Senate committee dealing with the subject.

In the last years of the nineteenth century, a confluence of factors accelerated the canal project and led to the last-minute shift to Panama as the preferred site for it. In 1896 the Republicans gained control of the White House and Congress, cutting the power of southern Democrats to set the national agenda and dictate regionally tilted preferences such as the Nicaraguan canal route. A strong economic recovery from the 1893 depression allowed the federal government to afford a hugely expensive project like the canal. High railroad freight charges imposed through monopolistic pricing power evoked rising resentment by customers who saw an isthmian canal as a promising alternative for long-distance shipments. The Spanish-American War gave the nation new naval bases in the Caribbean and across the Pacific that needed shorter linkage by sea than the interminable voyage around Cape Horn. President McKinley told Congress in his annual message in December 1898 that a canal was "demanded by the annexation of Hawaii [a few months earlier] and the prospective expansion of our influence and

commerce in the Pacific." Chambers of commerce, boards of trade, and resolutions by state legislatures in New York, California, South Carolina, and
Louisiana endorsed the idea. In 1899 the government created the Isthmian
Canal Commission to make a final, definitive study of where the canal
should be located. And in 1901 the new Secretary of State, John Hay, lately
ambassador to Britain, removed a thorny obstacle to the canal project by
persuading London to lay aside the fifty-year-old Clayton-Bulwer pact forbidding either nation from going it alone in the isthmus. It was not a disclaimer that could have been issued unilaterally by the U.S. government; it
represented, rather, a tactical retreat by British policymakers who calculated
that their global activities already faced enough challenges—by the Boers
in South Africa, the rising naval power of Germany and Japan, the Russian
push against China, and the rebellious Boxers—and they would do well to
recognize the Caribbean as an American lake. Under Hay's treaty with
Julian Pauncefote, Britain's ambassador to Washington, the United States
was authorized to build, own, operate, and defend a Central American canal
on the proviso that it would be forever open to British shipping.

Developments on the isthmus at first seemed to work against Panama's
aspirations to host the canal. Colombia was rocked by growing civil strife,
culminating in the War of a Thousand Days (1899–1902), in which constant guerrilla fighting took upwards of 100,000 lives. The turmoil provided an opportunity for nationalists in Panama, where enmity toward the
government in Bogotá had been growing since the Colombian constitution of 1886 imposed unprecedented central authority over the isthmian
province, then the beneficiary of a torrent of French money being expended
on de Lesseps's massive building project. By the dawn of the new century,
even with the canal construction in abeyance, the independence movement
in Panama was deepening as liberal, antigovernment forces took virtual
control over rural areas. The province was ready tinder for a revolution, but
somebody had to strike the match—and somebody had to keep Colombian
troops from swarming in and smothering the blaze.

Such political combustibility was hardly conducive to Panama's chances
of being selected as the site for a U.S.-built canal just at the moment when
the exuberant new (and youngest-ever) President, Theodore Roosevelt, was
embracing the idea. In his first annual message to Congress in December
1901, he reinforced his assassinated predecessor's advocacy of the canal by
declaring, "No single great material work which remains to be undertaken
on this continent is of such importance to the American people." All the
signs, though, pointed toward politically stable Nicaragua as the logical
site—until the New Panama Canal Company, with Bunau-Varilla in Paris

pulling the strings, engaged the costly services of a cunning New York attorney to lobby Washington officials and the government's Canal Commission members to revise their thinking.

Cool, dapper, theatrical William Nelson Cromwell—he insisted on using all three names, perhaps to gild his impoverished youth in Brooklyn—had apprenticed as a lowly accountant for a railroad company, worked his way through Columbia Law School, and soon found employment on Wall Street. Cromwell had a quick mind and a lash for a tongue that could lacerate and obfuscate with equal facility. His legal acumen was garnished by a wizardry with figures and a gift for rapid shorthand. After just three years in practice, he formed a partnership with older trial attorney Algernon Sullivan; the firm, a powerhouse catering to elite corporate clients, still bears their names. The nervy Cromwell—some found him crassly forward—represented a number of the most powerful businesses in the nation, including the Northern Pacific and Southern Pacific railroads and J. P. Morgan's United States Steel Corporation, which he helped organize. Among Cromwell's small-fry clients was the still-operating Panama Railroad Company, which he superintended from New York. Several of the rail line's officials were among the leaders of the surging independence movement in the isthmus. Their potential value as revolutionists was not lost on Cromwell when the New Canal Company, owner of the Panama Railroad, called on him to intervene in Washington, where he was well connected, to plead its case.

Among Cromwell's first maneuvers—subtlety not being his strong suit—was a $60,000 contribution to McKinley's 1900 reelection campaign, chaired by Mark Hanna, who by then happened to be the most powerful man in the U.S. Senate. It was at Hanna's insistence that the Republican national platform that year called for the government to build an isthmian canal without reference to a preferred site. Cromwell then went to work on the federal Canal Commission, whose members he lured on an extended junket to Paris, where they were royally treated and, with the help of Bunau-Varilla, thoroughly schooled in canalogy. On one hand, the New Company's advocates itemized the alleged shortcomings of Nicaragua as a canal site—most notably, the route there would be three times as long, the San Juan River was too shallow for deep-keeled vessels and its course too crooked for easy navigation, and the region was studded with active volcanoes (as illustrated on Nicaragua's postage stamps, which were passed around to the American visitors) that could at any moment rain disaster on canal construction. On the other hand, the New Company's Panama route, shorter, quicker, and easier to traverse by the planned new system of tiered locks, offered an already partially built canal that would be less costly and time-consuming to complete than a Nicaraguan canal started from scratch. Besides, the New Company was offering the United States all those buildings and all that equipment it had kept well oiled and functional—huge pumps, a forest of cranes, herds of excavators, a railroad—as well as the Colombian government's license to build the canal across Panama. And it could all be purchased by the American government for the sacrifice price of $109 million.

Back home, the Canal Commission reflected and issued its final report. It recommended the Nicaraguan route, even though it conceded the engineering advantages of the shorter canal through Panama and the considerably lower estimated construction cost of $144 million (against about $185 million to build in Nicaragua). The hang-up was the New Company's bailout price of $109 million for its assets, which made the total cost of the Panamian project some 37 percent higher. Cromwell and Bunau-Varilla pressed the New Company stockholders to lower their asking price drastically—to $40 million—so the Panama Canal would cost no more, and perhaps a bit less, than the projected price in Nicaragua. After an acrimonious meeting in Paris, the New Company investors conceded that $40 million was a lot more than nothing, which was that their assets would be worth if the Americans proceeded to build in Nicaragua. This concession was enough to convince the U.S. Canal Commission to reverse itself and recommend Panama for the site. The House of Representatives, though, voted almost unanimously for the Nicaragua option.

William Nelson Cromwell, with the Canal Commission experts now on his side, called on still bigger guns. One was his close acquaintance, Republican kingpin Mark Hanna, the nearest anyone had ever become to a national party boss, who agreed to spearhead the case for Panama in the Senate. The other was Teddy Roosevelt. The new President was committed to extending the nation's power, prestige, and moral leadership through its military and commercial prowess, and an isthmian canal would quicken that ascendancy. For him, Panama was clearly the route to take, all factors considered, and the United States already had a preferential arrangement with Colombia in the Bidlack Treaty, guaranteeing its right of transit across the isthmus. Sealing the deal ought to be a simple enough diplomatic matter. The Rough Rider in the White House had saddled up.

The political formula devised to sway Congress was a bill introduced by Senator John Spooner, a Wisconsin Republican with close ties to both Hanna and Cromwell, and meant to console Alabama's splenetic Senator Morgan. Under the Spooner proposal, the government was to buy out the

French stockholders of the New Canal Company for the reduced $40 million price tag and work out a final understanding with Colombia, granting the United States perpetual ownership of the canal and full jurisdiction over a buffer strip of territory on both sides of the waterway for its full fifty-mile length. If either the New Company or the Colombian government balked at these arrangements, Secretary of State Hay would proceed at once to negotiate a canal deal with the government of Nicaragua.

The debate in the Senate over the Spooner bill in June 1902 was heated. And then Mark Hanna, in failing health, limped to the Senate rostrum and, with the help of notes provided by Cromwell and Bunau-Varilla, clinched the case for Panama. He was a trained businessman, Hanna noted, and if you removed sentiment from the issue and examined it as a straight, coldly calculated financial and technical proposition, there was no contest. As to the political volatility in Panama that some backers of the Nicaraguan option stressed, well, to be honest, all of Central America was unstable, but the canal would bring prosperity and tranquility to the region, and the sooner the better. The Spooner bill carried and, with some armtwisting, the House fell in line.

It was now up to John Hay to get the regime in Bogotá to sign on. The Secretary of State, who had had the benefit of a rarefied education in politics and human nature while serving in the White House as Abraham Lincoln's devoted wartime secretary, ran into a surprisingly cranky response from the Colombians. Fearful that the fiery American President would ride roughshod over their sovereignty, they insisted that the Bidlack Treaty had not granted the United States the license or any land for building a canal across the isthmus, and if Washington was prepared to pay the New Company $40 million for its equipment and the concession it had been awarded by Colombia, the Bogotá government was entitled to no less, and perhaps more, as well as an annual rental charge once the canal was operating. When Hay objected, the Colombians said they would settle for a part of the price to be paid the New Company, but Cromwell flatly rejected the request. As a conciliatory gesture, Hay offered the Colombian envoy $10 million for the right to build the canal and operate it for 100 years plus an annual rental of $250,000; the United States would also gain full jurisdiction over a six-mile-wide protective strip of territory enclosing the passageway. To lend luster to the take-it-or-leave-it offer, Hay reminded the Colombian envoy, Tomás Herrán, that the United States would at once take its canal plans to Nicaragua if Bogotá declined the deal. Glumly, Herrán capitulated.

Herrán's countrymen, however, would not. When the Hay-Herrán Treaty draft reached Bogotá, the monetary offer struck Colombian officials as insultingly paltry and the rest of the terms inadequately protective of their national rights. Prospects for ratification of the treaty by the volatile Colombian Senate were far from bright during the spring and summer of 1903. Hay bristled and, with un-Lincolnesque pugnacity, instructed his envoy in Bogotá to advise the government there that its rejection of or undue delay in passage of the canal treaty would so badly compromise amicable relations between the two countries that "action might be taken by the Congress next winter which every friend of Colombia would regret." That sounded suspiciously like an invasion threat, which some federal officials and experts in international law argued was justified, under an expansive reading of the Bidlack Treaty, to enforce the alleged U.S. right-of-way by building a canal or whatever else it wanted across the isthmus. Cromwell, though, had what he felt was a better weapon at his client's—and his country's—disposal and almost certainly revealed it to the President: the attorney's intelligence pipeline to officials at the Panama Railroad and their associates heading up the independence movement in the isthmus were ready to act if given material support. Cromwell did not as yet need to seek such a commitment from the President, but the possibility of U.S. complicity in a full-scale insurgency might be enough to bring the Colombians to their senses. Emerging from a mid-June meeting at the White House, Cromwell contacted a reporter from Joseph Pulitzer's *New York World,* and in a freewheeling background interview the peppery Wall Street lawyer said he guessed that if the Senate in Bogotá rejected the Hay-Herrán Treaty, Panama would declare its independence from Colombia, and the United States would be free to make a canal agreement with the new government in Panama City. This scenario was given prompt and prominent display in the *World.*

The only thing wrong with Cromwell's veiled threat was that under the Bidlack Treaty, the United States was duty-bound to safeguard Colombia's sovereignty over the isthmus—and thus to oppose with military force an uprising by the Panamanians. But White House and State Department thinkers began formulating a rationale for evading this apparent obligation. The guarantee in the treaty, they argued creatively, was always intended to apply only to *foreign* threats to Colombian sovereignty over Panama; it could not possibly have been intended to place the United States in the role of an intervening party in a purely domestic quarrel—unless, that is, a civil conflict endangered any mode of transit that had been built across the isthmus, such as the Panama Railroad, which, under the treaty, the United States had solemnly pledged to protect. This line of argument seemed to mean that U.S. forces could fulfill the treaty obligation to maintain the safety of the railroad by keeping Colombian government troops from subduing Panamanian secessionists.

By early August, while the Colombian Senate remained locked in debate, the leader of the Panamanian independence movement, seventy-year-old Manuel Amador, who served as chief physician for the Panama Railroad when not a political activist, arrived in New York to meet with Cromwell. Dr. Amador's mission was to seek $6 million for gunboats to keep Colombian reinforcements out of Panama and other weapons to overcome the small government garrison already in place. As important, he sought a firm pledge of support, both diplomatically and militarily, for Panama's independence by the U.S. government. His effort was interrupted by the news from Bogotá that the Colombian Senate had rejected the canal treaty unanimously. The vote may have been an earnest outcry of national pride against high-handed treatment by the powerful North American giant, but it sealed Panama's future. Secessionists conspiring in the isthmus had now been handed their most telling grievance yet. By scuttling the treaty that the Americans had offered, Colombia was depriving the province of Panama of its resurrected chance to become a world commercial link and to enjoy a prosperous future. The fight was on. And its most potent combatant was about to join the fray. "Those contemptible little creatures in Bogotá," Theodore Roosevelt sputtered in a note to Secretary Hay, who agreed with the President that the Colombians were just trying to extort more money from the United States for the right to build the canal. "We may have to give a lesson to those jack rabbits," T.R. added, always up for a hunt.

Just when Dr. Amador's mission in New York should have borne fruit, he showed himself miscast for the role of dynamic promoter of the Panamanian revolution. While en route to America, he had let slip the purpose of his mission in a shipboard conversation with a leading journalist from the isthmus, who, as a government loyalist, passed on the word to Colombia's consul in New York. Cromwell was soon advised that his client, the New Canal Company, would forfeit its franchise to build the waterway if he colluded with the Panamanian nationalists. Cromwell hurriedly summoned Bunau-Varilla from Paris, and the suave, energetic Frenchman, by then publisher of the influential journal *Le Matin,* thereafter superseded Amador as the principal communicator between the U.S. government and the secessionist junta in Panama. Bunau-Varilla, a surefooted operator with an elaborate, dark-red mustache that he waxed to two fine points and made him hard to miss, headed to Washington, where Cromwell opened doors for him. The Frenchman already had an invaluable contact in Assistant Secretary of State Francis B. Loomis, whom he had befriended years earlier when the American was on a diplomatic posting. In short order the agent provocateur had an audience with Hay and on October 10 with Roosevelt himself.

Bunau-Varilla reported to the President that the secessionists were ready to strike and only awaited word whether the United States would assist the rebel forces, now that Colombia's foolish rejection of the Hay-Herrán Treaty had violated the Americans' alleged right to build an isthmian canal based on their undisputed right of transit. Once in power, of course, the insurgents would gladly sign the canal treaty under the same terms Bogotá had refused. Bunau-Varilla said he knew the President would probably not be able to answer him directly, but Roosevelt, who took his visitor to be "a very able fellow," later recounted to a friend, "I have no doubt that he was able to make a very accurate guess, and to advise his people accordingly." Within days Roosevelt received a corroborative report from two U.S. Army intelligence officers just back from Panama on secessionist sentiment there and the state of readiness by the nationalist leadership. Then the President set American forces into motion. Four navy ships were to head south from San Francisco on October 22, purportedly on a training exercise, with the U.S.S. *Boston,* pivotal to the *haole* coup in Honolulu ten years earlier, proceeding directly to Panama City on the Pacific coast and the rest to follow as directed. Simultaneously, the *Nashville* from the Atlantic squadron was to speed to Colón, the Caribbean terminus of the Panama Railroad, and prevent "any armed force with hostile intent" (that is, Colombian soldiers) from landing. The *Dixie,* at Guantánamo, was to follow with 400 marines on board, and other ships would be deployed to shield both Panamanian coasts. When Bunau-Varilla called on Hay at his Lafayette Square home on October 16, the Secretary of State told him none too coyly that U.S. warships were already under orders to converge on the isthmus.

The Frenchman hurried back to New York to apprise Dr. Amador and present him with a kind of do-it-yourself instant revolution kit (including the proposed text for a Panamanian constitution and, for good measure, a design for a new national flag) and $100,000 in cash, courtesy of the New Canal Company, for bribes to be distributed in the right places. The physician then sailed for Panama with assurances that his newly independent regime, once the canal treaty was sealed, would receive the $10 million Colombia had spurned and could use it to establish a solvent government. But nothing had been committed to paper by any U.S. government official; the Panamanians would have to proceed on trust—and they did.

IT WAS A VERITABLE COMIC-OPERA revolution and, happily, one just as bloodless. The provincial governor of Panama, sympathetic with the secessionist movement, made no move to halt it. The young, ambitious general in charge of the government garrison there was purchased for $65,000, a fortune at that time in that place, and his men each given $50. Now the insurgents had an army. When 500 crack Colombian troops landed at Colón before the *Nashville* could intervene, their commander and his top officers were gulled by Panama Railroad officials, all of them leading secessionists, into riding a special train to the other end of the line, Panama City, where the uprising was expected. Other trains were to follow shortly, bringing the main body of troops. But no other trains were provided; the head of the government expeditionary force had been severed from its body, and the success of the rebellion was all but ensured. The *Nashville*'s commander, after landing about forty U.S. troops, convinced the ranking officer of the now leaderless Colombian force—with the help of an $8,000 gratuity from the secessionists—that there was no point in engaging the rebels since a huge host of American ships and soldiers was about to descend on Panama, guns blazing. The shanghaied Colombian commander, recipient of a $35,000 payoff (his chief aides got $10,000 apiece), was reunited with his troops, and, glad to be spared certain doom when the Americans arrived, all of them reboarded their ship and sailed home.

"Yesterday we were but the slaves of Colombia; today we are free," Dr. Amador, interim first president of Panama, declared at the independence ceremonies. "President Roosevelt has made good—*viva* President Roosevelt!" A U.S. Army major helped raise the new nation's flag (it had a different design from the one suggested by Bunau-Varilla) over Colón on November 6. A few days later the State Department granted diplomatic recognition to the little isthmian republic and pointedly told the Colombian government the secession was a fait accompli. To reinforce the point, 2,000 U.S. troops were on guard in Panama by December and no fewer than nine warships were patrolling its coastline on both oceans. Trying to justify his government's flagrant disregard of its long treaty obligation to protect—not remove—Colombia's sovereignty over Panama, Secretary Hay contended the President had followed "the only course he could have taken in compliance with our treaty rights and obligations" and suggested that a plebiscite in Panama would surely approve of the secession. Hay was no doubt right about popular sentiment in the isthmus favoring independence, but that hardly justified the U.S. intervention; it might, though, have partially excused Washington for tardiness in supporting Colombia's suppression of the insurgency. Had Roosevelt been genuinely concerned about honoring American treaty commitments in preference to roughing up "those jack rabbits" in Bogotá, he might well have offered them a better price for rights to build and run the canal as the United States saw fit.

Since Bunau-Varilla had delivered the goods for them, the new rulers of

Panama deferred to his insistence that he negotiate the canal treaty in their (as well as the New Canal Company's) behalf. The savvy Frenchman knew that for the Senate to ratify any such pact, the American government would have to be granted ironclad control over the construction and operation of a canal running through the midst of such a politically turbulent country. Thus, in return for the U.S. guarantee of Panama's independence and the same financial package Colombia had rejected, Bunau-Varilla agreed to the cession "in perpetuity" of a zone of land and water ten miles wide from ocean to ocean, comprising 553 square miles, for the construction, mainte-nance, and defense of an interoceanic canal. To hammer home the extent of the concession, the treaty said Panama would hand over "all the rights, power, and authority within the [canal] zone . . . which the United States would possess and exercise if it were the sovereign of the territory," includ-ing the unilateral right of American soldiers to protect the canal and the duty-free import of whatever goods and materials were "necessary and con-venient" for U.S. employees of the canal authority.

The treaty was not just a commercial concession; it was intended, like the lately adopted Cuban constitution, to make a new, small, strategic His-panic republic dependent on the United States. The Canal Zone was the cen-tral corridor and core of the newly liberated nation, but while it technically belonged to Panama, as a practical matter it was an American colonial enclave. The new secessionist regime in Panama City, shaken by the sever-ity of the treaty's strictures, knew that the only alternative to acceptance was a Colombian firing squad. Democrat William Randolph Hearst's papers called the Republican administration's conduct in Panama "perfidious," and the *New York Times* branded the Canal Zone "stolen property," a heist pulled off not by patriots but by promoters and lobbyists, and "encouraged, made safe, and effectuated" by the government of the United States.

Teddy Roosevelt would have none of that. With his usual immoderation when aroused, he dismissed his critics as "a small body of shrill eunuchs" and went on to claim, in submitting the canal treaty to the Senate, that "no one connected with this Government had any part in preparing, inciting, or encouraging the late revolution on the Isthmus of Panama . . . [or] had any knowledge of the revolution except such as was accessible to any person of ordinary intelligence who read the newspapers and kept up an acquaintance with current affairs." The magnitude of that whopper was revealed by Roo-sevelt himself when he later wrote his friend Henry Cabot Lodge that he was the man with the plan to separate Panama from Colombia—it "was done by me without the aid or advice of anyone else"—and suggested to his Secretary of War, William H. Taft, that he deserved most credit as President for "my action seizing the psychological moment to get complete control of Panama." Or, as he would boast (and confess) in a famous speech he gave at Berkeley shortly after leaving office, while others dithered over the canal, "I took the isthmus."

Chest-thumping aside, Roosevelt would justify his actions by two arguments. First, as he wrote in his 1913 autobiography, "[w]e gave the people of Panama self-government and freed them from subjugation to alien oppressors." But to characterize the people of Panama as self-governing after accepting the canal treaty was like suggesting *Homo sapiens* could stand without a spinal column; Panama had, in reality, traded one form of subjugation for another and would pay for it for the next ninety-five years. Roosevelt's second, grander apologia can be found in his annual address to Congress at the end of 1903: "If ever a government could be said to have received a mandate from civilization to effect an object the accomplishment of which was demanded in the interests of mankind, the United States holds that position" with regard to its intervention in Panama. It was not American self-interest or hubris that had driven Roosevelt to grab the single most valuable strip of real estate in the Western Hemisphere; he did it for the good of all the world—and, oh, yes, the Panamanians. A century later, another Republican President of comparable swagger but fewer redeeming virtues would act with a similar assertion of rectitude in deploying the U.S. military to remove a megalomaniac ruler in the Middle East, but civilization had no more given him a mandate "in the interests of mankind" than it had to T.R.

The Senate, however, approved the Panama treaty by a lopsided 66–14 vote, and in May 1904 the President promised that "in asserting the equivalent of sovereignty over the canal strip, it is our full intention that the rights . . . shall be exercised with all proper care for the honor and interests of the people of Panama." But they never were.

For his not quite inestimable services enabling the New Panama Canal Company to sell its assets to the American government, William Nelson Cromwell submitted a legal bill to Paris for $800,000. He was paid $200,000, plus reimbursement for the thoughtful $60,000 contribution he had put in Mark Hanna's pocket for the 1900 McKinley-Roosevelt election campaign.

RETURNING TO THE CANAL SITE that had sat untouched for fifteen years, the U.S. Army Corps of Engineers began operations by draining swamps and otherwise improving sanitation and health conditions, building a giant dam to control the flow of the Chagres River that had flooded regularly in the de Lesseps years of construction, and adopted a design using seven immense locks allowing vessels to make the fifty-one-mile passage in eight hours. To complete the labor required excavation and removal of enough earth and stone, according to one estimate, to build the equivalent of 100 great pyramids the size of Cheop's. At its peak in 1913 the canal workforce reached more than 43,000, many from Barbados. The death toll dropped from 20 percent during the earlier French management to a fraction thereof, but that still came to some 5,600 fatalities. By the time it opened, eleven days after the outbreak of the First World War, the canal had cost the U.S. government $388 million and qualified as the most ambitious man-made creation since the Great Wall of China. As vital connective tissue, the canal would immeasurably strengthen America's expansive economy and military capability.

But it did not bring utopia to the people of Panama. The Canal Zone was operated as a restricted if not entirely closed enterprise for the benefit of its American residents and their few favored locals among the white elite. Only 15 percent of the white-collar jobs went to Panamanians, who were rarely trained for managerial or technical positions. The pay differential between U.S. citizens and the natives was glaring, and local merchants could not penetrate the zone marketplace, which was dominated by a U.S. government-backed commissary. Operating behind their cordon sanitaire, zone officials, like American policymakers generally in dealing with less developed nations, favored reactionary elements set on squelching social ferment—in Panama's case, oligarchic regimes in thrall to the wealthy and often wedded to military cadres under orders to suppress the legitimate grievances of the masses. The result throughout most of the twentieth century, even as the canal prospered, was that surrounding Panama remained a colonial Jim Crow society, backward economically and unstable politically, its governance plagued by fraudulent elections and corrupt administrations, with intermittent efforts, like those by Omar Torrijos in the 1970s, to bring social reforms. What united all segments of the country, though, was the hope of escaping from the domination of the United States, the taloned colossus that loomed over them.

That theoretically benevolent oversight had grown into a fixed policy of the United States announced in 1904 by the President and quickly labeled the Roosevelt Corollary. A unilateral extension of the unilateral Monroe Doctrine, this assertion of interventionist entitlement was patterned on the concessions yielded under duress by the fledgling republics of Cuba and Panama and allowing their Yankee liberators to police their conduct and

step in whenever it veered out of control. Frequently thereafter, usually citing the endangerment of foreign creditors (which mostly meant American
investors) and their property, U.S. forces intervened in and sometimes temporarily occupied Caribbean countries powerless to resist them: Cuba in
1906 and 1917; Nicaragua, where Washington installed a puppet regime to
replace the bankrupt government in 1909 and sent in the marines three years
later; Haiti, designated a U.S. protectorate in 1915; the Dominican Republic, taken over by American soldiers in 1916; and Panama, where the United
States exercised its treaty rights and interceded on eight occasions over the
course of the century. The final time, in 1989, 24,000 U.S. airborne troops
invaded to take out Manuel Noriega, who had turned Panama into a police
state and partner of the Medellín drug cartel. In the fighting, the number of
Panamanian soldiers and civilians killed reportedly approached 3,000, and
the collateral property damage was heavy—a toll that the UN Security
Council condemned as unjustifiable. This "Big Stick" policy first wielded
by Roosevelt was extended at times and a bit more subtly to other Latin
American lands, using dollar diplomacy as well as covert intelligence operations against regimes deemed destabilizing or intolerably anti-American,
such as Salvador Allende's in Chile. At no time, though, did the United
States act to annex all or part of any offending Latin nation.

Teddy Roosevelt may never have expressed qualms about throwing his
weight around the Caribbean and generally exhibiting America's combat-
ready biceps for global acclaim, but his compatriots did on one notable
occasion. In 1922, a respectful three years after the scrappy Roosevelt's
death, Congress voted an apologetic $25 million payment to Colombia "to
remove all misunderstandings" arising from U.S. behavior in facilitating the
Panamanian revolution.

The United States paid up as well for another egregious discourtesy it
had committed in the Caribbean—the 1867 cancellation by a vindictive
Congress of William Seward's treaty to buy two of the Virgin Islands from
Denmark for $7.5 million. With the security of the future Panama Canal in
mind, Roosevelt tried twice to revive the deal—the first time in 1902, when
rumors reached him that the newly assertive German government was trying
to pry the islands loose from neighboring Denmark, but Congress was too
caught up with Cuba and the Philippines to care. Five years later T.R.
instructed his ambassador to Denmark to press the matter and learn what the
price would be, but the Danes were scornful of the prevailing American
ethos and fearful for the well-being of the islands' mostly black residents if
ownership was sold to the United States. The opening of the canal and onset
of World War I inspired a sudden sense of urgency in Washington over

obtaining the Virgin Islands (all of them, not just two, as Seward's aborted 1867 treaty had provided). The 1915 sinking of the British liner *Lusitania,* with many Americans aboard, by a German submarine—Roosevelt called it "murder on the high seas"—led to renewed fears that Kaiser Wilhelm's diplomats were trying to engineer a forced sale by Denmark and obtain a naval base right in the middle of the Caribbean, posing a constant peril to U.S. shipping. If Germany won the war, it would likely absorb Denmark and the Virgin Islands with it, the Danish envoy to Washington was advised, in which case the United States—"with the greatest reluctance"—would have to seize and annex the islands, so why not sell them willingly to the Americans? Copenhagen saw the point and, thus invited, put its selling price at $27 million. The deal was sealed in 1917 for $2 million less. Ten years later, Virgin Islanders were granted U.S. citizenship, but they could not choose their own governor until 1970. The Virgins were never needed as a naval base, but their pristine waters made the nine-island group a holiday mecca, with tourism providing 70 percent of the employment for the 125,000 residents (as of the 2000 census).

The only U.S. territorial acquisition since then has been the Northern Mariana Islands, slightly larger (184 square miles) and less populous (80,000) than the Virgin Islands and located about 1,000 miles east of the Philippines in Micronesia. They were declared a UN trusteeship after World War II and administered by the United States, which had wrested them from Japanese occupation. The best known of the Northern Marianas is Tinian, from which an American plane flew to drop an atomic bomb on Hiroshima and, three days later, Nagasaki, obliterating both but ending the war against Japan. The islands became official American territory in 1985. Saipan, the largest of them, thrived as a haven for garment manufacturers' sweatshops, exploiting Asian immigrant laborers whose employers had become legally entitled to apply a "Made in the USA" label to their products.

By the second half of the twentieth century, the Panama Canal and the zone encasing it remained the only remnant of an American colonial impulse that surfaced with the seizure of the Philippines and sank within a generation. And the canal did not signal a rebirth of the territorial voracity that had marked the first century of the nation's existence. It served, rather, as a mechanism to power American economic expansion under private corporate auspices and demonstrate beyond further doubt that the United States stood at or near the zenith of the great powers of the world. But the canal and the way it was operated under the 1904 treaty with Panama had locked the little Central American state into a love-hate relationship with its feudal lords in Washington, and even though the treaty was occasionally liberalized, resentment festered as the century lengthened and life for Panamanians outside the Canal Zone grew no better. Nationalist protests in the early 1960s turned violent and deadly, and worse were threatened.

By 1964 President Lyndon Johnson came to two conclusions about the canal. The first was that its commercial and military value to the United States had declined. American business preferred eighteen-wheelers on superhighways and air freight to move goods between the two coasts; by the 1970s less than 1 percent of the U.S. gross domestic product passed through the canal. It was too small, moreover, to accommodate state-of-the-art aircraft carriers and supertankers, and nuclear submarines avoided it for security reasons. Besides, it was highly vulnerable to long-distance missile attack or sabotage by terrorists. All of which helped Johnson reach his second conclusion: it was time to show respect for the national pride and sovereignty of a small republic by gradually yielding control over the Canal Zone to Panama and meanwhile training its citizens to take over the canal's operation—so long, of course, as the United States retained the right to intervene if the freedom of passage through the great waterway was ever compromised.

The proposed giveback treaty, evolving over several years of negotiation, aroused such an outcry, especially from chauvinists and others lamenting the loss of American stature in the wake of the traumatizing defeat in Vietnam, that no agreement crystallized until the late 1970s. The opposition's view was most compactly and unambiguously summarized at the time by conservative Republican presidential hopeful Ronald Reagan: "We bought it. We built it. We paid for it. It's ours, and we're going to keep it." Reagan, whatever his other virtues, was less than fastidious about his facts: the United States had never bought the canal or the zone around it, and neither was it ever "ours"—they had been rented under a long-term lease. The debate, fortunately, was not strictly partisan. Former Republican Presidents Richard Nixon and Gerald Ford, both more moderate than the doctrinaire Reagan and more sophisticated in their approach to international affairs, had endorsed the turnover treaty. In the end, though, it took the maximum effort of the sitting President, Jimmy Carter, to accomplish the task. A man of high principles but short of fire to forge them into public policy, Carter understood that a nation's greatness could be measured not only by its power and wealth but by its magnanimity as well. He risked all his political capital on the canal treaty and won Senate ratification in 1978 by a vote of 68 to 32, just one vote over the required two-thirds majority. The pro-treaty votes by several Democratic Senators cost them their seats, and Carter's courageous advocacy of the transfer contributed to his failed reelection bid in 1980.

It was altogether fitting, then, that the former President from Georgia should be on hand twenty-one years later at the noonday ceremony on December 14, 1999, in which the United States formally relinquished control of the canal. The event "removed the onus of maintaining a colonial enclave in a country whose people opposed it," commented the *New York Times,* and marked "a profound and welcome evolution of American power as the century comes to a close."

It was entirely unfitting, on the other hand, that the incumbent President of the United States, Bill Clinton, renowned for demonstrably feeling the pain of life's unfortunates, chose to absent himself from an event of such importance to the dignity of long-anguished Panama. This gross incivility was due, White House aides explained vaguely, to "scheduling difficulties." Clinton never apologized for his truancy or, certainly, for U.S. conduct in long running the Canal Zone like an antebellum plantation, just as he had failed two years earlier, when placing a wreath at the memorial to the Boy Heroes of Chapultepec in Mexico City, to acknowledge American belligerency in fomenting the Mexican War. The most likely reason for Clinton's absence in Panama, according to inside-the-Beltway punditry, was the political fallout he feared from calling prominent attention to the occasion and handing Republican ultranationalists a juicy campaign issue on the eve of the 2000 election season. Compounding the insult, Secretary of State Madeleine Albright chose to cancel her planned appearance at the canal ceremony in order to attend Mideast peace talks in Washington. Remarked an aide to Panama's president, Miryea Moscoso, "What a way to mess up something beautiful." In keeping with this sour note, the designated singer at the historic event mangled the words of "The Star-Spangled Banner."

DESPITE THE ILL GRACE with which it was accomplished, the surrender of the Panama Canal at the close of what was deservedly called the American Century marked a level of maturation no less noteworthy than the nation's abandonment of unbridled territorial expansion a century earlier. Many historians have identified the Spanish-American War and the McKinley-Roosevelt era as an escalation from dormant manifest destiny ideology to imperialist adventurism, aping the European powers in their last spasm of colonialism as they grabbed up what Henry Cabot Lodge called "the waste places of the earth." But as strong an argument can be made that although the United States had been greatly tempted to do so—and for a dismal interlude had succumbed to this sort of contemptible bullying in the Philippines—the nation chose instead to turn away from annexing additional large portions of real estate, as it did in renouncing any intention to own Cuba. When the western frontier closed at the sunset of the nineteenth century, Americans were satisfied that they needed no more physical space to ensure their prosperity and security. They chose to sublimate their compulsively acquisitive drive by redirecting it from the massive accumulation of land they claimed as their just (and destined) reward—no matter that such acts usually required liberating the soil by force from its nominal occupants—to other forms of expansionism.

In making this transfer they proved no less fabulously successful than they had been in asserting dominion over a gigantic territory in a blink of eternity's eye. The economic growth of the United States so far outstripped the rest of the world's that by the year 2000 its gross domestic product was larger than that of the next three most productive nations combined. Americans, accounting for not even 5 percent of the world's population, consumed nearly one-third of all the resources used on earth annually in their orgiastic pursuit of material goods and comforts. Their phenomenal dynamism generated so much cash flow that many were convinced the nation was capable of indefinitely sustaining huge trade deficits and an astronomical national debt without unduly endangering its solvency—as if its creditors were the ones who could not afford to let it perish, no matter how irresponsibly it behaved.

In expanding its military power, the United States proved similarly peerless—and spendthrift. It fought more wars (at times with mixed results because it brought less than maximum force to bear) than any other nation but never for the sake of territorial aggrandizement. Its forces selectively eradicated monstrous tyrants and murderous regimes, though at times faltered in the swamps of ideology. It developed doomsday weapons to deter all foreign governments from threatening its security. And to maintain its death-dealing supremacy, it lavished as much money on its war machine as the rest of the world combined did on theirs, all the while stinting on the care of its own people's bodies and minds.

In the realm of science and technology, American inventiveness was no less wondrously expansive. In biochemistry, pharmacology, medical devices and procedures, cybernetics and telecommunications, air and space travel, and astrophysics it pioneered advances undreamed of by Benjamin Franklin or Thomas Jefferson, men of questing minds. And the influence of American popular culture—its music, arts, media, apparel, celebrities, even its manner of speaking and eating—have become, for better or worse, virtu-ally inescapable anywhere on earth.

So much showy success inevitably brought envy and loathing among the onlookers and a swollen ego and preening sense of entitlement in the perpe-trator. It is understandable, of course, that Americans, many of them faith-professing people, should have reasoned that if they had not deserved their beautiful land, overflowing abundance, and preeminence among nations, the Supreme Being or moral design of the cosmos would not have bestowed such gifts. Nor, to be sure, have Americans been altogether negligent in expressing gratitude for their fortunate condition; at times they have been hugely generous with their blood, coin, and kindness toward others in need or distress, though often with a price or ulterior purpose attached—no one ever mistook them for saintly. Perhaps more than most other people, they have seemed refreshingly candid and self-critically funny. Yet they have also shown themselves to be fully capable of callous neglect toward those among them unblessed by their genes or family circumstances and of petu-lance toward those abroad who question their values, dispute their policies, and accuse them of indifference to the delicate ecosystem of the planet. Americans' matchless achievements, in short, have not yet made them the kinder, gentler people that President George Bush *père* once called on them to become. But then, kindness and gentleness are not what got them where they are.

Still, many in the great republic are mindful of its gathering challenges. Systemic inequities, evidenced by the cruel and growing gap between the grossly affluent and the desperately struggling, have polarized American society, created a permanent underclass of the disaffected, and cast liberty and social justice as antagonists to, not twin pillars of, the national creed. The battlefields of Korea, Vietnam, Lebanon, Somalia, and Iraq have dis-closed the limitations of American weaponry and the folly of trying to police a fractious world by firepower. The collaborative skills and historic resources of the European nations, the disciplined craftsmanship of the Japanese, and the sudden awakening of China, India, and other thronged societies from their arrested development have inevitably eroded American economic supremacy. Catastrophes of nature have struck hard blows at home as well in those "waste places of the earth"; pandemics threaten, while official U.S. policy clings to the delusion that global warming is humbug. At the opening of the twenty-first century Americans were jolted from their complacent assumption that they were immune from suicidal international terrorism. The resulting post-traumatic stress syndrome was shamelessly preyed upon by national leaders who failed—or chose not—to recognize that fanatic hatred of the United States was harbored not within the boundaries of alien states so much as within the confines of the pathological human mind—and that to wage retributive war on the former would only further inflame the latter.

But new and perhaps wiser leaders will follow. They may yet guide Americans to see that, having risen so high and mighty by seizing every opportunity their fortunate geography presented to them and then creating new modes of growth to enrich their own—and the world's—existence, they cannot sustain their primacy by claiming entitlement to mastery abroad and continuing to neglect the social pathogens stalking their homeland. Destiny has never been fond of lingering in one place, or favoring one people, forever.

APPENDIX

Principal Acquisitions of Territory by the United States

Territory	Date and How Acquired	Land Area in Square Miles
Original boundaries	1783: Treaty of Paris	895,415
Louisiana Territory	1803: Purchased from France	909,380
Florida	1819: Purchased from Spain	58,666
Republic of Texas	1845: Annexed by Congress	388,687
Oregon Territory	1846: Treaty with Britain	286,541
Mexican cession	1848: Treaty of Guadalupe Hidalgo	529,189
Gadsden Purchase	1853: Treaty with Mexico	29,670
Alaska	1867: Purchased from Russia	570,374
Hawaii	1898: Annexed by Congress	6,423
Puerto Rico	1898: Treaty with Spain	3,427
Guam	1898: Treaty with Spain	210
American Samoa	1900: Annexed by Congress	77
Virgin Islands	1917: Purchased from Denmark	134
Northern Marianas	1947: UN Trusteeship	179
	1976: Covenant by Congress	
Total U.S. Territory		3,540,305

Source: U.S. Departments of Interior and Commerce

ACKNOWLEDGMENTS

EACH OF THE HISTORICAL EPISODES explored in this book has generated a considerable body of literature—so much so that my own reading had to be supplemented by the efforts of several research assistants who worked with me over a period of five years. Collectively, our source readings included hundreds of books and a like number of articles from newspapers, scholarly journals, and other periodicals, to the extent that a conscientious listing of them all would probably require an appendix half as long as the text itself. There was, moreover, a good deal of overlap in this material, so that providing conventional academic footnoting would have been both unwieldy and beside the point. What I have attempted here is a narrative— of a scope not previously undertaken in a single volume, to my knowledge—that seeks to convey step-by-step how and why the American nation acquired its territorial domain. This rendering, while necessarily synthesizing earlier works, is not dependent on or limited by any of them for the judgments and characterizations of the events, policies, and personal conduct described here. The book is intended to be the distillation of a historical process, refracted by the author's thematic stress on land accumulation as the nurturing engine and compelling impulse in ruthlessly transforming a spectacular wilderness into a mighty state.

While assuming full responsibility for the text, I wish to acknowledge the substantial assistance I was given by skilled researchers, the majority of them at the time graduate students in the Department of History at the University of California at Berkeley. Foremost among these was Ruben Flores, whose diligence and insights were of particular value. Dan Geary, another former UC Berkeley graduate student, though he was involved in the project for a shorter period, also provided me with astute memoranda. Two other Berkeley grad students, Heather Norby and Dee Beelenberg, were useful contributors, along with Rebecca Voigt Krawiec of Oakland. Most of all, I am grateful for the incalculable and dedicated labors that my wife, Phyllis, contributed to this effort. These included voluminous readings and memoranda on, among other subjects, the native Americans, the Louisiana Purchase, Andrew Jackson, and the acquisitions of Alaska and the Virgin

Islands. Her enthusiasm sustained the project from the first, and it was she who suggested the main title.

I am greatly appreciative as well to those who reviewed the manuscript and offered me their suggestions—Joseph E. Illick III, Gene Marine, Ruben Flores, and Phyllis Kluger. The late and greatly lamented Reggie Zelnik provided me with entrée to the History Department at Berkeley. And a legion of staff members at the University of California's Doe Library were patiently helpful.

Finally, I am indebted to my editor at Knopf, Jonathan B. Segal, who encouraged this effort from the first and constructively examined the text with uncommon caring. Knopf's copyediting department also provided expert scrutiny of the manuscript.

R.K.
Berkeley, California

BIBLIOGRAPHICAL NOTES

WHAT FOLLOWS is a selected list of sources, broken down on a chapter-by-chapter basis, that were most helpful to me. Those books and articles of particular value and essential reading for any serious student of the subject are marked with an asterisk (*) at the end of the citation. In the cases where a source is listed for more than one chapter, it is followed by a parenthetical reference to the notes for the chapter in which it was initially cited. In most cases where an excerpt appears in the text, its source is given either in the main narrative or following the bibliographical listing for the chapter for which it appears, along with an occasional remark about sources of surpassing importance. Some quoted material is unreferenced because it appears in multiple texts, all of them given in the bibliography.

Preface

President Clinton's visit to the monument for the Boy Heroes of Chapultepec was reported in the *New York Times* on May 6, 1997, and in *Newsday* the following day.

Robert Frost's poem "The Gift Outright," excerpted on p. xiv, was first published in his 1942 collection, *A Witness Tree* (Henry Holt), and later included in a larger collection, *The Road Not Taken* (Holt, 1949, 1951). The poem gained global attention at the 1961 presidential inauguration of Frost's fellow New Englander, John F. Kennedy, when inclement conditions and failing eyesight prevented the poet from reading a new work he had written for the occasion, and he was forced to recite "The Gift Outright" from memory.

CHAPTER I: *An empty sack cannot stand upright (1500–1750)*

Bakeless, John. *The Eyes of Discovery.* Dover, 1961.

Billington, Ray Allen. *Land of Savagery, Land of Promise: The European Image of the American Frontier.* Norton, 1981.

Boorstin, Daniel J. *The Americans: The Colonial Experience.* Random House, 1959.

Cherry, Conrad, ed. *God's New Israel: Religious Interpretations of American Destiny.* University of North Carolina, 1998.

Dabney, Virginius. *Virginia: The New Dominion.* Doubleday, 1971.

DeVoto, Bernard. *The Course of Empire.* Houghton Mifflin, 1952.

Faragher, John M., ed. *A History of the American People.* Prentice-Hall, 1999.

Farb, Peter. *Face of North America.* Harper & Row, 1963.

Friedenberg, Daniel M. *Life, Liberty and the Pursuit of Land: The Plunder of Early America.* Prometheus, 1992.*

Harris, Marshall. *Origin of the Land Tenure System.* Iowa State College, 1953.*

Hinsdale, B. A. *The Old Northwest.* Silver, Burdett, 1899.

Horsman, Reginald. *Race and Manifest Destiny.* Harvard, 1987.*

Jefferson, Thomas. *Notes on the State of Virginia.* Harper Torchbooks, 1964.

Landes, David. *The Wealth and Poverty of Nations.* Norton, 1998.*

Meinig, D. W. *The Shaping of America.* Vol. 1: *Atlantic America, 1492–1800.* Yale, 1986.*
Muzzey, David Saville. *A History of Our Country.* Ginn, 1950.
Pagden, Anthony. *Spanish Imperialism and the Political Imagination.* Yale, 1990.
Palmer, R. R., and Joel Colton. *A History of the Modern World.* Knopf, 1961.
Turner, Frederick Jackson. *The Frontier in American History.* University of Arizona, 1997.*
Wright, J. Leitch. *Anglo-Spanish Rivalry in North America.* University of Georgia, 1971.

Page 29: The recruitment pamphlet excerpt appears on p. 87 of Harris, *Origins of the Land Tenure System.*

Page 40: For detailed treatment of the land plunder committed by colonial officials, see Friedenberg, *Life, Liberty, and the Pursuit of Land.*

Page 43: Jefferson's view on the primacy of land and farming over all other earthly possessions and occupations was famously asserted in his *Notes on the State of Virginia* (see p. 157 of the edition cited above).

Page 45: Revisionist historians, in faulting *The Frontier in American History* for romanticizing the virtues of the western pioneers, have generally overlooked the rapacious nature of those early homesteaders that Turner points out (see pp. 269–74 of the edition cited above) and that I cite here as a central premise of this book. Americans' seizure and taming of their land were far more a painful conquest than a love affair consummated by mutual consent.

CHAPTER 2: *The Poor Richards arise (1750–1776)*

Anderson, Fred. *Crucible of War: The Seven Years' War and the Fate of Empire in British North America, 1754–1766.* Knopf, 2000.
Aptheker, Herbert. *The American Revolution.* International Publishers, 1960.
Bailyn, Bernard. *The Ideological Origins of the American Revolution.* Harvard, 1967.*
———. *The Peopling of British North America: An Introduction.* Knopf, 1986.
Boorstin, Daniel J. *The Lost World of Thomas Jefferson.* University of Chicago, 1948.
Brands, H. W. *The First American: The Life and Times of Benjamin Franklin.* Anchor, 2000.
Burstein, Andrew. *Sentimental Democracy.* Hill & Wang, 1999.
Christie, I. R. *Crisis of Empire: Great Britain and the American Colonies, 1754–83.* Norton, 1967.
Clark, Ronald W. *Benjamin Franklin: A Biography.* Random House, 1983.
Higham, John, ed. *The Reconstruction of American History.* Harper, 1962.
Isaacson, Walter. *Benjamin Franklin.* Simon & Schuster, 2003.
Middlekauff, Robert. *Benjamin Franklin and His Enemies.* University of California, 1996.
Morgan, Edmund S. *The Birth of the Republic, 1763–89.* University of Chicago, 1956.*
Tunis, Edwin. *Frontier Living.* Crowell, 1961.
Van Doren, Carl. *Benjamin Franklin.* Viking, 1938.*
Wright, Esmond. *Franklin of Philadelphia.* Harvard, 1986.
Zinn, Howard. *A People's History of the United States.* HarperPerennial, 1995.

Page 55: Franklin's extraordinary prescience about a boundless American future is richly developed in Van Doren's *Benjamin Franklin,* which remains the best biography on him.

Page 77: Franklin's deep involvement with Philadelphia speculators in western land is treated in depth in Chapter II of Abernethy's *Western Lands and the American Revo-*

lution (cited in full below in Chapter 5 notes). See especially pp. 30–33 for his efforts to beguile Shelburne into supporting the scheme to establish new colonies beyond the Appalachians.

CHAPTER 3: *Thinking large (1776–1782)*

Bancroft, George. *History of the United States from the Discovery of the American Continent.* Vol. X. Little, Brown, 1874.

Bemis, Samuel F. *The Diplomacy of the American Revolution.* Appleton-Century, 1925.

Bobrick, Benson. *Angel in the Whirlwind: The Triumph of the American Revolution.* Simon & Schuster, 1997.*

Cummins, Light Townsend. *Spanish Observers and the American Revolution, 1775–1783.* Louisiana State University, 1991.

Fitzmaurice, Lord. *Life of William, Earl of Shelburne.* 2 vols. Macmillan, London, 1912.

Franklin, Benjamin. *The Autobiography.* Vintage, 1990.

Giunta, Mary, et al., eds. *Documents of the Emerging Nation, U.S. Foreign Relations, 1775–1789.* Scholarly Resources, 1998.

Hibbert, Christopher. *George III: A Personal History.* Viking, 1998.

Johnson, Herbert A. *John Jay: Colonial Lawyer.* Garland, 1989.

Mackesy, Piers. *The War for America, 1775–83.* University of Nebraska, 1964.

McCusker, John. *How Much Is That in Real Money?* Oak Knoll, 2001.

Price, Roger. *A Concise History of France.* Cambridge, 1993.

Rappaport, Armin, ed. *Sources in American Diplomacy.* Macmillan, 1966.

Smith, Henry Nash. *Virgin Land: The American West as Symbol and Myth.* Harvard, 1950.

Varg, Paul A. *Foreign Policies of the Founding Fathers.* Michigan State University, 1963.

Weber, David J. *The Spanish Frontier in North America.* Yale, 1992.

DOCUMENTS

For John Adams's "Plan of Treaties," the first proposed peace terms by the United States, urging cession of all British North American colonies, see *Journals of Congress,* Sept. 17, 1776, article IX. For Congress's evolving instructions to its diplomats on acceptable peace terms, see *Journals* for Feb. 23, 1779; Aug. 4, 1779; Sept. 9, 1779; Oct. 4, 5, 6, and 18, 1780; Feb. 15, and June 5, 8, 9, and 12, 1781.

ARTICLES

Dull, Jonathan. "Franklin the Diplomat: The French Mission." American Philosophical Society, 1982; included in the society's *Transactions,* vol. 72, part I, 1–72.

Fisher, James. "A Forgotten Hero Remembered, Revered, and Revised: The Legacy and Ordeal of George Rogers Clark." *Indiana Magazine of History,* vol. 92 (June 1996).

Hutson, James H. "Intellectual Foundations of Early American Diplomacy." *Diplomatic History,* vol. I, no. 1 (Winter 1977), 1–19.

Lewis, Anthony Marc. "Jefferson and Virginia's Pioneers." *Mississippi Valley Historical Rev.,* vol. 34, no. 4 (March 1948), 551–88.

Page 84: The excerpt from the Freneau-Brackenridge poem appears on p. 9 in the prologue of Smith's *Virgin Land,* cited above.

Page 85: For Hamilton's charge of British jealousy over America's bounty, see Boorstin's *The Americans: The Colonial Experience,* p. 98.

Page 109: Bancroft's filigreed denunciation of Spain's opposition to U.S. expansionist hopes appears on p. 192 of vol. X of his history of the nation, cited above.

Page 120: For Philip Schuyler's Jan. 20, 1780, letter to New York State Assembly, see *Letters of Members of the Continental Congress,* vol. V (Carnegie Institution, 1931), pp. 20–22.

CHAPTER 4: *The kings outfoxed (1782–1783)*

Bailey, Thomas. *A Diplomatic History of the American People,* ch. 4. Prentice-Hall, 1980.

Bemis, Samuel F., ed. *The American Secretaries of State and Their Diplomacy.* Vol. I: *Robert R. Livingston and John Jay.* Knopf, 1927.

———. *A Short History of American Foreign Policy and Diplomacy.* Holt, 1959.

Fitzmaurice, Lord. *Life of William,* cited in ch. 3.

Gottschalk, Louis. *Lafayette and the Close of the American Revolution.* University of Chicago, 1942.

Hoffman, Ronald, and Peter J. Albert, eds. *Peace and the Peacemakers: The Treaty of 1783.* University Press of Virginia, 1986.

Jay, John. *The Correspondence and Public Papers of John Jay.* Vol. II: 1781–1782, ed. Henry P. Johnston. Putnam's, 1891.

Jones, Howard. *The Course of American Diplomacy from the Revolution to the Present.* Franklin Watts, 1985.

McCullough, David. *John Adams.* Simon & Schuster, 2001.

Monaghan, Frank. *John Jay.* Bobbs-Merrill, 1935.

Morris, Richard B. *The Peacemakers: The Great Powers and American Independence.* Harper & Row, 1965.*

Murphy, Orville T. *Charles Gravier, Comte de Vergennes.* State University of New York, 1982.

Pellew, George. *John Jay.* Chelsea House, 1980.

Schiff, Stacy. *A Great Improvisation: Franklin, France, and the Birth of America.* Holt, 2005.

Schoenbrun, David. *Triumph in Paris: The Exploits of Benjamin Franklin.* Harper & Row, 1976.

Winsor, Justin, ed. *Winsor's History of America,* vol. VII; see chapter II, "The Peace Negotiations, 1782–1783," by John Jay (the jurist-diplomat's grandson). Houghton Mifflin, 1888.

ARTICLES

Crout, Robert Rhodes. "In Search of a 'Just and Lasting Peace': The Treaty of 1783, Louis XVI, Vergennes, and the Regeneration of the Realm." *International History Rev.,* vol. 3 (Aug. 1983), 364–98.

Dull, Jonathan R. "Franklin the Diplomat: The French Mission." *Transactions of the American Philosophical Society,* vol. 72, part 1 (1982).

Richard Morris's *The Peacemakers* is by far the richest account of the complex negotiations that led to the Treaty of 1783 and gave the United States far broader boundaries than its statesmen could reasonably claim.

CHAPTER 5: *Owning the wilderness (1783–1800)*

Abernethy, Thomas P. *Western Lands and the American Revolution.* Appleton-Century, 1937.

Aeon, Stephen. *How the West Was Lost: The Transformation of Kentucky from Daniel Boone to Henry Clay.* Johns Hopkins, 1996.

Axelrod, Alan. *Chronicle of the Indian Wars: From Colonial Times to Wounded Knee.* Prentice-Hall, 1993.

Beard, Charles A. *An Economic Interpretation of the Constitution of the United States.* Free Press, 1941.

Bellesiles, Michael A. *Revolutionary Outlaws: Ethan Allen and the Struggle for Independence on the Early American Frontier.* University Press of Virginia, 1993.

Bemis, Samuel F. *A Diplomatic History of the United States.* Holt, 1936.

———. *Jay's Treaty: A Study in Commerce and Diplomacy.* Yale, 1962.

———. *Pinckney's Treaty: America's Advantage from Europe's Distress.* Yale, 1960.

Berkhofer, Robert F., Jr. *The White Man's Indian: Images of the American Indian from Columbus to the Present.* Vintage, 1979.

Brown, Dee. *Bury My Heart at Wounded Knee: An Indian History of the American West.* Holt, Rinehart & Winston, 1970.

Combs, Jerald A. *Jay's Treaty: Political Background of the Founding Fathers.* University of California, 1970.

Deloria, Vine, Jr. *Custer Died for Your Sins: An Indian Manifesto.* University of Oklahoma, 1988.*

DeRosier, Arthur H., Jr. *The Removal of the Choctaw Indians.* Harper Torchbooks, 1972.

Dick, Everett. *The Lure of the Land: A Social History of the Public Lands from the Articles of Confederation to the New Deal.* University of Nebraska, 1990.

Drinnon, Richard. *Facing West: The Metaphysics of Indian Hating and Empire Building.* University of Minnesota, 1980.

Friedenberg, Daniel M. *Life, Liberty,* cited in ch. 1.

Hibbard, Benjamin H. *A History of the Public Land Policies.* University of Wisconsin, 1965.

Hinsdale, B. A. *Old Northwest,* cited in ch. 1.*

Jay, John. *Correspondence and Public Papers of John Hay,* ed. Henry P. Johnston. Vol. IV. Putnam's, 1893.

Koning, Hans. *The Conquest of America: How the Indian Nations Lost Their Continent.* Monthly Review, 1993.

Linklater, Andro. *Measuring America: How an Untamed Wilderness Shaped the United States and Fulfilled the Promise of Democracy.* Walker, 2002.

McCoy, Drew. *The Elusive Republic: Political Economy in Jeffersonian America.* University of North Carolina, 1980.

Magrath, C. Peter. *Yazoo: Law and Politics in the New Republic, The Case of* Fletcher v. Peck. Brown University, 1966.

Morgan, Edmund S. *Birth,* cited in ch. 2.

Morris, Richard B. *The Forging of the Union, 1781–1789.* Harper & Row, 1987.

Morrisey, Charles T. *Vermont: A Bicentennial History.* Norton, 1981.

Nabokov, Peter, ed. *Native American Testimony: A Chronicle of Indian-White Relations from Prophecy to the Present.* Penguin, 1991.

Nasatir, Abraham P. *Borderland in Retreat: From Spanish Louisiana to the Far Southwest.* University of New Mexico, 1976.

Nobles, Gregory H. *American Frontiers: Cultural Encounters and Continental Conquest.* Hill and Wang, 1997.

North, Douglas C. *The Economic Growth of the United States, 1790–1860.* Prentice-Hall, 1961.

Onuf, Peter S. *Statehood and Union: A History of the Northwest Ordinance.* Indiana University, 1997.

Rappaport, Armin, ed. *Essays in American Diplomacy,* ch. 2, "The Jay Treaty: The Origins of the American Party System," by Joseph Charles. Macmillan, 1967.

Rohrbough, Malcolm J. *The Land Office Business: The Settlement and Administration of American Public Lands, 1789–1837.* Oxford, 1968.

———. *The Trans-Appalachian Frontier.* Oxford, 1978.

Shalhope, Robert E. *Bennington and the Green Mountain Boys: The Emergence of Liberal Democracy in Vermont, 1760–1850.* Johns Hopkins, 1996.

Thompson, Charles Miner. *Independent Vermont.* Houghton Mifflin, 1942.

Washburn, Wilcomb E., ed. *The Indian and the White Man.* Anchor, 1964.

Weeks, William E. *Building the Continental Empire: American Expansion from the Revolution to the Civil War.* Ivan R. Dee, 1996.

Williamson, Chilton. *Vermont in Quandary, 1763–1825.* Vermont Historical Society, 1949.

DOCUMENTS

In *Journals of Continental Congress* (Edward Burnett, ed.), see vol. 25, pp. 690–92, on need to establish temporary government in the West; vol. 26, pp. 274–79, on Ordinance of 1784; vol. 28, pp. 375–81, for text of Ordinance of 1785; vol. 32, pp. 334–43, for text of Northwest Ordinance of 1787.

ARTICLES

Bemis, Samuel F. "Jay's Treaty and the Northwest Boundary Gap." *American Historical Rev.,* vol. 27, no. 3 (April 1922), 465–84.

———. "The London Mission of Thomas Pinckney." *American Historical Rev.,* vol. 28, no. 2 (Jan. 1923), 228–47.

Berkhofer, Robert F., Jr. "Jefferson, the Ordinance of 1784, and the Origins of the American Territorial System." *William and Mary Quarterly,* vol. 29, no. 2 (April 1972), 231–62.

Horsman, Reginald. "Thomas Jefferson and the Ordinance of 1784." *Illinois Historical Jour.,* vol. 79 (Summer 1986), 99–112.

Jensen, Merrill. "The Cession of the Old Northwest." *Mississippi Valley Historical Rev.,* vol. 23, no. 1 (June 1936), 27–48.*

———. "The Creation of the National Domain, 1781–1784." *Mississippi Valley Historical Rev.,* vol. 26, no. 3 (Dec. 1939), 323–42.*

McCormick, Richard P. "The Ordinance of 1784." *William and Mary Quarterly,* vol. 50, no. 1 (Jan. 1993), 112–22.

Onuf, Peter. "Toward Federalism: Virginia, Congress, and the Western Lands." *William and Mary Quarterly,* vol. 34, no. 3 (July 1977), 353–74.*

Pease, Theodore. "The Ordinance of 1787." *Mississippi Valley Historical Rev.,* vol. 25 (Sept. 1938), 167–80.

Whitaker, Arthur P. "The Commerce of Louisiana and the Floridas at the End of the Eighteenth Century." *Hispanic American Historical Rev.,* vol. 8, no. 2 (May 1928), 190–203.

———. "New Light on the Treaty of San Lorenzo: An Essay in Historical Criticism." *Mississippi Valley Historical Rev.,* vol. 15, no. 4 (March 1929), 435–54.

Page 199: Robbins's astute remarks on squatters' exemption rights appeared in the December 1933 issue of the *Mississippi Valley Historical Rev.*

CHAPTER 6: *For a nice little kingdom in Tuscany (1800–1803)*

Adams, Henry. *The Formative Years: A History of the United States During the Administrations of Jefferson and Madison.* Vol. 1. Scribner's, 1890.

Asprey, Robert. *The Rise of Napoleon Bonaparte.* Basic Books, 2000.

Barbé-Marbois, François. *The History of Louisiana, Particularly on the Cession of That Colony to the United States of America.* Carey and Lea, 1830.*

Brant, Irving. *James Madison, Secretary of State, 1800–1809.* Bobbs-Merrill, 1953.

Butterfield, Herbert. *Napoleon.* Collier, 1962.

Cerami, Charles A. *Jefferson's Great Gamble: The Remarkable Story of Jefferson, Napoleon, and the Men Behind the Louisiana Purchase.* Sourcebooks, 2003.

Dangerfield, George. *Chancellor Robert R. Livingston of New York, 1746–1813.* Harcourt, Brace, 1960.

DeConde, Alexander. *This Affair of Louisiana.* Scribner's, 1976.

Ellis, Joseph J. *American Sphinx: The Character of Thomas Jefferson.* Knopf, 1997.

Halliday, E. M. *Understanding Thomas Jefferson.* HarperCollins, 2001.

Hermann, Binger. *The Louisiana Purchase and Our Title West to the Rocky Mountains: A Review of Annexation by the United States.* U.S. Government Printing Office, 1900.

Johnson, Paul. *Napoleon.* Viking/Penguin, 2002.

Koch, Adrienne. *Jefferson and Madison: The Great Collaboration.* Knopf, 1950.

Kukla, Jon. *A Wilderness So Immense: The Louisiana Purchase and the Destiny of America.* Knopf, 2003.*

Laussat, Pierre-Clément de. *Memoirs of My Life to My Son During the Years 1803 and After, Which I Spent in Public Service in Louisiana as Commissioner of the French Government for the Retrocession to France of That Colony and for Its Transfer to the United States.* Louisiana State University, 1978.

Lyon, E. Wilson. *Louisiana in French Diplomacy.* University of Oklahoma, 1934.

———. *The Man Who Sold Louisiana: The Career of François Barbé-Marbois.* University of Oklahoma, 1942.

Malone, Dumas. *Jefferson the President: First Term, 1801–1805.* Little, Brown, 1970.*

Matthews, Richard K. *The Radical Politics of Thomas Jefferson.* University Press of Kansas, 1984.

Meinig, D. W. *The Shaping of America.* Vol. 2: *Continental America, 1800–1867.* Yale, 1993.*

Pitot, James. *Observations on the Colony of Louisiana from 1796 to 1802.* Louisiana State University, 1979.

Richard, Carl J. *The Louisiana Purchase.* University of Southwestern Louisiana, 1995.

Sprague, Marshall. *So Vast, So Beautiful a Land: Louisiana and the Purchase.* Little, Brown, 1974.*

Thompson, J. M. *Napoleon Bonaparte: His Rise and Fall.* Basil Blackwell, 1952.

Tucker, Robert W., and David Hendrickson. *Empire of Liberty: The Statecraft of Thomas Jefferson.* Oxford, 1990.

Weber, David J. *The Spanish Frontier in North America.* Yale, 1992.

ARTICLES

Adams, Mary P. "Jefferson's Reaction to the Treaty of San Ildefonso." *Jour. of Southern History,* vol. 21, no. 2 (May 1955), 173–88.*

Aiton, Arthur S. "The Diplomacy of the Louisiana Cession." *American Historical Rev.,* vol. 36, no. 4 (July 1931), 701–20.

Carson, David. "The Role of Congress in the Acquisition of the Louisiana Territory." *Louisiana History,* vol. 26, no. 4 (1985), 469–83.

Keller, Christian B. "Philanthropy Betrayed: Thomas Jefferson, the Louisiana Purchase, and the Origins of Federal Indian Removal Policy." *Proceedings of the American Philosophical Society,* vol. 144, no. 1 (March 2000), 39–66.

Whitaker, Arthur P. "The Retrocession of Louisiana in Spanish Policy." *American Historical Rev.,* vol. 39, no. 3 (April 1934), 454–76.

No sources were more valuable to me than the first two volumes of Donald W. Meinig's *The Shaping of America: A Geographical Perspective on 500 Years of History* (Yale, 1986 and 1993), an extraordinarily rich, interdisciplinary treatment of a vast subject. For all its detail, it is readily digestible by nonscholars.

CHAPTER 7: *Everything he does is rapid as lightning (1803)*

Ariaga Weiss, Victor Adolfo. "The Domestic Opposition to the Louisiana Purchase: Anti-expansionism and Republican Thought." Ph. D. diss., University of Virginia, 1993. [Available from University Microfilms International.]

Brown, Everett. *The Constitutional History of the Louisiana Purchase, 1803–1812.* University of California, 1920.

Wallace, Anthony F. *Jefferson and the Indians.* Harvard, 1999.*

ARTICLES

Balleck, Barry. "When the Ends Justify the Means: Thomas Jefferson and the Louisiana Purchase." *Presidential Studies Quarterly,* vol. 22, no. 4 (1992), 679–96.

Carson, David. "Blank Paper of the Constitution: The Louisiana Purchase Debates." *Historian,* vol. 54, no. 3 (1992), 477–90.

Farnham, Thomas. "The Federal-State Issue and the Louisiana Purchase." *Louisiana History,* vol. 7, no. 1 (1968), 7–30.

Knudson, Jerry. "Newspaper Reaction to the Louisiana Purchase." *Missouri Historical Rev.,* vol. 63, no. 2 (1969), 182–215.

Page 276: Napoleon's reasons for selling Louisiana to the Americans in his reported conversation with Talleyrand are discussed on pp. 29–30 of Carl Richard's *The Louisiana Purchase* (see ch. 6 sources).

Page 279: Johnson's rebuke of Napoleon's decision to sell Louisiana appears on p. 95 of his short, lively biography on the First Consul and self-crowned emperor (cited in ch. 6 notes).

Page 297: Wallace's indicting judgment of Jefferson's seminal role in the Indian removal policy of the U.S. government is on p. 275 of his book cited above. The anonymous citizen's letter expressing a brutally realistic assessment of the price to be paid in blood—mostly by the native Americans—for the Louisiana Purchase is quoted by Ariaga Weiss on p. 138 of his dissertation cited above.

Page 298: Jefferson's letter explaining his tortured turn to expediency in rationalizing his qualms over the constitutionality of the purchase appears on p. 320 of the fourth volume of Malone's monumental, if sometimes doting, biography (cited in ch. 6 notes) of the third President.

CHAPTER 8: *From motives of purest patriotism (1803–1823)*

Adams, Henry. *The Formative Years: A History of the United States During the Administrations of Jefferson and Adams.* Vol. 2. Scribner's, 1890.*

Bemis, Samuel F. *John Quincy Adams and the Foundations of American Foreign Policy.* Knopf, 1956.*

Brands, H. W. *Andrew Jackson: His Life and Times.* Doubleday, 2005.

Buchanan, John. *Jackson's Way: Andrew Jackson and the People of the Western Waters.* Wiley, 2001.

Dangerfield, George. *The Awakening of American Nationalism, 1815–1828.* Harper & Row, 1965.

Graves, Donald E. *Field of Glory: The Battle of Crysler's Farm, 1813.* Robin Brass Studio, 1999.

Green, Michael D. *The Politics of Indian Removal: Creek Government and Society in Crisis.* University of Nebraska, 1962.

Hickey, Donald. *The War of 1812: A Forgotten Conflict.* University of Illinois, 1989.

Hindle, Wendy. *Castlereagh.* Collins, 1981.

Johnson, Dorothy O., and Charles M. Gates. *Empire of the Columbia.* Harper & Row, 1967.

Marshall, Thomas Maitland. *A History of the Western Boundary of the Louisiana Purchase, 1819–1841.* University of California, 1914.

Merk, Frederick. *The Oregon Question: Essays in Anglo-American Diplomacy and Politics.* Harvard, 1967.

Milner, Clyde A. II, et al. *The Oxford History of the American West.* Oxford, 1994.

Myers, Gustavus. *History of the Great American Fortunes.* Modern Library, 1936.

Nagel, Paul C. *John Quincy Adams: A Public Life, a Private Life.* Harvard, 1997.*

Nobles, Gregory H. *American Frontiers: Cultural Encounters and Continental Conquest.* Hill & Wang, 1997.

North, Douglas C. *The Economic Growth of the United States, 1790–1860.* Norton, 1966.

Owsley, Frank. *Struggle for the Gulf Borderlands: The Creek War and the Battle of New Orleans, 1812–1815.* University of Florida, 1981.

Perkins, Bradford. *Castlereagh and Adams: England and the United States, 1812–1823.* University of California, 1964.

Pickles, Tim. *New Orleans, 1815.* Osprey, 1993.

Remini, Robert V. *Andrew Jackson.* Twayne, 1966.

———. *The Legacy of Andrew Jackson: Essays on Democracy, Indian Removal, and Slavery.* Louisiana State University, 1988.

Smith, Joseph B. *The Plot to Steal Florida: James Madison's Phony War.* Arbor House, 1983.

Stagg, J. C. A. *Mr. Madison's War: Politics, Diplomacy, and Warfare in the Early American Republic, 1783–1830.* Princeton, 1983.

Takaki, Ronald T. *Iron Cages: Race and Culture in Nineteenth-Century America.* Knopf, 1979.

Ward, John William. *Andrew Jackson: Symbol for an Age.* Oxford, 1955.

Weeks, William E. *John Quincy Adams and the American Global Empire.* University Press of Kentucky, 1992.

ARTICLES

Ambler, Charles. "The Oregon Country, 1810–1830: A Chapter in Territorial Expansion." *Mississippi Valley Historical Rev.,* vol. 30, no. 1 (June 1943), 3–24.

Campbell, Gordon T. "Some Patterns of Land Speculation in the Old Southwest." *Jour. of Southern History,* vol. 15, no. 4 (Nov. 1949), 463–77.

Egan, Clifford. "The Origins of the War of 1812: Three Decades of Historical Writing." *Military Affairs,* vol. 39, no. 2 (April 1974), 72–75.

Hacker, Louis M. "Western Land Hunger and the War of 1812." *Mississippi Valley Historical Rev.,* vol. 10, no. 4 (March 1924), 365–95.*

Horsman, Reginald. "On to Canada: Manifest Destiny and U.S. Strategy in the War of 1812." *Michigan Historical Rev.,* vol. 12 (Fall 1987), 1–24.*

Robbins, Roy M. "Preemption—A Frontier Triumph." *Mississippi Valley Historical Rev.,* vol. 18, no. 3 (Dec. 1931), 331–49.*

Shafer, Joseph. "The British Attitude Toward the Oregon Question." *American Historical Rev.,* vol. XVI (1911), 273–99.

Page 313: The Henry Adams excerpt appears on p. 736 of his *The Formative Years.*

Page 316: Remini's apologist comment that Jackson is no longer regarded as "a mad racist intent on genocide" against the Indians appears on p. 45 of *The Legacy of Andrew Jackson.*

Page 336: Jackson's statement to Calhoun of his intended disposal of Spanish authority in Florida is quoted on p. 48 of Dangerfield's *The Awakening of American Nationalism.*

CHAPTER 9: *Big Drunk wins the day (1821–1836)*

Barker, Eugene C. *The Life of Stephen F. Austin.* University of Texas, 1926.

———. *Mexico and Texas, 1821–1835.* P. J. Turner, 1928.

Binkley, William C. *The Expansionist Movement in Texas, 1838–1850.* University of California Publications in History, vol. 13. University of California, 1925.*

Brands, H. W. *Lone Star Nation: How a Ragged Band of Volunteers Won the Battle for Texas Independence—and Changed America.* Doubleday, 2004.

Campbell, Randolph B. *Sam Houston and the American Southwest.* HarperCollins, 1993.

Cantrell, Gregg. *Stephen F. Austin, Empresario of Texas.* Yale, 1999.

De Bruhl, Marshall. *Sword of San Jacinto: A Life of Sam Houston.* Random House, 1993.

Dobie, Frank J. *The Flavor of Texas.* Dealey and Lowe, 1936.

Fehrenbach, T. R. *Lone Star: A History of Texas and the Texans.* Collier, 1968.

Fletcher, David M. *The Diplomacy of Annexation: Texas, Oregon, and the Mexican War.* University of Missouri, 1973.*

Friend, Llerena B. *Sam Houston: The Great Designer.* University of Texas, 1969.

Hardin, Stephen L. *Texan Iliad: A Military History of the Texas Revolution, 1835–1836.* University of Texas, 1994.

Hogan, William Ransom. *The Texas Republic: A Social and Economic History.* University of Texas, 1946.

Lack, Paul D. *The Texas Revolutionary Experience: A Political and Social History.* Texas A&M, 1992.

Long, Jeff. *Duel of Eagles: The Mexican and U.S. Fight for the Alamo.* Morrow, 1990.

Lord, Walter. *A Time to Stand.* Harper, 1961.

Merk, Frederick. *Slavery and the Annexation of Texas.* Knopf, 1972.

Reichstein, Andreas V. *Rise of the Lone Star: The Making of Texas.* Texas A&M, 1989.

Rives, George L. *The United States and Mexico, 1821–1848.* Scribner's, 1913.

Simpson, Lesley Byrd. *Many Mexicos.* University of California, 1941.

Stevens, Donald Faithian. *Origins of Instability in Early Republican Mexico.* Duke, 1991.

Weber, David J. *The Mexican Frontier, 1821–1846: The American Southwest Under Mexico.* University of New Mexico, 1982.

Weems, John Edward. *Dream of Empire: A Human History of the Republic of Texas, 1836–1846.* Simon & Schuster, 1971.*

ARTICLES

Barker, Eugene C. "President Jackson and the Mexican Revolution." *American Historical Rev.,* vol. 12 (July 1907), 788–809.

———. "The United States and Mexico, 1845–1837." *Mississippi Valley Historical Rev.,* vol. 1 (June 1914), 3–30.

Lebergott, Stanley. "The Demand for Land: The United States, 1820–1860." *Jour. of Economic History,* vol. XLV, no. 2 (June 1985), 181–212.

Merk, Frederick. "A Safety Valve Thesis and Texan Annexation." *Mississippi Valley Historical Rev.,* vol. 49 (Dec. 1962), 13–36.

Fletcher's *The Diplomacy of Annexation* is the essential text for a clear understanding of the U.S. government's policy of territorial aggrandizement in the 1845–50 period. The collective works of Frederick Merk and Reginald Horsman are also indispensable for an objective appraisal of the political and emotional drives behind the expansionist movement.

Page 360: Terán's prescient assessment that prospering Texas would soon break away from Mexico unless its separatist inclinations were forcefully checked appears in Brands's lively *Lone Star Nation* on p. 151.

Page 377: For more on Austin's destitute condition after devoting his life to the successful colonization of Texas, see *Lone Star Nation,* p. 174. Cantrell's biography is a worthy rendering of the republic's founding father, who ultimately attained neither wealth nor power.

Page 388: Houston's ambivalence on annexation as expressed in the excerpted letter to Jackson is cited in Brands, *Lone Star Nation,* p. 403.

Page 398: Greeley's plaintive screed against his countrymen's lust "[t]o grasp more and more of the face of the earth" is cited on p. 159 of Merk's *Slavery and the Annexation of Texas.*

CHAPTER 10: *Polking John Bull in the eye (1836–1847)*

Bergeron, Paul H. *The Presidency of James K. Polk.* University Press of Kansas, 1987.

Clark, Malcolm, Jr. *Eden Seekers: The Settlement of Oregon, 1818–1862.* Houghton Mifflin, 1981.

DeVoto, Bernard. *The Year of Decision: 1846.* Little, Brown, 1943.*

Fletcher, David M. *Diplomacy of Annexation,* cited in ch. 9.*

Haynes, Sam W. *James K. Polk and the Expansionist Impulse.* Longman, 1997.

Jones, Howard. *To the Webster-Ashburton Treaty: A Study in Anglo-American Relations, 1783–1843.* University of North Carolina, 1977.

Le Duc, Thomas. "The Maine Frontier and the Northeastern Boundary Controversy." *American Historical Rev.,* vol. 53, no. 1 (Oct. 1947), 30–41.

Lomask, Milton. *The Slender Reed: The Life of James K. Polk.* Farrar Straus & Giroux, 1966.

Merk, Frederick. *Manifest Destiny and Mission in American History.* Harvard, 1995.*

———. *Oregon Question,* cited in ch. 8.

Parkman, Francis. *The Oregon Trail.* Doubleday, 1945.

Rappaport, Armin. *Essays in American Diplomacy,* cited in ch. 5.

Seigenthaler, John. *James K. Polk.* Times Books, 2003.

Sellers, Charles G. *James K. Polk.* Vol. 2: *The Continentalist, 1843–1846.* Princeton, 1966.*

Unruh, John D., Jr. *The Plains Across: The Overland Emigrants and the Trans-Mississippi West, 1840–1860.* University of Illinois, 1979.

Van Alstyne, R. W. *The Rising American Empire.* Oxford, 1960.

Walker, Dale L. *Pacific Destiny: The Three-Century Journey to the Oregon Country.* Forge/Tom Doherty Associates, 2000.

Webb, Walter Prescott. *The Great Frontier.* University of Texas, 1952.

Weinberg, Albert K. *Manifest Destiny: A Study of Nationalist Expansionism in American History.* Johns Hopkins, 1935.*

Charles Sellers's two-volume biography of Polk, though put aside by the author before he had dealt with the war against Mexico, remains the most authoritative work on a personally uninteresting statesman who did extraordinary things when he became President. DeVoto's stylized and often cryptic narrative of the two-year-long "year of decision" is an enduring testament to this most literary of American historians. Weinberg's encyclopedic approach and Merk's more incisive handling are complementary reading for any student of the "manifest destiny" claim. My own view, expressed throughout this work, is that American territorial aggrandizement was no more a manifestation of destiny than the divine right of any king who ever reigned.

Page 401: The anonymous poem "Come Out to the West" is quoted by Ephraim D. Adams on p. 83 of ch. 5, "Manifest Destiny—An Emotion," in *Essays in American Diplomacy,* edited by Armin Rappaport.

Page 402: The *Albany Argus* editorial positing a link between the superb American landscape and the great ambitions of those who peopled it is cited on p. 55 of Merk's *Manifest Destiny.*

Page 425: Polk's view that the only way to obtain justice from Britain was to stand up firmly against it is quoted on p. 358 of Sellers's second volume on the Tennessean's life.

CHAPTER 11: *The lost virtue of their better days (1846–1850)*

DeVoto, Bernard. *Year of Decision,* cited in ch. 10.

Drexler, Robert W. *Guilty of Making Peace: A Biography of Nicholas Trist.* University Press of America, 1991.*

Dusinberre, William. *Slavemaster President: The Double Career of James Polk.* Oxford, 2003.

Fletcher, David M. *Diplomacy of Annexation,* cited in ch. 9.

Fuller, John Douglas Pitts. *The Move for the Annexation of All Mexico, 1846–1848.* Johns Hopkins, 1936.

Griswold del Castillo, Richard. *The Treaty of Guadalupe Hidalgo: A Legacy of Conflict.* University of Oklahoma, 1983.

Henry, Robert S. *The Story of the Mexican War.* Bobbs-Merrill, 1950, 1961.

Holliday, J. S. *Rush for Riches: Gold Fever and the Making of California.* University of California, 1999.

Horsman, Reginald. *Race,* cited in ch. 1.

Johnson, David Alan. *Founding the Far West: California, Oregon and Nevada, 1840–1890.* University of California, 1992.

Manning, William R., ed. *Diplomatic Correspondence of the United States: Inter-American Affairs, 1831–1860.* Vol. VIII: *Mexico, 1831–1848.* Carnegie Endowment for International Peace, 1937. See pp. 984–1020.

Merk, Frederick. *Manifest Destiny,* cited in ch. 10.

Meyer, Michael C., and William I. Sherman. *The Course of Mexican History.* Oxford, 1983.

Ohrt, Wallace. *Defiant Peacemaker: Nicholas Trist in the Mexican War.* Texas A&M, 1997.

Rives, George L. *United States and Mexico,* cited in ch. 9.

Roberts, David. *A Newer World: Kit Carson, John C. Frémont, and the Claiming of the American West.* Touchstone, 2000.

Schmitt, Karl M. *The United States and Mexico, 1821–1973: Conflict and Coexistence.* Wiley, 1974.

Schroeder, John H. *Mr. Polk's War: American Opposition and Dissent, 1846–1848.* University of Wisconsin, 1973.

Singletary, Otis A. *The Mexican War.* University of Chicago, 1960.

Starr, Kevin. *Americans and the California Dream, 1850–1915.* Oxford, 1973.

Vazquez, Josefina Z., and Lorenzo Meyer. *The United States and Mexico.* University of Chicago, 1985.

Walker, Dale L. *Bear Flag Rising: The Conquest of California, 1846.* Forge, Tom Doherty Associates, 1999.*

Weems, John Edward. *To Conquer a Peace: The War Between the United States and Mexico.* Doubleday, 1974.*

Page 434: Starr's volumes on California history are a good starting point for any student of the subject. The quotation here comes from *Americans and the California Dream,* p. 7.

Page 468: The *New York Sun* editorial ran October 27, 1847. The *Philadelphia Public Ledger*'s comment was made December 1, 1847.

Page 476: The poignant excerpt from the Mexican peace commissioners' report to their Congress urging acceptance of the painful Treaty of Guadalupe Hidalgo was translated for this book by my research assistant, Ruben Flores, now on the Kansas University faculty.

CHAPTER 12: *A wolf couldn't make a living on it* (1850–1854)

Cline, Howard F. *The United States and Mexico.* Rev. ed. Atheneum, 1973.

Cooper, William J. *Jefferson Davis, American.* Knopf, 2000.

Davis, William C. *Jefferson Davis: The Man and His Hour.* HarperCollins, 1991.

Gara, Larry. *The Presidency of Franklin Pierce.* University Press of Kansas, 1991.

Garber, Paul N. *The Gadsden Treaty.* University of Pennsylvania, 1923.*

Griswold del Castillo, Richard. *Treaty of Guadalupe Hidalgo,* cited in ch. 11.

McCardell, John. *The Idea of a Southern Nation: Southern Nationalists and Southern Nationalism, 1830–1860.* Norton, 1991.

Potter, David M. *The Impending Crisis, 1848–1861.* Harper & Row, 1976.

Rippy, J. Fred. *The United States and Mexico.* Knopf, 1926.

ARTICLES

Hodder, Frank H. "The Railroad Background of the Kansas-Nebraska Act." *Mississippi Valley Historical Rev.,* vol. 12, no. 1 (June 1925), 3–22.*

Robertson, Jere W. "The South and the Pacific Railroad." *Western Historical Quarterly,* vol. 5, no. 2 (April 1974), 163–86.

Page 496: Former Governor Hammond's withering appraisal of Gadsden is given on p. 82 of Garber's *The Gadsden Purchase.*

CHAPTER 13: *The great white elephant sale* (1854–1867)

Andrews, C. L. *The Story of Alaska.* Caxton Printers, 1936.

Bancroft, Frederic. *The Life of William H. Seward.* Harper, 1900.

Bolkhovitnow, Nikolai N. *Russian-American Relations and the Sale of Alaska, 1834–1867.* Limestone Press, 1996.*

Clark, Henry W. *History of Alaska.* Macmillan, 1930.

Creighton, Donald. *The Story of Canada.* Macmillan Canada, 1959.

Gruening, Ernest. *The State of Alaska.* Random House, 1954.*

Haas, William H., ed. *The American Empire: A Study of the Outlying Territories of the United States.* University of Chicago, 1940.

Harsha, D. A. *The Life of Charles Sumner.* Dayton and Burdick, 1856.

Hedin, Robert, and Gary Holthaus, eds. *Alaska: Reflections on Land and Spirit.* University of Arizona, 1989.

Holbo, Paul S. *Tarnished Expansion: The Alaska Scandal, the Press and Congress, 1867–1871.* University of Tennessee, 1983.

Huculak, Mukhaylo. *When Russia Was in America.* Mitchell Press, 1971.

Hulley, Clarence C. *Alaska 1741–1953.* Binfords & Morty, 1953.

Hunt, William R. *Alaska, a Bicentennial History.* Norton, 1976.

Jensen, Ronald J. *The Alaska Purchase and Russian-American Relations.* University of Washington, 1975.*

Kushner, Howard. *Conflict on the Northwest Coast: American-Russian Rivalry in the Pacific Northwest, 1790–1867.* Greenwood, 1975.

McNaught, Kenneth. *The Pelican History of Canada.* Penguin, 1969.

Paolino, Ernest N. *The Foundations of the American Empire: William Henry Seward and U.S. Foreign Policy.* Cornell, 1973.

Saul, Norman E. *Concord and Conflict: The United States and Russia, 1867–1914.* University Press of Kansas, 1996.

Sgroi, Peter P. *Why the United States Purchased Alaska.* University of Alaska, 1970.

Sherwood, Morgan B., ed. *Alaska and Its History.* University of Washington, 1967.

Storey, Moorfield. *Charles Sumner.* Houghton Mifflin, 1900.

Taylor, John M. *William Henry Seward, Lincoln's Right Hand.* HarperCollins, 1991.

Thomas, Benjamin Platt. *Russo-American Relations, 1815–1867.* Johns Hopkins, 1930.

Underwood, John J. *Alaska, an Empire in the Making.* Dodd, Mead, 1913.

Van Deusen, Glyndon G. *William Henry Seward.* Oxford, 1967.*

ARTICLES

Dunning, William A. "Paying for Alaska." *American Historical Rev.,* vol. 27, no. 3 (April 1920), 385–98.

Gilbert, Benjamin F. "The Alaska Purchase." *Journal of the West,* vol. 3, no. 1 (1964).

Golder, Frank A. "The Purchase of Alaska." *American Historical Rev.,* vol. 25, no. 3 (April 1920), 411–25.

Snell, James G. "The Frontier Sweeps Northwest: American Perceptions of the British American Prairie West at the Point of Canadian Expansion (Circa 1870)." *Western Historical Quarterly,* vol. 11, no. 4 (Oct. 1980), 381–400.

DOCUMENTS

"Speech of Hon. Charles Sumner of Massachusetts on the Cession of Russian America" before U.S. Senate, April 8, 1867. Printed as a pamphlet at *Congressional Globe* office, 1867.

Speech of Hon. Nathaniel P. Banks of Massachusetts in U.S. House of Representatives, June 30, 1868. Appendix to the *Congressional Globe,* 40th Congress, 2nd session, 385–92.

Page 533: Sumner's explanation to a friend about why he threw his critical support behind the Alaska purchase treaty is given on p. 339 of Storey's biography. In contrast to this letter, his speech on the floor of the Senate suggests Sumner had become, on reflection, a strong advocate of the acquisition.

CHAPTER 14: *Treachery in the tropics (1869–1902)*

Faulkner, Harold U. *Politics, Reform and Expansion, 1890–1900.* Harper & Bros., 1959.*

Freidel, Frank. *The Splendid Little War.* Little, Brown, 1958.

Joesting, Edward. *Hawaii: An Uncommon History.* Norton, 1972.

Kuykendall, Ralph S. *The Hawaiian Kingdom.* Vol. III: *1874–1893, The Kalakaua Dynasty.* University of Hawaii, 1967.*

LaFeber, Walter. *The New Empire: An Interpretation of American Expansion, 1860–1898.* Cornell, 1998.*

Leech, Margaret. *In the Days of McKinley.* Harper & Bros., 1959.

May, Ernest R. *Imperial Democracy: The Emergence of America as a Great Power.* Harcourt Brace, 1961.*

Morris, Edmund. *The Rise of Theodore Roosevelt.* Coward-McCann, 1979.

O'Toole, G. J. A. *The Spanish War: An American Epic—1898.* Norton, 1984.*

Schoultz, Lars. *Beneath the United States: A History of U.S. Policy Toward Latin America.* Harvard, 1998.

Van Alstyne, R. W., *Rising American Empire,* cited in ch. 10.

ARTICLES

Bailey, Thomas A. "The United States and Hawaii During the Spanish-American War." *American Historical Rev.,* vol. 36, no. 3 (April 1931), 552–60.

Clow, Frederick R. "Our Commercial Relations with the Hawaiian Islands." *Jour. of Political Economy,* vol. 1, no. 2 (March 1893), 280–84.

Field, James A., Jr. "American Imperialism: The Worst Chapter in Almost Any Book." *American Historical Rev.,* vol. 83, no. 3 (June 1978), 644–68.

Hofstadter, Richard. "Cuba, the Philippines, and Manifest Destiny." From *The Paranoid Style of American Politics* (Knopf, 1952), reprinted as ch. 9 in *Essays in American Diplomacy,* ed. Armin Rappaport et al. (Macmillan, 1967).*

Jones, Stephen B., and Klaus Mehnert. "Hawaii and the Pacific: A Survey of Political Geography." *Geographical Rev.,* vol. 30, no. 3 (July 1940), 358–75.

La Croix, Sumner J., and Christopher Grandy. "The Political Instability of Reciprocal Trade and the Overthrow of the Hawaiian Kingdom." *Jour. of Economic History,* vol. 57, no. 1 (March 1997), 161–89.

Lauck, W. Jett. "The Political Significance of Reciprocity." *Jour. of Political Economy,* vol. 12, no. 4 (Sept. 1904), 495–524.

Nichols, Jeanette P. "The United States Congress and Imperialism, 1861–1897." *Jour. of Economic History,* vol. 21, no. 4 (Dec. 1961), 526–38.

Osborne, Thomas J. "Empire Can Wait: American Opposition to Hawaiian Annexation, 1893–1898." *Reviews in American History,* vol. 10, no. 3 (Sept. 1982), 374–79.

Pratt, Julius W. "The 'Large Policy' of 1898." *Mississippi Valley Historical Rev.,* vol. 19, no. 2 (Sept. 1932), 219–42.*

Russ, William A., Jr. "Hawaiian Labor and Immigration Problems Before Annexation." *Jour. of Modern History,* vol. 15, no. 3 (Sept. 1943), 207–22.

Smith, Theodore C. "Expansion After the Civil War, 1865–71." *Political Science Quarterly,* vol. 16, no. 3 (Sept. 1901), 412–36.

Tate, Merze. "Hawaii: A Symbol of Anglo-American Rapprochement." *Political Science Quarterly,* vol. 79, no. 4 (Dec. 1964), 555–75.

Twain, Mark. "To the Person Sitting in Darkness." *North American Review,* Feb. 1901, 161–76.*

Page 558: For commissioner James Blount's curious failure to interview members of the 1893 Hawaiian revolutionary junta or officers of the *Boston,* whose troops were sent ashore to assure the success of the coup, see Kuykendall, *The Hawaiian Kingdom,* pp. 628, 647.

Page 574: *The Literary Digest* poll of U.S. newspaper editors' views on the disposition of the Philippines is noted in Zakaria's *From Wealth to Power* (see ch. 15 bibliography below) on p. 160. McKinley's account of how God answered his prayers for guidance on the Philippines question is elaborated on by May's *Imperial Diplomacy* at p. 253.

CHAPTER 15: *The so-called mandate of mankind (1903–1999)*

Beale, Howard K. *Theodore Roosevelt and the Rise of America to World Power.* Johns Hopkins, 1956.

LaFeber, Walter. *The Panama Canal: The Crisis in Historical Perspective.* Oxford, 1989.*

Leonard, Thomas M. *Panama, the Canal, and the United States: A Guide to Issues and References.* Regina Books, 1993.

Lindsay-Poland, John. *Emperors in the Jungle: The Hidden History of the U.S. in Panama.* Duke, 2003.

Major, John. *Prize Possession: The United States and the Panama Canal, 1903–1979.* Cambridge, 1993.

McCain, William D. *The United States and the Republic of Panama.* Russell & Russell, 1965.

McCullough, David. *The Path Between the Seas: The Creation of the Panama Canal, 1870–1914.* Simon & Schuster, 1977.*

Parton, James. *The Danish Islands: Are We Bound in Honor to Pay for Them?* Ticknor and Fields, 1869.

Tansill, Charles C. *The Purchase of the Danish West Indies.* Johns Hopkins, 1932.

Weinstein, Edwin A. *Cultural Aspects of Delusion: A Psychiatric Study of the Virgin Islands.* Free Press, 1962.

Zakaria, Fareed. *From Wealth to Power: The Unusual Origins of America's World Role.* Princeton, 1998.

A Note on Maps

The maps in this book were created especially for it by Joshua Borkowski, a member of the Cartography Group of the Department of Geography at the University of California in Berkeley under the guidance of the author and the supervision of Darin Jensen, staff cartographer and lecturer. The maps dealing with the boundaries of colonial Virginia, the states' western land claims and cessions to Congress, the boundaries of the new United States established at the close of the War for Independence, and the changing shape and extent of Texas between 1830 and 1850 are based on Goode's Homolosine projection; those dealing with the U.S. western boundary as settled with Spain in 1819 and the Mexican Cession of 1848 are based on the Boggs Eumorphic projection; the map of the Louisiana Purchase is based on the Lambert Conformal projection; the map of the Oregon Country and the boundary settlement of 1846 is based on the Robinson projection; the map of the Gulf of Mexico and Caribbean Sea is based on the Sinusoidal projection; and the map of Alaska is based on the Berghaus Star Polar projection.

INDEX

Italicized page numbers refer to the maps.

Aberdeen, George Hamilton-Gordon, Lord, 406–13
  California and, 437, 451
  Oregon and, 408–13, 416–20, 427–31
  Texas and, 387, 389, 424
Abernethy, Thomas P., 78
absentee landlords, 40–1, 49
Adams, Henry, 312–13
Adams, John, 133, 229, 272, 432
  Netherlands mission of, 125–6, 131, 135, 146, 165–6
  Paris Treaty and, 165–70, 172–4, 176, 318
  Revolutionary War and, 85, 104–5, 124–7, 146, 152, 173
  U.S.-French relations and, 104–5, 234–5
Adams, John Quincy, 337–50, 391–2, 407, 432, 435, 544
  and acquisition of Florida, 333–5, 339–48
  clarifying U.S. western boundaries and, 325, 328–31, 337–44, *343,* 346–7, 353–4, 358, 392, 403, 428
  Oregon and, 402–4, 420–2, 428–9
  Texas and, 353–4, 358, 380, 389, 397–8, 428
  and War of 1812, 318–19, 321
Adams, Samuel, 74, 80–1
Adams-Onís Treaty, *343,* 346–9, 353, 358, 378, 391–2, 408–9, 417–18, *472*
Agassiz, Louis, 531, 533–4
Age of Discovery, xvi–xvii, 3–5, 7–8, 50
Age of Enlightenment, xvi, 7, 34, 91–2, 103, 193
agriculture, 184–6, 195, 210, 304, 319, 405–7, 426, 461, 488, 502, 516, 546–7, 559–60, 571
  Alaska and, 510, 523, 537–8, 541
  California and, 433–4, 476
  in colonial period, 14–15, 17–19, 21, 28–31, 33–6, 39–41, 43–4, 46–50, 53, 56, 59–60, 65, 72, 82–3
  Cuba and, 544, 560, 577
  Haiti and, 236–7, 256
  Hawaii and, 549–51, 553–4, 573
  Jefferson and, 253–4, 306, 324–5, 390–1

Louisiana and, 235, 240, 249, 255, 260–1, 267, 276, 296
  Mexico and, 351–2
  of native Americans, 296–7
  Oregon and, 401, 405–6, 417, 428
  Paris Treaty and, 160–1, 170
  railroads and, 485, 580
  Revolutionary War and, 86, 90, 93, 114, 118, 172
  slavery and, 33–4, 481
  Texas and, 356–7, 360, 379, 382
  see also land, land ownership
A. G. Sloo and Associates, 494–5, 500, 503
Aguinaldo, Emilio, 569, 574–5
Alabama, 228, 348, 487, 585, 588
  native Americans and, 316–17, 333
Alamo, 368, 371–3, 375, 458
Alaska, xiii, 326, 518, 520–43, 557, 573
  climate of, 508, 523, 530, 532, 534, 538
  press on, 531–2, 535–6
  Russia and, 404, 507–16, 520–39
  topography of, 507, 523, 531, 538
  U.S. acquisition of, 507, 509–16, 520–3, *522,* 525–40, 543, 548, 622n
  U.S. neglect of, 540–1
Albany, N.Y., 56–7, 62, 120, 257, 300
Albright, Madeleine, 600
Aleutian Islands, 326, 402, 548
  Alaska and, 326, 508, 511, 521, *522,* 535, 541
Alexander I, Tsar of Russia, 319, 338, 402–3
Alexander II, Tsar of Russia, 509, 512–16, 526–7, 532–3, 535
Alexander VI, Pope, xvii, 13
Allen, Ethan, 86, 205–8
Allen, Ira, 207–8
Amador, Manuel, 591–3
American Century, 600–2
American Philosophical Society, 53, 254
American Revenue Act (Sugar Act), 68–9, 75
American Samoa, 571
Ames, Fisher, 289
Amiens, Treaty of, 250, 271

Amity and Commerce, Treaty of, 106, 247
Anglicans, 14, 17–18
Anglo-American Convention of 1818, 332
Appalachian Mountains, 56, 63, 95–6, 98,
　　114, 118–19, 184–6, 191, 230, 273,
　　296
　　and Declaration of Independence, 92–3
　　land rushes and, 185, 200
　　Paris Treaty and, 159, 161, 164, 167
　　Proclamation Line and, 65, 76, 137, 148,
　　　186
　　Revolutionary War and, 95, 105, 109, 118,
　　　129, 134, 148–50, 154
　　Virginia backland settlement and, 208–9,
　　　211
Aranda, Don Pedro Pablo Abarca de Bolea,
　　Conde de, 140–1, 148–50, 155, 157,
　　167
Arctic Ocean, 404, 511, 530, 542
Ardrey, Robert, 45
Arkansas, 349, 365, 400, 501
Army, U.S., 439, 490
　　and acquisition of Florida, 335–6, 345
　　and acquisition of New Mexico, 448–9,
　　　455
　　Alaska and, 540–1
　　Cuba and, 568, 577–8
　　Guadalupe treaty disputes and, 492, 496,
　　　500
　　Mexican War and, 441–3, 447–51, 454–63,
　　　465, 468–71, 474–5, 477
　　Panamanian revolution and, 592–3
　　Philippines and, 570, 575
　　and settlement of California, 435–6
　　Spanish-American War and, 568–70,
　　　572–3
　　and War of 1812, 313–15, 317, 322–4
Army Corps of Engineers, U.S., 595–6
Arnold, Benedict, 86, 210
Articles of Confederation, U.S., 96–7,
　　99–100, 110–11, 121–2, 139, 182, 192,
　　196–7, 292
　　ratification of, 122, 189
Ashburton, Alexander Baring, Lord, 407
Asia, Asians, 26, 154, 244, 330–1, 435, 477,
　　548, 598
　　Alaska and, 512, 521, 522, 531, 534, 538
　　canals and, 580, 583, 585
　　Hawaii and, 551–4, 557–8, 560, 562–3,
　　　573
　　Oregon Country and, 400–2, 408
　　Philippines and, 569–70, 574–5
　　railroads and, 484–6
　　Russia and, 508–9, 511–12, 515
Astor, John Jacob, 327–8
Austin, Moses, 354–6

Austin, Stephen, 355–63, 365–8, 377, *386,*
　　619*n*
Austria, 123–4, 154, 241, 247, 250, 291,
　　330
　　Napoleon's defeat of, 239, 243, 245,
　　　275
　　Russian relations with, 508–9, 515

Báez, Buenaventura, 545
Bagot, Charles, 329–30
Baja California, 464, 467, 475, 495,
　　498–500
Baltimore, Cecil Calvert, Lord, 20, 24, 100
Baltimore, Md., 321, 389, 392, 489
Baltimore & Ohio Railroad, 378, 477
Bancroft, George, 109–10, 413, 436
Bank of the United States, 325, 381, 385,
　　413
Banks, Nathaniel, 535, 538–9
Barbé-Marbois, François, 156, 277–9,
　　281–8, 295
Bartlett, John, 491–2
Basle, Treaty of, 227, 237
Batista, Fulgencio, 578
Bemis, Samuel Flagg, 345
Bennett, James Gordon, 531–2
Benton, Thomas Hart, 436
　　Oregon and, 420–2, 425–6, 430
　　railroads and, 486–7
　　and Texan annexation and statehood,
　　　395–6
Bering Strait, 402, 404, 408, 511, 531
Beveridge, Albert, 576
Biddle, James, 330
Bidlack, Benjamin, 581
Bidlack Treaty, 581–3, 588–90
Bigelow, John, 539
Bill of Rights, U.S., 197
Black, James, 425
blacks, 6, 50, 249, 323, 352, 517–20, 581
　　civil rights and, 517–19
　　Dominican Republic and, 544–6
　　Haiti and, 236–7, 246, 250–1, 256, 262–3,
　　　277–8, 290
　　see also slavery, slaves, slaveholders
Blackstone, Sir William, 63, 75
Blaine, James G., 554–5
Blount, James H., 557–8
Blount, William, 212
Board of Trade and Plantations, British, 56,
　　63–4, 82
Bonaparte, Joseph, 263–6, 276–7, 292
Bonaparte, Lucien, 263, 276–7
Bonaparte, Napoleon, *see* Napoleon I,
　　Emperor of France
Booth, John Wilkes, 505–6

Boston, Mass., 50, 53, 69–70, 79–81, 147,
   221, 325, 400, 409, 434, 532
   Revolutionary War and, 86, 89, 172–3
   Tea Act and, 79–80
   Townshend Revenue Acts, 74, 79
Boston, U.S.S., 556, 558, 592
Boston Massacre, 79
Boston Tea Party, 81
Boundary Act, 480
Brackenridge, Henry, 84–5
Breckinridge, John, 272, 294
British, *see* Great Britain, British
British Columbia, 326, 392, 431, 509, 513,
   524–5
British Guiana, 560–2
British North America Act, 524–5
Brown, Lancelot "Capability," 75
Bryan, William Jennings, 562
Buchanan, James, 457, 504, 545
   Alaska and, 512–13
   Mexican War and, 445–7, 463–4, 466–7,
      470, 473–4, 476
   Oregon and, 411–12, 416–19, 427–31
   Texas boundary disputes and, 439–40, 492
Buena Vista, Battle of, 462, 490
Bulwer, Sir Henry, 494, 583
Bunau-Varilla, Philippe, 585–9, 591–4
Bunker Hill, Battle of, 89
Burgoyne, John, 90–1, 103, 318
Burnet, David, 371, 373–4, 376
Bush, George W., 429–30
Bute, John, 64, 66, 131
Butler, Andrew, 529
Byrd, William, 38

Cabot, John, 13
Cadwallader, Colden, 204–5
Calhoun, John C., xii, 496
   Mexican War and, 468–9
   Oregon and, 412, 416–17, 426, 429–30
   Seminole War and, 334–7
   Texas and, 388–9, 408, 411
California, 326, 385, 401, 409, 422, 425,
   482–3, 496, 553, 569, 574, 583, 586
   Alaska and, 510–13, 520, 527–8, 532, 534,
      538–9, 541
   boundary issues and, 342, 440, 458
   discovery of gold in, 478–9, 482, 487, 511,
      549, 581
   Hawaii and, 548–50, 555
   Mexican War and, 433, 437–8, 445–6,
      451–7, 460, 464, 467–8, 471, 475–8
   Mexico and, 415, 433–8, 446, 451–3, 479,
      482
   railroads and, 486–7, 490, 501, 504
   settlement of, 433–7, 452

   statehood gained by, 500–1, 549
   U.S. acquisition of, 413, 415, 433, 435–7,
      445–6, 448, 451–7, 459–61, 464, 468,
      471, 475–80, 513, 581
Canada, xiii, 11–13, 59–66, 94–5, 182–3,
   217–20, 222, 224, 235–6, 277, 332–3,
   350, 419–20, 448, 560
   Alaska and, 525–6, 531–2, 538, 540
   clarifying U.S. western boundaries and,
      326, 328–30, 342, 346
   economic evolution of, 547–8
   and French and Indian War, 59–61, 63,
      137–8, 143
   and French New World arrival and colo-
      nization, 8–9, 11–12, 49
   home rule gained by, 523–5
   Jay's Treaty and, 219–20
   Louisiana and, 236, 255, 266, 299
   native Americans and, 218, 302–3, 305
   Oregon and, 391–2, 402, 405–6, 422, 429,
      431
   Paris Treaty and, 160–2, 164–5, 168–9,
      172, 178–9, 183, 217–18, 261, 303
   Proclamation Line and, 64–6
   proposed U.S. acquisition of, 308–9
   Quebec Act and, 83, 85–7, 113
   Revolutionary War and, 85–7, 90, 95, 105,
      109, 113, 115, 119, 128, 133–7, 140,
      143–4, 153, 157, 206
   U.S.-French relations and, 105, 109
   U.S. invasion of, 308–14, 319–20, 333
   and War of 1812, 311–14, 317–22, 324,
      326, 353
canals, 485, 488
   across Mexico, 464, 467, 483, 493–6,
      498–500, 503
   military importance of, 561–2, 579–80,
      584–5, 596, 599
   across Panama, *see* Panama Canal
   railroads and, 580, 585
Canal Zone, 594–6, 599–600
Caribbean Sea, 4, 20, 49, 108, 139, 177, 201,
   218, 227, 235, 256, 265, 279, 304,
   543–5, 561–2, 570, 578–9, 581–3, *582,*
   592, 596–8
   and French and Indian War, 58, 60–1
   and French interest in Haiti, 270, 274
   and French reacquisition of Louisiana,
      246–7, 261, 263, 268
   isthmian canal and, 585–6
   Roosevelt Corollary and, 596–7
Carleton, Guy, 218
Carlos III, King of Spain, 211, 226, 249
   anti-U.S. trade practices and, 183–4
   Jay's Spanish mission and, 115, 117
   Paris Treaty and, 177, 201

Carlos III, King of Spain *(continued)*
 Revolutionary War and, 105, 107–8, 117, 140, 156
Carlos IV, King of Spain, 225
 and French reacquisition of Louisiana, 240–2, 246–8, 259, 262, 265–9
 New Orleans crisis and, 268–9
Carondelet, François-Luis Hector, Baron de, 225
Carson, Christopher "Kit," 436, 456, 500
Carter, Jimmy, 599–600
Castlereagh, Robert Stewart, Viscount, 333, 345, 349
 clarifying U.S. western boundaries and, 330–1, 340
 and War of 1812, 318–22
Castro, Fidel, 578
Catherine II (the Great), Empress of Russia, 123–4
Catholicism, Catholics, xvii, 27, 49, 59, 82, 87, 108, 246, 248, 289, 352–4, 359–60, 401, 426, 563
 and British New World arrival and colonization, 14, 16–17, 20
 Mexico and, 352–3, 360, 366
 Texas and, 354, 356, 359
 U.S.-Spanish relations and, 116, 118
Central America, 4, 579–89, 599
Cerro Gordo, Battle of, 463
Chapultepec, Battle of, xi, 469, 600
Chapultepec, monument to Mexico's Boy Heroes of, xi–xii, 600
Charles II, King of Great Britain, 20, 203
Charleston, S.C., 160n, 221, 483–6, 498
 railroads and, 483–4, 486, 489
 Revolutionary War and, 120, 136, 172
Charleston, U.S.S., 570
Cherokees, 62, 184, 229, 297, 305, 317
 Houston's relationship with, 364–5
 North Carolina backlands and, 212–13
Chesapeake, U.S.S., 307, 329
Chesapeake Bay, 19, 31, 97, 127–8, 320
 colonial boundaries and, 23–4
Chicago, Ill., 223, 486–7, 496, 501–2
China, xiii, 15, 45, 326, 331, 385, 408, 484, 534, 546–8, 558–9, 563, 586, 602
 immigration from, 547, 551
 Philippines and, 565, 569
 Russia and, 508–9, 511
Chittenden, Thomas, 207–8
Christianity, Christians, 4–5, 9, 27, 581
 Hawaii and, 549, 553–4
 native Americans and, 34–5
 Philippines and, 574–6
Civil War, 457, 504–5, 507, 514–15, 519, 521, 524, 529, 531, 538, 543, 546–7, 583

Clark, George Rogers, 112–14, 148, 210
Clark, William, 301, 327–9, 435
Clay, Henry, xii, 413, 580
 Texas and, 389–90, 393–4
Clayton, John M., 492–4, 583
Clayton-Bulwer Treaty, 494, 498–9, 583, 586
clergy, xv–xvii, 11–14, 238
 and Age of Discovery, xvii, 3–4
 and British New World arrival and colonization, 13–14
 and French New World arrival and colonization, 9, 11–12
 revolutionary thought and, xv–xvi
 and Spanish New World arrival and colonization, 5–6, 9, 13
Cleveland, Grover, 557–61
 Cuba and, 560–1
 Hawaii and, 557–60, 563, 567
Clinton, Bill, xi–xii, 600
Clinton, George, 205, 207
Colombia, 580–4, 588–95
 Panamanian war against, 586, 590–5, 597
colonies, colonists, colonial period, American, xiii–xiv, 9–89, 352, 354, 360–1, 368, 480
 abuse of power in, 37–42
 and Age of Discovery, xvii, 13–14
 agriculture in, 14–15, 17–19, 21, 28–31, 33–6, 39–41, 43–4, 46–50, 53, 56, 59–60, 65, 72, 82–3
 boundaries of, 23–6, 25, 38
 and British arrival in New World, 6, 9–23, 27–32, 35–6
 character of, 42–6, 51, 610n
 commerce and, 15, 29, 33–4, 43, 45–50, 53–5, 58–61, 68, 71–81, 83, 106, 138
 finances of, 53–5, 59, 63, 66–9, 72, 84, 88
 Franklin and, 52–8, 60–1, 71–3
 and French and Indian War, 57–63, 67–9, 85, 94–5, 133, 136–8, 172, 265
 French relations with, 39, 56
 governments in, 21–3, 36–8, 41, 47–8, 51
 land in, 9–11, 13, 17–23, 28–45, 48, 51, 53–5, 58–60, 63–7, 75–8, 81–6, 94–5, 133, 136–8, 148, 186, 265, 610n
 and liberality of British monarchy, 26–7
 living standards in, 50–1
 native Americans and, 32, 34–6, 38–40, 44, 46, 56–69, 72, 76–8, 82, 85, 94–5, 133, 136–8, 222–3, 265
 Proclamation Line and, 64–8, 75–6, 137
 Quebec Act and, 82–3
 Revolutionary War and, 78, 85–9
 slavery in, 32–6, 39–40, 44, 46, 62, 83, 88
 Stamp Act and, 69–75, 79, 81–2
 Sugar Act and, 68–9, 75

Tea Act and, 79–81
uniting of, 52, 55–8, 61–2, 71, 74
Colorado, 480
    clarifying U.S. western boundaries and,
        344, 346
    Texas boundary dispute and, 439–40
Colorado River, 355, 447, 475, 499
    clarifying U.S. western boundaries and,
        339, 341–2
Columbia River, 484
    clarifying U.S. western boundaries and,
        326–31, 341–6, 392
    Oregon and, 392, 401–6, 408–13, 416–18,
        420, 427, 429–31
Columbus, Christopher, 5, 13, 36, 227
Comanches, 353, 357, 397, 492
    Houston's mission to, 365–6
"Come Out to the West," 401, 620n
commerce, xv, 26, 90–2, 187–9, 193,
        198–202, 214, 224–31, 239–41, 244,
        267–76, 301, 306–12, 340, 381–5, 413,
        426–7, 476–7, 500–1, 544–55, 558–63,
        569–71, 588
    and acquisition of Florida, 304, 333
    and Age of Discovery, 3–4
    Alaska and, 508–9, 513, 520–3, 522, 526,
        534, 538, 541–2
    anti-U.S. trade practices and, 182–4, 188,
        198, 201, 216–19, 226, 231, 233–4, 272,
        307–12, 318–20, 325, 329, 332, 519
    California and, 434–5, 459, 476, 511
    clarifying U.S. western boundaries and,
        327, 331
    in colonial period, 6–9, 11–20, 29, 33–4,
        43, 45–50, 53–5, 58–61, 68, 71–81, 83,
        106, 138
    Cuba and, 544, 561, 563, 577–8
    and Declaration of Independence, 91–2
    Georgia backland settlement and, 229–30
    of Great Britain, 12–20, 46–50, 55, 58–61,
        68, 73, 75–6, 83, 106, 123–4, 135, 144,
        255, 524
    Haiti and, 236–7, 256
    Hawaii and, 548–55, 558, 560, 562
    isthmian canal and, 493–4, 580, 586, 599
    Jay's Treaty and, 219–22, 233, 307
    land rushes and, 187, 200
    Louisiana and, 62, 113–14, 235, 240,
        246–8, 251, 253, 260–1, 263, 267–9,
        276, 278–9, 287, 296
    Mexico and, 351–2, 359
    New Orleans and, 236, 240–1, 255,
        267–75, 280, 284, 286, 289–90
    Oregon and, 400–5, 408–10, 427, 429, 431
    Panama and, 581–3
    Paris Treaty and, 159, 162, 165, 171, 177

Philippines and, 569–70, 576
Pinckney's Treaty and, 227–8
    post–Revolutionary War U.S.-Spanish
        relations and, 201–2, 210, 224–5,
        227–8
    public land sales and, 198–9
    railroads and, 483–6, 490, 501, 580
    Revolutionary War and, 90, 106, 114–15,
        117–19, 129, 138–9, 141–2, 144, 154,
        158
    Texas and, 381–4, 389–90, 392–3, 396,
        435
    U.S.-French relations and, 105, 233–5
    U.S. naval policy and, 559, 562
    and War of 1812, 311–12, 314, 318–20,
        325
Compromise of 1850, 481, 487, 489, 518
Congress, U.S., xii, 41, 215, 223, 228–30,
        315, 346–9, 364–5, 371, 380–1, 385,
        387–91, 410–14, 416, 420–31, 436,
        479–81, 506–7, 515–17, 561–3, 571–3
    Alaska and, 510–13, 516, 520, 526–41,
        622n
    anti-U.S. trade practices and, 307–8
    Cuba and, 545, 561, 566–7, 578, 597
    Dominican Republic and, 545–7
    Florida and, 303, 305, 344, 346
    Georgia backland settlement and, 229–30
    Hawaii and, 550, 553, 557–8, 563, 572–3
    isthmian canal and, 581, 585–90, 594–5
    Johnson's relations with, 517, 520–1, 526,
        528, 531, 536–9
    land ceded by states to, 292, 305, 472
    Louisiana and, 257, 264–5, 273, 282, 288,
        292–5, 298–300
    Mexican War and, 431, 442–4, 446–8, 461,
        471, 476–7, 480
    New Orleans crisis and, 271–3, 275
    Oregon and, 395, 405–6, 410, 412–13,
        420–2, 425–31
    Panamanian revolution and, 595, 597
    Paris Treaty and, 217, 219
    public land sales and, 305, 356, 365
    Puerto Rico and, 571–2
    railroads and, 483–6, 490–2, 500–4
    slavery and, 348–9, 461, 480
    Spanish-American War and, 567, 575
    Texas and, 365, 373, 379, 381, 386,
        387–90, 393–7, 399, 411–14, 423, 438,
        459, 480–1, 510
    U.S.-French relations and, 234, 252
    and U.S. invasion of Canada, 308–10
    Virgin Islands and, 535–6, 597
    and War of 1812, 312, 319
    see also Senate, U.S.
Congress of Vienna, 319

Connecticut, 20, 24, 82, 90, *190,* 302, 354
  New England frontier and, 203, 205
  western land claims of, 93–4, 96, 120
Connecticut River, 20, 38, 160
  New England frontier and, 203–4, 207
Constantine, Grand Duke, 509, 512–15
Constitution, U.S., 100, 207, 211, 213–15,
    221, 229, 232, 254, 271–2, 288–9,
    292–6, 308, 385, 422, 448, 485, 517–18,
    521, 535
  genius of, 214–15
  Louisiana Purchase and, 292–5, 298, 379
  slavery and, 197, 215, 414, 480, 517
  Texas and, 379, 395
Continental Army, U.S., 197, 210
  demobilization of, 182–3
  Revolutionary War and, 89–90, 101,
    111–12, 122, 124–5, 127–8, 130, 146,
    173, 205
Continental Congress, U.S., 91–2, 95–7,
    110–22, 182, 185, 187–91, 206–13, 257
  land ceded by states to, 120–2, 189–91,
    190, 202, 208–9, 212–13
  New England frontier and, 206–8
  Northwest Territory and, 195, 197–8
  Paris Treaty and, 159, 161–2, 164–5,
    170–1, 173–4, 176
  Revolutionary War and, 85–8, 95, 97,
    101–2, 104, 106, 110, 112, 114–15,
    117–18, 122, 124–7, 130–1, 134–5, 137,
    139–40, 142–3, 146, 148–50, 152, 155,
    157, 210
  states' western land claims and, 96–101,
    111–13, 115, 117–19
  U.S-Spanish relations and, 200–1
Continental Divide, 402, *421*
continentalism, 309, 325, 546
Convention of Aranjuez, 110, 247
Convention of 1800, 235, 247
Cook, James, 226, 326, 548
Corn Laws, 426–8, 431, 524
Cornwallis, Lord Charles, 127–8, 173
Corpus Christi, Tex., 397, 439
Cos, Martín Perfecto de, 368–9, 372
cotton, 315, 324, 348, 353, 378, 488, 504,
    518, 585
  Texas and, 356–7, 360, 382, 389
Creeks, 62, 184, 201, 212, 222–4, 229,
    304–5, 316–17, 321, 335, 364
Crimean War, 508–9, 511–14, 536–7
Crockett, Davy, 316, 371
Cromwell, William Nelson, 587–91
Crusades, 4–5
Cuba, 154, 227, 248, 293, 304, 334, 458, 495,
    560–9, 571–5, 577–80, 594, 601
  civil war in, 560–1, 563–8

Roosevelt Corollary and, 596–7
  Spanish-American War and, 565–9, 571–3
  U.S. interest in, 543–5
  U.S. occupation of, 577–8
Cumberland River, *149*
Cushing, Caleb, 490
Custer Died for Your Sins (DeLoria), 222

Dana, Richard Henry, 436, 445
Davis, Jefferson, 490, 496, 503
Declaration of Independence, 91–3, 99–100,
    119, 257, 463
Declaratory Act, 73–5
Decrès, Denis, 277, 279
Delaware, 20, 38, 97, 196, 208
Delaware Nation, 222–3
Deloria, Vine, Jr., 222
democracy, 87, 92, 100, 105, 179, 215, 252,
    301, 322, 324, 334, 344, 349, 370,
    376–7, 432, 469, 482, 497–8, 540, 547,
    563, 573–4, 576
  and character of American colonists, 43–4
  and federalization of western lands,
    189–91
  France and, 232–3
  Hawaii and, 551–2, 558, 573
  Louisiana Purchase and, 289, 296, 299
  Mexican War and, 445–6
  Mexico and, 351–2, 359, 366, 465
  Revolutionary War and, 107, 109, 123,
    126, 142
  and U.S. invasion of Canada, 310–11
Democratic Party, Democrats, 385, 389–95,
    410–15, 432, 436, 461, 486–7, 502, 516,
    545, 562–3, 585, 600
  Hawaii and, 557, 563
  Mexican War and, 447, 476
  Oregon and, 392, 410–13, 415, 419–20
  railroads and, 483, 487, 489, 491–2
  Texas and, 380, 389–91, 393, 395
Denmark, 519, 527, 535, 545, 597–8
Detroit, Mich., 62, 78, 113, 223, 313
De Voto, Bernard, 449–50
Dewey, George, 565, 568–9, 572
Díaz, Porfirio, 547
Dickinson, John, 74, 99
Discourse on Western Planting (Hakluyt),
    14–15
Dodge, Augustus, 501–2
Dole, Sanford Ballard, 555–6, 558, 563, 573
Dominican Republic, 520, 544–6, 597
Donation Land Claim Act, 431
Douglas, Stephen A., 486–7, 501–4
Drake, Francis, 13–14, 326, 329
Du Pont de Nemours, Pierre S., 259–60,
    271

East India Company, 49, 76, 79–80

Edwards, Jonathan, 45

Egremont, Charles Wyndham, Earl of, 64

Egypt, 239–40, 271, 275–6
   Napoleon's expedition to, 240, 244–6, 250, 276, 279

Elizabeth I, Queen of Great Britain, 13–19, 326

El Paso, Tex., 424, 440, 464, 474–5, 487, 491–2, 499

Era of Good Feelings, 325, 349

"Essay on the Advantages to Be Derived from Colonies Under Present Conditions" (Talleyrand), 239

Everett, Edward, 409–13, 416–18, 420, 427–30

expansionism, U.S., 183–9, 292, 310–12, 315, 325, 345, 390–3, 407–8, 430–2, 436, 461, 482, 484, 489, 495, 518, 547–8, 559, 562–3, 598
   Alaska and, 534, 543
   in American Century, 600–1
   Canadian home rule and, 523–5
   Cuba and, 563, 577
   Hawaii and, 551, 555, 557
   land hunger in, xvii–xviii, 154, 230
   land rushes and, 184–9, 199–200, 230–1
   Louisiana and, 240–1, 248, 255, 260, 264, 280, 289, 295–6, 379
   Mexican War and, 442–4, 447, 468, 476
   Oregon and, 392, 403, 408, 410–13, 415, 420–2, 426, 428, 430–1, 468
   Paris Treaty and, 177, 183–4
   racism and, 305–6
   Revolutionary War and, 118, 153–4
   Texas and, 379–81, 385, 390, 392–3, 395, 510
   and U.S. invasion of Canada, 310, 312
   and War of 1812, 311–12
   see also manifest destiny

Fallen Timbers, Battle of, 223, 228

Family Compact, 105, 108

farms, farmers, *see* agriculture

Farnham, T. J., 445

federalism, 187, 525
   Constitution and, 214–15
   Louisiana Purchase and, 293–4, 296
   Mexico and, 352, 360

Federalist Party, Federalists, 254, 310
   Louisiana Purchase and, 289–90
   New Orleans crisis and, 271–2
   U.S.-French relations and, 233–4

Federal Land Act of 1785, 193–4, 197, 222

Ferdinand VII, King of Spain, 334, 338, 340, 344, 346–9, 363

feudalism, xv–xvii, 26–8, 67, 100, 245, 301, 351, 433, 509, 558, 581, 599
   colonial period and, 6, 9, 17–18, 28, 30, 37

Fillmore, Millard, 489, 491–2, 494

Fitzherbert, Alleyne, 141, 154, 174

Fletcher v. Peck, 230

Florida, Floridas, 61, 72, 183, 229, 252, 255, 317, 399, 448, 486, 519, 574
   Louisiana and, 248, 260–2, 265, 286, 290–2, 303
   New Orleans crisis and, 272, 274
   Paris Treaty and, 159, 160*n*, 163, 177
   post–Revolutionary War U.S.-Spanish relations and, 224–5
   Proclamation Line and, 64–5
   Revolutionary War and, 85, 105, 107–9, 114–15, 142, 148, *149,* 151, 154
   slavery and, 304–5, 333–4, 336, 345, 349
   statehood gained by, 460–1
   U.S. acquisition of, 260–1, 265–6, 272–3, 280–4, 292–3, 303–6, 314, 333–48, 354, 544
   and War of 1812, 314, 323

Floridablanca, Conde de, 148, 225
   Revolutionary War and, 107–10, 117, 119, 140, 156

Fort Brown, 441–2, 449–50

Fort Dummer, 203

Fort Duquesne (Fort Pitt), 57, 62

Fort Erie, 321

Fort George, 328, 330, 346, 405

Fort Jackson, Treaty of, 317, 321, 333, 335

Fort McHenry, 321

Fort McIntosh, Treaty of, 222

Fort St. Joseph, 148

Fort Ticonderoga, 86, 119, 205–6

Fort Vancouver, 405–6, 408

Fox, Charles James, 129, 131, 136, 138–41, 146

France, French, 26, 121–41, 203, 224–9, 231–95, 322–3, 379, 406, 435, 539, 559
   and Age of Discovery, xvii, 7–8
   anti-U.S. trade practices and, 231, 233–4, 308, 312
   British relations with, 9–11, 14, 49–50, 56, 101–6, 109, 122–4, 131, 138–40, 150, 154–7, 162–3, 166, 174–7, 216–19, 226, 233, 236, 238, 241, 244, 246–7, 250–1, 255–6, 259, 261, 270–1, 275–80, 282, 285, 288, 290–2, 307–9, 318, 322, 330
   clarifying U.S. western boundaries and, 338, 344
   in colonial period, 7–12, 14–15, 22, 28, 31, 34, 39, 47, 49, 53, 56–7, 61–2, 64, 66–7, 76–7, 82–3
   Cuba and, 544–5

France, French *(continued)*
  Franklin and, 53, 56, 102–4, 106, 115, 117,
    125, 130–6, 174–6, 179, 218
  Gibraltar defeat of, 162–3
  Haiti and, 236–7, 246–7, 250–1, 255–6,
    258–9, 261–3, 265, 270, 274–80, 290
  Hawaii and, 520, 549–50
  Jay's Treaty and, 233–4
  Jefferson's mission to, 195, 253, 259
  Livingston's mission to, 258–61, 263–6,
    268, 271–4, 291–2, 295, 300
  Louisiana and, 10–12, 61–2, 94, 227, 236,
    239–42, 246–53, 255–94, *283,* 300, 303,
    344, 347
  Napoleon's coup d'état in, 242, 245
  Napoleon's Egyptian expedition and,
    244–5, 250
  New Orleans crisis and, 267–72, 274, 284,
    286
  Panama Canal and, 583–7, 589, 591, 595–6
  Paris Treaty and, 159, 162–8, 170–7, 180
  Revolutionary War and, 85–6, 101–6,
    108–10, 112–15, 122–41, 144–7, *149,*
    150–7, 174–5, 177, 232–3, 279, 286
  Russian relations with, 508–9, 514–15
  Spanish relations with, 7–8, 10–11, 105–6,
    108–10, 114, 125, 128, 131, 150, 156–7,
    162–3, 166, 176, 224–8, 233, 237–41,
    246–51, 280, 291–2
  Texas and, 354, 382–3, 396–7
  U.S. relations with, 85, 101–6, 108–10,
    115–16, 121–3, 125, 129, 131–6, 140–1,
    144, 146–7, 151–7, 159, 163, 165–6,
    168, 174–7, 217, 232–5, 247, 250–3,
    257–66, 268–9, 271–8, 280, 285–6, 290,
    295, 308, 310, 312, 514
Franklin, Benjamin, 46, 52–8, 71–8, 83–4,
  98–9, 201, 432, 601
  colonial commerce and, 53–5, 58, 60–1, 73
  and colonists' relations with native
    Americans, 77–8
  France and, 53, 56, 102–4, 106, 115, 117,
    125, 130–6, 174–6, 179, 218
  and French and Indian War, 60–1
  Hutchinson affair and, 80–1, 175
  Illinois Company and, 76–8, 81, 610n–11n
  illnesses of, 153, 155, 166–7
  intercolonial union advocated by, 52, 55–8,
    61–2
  Jay's relationship with, 151–2, 157, 169,
    180
  last will and testament of, 179–80
  Paris Treaty and, 159–62, 164–72, 174–8,
    180, 261
  population studies of, 54–5, 60
  public service of, 52–5

  reprimand of, 81, 103, 147, 172, 175
  Revolutionary War and, 102–4, 106, 115,
    117, 125–7, 130–9, 141–8, 151–5, 157
  Shelburne's relationship with, 75–8, 83,
    130–2, 138, 141, 178
  Stamp Act and, 71–4
Franklin, William, 77–8, 164
Freamer, James, 473
Frémont, Jessie Benton, 436, 452
Frémont, John Charles, 435–7, 478, 498
  Mexican War and, 437, 446, 452–4, 457
French and Indian War, 57–63, 67–9, 85,
  94–5, 118–19, 172
  land and territorial issues in, 58–60, 63,
    94–5, 133, 136–8, 265
  and Treaty of 1763, 67, 115, 118, 136–8,
    143, 183, 255, 265
French Revolution, 214, 232–3, 237–8, 242,
  245–6
Freneau, Philip, 84–5
Frontier in American History, The (Turner),
  610n
Frost, Robert, xiii–xiv, 609n
Fugitive Slave Law, 481
Fulton, Robert, 300

Gadsden, James, 485–90, 496–503
  Mexican mission of, 489–90, 496–501, 503
  railroads and, 485–7, 489–90, 496–502
Gadsden Purchase, *472,* 499–504, 523
Gage, Thomas, 82, 173
Gaines, Edmund, 334–5
Gallatin, Albert, 252, 293, 319, 404–5
Gálvez, Bernard de, 113–15, 118
García Condé, Pedro, 491–2
Gardoqui, Don Diego de, 200–2, 210, 218,
  273
Gates, Horatio, 210, 257
Genet, Edmond "Citizen," 233, 254
George III, King of Great Britain, 64–8, 78,
  91, 102–4, 218–20, 225, 307
  Paris Treaty and, 158, 172, 178
  Proclamation Line and, 65–8, 137
  Quebec Act and, 82–3
  Revolutionary War and, 86, 88–9, 103–4,
    106, 108, 123, 128–31, 134, 137, 141,
    147, 158, 370
  Stamp Act and, 70–1
  and War of 1812, 320, 322
Georgia, 10, 23, 65, 71, 122, 160n, 184, 201,
  208, 213, 224, 356, 383, 557, 600
  and acquisition of Florida, 304–5, 333–4
  backland settlement of, 228–30, 302, 305
  native Americans and, 62, 229, 316–17,
    333–4
  Revolutionary War and, 93–4, 148

Gérard de Rayneval, Conrad-Alexandre, 109
Gérard de Rayneval, Joseph-Mathias, 150–1, 156–7, 163, 167, 171, 175
Germany, Germans, 16–17, 32, 50, 90, 245–6, 354, 514, 571, 586
 Seven Years' War and, 58, 63
 Virgin Islands and, 597–8
Gettysburg, Battle of, 409, 505
Ghent, Treaty of, 318–22, 328, 330, 332–3, 335
Gibraltar, 241, 544
 British victory at, 162–3, 168
 Revolutionary War and, 108–10, 128, 154, 156
Giddings, Joshua R., 444, 500
"Gift Outright, The" (Frost), xiii–xiv, 609*n*
Gila River, 467, 475, 491, 499
Gilbert, Humphrey, 13
Gillespie, Archibald H., 446, 452, 454–7
Godoy, Manuel de, 225–8
 and French reacquisition of Louisiana, 240–1, 248–9, 265–7
Goliad, Battle of, 372–3, 375, 458
Gorchakov, Prince Alexander, 509, 512–16, 537
Grant, Ulysses S., 477, 543, 545–6, 583
Grasse, Comte de, 127–8, 139, 163
Gray, A. B., 491
Gray, Robert, 326–8
Great Britain, British, xiii, 46–61, 181–9, 197, 209, 270–3, 302–5, 354, 361, 368, 424–33, 477–8, 482, 518, 521–6, 544–50, 560–2, 565, 571, 585–6, 598
 Alaska and, 509, 511–12, 521, 524–6, 534, 538, 540
 anti-U.S. trade practices of, 182–3, 188, 201, 216–18, 226, 231, 233, 272, 307–12, 318–20, 325, 329, 332
 and Battle of New Orleans, 322–4, 332–3, 411, 420
 California and, 435–7, 446, 451, 453–4
 Canadian home rule and, 523–5
 clarifying U.S. western boundaries and, 325–32, 339–47, 391–2, 403
 commerce of, 12–20, 46–50, 55, 58–61, 68, 73, 75–6, 83, 106, 123–4, 135, 144, 255, 524
 Cuba and, 544–5
 and Declaration of Independence, 91–3, 100
 emigration encouraged by, 31–2, 50
 Franklin and, 52–8, 60–1, 71–5, 77–8, 80–1, 103, 147, 172, 175
 French relations with, 9–11, 14, 26–8, 49–50, 56, 101–6, 109, 122–4, 131, 138–40, 150, 154–7, 162–3, 166, 174–7,
216–19, 226, 233, 236, 238, 241, 244, 246–7, 250–1, 255–6, 259, 261, 270–1, 275–80, 282, 285, 288, 290–2, 307–9, 318, 322, 330
 Gibraltar victory of, 162–3, 168
 Hawaii and, 520, 549–50, 560
 isthmian canal and, 493–5, 498–9
 Jay's Treaty and, 219–22, 224, 226, 228, 233, 307
 land distribution in, 28, 40
 land rushes and, 187, 200
 liberality of monarchy of, 26–7
 Louisiana and, 236, 241, 247–9, 251, 255, 259, 261, 264, 271, 275–82, 285, 288, 291, 303, 347
 Loyalists of, 79–81, 88, 93, 122, 132–4, 136–7, 139, 144, 152–3, 155, 160*n*, 162, 164–7, 169–75, 183, 185, 187, 204, 217, 219, 318
 Massachusetts occupied by, 81–2
 Mexican relations with, 418, 422, 424, 426, 435, 437, 442, 451, 458, 467, 493–4, 498–9
 Mexican War and, 431, 442, 447, 453–4, 458, 465, 473
 Napoleon's Egyptian expedition and, 244, 250
 native Americans and, 14–15, 19, 31, 35–6, 56, 222–3, 302–3, 305, 308–10, 321, 337
 New England frontier and, 202–7
 Oregon and, 391–2, 401–13, 415–22, 425–31, 433, 435–7, 442, 459, 477, 508
 Panama and, 581–3, 585
 Paris Treaty and, 158–79, 182–3, 216–18, 220–1, 257, 261, 303, 329
 Proclamation Line and, 64–7, 76, 136–7, 143, 148, *149*, 186
 Quebec Act and, 82–3, 85–7
 Revolutionary War and, 52, 85–90, 92–8, 101–14, 117–20, 122–5, 126*n*, 127–8, 129–58, *149*, 173, 181, 202, 204–6, 212, 223, 256, 261, 315, 318, 370, 420
 Russian relations with, 508–12, 514–15
 Spanish relations with, 13–16, 18, 105–8, 110, 122, 131, 139, 154, 156, 162–3, 177, 184, 224–8, 235–6, 240–1, 248, 271, 292, 330, 339–40, 344–5, 349
 Texas and, 379–90, 392–3, 396–7, 424, 435, 437
 and U.S. acquisition of Florida, 304, 340, 345
 and U.S. invasion of Canada, 308–13
 and War of 1812, 311–14, 317–24, 332–3, 420
 see also colonies, colonists, colonial period, American

Great Lakes, 24, 66, 87, 120, 183, 198, 218, 255, 332, 420, 448, 518
  and French and Indian War, 58, 60
  and French New World arrival and colonization, 8, 10–11
  native Americans and, 62, 302, 321
  Paris Treaty and, 158–61, 168–9, 171
  railroads and, 484, 501
  Revolutionary War and, 109, 137, 142–3, 150, 155–6
  and U.S. invasion of Canada, 309, 311, 314
  and War of 1812, 314, 321–2
Greeley, Horace, 398, 518, 531, 534–6, 619*n*
Greenville, Treaty of, 223
Grenville, George, 66, 68–9, 138, 219
Grenville, Thomas, 138–41, 146
Grenville, Treaty of, 321
Grenville, William Wyndham, 219–21
Groce, James, 360–1
Guadalupe Hidalgo, Treaty of, *472,* 476, 478, 480
  disputes arising from, 491–3, 496–500
Guadeloupe, 60–1, 139, 236
Guam, 570, 575
Guantánamo Bay, 580, 592
Gulf of California, 475, 495, 499, 503
Gulf of Mexico, 8, 10, 229, 235, 240, 265–6, 277, 430, 467, 487, 499, *582*
  and acquisition of Florida, 304–5, 333
  and Battle of New Orleans, 323, 420
  and clarifying U.S. western boundaries, 339, 341–2, 353, 358
  and Louisiana, 248, 260, 266, 268, 299
  and Mexican War, 441–2, 446, 459–62, 473
  and Paris Treaty, 159, 160*n*, 177
  and postwar U.S.-Spanish relations, 224, 226
  and Revolutionary War, 107, 114–15, 118, 125, 128, 150, 156–7
  and Texas, 355, 359, 368–9, 372, 388, 438
Gwin, William M., 511–13, 527

Hacker, Louis M., 311
Haiti, 240, 544, 597
  France and, 236–7, 246–7, 250–1, 255–6, 258–9, 261–3, 265, 270, 274–80, 290
Hakluyt, Richard, 13–15
Haldimand, Sir Frederick, 183
Hamilton, Alexander, 84–5, 200, 218, 230, 254
  New England frontier and, 207–8
  New Orleans crisis and, 271–2, 289–90
Hammond, James H., 496
Hanna, Marcus A., 562, 564, 587–9, 595
Hargous brothers, 493–5, 499

Harrisburg, Tex., 374
Harrison, Benjamin, 555, 557, 559
Harrison, William Henry, 302–3, 314, 385
Harsha, D. A., 533
Havana, 114, 265, 337, 464
  and sinking of *Maine,* 565–7, 579
Hawaiian Islands, 208, 435, 495, 520, *522,* 548–60, 562–4, 571–4
  insurgency in, 556–8, 573
  military value of, 550, 553–5, 558–9, 573
  monarchy of, 550–2, 554–8, 573
  racial friction in, 551, 554, 558
  as republic, 552, 556, 558
  statehood gained by, 549, 573
  U.S. annexation of, 549–50, 553–5, 557–60, 563–4, 567, 572–4, 580, 585–6
  as U.S. protectorate, 549, 557
Hawkesbury, Robert Jenkinton, Lord, 255
Hay, John, 536, 568, 586, 589–92
Hay-Herrán Treaty, 589–90, 592
headright grants, 30–1, 33, 38–9
Hearst, William Randolph, 561, 594
Henderson, Richard, 98
Henry, Patrick, 70, 100–1, 112, 114
Henry VIII, King of Great Britain, 14, 17
Herrán, Tomás, 589
Herrera, José Joaquín de, 423–5, 439–40, 471
Higby, William, 538–9
Hobbes, Thomas, 27, 37
Homestead Laws, 516, 546
Horseshoe Bend, Battle at, 316–17, 364
House of Burgesses, Va., 21, 37, 39, 70
House of Representatives, U.S., *see* Congress, U.S.
Houston, Samuel, 363–6, 476
  and Texan annexation and statehood, 365, 378, 381, 385–8, 396–7, 399, 619*n*
  Texan presidency of, 377, 381–7, 390
  and Texan secession from Mexico, 365–6, 368–77, 382, 442
Hudson River, Hudson River Valley, 39, 50, 90, 103, 203, 257, 300–1, 318, 402
Hudson's Bay Company (the Bay), 49, 327–8, 508
  Canadian home rule and, 524–5
  Oregon and, 405–6, 408, 410, 413, 418, 427, 430–1
Huguenots, 32, 50, 63, 116, 151
Hull, William, 309–10, 312–13
Hutchinson, Thomas, 79–81, 175

Illinois, 11, 66, 167, 302, 348, 486–7
  railroads and, 501, 504
  Revolutionary War and, 112–14, 148

Illinois Company, 76–8, 81, 98, 610*n*–11*n*
indentured servants, 93, 249
    colonial land distribution and, 30–3, 40
    Hawaii and, 551, 553
Indiana, 66, 148, 198, 302, 348, 486, 576
*Influence of Sea Power upon History,
    1660–1783, The* (Mahan), 559
Intercourse Act of 1790, 223
Interest of Great Britain Considered, The
    (Franklin), 60–1
Iowa, 400, 487, 501, 504
Ireland, Irish, 32, 38, 49–50, 63, 75, 426, 437,
    506, 518
Iroquois, 56–7, 62, 93–4, 119, 222
"Is It Advantageous to France to Take
    Possession of Louisiana?" (Livingston),
    263–4
Italy, 26, 234, 247, 249, 514
    Napoleon's campaigns in, 239, 241, 243,
        245
    Seven Years' War and, 58, 63

Jackson, Andrew, 214, 358, 385, 388–9, 435,
    464, 486, 496, 516, 543–4
    and acquisition of Florida, 333, 335–7,
        339–48
    and Battle of New Orleans, 322–4, 332–4,
        376
    Houston's relationship with, 364–6, 372–3,
        376–7, 381
    native Americans and, 315–17, 334–7,
        340, 347, 364, 400
    Polk's relationship with, 391, 415, 417,
        433, 478
    Texas and, 365–6, 372, 377, 379–81, 388,
        391
    and War of 1812, 317, 322–4, 364
Jamaica, 20, 50, 108, 132, 139, 147, 163
James I, King of Great Britain, 19, 35
Japan, Japanese, 507, 570, 586, 598, 602
    Alaska and, 511, 521, *522*, 541
    Hawaii and, 551, 553, 563
    Philippines and, 576–7
Jay, John, 253, 257–8, 277
    anti-U.S. trade practices and, 218–19
    Franklin's relationship with, 151–2, 157,
        169, 180
    Gardoqui and, 200–2, 210, 218, 273
    Paris Treaty and, 158–61, 163–71, 176,
        178–80, 200, 218–19, 221
    Revolutionary War and, 115–17, 125–7,
        131, 135–6, 140–2, 145–53, 155–8
    Spanish mission of, 115–17, 125, 131,
        135–6, 140, 200, 226
Jay's Treaty, 216, 218–24, 226, 228, 233–4,
    307

Jefferson, Thomas, 33, 48, 97, 100–1, 165*n*,
    180, 200, 211, 231, 251–61, 270–4,
    291–301, 316–17, 319, 349, 432, 580,
    601
    agrarianism of, 253–4, 306, 324–5,
        390–1
    anti-U.S. trade practices and, 307–10
    and character of American colonists,
        43–4, 610*n*
    and claims to Texas, 353–4
    clarifying U.S. western boundaries and,
        339, 378, 392
    and Declaration of Independence, 91–2
    and federalization of western lands,
        189–92, 194–7
    and French interest in Haiti, 255–6, 258
    French mission of, 195, 253, 259
    Louisiana and, 252–3, 255–61, 264–6,
        268, 272–4, 284, 287, 289, 291–300,
        303, 339, 347, 543
    on Mississippi region, 253–5
    on native Americans, 296–7, 316
    New Orleans crisis and, 268, 270–3
    Northwest Territory and, 197–8
    public land sales and, 192–3, 254, 256–7
    Revolutionary War and, 112, 114, 125–6,
        131
    Trist and, 463–4
    and U.S. invasion of Canada, 308–9
Johnson, Andrew, 506–7, 516–21
    Alaska and, 516, 520, 525–8, 531–2,
        536–9
    congressional relations of, 517, 520–1,
        526, 528, 531, 536–9
    Seward's relationship with, 517–19, 526,
        539
Johnson, Lyndon, 599
Johnson, Paul, 279
Johnson, Richard M., 309
Johnson, William, 38, 78
joint-stock companies, 19
Jones, Joseph, 121

Kalakaua, David, King of Hawaii, 550–2,
    554, 556
Kansas, 346, 480, 502, 504, 529, 533
Kansas-Nebraska Act, 500, 502–4, 518
Kearny, Stephen W., 449, 455–7
Kennedy, John F., xiii, 609*n*
Kentucky, 85, 98, 112, 207, 209–12, 230,
    254, 272, 302, 314*n*, 319, 324, 355–6,
    390
    and federalization of western lands,
        191–3
    New Orleans crisis and, 267–8
    separation of Virginia and, 209–11

King, Rufus, 252, 255
Kipling, Rudyard, 576

Lafitte, Jean, 323
Lake Champlain, 183, 217
    New England frontier and, 203, 205
    and War of 1812, 318, 321
Lake Nipissing, 137, 160–1, 168
Lake of the Woods, 169, 303, 329–31, 403
La Luzerne, Anne-César, Chevalier de, 125,
    162, 171
Lamar, Mirabeau Buonaparte, 383–4, 387
land, land ownership, xiv–xvii, 27–45, 73,
    90–101, 104–25, 201–14, 273, 458–62,
    545–8
    and acquisition of Florida, 304–5, 333,
        347–8
    and Age of Discovery, xvi–xvii, 3–4
    Alaska and, 507, 520–3, 528–30, 532,
        540, 543
    California and, 342, 433, 437, 440, 453,
        458, 479
    clarifying U.S. western boundaries
        and, 325–33, 337–47, *343*, 349, 351,
        353–4, 358, 378, 391–2, 402–9,
        417–18, 428
    in colonial period, xiv, xvi–xvii, 5–6, 9–11,
        13, 17–23, 28–45, 48, 51, 53–5, 58–60,
        63–7, 75–8, 81–6, 94–5, 133, 136–8,
        148, 186, 265, 610n
    Cuba and, 561, 563, 566–7, 569, 578
    and Declaration of Independence, 91–3
    federalization of, 189–97, *190*, 230, 254
    Gadsden and, 496–504, 523
    Georgia backland settlement and, 228–30
    Guadalupe treaty disputes and, 491–3,
        496–9
    Hawaii and, 549, 551–2, 554–6, 558, 563,
        573
    isthmian canal and, 493–6
    Jay's Treaty and, 219–21, 233
    Louisiana and, 240, 256–7, *283*, 284–5,
        288–97, 299, 303, 306
    Mexican War and, 438, 444–5, 447,
        458, 460–2, 465–9, 471, *472*, 473–81,
        487
    Mexico and, 351, 353
    native Americans and, 32, 34–6, 40, 62,
        93–4, 99–100, 119–21, 185–6, 189, 193,
        198, 209–10, 212–14, 222–4, 302–3,
        305, 308–10, 315–17, 326, 328, 333,
        337, 400, 492, 496–9, 501
    New England frontier and, 202–9
    North Carolina backland settlement and,
        208, 211–14, 229
    of older families, 301–2

    in Old World, xiv–xvi, 32
    Oregon and, 392, 400–6, 408–12, 415–17,
        422, 426, 428–31
    Panama Canal and, 589, 594–5
    Paris Treaty and, 158–65, 167–9, 171–5,
        177, 179–80, 183–4, 196, 201, 207, 212,
        217–21, 226, 240, 253, 261, 292, 303,
        329
    and postwar dispensation for Loyalists,
        160n, 162, 164–7, 169–74, 217, 219
    public sales of, 188–9, 192–4, 198–9, 202,
        208–9, 211–13, 229, 254, 256–7, 302,
        305, 348, 356, 365, 377, 379, 381, 486,
        518, 521, 540
    Quebec Act and, 82–3, 85–6, 137, 142,
        148, 155, 164
    railroads and, 483–90, 500–2
    Revolutionary War and, 85–6, 88, 90–9,
        104–15, 117–25, 128–9, 132–40, 142–4,
        146, 148–58, *149*, 173, 187–8, *190*, 191,
        212–13, 370, 612n
    Spanish-American War and, 567, 569–70
    Talleyrand on, 238–9
    and territory ceded to Congress, 120–2,
        189–91, *190*, 202, 208–9, 212–13, 292,
        305, *472*
    Texas and, 353–8, 365–7, 370, 378–82,
        386, 389, 392–5, 397, 422–5, 438–41,
        467, 480–1, 491–2, 499
    U.S.-French relations and, 105, 109–10,
        115, 235
    and U.S. invasion of Canada, 309, 311,
        313, 319
    Virginia backland settlement and, 208–9,
        211
    and War of 1812, 311, 313, 315, 319–20,
        322, 324, 326, 328, 335, 353
    and western claims of states, 93–101,
        111–13, 119–21, 137, 142–3, 148, 161,
        185
    see also agriculture; expansionism, U.S.
Land Ordinance of 1784, 191, 194–7, 212
Lansdowne, Marquis of, *see* Shelburne,
    William Petty Fitzmaurice, Earl of
Larkin, Thomas O., 434, 437, 446, 453
La Salle, Robert Cavelier, Sieur de, 10, 299,
    338
Laurens, Henry, 126, 131, 165n, 173
Leclerc, Charles, 250–1, 274
    and French attempted acquisition of Haiti,
        250, 255, 258, 262–3, 265
Lee, Richard Henry, 100–1, 187
Lee, Robert E., 475
Lesseps, Ferdinand de, 583–6
Letters from a Pennsylvania Farmer (Dickinson), 74

Lewis, Meriwether, 254, 271, 301, 327–9, 435
Liliuokalani, Queen of Hawaii, 554–8
Lincoln, Abraham, 399, 505–7, 514, 516–18, 536, 546, 589–90
Livingston, Robert R., 257–61, 277
  French mission of, 258–61, 263–6, 268, 271–4, 291–2, 295, 300
  Louisiana and, 258–61, 263–6, 268, 273–5, 281–8, 291–2, 295, 300
  New Orleans crisis and, 271–2, 274
  Paris Treaty and, 162, 168, 170, 176, 257
  Revolutionary War and, 157, 257
Lodge, Henry Cabot, 562, 564, 574, 594, 600
Long, John, 564–5
Los Angeles, Calif., 454–7
Louis XIV, King of France, 10, 12, 47, 102, 116
Louis XVI, King of France, 233, 235, 238
  and Paris Treaty, 175–7
  and Revolutionary War, 102–3, 105–6, 125–6, 130, 138, 140, 156
Louisiana, 184, 210–11, 233, 235–7, 254–86, 305, 318, 461–3, 543, 586
  clarifying U.S. western boundaries and, 328–9, 338–9, 342–4
  France and, 10–12, 61–2, 94, 227, 236, 239–42, 246–53, 255–71, 274–5, 277–8, 281, 291, 299
  Mexican War and, 461–2
  Napoleon and, 240–1, 246–50, 253, 255–65, 268–71, 273–86, 288–92, 294–5, 298, 300
  Pinckney's Treaty and, 228, 240
  postwar U.S.-Spanish relations and, 224–5, 228
  slavery and, 289, 293, 298, 348–9
  Spain and, 61–2, 94, 113–14, 235–6, 240–2, 246–9, 251–3, 255, 258–63, 265–71, 276, 281, 290–2, 295, 299, 303, 344, 347
  Texas and, 299, 303, 354, 356, 370, 373, 388
Louisiana Purchase, 264–8, 272–301, 311, 346–7, 400
  clarifying U.S. western boundaries and, 329, 331, 338–9, 341, 344, 346, 351, 354, 392
  Congress and, 257, 264–5, 273, 282, 288, 292–5, 298–300
  Constitution and, 292–5, 298, 379
  domestic U.S. reactions to, 289–90, 295, 298
  France and, 272–94, 283, 300, 303, 344, 347
  Great Britain and, 275–82, 285, 288, 291, 303, 347

Jefferson and, 252–3, 255–61, 264–6, 268, 272–4, 284, 287, 289, 291–300, 303, 339, 347, 543
  and land and territorial issues, 240, 256–7, 283, 284–5, 288–97, 299, 303, 306
Lusitania, sinking of, 598
Luther, Martin, xv–xvi

Mackenzie, Alexander, 303, 327, 329
Madison, James, 33, 126, 206, 215, 221, 305, 317–19, 324–5, 349, 464
  anti-U.S. trade practices and, 218, 308
  Louisiana and, 256, 260, 266, 273–5, 278, 281–4, 286–7, 289–92, 295, 300
  New Orleans crisis and, 270, 273
  and War of 1812, 312, 317–18
Mahan, Alfred Thayer, 559–62, 564, 584
Maine, 55, 86, 185, 198, 239, 348–9, 385
  boundaries of, 407–8
  Paris Treaty and, 160, 164, 180
  Revolutionary War and, 124–5, 137
  and War of 1812, 318, 320–2
Maine, U.S.S., sinking of, 565–7, 579
Malta, 244, 250, 271, 544
manifest destiny, xii–xiii, xvii, 398, 444, 518, 523, 547, 600, 620*n*
  Alaska and, 511, 513
  Oregon and, 401–2, 428
Manila, 564, 569–70
Manila Bay, Battle of, 568, 572
manufacturing, 118, 144, 169, 218, 224, 231, 393–4, 476, 546–7, 571
  anti-U.S. trade practices and, 182–3, 325
  British mercantilism and, 46–8, 55, 58–61
  and French and Indian War, 59–61
  railroads and, 485, 580
  Stamp Act and, 70–2
Marcy, William L., 489–90, 496, 511
  Mexican War and, 449–51, 473
  railroads and, 496, 498
Maria Luisa, Queen of Spain, 225, 241–2, 247, 262
Mary I, Queen of Great Britain, 14
Maryland, 20, 23–4, 29, 38, 121–2, 210, 217
  Revolutionary War and, 97, 111
  western land claims and, 97–101, 111, 119
Mason, Richard, 479
Massachusetts, 23, 35, 42, 57, 69, 71, 79–82, 96, 160, 175, 182, 190, 195, 198, 209, 289, 293, 302, 311, 318, 342, 349, 355, 409, 512, 529, 533, 538, 562
  British occupation of, 81–2
  Hutchinson affair and, 79–80
  New England frontier and, 202–3, 205–6
  Revolutionary War and, 90, 93–4, 137, 362–3

Matamoros, 425, 442, 450
Mather, Cotton, 35
Maury, Matthew, 419–20
McCulloh, Henry, 38
McGillivray, Alexander, 222–3
McKinley, William, 562–9, 571–8, 595, 600
    Cuba and, 563–4, 566–7, 577–8
    Hawaii and, 563, 572–3, 585–6
    isthmian canal and, 585–7
    Philippines and, 569, 573–7
McKinley tariff, 552–3
McLane, Louis, 417–18, 427–31
Memphis, Tenn., 184, 485–6, 489, 501
mercantilism, *see* commerce
Mermentau River, 338–9
Mesilla Valley, 491–2, 496, 499, 501, 504
metes and bounds system, 42
Mexican War, xi–xii, 431, 437–81, 487,
        489–91, 544, 600, 620*n*
    California and, 433, 437–8, 445–6, 451–7,
        460, 464, 467–8, 471, 475–8
    casualties in, 442, 450–1, 456–8, 462–3,
        469, 476
    inland combat in, 460–3, 465–6, 468–71
    New Mexico and, 447–9, 455–6, 460, 464,
        467–8, 471, 475, 477–8, 480
    in northern Mexico, 441–3, 449–51,
        457–60, 462
    peace negotiations in, 458, 463–8, 470–7,
        472
    public opinion on, 442–3, 468–9
    slavery in territory acquired in, 460–2,
        467–8, 471, 476, 479–81
    start of, 442–3
    Texas and, 438–43, 457, 461–2, 464,
        466–8, 470, 472, 473–5, 480
    U.S. motives and provocations in, 438–47
Mexico, 113, 155, 201, 211, 224–6, 246, 262,
        349, 351–63, 401, 403, 418–19, 422–6,
        432–83, 567, 574
    anti-immigration laws of, 361, 365, 367
    British relations with, 418, 422, 424, 426,
        435, 437, 442, 451, 458, 467, 493–4,
        498–9
    California and, 415, 433–8, 446, 451–3,
        479, 482
    cession of, xii, 472, 475–7, 480–1
    clarifying U.S. western boundaries and,
        339, 342, 358, 408
    economic evolution of, 547–8
    Gadsden and, 489–90, 496–501, 503,
        523
    Guadalupe treaty disputes and, 491–3,
        496–8
    independence gained by, 351–2, 355,
        359–60, 362, 433, 440

isthmian canal and, 464, 467, 483, 493–6,
        498–500, 503
    Oregon Country and, 409, 418
    proposed U.S. annexation of, 468–9, 510
    railroads and, 486–7, 489–90, 495–9, 501
    Spain and, 4–7, 224–5, 236, 351–5, 359,
        363
    Texas and, 354–63, 365–79, 381–9, *386,*
        393, 395–7, 411, 414, 418, 422–5, 434,
        438–43, 451, 458–9, 464, 466–8, 470,
        473–5, 494, 691*n*
Mexico City, 6, 305, 352, 360, 424, 498, 503,
        600
    California and, 435, 437
    Mexican War and, 446, 458, 460, 462–3,
        465–6, 468–73, 475–6
    Texas and, 354, 362–3, 366–7, 369, 376,
        383, 393, 397, 439
Michaux, André, 254, 271
Michigan, 66, 309–10, 313, 486, 501
Midway Islands, 520
Minnesota, 66, 169, 220, 329–30
Minorca, 108–10, 128, 177, 250
Miró, Esteban, 210–11
Mississippi River, Mississippi River Valley,
        56, 64, 92–6, 112–15, 198, 200–2,
        210–12, 224–30, 235–6, 271, 295–7,
        299–305, 353, 356, 400, 414, 432, 445,
        464, 489–90, 492–3, 501, 510–11, 517
    and acquisition of Florida, 303–5, 348
    anti-U.S. trade practices and, 183–4
    clarifying U.S. western boundaries and,
        327, 329–32, 338–9, 344
    and Declaration of Independence, 92–3
    and French and Indian War, 59–61, 95,
        136–7, 183, 265
    and French New World arrival and colo-
        nization, 7–8, 10, 12
    Georgia backland settlement and, 228–30
    Illinois Company and, 77–8
    Jay's Treaty and, 220–2, 224
    Jefferson on, 253–5
    Louisiana and, 61–2, 240, 246, 251, 253,
        256, 260–4, 266–9, 279–80, 287–8, 290,
        293, 295–6, 299, 303
    New Orleans crisis and, 267–9
    Paris Treaty and, 158–62, 165, 167–9, 177,
        220, 226, 303
    Pinckney's Treaty and, 227–8
    post–Revolutionary War U.S.-Spanish
        relations and, 201–2, 210–11, 224–8,
        253
    railroads and, 485–7, 489, 492
    Revolutionary War and, 85, 95, 105, 107,
        109–10, 113–15, 117–19, 125, 128, 130,
        134, 137, 142–3, 146, 148–51, 155–7

Spanish-French relations and, 7–8
and U.S. invasion of Canada, 309, 311
Virginia backland settlement and, 208, 210
and War of 1812, 314, 317–18, 320, 322–3
Missouri, 299, 342, 355, 395, 400, 420, 449
railroads and, 487, 501, 504
slavery and, 348–9
Missouri Compromise, 349, 380, 392, 395, 460–1, 468, 480, 500–2
Missouri River, Missouri River Valley, 10, 251, 400, 501
clarifying U.S. western boundaries and, 327–8, 338–9, 341, 344, 346
expeditions up, 254, 327
Louisiana and, 61, 299
Mitchell, Billy, 541
Mitchell, Thomas, 209
Mobile, Ala., 114, 248, 265
railroads and, 487, 489
and War of 1812, 315, 323
Monroe, James, 196, 221, 324–5, 347–50, 404, 432
and acquisition of Florida, 333–7, 340, 344–6, 348
clarifying U.S. western boundaries and, 330–1, 342–4, 347
Louisiana Purchase and, 272–4, 282–8, 295, 300
U.S.-French relations and, 233–4
and War of 1812, 320–1
Monroe Doctrine, 350, 411, 493, 544, 560
Roosevelt Corollary to, 596–7
Montana, 331, 341, 392
Monterey, Calif., 434, 437, 486, 548
Mexican War and, 446, 453, 457, 468
Monterrey, Battle of, 457–8
Montreal, 59, 86, 160, 211, 310, 327, 405
and War of 1812, 318, 321
Morales, Juan Ventura, 267–70, 272
Morgan, John Tyler, 585, 588
Morris, Richard, 151–2, 612*n*
Morris, Robert, 99, 229
Moscoso, Miryea, 600

Napoleon I, Emperor of France, 239–53, 307–10, 330, 334, 338, 362, 514, 559
anti-U.S. trade practices and, 308, 312
authoritarianism of, 245–6, 250, 277
coup d'état of, 242, 245
defeat of, 318–19
Egyptian expedition of, 240, 244–6, 250, 276, 279
French-British relations and, 275–8, 288, 290, 309

Haiti and, 246, 250, 256, 261–2, 274–6, 278, 280, 290
Italian campaigns of, 239, 241, 243, 245
Louisiana and, 240–1, 246–50, 253, 255–65, 268–71, 273–86, 288–92, 294–5, 298, 300
New Orleans crisis and, 268–9, 274
Talleyrand's relationship with, 242, 244–5
U.S.-French relations and, 234–5
and U.S. invasion of Canada, 309–10
Napoleonic Wars, 231, 306, 322, 351
Nashville, U.S.S., 592
Natchez, Miss., 11, 114, 226, 230
native Americans, xiii–xiv, xvii, 133–4, 183–6, 201–2, 212–15, 218–24, 236, 254, 257, 302–5, 425, 444–5, 466, 478, 481, 487, 506–8, 518, 568, 574
and acquisition of Florida, 304–5, 333–7, 340, 345, 347
Alaska and, 507–8, 513–14, 521, 532, 534, 538, 540–1
California and, 433–4, 452, 454, 456
in colonial period, 4, 8–11, 32, 34–6, 38–40, 44, 46, 56–69, 72–3, 76–8, 82, 85, 94–5, 133, 136–8, 222–3, 265
Georgia and, 62, 229, 316–17, 333–4
Great Britain and, 14–15, 19, 31, 35–6, 56, 222–3, 302–3, 305, 308–10, 321, 337
Jay's Treaty and, 219–21, 223
and land and territorial issues, 32, 34–6, 40, 62, 93–4, 99–100, 119–21, 185–6, 189, 193, 198, 209–10, 212–14, 222–4, 302–3, 305, 308–10, 315–17, 326, 328, 333, 337, 400, 492, 496–9, 501
Louisiana and, 61, 266, 293–4, 296–8
Mexico and, 113, 351–3, 359, 369
New Mexico and, 447, 449
Paris Treaty and, 167, 217–18
Pinckney's Treaty and, 227, 336
Revolutionary War and, 86, 93–4, 111–12, 114, 118, 133, 148, *149,* 151, 154–6, 172–3, 212, 222–3
Spain and, 4–8, 11, 34, 61, 201, 305, 353
Texas and, 353–4, 357, 359, 377, 382–3, 389, 397, 400
treatymaking with, 222–4, 228–9, 302, 305, 317, 321, 333, 365, 400
U.S. battles with, 218, 223, 228, 315–17, 334–7, 340, 347, 364, 400
and U.S. invasion of Canada, 308–10, 313, 314*n*
and War of 1812, 313–14, 317, 320–2, 324, 335
Navigation and Trade Acts, 46, 57–8, 91, 106, 138, 144, 162, 179

Navy, U.S., 330, 419, 519–20, 568–74
    Cuba and, 562, 564–6, 579–80
    Hawaii and, 550, 553–6, 558, 562, 573
    and importance of Central American canal,
        579–80, 584–5, 599
    Mahan on, 559–62, 564, 584
    Mexican War and, 437–8, 442, 446, 453–6,
        460, 462
    Panamanian revolution and, 592–3
    Philippines and, 564–5, 568–70, 572, 574
    Spanish-American War and, 559, 565–6,
        568–71
    and War of 1812, 314, 321
Nebraska, 487, 501–2, 562
Necker, Jacques, 122–3
Nelson, Horatio, 244, 292
Netherlands, 12, 16–17, 20, 26, 32, 74,
        109, 116, 139, 271, 276, 319, 383,
        407, 548
    Adams's mission to, 125–6, 131, 135,
        146, 165–6
    British mercantilism and, 49–50
New Brunswick, 407–8, 525
New England, 125–6, 135, 193, 229, 308,
        314, 318, 325, 413, 489, 544, 546–8
    Alaska and, 532, 538
    in colonial period, 19–22, 27, 29–31, 34,
        37, 40, 48, 50, 62, 65, 74, 83
    frontier of, 202–9, 211–12
    land rushes and, 185, 200
    Louisiana Purchase and, 289, 295, 297
    Paris Treaty and, 169, 172, 179
    Revolutionary War and, 86, 90, 94, 156
    slavery and, 62, 380, 385
Newfoundland, 8, 13, 49, 85, 109, 130, 525
    and French and Indian War, 61, 138
    Paris Treaty and, 161, 169, 172, 179, 320
    Revolutionary War and, 143–4, 146, 156
New France, 9–12, 136, 251
New Hampshire, 38, 47, 90, 160, *190,* 489
    New England frontier and, 202–8
New Jersey, 20–1, 50, 71, 77, 89, 97–8, 116,
        125, 185, 192, 208, 446, 478
New Mexico, 248, 326, 352–3, 484, 497,
        500–2, 574
    boundaries of, 467, 480–1
    clarifying U.S. western boundaries and,
        344, 346
    Mexican War and, 447–9, 455–6, 460, 464,
        467–8, 471, 475, 477–8, 480
    railroads and, 487, 491, 500–1
    Texas and, 378, 383–5, 424–5, 439–40
    U.S. acquisition of, 447–9, 455, 459–61,
        464, 468, 471, 475, 477–8
New Orleans, Battle of, 321–4, 332–4, 376,
        411, 420

New Orleans, La., 65, 159, 198, 210–11,
        233, 299–300, 360, 372, 376, 387, 424,
        489
    and acquisition of Florida, 304–5, 333
    Austin and, 355–6
    clarifying U.S. western boundaries and,
        338, 344
    closed to U.S. shipping, 267–75, 280, 284,
        286, 289–90
    and French New World arrival and colo-
        nization, 8, 11
    and French reacquisition of Louisiana,
        249, 251, 256, 260–2, 264–5, 267–70,
        274
    isthmian canal and, 493–4, 580
    Louisiana Purchase and, 282, 286–7,
        289–90, 299
    Pinckney's Treaty and, 227–8, 267–8
    Revolutionary War and, 114–15
    Spain and, 62, 113–14, 224–5, 227, 236,
        240–1, 255, 267–70, 272, 275, 280,
        289–90
    U.S. acquisition of, 260–1, 264–6, 268,
        272–3, 275, 278–85, 293
    and War of 1812, 314–15, 318, 321–4,
        332–3
New Spain, 6–7, 61, 107, 113, 156, 224,
        248
    see also Mexico
New World, xiii–xiv, xvi–xvii, 42, 68, 95,
        105–7, 182, 222, 224, 226–7, 235, 239,
        292, 304, 308, 332–4, 338, 349, 381,
        415, 514, 547, 580
    and Age of Discovery, xvi–xvii, 3–4
    British arrival and colonization of, 6, 9–23,
        27–32, 35–6
    Cuba and, 543–4
    Franklin and, 54–5, 60–1
    French arrival and colonization of, 7–12,
        15, 22, 28, 31, 34, 49
    Louisiana and, 241, 248, 251, 259, 262–3,
        270–1, 275–6, 279–80, 282
    Paris Treaty and, 159, 172, 174–5
    Revolutionary War and, 106–7, 126, 140
    Spanish arrival and colonization of, 4–16,
        18, 22–3, 28, 31, 34
    and U.S. acquisition of Florida, 333–4
New York, 116, 160, 185, *190,* 196–8, 201–9,
        217, 222–3, 257–8, 265, 300–1, 308,
        314, 318, 328, 365, 391, 394, 398,
        401–2, 484, 491–5, 506, 510, 514, 518,
        531, 537, 545, 557, 560, 564, 568, 583,
        586–7, 591–2
    in colonial period, 20–1, 24, 38–9, 48, 50,
        62, 69, 71, 77
    New England frontier and, 202–9, 211

Revolutionary War and, 89–91, 93–4, 127, 136, 206
western territory claimed by, 93–4, 96, 119–20
Nicaragua, 562, 581–9, 597
Nipissing line, 161, 168
Nonintercourse Act, 307
Noriega, Manuel, 597
North, Lord Frederick, 129–30
Revolutionary War and, 103–4, 122, 127, 129
Tea Act and, 79, 81
North America, 3, 13, 49, 59–61, 64, 76, 224–6, 235–6, 309, 432
Alaska and, 507, 509, 533–4
Canadian home rule and, 523–4
clarifying U.S. western boundaries and, 329–30, 332, 338
and French and Indian War, 59, 136–8
and French New World arrival and colonization, 8–11
and French reacquisition of Louisiana, 246–7, 249, 255, 257
Louisiana Purchase and, 280–1, 288–9, 292, 300
Oregon and, 391–2, 402, 404–5, 411, 413, 420–2, 428–9
Paris Treaty and, 159, 160n, 161
Revolutionary War and, 144–5, 148–51, 154–6, 158
U.S.-French relations and, 104–5, 235
and War of 1812, 318–20
North Carolina, 10, 15, 47, 55, 62, 86, 93–4, 98, 132, 185, 315
abuse of power in, 39–40
colonial boundaries of, 24, 38
public land sales of, 208, 211–12
Revolutionary War and, 93–4, 144
settlement of backland of, 208, 211–14, 229
Northern Mariana Islands, 598
Northwest, Northwest Territory, 193–5, 197–8, 223, 326–32, 341–7, 511
Northwest Ordinance, 195–7, 213, 293
Notes on the State of Virginia (Jefferson), 33, 44
Nova Scotia, 13, 49, 64, 85, 109, 309, 318, 525
Paris Treaty and, 160–1, 169, 172, 180
Revolutionary War and, 137, 144
Nueces River, Nueces Strip, 397, 423, 438–9, 441–3, 466–8

"Observations Concerning the Increase of Mankind, Peopling of Countries, Etc." (Franklin), 54

O'Hara, Charles, 128
Ohio, 66, 167, 196, 222–4, 230, 444, 486, 500, 562
Ohio Company, 56–7, 199
Ohio River, Ohio River Valley, 56–9, 62, 142–4, 228, 239, 254, 263, 293, 302–3, 310–11
and federalization of western lands, 189–91
and French and Indian War, 57–9, 95
and French New World arrival and colonization, 10–11
Illinois Company and, 76, 78
land rushes and, 185–6, 200
New Orleans crisis and, 267–8
Paris Treaty and, 164, 183
Proclamation Line and, 64, 66
Quebec Act and, 82, 85–6, 137, 148
railroads and, 485, 487
Revolutionary War and, 94–5, 111–14, 142–3, 148, *149*, 151, 155, 157
slavery and, 197–8, 213, 348
Virginia backland settlement and, 208–9
and War of 1812, 311, 320
and western claims of states, 94–6, 98, 100–1, 111, 119, 121
oil, 542, 547–8
Oklahoma, 222, 299, 346, 349, 501
Old World, xiii–xvii, 40, 49, 85, 87, 92, 174, 185, 290, 301, 332, 349, 444, 514, 560, 569
and acquisition of Florida, 305–6
and Age of Discovery, xvi–xvii, 3–4
and character of American colonists, 42–4, 51
land in, xiv–xvi, 32
Revolutionary War and, 110, 124, 126, 151, 154, 156
U.S.-French relations and, 234–5
Olympic Peninsula, 404, 408
Onís, Luis de, 337–49
clarifying U.S. western boundaries and, 337–44, *343*, 346, 349
and U.S. acquisition of Florida, 337, 339–48
Ontario, 85, 109, 137, 183, 303, 420, 524–5
Paris Treaty and, 160–1
and War of 1812, 320, 322
Ontario, U.S.S., 330, 345–6
"On the Rising Glory of America" (Freneau and Brackenridge), 84–5
Oregon, Oregon Country, 326, 342, 395, 400–22, 452, 459–61, 466, 468, 513, 581
fixing borders of, 391–2, 402–22, *421*, 425–31, 433, 444

Oregon, Oregon Country *(continued)*
  Great Britain and, 391–2, 401–13, 415–22,
    425–31, 433, 435–7, 442, 459, 477, 508
  settlement of, 401, 405–6, 408, 410–11,
    413, 416–17, 430–1, 435–6
  statehood gained by, 414, 431
Oregon, U.S.S., 579
Oregon Trail, 392, 401, 413, 434
Ostend meeting, 545
O'Sullivan, John Louis, 398, 401–2
Oswald, Richard
  Paris Treaty and, 158–60, 162–6, 169–71,
    173–4
  Revolutionary War and, 132–9, 141–7,
    150, 152–4, 158
Otis, James, 69–71
Ottawas, 62, 222
Ottoman Empire, 67, 123, 239, 275

Paine, Lewis, 505–6
Paine, Thomas, 121
Pakenham, Edward, 322, 324
Pakenham, Richard, 411–12, 417–19, 427
Palo Alto, Battle of, 450
Panama, xii, 519, 580–95
  guerrilla war in, 586, 590–5, 597
  railroads and, 581–4, 587, 590–3
  Roosevelt Corollary and, 596–7
  secession from Colombia of, 590–2
Panama Canal
  Bunau-Varilla and, 585–9, 591–4
  Canal Zone and, 594–6, 599–600
  construction of, 251, 578, 595–6
  diplomacy on, 581–95, 598–9
  Lesseps and, 583–6
  Virgin Islands and, 597–8
Panic of 1819, 356
Panic of 1837, 381
Panic of 1893, 566, 584
Paredes, Mariano
  Mexican War and, 441–2, 445–6, 451,
    458
  Texan boundary dispute and, 423–5
Paris, Treaty of (1763), 67, 115, 118, 136–8,
  143, 183, 255, 265
Paris, Treaty of (1783), 158–85, 200–1,
  216–21, 257, 318, 612n
  dispensation for Loyalists in, 160n, 162,
    164–7, 169–74, 217, 219
  drafting of, 158–64, 167
  land and territorial issues in, 158–65,
    167–9, 171–5, 177, 179–80, 183–4, 196,
    201, 207, 212, 217–21, 226, 240, 253,
    261, 292, 303, 320, 329
  ratification of, 165, 174, 182, 185
  on recognizing U.S. sovereignty, 158, 200

  on repayment of prewar debts, 164–7,
    169–71, 174, 217, 219, 221
  secret article to, 160n
  signing of, 174–6
  as U.S. diplomatic triumph, 178, 181
  violations of, 183, 217–19
Parliament, British, 27, 64, 66–76, 78–9,
  81–2, 89, 91, 95, 98, 174–5, 189, 218,
  437
  British mercantilism and, 46–7, 55, 106
  and British New World arrival and colo-
    nization, 18, 21–22
  Canadian home rule and, 523–5
  colonial governments and, 21–2
  Franklin and, 52, 55, 57, 72–3
  Oregon and, 405, 415, 422, 428, 431
  Paris Treaty and, 164, 170–2, 174, 178–9,
    182
  Proclamation Line and, 66–8
  Quebec Act and, 82, 142
  Revolutionary War and, 106, 127–8,
    130–2, 134, 139, 141–3, *149*, 153–4,
    156, 158
  Stamp Act and, 69–73
Parma, 241, 247, 265, 280
Parma, Luis, Duke of, 241, 247, 262, 265
Peacemakers, The (Morris), 151–2, 612n
Pearl Harbor, 550, 553, 555, 559, 573
Peel, Sir Robert, 406, 410–12, 415–16,
  419–22, 425–31
Peña y Peña, Manuel de la, 471–4
Peninsular War, 292, 305
Penn, William, 20, 23–4, 32, 34, 60, 100
Pennsylvania, 10, 20, 23–4, 48, 50, 56–8, 62,
  76–7, 98–9, 120, 185, 195, 198, 210,
  272, 277, 319, 378, 394, 411, 416, 445,
  461, 529
  Franklin and, 52–4, 60, 71, 77
  and French and Indian War, 58, 60
  paper currency issued by, 53–4
  Revolutionary War and, 89, 94, 125
Pensacola, Fla., 6, 114, 248, 304, 323
  and acquisition of Florida, 333, 337, 340
Perkins, Benjamin, 536–7
Peru, 5, 7, 155
Philadelphia, Pa., 50, 98–9, 115–16, 119–20,
  122, 132–3, 144, 146, 196–7, 209–10,
  226, 229, 277, 352
  Franklin and, 52–3, 55, 74, 76, 78
  Paris Treaty and, 162, 170–1
  railroads and, 483–4
  Revolutionary War and, 86, 156, 172
Philip II, King of Spain, 13–16
Philippine Islands, 564–5, 572–7, 597–8
  guerrilla war in, 565, 569–70, 575–6
  Spanish-American War and, 568–70, 572

U.S. occupation of, 573–6, 598, 601
as U.S. territory and commonwealth, 576, 580
Pichon, Louis-André, 274–5, 288–9
Pierce, Franklin, 495–7, 503–4
Cuba and, 544–5
Gadsden and, 489–90, 499, 503
Hawaii and, 549–50
isthmian canal and, 495–6, 503
railroads and, 489–90, 493, 495
Pinckney, Charles, 202
Pinckney, Charles Cotesworth, 234, 257, 266
Pinckney, Thomas, 226–8, 240
Pinckney's Treaty (Treaty of San Lorenzo), 226–9, 240, 267–8, 336
Pitt, William, the Elder, 64, 71, 73, 76, 78, 127
Pius VII, Pope, 246, 250
Plains of Abraham, 59, 87
Plattsburgh, N.Y., 321
Point Comfort, Va., 25
Point Isabel, Tex., 449–50
Poland, 514–15
Polk, James K., 390–7, 412–33, 441–51, 461, 489, 495–6, 498–9, 518, 567, 620n
and acquisition of New Mexico, 447–9, 477–8
Alaska and, 510, 512
background of, 390–1, 393–4
California and, 413, 415, 433, 435–7, 445–8, 476–9
inaugural address of, 414–17
Mexican War and, 431, 433, 437–8, 441–7, 451, 457–9, 463, 468, 470–8, 544
Oregon and, 392, 395, 412–22, 425–30, 433, 436, 477
Scott's relationship with, 448, 450
Texas and, 392–3, 395–7, 413, 420–4, 433, 436, 438–9, 441, 443, 477, 481
Pontiac, 62
Popov, Andrei A., 513
preemption, preemptive rights, 199, 257
Proclamation Act, Proclamation Line, 64–8, 75–8, 85–6, 98, 136–7, 143, 148, 149, 162, 186
Protestantism, Protestants, 4, 7, 9, 14, 16–17, 27, 32, 50, 77, 105, 248, 359, 512
"Public Good" (Paine), 121
Puerto Rico, 569, 571–2, 575
Puget Sound, 524
clarifying U.S. western boundaries and, 327, 330–1
Oregon and, 403–6, 408–9, 411, 430–1
Puritanism, Puritans, 16, 20, 27, 29, 35, 45, 79, 325, 342

Quadruple Alliance, 330, 333
Quakers, 20, 27, 103
Quartering Act, 70, 75, 79
Quasi-War, 234
Quebec, 59, 72, 85–7, 109, 134, 309, 318, 524–5
and French New World arrival and colonization, 9, 11
Paris Treaty and, 160–1, 164, 168
Proclamation Line and, 64–5, 137, 143, 162
Revolutionary War and, 86–7, 95, 128, 137, 143, 206
Quebec Act, 82–3, 85–7, 113, 137, 142, 148, 155, 164
quit-rents, 30–1, 38–40

railroads, 378, 483–93, 495–504, 518, 521, 580–5
construction of, 483–4, 487, 500–1, 504, 546–7
Gadsden and, 485–7, 489–90, 496–502
Guadalupe treaty disputes and, 491–2
isthmian canal and, 580, 585
Panama and, 581–4, 587, 590–3
Whitney's plan for, 484–6
Raleigh, Walter, 14–15, 18
Randolph, John, 310
Reagan, Ronald, 599
Reconstruction, 517, 533, 536, 583
Remini, Robert V., 316
republicanism, 92, 100, 105, 182, 192, 229, 319, 482
Alaska and, 534, 540
Jefferson and, 254, 272, 324–5, 390–1
Louisiana Purchase and, 289, 293, 296
Mexican War and, 445–6
Mexico and, 352, 362–3
Napoleon and, 242–3, 246, 252
Revolutionary War and, 108–9
Republican Party, Republicans, 254, 258, 272–3, 310, 312, 457, 504, 506–7, 517–18, 529, 535–7, 557, 567–8, 594–5, 599–60
isthmian canal and, 585, 587–8, 594
Johnson's relations with, 517, 520–1, 526, 536–7
Louisiana Purchase and, 289–90, 294
U.S. naval policy and, 561–2
Resaca de la Palma, Battle of, 450
Revolutionary War, 43, 52, 78, 85–182, 185, 204–6, 210, 226, 256–7, 259, 261, 301, 309–10, 312, 318, 325, 362–3, 370–1, 420, 555
British military superiority in, 87–9, 101, 256

Revolutionary War *(continued)*
  British military tactics and strategy in, 89–90, 101, 111–12, 127, 143–4, 370
  Clark and, 112–14, 148
  crimes in, 133–4, 143–4, 172–3
  finances in, 87, 92–3, 95, 98–9, 101–4, 125, 155, 177–9, 182, 212, 215
  France and, 85–6, 101–6, 108–10, 112–15, 122–41, 144–7, *149*, 150–7, 174–5, 177, 232–3, 279, 286
  and land and territorial issues, 85–6, 88, 90–9, 104–15, 117–25, 128–9, 132–40, 142–4, 146, 148–58, *149*, 173, 187–8, *190*, 191, 212–13, 370, 612*n*
  native Americans and, 86, 93–4, 111–12, 114, 118, 133, 148, *149*, 151, 154–6, 172–3, 212, 222–3
  New England frontier and, 202, 204–7
  peace negotiations in, 85, 93, 106, 108–9, 111, 113–15, 122–7, 129–58, 612*n*
  prisoners in, 125, 126*n*, 131, 165*n*, 173, 206, 315
  recognizing U.S. sovereignty and, 125–6, 131, 133, 135–6, 138–43, 145–7, 150–4, 157–8
  Spain and, 105–10, 113–19, 122–3, 125, 128, 131–2, 135–6, 139–41, 148–52, *149*, 200, 265
  U.S. military tactics and strategy in, 89–91, 101, 122, 127–8, 256, 371
  see also Paris, Treaty of (1783)
Rhea, John, 335
Rhode Island, 20, 97, 124, 208, 293, 305, 491
Rio Grande, Rio Grande Valley, 36, 113, 378
  clarifying U.S. western boundaries and, 339, 353–4, 358
  Guadalupe treaty disputes and, 491, 499
  Mexican War and, 431, 441–3, 449–50, 458–9
  Texas and, 369, 371, 376, 383–4, 397, 423–5, 438–40, 443, 464, 467–8, 470, 473–5, 480
Roanoke Island, 15, 18
Robbins, Robert M., 199
Rochambeau, Jean-Baptiste-Donatien de Vimeur, Comte de, 124, 127–8
Rockingham, Lord, 131, 136, 141
Rocky Mountains, 109–10, 235, 251, 254, 434, 436, 487, 491, 498, 501
  clarifying U.S. western boundaries and, 327–8, 331–2, 339, 341–2, 346, 351, 403
  Oregon and, 391–2, 401, 403, 409–10
Rodney, George, 139

Rodriguez Creek, 323–4
Roosevelt, Theodore, 563–5, 574–5, 600
  Cuba and, 564, 568
  Hawaii and, 563–4
  isthmian canal and, 586, 588–95
  Panamanian revolution and, 591–5, 597
  Spanish-American War and, 568, 575
  Virgin Islands and, 597–8
Roosevelt Corollary, 578, 596–7
Ross, James, 272
Rousseau, Jean-Jacques, 103, 277
Russia, xiii, 246, 279, 291, 319, 330, 416, 426, 440, 507–16, 547, 585–6
  Alaska and, 404, 507–16, 520–39
  clarifying U.S. western boundaries and, 326, 328, 332, 342
  Crimean War and, 508–9, 511–14, 536–7
  Oregon and, 391–2, 402–4, 409
Russian-American Company (RAC), 402, 508–11, 513–15, 520, 527–8

Sacramento Valley, 434, 436, 452, 478–9
St. Clair, Arthur, 197–8, 210
St. John River, 160, 164, 169
St. Lawrence River, St. Lawrence River Valley, 86, 159–62, 246, 303, 407
  and French and Indian War, 58–60, 136–7
  and French New World arrival and colonization, 8–9, 12
  Paris Treaty and, 159–61
  Revolutionary War and, 109, 156
  and U.S. invasion of Canada, 309, 311
St. Louis, Mo., 184, 210, 328, 401
  railroads and, 486–7, 501
Saints, Battle of the, 139
Saltillo, 357, 359, 462
San Antonio, Tex., 354, 357, 360, 367–9, 384, 457
  and Texan secession from Mexico, 368–9, 371–2
San Diego, Calif., 487, 509
  Mexican War and, 454, 456, 464, 467, 475
San Francisco, Calif., 453, 495, 514, 524, 550, 570, 579
  Alaska and, 511–12, 520–1, *522*, 527–8, 534, 541
  and discovery of gold, 478–9
  railroads and, 487, 501
San Francisco Bay, 326, 403, 408, 424, 486
  Mexican War and, 438, 453, 466
San Ildefonso, Treaty of, 247–9, 251, 258, 262, 265, 267–9, 291
San Jacinto, Battle of, 374–7, 379, 383
San Juan Hill, Battle of, 568

San Lorenzo, Treaty of (Pinckney's Treaty), 226–9, 240, 267–8, 336
San Luis Potosí, 459, 462
San Pascual, Battle of, 456–7
Santa Anna, Antonio López de, 366–76, 397, 465–74, 493, 496–500
    California and, 434, 437
    capture of, 375–6
    despotism of, 366–7, 370–1, 375, 423, 458, 497–8, 500, 503
    Gadsden and, 497–500, 503
    Mexican War and, 458–9, 462–3, 465–71, 474
    railroads and, 497–8, 503
    rise to power of, 362–3, 366
    Texas and, 363, 366, 368–76, 379, 388, 393, 395, 458
Santa Fe, N.Mex., 6, 352–3, 447–9, 480
    Texas and, 378, 384, 424–5, 439
    U.S. invasion of, 449, 455–6
Santa Fe Trail, 383, 449, 455
Santa Rita de Cobra Mountains, 491
Santiago, Battle of, 572–3, 579
Saratoga, Battle of, 103, 106, 119
Schuyler, Philip John, 119–20
Scott, Winfield T., 448–50, 489, 492, 568
    Mexican War and, 457, 461–6, 468–74, 477
    Polk's relationship with, 448, 450
    Trist's relationship with, 465, 473
Sellers, Charles, 396, 620n
Seminoles, 304, 317, 448
    and U.S. acquisition of Florida, 333–7, 345, 347
Seminole War, 334–7, 340, 347
Senate, U.S., 215, 221, 315, 319, 393–4, 416, 436, 445, 476–7, 489–94, 506, 516, 518, 526–38, 562, 574
    Gadsden Purchase and, 499–500, 502–3
    isthmian canal and, 493–4, 500, 503, 581, 585, 587–90, 594–5
    and return of Canal Zone, 599–60
    see also Congress, U.S.
Seven Years' War, 58–60, 63, 106, 108, 113
Sevier, John, 212–14
Seward, Frederick, 505–6, 529
Seward, William H., 505–7, 514–23
    Alaska and, 507, 510–11, 515–16, 520–3, 525–33, 535–7, 539–42
    attempted assassination of, 505–6
    Johnson's relationship with, 517–19, 526, 539
    Virgin Islands and, 519–20, 527, 535–6, 545, 597
Shawnees, 302, 314n
Shays's Rebellion, 195

Shelburne, William Petty Fitzmaurice, Earl of, 63–6, 70, 73, 219, 238, 319
    censuring of, 179, 182
    Franklin's relationship with, 75–8, 83, 130–2, 138, 141, 178
    Illinois Company and, 77–8
    Paris Treaty and, 158–60, 162–5, 167–8, 170–1, 173, 178–9, 261
    Proclamation Line and, 64–6, 75–6
    Revolutionary War and, 78, 130–6, 138–9, 141–4, 146–7, 152–8
Shelby, Evan, 213
Shenandoah, 515, 519
Shirley, William, 57
"Short Hints Towards a Scheme for Uniting the Northern Colonies" (Franklin), 56
Sitka, 402–3, 508, 527, 535, 539–40, 548
slavery, slaves, slaveholders, 132, 172, 185, 200, 213, 227, 278, 315–16, 342, 399, 416, 478–81, 488–90, 496, 512
    abolition of, 197, 337, 380, 385, 394, 443–4, 516–18
    in colonial period, 5–6, 32–6, 39–40, 44, 46, 62, 83, 88
    Constitution and, 197, 215, 414, 480, 517
    Cuba and, 544–5
    emancipation of, 506–7, 510, 517–18
    and federalization of western lands, 192, 197
    Florida and, 304–5, 333–4, 336, 345, 349
    Gadsden Purchase and, 499–500
    Louisiana and, 289, 293, 298, 348–9
    New England frontier and, 206–7
    opposition to, 380, 385, 388–90, 394–5, 414, 426, 428, 443–4, 461, 467–8, 479–81, 488–9, 499, 502, 504, 529, 544
    Paris Treaty and, 158, 170
    prohibition of, 192, 197–8, 340, 355
    railroads and, 483, 502
    runaway, 304–5, 333–4, 336, 362, 481
    in territory acquired in Mexican War, 460–2, 467–8, 471, 476, 479–81
    Texas and, 349, 356–7, 359–62, 367, 378, 380, 385, 388–90, 392, 395, 414, 426, 428
Slidell, John, 435
    Mexican War and, 442–3, 463, 471, 475
    Texas and, 424–5, 439–41, 443
Sloat, John D., 437–8, 446, 453–4
Smith, Adam, 75, 83
Sonoma, Calif., 452–3
Sonora, Calif., 454, 467, 475, 495, 498–9
South, 185, 193, 206, 289, 304–6, 342, 348–9, 378, 426, 432, 496–7, 500–2, 507, 512, 516–19, 525, 529, 531–3, 535–6, 544, 546

South *(continued)*
  and acquisition of Florida, 304–5, 333, 335–6
  Johnson and, 516–17
  land rushes and, 187, 200
  Mexican War and, 443, 460–1, 468, 480
  post–Revolutionary War U.S.-Spanish relations and, 201–2
  railroads and, 483, 485–92, 497, 501–2, 504
  Revolutionary War and, 120, 122, 127, 146, 173, 226
  Texas and, 357, 389, 391
  War of 1812 in, 314–15, 317–18, 320–4
South America, 6, 201, 342, 344, 384, 548, 580, 597
South Carolina, 10, 23–4, 47, 55, 62, 126, 132, 173, 185, 202, 215, 226, 237, 310, 377, 496, 529, 586
  abuse of power in, 39–40
  Revolutionary War and, 93–4, 144
South Carolina Railroad, 485, 490
Southern Pacific Railroad, 504, 587
Southwest, clarifying U.S. boundaries in, 328–9, 332, 337–47, 349, 351, 353–4, 358, 392, 408–9, 417–18
Spain, Spanish, 26, 49, 59, 64, 78, 82, 94–5, 223–9, 381, 467, 492, 508, 579–81
  and Age of Discovery, xvii, 4–5
  anti-U.S. trade practices and, 183–4, 198
  arrival and colonization of New World by, 4–16, 18, 22–3, 28, 31, 34
  British relations with, 13–16, 18, 105–8, 110, 122, 131, 139, 154, 156, 162–3, 177, 184, 224–8, 235–6, 240–1, 248, 271, 292, 330, 339–40, 344–5, 349
  California and, 433–4, 479, 482
  clarifying U.S. western boundaries and, 325–6, 328–9, 332, 337–47, 343, 349, 351, 353–4, 358, 392, 409, 417–18, 472
  Cuba and, 495, 543–5, 560–1, 563, 565–9, 572–5, 579
  Florida and, 280, 303–6, 333–7, 339–48, 354, 544
  French relations with, 7–8, 10–11, 105–6, 108–10, 114, 125, 128, 131, 150, 156–7, 162–3, 166, 176, 224–8, 233, 237–41, 246–51, 280, 291–2
  Gibraltar defeat of, 162–3
  Guam and, 570, 575
  Haiti and, 236–7, 240, 246
  Jay's mission to, 115–17, 125, 131, 135–6, 140, 200, 226
  Jay's Treaty and, 224, 226
  land rushes and, 187, 200

Louisiana and, 61–2, 94, 113–14, 235–6, 240–2, 246–9, 251–3, 255, 258–63, 265–71, 276, 281, 290–2, 295, 299, 303, 344, 347
Mexico and, 4–7, 113, 224–5, 236, 351–5, 359, 363
native Americans and, 4–8, 11, 34, 61, 201, 305, 353
New Orleans and, 62, 113–14, 224–5, 227, 236, 240–1, 255, 267–70, 272, 275, 280, 289–90
Oregon and, 391, 402, 405
Panama and, 580–1
Paris Treaty and, 159, 160*n*, 162–4, 167, 176–7, 183–4, 200–1, 226, 240
Philippines and, 564–5, 568–70, 572, 574–5
Pinckney's Treaty and, 226–9, 240, 267–8, 336
Puerto Rico and, 571, 575
Revolutionary War and, 105–10, 113–19, 122–3, 125, 128, 131–2, 135–6, 139–41, 148–52, *149,* 200, 265
and separation of Kentucky and Virginia, 210–11
Texas and, 7–8, 354–5, 397, 423, 438
U.S. relations with, 109–10, 114–19, 125, 131–2, 135–6, 140–1, 148, 159, 166, 177, 183–4, 198, 200–2, 209–11, 224–9, 235–6, 240–1, 248, 253, 255, 266–70, 273, 275, 280, 289–92, 333–49
Virginia backland settlement and, 209–10
and War of 1812, 314–15, 318, 323–4
Spanish-American War, 559, 565–75, 579–80, 585, 600
  Cuba and, 565–9, 571–3
  Philippines and, 568–70, 572
Spooner, John, 588–9
Spottswood, Alexander, 39
Spreckels, Claus, 553
squatters, 95, 208, 254, 257, 289, 302, 357, 400–1, 510
  California and, 434, 479
  in colonial period, 32, 40–1, 65, 76, 82–3
  Georgia backland settlement and, 229–30
  land rushes and, 186–8
  public land sales and, 192–4, 199, 365
  Texas and, 360–1, 367
Stamp Act, 69–75, 79, 81–2, 131, 209, 219
Stanton, Edwin, 521, 536
Stanwix, Treaty of, 222
Starr, Kevin, 434–5
State Department, U.S., 271, 347, 440, 492–4, 505, 555, 580
  Alaska and, 525, 528–31
  Guadalupe treaty disputes and, 492, 497

isthmian canal and, 493–4, 590
Mexican War and, 458, 463–4, 477
Oregon and, 391, 408
Panamanian revolution and, 590, 593
states' rights, 272, 298, 385, 388, 390–1, 414, 481, 483, 488, 516
Stevens, John L., 554–8
Stevens, Thaddeus, 529, 535, 538–9
Stockton, Robert F., 446, 454–7
Stoeckl, Edouard de, 511–14
Alaska and, 511–13, 516, 525–30, 532–3, 535, 537–9
Strachey, Henry, 165–8, 170–1, 174
Suez Canal, 583–4
sugar, 48, 58, 60, 227, 236, 244, 360, 544, 571
Hawaii and, 549–51, 553–4
Sugar Act (American Revenue Act), 68–9, 75
"Summary View of the Rights of British America" (Jefferson), 91–2
Sumner, Charles, 477
Alaska and, 529–35, 538, 540–2, 622*n*
Dominican Republic and, 545–6
Supreme Court, U.S., 230, 258
Sutter, John A., 434, 436, 452, 478–9

Talleyrand-Périgord, Charles-Maurice de, 237–42, 244–50, 258–9
colonization advocated by, 239–40, 244, 246, 248, 261
Louisiana and, 240–1, 246–50, 255, 258, 261–3, 265–6, 268–9, 274, 276–7, 281–6, 291
Napoleon's relationship with, 242, 244–5
New Orleans crisis and, 268–9
U.S.-French relations and, 234–5
U.S. visit of, 238–9, 246, 248, 276
tariffs, taxes, 91, 116, 132–4, 182, 187, 207, 209, 220, 225, 325, 361–2, 385, 390–1, 393–4, 413, 426, 434, 474, 488, 540, 562, 566
in colonial period, 47–8, 51, 56–8, 66, 68–75, 79–83, 95
Hawaii and, 549–53
Napoleon and, 245, 250
Puerto Rico and, 571–2
Revolutionary War and, 106, 132–3
Texas and, 362, 367, 370, 382
Taylor, John M., 519
Taylor, Zachary, 481
Mexican War and, 441–3, 449–51, 457–9, 462
Texas boundary dispute and, 423, 425, 439, 441, 443
Tea Act, 79–81

Tecumseh, 302–3, 314*n*, 321
Tehuantepec
canal building in, 483, 493–6, 498–500, 503
Mexican War peace negotiations and, 464, 467
Teller Amendment, 567, 571, 576
Tennessee, Tennesseans, 86, 224, 230, 267, 302, 324, 333, 356, 390–1, 413–14, 425, 487, 507, 516, 544
and acquisition of Florida, 304–5, 335–6
creation of state of, 211–14
Houston's background and, 363–5, 368
native Americans and, 315–16
Tenure of Office Act, 520–1, 536
Terán, Manuel de Mier y, 360–1, 619*n*
terrorism, 602–3
Texas, 211, 349, 353–63, 365–400, 433–43, 473–7, 574
annexation and statehood of, 365, 377–81, 383, 385–99, 408, 410–14, 418, 420–4, 426, 428, 433, 436, 438–41, 443, 459–61, 464, 466–8, 477, 480–1, 510, 572, 619*n*
boundaries of, 353, 378, 384, *386*, 388, 392, 395–7, 399, 423–5, 438–43, 447, 464, 466–8, 470, *472*, 473–5, 480–1, 491–2, 499
clarifying U.S. western boundaries and, 339, 341–6, 392
early U.S. claims to, 353–4
Great Britain and, 379–90, 392–3, 396–7, 424, 435, 437
independence of, 422, 424
Louisiana and, 299, 303, 354, 356, 370, 373, 388
Mexican War and, 438–43, 457, 461–2, 464, 466–8, 470, *472*, 473–5, 480
Mexico and, 354–63, 365–79, 381–9, *386*, 393, 395–7, 411, 414, 418, 422–5, 434, 438–43, 451, 458–9, 464, 466–8, 470, 473–5, 494, 619*n*
native Americans and, 316, 353–4, 357, 359, 377, 382–3, 389, 397, 400
New Mexico and, 378, 383–5, 424–5, 439–40
railroads and, 486–7, 491, 500–1
as republic, 371–97, *386*, 440, 481, 552
size of, 379, 521
Spain and, 7–8, 354–5, 397, 423, 438
U.S. colonization of, 354–63, 365–8, 377, 380, *386*, 434–5, 467, 494, 619*n*
Texas Boundary Act, 438–9
Thames, Battle of the, 314
Thurston, Lorrin, 555–6
Tidewater region, 19, 24, 56, 121, 209

tobacco, 33, 47–8, 50, 118, 170, 182, 200–1, 211
Toronto, 313–14, 320
Toussaint L'Ouverture, François Dominique
  death of, 263, 274
  and French attempted acquisition of Haiti, 250–1, 256, 259, 262–3, 290
  Spanish overthrown by, 237, 246
Townshend, Charles, 69, 73–4, 76–8
Townshend Revenue Acts, 74, 79
Treaty of 1763, 67, 115, 118, 136–8, 143, 183, 255, 265
Treaty of 1783, *see* Paris, Treaty of (1783)
Trist, Nicholas P., 493
  Mexican War and, 463–8, 470–4, 476–7
  Scott's relationship with, 465, 473
Turgot, Anne-Robert-Jacques, 101–2, 122, 177
Turkey, Turks, 45, 67, 239, 244, 250, 275, 508–9
Turner, Frederick Jackson, 44, 610*n*
Tuscany, 247, 249, 262, 280, 291
Twain, Mark, 515, 569–70, 575–6
Two Years Before the Mast (Dana), 436
Tyler, John, 408–14
  Oregon and, 391–2, 409–13, 417
  Texas and, 385–98, 410–11, 413–14, 572

Uncle Tom's Cabin (Stowe), 481
Union Act, 523
United Nations, 597–8
United States
  expected dissolution of, 214
  finances of, 92–3, 98–100, 103–4, 114, 117, 122, 125–6, 135–6, 143, 155, 164–7, 169–71, 174, 177, 179, 182–4, 186–8, 192, 199, 207, 212–13, 215–17, 219–21, 231, 233, 252, 254, 286, 306–8, 314, 318, 324–5, 356, 377, 381, 385, 389, 391, 394–7, 401, 413, 425, 460, 476–7, 487–8, 507, 518, 536, 546–8, 561, 566, 575, 584–5, 601
  independence declared by, 89, 91–3, 100, 110
  political incoherence of, 181–2, 184, 214
  racism in, 445, 460, 478, 549, 552, 557, 563, 574, 576
  recognizing sovereignty of, 125–6, 131, 133, 135–6, 138–43, 145–7, 150–4, 157–8, 200
Upshur, Abel, 385–7
Utah, 425, 440, 481, 487, 502

Vallejo, Mariano, 452–3
Van Buren, Martin, 380–1, 389–91
Vancouver, George, 326–7

Vancouver Island, 225–6, 550
  Oregon Country and, 403, 405, 408–12, 416–18, 429, 431
Vandalia, 98, 101, 121
Van Doren, Carl, 55
Van Rensselaer, Stephen, 301
Vaughan, Benjamin
  Paris Treaty and, 161–3
  Revolutionary War and, 147–8, 154, 157–8
Venezuela, 560–2
Veracruz, 225, 362, 446, 493
  Mexican War and, 460, 462–3, 470, 473, 477
Vergennes, Charles Gravier, Comte de, 67, 115–16, 235, 259, 277
  Paris Treaty and, 162–3, 166, 170–1, 175–7
  Revolutionary War and, 102–6, 108–10, 115, 122–6, 132–3, 135, 138, 140–1, 145–6, 150, 152, 155–7
Vermont, *190,* 202, 204–9, 211–12
Victoria, Queen of Great Britain, 513
Virginia, 10, 52, 56–7, 74, 165*n*, 207–12, 217, 231, 252–4, 257, 272, 281, 289, 320, 325, 329, 385–7, 463–4
  abuse of power in, 37–9
  and British New World arrival and colonization, 19, 21
  and character of American colonists, 43–4
  Clark's expedition and, 112–13
  colonial boundaries of, 23–4, *25,* 38
  colonial government of, 21, 23, 37–8
  and federalization of western lands, 189–91, 196
  Jefferson's agrarian convictions and, 253–4
  land distribution in, 29–31, 33
  native Americans and, 35, 62, 209–10, 212
  public land sales and, 198, 208–9
  Quebec Act and, 82–3, 85–6, 137
  Revolutionary War and, 85–6, 93–4, 98, 111–13, 125, 127–8, 137, 143, 148
  settling backland of, 208–12, 254
  territory ceded to federal government by, 121–2, 189–91, *190,* 208–9
  western territory claimed by, 85–6, 93–4, 96–101, 111–13, 119–20, 137, 143, 148, 161, 185, *190*
Virgin Islands, 519–20, 527, 535–6, 545, 597–8

Wake Island, 570
Walker, Robert J., 445, 510–11, 518
  Alaska and, 510, 538–9
Walker, William, 498
Wallace, Anthony F. C., 297
Walpole, Horace, 179

War Department, U.S., 334, 439, 573
and War of 1812, 312–14, 317, 323
War Hawks, 308–9, 312, 319
War of 1812, 211, 311–15, 317–26, 364, 420,
    448, 514, 523
and British anti-U.S. trade practices,
    311–12, 318–20
British military tactics and strategies in,
    318, 320–1
and Canada, 311–14, 317–22, 324, 326,
    353
land and territorial issues in, 311, 313, 315,
    319–20, 322, 324, 326, 328, 335, 353
and New Orleans, 314–15, 318, 321–4,
    332–3
peace negotiations in, 318–22, 328
in South, 314–15, 317–18, 320–4
U.S. mismanagement of, 312–14, 317, 324
War of a Thousand Days, 586
War of the Spanish Succession, 49, 108
Washington, 392, 431
and acquisition of California, 436–7
Alaska and, 520, 526
clarifying U.S. western boundaries and,
    326, 330
Oregon Country and, 403–4
Washington, D.C., 429–32, 435, 481, 512,
    566, 591, 593
Alaska and, 516, 526, 528, 531, 538–40
Hawaii and, 549–50, 552–3, 555–8
Mexican War and, 456–7, 459, 465, 468,
    470, 473–5
Oregon Country and, 406, 411, 417–19,
    429–31
Texas and, 368, 372–3, 439
and War of 1812, 318, 320–1
Washington, George, 57, 83, 182, 195,
    210–11, 215–18, 221–3, 254, 258, 325,
    347
anti-U.S. trade practices and, 217–18, 233
Jay's Treaty and, 221–2
land rushes and, 186–9, 200
New England frontier and, 205–7
Revolutionary War and, 52, 86, 89–90, 93,
    95, 101, 103–4, 111–12, 124–5, 127–8,
    146, 205–6, 210, 256, 370–1
U.S.-French relations and, 104, 233–4
Wayne, Anthony, 211, 218, 223, 228
Wealth of Nations, The (Smith), 83
Webster, Daniel, xii, 385
Maine–New Brunswick border and, 407–8
Mexican War and, 476, 480
Oregon and, 407–8

Webster-Ashburton Treaty, 407
Wellington, Duke of, 322, 406, 412, 420,
    428
Wentworth, Benning, 38, 202–4
Wentworth Grants, 203–8
West
agrarianism of, 306
clarifying U.S. boundaries in, 325–33,
    337–47, *343*, 349, 351, 353–4, 358, 378,
    391–2, 402–9, 417–18, 428, *472*
Western Lands and the American Revolution
    (Abernethy), 78
West Indies, 11, 48–51, 74, 127–8, 132, 160*n*,
    163, 236, 255, 561–2
anti-U.S. trade practices and, 182, 216
British mercantilism and, 49–50
Jay's Treaty and, 219–20
Revolutionary War and, 102, 105, 138–9
Weyler, Valeriano, 560–1
Whig Party, Whigs, 385, 393–4, 408, 410,
    413, 432, 436, 448, 451, 489, 491–2,
    500
Mexican War and, 443–4, 476
Oregon and, 416, 426, 430
Texas and, 380, 389–91, 393, 439
"White Man's Burden, The" (Kipling), 576
Whitman, Walt, xii, 444
Whitney, Asa, 484–6
Wilkes, Charles, 406
Wilkes, John, 78
Wilkinson, James, 225, 299
and separation of Kentucky and Virginia,
    210–11
and War of 1812, 314–15
Willamette River, Willamette Valley, 401,
    405–6
Wilmot, David, 461
Wilmot Proviso, 467, 479–80
Winthrop, John, 35, 42, 45
World War I, 596–8
World War II, 541, 570–1, 576–7, 598
Worth, William J., 457

XYZ Affair, 234

Yazoo Grants, 228–30, 302
Year of Decision—1846, The (De Voto),
    449–50
York, James, Duke of, 20, 24, 38, 203
Yorktown, Battle of, 127–30, 139

Zacatecas, 366–7
Zedillo, Ernesto, xi–xii

A NOTE ABOUT THE AUTHOR

RICHARD KLUGER is a native of Paterson, New Jersey, grew up in Manhattan, and graduated from the Horace Mann School and Princeton University. He began his writing career as an editor at the *Wall Street Journal* and reporter for the *New York Post* and *Forbes* magazine before becoming literary editor of the *New York Herald Tribune.* He later entered book publishing and served as executive editor of Simon & Schuster, editor in chief at Atheneum, and publisher of Charterhouse Books, then turned to writing books full-time. He is the author of three other works of social history—*Simple Justice,* an account of the epochal 1954 decision by the Supreme Court outlawing school segregation, and *The Paper,* about the life and death of the *Herald Tribune,* both of which were nominated for the National Book Award in history, and *Ashes to Ashes,* a history of the cigarette industry and smoking-related health issues, which was awarded the 1997 Pulitzer Prize for general nonfiction. The best known of his six novels are *Members of the Tribe* and *The Sheriff of Nottingham.* Kluger and his wife, Phyllis, have two sons and six grandsons, co-authored two novels, and now live in Berkeley, California.

A NOTE ON THE TYPE

THE TEXT of this book was set in a typeface called Times New Roman, designed by Stanley Morison for *The Times* (London) and introduced by that newspaper in 1932.

Among typographers and designers of the twentieth centruy, Stanley Morison was a strong forming influence, as typographical advisor to the Monotype Corporation of London, as a director of two distinguished English publishing houses, and as a writer of sensibility, erudition, and keen practical sense.

In 1930 Morison wrote: "Type design moves at the pace of the most conservative reader. The good type-designer therefore realizes that, for a new font to be successful, it has to be so good that only very few recognized its novelty. If readers do not notice the consummate reticence and rare discipline of a new type, it is probably a good letter." It is now generally recognized that in the creation of Times Roman, Morison successfully met the qualifications of his theoretical doctrine.

Composed by North Market Street Graphics,
Lancaster, Pennsylvania
Printed and bound by Berryville Graphics,
Berryville, Virginia